COMMON ELEMENTS

Name	Symbol	Approx. At. Wt.	Common Ox. Nos.	Name	Symbol	Approx. At. Wt.	Common Ox. Nos.
Aluminum	Al	27.0	+3	Magnesium	Mg	24.3	+2
Antimony	Sb	121.8	+3,+5	Manganese	Mn	54.9	+2,+4,+7
Arsenic	As	74.9	+3,+5	Mercury	Hg	200.6	+1,+2
Barium	Ba	137.3	+2	Nickel	Ni	58.7	+2
Bismuth	Bi	209.0	+3	Nitrogen	N	14.0	−3,+3,+5
Bromine	Br	79.9	−1,+5	Oxygen	O	16.0	−2
Calcium	Ca	40.1	+2	Phosphorus	P	31.0	+3,+5
Carbon	C	12.0	+2,+4	Platinum	Pt	195.1	+2,+4
Chlorine	Cl	35.5	−1,+5,+7	Potassium	K	39.1	+1
Chromium	Cr	52.0	+2,+3,+6	Silicon	Si	28.1	+4
Cobalt	Co	58.9	+2,+3	Silver	Ag	107.9	+1
Copper	Cu	63.5	+1,+2	Sodium	Na	23.0	+1
Fluorine	F	19.0	−1	Strontium	Sr	87.6	+2
Gold	Au	197.0	0,+3	Sulfur	S	32.1	−2,+4,+6
Hydrogen	H	1.0	−1,+1	Tin	Sn	118.7	+2,+4
Iodine	I	126.9	−1,+5	Titanium	Ti	47.9	+3,+4
Iron	Fe	55.8	+2,+3	Tungsten	W	183.8	+6
Lead	Pb	207.2	+2,+4	Zinc	Zn	65.4	+2

COMMON IONS AND THEIR CHARGES

Name	Symbol	Charge	Name	Symbol	Charge
Aluminum	Al^{+++}	+3	Lead(II)	Pb^{++}	+2
Ammonium	NH_4^+	+1	Magnesium	Mg^{++}	+2
Barium	Ba^{++}	+2	Mercury(I)	Hg_2^{++}	+1
Calcium	Ca^{++}	+2	Mercury(II)	Hg^{++}	+2
Chromium(III)	Cr^{+++}	+3	Nickel(II)	Ni^{++}	+2
Cobalt(II)	Co^{++}	+2	Potassium	K^+	+1
Copper(I)	Cu^+	+1	Silver	Ag^+	+1
Copper(II)	Cu^{++}	+2	Sodium	Na^+	+1
Hydronium	H_3O^+	+1	Tin(II)	Sn^{++}	+2
Iron(II)	Fe^{++}	+2	Tin(IV)	Sn^{++++}	+4
Iron(III)	Fe^{+++}	+3	Zinc	Zn^{++}	+2
Acetate	$C_2H_3O_2^-$	−1	Hydroxide	OH^-	−1
Bromide	Br^-	−1	Hypochlorite	ClO^-	−1
Carbonate	CO_3^-	−2	Iodide	I^-	−1
Chlorate	ClO_3^-	−1	Nitrate	NO_3^-	−1
Chloride	Cl^-	−1	Nitrite	NO_2^-	−1
Chromate	$CrO_4^=$	−2	Oxide	$O^=$	−2
Fluoride	F^-	−1	Permanganate	MnO_4^-	−1
Hexacyanoferrate(II)	$Fe(CN)_6^{\equiv}$	−4	Peroxide	O_2^-	−2
Hexacyanoferrate(III)	$Fe(CN)_6^{\equiv}$	−3	Phosphate	$PO_4^{\equiv}$	−3
Hydride	H^-	−1	Sulfate	$SO_4^=$	−2
Hydrogen carbonate	HCO_3^-	−1	Sulfide	$S^=$	−2
Hydrogen sulfate	HSO_4^-	−1	Sulfite	$SO_3^=$	−2

The Holt Chemistry Program

MODERN CHEMISTRY

Metcalfe, Williams, and Castka

Supplementary Materials for MODERN CHEMISTRY

MODERN CHEMISTRY Teacher's Guide
Laboratory Experiments in Chemistry
Exercises and Experiments in Chemistry
Tests in Chemistry
Alternate Tests in Chemistry

Other Supplementary Materials

Scientific Experiments in Chemistry, Manufacturing Chemists' Association
Semimicro Chemistry, DeBruyne, Kirk, and Beers
Chemistry Problems, Castka
Radioactivity: Fundamentals and Experiments, Hermias and Joecile
Life and the Physical Sciences, Morowitz
A Tracer Experiment, Kamen
Viruses, Cells, and Hosts, Sigel and Beasley
Photosynthesis, Rosenberg
Chemistry in the Space Age, Gardner

MODERN

H. Clark Metcalfe

John E. Williams

Joseph F. Castka

CHEMISTRY

Holt, Rinehart and Winston, Inc.

New York • Toronto • London

H. Clark Metcalfe

Teacher of chemistry in the Winchester-Thurston School, 555 Morewood Ave., Pittsburgh, Pennsylvania; and Science Consultant for the Wilkinsburg School District, Wilkinsburg, Pennsylvania.

John E. Williams

Teacher of chemistry in the Newport Harbor High School, Newport Beach, California.

Joseph F. Castka

Chairman of the Science Department, Martin Van Buren High School, New York City; and Associate Professor of General Science and Chemistry, C. W. Post College, Long Island University.

Charles E. Dull

Author of the original editions of MODERN CHEMISTRY, deceased, was Head of the Science Department, West Side High School; and Supervisor of Science, Junior and Senior High Schools, Newark, New Jersey.

The color photograph on the cover was produced by Aaron Heller.

66VH

PREFACE

MODERN CHEMISTRY is designed to meet the various curriculum requirements for an introductory course in chemistry. This revision continues the sound policy of classroom development by practicing teachers which has characterized MODERN CHEMISTRY from its first edition.

To enable students to study chemistry in a modern theoretical development, this edition has been completely reorganized and rewritten. The presentation of chemical theory occupies nearly the first two-thirds of the text; descriptive chemistry, with emphasis on the structure and periodicity of the elements, follows the theoretical material. A single unit on organic chemistry appears near the middle of the text.

Significant changes in this edition of MODERN CHEMISTRY include a more detailed presentation of the use of significant figures together with a discussion of precision and accuracy; early introduction and continuous emphasis of the roles of energy and entropy changes in chemical reactions; development of the mole concept in Chapter 3, and continual use thereafter; detailed treatment of the concept of equilibrium at various points during the presentation of chemical theory and inclusion of solubility equilibria for the first time; an explanation of quantum numbers together with experimental evidence for the electron configurations of the atoms; use of the concepts of oxidation and reduction in terms of electron transfer throughout the text; elimination of descriptive chemistry of oxygen and hydrogen because this material now is presented in many high school science courses; expanded kinetic theory explanation of the properties of solids, liquids, and gases; adoption of modern U.S. thermochemical sign and notation conventions; treatment of organic chemistry in a single unit, with more detailed chapters on organic substitution compounds and natural organic compounds. New chapters on chemical kinetics and the descriptive chemistry of the elements of period three of the Periodic Table are included.

Many other significant changes have been made in the text at the suggestion of teachers and students who have used the previous edition, and from the authors' own teaching experience. The areas of introductory chemistry which the authors consider to be fundamental are treated in detail. However, no attempt has been made to produce a text which is encyclopedic in nature or which includes an unnecessary multiplicity of topics.

Teachers will find ample material in MODERN CHEMISTRY for an outstanding college-preparatory course, or for an introductory course at the junior-college level. For those students who do not plan to go beyond this course in science, there is sufficient elementary theory and interest-arousing descriptive material for a complete and thorough program. It has been the authors' purpose to include more material than can be covered in one year, thus permitting a wide choice of topics and allowing for selective emphasis. Teachers should feel free to choose those topics which best meet their needs. As a guide in the selection of material, some sections and paragraphs, and certain questions and problems, have been marked with the symbol (▶). These sections are intended only for the better students. The needs of the average student are amply provided for in the unmarked material which constitutes the major portion of the text.

Careful attention has been given to teaching and learning aids. The inductive approach, so helpful to teachers and students alike, has been used wherever possible. The language of chemistry has been made clear and meaningful. Chemical words and terms when first used in the text appear in *boldface italics*, and are defined and pronounced. In addition, an extensive *Glossary* appears at the back of the book and includes definitions of all words and terms presented in the text. The complete *Appendix*, also in the back of the book, contains tables of useful data.

The material for each chapter concludes with a *Review Outline; Questions* based on the text itself, graded according to difficulty in *Groups A* and *B;* and *Problems*, also graded in *Groups A* and *B.* The average student should master all the *Group A* questions and problems; the better student will be able to do both.

Because of their great learning value, line drawings are used extensively. The text is also illustrated with many fine photographs, chosen with great care for their teaching value.

The text was written by H. Clark Metcalfe and John E. Williams. Joseph F. Castka was mainly responsible for the preparation of all supplementary materials to accompany the text, including the Teacher's Guide, EXERCISES AND EXPERIMENTS IN CHEMISTRY, LABORATORY EXPERIMENTS IN CHEMISTRY, and TESTS and ALTERNATE TESTS IN CHEMISTRY.

The following teachers have been kind enough to read the entire manuscript or special parts of it, and have offered invaluable assistance by their helpful criticisms:

Dr. Morris Abramson, Flushing High School, Flushing, New York;

Dr. Jay Erickson, Associate Professor of Chemistry, Teachers College, Columbia University, New York City;

Mr. Edward Kassig, Chairman of the Science Department, Broad Ripple High School, Indianapolis, Indiana;

Dr. David A. Shirley, Department of Chemistry, University of Tennessee, Knoxville, Tennessee;

Mr. Richard Trump, Head of the Science Department, Ames High School, Ames, Iowa;

Mr. Robert Watson, Chemistry Coordinator, North Central High School, Indianapolis, Indiana

The authors also acknowledge with thanks the work of Felix Cooper, who prepared the text illustrations and Frances Orkin, who obtained the photographs.

CONTENTS

MODERN CHEMISTRY

Chapter One

THE SCIENCE OF CHEMISTRY

INTRODUCTION

1. Chemistry: a physical science. Man's nature is such that he seeks for order in his environment, and while seeking, invents and generalizes. Through the ages he has learned many things about himself and his environment. However, not until he started recording his discoveries and observations and communicating his ideas did modern science, as such, begin.

Early scientists began to organize and classify their information into areas of similarity from which they could derive broad generalizations and devise models of behavior. This organized knowledge has developed into the fundamental sciences with which we are familiar today. Each important discovery suggests new avenues of investigation. These lead to the expansion of scientific knowledge at an ever-increasing rate.

All the sciences may be grouped into two large divisions: the *biological sciences,* which are concerned with living things, their structure, life processes, and environment; and the *physical sciences,* which deal with the natural relationships about us. An understanding of basic concepts in the sciences helps us to recognize and appreciate the order in nature.

Chemistry is the science dealing with the structure and composition of materials and the changes in composition of these materials.

Physics is the science which is concerned primarily with the study of matter and energy. It seeks to explain the behavior and interrelationships of matter and energy in the universe.

Mathematics is the science of our number system. It gives us a means of expressing the relationships we observe in nature and of performing useful and necessary computations. Mathematics is often called the *language of the sciences.*

During the present century chemistry has played an important part in the study of the life sciences. As a result, there is an increasing merger of chemical research with the other sciences. Substantial knowledge of complex chemical structures has enabled chemists to make major contributions toward the ultimate understanding of life processes. This is the realm of *biochemistry*, a blend of biology and chemistry.

There are many important areas of modern scientific endeavor which stem from the fundamental sciences. Among these are *physical chemistry*, which combines the principles and techniques of physics and chemistry. *Biophysics* makes use of both biology and physics in the study of living things.

2. Keystones of modern chemistry. The initial concept of modern chemistry, that elements are the basic stuff of which all things are made, was under development in France at about the time of the American revolution. In 1778 **Antoine Lavoisier** (la-*vwah*-zee-ay) demonstrated that oxygen was the active fraction of the air involved in ordinary combustion processes. This set the stage for a better understanding of chemical changes and for a determined search for chemical elements. Through the efforts of a long line of investigators, some ninety elements were recognized. By 1920 most of these had been isolated and their properties studied.

Lavoisier was followed closely by **John Dalton** of England who, in 1808, conceived elements as consisting of chemically indivisible particles he called *atoms*. In 1811 the Italian physicist, **Amadeo Avogadro,** formulated some general laws describing the behavior of combined atoms, or *molecules*. Then in 1852, Great Britain's **Sir Edward Frankland** proposed the first useful explanation of the manner in which these atoms combined to form molecules. Chemistry was soon to be recognized as the architecture of molecules.

The first great chemical architect was **Friedrich Kekulé** of Germany. In 1858, he explained the formation of the carbon skeletons of long-chain and ring molecules of organic compounds. From this beginning chemists have continued to construct a great variety of useful molecules in the forms of drugs, dyes, explosives, fibers, plastics, and solvents.

The first Nobel Prize in chemistry was given to **Jacobus H. van't Hoff** of Hol-

1-1 Dr. Robert Woodward, is the brilliant architect of many of the most complex molecules yet synthesized. He was the 1965 recipient of the Nobel prize in chemistry for his synthesis of chlorophyll. A research project he now directs at Harvard University may lead to the laboratory production of vitamin B-12. (Harvard University)

land in 1901 for his pioneering work in developing the laws of reactions and solutions. Germany's **Emil Fischer** received the second Nobel Prize in chemistry in 1902 for his work on the structure of sugars and proteins. Sweden's **Svante Arrhenius,** about whom you will learn more in Unit 5, was awarded the third Nobel Prize in 1903 for his theory explaining the behavior of electrolytes in solution.

Later, in 1909, the Nobel Prize went to the German chemist **Wilhelm Ostwald** for his work in catalysis, a technique of tremendous importance in industrial chemistry. Ostwald is sometimes referred to as the father of physical chemistry. The Swiss chemist, **Alfred Werner,** received the Prize in 1913 for his studies of the structure of complex compounds. The first American chemist to win the Nobel Prize was **Theodore Richards.** He was selected in 1914 for his precise determination of atomic weights. In 1920 a German, **Walther Nernst,** was awarded the Nobel Prize for his discoveries in thermodynamics.

Marie Curie was awarded the Nobel Prize in 1911 for her discovery of the radioactive elements radium and polonium. This was probably the most important contribution to modern chemistry since Lavoisier introduced the modern concept of elements. No longer was the atom to be considered impregnable; here were atoms of elements which burst apart giving off tiny particles and high-energy radiations. Thus a chemist opened a whole new realm for exploration by physicists, the structure within the atom.

The list of Nobel Prizes, while not infallible, gives a rough indication of the creative effort in chemistry being put forth by scientists of the various nations of the world. Up to the end of World War II only three American chemists had been awarded this prize. Seventeen German, six British, and six French chemists had been selected also. In eighteen years following World War II, however, nine Americans became Nobel Prize winners in chemistry. Meanwhile seven British chemists, four German, one French, and one Russian were so recognized.

3. Methods of science. In some instances, important scientific discoveries have come about quite by accident. In others, they have been the result of brilliant new ideas. However, most of our scientific knowledge is the result of carefully planned investigations carried on by trained scientists. Their techniques, known as *scientific methods,* are simply *logical approaches to the solution of problems which lend themselves to investigation.* Scientific methods require strict honesty, the ability to withhold a decision until all the evidence is in, and the desire for truth.

Scientists believe without question in the orderliness in nature—that everything in the universe behaves in an orderly way, and that man can discover and understand natural rules of behavior. Chemists, like other scientists, strive to explain a large number of related observations in terms of *broad principles* or *generalizations.* All basic scientific research is devoted to the discovery of these principles. *The generalizations which describe behavior in nature are called **laws** or **principles.*** Natural laws tell us what relations do occur in nature; they *do not* tell us what relations *must* occur. The laws of science may be expressed by concise statements or by means of mathematical formulas.

One of the distinguishing qualities of man is his curiosity. This causes him to ask two important questions: *"what?"* and *"why?"* When a scientist observes an event or situation in nature, called a *phenomenon,* he seeks the answers to these questions by carrying out systematic, disciplined, and persistent investigations.

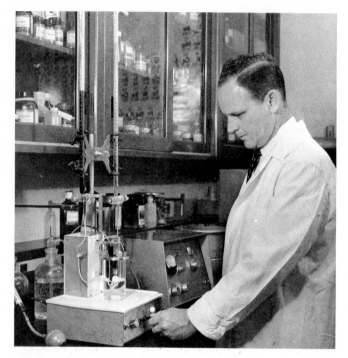

1-2   Chemistry is an experimental science. (Fisher Scientific Company)

We usually recognize four distinct phases in the application of scientific methods: *observing, generalizing, theorizing,* and *testing.*

1. Observing. The scientist accumulates as much reliable data as possible about an observed phenomenon, his initial interest being in *what* actually occurs. These data may come from direct observations, from a search of scientific literature for information previously reported, and from well-planned and skillfully executed experiments.

Observations are of little value unless they are made carefully and skillfully. Chemists know that observing is most productive when the conditions which affect the observations are brought under their control. Thus, observing is generally done in the *laboratory* where conditions can be controlled at the discretion of the observer. *A sequence of observations carried out under controlled conditions is called an **experiment.*** Experimentation provides the foun-

dation upon which modern science is built.

2. Generalizing. The scientist organizes the accumulated data and looks for relations between them. Relations that he discovers may enable him to formulate a broad generalization describing what does occur. When well established by abundant supporting data, this generalization may be recognized as a new law or principle which states what the behavior is.

3. Theorizing. When the scientist knows what occurs he is ready to move on to the more stimulating task of determining *why* the phenomenon occurs. A creative imagination may enable him to develop a plausible explanation and to construct a simple physical or mental model which will relate the observed behavior to familiar and well-understood phenomena. *A plausible explanation of an observed natural phenomenon in terms of a simple model which has familiar properties is called a **theory.***

4. Testing. Once a seemingly satisfactory theory is developed, it must be tested and retested to establish its validity. In fact, the scientist continually tests observational and experimental data and predictions based on known principles by subjecting them to new and ingenious experiments. A theory is retained only so long as it is useful. It may be discarded or modified as a result of new experimentation. A theory that stands up under scientific testing is a valuable asset to scientists because it stimulates the imagination and serves as a basis for predicting behavior not previously investigated. This is the heart of the scientific method and the real stimulus for the tremendous growth of science.

The principles of chemistry are studied most effectively and understood most easily when the laws and experimental evidence making up a body of related knowledge are brought together to form a general theory concerning the behavior of matter. In this way the term "theory"

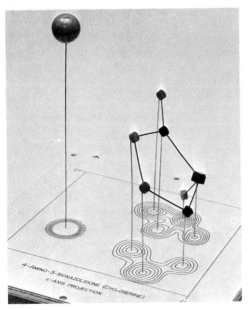

1-3 A physical model is often used by chemists to help them understand the behavior of matter. (Ray Pepinsky, Crystal Research Laboratory)

is often used by chemists in a broad sense. Some examples of chemical theories which you will soon study in this sense are the *kinetic theory*, the *atomic theory*, and the *theory of ionization*.

MATTER AND ENERGY

4. Concept of matter. All materials about us consist of matter. With our senses—sight, touch, taste, and smell—we recognize various kinds of matter. This book, your desk, the air you breathe, the water you drink are examples of matter. Some kinds of matter are easily observed. A stone or a piece of wood may be seen and held in the hand. Other kinds of matter are recognized less readily, such as the air or even water in a quiet pool. However, we ride on compressed air in automobile tires. We know of the tremendous damage which can be caused by rapidly moving air.

We say that *matter is anything which occupies space and has mass*. Matter possesses *inertia*, a resistance to change of position or motion. The concept of inertia as a property of matter is quite important in the study of physics and chemistry. Imagine a basketball being used in a bowling alley as a substitute for a bowling ball. The effect on the pins would not be the same at all. Although they are approximately the same size, the bowling ball contains more matter than the basketball. Its inertia is correspondingly higher and thus its tendency to remain in motion, once set in motion, is greater.

Matter may be acted on by *forces* which may set it in motion, or change its motion. While all these statements are descriptive of matter, they do not provide us with a completely satisfactory definition. Scientists, with their great knowledge of the properties and behavior of matter, are not able to define it precisely.

1-4 A new product of chemical research being checked for uniformity of texture, color, and thickness. (E. I. duPont de Nemours & Co.)

5. Mass and weight. *The quantity of matter which a body possesses is known as its* **mass.** If we try to move an object which is at rest, we notice that it resists our effort. If we try to stop the object once it is moving, we notice that it resists this effort also. Its mass is the measure of this resistance to change of position or motion. Thus *mass is the measure of the inertia of the body* and is responsible for it.

Mass is also responsible for the *weight* of the body. **Weight** *is the measure of the earth's attraction for a body.* If we were to attach an object to a spring balance we would find that it weighs less at high altitudes than it does on the surface of the earth. On the other hand, its mass remains unchanged; *the mass of a body is constant.*

Mass is usually measured by comparison with known masses (see Fig. 1-5). If the masses of two bodies are the same they will have equal weights while in the same location. Thus the mass of a body, when determined by "weighing" it on a platform balance, is sometimes incorrectly referred to as its "weight." This practice is common throughout chemistry and should not be confusing if the meanings of the terms *mass* and *weight* are understood. Chemists are primarily concerned with measurements of mass, and we shall use the term *mass* in its proper meaning.

6. Density of matter varies. Matter occupies space and therefore has volume. From our everyday experiences we recognize that materials have different masses. We say that lead is heavy and that cork is light. This has little meaning unless we have in mind equal volumes of lead and cork. *The mass of a unit volume of a material is called its* **density,** which is expressed by the equation

$$D = \frac{m}{V}$$

where m is the mass of a material and V is its volume, D is its density. The basic unit of mass in chemistry is the *gram* (g) and of volume is the *cubic centimeter* (cm³). Thus, density may have the dimensions g/cm³. By comparing the masses of equal volumes of materials we are able to see that the density of different kinds of matter varies. Thus one cubic centimeter of lead, having a mass of 11.34 grams, is nearly 50 times more dense than one cubic centimeter of cork having a mass of 0.24 gram (see Fig. 1-6).

$$D_{lead} = \frac{m}{V} = \frac{11.34 \text{ g}}{cm^3}$$

$$D_{cork} = \frac{m}{V} = \frac{0.24 \text{ g}}{cm^3}$$

7.   Three states of matter.   We call a block of ice a solid. It may melt and form a liquid. As it evaporates, liquid water changes into a vapor or gas. Iron, too, is a solid but it may be melted and converted into a liquid. When iron is boiled, it forms iron vapor. Materials exist either in the *solid, liquid,* or *gaseous* state and may undergo a change from one state to another under suitable conditions.

A block of wood placed on a table keeps its shape and its volume. To change its shape or its volume you would have to use considerable external force on the block. A solid does not need lateral (side) support to prevent it from losing its shape. *Solids have both a definite volume and a definite shape.*

Suppose we pour water on top of a table. The water is not rigid; it flows out over the surface. A liquid must have lateral support to retain its shape. For that reason a liquid takes the shape of its container. We find, however, that a liquid has a definite volume if we try to put a quart of milk into a pint bottle. Therefore we conclude that *liquids have a definite volume, and that they take the shape of their containers.*

If we inflate an automobile tire, we find

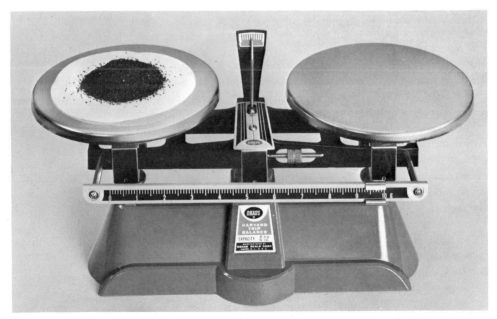

1-5   The combined mass of the materials on the left pan is 9.7 grams because they counter-balance this known mass indicated by the slider position on the beam. (Ohaus Scale Corp.)

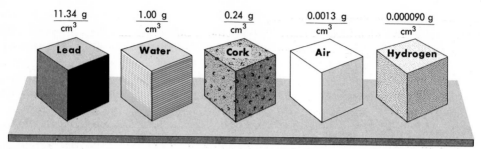

$\dfrac{11.34\ g}{cm^3}$	$\dfrac{1.00\ g}{cm^3}$	$\dfrac{0.24\ g}{cm^3}$	$\dfrac{0.0013\ g}{cm^3}$	$\dfrac{0.000090\ g}{cm^3}$
Lead	Water	Cork	Air	Hydrogen

1-6 Equal volumes of different materials do not necessarily have the same mass.

that the air takes the shape of the tire, which is its container. The tire is really full of air, but if a blow-out occurs, the escaping air expands in volume. A pint of liquid does not expand and form a quart if it is put into a quart bottle. However, a pint of air would expand and occupy all that space if it were placed in a really empty quart bottle. *Gases have neither a definite volume nor a definite shape.* This makes it difficult to measure the volume of gases. If they are warmed, they expand decidedly, but their volume is reduced when the pressure on them is increased. In measuring gas volumes, we must specify *both the temperature and the pressure* to which they are subjected.

Both liquids and gases are known as *fluids.* These are materials that flow readily and require vessels to contain them. We think of solids as being rigid, yet none is perfectly rigid. Butter, for example, may not be very solid on a warm summer day. Similarly, there are no perfectly fluid materials. Molasses, water, and carbon dioxide may be observed to flow, but certainly at different rates.

Liquids, having a definite volume, can have a free surface; that is, a surface unbounded by the container. Thus water may be contained in an open vessel. The free (upper) surface of a liquid lies in a plane perpendicular to the force acting on it. In the normal case of a liquid at rest, this force is gravity and the free sur-

face of the liquid lies in the horizontal plane. For ordinary purposes, matter in the gaseous state must be bounded on all sides by a container. Gases are fluids which do not have a free surface.

Fluids which cannot exist as liquids having a free surface at ordinary conditions of temperature and pressure are correctly termed *gases.* *Vapor is the term used for the gaseous state of fluids which exist as liquids under normal conditions.* Thus we speak of water *vapor* and oxygen *gas.*

The structure of a solid is generally well ordered. The particles of the material are closely packed and rigidly bound into fixed positions to give it its size and shape. The particles of a liquid are also closely packed (when a solid melts its volume changes very little), but they are not bound to fixed positions. A liquid has fluidity; its structure is less orderly than that of a solid and is without shape. The particles of a gas are widely dispersed in a completely random, disorganized fashion.

8. Properties of matter. We are able to identify matter and determine its usefulness by studying its properties. Chemists are concerned with the materials that compose matter. Many liquids, including water, are colorless. Some colorless liquids have distinctive odors; water is odorless. Water freezes at 0° Celsius, boils at 100° Celsius (at standard pressure), and has a density of 1 gram per cubic centimeter at 4° Celsius. Since no other liquid exhibits exactly these same characteristics, liquid water is easily identified. *Properties of matter useful in identifying it are called* **specific** *(or* *characteristic)* **properties.** The most useful specific properties are those that lend themselves to quantitative measurements and can be expressed as a number of units. The specific properties of materials may be organized under two general headings: *physical*, and *chemical*.

Physical properties include *color, odor, solubility, density, hardness, melting* and *boiling points*, and *crystalline* or *amorphous forms*. These physical properties do not apply equally to all states of matter. For example, hardness and crystalline form are not properties of fluids. Similarly, odor is of little value in describing many solids. **Physical properties** *are those which can be determined without causing a change in the identity of a material.*

Under chemical properties we include *chemical activity*, or behavior with other materials. Some materials are *active*, reacting vigorously with others. Some other materials are *inactive*. These inactive materials do react, but not very readily, with others. Still other materials are said to be *inert*. These do not react under ordinary conditions of chemical reactions. In our study of chemical properties, we shall be interested to know whether a material burns. We shall also inquire how it reacts with air, with water, with acids, and with alkalies. **Chemical properties** *are those which pertain to the behavior of a material in changes in which its identity is altered.*

9. Concept of energy. We find much the same difficulty in defining energy as we did in defining matter. Scientists know a great deal about energy and how it may be used but they cannot define it precisely. **Energy** *is usually defined as the capacity for doing work.* It is associated with matter but is not a form of matter. We have no knowledge of matter which does not possess energy.

10. Forms of energy. Our most common forms of energy are *mechanical energy* and *heat energy*. Mechanical energy may be of two types: **potential energy** *or the energy of position,* and **kinetic energy** *or*

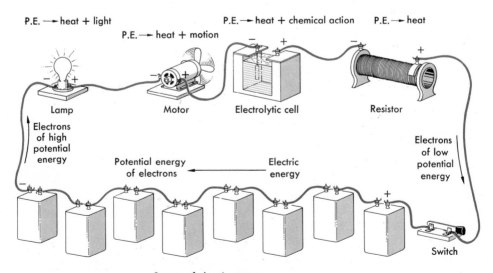

Source of electric energy

1-7   Energy transformation

the energy of motion. Thus water held behind a dam has potential energy due to its elevated position. As the water is released from the dam it acquires kinetic energy due to its motion. Heat energy is released whenever fuels are burned. Practically all our industrial power is provided by heat energy from burning fuel and from the kinetic energy of falling water.

Other forms of energy are *electric energy*, *chemical energy*, *radiant energy*, and *nuclear energy*. Chemical energy is a basic concern of chemistry. Radio waves, infrared and ultraviolet radiations, visible light, X rays, and gamma rays are examples of radiant energy. Nuclear energy is being developed as a source of industrial power.

We may convert or *transform* one form of energy into another. As an example, we may burn coal to produce energy. Some of the chemical energy of the coal and the oxygen of the air is released as heat during the burning action. The heat energy may be transferred to water so that it is converted to steam. The steam can then drive a turbine to produce mechanical energy. A dynamo may be turned to generate electric energy. This may then be transformed into heat and radiant (light) energy in an incandescent lamp or carbon arc. It may also be transformed into mechanical energy in an electric motor which drives a clock or a locomotive. It is the transformation of energy that is usually observed. Our means of measuring energy is to measure the *energy change* during an energy transformation.

11. Conservation of matter and energy. About 54 years ago Albert Einstein (1879–1955) suggested that matter and energy are related. This relationship is shown by his famous equation $E = mc^2$. E represents the amount of energy, m the amount of matter, and c is a constant equal to the velocity of light. Many experiments during the last 35 years have estab-

1-8 The Law of Conservation of Matter and Energy is demonstrated in the explosion of this nuclear device at a Nevada test site. (Lookout Mountain Laboratory, USAF)

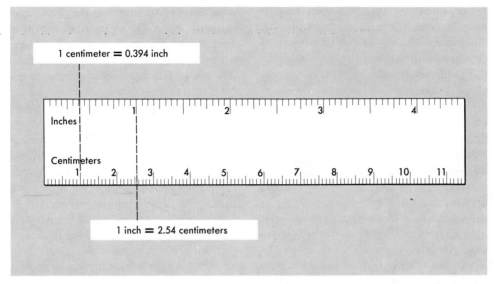

1 centimeter = 0.394 inch

Inches

Centimeters

1 inch = 2.54 centimeters

1-9   The centimeter is nearly 0.4 of an inch in length.   One inch equals 2.54 centimeters.

lished the truth of this relationship.

Matter can be converted to energy and energy to matter. The conversion factor, c^2, is involved in both transformations. Indeed, the amount of matter is changed if the amount of energy is changed. Thus matter and energy are not two different physical quantities, which we can define independently. Instead, *they may be considered to be two different forms of the same physical quantity.* The facts are formulated into a law of science known as the ***Law of Conservation of Matter and Energy.*** This law may be stated formally: *matter and energy are interchangeable; and the total matter and energy in the universe is constant.*

Chemical reactions are always accompanied by an energy change. Either energy is released or it is acquired. Only in nuclear reactions involving a tremendous quantity of energy, such as the explosion of a hydrogen bomb, does the amount of matter transformed into energy become significant. Ordinary chemical reactions involve such small matter changes that they go undetected. For all ordinary purposes such matter losses may be ignored. We may then recognize the following generalization: *in an ordinary chemical change, the total mass of the reacting materials is equal to the total mass of the products.* It follows that, in such changes, *energy is conserved.*

MEASUREMENTS IN CHEMISTRY

12.   Metric system.   The study of science could not be precise without a suitable system of measurement. The English system, which we use in our daily activities, presents many disadvantages in scientific measurements. It is a system which, in a sense, just grew up. Its chief disadvantage is that there are no simple numerical relationships between the different units.

The *metric system*, with which you may already be familiar, was developed in France near the end of the eighteenth century. It is used in scientific work throughout the world and is in general use in practically all countries except the United

States, Great Britain, and other English-speaking countries. Certain industries in the United States, particularly pharmaceutical manufacturers, are now adopting the metric system for general use. *It is a decimal system that has simple numerical relationships between units.* The disadvantage in its everyday usage is that the basic units do not have the practical magnitudes of those of the English system. Also, they do not lend themselves to the convenient custom of reducing by halves, quarters, eighths, sixteenths, etc.

13. Units of the metric system. The metric system includes measures of *length, capacity,* and *mass.* The basic unit of length is the *meter* (m), of capacity is the *liter* (l), and of mass is the *gram* (g). Prefixes are used with these units to complete the system. Latin prefixes are employed to identify *descending* multiple values. These are *deci-* (0.1), *centi-* (0.01), and *milli-* (0.001). Greek prefixes are used to identify *ascending* multiple values: *deka-* (10), *hecto-* (100), and *kilo-* (1000). The prefixes shown in the brief table of metric equivalents will be used throughout your study of chemistry. It will be helpful to memorize them.

BRIEF TABLE OF METRIC EQUIVALENTS

Length

10 millimeters (mm)	= 1 centimeter (cm)
100 centimeters	= 1 meter (m)
1000 meters	= 1 kilometer (km)

Capacity

1000 milliliters (ml)	= 1 liter (l)
1000 liters	= 1 kiloliter (kl)

Mass

1000 milligrams (mg)	= 1 gram (g)
1000 grams	= 1 kilogram (kg)

As originally conceived, the metric system was to be based on natural standards with the meter as the fundamental unit. The originators of the metric system in-tended that the meter should be one-millionth of the north polar quadrant of the Paris meridian. However, they found later that they could compare two meter bars with each other with greater precision than they could relate them to the earth's quadrant. Accordingly, *the standard meter is commonly defined as the distance between two parallel lines engraved on a platinum-iridium bar preserved at the International Bureau of Weights and Measures near Paris.*

The standard-meter bar is a physical instrument. If it should be damaged, lost, or destroyed, there would be no primary standard of this fundamental metric unit. Accordingly, the International Conference on Weights and Measures has defined a *nondestructible* standard meter which any laboratory that has the proper equipment can reproduce as a primary standard. By this new definition, the meter is described in terms of the orange-red spectral line of light emitted from excited atoms of an isotope of krypton (krypton-86). The meter is 1,650,763.73 times the wavelength of this line.

The meter is slightly longer than the English yard, being equal to 39.37 inches or 3.28 feet. One inch is 2.54 centimeters. This is now a defined relationship, being taken as 2.540000000 centimeters per inch.

One gram was intended to be the mass of 1 cubic centimeter (cm^3) of water at 4° C, the temperature at which it is most dense. Again it was found that the masses of two metal kilogram cylinders could be compared with each other more precisely than either cylinder could be related to the mass of 1000 cubic centimeters of water. *The gram is now defined as one thousandth of the mass of the standard kilogram resting in the International Bureau of Weights and Measures.* The gram is a small unit equal to 0.035 ounce. One pound is approximately 454 grams; one kilogram is approximately 2.2 pounds.

1-10   Some comparisons between the English and metric systems. The liter is slightly larger than the U.S. liquid quart, and the kilogram is more than twice as heavy as the avoirdupois pound.

*The **liter** is a special name for a cubic decimeter.* Since a cubic decimeter is equal to 1000 cm³, a container having a capacity of 1 liter holds 1000 cubic centimeters of liquid when full. One milliliter (1 ml) is then equivalent to one cubic centimeter (1 cm³). Because the volumes of liquids and gases are commonly measured in flasks and other containers graduated in capacity units, their measured volumes are most conveniently expressed in milliliter, liter, and kiloliter (capacity) units. This is a standard practice in chemistry and will be followed generally in this book.

Since water is a universal standard, the remarkable simplicity of the metric system can be seen in the following table.

VØLUME–MASS RELATIONS

> **1 liter of water has 1000 cm³ volume and a mass of 1 kg**
>
> **1 ml of water has 1 cm³ volume and a mass of 1 g**

Density is a measurable property of matter which we can employ to illustrate the use of metric units. It has been defined in Section 6 as the *mass per unit volume* of a material. If mass is measured in *gram* units and volume in *cubic centimeter* units, density is expressed in *grams per cubic centimeter* (g/cm³).

Suppose the mass of one cubic centimeter of lead is determined to be 11.34 grams. Then the mass of *the same volume* of cork is found to be 0.24 gram. Since these measurements of mass involve equal volumes of the two materials, we can compare their *densities*. Thus, lead is nearly 50 times more dense than cork.

$$D_{lead} = \frac{m}{V} = \frac{13.34 \text{ g}}{cm^3}$$

$$D_{cork} = \frac{m}{V} = \frac{0.24 \text{ g}}{cm^3}$$

Matter in the gaseous state has a very low density compared to solids and liquids. Consequently, expressions of density in grams per cubic centimeter would involve inconveniently small numbers in the case of gases. Chemists prefer to state the densities of gases in *grams per liter*. For example, under standard conditions of temperature and pressure, oxygen gas has a density of 1.43 g/l and air (a mixture of gases) has an average density of 1.29 g/l.

$$D_{oxygen} = \frac{m}{V} = \frac{1.43 \text{ g}}{1}$$

$$D_{air} = \frac{m}{V} = \frac{1.29 \text{ g}}{1}$$

The unit structure of a measured quantity indicates its *dimensions*. Thus, density has the dimensions "g/cm³" when expressed as a property of a solid or liquid. It has the dimensions "g/l" when expressed as a property of a gas.

14.   Temperature and heat.   Temperature and heat are different, but related, physical quantities. It is important that the subtle distinction between them be understood. Just as we might push an object to estimate its mass or lift it to estimate its weight, we may touch an object to determine its *hotness* or *coldness* and describe the sensation with a term such as hot, warm, tepid, cool, or cold. Thus our sense perceptions of hotness and coldness are used to assign a property called *temperature* to the object.

Our temperature sense, while generally useful, may be quite unreliable under some conditions. If the hand is held in cold water and then placed in tepid water, the tepid water will feel warm. However, if the hand had been in hot water, the tepid water would feel cool.

This suggests that the temperature sensation depends on the transfer of heat energy to the hand or away from it. If a system, a body of matter, has a higher temperature than its surroundings, energy flows away from the system. If the temperature of the system is lower than its surroundings, energy flows to the system. This energy, *while in transit*, is called *heat*. *Heat is the energy transferred between two systems that is associated exclusively with the difference in temperature between the systems. The temperature of a system is a measure of its ability to transfer heat to, or acquire heat from, other systems.*

When two systems with different temperatures are in contact, heat energy will flow from one to the other. *Temperature* is the property that determines the direction of the heat transfer. The warmer system

cools as it gives up heat and the cooler system warms as it acquires heat (assuming that neither system experiences a change of state). As the temperatures of the two systems become equal no further transfer of heat occurs and they are said to be in *thermal (heat) equilibrium*. It follows that *systems in thermal equilibrium have the same temperature.*

Heat and temperature are different physical quantities that can be sensed qualitatively. However, to determine them quantitatively we must perform operations which involve measurable quantities and are independent of our sense perceptions. Heat is measured as a *quantity of energy*, whereas temperature indicates the heat intensity of a body of matter. A burning match and a camp fire might be at the same temperature but the quantities of heat given up are quite different.

15.   Measuring temperature.   A number of properties of matter vary with temperature and can be used in the measurement of temperature. For example, most materials expand when they are warmed and contract when cooled. Our most familiar temperature-measuring instrument, the mercury thermometer, is based on the nearly linear expansion and contraction of liquid mercury with changing temperature.

In the construction of a thermometer, both a temperature scale and a method of calibrating the thermometer in terms of this scale must be specified. Mercury thermometers for scientific use are commonly calibrated in the **Celsius** temperature scale (formerly called the centigrade scale). This scale was devised by a Swedish astronomer, Anders Celsius (1701–1744). He established his scale by defining two *fixed points:* the normal freezing point of water, the *ice point*, as **0 degrees** (0° C) and the normal boiling point of water, the *steam point*, as **100 degrees** (100° C).

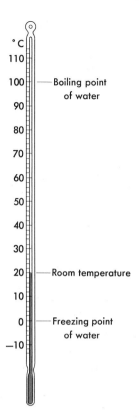

°C
110
100 ——Boiling point
         of water
90
80
70
60
50
40
30
20 ——Room temperature
10
0 ——Freezing point
        of water
—10

1-11 The Celsius thermometer is widely used in scientific work. Compare the temperatures shown here with those on the common Fahrenheit thermometer.

The interval between the ice point and the steam point is divided into 100 equal parts, each representing a temperature change of 1 C°. The same scale divisions may be extended beyond the two fixed points to provide for temperature readings below 0° and above 100°. See Fig. 1-11.

In modern thermometry only one fixed point is defined as a standard for setting up a temperature scale. It is the *triple point of water*, a single condition of temperature and pressure at which the solid, liquid, and gaseous states of water can exist simultaneously (in equilibrium). The temperature of the triple point of water on the Celsius scale is 0.01° C. We will discuss the construction of an *absolute* tem-

perature scale from the standard fixed point in our study of gases, Chapter 9.

16. Measuring heat. Heat causes an increase in the temperature of matter to which it is added and a decrease in the temperature of matter from which it is removed, providing the process is not accompanied by a change of state. The experimental determination of a number of properties of matter, called *thermal properties*, requires the measurement of quantities of heat. Among these properties are heat capacity, heat of fusion, heat of vaporization, heat of combustion, heat of reaction, heat of formation, and heat of solution. The measurement of thermal properties is called *calorimetry*.

The basic unit commonly used by chemists to measure quantities of heat energy is the *calorie*. *The **calorie** is traditionally defined as the quantity of heat required to raise the temperature of 1 gram of water through 1 Celsius degree.* However, the equivalence of heat and work as two forms of energy is now definitely established. Today, because the heat required to raise the temperature of 1 gram of water through 1 Celsius degree varies slightly with the temperature of the water, the calorie is defined more precisely in terms of a work unit, the *joule*.

1 calorie = 4.1840 joules

The calorie is a very small unit of heat and is sometimes inconvenient to use. A larger unit, the *kilocalorie* (1000 calories) is often used. *The **kilocalorie** (kcal) is the quantity of heat required to raise the temperature of 1 kilogram of water through 1 Celsius degree.*

1 kcal = 10^3 cal
1 kcal = 4.18 × 10^3 joules

The kilocalorie is the large Calorie used in dietetics.

▶ **17. Uncertainty in measurements.** Chemistry is an experimental science. The measurement of numerous physical quantities such as length, mass, volume, and temperature is an important part of the experimental process. *Unfortunately the measurement of any physical quantity is subject to some uncertainty.* If a measurement is to have much worth, some idea regarding its *reliability* is essential. To this end, the complete expression of a measured quantity must include the number, the units, and some indication of how reliable the number is.

Contributions to the uncertainty in measurements fall into two general categories: *limitations in accuracy* and *limitations in precision.* The dictionary assigns about the same meaning to the terms *accuracy* and *precision.* However, with reference to measurement data, each has a meaning that is quite distinct. It is essential that this distinction be clearly recognized.

Accuracy denotes the nearness of a measurement to its accepted value. It refers to the correctness of measurement data. Accuracy is expressed in terms of *error.* Such errors may be *absolute* or *relative.*

An *absolute error* can be expressed by

$$E_a = O - A$$

where the absolute error E_a is the difference between the observed value O and the accepted value A. In quantitative laboratory experiments we shall refer to absolute errors as *experimental errors.*

In one such experiment you will decompose a measured quantity of potassium chlorate to determine the percentage of oxygen in the substance. Suppose your experimental result is 38.02% oxygen. The accepted value is known to be 39.16%. Thus your experimental (absolute) error is

$$E_a = 38.02\% - 39.16\% = -1.14\%$$

The sign of the error may be retained if you wish to indicate whether the result is low or high. Observe that the dimensions of absolute errors are those of the observed and accepted values. If O and A are expressed in grams, degrees Celsius, or milliliters, then E_a will have grams, Celsius degrees, or milliliters as its dimension.

A *relative error* is a more generally useful quantity than an absolute error. This is commonly expressed as a percentage, the accepted value being used as the basis for comparison. In experimentation, relative errors are often referred to as *percentage errors.* The relative error E_r is calculated as follows:

$$E_r = \frac{E_a}{A} \times 100\%$$

Consider again the data from which we determined the absolute error. The percentage (relative) error is

$$E_r = \frac{38.02\% - 39.16\%}{39.16\%} \times 100\%$$

$$E_r = \frac{-1.14\%}{39.16\%} \times 100\% = -2.91\%$$

As in the case of absolute errors, the sign of the relative error merely indicates whether the result is low or high.

Observe that the true or accepted value of a measured quantity is used to determine both the absolute error and the relative error. Thus, the accuracy of a measurement can be determined only if the accepted value of that measurement is available.

Precision is the agreement between the numerical values of two or more measurements that have been made in the same way. Precision refers to the reproducibility of measurement data or the degree of detail—that is, the ± uncertainty—involved. It conveys nothing about accuracy. Precision is expressed in terms of *deviation.* We will consider two simple forms of deviation, *absolute* and *relative*.

An *absolute deviation* D_a is the difference between an observed value O and the arithmetic mean (average) M for the set of several identical measurements.

$$D_a = O - M$$

In an experiment similar to the one described previously, suppose three identical samples of potassium chlorate are decomposed and the mass of oxygen determined to be 3.87 g, 3.95 g, and 3.89 g for the set. On the assumption that there is an equal chance for the individual values to be high and low, we will take the average for the set as the "best" value. This is found to be 3.90 g.

The deviations of the individual values *from this average* can be calculated from the expression for D_a given above. The average of these deviations provides us with a measure of the precision of the experiment. These results are presented in the following table. Observe that we do not take into account the sign of the individual deviation since we are concerned only with its absolute magnitude.

AVERAGE DEVIATION OF A SET OF MEASUREMENTS

Sample	Mass of Oxygen	Deviation
1	3.87 g	0.03 g
2	3.95 g	0.05 g
3	3.89 g	0.01 g
Average	3.90 g	0.03 g

The uncertainty in the measurements data is ±0.03 g and the mass of oxygen derived from the set of experimental data can be expressed as 3.90 ± 0.03 g.

A *relative deviation* D_r may also be used to express the precision of the set of experimental data. This is calculated as a *percentage average deviation* based on the average value M for the set.

$$D_r = \frac{D_{a(\text{ave})}}{M} \times 100\%$$

$$D_r = \frac{0.03 \text{ g}}{3.90 \text{ g}} \times 100\% = 0.8\%$$

The uncertainty can now be expressed as ±0.8% and the mass of oxygen may be recorded as 3.90 g ± 0.8%. Uncertainties in measured quantities of different magnitudes can be compared more clearly when expressed as relative rather than absolute deviations.

If several different measurements are combined to yield a final result, the manner in which the individual deviations affect the result depends on the nature of the computation. When measured quantities are added or subtracted, the uncertainty in the result is the sum of the *absolute* deviations of the individual measurements. In multiplication and division, the uncertainty in the result is the sum of the *relative* deviations of the individual measurements.

The reproducibility of a measurement would not ordinarily be expected to exceed the tolerance of the instrument used. Tolerances of laboratory instruments are generally known and can serve to indicate the precision obtainable with these instru-

1-12 An equal-arm platform balance for ordinary use in the laboratory. Its sensitivity is 0.1 gram. (Ohaus Scale Corp.)

ments. Of course this assumes that the device is used properly and gross human errors are not included in the measurement. A list of common laboratory instruments is given in the following table together with typical tolerances shown as ± uncertainties.

TYPICAL UNCERTAINTIES

INSTRUMENT	UNCERTAINTY
Platform balance	±0.1 g
Centigram balance	±0.01 g
50 ml buret	±0.10 ml
50 ml gas measuring tube	±0.10 ml
10 ml graduated cylinder	±0.1 ml
50 ml graduated cylinder	±0.4 ml
5 ml pipet	±0.01 ml
10 ml pipet	±0.02 ml
15 cm ruler (grad. in mm)	±0.01 cm
− 1 to 101° C thermometer	±0.1 C°
100 ml volumetric flask	±0.08 ml
250 ml volumetric flask	±0.12 ml
1000 ml volumetric flask	±0.30 ml

18. Significant figures. Suppose the mass of a sample measured on a platform balance is determined to be 25.2 g. The balance is precise to the nearest 0.1 g so the precision of the measurement may be shown by recording the mass as 25.2 ± 0.1 g. The deviation of ±0.1 g indicates that the digit in the first decimal place of the measurement is subject to uncertainty; those to the left of it are certain.

As a matter of convenience, the ±0.1 is often omitted with the understanding that there is uncertainty in the last digit of the measurement. The recorded value, 25.2 g, then consists entirely of figures that have physical significance—that is, *significant figures*. *Significant figures in a number comprise all digits known with certainty plus the first digit that is uncertain.* The position of the decimal point is irrelevant.

The method of significant figures provides us with a third way to indicate the precision of a measurement. It is less informative than our previous methods in which ± uncertainties are shown as either

absolute or relative deviations, to the extent that the uncertainty of the last digit is not specified. However, the method of significant figures is more convenient and more widely used. It is satisfactory for our purposes in chemistry and is the method we shall use.

In the absence of any qualifying information about a measuring instrument, such as its tolerance, we may assume that the last digit (the uncertain digit) of a measurement is known to within plus or minus one unit. For example, the value for π expressed to three significant figures is *3.14*. The digit in the second decimal place is uncertain. We infer that the true value lies somewhere between *3.13* and *3.15*.

We have seen how the precision of the average value for a set of measurements can be expressed in terms of average deviation (Section 17). The average deviation

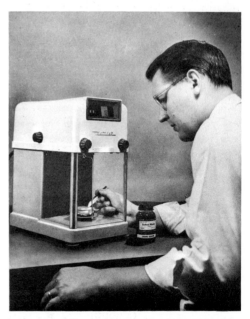

1-13 A modern analytical balance which provides high precision and rapid readout. Its sensitivity may be 0.0001 gram. (Fisher Scientific Company)

also reveals the number of digits we are entitled to include in the average value of the set when its precision is denoted by the method of significant figures.

To illustrate this, we will assume that a set of measurements includes the following individual values: 36.64 g, 36.55 g, 36.62 g, and 36.41 g. The average for the set appears to be 36.555 g. The average deviation of the individual values from this mean value is ±0.075 g. Clearly, the digit in the second decimal place of the mean is subject to uncertainty. If we are uncertain about the value in the second decimal place, we can have no notion whatsoever about values in succeeding decimal places. Therefore, we are forced to round off the average value to the second decimal place. Will this be 36.55 g or 36.56 g? A good rule to follow here is: *always round to the nearest even number.* Thus 36.56 g is the "best" value for the set. The last digit has uncertainty and limits the precision of the value to four significant figures.

Suppose you wish to determine the volume of a metal block. Your measuring instrument is a meter stick having 1 mm divisions. You find the sides to be 3.54 cm, 4.85 cm, and 5.42 cm, estimating the value of the last digit in each case. You may be reasonably sure of these measurements. However, you can have no idea of the digit which should occupy the next decimal place. Each measurement thus consists of two *certain figures* and one *doubtful figure,* or three *significant figures.* The area of one surface is

3.54 cm $\times$ 4.85 cm = 17.**1690** cm²

Recognizing that the product of anything multiplied by a doubtful figure is also doubtful, and that only one such figure may be carried, the result is rounded to 17.**2** cm².

The volume of the block then becomes

17.**2** cm² $\times$ 5.42 cm = 93.**224** cm³

Again the result is properly expressed as 93.**2** cm³, the volume of the metal block. Had all of the doubtful figures been retained throughout the computation, the volume would be expressed as 93.**055980** cm³. Obviously this precision, millionths of a cubic centimeter, cannot be obtained with a meter stick graduated in tenths of a centimeter. *Merely assuming more decimal places does not improve the accuracy or the precision of the measurement.*

In the measurements and computations given, the number of significant figures is easily recognized since all figures used are nonzero digits. It is not so easy to determine when the zeros in an expression are significant. For example, the mean distance to the moon is known to six significant figures to be 238,854 mi. This distance is more commonly expressed as 239,000 mi, being precise to *three* significant figures. The three zeros which follow the 9 merely serve to locate the (understood) decimal point. Similarly, a measured length of 0.00531 cm is precise to *three* significant figures, the zeros being used to locate the decimal point. However, the measurements 104.06 m and 100.60 m contain *five* significant figures. The question naturally arises: when are zeros significant?

Of course, the person who reads an instrument while making a measurement knows whether a zero appearing in his expression is significant. However he must follow accepted rules concerning significant figures if he is to communicate the information properly to others who may use the data. In order to overcome the difficulties of communication where zeros are included in the expression of a measured quantity, the following rules for determining the number of significant figures have been established and will be used throughout this book:

1. All nonzero digits **are** *significant:* 127.34 g contains *five* significant figures.

2. All zeros between two nonzero digits **are** *significant:* 120.007 m contains *six* significant figures.

3. Unless specifically indicated by the context to be significant, *all zeros to the left of an understood decimal point but to the right of a nonzero digit* **are not** *significant:* 109,000 km contains *three* significant figures.

4. All zeros to the left of an expressed decimal point and to the right of a nonzero digit **are** *significant:* 109,000. km contains *six* significant figures.

5. All zeros to the right of a decimal point but to the left of a nonzero digit **are not** *significant:* 0.00476 kg contains *three* significant figures. (The single zero conventionally placed to the left of the decimal point in such an expression is never significant.)

6. All zeros to the right of a decimal point and to the right of a nonzero digit **are** *significant:* 0.04060 cm and 30.00 mg contain *four* significant figures.

Uncertainty is inherent in any experimental procedure. Accuracy of a measurement can be determined only if true, or accepted values of the measurement are known. However, precision can always be expressed by the proper use of significant figures. Judgment based on precision alone must be considered with caution.

19. Exponential notation. In science we often encounter numbers which are extremely large or exceedingly small.

The speed of light is approximately 30,000,000,000 centimeters per second. The speed of light in a vacuum generally accepted as accurate to *seven* significant figures is 29,979,250,000 cm/sec. The mass of the earth is about 6,000,000,000,-000,000,000,000,000 grams. The mass of an electron is 0.000,000,000,000,000,-000,000,000,000,910,91 gram. The wavelength of yellow light is about 0.000059 cm. These numbers have little meaning in the ordinary sense. To save having to write many zeros, we can express such numbers as powers of 10. This *exponential notation* has the form

$$M \times 10^n$$

where M is a number having one digit to the left of the decimal point and n is a positive or negative integer.

We may now write the unusual quantities already given in exponential form as shown in the table below.

To change a number into exponential notation form:

1. Determine M by moving the decimal point so that you leave only one nonzero digit to the left of it.

2. Determine n by counting the number of places you have moved the decimal point; if moved to the left, n is positive; if to the right, n is negative. The laws of exponents apply in computations involving numbers expressed in exponential form.

When a number is written in the form $M \times 10^n$ all the digits, zero and nonzero, expressed explicitly in M are significant. This enables us to tell at a glance the

NUMBERS IN EXPONENTIAL–NOTATION FORM

30,000,000,000 cm/sec = 3×10^{10} cm/sec

29,979,250,000 cm/sec = 2.997925×10^{10} cm/sec

6,000,000,000,000,000,000,000,000,000 g = 6×10^{27} g

0.000,000,000,000,000,000,000,000,000,910,91 g = 9.1091×10^{-28} g

0.000059 cm = 5.9×10^{-5} cm

1000. = 1.000×10^3

1000 = 1×10^3

number of significant figures and the accuracy implied in an indicated measurement to a degree of certainty that may not be possible using the ordinary system of notation.

The distance from the earth to the sun, 93,005,000 mi, cannot be expressed in ordinary notation to three significant figures without confusion. However using the exponential notation, this distance may be shown to have three significant figures as 9.30×10^7 mi with complete clarity.

20. Operations with significant figures. The results of mathematical operations involving laboratory measurements can be no more precise than the measurements themselves. Accordingly, certain precautions must be observed when performing calculations in order to avoid implying greater precision in the results than was originally obtained in the measurements. The following rules, while not infallible, are valid for most practical purposes and should be adopted where the context does not indicate otherwise.

1. Addition and subtraction. Remembering that the rightmost significant figure in a measurement is uncertain, *the rightmost significant figure in a sum or difference occurs in the leftmost place at which the doubtful figure occurs in any of the measurements involved.* The example of an addition which follows will help you to visualize this rule.

20.63 cm	leftmost place of doubtful
6.6 cm	figure in measurements
3.786 cm	involved in addition
31.016	
	rightmost significant
	figure in the sum

The sum 31.016 should then be recorded as 31.0 cm, the best expression for the answer to this addition problem. If, for example, the leftmost place where a doubt-

ful figure occurs is in the hundredths place (second place to the right of the decimal point), the sum or difference should be rounded to the nearest hundredth. When working with numbers expressed in exponential notation, all terms must be converted to the same power of ten before adding or subtracting.

2. Multiplication and division. Three points previously discussed in Section 18 must be remembered in operations involving multiplication and division: (*a*) The rightmost significant figure in a measurement is uncertain. (*b*) The product of any number multiplied by a doubtful digit is also uncertain. (*c*) Only one doubtful digit is retained in the result. Therefore, *the product or quotient is precise to the number of significant figures contained in the least precise factor.* The result in either operation should be rounded to the same number of significant figures contained in the factor that has the least number of significant figures. In an expression in which both multiplications and divisions occur, the multiplications should be performed first. The result should be rounded to the proper number of significant figures on completing each multiplication or division operation.

In multiplication or division operations with numbers expressed in exponential form, the *M* portions are handled as described above, keeping in mind that all digits are significant. The laws of exponents govern the multiplication and division of the 10^n terms. In multiplication the exponents are added:

$$10^3 \times 10^4 = 10^7$$
$$10^6 \times 10^{-2} = 10^4$$
$$10^4 \times 10^{-6} = 10^{-2}$$

In division the exponent of the divisor is subtracted from the exponent of the dividend:

$$10^3 \div 10^2 = 10^1$$
$$10^4 \div 10^{-3} = 10^7$$
$$10^{-5} \div 10^2 = 10^{-7}$$

Number expressions that are not the result of measurements should not be interpreted as having limited accuracy. Such numbers, when included in a computation with laboratory measurements, do not enter into the determination of the number of significant figures in the result. As an example, the freezing point of water is *defined* as 0° C. This is exactly zero and could be written with as many zero digits to the right of the decimal point as desired. A thermometer *reading*, of course, is a measurement and would have limited accuracy, being written with the number of significant figures the instrument is capable of yielding. Similarly, a triangle has *exactly* three sides. If one side of an equilateral triangle is measured to a precision of four significant figures and then multiplied by the number of sides, the number of significant figures in the product remains the same as that of the original measurements.

21. Operations with units. Measurements are always expressed as a significant number of some kind of units: 12.5 g, 6.7 cm, 10.0 sec, 42.1° C, 0.09 g/l, etc. Both the number and the unit are essential parts of the expression since the choice of unit affects the magnitude of the number. A measurement determined to three significant figures to be 1.30 m would be written as 130. cm if the centimeter unit rather than the meter unit had been used.

$$1.30 \cancel{\text{ m }} \times \frac{100 \text{ cm}}{\cancel{\text{m}}} = 130. \text{ cm}$$

Observe that the expression 100 cm/m is arrived at by definition, not by measurement. Thus, it is exactly 100 cm and does not affect the significance of the measurement. Had the measurement been determined to two significant figures to be 1.3 m, it would then be written as 130 cm when converted to the centimeter unit.

$$1.3 \cancel{\text{ m }} \times \frac{100 \text{ cm}}{\cancel{\text{m}}} = 130 \text{ cm}$$

Thus 1.30 m is equivalent to 130. cm and 1.3 m is equivalent to 130 cm.

Because of the multiplicity of units and the fact that the expression of a physical measurement requires *both* a number and a unit, chemistry students will avoid confusion and errors in computations by adopting the practice of *always* writing the unit with the number to which it belongs. Usually the "cancellation" of units in an expression leads directly to the proper unit for the answer. The technique of unit cancellation is sometimes referred to as dimensional analysis. This method of writing and solving expressions, illustrated in the following sample problems, will be used in problem work in this book through Chapter 8. Beyond that point it will be assumed that the student will carry on his own dimensional analysis.

Sample Problem

A chemistry student was required to determine the density of an irregularly shaped sample of lead. He first weighed it on a balance sensitive to 0.01 g and found its mass to be 49.33 g. He then immersed the lead in water contained in a cylinder graduated in one-tenth milliliter divisions and observed that it displaced 4.35 ml of water (the 0.05 ml being estimated).

Solution

The student recalled from his study of general science that a body immersed in a liquid displaces its own volume. Since the volume of a solid is normally expressed in cubic measure, the equivalency of the milliliter and the cubic centimeter is used to convert the volume to cubic centimeters.

$$1 \text{ cm}^3 = 1 \text{ ml}$$

$$4.35 \text{ ml} \times \frac{1 \text{ cm}^3}{\text{ml}} = 4.35 \text{ cm}^3$$

By definition:

$$D = \frac{m}{V}$$

$$D = \frac{49.33 \text{ g}}{4.35 \text{ cm}^3} = 11.34 \text{ g/cm}^3$$

Observe that the indicated division has been carried to the hundredths place. It should next be rounded to the nearest tenth to give the proper number of significant figures in the answer.

A more appropriate way to set up this solution would be as follows:

$$D = \frac{m}{V}$$

$$D = \frac{49.33 \text{ g}}{4.35 \text{ ml} \times 1 \text{ cm}^3/\text{ml}} = 11.3 \text{ g/cm}^3$$

Sample Problem

What is the concentration of sodium chloride (table salt), in grams of salt per gram of solution, if 400. mg of the salt is dissolved in 100. ml of water measured at 65° C?

Solution

The problem requires that the concentration be expressed in grams of salt per gram of solution. The mass of solution is the sum of the mass of the water used and the mass of the salt added. Thus, the volume of water must be converted to mass of water. To make this conversion the density of water at 65° C must be known.

The table in a chemistry handbook giving density of water over a range of temperatures shows that water has a density of 0.981 g/ml at 65° C.

By definition: $D = \dfrac{m}{V}$

Solving for m: $m = DV$

Substituting: $m = 0.981 \dfrac{\text{g}}{\text{ml}} \times 100. \text{ ml} = 98.1 \text{ g}$

(Observe that the ml units "cancel" leaving g which is the proper unit for the answer.)

The mass of the salt is given in milligrams and the mass of the water is in grams. Since milligrams and grams cannot be added, the milligrams of salt must be converted to grams.

By definition:
$$1 \text{ mg} = 0.001 \text{ g}$$
$$400. \text{ mg} \times \frac{0.001 \text{ g}}{\text{mg}} = 0.400 \text{ g of salt added.}$$

(Observe that 0.001 g is an exact number derived by definition and is not a measurement precise only to one significant figure.)

$$\textbf{Mass of solution} = 98.1 \text{ g} + 0.400 \text{ g} = 98.5 \text{ g}$$

(Recall the rule for addition of significant figures to recognize that the sum is 98.5 g and *not* 98.500 g.)

Since 0.400 g of salt is present in 98.5 g of solution, there is

$$\frac{0.400 \text{ g}}{98.5} \text{ of salt in 1 g of solution}$$

or   **0.00406 g salt/g solution**

REVIEW OUTLINE

You will find a review outline like this one at the end of each chapter in this book. It consists of a list of the important topics and terms in the order in which they appear in the chapter. This outline should be useful to you as a guide for vocabulary review and for preparation of study notes. When your class has completed its study of the chapter, the outline may serve as a basis for review before a quiz or examination.

The number in parentheses following a topic in the outline refers to the section number of the chapter within which this topic is developed. This should make it easier to locate a specific concept that you may wish to reexamine while preparing notes.

Scientific methods
    Natural laws (3)
    Phases of scientific methods (3)
    Importance of experiments (3)

Concept of matter
    Nature of inertia (4)
    Measure of inertia (5)
    Distinction between mass and weight (5)
    Density (6)

QUESTIONS

Group A

1. Why is chemistry considered to be a fundamental science?
2. What distinguishes (*a*) a solid from a liquid? (*b*) a liquid from a gas?
3. What properties of materials are classed as physical properties? *observable*
4. What properties of materials are classed as chemical? *P 9*
5. What three basic units of the metric system are used in chemistry?
6. Name six prefixes used in the metric system and indicate what each one means.
7. Why is the study of chemistry concerned with energy?
8. In scientific work what are the advantages of the metric system over the English system? *it is conventional*
9. What metric units would you use to represent: (*a*) the area of the cover of this book; (*b*) a family's daily milk supply; (*c*) your own weight; (*d*) the length of the eye of a darning needle; (*e*) the speed of a moving automobile?
10. What disadvantage would we encounter in the everyday use of the metric system in place of our English system of weights and measure?
▶ 11. Distinguish between accuracy and precision as they pertain to measurements.
12. (*a*) What is the distinction between heat and temperature? (*b*) In what unit is each measured?

Group B

13. Prepare a list of new chemical products which you have read about in newspapers and magazines.
14. (*a*) List five common materials used in the kitchen in your home. (*b*) What properties does each have which makes it suitable for its particular use?
15. Why are both liquids and gases considered to be fluids?
16. What determines whether a certain property of a material is classed as physical or chemical?
17. Why does our sense of touch give us the most direct evidence of the existence of matter?
18. A weighing was made on a platform balance which was graduated in 0.1 g units and was sensitive to 0.01 g. The mass was recorded as 73.14 g. (*a*) How many significant figures are in this measurement? (*b*) Which digit would be called a doubtful figure?
19. Volume is a property of a material. (*a*) Is it a specific property? (*b*) Is mass a specific property? (*c*) Is the ratio of mass to volume a specific property? Explain.
20. Your laboratory partner was given the task of measuring the length of a box (approximately 5 in.) as accurately as possible using a meter stick graduated in millimeters. He supplied you with the following measurements: 12.65, 12.6 cm, 12.65 cm, 12.655 cm, 126.55 mm, 12 cm. (*a*) State which one of the measurements you would accept, giving the reason, (*b*) Give your reason for rejecting each of the others.
21. Copy each of these measurements and underscore all significant figures in each (*do not mark in this book*): (*a*) 127.50 km; (*b*) 1200 m; (*c*) 90027.00 cm³; (*d*) 0.0053 g; (*e*) 670. mg; (*f*) 0.0730 g; (*g*) 43.050 1: (*h*) 300900 kg; (*i*) 0.147 cm; (*j*) 6271.9 cm².
22. Explain why the unit of any measurement should be written in a mathematical expression with the number to which it belongs.
▶ 23. A thermometer is graduated in 1° intervals. In the absence of any tolerance data, what uncertainty would you assume to be associated with each temperature reading?
▶ 24. You may use a laboratory balance that has a sensitivity of 0.01 g. Does this indicate an uncertainty in terms of a limitation in accuracy or precision? Explain.

PROBLEMS   See Table 1, Appendix

Group A

1. How many millimeters are there (*a*) in 1 centimeter? (*b*) in 1 meter? (*c*) in 1 kilometer?
2. How many centimeters are there (*a*) in 1 foot? (*b*) in 2 meters? (*c*) How many inches are there in 1 meter?
3. How many milliliters are there in (*a*) 2 liters? (*b*) 10 liters? (*c*) How many liters are there in 1 m³?

4. Calculate the number of milligrams (*a*) in 0.4 kilogram; (*b*) in 1 pound. (*c*) How many grams are there in 2 kilograms?

5. (*a*) What is your height in meters? (*b*) What is your mass in kilograms?

6. A Florence flask has a capacity of 2.50×10^2 ml. (*a*) What part of a liter is this? (*b*) How many grams of water will the flask hold?

7. The distance to the sun is approximately 93,000,000 miles. Express this in exponential notation form.

8. The thickness of an oil film on water is about 0.0000005 cm. Express this in exponential notation form.

Group B

9. A cubic box holds 1000. g of water. (*a*) What is the volume of the box in milliliters? (*b*) in cubic centimeters? (*c*) What is the length of one side in centimeters? (*d*) in meters?

10. A test tube in the laboratory is 125 mm long and 25.0 mm in diameter. (*a*) Neglecting the fact that the bottom of the test tube is rounded, calculate its capacity in milliliters. (*b*) How many grams of water will it hold?

11. Each member of a class of 24 students needs 8.600 g of sodium chloride for an experiment. The instructor sets out a new one-pound jar of the salt. How many grams should be left at the end of the laboratory period?

12. A 1-liter graduated cylinder has an inside diameter of 8.24 cm. There is a 52-mm ungraduated portion at the top. What is the total height of the cylinder in centimeters?

13. The density of mercury, to three significant figures, is 13.6 g/ml. (*a*) What is the mass of 8.20 ml of mercury? (*b*) What volume would 120. g of mercury occupy?

14. Express the distance 152.20 cm in each of the following units showing the conversion computation in each case: (*a*) meters; (*b*) millimeters; (*c*) kilometer; (*d*) inches.

15. Chemists have determined that 18.0 g of water consists of 6.02×10^{23} molecules. Assuming that a teaspoon holds 3.70 ml of water, determine the number of water molecules the teaspoon can hold.

16. Suppose that you are able to remove individual molecules of water from the teaspoon of Problem 15 at the rate of 1 molecule per second. How many years would be required to empty the spoon?

Chapter Two

MATTER AND ITS CHANGES

COMPOSITION OF MATTER

1. Three general classes of matter.
We are familiar with many different kinds
of materials. To study materials without
first organizing them into similar groups
would be difficult and would require much
effort and time. Chemists have found that
all forms of matter may be divided into
three general groups on the basis of their
properties. These three general classes
into which all forms of matter may be
divided are *elements*, *compounds*, and *mixtures*.

2. Mixtures. If we examine a piece
of granite closely with a hand lens, we
can see three different crystalline materials: quartz, feldspar, and mica. The
properties of each differ greatly. *A material
which has parts with different properties is said
to be* **heterogeneous** (het-er-oh-*jee*-nee-us).

The properties of quartz are the same
regardless of its source. One part of a
piece of quartz has the same properties
as every other part. This is also true of
feldspar and mica. *A material which has
similar properties throughout is said to be*
homogeneous (hoh-muh-*jee*-nee-us). Heterogeneous materials are *mixtures* of homogeneous materials.

All mixtures are not heterogeneous,
however. When sugar is dissolved in water,
the resulting solution has similar properties
throughout. Thus the solution is homogeneous. We may increase the amount of
sugar or water, but we still have a homogeneous mixture of the two materials. The
solution has the sweet taste of the sugar it
contains. The water may be removed by
evaporation and the sugar recovered in its
original form. Solutions are therefore homogeneous mixtures. Air is a gaseous solution. Alloys are usually solid solutions.
A **mixture** *is a material consisting of two or
more kinds of matter, each retaining its own
characteristic properties.*

**3. Substances include compounds
and elements.** It has already been
stated that materials with similar properties throughout are homogeneous. In
chemistry, *a* **substance** *is a homogeneous
material consisting of one particular kind of*

matter. Both the sugar and the water of a sugar-water solution are substances. Unlike the granite which has the different properties of quartz, feldspar, and mica, the properties of sugar cannot be attributed to anything but the sugar itself and are due to its particular composition. Furthermore, *a substance has a definite chemical composition*.

Suppose we were to place a small quantity of sugar in a test tube and heat it over a low flame. The substance would melt and change color. Finally a charred black mass would remain in the bottom of the test tube, and drops of a clear colorless liquid would be seen around the cooler open end. This black substance can be shown to be carbon and the liquid to be water. The properties of the sugar no longer exist. Instead we observe the properties of two different substances. The process could be repeated and the sugar would be observed to decompose in the same way yielding the same proportions of carbon and water. Sugar may be recognized as a complex substance showing a consistent composition, called a compound. *A compound is a substance which may be decomposed into two or more simpler substances by ordinary chemical means*.

Chemists are able to decompose water into two simpler substances, hydrogen and oxygen. Thus water is a compound. Chemists have not succeeded, however, in decomposing carbon, hydrogen, or oxygen into any simpler substances. We conclude that these are elementary substances or *elements*. *Elements are substances which cannot be further decomposed by ordinary chemical means*. Elementary substances cannot be further broken down or simplified by the usual methods of carrying out chemical reactions—by application of heat, light, or electric energy.

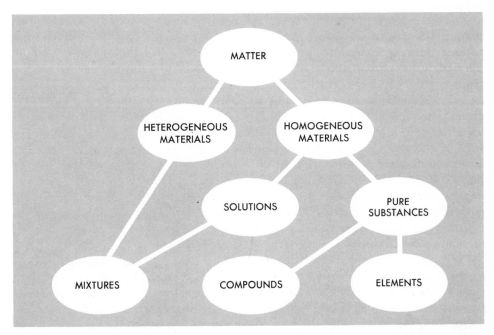

2-1 All matter is divided into three general classes: elements, compounds, and mixtures.

4. Relative scarcity of elements in nature. One of the most fascinating facts of science is that all matter is composed of about 100 elements. Approximately 90 elements are known to occur in a free or combined state in the earth's crust in detectable amounts. The atmosphere consists almost entirely of two elements, nitrogen and oxygen. Water, which covers such a great portion of the surface of the earth, is a combination of hydrogen and oxygen. It is true, however, that natural water contains many dissolved substances.

Only about 30 elements are well known. The relative distribution (by weight) of the 10 most abundant elements in the atmosphere, lakes, rivers, and oceans, and the earth's crust is:

DISTRIBUTION OF ELEMENTS BY WEIGHT

Oxygen	49.5%	Sodium	2.6%
Silicon	25.8%	Potassium	2.4%
Aluminum	7.5%	Magnesium	1.9%
Iron	4.7%	Hydrogen	0.9%
Calcium	3.4%	Titanium	0.6%
		All other elements	0.7%

Some elements would change positions relative to other elements in the table if the basis for comparison were changed. On a relative-number-of-particles basis, for example, hydrogen would appear ahead of aluminum.

A few elementary substances such as gold, silver, copper, and sulfur, have been known since ancient times. During the Middle Ages and the Renaissance which followed, more elements were discovered. Through the years, scientists have added even more elements to the list as a result of improved research techniques.

There are 103 known elements at the time of this writing. The discovery of element 104 was reported by Russian scientists in September 1964. However, during the time this manuscript was in preparation, no reports of experiments confirming the synthesis of this new element were published. The theoretical possibility of eventually extending the number to 118, or even beyond 137, has been suggested. However, present evidence indicates that the number may not exceed 110.

The 92 elements ranging from hydrogen to uranium are traditionally known as *natural elements*. They constitute the pre-Atomic Age list of elements. Atomic bomb research during World War II led to the synthesis of *neptunium* named for the planet Neptune, and *plutonium* named for Pluto. These were followed by *americium* (am-er-*ih*-see-um) named for America, curium (*ku*-ree-um) named in honor of Madame Curie, *berkelium* (*berk*-lee-um) for Berkeley (the site of the University of California), and *californium* for the University and the State. More recently *einsteinium* named for Albert Einstein, *fermium* named for Enrico Fermi, *mendelevium* (men-del-*ev*-ee-um) named for Dimitri Mendeleyev (men-deh-*lay*-eff) brought the total to 101.

In the summer of 1957 a team of American, British, and Swedish scientists working at the Nobel Institute in Sweden an-

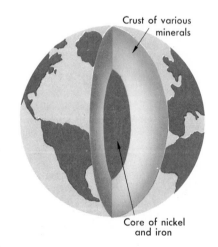

2-2 The core of the earth is believed to be composed of nickel and iron.

Crust of various minerals

Core of nickel and iron

2-3 Plutonium being prepared for fabrication into atomic reactor fuel. (General Electric)

nounced the discovery of element 102 and suggested the name *nobelium*. Careful experiments by other scientists failed to confirm this discovery.

In 1958 a research group at the Lawrence Radiation Laboratory of the University of California produced *nobelium* and identified it by chemical means. In 1961, element 103 was produced by scientists at this same laboratory. The name *lawrencium* has been assigned to element 103 in honor of Dr. Ernest O. Lawrence, the inventor of the cyclotron, and the founder of the laboratory in which the element was produced.

5. Two general classes of elements. Elements differ enough in their properties so that chemists recognize two general classes, *metals* and *nonmetals*.

Metals. Some elements have a luster similar to that of steel or silver. They reflect heat and light readily and conduct heat and electricity remarkably well. Some are ductile and can be drawn into wire, or malleable and can be hammered into thin sheets. Elements which have such properties are known as *metals.* Some examples of metals are: gold, silver, copper, zinc, sodium, potassium, titanium, magnesium, calcium, and aluminum. Mercury is a liquid metal.

Nonmetals. These are usually poor conductors of heat and electricity. They cannot be hammered into sheets or drawn into wire because they are usually too brittle. Sulfur is an example of a nonmetal. Some nonmetals such as iodine, carbon, and phosphorus are solid at room temperatures. Bromine is a liquid nonmetal. Others are gaseous, as oxygen, nitrogen, chlorine, and neon.

Some borderline elements have certain properties characteristic of metals and other properties characteristic of nonmetals. Arsenic, antimony, silicon, and germanium are examples of this type. They are sometimes called *metalloids.*

6. Chemical symbol. Jöns Jaköb Berzelius (1779–1848), a Swedish chemist, was the first to use letters as symbols for

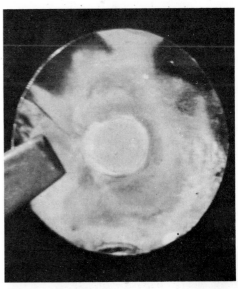

2-4 Californium, element number 98, was discovered in 1950. (Lawrence Radiation Laboratory)

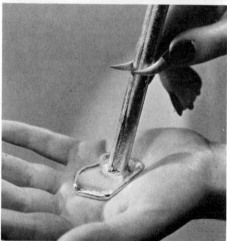

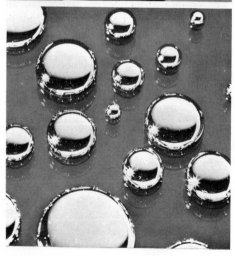

elements to replace the crude picture system used by the alchemists in the Middle Ages. Berzelius used the first letter of the name of an element as its symbol. For example, the letter **O** represents oxygen, and the letter **H** represents hydrogen.

Since there are over 100 elements known, and there are only twenty-six letters in our alphabet, the names of several elements must begin with the same letter. In this event, Berzelius suggested using the second letter of the name of the element with the first letter, or the first letter with some other letter whose sound is conspicuous when the name of the element is pronounced. For example, the symbol for carbon is **C**; for calcium, **Ca**; for chlorine, **Cl**; for chromium, **Cr**; and for cobalt, **Co**. The first letter of a symbol is *always* a capital, but the second letter of a symbol is *never* capitalized. For example, **Co** is the symbol for cobalt, but **CO** is the formula for the compound *carbon monoxide*, composed of the two elements carbon and oxygen.

In several cases, the symbol for an element is derived from the Latin name of the element. For example, the symbol for iron is **Fe,** from the Latin *ferrum.* **Pb,** the symbol for lead, comes from the Latin *plumbum.* The symbols for silver, **Ag,** and sodium, **Na,** come from the Latin, *argentum* and *natrium.*

7. Significance of a symbol.   A chemical symbol is more than an abbreviation; it has quantitative significance. When we use the symbol **O**, it first of all

2-5 Sulfur (top) is a nonmetallic element that occurs as yellow rhombic crystals in its ordinary form. The metallic element gallium (center) will melt in your hand but will not boil until heated to about 2000° C. Mercury (at the bottom) is the only metallic element that is liquid at room temperature.

means oxygen. More than that, it means *one atom* of oxygen. The expression **2O** means 2 atoms of oxygen; **5O** means 5 atoms of oxygen. Similarly **Fe** means 1 atom of iron; **3Fe,** 3 atoms of iron; and **10Fe,** 10 atoms of iron. The atom is the smallest particle of an element that can enter into combination with other elements. Just as a mason uses different kinds of bricks to build houses, so the chemist uses different kinds of atoms to build chemical compounds. The symbol of an element will acquire additional significance as your study of chemistry progresses.

8. Compounds differ from mixtures. When matter is made up of two or more elements, they may either be mixed mechanically or combined chemically. The material is either a *mixture* or a *compound* depending on what happened to the elements. If it is a mixture, the properties of each of the elements present can be recognized. On the other hand, if the elements are chemically combined, a complex substance with its own characteristic properties is observed.

Suppose some powdered sulfur and some iron powder are mixed thoroughly on a sheet of paper. There is no evidence of chemical action; no light is produced and no heat is given off. The two substances may be mixed in any proportion. It is possible to use a large amount of iron and a small amount of sulfur or a large portion of sulfur and a small portion of iron.

If the paper containing this mixture is moved back and forth over a strong magnet, the iron particles can be separated from the sulfur. When a small portion of the mixture is put in hydrochloric acid, the iron reacts with the acid and disappears from view leaving the sulfur unaffected. When another portion of the mixture is put in liquid carbon disulfide, the

sulfur dissolves leaving the iron powder unchanged.

In each of these tests the properties of iron and sulfur persist. This is typical of a mixture; the components do not lose their identity. They may be mixed in any proportion without evidence of chemical activity.

It is possible to cause the iron and sulfur to unite chemically to form a compound. Suppose these two elements are mixed intimately in the ratio of 7 g iron to 4 g sulfur and the mixture is heated in a test tube over a Bunsen flame. With a rise in temperature the mixture begins to glow. Even after its removal from the flame, the mixture continues to react and the whole mass soon becomes red hot. *Both heat and light are produced during the chemical action in which sulfur unites with iron to form a compound.*

After the reaction has ceased and the product has been removed, careful examination shows that it no longer resembles either the iron or the sulfur. Each element has lost its characteristic properties. The iron cannot be removed by a magnet. The sulfur cannot be dissolved out of the product with carbon disulfide. Hydrochloric acid acts on the mixture of iron and sulfur to produce hydrogen, an odorless gas. It acts on this new product to produce hydrogen sulfide, a gas with a distinctive (rotten egg) odor. *A new substance with a new set of properties has been formed.*

Chemical analysis of this new product shows that it is made up of seven parts by weight of iron to four parts by weight of sulfur. *A compound is always made up of the same elements in a definite proportion by weight.* For example, the new compound, which may be called *iron sulfide,* is composed of 63.5% iron and 36.5% sulfur. That does not mean that this compound could not be made by starting with eight parts of iron and four parts of sulfur. It does mean that in such a case, one part by weight of iron would remain as an unused surplus after the seven parts of iron had combined with four parts of sulfur to form iron sulfide.

The differences between a mixture and a compound are summarized in the table below.

9. Law of Definite Composition. Louis Proust (1755–1826), a French chemist, was one of the first to observe that elements always combine with one another in a definite ratio by weight. About fifty years later, Jean Servais Stas, a Belgian chemist, performed a series of precise experiments which confirmed this observation. We now recognize the work of Proust as the *Law of Definite Composition: every compound has a definite composition by weight.*

Because of the Law of Definite Composition, a manufacturer of chemical compounds can find out just how much of each constituent to use in making each compound.

10. Common examples of mixtures and compounds. Air is a mixture. Its composition varies somewhat in different localities. Other familiar examples of mixtures include substances such as baking powders, concrete, and various kinds of soil. There is practically no limit to the number of possible mixtures. They may be made up of two or more elements, of two or more compounds, or of both elements and compounds. For example, brass is a mixture of two elements, copper and zinc. Common gunpowder is a mixture of two elements, carbon and sulfur, with a compound, potassium nitrate. A solution of common salt is a mixture of two compounds, sodium chloride and water.

Some of our large dictionaries define almost a half-million words, all formed from one or more of the 26 letters that make up our alphabet. Try to imagine the number of compounds it would be possible to make from 100 or more elements. However, some elements do not unite readily with others to form compounds. Only three elements are now known which form no compounds. There are enough elements that do combine, however, to form the *several hundred thousand* compounds known to chemists. Water, table salt, sugar, alcohol, baking soda, ether, glycerol, turpentine, cellulose, nitric acid, and sulfuric acid are examples of some common compounds.

The simplest compounds are made up of two different elements; iron sulfide is such a compound. Carbon dioxide is composed only of carbon and oxygen. Table salt consists of sodium combined with chlorine. Sodium is an active metallic element which must be protected from contact with air and water. Chlorine is a poisonous gas. But when combined chemically, the two form common table salt.

DIFFERENCES BETWEEN A MIXTURE AND A COMPOUND

MIXTURE	COMPOUND
1. In a mixture, the components may be present in any proportion.	1. In a compound, the constituents always have a definite proportion by weight.
2. In the preparation of a mixture, there is no evidence of any chemical action taking place.	2. In the preparation of a compound, evidence of chemical action is usually apparent (light, heat, etc.)
3. In a mixture, the components do not lose their identity. They may be separated by physical means.	3. In a compound, the constituents lose their identity. They can be separated by chemical means only.

Many compounds are composed of no more than three different elements. Carbon, hydrogen, and oxygen are the constituents of sugar. These same three elements, combined in different proportions, form many other compounds having decidedly different properties.

CHANGES IN MATTER

11. Physical changes. Ice melts, water boils, liquids freeze, glass breaks, and sugar dissolves in water. We may heat a piece of platinum wire until it glows. In all these cases matter undergoes some change. Its form may be different or it may have experienced a change of state or energy. However, in no case has the matter lost its identity. Sometimes by a reversal of the action which caused the change, the material may be restored to its original form and the same identifying properties are again readily recognized.

These are examples of *physical changes.* In such changes only alterations in physical properties are apparent; the composition of the material is not changed. *Physical changes are those in which the identifying properties of substances remain unchanged.*

Modern ideas concerning solutions suggest that some types of physical changes may involve intermediate processes which are not physical in nature. These ideas will be treated in Chapter 12.

12. Chemical changes. You know that wood burns, iron rusts, silver tarnishes, milk sours, plants decay, and acids react with metals. In each of these actions the identifying properties of the original substance are altered; new substances with different properties are recognized. Changes occur which alter the composition of matter. *Chemical changes are those in which new substances with new properties are formed.*

Chemical action may involve the combining of atoms of elementary substances to form compounds. Complex substances may be broken down into simpler compounds or into the elements which compose them. Compounds may react with other compounds or elements to form new and different compounds. *The science of chemistry is concerned specifically with the chemical changes of substances and with methods of controlling these changes.*

13. Chemical changes involve energy. Chemical changes are always accompanied by energy changes. Substances possess energy because of their composition and structure. This is a kind of potential energy which chemists generally refer to as *chemical energy.* The products of chemical changes are different in composition and structure from the original substances and thus will have larger or smaller amounts of chemical energy. If the amount is smaller, energy will be *liberated* during the change, usually in the form of *heat* and sometimes *light* or *electric energy.* If the amount of chemical energy is larger, energy will be *absorbed* during the change.

Calcium carbide is produced in the intense heat of the electric furnace. Carbon disulfide is formed when hot sulfur vapor is passed over white-hot carbon in an electric furnace. Heat energy is absorbed continuously while such chemical actions are taking place. *Any chemical change which absorbs heat energy as it progresses is said to be endothermic.*

Some chemical changes are of importance because of their products. Others are carried out because of the energy which is released. In the burning of fuels, large amounts of heat energy are released rapidly. Many similar changes occur in nature, but take place so slowly that the evolution of heat is not noticed. *Any chemical change which liberates heat energy as it*

2-6   An astronaut is launched into space atop a huge rocket. (NASA)

proceeds is said to be **exothermic.** The majority of chemical changes which occur in nature are exothermic. The photosynthesis process of green plants is a notable exception; this reaction is endothermic.

In the burning of fuels, light energy usually accompanies the release of heat. A photoflash lamp is designed to release a maximum amount of energy as light. The final proof of a chemical change rests with the analysis of the products. However, the evolution of heat and light usually offers evidence that chemical action is taking place.

The explosion of dynamite or gunpowder is a chemical change that produces *mechanical energy.* Similarly, the explosion of gasoline vapor mixed with air in the cylinder of an automobile engine is an example of chemical action.

In the flashlight cell the zinc cylinder is acted on chemically when the cell is in use. *Electric energy* is produced by this action and indicates that the chemical change is taking place within the cell.

The *production of a gas* is usually evidence that chemical action is taking place. We must be careful, however, to avoid mistaking the boiling of a liquid, the escaping of a dissolved gas from solution, or the escaping of gas from the pores of a solid, for chemical action.

In many cases an insoluble solid is formed by adding one solution to another. The *formation of an insoluble solid, called a precipitate,* may show that a chemical change has taken place as the solutions are mixed.

Chemists use several agents to bring about chemical changes or to control those which have already started. Some type of energy is often used.

1. Heat energy. A match is kindled by rubbing it over a rough surface to warm it by friction. By holding the lighted match to a piece of paper we may start the paper burning. The heat from the burning match is used to start this chemical change. It is, however, an exothermic action and we do not need to continue furnishing heat in order to keep the paper burning. Many chemical actions which occur in the preparation of foods are endothermic. Heat is supplied to keep these reactions going. As a rule, increasing the temperature hastens the speed of chemical changes. *Each increase in temperature of 10 C° approximately doubles the rate of many chemical actions.*

2. Light energy. The process of photosynthesis, by which green plants manufacture food, requires light energy. When we open the shutter of a camera for only a fraction of a second, light falls on the sensitive film. This starts a chemical change in the film which enables us to develop a picture.

3. Electric energy. If a direct current of

electricity is passed through water containing a little acid, the water is decomposed into hydrogen and oxygen. We use this method of bringing about a chemical change when a storage battery is charged. Electric energy is used in plating one metal on another, in the extracting of aluminum and other metals from their ores, and in purifying some metals. Electricity is also used to produce heat for thermal processes, as in the electric furnace.

4. Solution in water. Baking powder is a mixture of two or more compounds. No chemical action occurs as long as the powder is kept *dry*. However, when water is added to baking powder, chemical action begins immediately and a gas is evolved. Many chemicals which do not react in the *dry* state begin to react as soon as they are dissolved in water.

5. Catalysis (kuh-*tal*-uh-sis). Some chemical changes may be promoted by *catalysts* (*kat*-uh-lists). These are specific agents which enable changes to occur that would otherwise be difficult or impractical to carry out. You will soon be preparing oxygen in the laboratory by heating a mixture of potassium chlorate and manganese dioxide. Without the manganese dioxide the preparation would have to be carried out at a higher temperature. Also, the gas would be produced more slowly. The manganese dioxide aids the action by its presence. It could be recovered in its original form at the conclusion of the experiment. *A catalyst is an agent which affects the rate of a chemical action without itself being permanently altered.*

Many chemical processes, such as the production of vegetable shortening, the manufacture of synthetic rubber, and the preparation of high-octane gasoline, depend on catalysis for their successful operation.

14. Reaction tendencies. We are not surprised to see a ball roll unaided down an incline. This is just what would be expected. The ball gives up potential energy in this process and achieves a more stable status at a lower energy level. We would be surprised, however, if it rolled up the incline by and of itself. From our experiences with nature we have come to recognize a basic rule for natural processes: *the tendency for processes to occur which lead to a lower energy state.* This tendency in nature is toward greater stability of a system.

The great majority of chemical reactions in nature are exothermic. Energy is liberated as they proceed and the products have less energy than the original reactants. With the above rule in mind, we expect exothermic reactions *to occur* **spontaneously,** that is, *to have the potential to proceed without the assistance of an external agency.* It should follow that endothermic reactions, in which energy is absorbed, would not occur spontaneously but would proceed only with the assistance of an external agency.

We do not have to look very far to find processes which go spontaneously with the absorption of energy. When steam is passed over hot carbon, carbon monoxide and hydrogen gases are produced and heat is taken up. The products are in a higher energy state than the reactants. The reaction is endothermic and our rule appears to have failed. Apparently the tendency of a reaction to proceed is not governed solely by this energy-change concept.

An ice cube melts spontaneously at room temperature. As the ice melts it acquires energy. The well-ordered form of the ice crystal is lost and the less orderly liquid state of water, a state of higher energy, is formed. Why does this occur? What we observe here is a tendency for

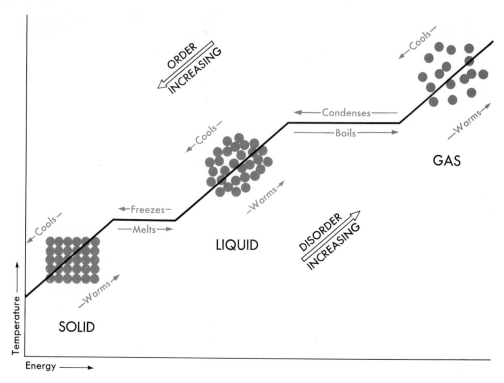

2-7   Changes of state.

the ice to move into the more disordered liquid state. This suggests a second basic rule for natural processes: *the tendency for processes to occur which lead to a more disordered state*. This tendency in nature is toward greater randomness in a system. *That property which describes the disorder of a system is called* **entropy.** The more disordered or random the state, the *higher* is the entropy. Liquid water has higher entropy than ice.

Thus, processes in nature are impelled in two ways: toward *lowest* energy and toward *highest* entropy. Where these two oppose each other, the dominant factor determines the direction of the spontaneous change. In the steam-plus-hot-carbon reaction, the temperature is high enough that the entropy factor overcomes the unfavorable energy change and the spontaneous endothermic reaction occurs.

If the ice cube had been subjected to a temperature below 0° C, it would not have melted. Liquid water placed in this environment would freeze. The temperature is low enough that the entropy-change factor loses out to the energy-change factor; heat is given up (lower energy) and the well-ordered ice crystal is formed (lower entropy).

15. Nuclear changes. New substances are produced during a chemical change by the rearrangement of the atoms of the original substances. In a *nuclear change* new substances with new properties are also produced. *However, in a **nuclear change,** the new substances are formed by changes in the identity of the atoms themselves.*

In nature some nuclear changes take place spontaneously. Radium atoms disintegrate in successive stages, finally becoming lead. Scientists are able to bring

about many important nuclear changes. clear reactions, both natural and artificial,
The synthetic elements named in Section will be discussed at greater length in
4 are products of nuclear changes. Nu- Chapter 31.

REVIEW OUTLINE

Classes of matter
    Mixtures (2)
    Compounds (3)
    Elements (3)
    Relative scarcity of elements (4)
    Classification of elements (5)
    Significance of the symbol (7)
    Law of Definite Composition (9)

Changes in matter
    Physical changes (11)
    Chemical changes (12)
    Spontaneous reactions (14)
    Energy change in reactions (13)
    Entropy change in reactions (14)
    Nuclear changes (15)

QUESTIONS

Group A

1. What are the three general classes of matter? *elements, compounds + mixtures*
2. Distinguish between matter and a substance.
3. Distinguish between a complex substance and an elementary substance.
4. (*a*) What are the two general classes of elements? (*b*) Do all elements fit *no* definitely into one of these classes? *metal + nonmetal.*
5. Distinguish between a compound and a mixture. *P 3 ¥ very important*
6. What are the five most abundant elements in the earth's surface environment? *P 30*
7. (*a*) What are the properties of metals? (*b*) of nonmetals? *P 3 /*
8. (*a*) How many elements are known? (*b*) How many were known prior to the atomic-bomb research of World War II? *92*
9. What is the meaning of a chemical symbol? *abreviation of an element.*
10. (*a*) List five familiar substances which you recognize to be elements. (*b*) List five which are compounds. (*c*) List five familiar mixtures.
11. What is the difference between a physical change and a chemical change?
12. How can a chemist usually increase the speed of a chemical change? *catalyst*
13. If two or more elements have symbols beginning with the same letter, how do we distinguish them?
14. If a symbol has two letters, (*a*) what is always true of the first letter? (*b*) what is always true of the second letter? *capital   small*

Group B

15. What difference in the properties of white sand and sugar would enable you to separate a mixture of the two substances?
16. How would you carry out the separation of the sand-sugar mixture of Question 15?
17. Why is a solution recognized as a mixture?
18. What is the meaning of the phrase "definite composition by weight"? *what it says*
19. Why is the Law of Definite Composition very important to chemists?
20. Consult the complete list of known elements appearing on the inside of the back cover of this book and compile a list of those about which you already have some knowledge. Give the name, symbol, and the pertinent bit of knowledge in column form.
21. Given two liquids, one a solution and the other a compound, how would you distinguish the solution from the compound?
22. Suppose you heat three different solids in open vessels and then allow them to cool. The first gains weight, the second loses weight, and the third remains the same. How can you reconcile these facts with the generalization that, in an ordinary chemical change, the total mass of the reacting materials is equal to the total mass of the products?
23. How can you explain the fact that gold, silver, and copper were known long before such metals as iron and aluminum?
24. Suppose you were given a sample of iodine crystals, a sample of antimony metal, and a sample of a mixture of iodine and antimony which had been ground together to form a fine powder of uniform consistency. Look up the physical and chemical properties of both iodine and antimony and list those for each element that you believe would be useful in separating and recovering them from the mixture. On the basis of these properties, devise a procedure which would enable you to separate the two elements from the mixture and recover the separate elements.
25. Which of these changes are physical and which are chemical? (*a*) burning coal; (*b*) tarnishing silver; (*c*) magnetizing steel; (*d*) exploding gunpowder; (*e*) boiling water; (*f*) melting shortening.
26. Which of the chemical changes listed in Question 25 are also exothermic?
27. Show by example how each of these produces chemical changes: (*a*) heat energy; (*b*) light energy; (*c*) electric energy.
28. What evidences usually indicate chemical action?
29. Can you suggest a reason why iron and sulfur unite in definite proportions to form iron sulfide?
30. How do you decide whether a certain change is physical or chemical?
31. What two basic tendencies in nature appear to influence reaction processes?
32. An ice cube melts at room temperature and water freezes at temperatures below 0° C. From these facts, what can you infer concerning the relationship between the temperature of a system and the influence of the entropy factor on the change which the system undergoes?

Chapter Three

ATOMIC STRUCTURE

1. Particle concept of matter. When you crush a lump of sugar you can see that it consists of many small particles of sugar. You may grind these particles into very fine powder, but each tiny piece is still sugar. Now suppose you dissolve the sugar in water. The tiny particles disappear completely. Even a microscopic examination of the solution does not reveal their presence. However, your sense of taste tells you that sugar is still present in the water solution. Similarly, you can detect the odor of gas escaping from an open gas valve. Yet you cannot see gas particles in the air of the room, even if you use the most powerful microscope. These and many similar observations have led scientists to believe that matter consists of particles and that the *ultimate particles* of matter must be exceedingly small.

Greek philosophers, as early as 400 B.C., believed that matter was indestructible. They also thought that it could be divided into smaller and smaller particles until a point was reached beyond which no further subdivision was possible. These

were the ultimate particles of the philosophers. Democritus (deh-*mock*-writ-us) (460–370 B.C.) called such particles *atoms*, from a Greek word meaning indivisible. This ancient philosopher derived his fundamental knowledge almost entirely from his own thinking. Modern scientific methods make use of experiments to reveal fundamental truths. Thus the ideas of early philosophers concerning matter have very little resemblance to our present knowledge of the nature of matter.

2. The atomic theory. The concept of ultimate particles, or atoms of matter, did not contribute to the development of science until the beginning of the nineteenth century. Between 1803 and 1808 in England, John Dalton (1766–1844) performed many chemical experiments, particularly with gases. He greatly extended man's ideas about atoms. Dalton was the first to realize that the nature and properties of atoms could be used to explain the Law of Definite Composition and the way and the proportions in which substances react with one another. These are the fundamental ideas of Dalton's *atomic theory*.

The atomic theory today embraces a much wider field of knowledge than Dalton's original theory. Modern atomic theory includes information concerning the structure and properties of atoms, the kinds of reactions they undergo, the kinds of compounds they form and the properties of these compounds. It also includes information about the mass, volume, and energy relationships in reactions between atoms.

An **atom** *is the smallest particle of an element that can exist either alone or in combination with other atoms of the same or of another element.* No one has ever directly observed atoms. However, the chemical and physical properties of matter lead scientists to formulate the following statements about atoms and their properties:

1. All matter is made up of very small particles called *atoms.*

2. Atoms of the *same element* are *chemically alike;* atoms of *different elements* are *chemically different.*

3. Individual atoms of an element may not all have the same mass. However, *the atoms of an element,* as it occurs naturally, *have,* for practical purposes, *a definite average mass that is characteristic of the element.*

4. Individual atoms of different elements may have nearly identical masses. However, *the atoms of different naturally occurring elements have different average masses.*

5. Atoms are not subdivided in *chemical reactions.*

3. The structure of the atom. For three quarters of a century scientists have been accumulating evidence about the structure of atoms. Some of this evidence has come from the study of radioactive elements like radium and uranium. Particle accelerators, the mass spectrograph, the X-ray tube, the spectroscope, and a variety of electronic devices have given additional information. From all this information scientists have developed a comprehensive theory of atomic structure. As indicated in Chapter 1, Section 3, this theory includes an explanation of the observed phenomena in terms of a model with familiar properties. This atomic structure model will be described in the following sections of this chapter. Remember as you read that this explanation is based on the best current interpretation of experiments on atomic structure. Further experiments may from time to time make revisions of the model necessary.

At the present time scientists recognize that atoms are not simple indivisible particles. Instead, they are composed of several different kinds of still smaller particles arranged in a rather complex way.

An atom consists of two main parts. *The positively charged central part is called the* **nucleus.** It is very small and very dense. Its diameter is about 10^{-13} cm. A more convenient unit for expressing atomic dimensions is the Ångström. 1 Ångström (Å) = 10^{-8} cm. Hence the diameter of a nucleus is about 10^{-5} Å. This is about one one-hundred-thousandth of the diameter of the atom itself, since atoms range from 1 Å to 5 Å in diameter.

Negatively charged particles, called *electrons,* move about the nucleus in more or less definite regions called **shells** or **energy levels.** About 1913 the Danish scientist Niels Bohr (1885–1962) compared the movement of electrons about the nucleus of an atom with the revolution of the planets around the sun. However, the paths of the electrons are now believed to be much less definite than the orbits of the planets. Electrons move about the nucleus of an atom much as bees move about in the area near their hive. Sometimes the electrons are near the nucleus, sometimes they are farther away. In this manner the electrons effectively occupy the relatively vast empty

3-1 The Danish scientist Niels Bohr in 1913 developed the theory that electrons move about the nucleus of an atom in orbits much as the planets revolve about the sun. (United Press International)

space around the nucleus. The electrons form an electron cloud about the nucleus which gives the atom its volume and excludes other atoms. Each atom is electrically neutral, since the total positive charge of the nucleus is equaled by the total negative charge of the electrons in the shells or energy levels.

4. The characteristics of electrons. *Electrons are negatively charged particles with a mass of 9.109 × 10⁻²⁸ g.* This is $\frac{1}{1837}$ of the mass of the most common type of hydrogen atom—the atom of lowest mass. Each electron has one unit of negative electric charge. Electrons were discovered as a result of investigations of the flow of electricity through an evacuated glass tube, made by an English scientist, J. J. Thomson (1856–1940), in 1897.

The electron is a very small particle.

Its radius is 2.818 × 10⁻¹³ cm or 2.818 × 10⁻⁵ Å. Regardless of the atom of which an electron is a part, all electrons are identical.

5. The nucleus of the atom. The nuclei of atoms of different elements are different. They always have different amounts of positive charge. They also have different masses, although the difference in mass between atoms of two different elements is sometimes very slight. A nucleus is made up of two kinds of particles, *protons* and *neutrons*.

Protons are positively charged particles with a mass of 1.673 × 10⁻²⁴ g, which is $\frac{1836}{1837}$ of the mass of the most common type of hydrogen atom. Thus, the proton accounts for most of the mass of this hydrogen atom because it has a nucleus consisting of a single proton with a single electron revolving about it. While a proton has much more mass than an electron, it is believed to be somewhat smaller. A proton has one unit of positive electric charge.

Protons were discovered in the early years of this century during the investigation of "positive rays" which appear when electricity flows through specially designed evacuated glass tubes. In any atom the number of electrons and protons is equal. Since protons and electrons have equal but opposite electric charges, an atom is electrically neutral.

Neutrons are neutral particles with a mass of 1.675 × 10⁻²⁴ g, which is about the same mass as a proton. They have no electric charge. The English scientist, James C. Chadwick (1891–   ), discovered neutrons in 1932.

Like electrically charged particles generally repel one another. Nevertheless, up to about one hundred protons can exist close together in a nucleus when up to about one hundred fifty neutrons are also present. When a proton and a neutron

PARTICLES IN AN ATOM

Name	Mass	Atomic Mass (See Section 11)	Mass Number (See Section 6)	Charge
Electron	9.109×10^{-28} g	0.0005486	0	−1
Proton	1.673×10^{-24} g	1.007278	1	+1
Neutron	1.675×10^{-24} g	1.008665	1	0

are very close to each other, there is a strong attraction between them. Proton-proton forces of attraction also exist when the protons are very close together. These short-range proton-neutron and proton-proton forces hold the nuclear particles together, and are referred to as nuclear forces.

6. The hydrogen atom. The most common type of hydrogen is sometimes called *protium*. It has atoms which consist of a nucleus composed of one proton, with one electron moving about it. This electron moves about the nucleus at a most probable distance corresponding to the innermost shell or lowest energy level which an electron can have. This shell or energy level is called the *K shell* or *1st energy level*. The sizes and distances between the particles of the protium atom may be better understood if we picture the nucleus (a proton) as being the size of a pinhead, 0.25 cm in diameter. Comparatively speaking, the electron, which is somewhat larger, revolves about the nucleus at an average distance of about 12 m away. This electron moves rapidly about the nucleus, effectively occupying the surrounding space.

The atomic number of an atom is the number of protons in the nucleus of that atom. An element consists of atoms all of which have the same number of protons in their nuclei; hence, they all have the same atomic number. (All the unexcited neutral atoms of an element have the same arrangement of electrons about their nuclei, too.) The element hydrogen consists of atoms with one proton in their nuclei.

Their atomic number, therefore, is 1. Any atom having the atomic number 1 contains one proton in its nucleus, and is a hydrogen atom.

In addition to protium, which makes up 99.985% of naturally occurring hydrogen, there are two other known forms of hydrogen atoms. One of these is *deuterium* which occurs to the extent of 0.015% in nature. It consists of a nucleus containing one proton and one neutron, with one electron moving about it. The third form of hydrogen is *tritium*. It is a radioactive form which exists in nature in very small amounts, but which can be prepared artificially by a nuclear reaction. Tritium atoms have a nucleus composed of one proton and two neutrons, with one electron moving about it.

These three kinds of atoms are all hydrogen atoms, since they possess a nucleus containing one proton. The atomic number is 1 in each case. However, because their nuclei contain different numbers of neutrons, these atoms have different masses. *Atoms of the same element which have different masses are called isotopes.*

All elements exist in two or more isotopic forms. These may occur naturally or may be artificially prepared. While isotopes have different masses, they do not differ significantly in chemical properties. See Table 2 in the Appendix for a list of isotopes of some of the elements.

In addition to the names given to the hydrogen isotopes, they may also be distinguished by their **mass numbers**. The **mass number** of an atom is the sum of the number of protons and neutrons in its nucleus.

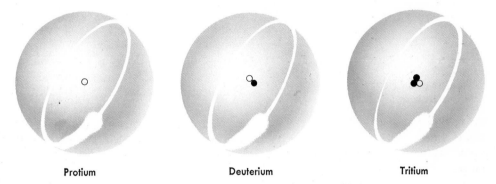

Protium   Deuterium   Tritium

3-2   The three isotopes of hydrogen: protium, deuterium, and tritium. Each has one proton in the nucleus and one electron moving about the nucleus in the 1st energy level. The only structural difference between them is the number of neutrons in the nucleus of each atom.

The mass number of protium is 1 (1 proton + 0 neutron), while that of deuterium is 2 (1 proton + 1 neutron) and of tritium is 3 (1 proton + 2 neutrons). Sometimes these isotopes are designated hydrogen-1, hydrogen-2, and hydrogen-3, respectively.

7.   The helium atom.   At the time of this writing, 104 different elements are known or reported to exist with atomic numbers ranging from 1 to 104. The elements may be arranged in the order of increasing atomic number. This simplifies the understanding of atomic structure. If the elements are arranged in this way, the nuclei of the atoms of one element differ from the nuclei of the atoms of the element preceding it by the addition of one proton.

The second element in order of complexity is helium. The atomic number of helium is 2, indicating that helium nuclei contain two protons. Natural helium exists as a mixture of two isotopes, helium-3, $1.34 \times 10^{-4}\%$, and helium-4 practically 100%. These forms of helium atoms contain 1 neutron and 2 neutrons respectively in their nuclei. (Remember that the number of neutrons in the nucleus of an atom may be determined by subtracting the atomic number from the mass number.) Moving about the helium nucleus

are two electrons, both in the *1st energy level*. These two electrons are all that can occupy this energy level. Thus hydrogen and helium constitute a first series of elements. In this first series, electrons enter the 1st energy level one at a time until it is filled with two electrons.

8.   The lithium atom.   Lithium exists as two isotopes, lithium-6 and lithium-7. Since the atomic number of lithium is 3, these types of atoms have 3 and 4 neutrons in their nuclei respectively. Surrounding the nucleus of lithium atoms are three electrons, since the number of protons and the number of electrons in any uncharged

3-3   A helium-4 atom is made up of a nucleus which consists of two protons and two neutrons. The two electrons are in motion in a region about this nucleus, and they fully occupy the 1st energy level of the atom.

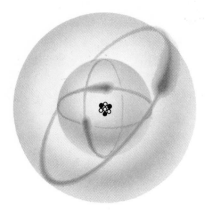

3-4 A lithium-7 atom has a nucleus consisting of three protons and four neutrons. Two electrons are in the 1st energy level and one is in the 2nd energy level. Lithium is the first element in the second series.

atom are equal. Two of these three electrons move in the 1st energy level. The third moves about the nucleus at a greater distance and with higher energy than the other two. It moves in the next larger shell or next higher energy level, which is called the *L shell* or *2nd energy level*. The 1st energy level can contain no more than two electrons. When it reaches this maximum of two electrons, additional electrons must enter other higher energy levels at correspondingly greater distances from the nucleus.

9.   Other atoms of the second series. The element with atomic number 4 is beryllium. Naturally occurring beryllium consists of only one form of atom, the beryllium-9 atom. Beryllium nuclei consist of four protons and five neutrons. The four electrons are arranged with two in the 1st energy level and two in the 2nd energy level. Next in order of atomic structure are the elements boron, carbon, nitrogen, oxygen, fluorine, and neon. Each successive element has one additional proton and may have one or two additional neutrons in its nucleus. Each has one additional

electron in the 2nd energy level. The element neon has a total of eight electrons in the 2nd energy level. Eight is the maximum number of electrons which the 2nd energy level can contain, so this element completes the second series.

The table of naturally occurring isotopes on page 47 contains information about the composition of the nucleus and the electron configuration of the atoms of the first and second series.

10.   The atoms of the third series. The elements in the third series are sodium, magnesium, aluminum, silicon, phosphorus, sulfur, chlorine, and argon. The atoms of these elements have a filled 1st energy level of two electrons and a filled 2nd energy level of eight electrons. Successive electrons enter the *M shell* or *3rd energy level* one at a time, until this level contains eight electrons in the atoms of the element argon.

11.   Atomic mass. The actual masses of individual atoms are very small. An atom of oxygen-16 has a mass of 2.65×10^{-23} g, while that of a protium atom is 1.67×10^{-24} g. These are inconveniently small numbers to use in chemical calculations. Consequently a system has been devised for indicating the *relative masses* of atoms in numbers that are easier for chemists to handle.

In order to set up a system of relative masses of atoms, one atom is assigned an arbitrary relative mass. The masses of all other atoms are then expressed in relation to this defined relative mass. In the system of relative masses designed by the world organizations of chemists and physicists, the carbon-12 atom is assigned a relative mass of exactly 12. Then an atom such as the protium atom, which has a mass about $\frac{1}{12}$ that of the carbon-12 atom, has a relative mass of about 1. The accurate value for the relative mass of protium atoms is 1.007825. *The mass of an atom expressed*

TABLE OF NATURALLY OCCURRING ISOTOPES

(First and Second Series of Elements)

Name of Isotope	Abundance	Atomic Number	Mass Number	Composition of Nucleus		Electron Configuration	
				Protons	Neutrons	1st energy level (K Shell)	2nd energy level (L Shell)
hydrogen-1 (protium)	99.985%	1	1	1	0	1	
hydrogen-2 (deuterium)	0.015%	1	2	1	1	1	
helium-3	0.00013%	2	3	2	1	2	
helium-4	~ 100%	2	4	2	2	2	
lithium-6	7.42%	3	6	3	3	2	1
lithium-7	92.58%	3	7	3	4	2	1
beryllium-9	100%	4	9	4	5	2	2
boron-10	19.6%	5	10	5	5	2	3
boron-11	80.4%	5	11	5	6	2	3
carbon-12	98.89%	6	12	6	6	2	4
carbon-13	1.11%	6	13	6	7	2	4
nitrogen-14	99.63%	7	14	7	7	2	5
nitrogen-15	0.37%	7	15	7	8	2	5
oxygen-16	99.759%	8	16	8	8	2	6
oxygen-17	0.037%	8	17	8	9	2	6
oxygen-18	0.204%	8	18	8	10	2	6
fluorine-19	100 %	9	19	9	10	2	7
neon-20	90.92%	10	20	10	10	2	8
neon-21	0.257%	10	21	10	11	2	8
neon-22	8.82%	10	22	10	12	2	8

relative to the carbon-12 = exactly 12 scale is the **atomic mass** *of the atom.* Thus 1.007825 is the atomic mass of protium. Deuterium atoms have a mass about $\frac{1}{6}$ that of carbon-12 atoms; thus their atomic mass is 2.01410. Oxygen-16 atoms have about $\frac{4}{3}$ the mass of carbon-12 atoms, and their atomic mass is 15.99491. Magnesium-24 atoms have about double the mass of carbon-12 atoms, so their atomic mass is 23.98504. In the same way the atomic masses of the isotopes of the other elements are determined by comparison with the mass of carbon-12 atoms. Atomic masses are quite accurately known, as

the values given as examples above indicate. The **mass number,** which indicates the total number of protons and neutrons in the nucleus of an atom, can also now be recognized as *the integer closest to the atomic mass.*

The masses of the sub-atomic particles may also be expressed on this atomic mass scale. The atomic mass of the electron is 0.0005486, of the proton is 1.007278, and of the neutron is 1.008665.

12. The Avogadro number and the mole. The number of atoms in the quantity of an isotope represented by its atomic mass in grams is important as a unit of measure in chemistry. This is the number of carbon-12 atoms in exactly 12 grams of this isotope; it is also the number of atoms in 1.007825 g of protium or in 15.99491 g of oxygen-16. Do you recognize that the number of atoms must be identical in these three cases since atomic masses are directly proportional to actual masses of isotopes?

Scientists have developed many direct and indirect ways for determining this number; its best present value is 6.02252 $\times 10^{23}$. This means that scientists have learned that there are 6.02252 $\times 10^{23}$ carbon-12 atoms in exactly 12 g of this isotope, 6.02252 $\times 10^{23}$ protium atoms in 1.007825 g of hydrogen-1, 6.02252 $\times 10^{23}$ oxygen-16 atoms in 15.99491 g of oxygen-16, and so on. This quantity, 6.02252 $\times 10^{23}$, is so important in science that it has been given a special name. It is called the *Avogadro number*, after an Italian chemist and physicist, Amadeo Avogadro (1776–1856). This constant is quite useful and should be remembered to at least three significant figures: 6.02 $\times 10^{23}$.

The amount of substance containing the Avogadro number of any kind of chemical unit is called a **mole** *of that substance.* Thus exactly 12 g of carbon-12 is a mole of carbon-12 atoms, 1.007825 g of hydrogen-1 is a mole of hydrogen-1 atoms, 15.99491 g of oxygen-16 is a mole of oxygen-16 atoms, and so on. The mole is also a very important unit of measure in chemistry. It will be used throughout this text.

13. Atomic weight. Naturally occurring elements usually exist as a mixture of several isotopes. Fortunately, the percentage of each isotope in the naturally occurring element is nearly always the same, regardless of the source of the element. Hence, the mass in grams of one mole of the *naturally occurring atoms* of an element indicates the "average relative mass" of these atoms on the same carbon-12 = ex-

actly 12 scale that was used for atomic masses. *The mass in grams of one mole of naturally occurring atoms of an element is called the* **gram-atomic weight** *of the element. The numerical portion of this quantity is the* **atomic weight** *of the element.*

Naturally occurring hydrogen consists of 99.985% hydrogen-1 atoms, atomic mass 1.007825, and 0.015% hydrogen-2 atoms, atomic mass 2.01410. Thus a mixture containing 1 mole of naturally occurring hydrogen atoms has a mass of 1.00797 g. This is the gram-atomic weight of hydrogen. The numerical portion, 1.00797, is the atomic weight of hydrogen. Similarly, naturally occurring carbon consists of 98.89% carbon-12, atomic mass exactly 12 (by definition), and 1.11% carbon-13, atomic mass 13.00335. One mole of atoms of this mixture has a mass of 12.01115 g. Thus 12.01115 g is the gram-atomic weight of carbon and 12.01115 is its atomic weight.

Atomic weights are important to the chemist because they indicate relative mass relationships between reacting elements. They enable him to predict the quantities of materials which will be involved in chemical reactions.

The Table of Atomic Weights on the inside of the back cover of this book (and in Table 3 of the Appendix) includes the most recent accurate figures. They are still revised occasionally when new data warrant. You need not memorize them. The approximate atomic weights given on the inside of the front cover (and in Table 4 of the Appendix) are sufficiently accurate for use in solving problems in high school chemistry. Your instructor may wish you to memorize some or all of these approximate values. For more sophisticated chemical work, the accurate atomic weights in the Table of Atomic Weights must always be used.

REVIEW OUTLINE

Atomic theory
  Ultimate particles of matter (1)
  Dalton's contribution (2)
  The atom (2)
  Properties of atoms (2, 3)

Atomic structure
  Nucleus: protons and neutrons (5)
  Shells or energy levels: electrons (3, 4)
  Atomic number (6)
  Isotopes (6)
  Mass number (6)
  Atomic mass (11)

Avogadro number
  Mole (12)
  Gram-atomic weight (13)
  Atomic weight (13)

QUESTIONS

Group A

1. What evidence is there that the particles of matter are very small?
2. What topics in chemistry are today included in the atomic theory?
3. What general statements may be made about the atoms of the elements and their properties?
4. (a) What are the main parts of an atom? (b) What particles are found in each part? (c) Describe each type of particle.
5. How does the size of the nucleus of an atom compare with the size of an atom?
6. What is a shell or energy level?
7. Describe the movement of electrons about the nucleus of an atom.
8. Describe the structure of each of the three isotopes of hydrogen.
9. (a) What is the atomic number of an atom? (b) How is it related to the number of electrons in a neutral atom?
10. If you know the number and kinds of particles in an atom, how can you calculate its mass number? $P + N$
11. An atomic nucleus contains 8 protons and 9 neutrons. About the nucleus move 8 electrons, 2 in the 1st energy level and 6 in the 2nd energy level. (a) What is the atomic number of this atom? (b) What is its mass number? (c) What is the name of this atom?
12. Which among the first ten elements exist naturally in only one form of atom?
13. What are isotopes?
14. What is the atomic mass of an atom?
15. (a) How many atoms are there in exactly 12 g of carbon-12? (b) What name is given to this number? (c) What name is given to the amount of substance containing this number of chemical units?

16. What is the atomic weight of an element?

17. What isotope is the standard for the atomic weight scale?

18. Why are atomic weights important to the chemist?

19. From the Table of Atomic Weights, find the atomic numbers and atomic weights of: (*a*) silver; (*b*) gold; (*c*) copper; (*d*) sulfur; (*e*) uranium.

20. What is the mass in grams of: (*a*) 2.00 moles of helium atoms; (*b*) 5.00 moles of boron atoms; (*c*) 0.500 mole of neon atoms; (*d*) 0.250 mole of magnesium atoms; (*e*) 0.100 mole of silicon atoms? Use the Table of Atomic Weights and follow the rules for significant figure calculations.

21. How many moles of atoms are there in: (*a*) 20.817 g of lithium; (*b*) 160. 93 g of sodium; (*c*) 3.995 g of argon; (*d*) 8.016 of sulfur; (*e*) 20.24 g of aluminum?

Group B

22. What did Dalton believe could be explained by knowledge of the nature and properties of atoms?

23. If you arrange the elements in order of increasing atomic number, how do successive elements differ in: (*a*) number of protons? (*b*) number of electrons? (*c*) number of neutrons?

24. Describe the electron configurations of the elements in the second series.

25. Copy and complete the following table *on a separate sheet of paper*.

Name of Isotope	Atomic Number	Mass Number	Composition of Nucleus		Electron Configuration		
			Protons	Neutrons	K	L	M
sodium-23	11	23	11	12	2	8	1
magnesium-24	12	24	12	12	2	8	2
aluminum-27	13	27	13	14	2	8	3
silicon-28	14						
phosphorus-31	15						
sulfur-32	16						
chlorine-35	17						
argon-40	18						

26. Chlorine exists in nature as chlorine-35, atomic mass 34.96885, and chlorine-37, atomic mass 36.96590. Its atomic weight is 35.453. What must be the approximate abundance in nature of these two isotopes?

27. The elements sodium, aluminum, and phosphorus have only one naturally occurring isotope. How will the atomic mass of this isotope and the atomic weight of the element compare?

28. (*a*) What is the relationship between an atom containing 10 protons, 10 neutrons, and 10 electrons, and one containing 10 protons, 11 neutrons, and 10 electrons? (*b*) What is the relationship between an atom containing 10 protons, 11 neutrons, and 10 electrons and one containing 11 protons, 10 neutrons, and 11 electrons?

29. Knowing the atomic mass of an isotope, how can the mass of a single atom of this isotope be calculated? *Divid by* 6.02×10^{23}

Chapter Four

ELECTRON CONFIGRATION OF ATOMS

▶**1. Theory that "opposites attract."** We have already described the atom as a nucleus, containing protons and usually neutrons, surrounded by electrons. The electrons move about the nucleus in more or less definite regions called shells or energy levels. Now we must consider the structure of the atom in more detail. We must learn how the electrons are arranged and held within the atom.

We recall that the nucleus has a positive charge due to its protons, and that a neutral atom contains an equal number of protons and negatively charged electrons. Thus we might expect electrons to be held in an atom by the attraction between oppositely charged particles. This is similar to the orbiting of a satellite about the earth. But instead of gravitational attraction which holds a satellite in orbit, the attraction of oppositely charged particles might be assumed to hold an electron in its path. However, scientists have observed that electrically charged particles moving in curved paths give off energy. If an electron moving about a nucleus continually

gave off energy, it should slow down, move nearer to the nucleus, and eventually fall into it. This is like the slowing down of a satellite by friction with the earth's upper atmosphere. As this occurs, the satellite falls toward the earth, and eventually burns up in the earth's atmosphere. We know that atoms do not collapse; electrons do not fall into the nucleus. Thus, the simple "opposites attract" theory is not satisfactory for explaining the motion of electrons about the nucleus of an atom.

▶**2. Electromagnetic radiation.** Light is a form of electromagnetic radiation. Other forms of electromagnetic radiation are X rays, ultraviolet and infrared light, and radio waves. Electromagnetic radiations are forms of energy which travel through space as waves. They move at the rate of 3.00×10^8 m/sec, the speed of light in a vacuum. For any wave motion, the speed equals the product of the frequency (the number of waves passing a given point in one second) and the wavelength. For electromagnetic radiation,

$$c = f\lambda$$

in which c is the speed of light, f is the frequency, and λ (lambda) is the wavelength.

Electromagnetic radiation, in addition to its wave characteristics, also has some properties of particles. Electromagnetic radiation is transferred to matter in units or *quanta* of energy called **photons.** The energy of a photon is proportional to the frequency of the radiation. Thus the energy of a photon and the frequency of the radiation are related by

$$E = hf$$

in which E is the energy of the photon, h is a proportionality constant called Planck's constant, and f is the frequency of the radiation. Planck's constant is identical for all types of electromagnetic radiation. Since energy is transferred to matter in photon units, the absorption of a photon by an atom increases its energy by a definite quantity, hf. An atom which has absorbed energy in this fashion is called an *excited* atom. When excited atoms radiate energy, the radiation must be evolved in photon units also.

▶3. **Spectra of atoms.** The radiation of energy by an excited atom may be represented by the equation

$$E_1 - E_2 = hf$$

in which E_1 is the energy of the excited atom, E_2 is its energy in its normal state, and hf is the energy of the photon of radiant energy emitted.

Atoms may be excited by such methods as subjecting them to a flame or to an electric arc. In returning to their normal states, excited atoms emit light of a color characteristic of their species. When this color is observed through a spectroscope,

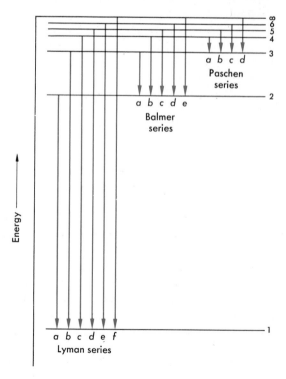

4-1 An electronic energy-level diagram for hydrogen showing some of the transitions which are possible in this atom.

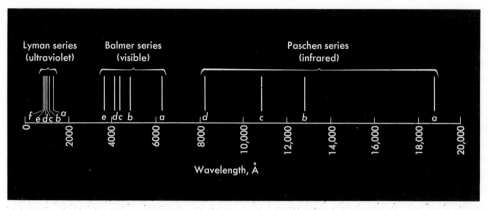

4-2 Representative lines in the hydrogen spectrum. The small letter below each line indicates which of the energy-level transitions in Figure 4-1 produces it.

it is found to consist of lines of particular colors. Such a spectrum is called a bright-line spectrum. It indicates that the light emitted by excited atoms has only very definite frequencies. Further, since the energy of a photon is dependent on the frequency of the radiation, only photons of definite energies are emitted.

Since the emitted photons have definite energies, representing differences between the energies of atoms before and after radiation, the energies of atoms themselves must be fixed and definite quantities. And because each species of atom has its own characteristic spectrum, each atom must have its own characteristic energy possibilities. Energy transitions within an atom must occur in jumps of discrete amounts of energy, rather than by a continuous change in energy.

Suppose we assume that the changes in energy of an excited atom on returning to its normal energy state are actually changes in the energy of its electrons. Then it is possible to devise a diagram which shows the electronic energy levels of the atom. Since the hydrogen atom is a simple atom with a simple spectrum, it was extensively studied in the early years of this century. Fig. 4-1 shows the elec-

tronic energy levels of the hydrogen atom and some of the transitions which are possible in this atom. These series of transitions correspond to series of spectral lines. See Fig. 4-2. The concept of electronic energy levels in the hydrogen atom was developed by Niels Bohr in 1913. The discrete energy levels of the atom indicate that the electron about the hydrogen nucleus can move only at certain distances from the nucleus and with only certain speeds.

This concept works well in explaining the spectra of one-electron particles like the hydrogen atom, but does not explain satisfactorily the spectra of more complex atoms.

4. Wave mechanics concept of an atom. During the past half century, the study of atomic structure has proceeded more mathematically. Through the work of theoretical physicists like Heisenberg, de Broglie, and Schroedinger, a complex mathematical picture of atomic structure has developed by the use of wave mechanics. While a detailed presentation of the fundamental concepts of wave mechanics is beyond the scope of this text, we can explain briefly some of its conclusions.

The motion of an electron about an atom is not in a definite path like that of the earth about the sun. It is impossible to determine the exact location of an electron without causing the electron to change its location. Thus we can indicate an electron's location only in terms of probabilities. This location is described by a *space orbital*, which may be thought of as a highly probable location in which an electron may be found. Thus the path of the single hydrogen electron is thought to lie within a hollow sphere of somewhat indefinite thickness which surrounds the nucleus. The mean radius of the sphere represents the most probable distance of the electron from the nucleus. This sphere is sometimes thought of as an *electron cloud*. The electron cloud gives size and shape to an atom, and prevents two free atoms (or portions of free atoms) from occupying the same space.

5. Quantum numbers. The mathematical expressions of wave mechanics indicate that each possible electronic orbital of an atom may be described by a set of four numbers, called *quantum numbers*. These numbers describe the orbital in terms of position with respect to the nucleus, shape, and spatial orientation. They also are related to the direction of spin and to the energy of the electron in each orbital.

The *principal quantum number* indicates the average distance of the electron from the nucleus of the atom. It is a positive integer, having values 1, 2, 3, and so on, and is the main energy level designation of an orbital. The 1st energy level is closest to the nucleus, with others at increasing distances. Electrons in the 1st energy level have the lowest energies; those in higher energy levels have increasingly greater energies. Sometimes, instead of using numbers, the energy levels are designated by letters, as K shell, L shell, M shell, etc.

The *secondary quantum number* indicates the shape of the orbital. The number of possible shapes is limited by the value of the principal quantum number. In the 1st energy level, an orbital of only one shape is possible; in the 2nd energy level, orbitals of two shapes are possible; in the 3rd energy level, orbitals of three shapes are possible, and so on. The letter designa-

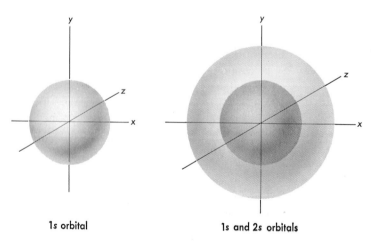

1s orbital   1s and 2s orbitals

4-3   Spatial orientation of *s* orbitals.

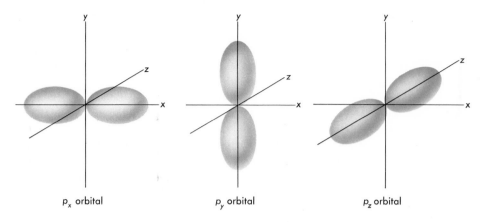

p_x orbital p_y orbital p_z orbital

4-4   The three spatial orientations of p orbitals.

tions for the first four secondary quantum numbers are *s*, *p*, *d*, and *f.* These are listed in order of ascending energies; so for a particular energy level, *s* orbitals have lower energy than *p* orbitals, and *p* orbitals have lower energy than *d* orbitals, and so on. Sometimes the *s* orbitals are called the *s* sublevel, the *p* orbitals the *p* sublevel, the *d* orbitals the *d* sublevel, etc.

The *magnetic quantum number* indicates the orientation in space of the electron cloud whose shape is given by the secondary quantum number. There is only one spatial orientation for an *s* orbital, while there are three for a *p* orbital, five for a *d* orbital, and seven for an *f* orbital. See Figs. 4-3 and 4-4.

The *spin quantum number* indicates the direction of spin of an electron. An elec-

tron spins on its axis, much as the earth does. There are two possibilities for spin, clockwise and counterclockwise. Thus for each of the *spatial orientations of orbitals* described by the first three quantum numbers, there are two possibilities for electron spin. Electrons of opposite spin in the same space orbital generally have about the same energy.

These four types of quantum numbers make it possible for us to classify the electrons in an atom. Furthermore, scientists have found that no two electrons in an atom have exactly the same quantum numbers; hence, they do not have exactly the same orbital. This means that no more than two electrons can occupy the same space orbital about an atom, and these must have opposite spins.

MAXIMUM NUMBER OF ELECTRONS IN ENERGY LEVELS

Principal Quantum Number, Energy Level, or Shell	Secondary Quantum Number (Letter designations)				Total
	Sublevels				
	s (1 space orbital)	*p* (3 space orbitals)	*d* (5 space orbitals)	*f* (7 space orbitals)	
1st or K	2				2
2nd or L	2	6			8
3rd or M	2	6	10		18
4th or N	2	6	10	14	32

6. Electron configurations of atoms of first three series. The quantum numbers which describe the arrangement of electrons about an atom are related to the energies of the electrons. The energies associated with the various electron orbitals are shown in Fig. 4-5. The most stable state of an atom is called its *ground state*. In this condition, the electrons have the lowest possible energies. If we know the number of electrons in an atom, it is possible to describe the electron configuration of its ground state, since electrons enter the various orbitals in a definite order starting with those of lowest energy.

Hydrogen has the electronic configuration designated $1s^1$, meaning that it has one electron (represented by the superscript) in the s sublevel of the 1st energy level. Helium has the electronic configuration $1s^2$, meaning that it has two electrons (represented by the superscript) in the s

sublevel of the 1st energy level. The two helium electrons must have opposite spins. Two such electrons of opposite spin in the same space orbital are called an *electron pair.*

Frequently other types of electronic notations are useful. One of these is the electron dot notation, in which hydrogen and helium are designated as

$$\textbf{H} \cdot \qquad \textbf{He} :$$

In this notation, the symbol denotes the element, and the dots indicate the number of outer-shell electrons. Another notation is the orbital notation

	1s		1s
H	◐	**He**	⊗

in which the occupation of a space orbital by one electron is represented as ◐, and by an electron pair is represented as ⊗.

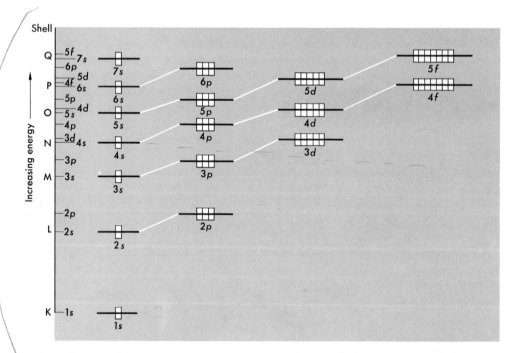

4-5 This chart shows the approximate relative energies of the atomic sublevels.

An empty circle, ○, indicates an unoccupied space orbital.

The elements in the second series have electrons entering the second energy level. Their ground state electron arrangements may be represented by electron configuration notation, electron dot notation, and orbital notation as shown in the following table. Note that the electron configuration notations and orbital notations show *all* of the electrons in the atom. However, the electron-dot notations show only the electrons in the *outer* shell or energy level.

Observe that electrons do not pair up in the $2p$ orbitals until each of the three $2p$ space orbitals is occupied by single electrons with parallel spins. An atom such as neon with the s and p orbitals of its outer energy level filled with eight electrons is said to have an outer shell consisting of an *octet*.

The electron configurations of the elements of the third series are similar to those of the second series with successive electrons entering the $3s$ and $3p$ space orbitals. (See Question 18 at the end of this chapter.)

▶**7. Atoms of the fourth series.** The atoms of the first two elements in the fourth series, potassium and calcium, have the same electron configuration in the first three energy levels as argon, $1s^2 2s^2 2p^6 3s^2 3p^6$. Electron-dot symbols for these elements are

K ·   Ca :

They show the entry of one or two electrons into the $4s$ sublevel. In the atoms of the next ten elements of this fourth series, the $3d$ sublevel is filled in successive steps by the entry of electrons into the atom structure. The distribution of electrons in the ground state of these atoms is given in the table shown at the top of the following page. The structures of both the chromium and copper atoms appear to be irregular, but the stability of a half-filled or completely filled $3d$ sublevel offsets what might be thought to be configurations of higher energy.

With the element zinc, the 3rd energy level is completely filled, and there are two electrons in the 4th energy level. The remaining six elements in the fourth

ELECTRON NOTATIONS OF ATOMS IN THE SECOND SERIES

Chemical Symbol	Electron Configuration Notation	Electron Dot Notation		Orbital Notation				
				1s	2s		2p	
Li	$1s^2 2s^1$	Li ·	Li	⊗	⊘	○	○	○
Be	$1s^2 2s^2$	Be :	Be	⊗	⊗	○	○	○
B	$1s^2 2s^2 2p^1$	Ḃ :	B	⊗	⊗	⊘	○	○
C	$1s^2 2s^2 2p^2$	· Ċ :	C	⊗	⊗	⊘	⊘	○
N	$1s^2 2s^2 2p^3$	· N̈ :	N	⊗	⊗	⊘	⊘	⊘
O	$1s^2 2s^2 2p^4$	· Ö :	O	⊗	⊗	⊗	⊘	⊘
F	$1s^2 2s^2 2p^5$	: F̈ :	F	⊗	⊗	⊗	⊗	⊘
Ne	$1s^2 2s^2 2p^6$	: N̈e :	Ne	⊗	⊗	⊗	⊗	⊗

STRUCTURE OF ATOMS IN THE FOURTH SERIES

Name	Symbol	Atomic Number	Number of Electrons in Sublevels							
			1s	2s	2p	3s	3p	3d	4s	4p
potassium	K	19	2	2	6	2	6		1	
calcium	Ca	20	2	2	6	2	6		2	
scandium	Sc	21	2	2	6	2	6	1	2	
titanium	Ti	22	2	2	6	2	6	2	2	
vanadium	V	23	2	2	6	2	6	3	2	
chromium	Cr	24	2	2	6	2	6	5	1	
manganese	Mn	25	2	2	6	2	6	5	2	
iron	Fe	26	2	2	6	2	6	6	2	
cobalt	Co	27	2	2	6	2	6	7	2	
nickel	Ni	28	2	2	6	2	6	8	2	
copper	Cu	29	2	2	6	2	6	10	1	
zinc	Zn	30	2	2	6	2	6	10	2	
gallium	Ga	31	2	2	6	2	6	10	2	1
germanium	Ge	32	2	2	6	2	6	10	2	2
arsenic	As	33	2	2	6	2	6	10	2	3
selenium	Se	34	2	2	6	2	6	10	2	4
bromine	Br	35	2	2	6	2	6	10	2	5
krypton	Kr	36	2	2	6	2	6	10	2	6

series, gallium, germanium, arsenic, selenium, bromine, and krypton, have completely filled 1st, 2nd, and 3rd energy levels. The electrons in the 4s and 4p sublevels are shown in these electron-dot symbols:

Ga: ·Ge: ·As: · Se: :Br: :Kr:

Krypton is the last member of the fourth series. It is a noble gas that has an octet in its 4th energy level.

STRUCTURE OF ATOMS IN THE FIFTH SERIES

Name	Symbol	Atomic Number	Number of Electrons in Sublevels										
			1s	2s	2p	3s	3p	3d	4s	4p	4d	5s	5p
rubidium	Rb	37	2	2	6	2	6	10	2	6		1	
strontium	Sr	38	2	2	6	2	6	10	2	6		2	
yttrium	Y	39	2	2	6	2	6	10	2	6	1	2	
zirconium	Zr	40	2	2	6	2	6	10	2	6	2	2	
niobium	Nb	41	2	2	6	2	6	10	2	6	4	1	
molybdenum	Mo	42	2	2	6	2	6	10	2	6	5	1	
technetium	Tc	43	2	2	6	2	6	10	2	6	6	1	
ruthenium	Ru	44	2	2	6	2	6	10	2	6	7	1	
rhodium	Rh	45	2	2	6	2	6	10	2	6	8	1	
palladium	Pd	46	2	2	6	2	6	10	2	6	10		
silver	Ag	47	2	2	6	2	6	10	2	6	10	1	
cadmium	Cd	48	2	2	6	2	6	10	2	6	10	2	
indium	In	49	2	2	6	2	6	10	2	6	10	2	1
tin	Sn	50	2	2	6	2	6	10	2	6	10	2	2
antimony	Sb	51	2	2	6	2	6	10	2	6	10	2	3
tellurium	Te	52	2	2	6	2	6	10	2	6	10	2	4
iodine	I	53	2	2	6	2	6	10	2	6	10	2	5
xenon	Xe	54	2	2	6	2	6	10	2	6	10	2	6

▶**8. Atoms of the fifth series.** The fifth series of elements, like the fourth, consists of eighteen elements. The first two of these, rubidium and strontium, have inner shells like krypton, $1s^2 2s^2 2p^6 3s^2 3p^6 3d^{10} 4s^2 4p^6$, and one or two electrons in the 5s sublevel.

Rb ·   **Sr :**

In the atoms of the next ten elements the five 4d sublevel orbitals become filled by the successive addition of electrons to the atom structure.

The atoms of the element cadmium have completely filled 1st, 2nd, and 3rd

energy levels, the 4s, 4p, and 4d sublevels filled, and two electrons in the 5s sublevel. The atoms of the remaining six elements of the fifth series, indium, tin, antimony, tellurium, iodine, and xenon have the first four energy levels like cadmium, but successive electrons enter the 5p sublevel, which has the next higher energy.

In: · Sn: · Sb: · Te: : I: : Xe:

Thus the entry of electrons into sublevels of two different energy levels proceeds in the fifth series in a manner similar

STRUCTURE OF ATOMS IN THE SIXTH SERIES

Name	Symbol	Atomic Number		Number of Electrons in Sublevels						
				4d	4f	5s	5p	5d	6s	6p
cesium	Cs	55		10		2	6		1	
barium	Ba	56		10		2	6		2	
lanthanum	La	57		10		2	6	1	2	
cerium	Ce	58		10	2	2	6		2	
praseodymium	Pr	59		10	3	2	6		2	
neodymium	Nd	60		10	4	2	6		2	
promethium	Pm	61		10	5	2	6		2	
samarium	Sm	62		10	6	2	6		2	
europium	Eu	63		10	7	2	6		2	
gadolinium	Gd	64		10	7	2	6	1	2	
terbium	Tb	65		10	9	2	6		2	
dysprosium	Dy	66		10	10	2	6		2	
holmium	Ho	67		10	11	2	6		2	
erbium	Er	68	Krypton	10	12	2	6		2	
thulium	Tm	69	Structure	10	13	2	6		2	
ytterbium	Yb	70	plus	10	14	2	6		2	
lutetium	Lu	71		10	14	2	6	1	2	
hafnium	Hf	72		10	14	2	6	2	2	
tantalum	Ta	73		10	14	2	6	3	2	
tungsten	W	74		10	14	2	6	4	2	
rhenium	Re	75		10	14	2	6	5	2	
osmium	Os	76		10	14	2	6	6	2	
iridium	Ir	77		10	14	2	6	9		
platinum	Pt	78		10	14	2	6	9	1	
gold	Au	79		10	14	2	6	10	1	
mercury	Hg	80		10	14	2	6	10	2	
thallium	Tl	81		10	14	2	6	10	2	1
lead	Pb	82		10	14	2	6	10	2	2
bismuth	Bi	83		10	14	2	6	10	2	3
polonium	Po	84		10	14	2	6	10	2	4
astatine	At	85		10	14	2	6	10	2	5
radon	Rn	86		10	14	2	6	10	2	6

to that of the fourth series. Xenon, the last member of the series, has an octet in its 5th energy level, and 4s, 4p, and 4d sublevels filled.

▶9. Atoms of the sixth series. The sixth series of atoms is much longer than the others. It consists of thirty-two elements. The atoms of the first two, cesium and barium, have inner energy levels like xenon and successive electrons in the 6s sublevel.

Cs·   **Ba:**

In the atoms of the next fourteen elements of the sixth series, the seven orbitals of the 4f sublevel are filled by the addition of successive electrons to the atom structure. In atoms of the element ytterbium, the 4th energy level has all of its sublevels filled with 32 electrons.

The atoms of the next ten elements of the sixth series have successive electrons

entering the five orbitals of the 5d sublevel, which have the next higher energies.

The atoms of the remaining six elements of this series, thallium, lead, bismuth, polonium, astatine, and radon, have the first four energy levels complete, and filled 5s, 5p, and 5d sublevels. The 6s and 6p electrons are shown in these electron-dot symbols.

Tl: ·Pb: ·Bi: ·Po: :At: :Rn:

Radon, the last member of the sixth series, has an octet in its 6th energy level, and 5s, 5p, and 5d sublevels filled.

▶10. Atoms of the seventh series. The seventh series of elements is an incomplete series of which only 17 elements are known. The arrangement of electrons in the 5th, 6th, and 7th energy levels is believed to be as shown in the following table.

STRUCTURE OF ATOMS IN THE SEVENTH SERIES

Name	Symbol	Atomic Number		Number of Electrons in Sublevels						
				4f	5d	5f	6s	6p	6d	7s
francium	Fr	87		14	10		2	6		1
radium	Ra	88		14	10		2	6		2
actinium	Ac	89		14	10		2	6	1	2
thorium	Th	90		14	10		2	6	2	2
protactinium	Pa	91		14	10	2	2	6	1	2
uranium	U	92		14	10	3	2	6	1	2
neptunium	Np	93		14	10	5	2	6		2
plutonium	Pu	94	Xenon	14	10	6	2	6		2
americium	Am	95	Structure	14	10	7	2	6		2
curium	Cm	96	plus	14	10	7	2	6	1	2
berkelium	Bk	97		14	10	8	2	6	1	2
californium	Cf	98		14	10	10	2	6		2
einsteinium	Es	99		14	10	10	2	6	1	2 ?
fermium	Fm	100		14	10	11	2	6	1	2 ?
mendelevium	Md	101		14	10	12	2	6	1	2 ?
nobelium	No	102		14	10	13	2	6	1	2 ?
lawrencium	Lw	103		14	10	14	2	6	1	2 ?

REVIEW OUTLINE

Evidence for electron energy levels
    "Opposites attract" theory (1)
    Electromagnetic radiation: photon (2)
    Atomic spectra: excited atom, bright-line spectrum (3)
    Wave mechanics: space orbital (4)
        Principal quantum number (5)
        Secondary quantum number (5)
        Magnetic quantum number (5)
        Spin quantum number (5)

Pattern of electron energy levels: ground state (6)

Electronic notations (6)
    Sublevel notation (6)
    Electron-dot notation: pair, octet (6)
    Orbital notation (6)

Series of elements
    Atoms of the first three series (6)
    Atoms of the fourth series (7)
    Atoms of the fifth series (8)
    Atoms of the sixth series (9)
    Atoms of the seventh series (10)

QUESTIONS

Group A

▶ 1. (*a*) What are electromagnetic radiations? (*b*) Give examples of forms of electromagnetic radiation.

▶ 2. (*a*) In what form do electromagnetic radiations travel through space? (*b*) In what form are they transferred to matter?

▶ 3. How is an excited atom produced?

▶ 4. What are the principal characteristics of the Bohr model of the hydrogen atom?

▶ 5. What is a space orbital?

   6. (*a*) What is an electron cloud? (*b*) What properties does it give an atom?

   7. What are the four kinds of quantum numbers and what does each indicate?

   8. (*a*) What is the shape of an *s* orbital? (*b*) How many *s* orbitals may there be in an energy level? (*c*) How many electrons can occupy such an orbital? (*d*) What characteristic must these electrons have? (*e*) Which is the lowest energy level having an *s* orbital?

   9. (*a*) What is the shape of a *p* orbital? (*b*) How many *p* orbitals may there be in an energy level? (*c*) How are they oriented with respect to one another? (*d*) Which is the lowest energy level having *p* orbitals?

10. (*a*) May two electrons in the same atom have exactly the same set of quantum numbers? (*b*) May two electrons occupy the same space orbital in an atom? (*c*) Under what conditions?

11. Distinguish between an atom in its ground state and an excited atom.

12. (*a*) What is an electron pair? (*b*) What is an octet?

Group B

▶13. What aspect of the "opposites attract" theory makes it unsatisfactory for explaining how electrons are held in an atom?

▶14. Derive the relationship between λ and E for an electromagnetic radiation.

▶15. Why must energy transitions within an atom occur in discrete amounts rather than as a continuous change?

16. (*a*) How many *d* orbitals may there be in an energy level? (*b*) How many *d* electrons may there be in an energy level? (*c*) Which is the lowest energy level having *d* orbitals?

17. (*a*) How many *f* orbitals may there be in an energy level? (*b*) How many *f* electrons may there be in an energy level? (*c*) Which is the lowest energy level having *f* orbitals?

18. On a separate sheet of paper copy and complete the following table for the atoms in the third series. *Do not write in this book.*

Chemical Symbol	Electron Configuration Notation	Electron-dot Notation	Orbital Notation
Na			
Mg			
Al			
Si			
P			
S			
Cl			
Ar			

19. How many electron pairs are there in the outer shell of each of the following atoms: (*a*) carbon; (*b*) krypton; (*c*) oxygen; (*d*) arsenic; (*e*) iodine?

20. Which of the atoms in Question 19 has an octet as an outer shell?

▶21. How many energy levels are partially or fully occupied in the mendelevium atom?

▶22. Why do the fourth and fifth series of elements contain 18 elements, rather than 8 as in the second and third series?

▶23. Why does the sixth series of elements contain 32 elements, rather than 18 as in the fourth and fifth series?

24. (*a*) Which energy level corresponds to the N shell? (*b*) What types of space orbitals may be found in this energy level? (*c*) How many of each type? (*d*) How many electrons may occupy each of these types of space orbitals? (*e*) How many electrons are needed to completely fill the N shell?

25. Which sublevels of the 3rd energy level are filled: (*a*) in the element argon; (*b*) in the element krypton?

▶ 26. What is a probable electron configuration for element 106?

Chapter Five

THE PERIODIC LAW

1. Value of classification of chemical elements. If you had to study the properties of each of the 104 chemical elements to have even an elementary knowledge of chemistry, the task would be great. However, if some elements had similar properties, and if they could be grouped together, it would not be too difficult to remember the distinguishing properties of the group. It might even be possible to remember some of the variations in properties among the members of the group, if the variations were to occur fairly regularly.

During the late eighteenth and early nineteenth centuries, chemists began to identify certain substances as chemical elements. They also recognized that there were similarities in the properties of some of these elements. They discovered that sodium and potassium were soft, silvery metals. They found that calcium, barium, and strontium could be prepared as elements by similar chemical changes; that sulfur, selenium, and tellurium formed similar chemical compounds; and that chlorine, bromine, and iodine were colored nonmetallic elements. But such isolated discoveries did not offer much promise of classifying all the known chemical elements into any unifying system.

2. Early attempts to classify elements. About 1800, chemists began to determine the atomic weights of some elements with fair accuracy. Attempts were soon made to classify the elements on this basis. As early as 1817, Johann Wolfgang Dobereiner (*doh*-ber-eye-ner) (1780–1849), noticed that the atomic weight of strontium was almost equal to the average of the atomic weights of calcium and barium. He later observed that the atomic weight of bromine was close to the average of the atomic weights of chlorine and iodine. Similarly, he found that the atomic weight of selenium was not too different from the average of the atomic weights of sulfur and tellurium. Dobereiner called such groups of elements *triads*.

In 1864 John A. Newlands (1838–1898)

arranged all the known elements in the order of their atomic weights. He then divided them into series of seven elements each. He made this division because the eighth element was found to have chemical properties similar to the first element of the preceding series. Hence, he made that element the first one in a second series. He tried to convince his colleagues of the usefulness of his *law of octaves*, but they merely laughed at his ideas.

Lothar Meyer (1830–1895) plotted a graph which was his attempt to group elements according to atomic weights.

3. Mendeleyev's Periodic Table. By 1869 Dmitri Mendeleyev (men-deh-*lay*-eff) (1834–1907)—the name is spelled in a variety of ways—had worked out a *Periodic Table of the Elements*. In this table the elements were arranged in the order of increasing atomic weights. The first two series or periods in Mendeleyev's system of classification contained *seven elements* each. The next three periods contained *seventeen elements* each. The Periodic Tables we use today are largely based on the pioneer work done by Mendeleyev.

When Mendeleyev first prepared his Periodic Table, he realized that all the elements were probably not yet discovered. For example, scandium, gallium, and germanium were unknown in Mendeleyev's day. He carefully studied the properties of the known elements. From this study he learned where to leave gaps in his table for those to be discovered later, and predicted that new elements would be discovered to fit these gaps. He also predicted the properties of these new elements. His predictions were later found to be quite accurate when compared with the actual properties of these elements.

Mendeleyev noticed, just as Newlands had, that the chemical properties of the elements recur at definite intervals. Therefore, he concluded that "the properties

of the elements are in periodic dependence on their atomic weights."

In Mendeleyev's table, the first two periods, or series, had seven elements before there was a recurrence of properties. In the third period, Mendeleyev found there were seventeen elements before there was recurrence of properties. Periods 4 and 5 were long series, too. The discovery of the noble gases, neon, argon, krypton, and xenon, by Sir William Ramsay (1852–1916) during the 1890's, together with the earlier discovered element, helium, added an additional element to each period in Mendeleyev's table.

4. Moseley determines atomic numbers. About 45 years after Mendeleyev's work on the Periodic Table, another important discovery was made which helped solve the problem of classifying elements. In Chapter 3 it was stated that the atomic

5-1 Dmitri Mendeleyev, a Russian chemist, worked out the first Periodic Table of the Chemical Elements. (SOVFOTO)

number of an element indicates the number of protons in the nuclei of its atoms. Henry Gwyn-Jeffreys Moseley (1887–1915), a brilliant young English scientist, used X rays to determine the atomic numbers of the elements.

X rays are electromagnetic radiations of high frequency and short wavelength. X rays are produced when high-speed electrons strike the metal target in an evacuated tube. Moseley found that the wavelengths of the X rays produced in such tubes depend on the kind of metal used as a target. Therefore, he used as targets various metals ranging in atomic weight from aluminum to gold. He found that the wavelengths of X rays became shorter as he used elements which have more of what are now recognized as protons in their nuclei. The higher the atomic number of an element, the shorter is the wavelength of the X rays produced when that element is used as a target within an X-ray tube.

Moseley found in some cases an unusual variation in the wavelengths of X rays between two successive elements. The variation was twice as great as his calculations justified. He concluded that in such cases an element was missing from the Periodic Table. Several elements have since been discovered which fill the gaps that Moseley indicated.

5. The Periodic Law. When the elements in a Periodic Table are placed in the order of increasing atomic numbers instead of in the order of increasing atomic weights, some of the problems of arrangement disappear. Arranged according to increasing atomic weights, potassium precedes argon. Yet, when arranged according to properties in the table, potassium follows argon. This is in agreement with the atomic numbers, argon 18, and potassium 19. A similar case is that of tellurium 52 and iodine 53.

As stated in Section 3, Mendeleyev concluded that the properties of elements are in periodic dependence on their atomic weights. Today, evidence shows that atomic numbers are better criteria for establishing the order of the elements. Mendeleyev's conclusion is now restated as the **Periodic Law:** *The physical and chemical properties of the elements are periodic functions of their atomic numbers.* In other words, the properties of elements go through a pattern of change, with elements of similar properties recurring after certain intervals, provided the elements are arranged in a table in the order of increasing atomic number.

6. Arrangement of the modern Periodic Table. The modern Periodic Table is shown on pages 68–69. Frequent reference to these pages as you study this section will help you to understand the Periodic Table and its importance in chemistry.

Each element is assigned a separate block in the table. In the center of the block is the chemical symbol for the element. Below the symbol is the atomic number of the element. Above the symbol is the atomic weight. To the right of each symbol are numbers which indicate the distribution of electrons in the shells of the atoms of this element. A horizontal row of blocks on the table is called a *period* or *series*. A vertical column is called a *group* or *family*.

Hydrogen, atomic number 1, is placed at the top of the table by itself because of its many unique properties. It is in the first column at the left of the table because it has one electron in its outermost shell. Helium, atomic number 2, is at the top of the extreme right-hand column. It is the simplest member of the group of generally inert elements known as the *noble gases*. Note that helium has two electrons in its K shell, and that with these two electrons, the K shell is complete. Hydrogen and helium comprise the first period of elements.

The second period consist. of eight elements: *lithium*, a soft silvery, active metal, whose atoms have one electron in their outer shell, the L shell; *beryllium*, a silvery metal, less active than lithium, whose atoms have two electrons in their L shell; *boron*, a black solid with few metallic properties, whose atoms have three electrons in their L shell; *carbon*, a solid element with very distinctive chemical properties intermediate between those of metals and nonmetals, four electrons in the L shell; *nitrogen*, a colorless gas, nonmetallic properties, five electrons in its L shell; *oxygen*, a colorless gas, strong nonmetallic properties, six electrons in its L shell; *fluorine*, a pale-yellow gas, very strong nonmetallic properties, seven electrons in its L shell; and *neon*, a colorless, inert gas, eight electrons in its L shell. Refer to the table of electronic arrangement of the elements in the Appendix.

In this brief description of the properties of these elements, it should be noted that they range from an active metallic element to an active nonmetallic element, while the last element in the period is inert. This variation in properties from metallic to nonmetallic is accompanied by an increase in the number of L-shell electrons from 1 to 7. The inert element neon has 8 electrons, an octet, in the L shell.

The third period also consists of eight elements: *sodium*, a soft silvery, active metal similar to lithium, one electron in its outermost shell, the M shell; *magnesium*, a silvery metal similar in properties to beryllium, two electrons in its M shell; *aluminum*, a silvery metal with some nonmetallic properties, three electrons in the M shell; *silicon*, a dark-colored nonmetallic element with some properties resembling carbon, four electrons in the M

shell; *phosphorus*, a nonmetallic solid element which forms compounds similar to those of nitrogen, five electrons in its M shell; *sulfur*, a yellow nonmetallic solid element, six electrons in its M shell; *chlorine*, a yellow-green gas with strong nonmetallic properties resembling those of fluorine, seven electrons in the M shell; and *argon*, a colorless, inert gas, eight electrons in its M shell.

Again, the elements range from strong metallic to strong nonmetallic properties as the number of electrons in the outer shell varies from 1 to 7. The element with an octet as its outer shell is a noble gas.

Notice that elements with similar properties have a similar arrangement of outer-shell electrons. They fall into the same group in the Periodic Table.

In Group I in the Periodic Table, we find the Sodium Family, a group of six similar, very active, metallic elements. Their atoms all have only one electron in the outermost shell. *Francium* is the most complex member of the Sodium Family. Its position in the Periodic Table indicates that it is probably the most active metal. Group II consists of six active metals whose chemical properties are very much alike. The atoms of each have two electrons in their outer shell. This is the Calcium Family. The most chemically active member of this family is *radium*.

The properties of elements in Group III vary from nonmetallic to metallic as the atoms become more complex. The atoms of this group have three electrons in their outer shell. The elements of Group IV vary in similar fashion; their atoms have four electrons in their outer shell. Atoms of elements of both of these groups have very stable inner shells.

Group V is the Nitrogen Family. *Nitrogen* and *phosphorus*, the elements in this family at the top of the table, are nonmetallic. The element *bismuth* at the bot-

METALS

TRANSITION ELEMENTS

	I	II							
1	1.00797 **H** 1 (1)								
2	6.939 **Li** 3 (2,1)	9.0122 **Be** 4 (2,2)							
3	22.9898 **Na** 11 (2,8,1)	24.312 **Mg** 12 (2,8,2)							
4	39.102 **K** 19 (2,8,8,1)	40.08 **Ca** 20 (2,8,8,2)	44.956 **Sc** 21 (2,8,9,2)	47.90 **Ti** 22 (2,8,10,2)	50.942 **V** 23 (2,8,11,2)	51.996 **Cr** 24 (2,8,13,1)	54.9380 **Mn** 25 (2,8,13,2)	55.847 **Fe** 26 (2,8,14,2)	58.9332 **Co** 27 (2,8,15,2)
5	85.47 **Rb** 37 (2,8,18,8,1)	87.62 **Sr** 38 (2,8,18,8,2)	88.905 **Y** 39 (2,8,18,9,2)	91.22 **Zr** 40 (2,8,18,10,2)	92.906 **Nb** 41 (2,8,18,12,1)	95.94 **Mo** 42 (2,8,18,13,1)	[99*] **Tc** 43 (2,8,18,14,1)	101.07 **Ru** 44 (2,8,18,15,1)	102.905 **Rh** 45 (2,8,18,16,1)
6	132.905 **Cs** 55 (2,8,18,18,8,1)	137.34 **Ba** 56 (2,8,18,18,8,2)	Lanthanide Series / 174.97 **Lu** 71 (2,8,18,32,9,2)	178.49 **Hf** 72 (2,8,18,32,10,2)	180.948 **Ta** 73 (2,8,18,32,11,2)	183.85 **W** 74 (2,8,18,32,12,2)	186.2 **Re** 75 (2,8,18,32,13,2)	190.2 **Os** 76 (2,8,18,32,14,2)	192.2 **Ir** 77 (2,8,18,32,15,0)
7	[223] **Fr** 87 (2,8,18,32,18,8,1)	[226] **Ra** 88 (2,8,18,32,18,8,2)	Actinide Series / [257] **Lw** 103 (2,8,18,32,32,9,2)						

Lanthanide Series

138.91 **La** 57 (2,8,18,18,9,2)	140.12 **Ce** 58 (2,8,18,20,8,2)	140.907 **Pr** 59 (2,8,18,21,8,2)	144.24 **Nd** 60 (2,8,18,22,8,2)	[147*] **Pm** 61 (2,8,18,23,8,2)	150.35 **Sm** 62 (2,8,18,24,8,2)	151.96 **Eu** 63 (2,8,18,25,8,2)

Actinide Series

[227] **Ac** 89 (2,8,18,32,18,9,2)	232.038 **Th** 90 (2,8,18,32,18,10,2)	[231] **Pa** 91 (2,8,18,32,20,9,2)	238.03 **U** 92 (2,8,18,32,21,9,2)	[237] **Np** 93 (2,8,18,32,23,8,2)	[242] **Pu** 94 (2,8,18,32,24,8,2)	[243] **Am** 95 (2,8,18,32,25,8,2)

OF THE ELEMENTS

Noble gases VIII

	III	IV	V	VI	VII	VIII
						4.0026 **He** 2 — (2)
	10.811 **B** 5 — (2,3)	12.01115 **C** 6 — (2,4)	14.0067 **N** 7 — (2,5)	15.9994 **O** 8 — (2,6)	18.9984 **F** 9 — (2,7)	20.183 **Ne** 10 — (2,8)
	26.9815 **Al** 13 — (2,8,3)	28.086 **Si** 14 — (2,8,4)	30.9738 **P** 15 — (2,8,5)	32.064 **S** 16 — (2,8,6)	35.453 **Cl** 17 — (2,8,7)	39.948 **Ar** 18 — (2,8,8)
58.71 **Ni** 28 — (2,8,16,2)	63.54 **Cu** 29 — (2,8,18,1)	65.37 **Zn** 30 — (2,8,18,2)	69.72 **Ga** 31 — (2,8,18,3)	72.59 **Ge** 32 — (2,8,18,4)	74.9216 **As** 33 — (2,8,18,5)	78.96 **Se** 34 — (2,8,18,6)
79.909 **Br** 35 — (2,8,18,7)	83.80 **Kr** 36 — (2,8,18,8)					
106.4 **Pd** 46 — (2,8,18,18,0)	107.870 **Ag** 47 — (2,8,18,18,1)	112.40 **Cd** 48 — (2,8,18,18,2)	114.82 **In** 49 — (2,8,18,18,3)	118.69 **Sn** 50 — (2,8,18,18,4)	121.75 **Sb** 51 — (2,8,18,18,5)	127.60 **Te** 52 — (2,8,18,18,6)
126.9044 **I** 53 — (2,8,18,18,7)	131.30 **Xe** 54 — (2,8,18,18,8)					
195.09 **Pt** 78 — (2,8,18,32,17,1)	196.967 **Au** 79 — (2,8,18,32,18,1)	200.59 **Hg** 80 — (2,8,18,32,18,2)	204.37 **Tl** 81 — (2,8,18,32,18,3)	207.19 **Pb** 82 — (2,8,18,32,18,4)	208.980 **Bi** 83 — (2,8,18,32,18,5)	[210*] **Po** 84 — (2,8,18,32,18,6)
[210] **At** 85 — (2,8,18,32,18,7)	[222] **Rn** 86 — (2,8,18,32,18,8)					

RARE EARTH ELEMENTS

157.25 **Gd** 64 (2,8,18,25,9,2)	158.924 **Tb** 65 (2,8,18,27,8,2)	162.50 **Dy** 66 (2,8,18,28,8,2)	164.930 **Ho** 67 (2,8,18,29,8,2)	167.26 **Er** 68 (2,8,18,30,8,2)	168.934 **Tm** 69 (2,8,18,31,8,2)	173.04 **Yb** 70 (2,8,18,32,8,2)
[247] **Cm** 96 (2,8,18,32,25,9,2)	[249*] **Bk** 97 (2,8,18,32,26,9,2)	[251*] **Cf** 98 (2,8,18,32,28,8,2)	[254] **Es** 99 (2,8,18,32,28,9,2)	[253] **Fm** 100 (2,8,18,32,29,9,2)	[256] **Md** 101 (2,8,18,32,30,9,2)	[254] **102** (2,8,18,32,31,9,2)

A value given in brackets denotes the mass number of the isotope of longest known half-life, or for those marked with an asterisk, a better known one.

tom of the table is metallic. *Arsenic* and *antimony* exhibit both metallic and non-metallic properties. Each of these atoms has five electrons in the outer shell, and has very stable inner shells.

Group VI is the Oxygen Family. The properties of the elements of this family vary from active nonmetallic to metallic as the atoms become more complex. The atoms of each element have six electrons in the outer shell and have very stable inner shells. The elements in Group VII, the Halogen Family, are very active nonmetals. Their atoms each have seven electrons in the outer shell, and have very stable inner shells. The most active member of the Halogen Family is its simplest element, *fluorine.* Thus we see that the activity of the elements ranges from the most active metal at the lower left corner of the Periodic Table to the most active nonmetal at the upper right corner.

Group VIII is the Noble Gas Family. With the exception of *helium* atoms, which have a pair of electrons as their outer shell, atoms of these elements have an octet as their outer shell. This is the greatest number of electrons found in an outer shell. These elements are generally chemically inert. A few compounds of krypton, xenon, and radon have been prepared.

The fourth period of elements is the first long period. In addition to the eight elements in Groups I to VIII, there are also ten *transition elements.* These are metallic elements whose atoms have one or two electrons in the outer shell. Successive electrons usually enter the group of 5 space orbitals of the $3d$ sublevel.

The fifth period of elements also includes ten transition elements, in which successive electrons enter the group of 5 space orbitals of the $4d$ sublevel. These elements are all metals.

The sixth period consists of thirty-two elements. In addition to the ten transition elements, there is a group of fourteen *rare earth elements.* These elements have almost identical chemical properties. They are called the *Lanthanide Series.* The *two* outer shells of these atoms are almost the same. Successive electrons enter the group of 7 space orbitals of the $4f$ sublevel, as the number of electrons in the 4th energy level increases from 18 to 32.

The seventh period of elements is at present an incomplete period. It is assumed to be similar to the sixth period. The rare earth elements in this period are called the *Actinide Series.* At present, eighteen members of the seventh period are known or reported.

In the Periodic Table the elements are roughly divided into metals, nonmetals, and noble gases. The line separating the metals from the nonmetals is a zigzag line running diagonally down and to the right near the right end of the table. The elements which border this zigzag line are the *metalloids*, which show both metallic and nonmetallic properties under different conditions.

7. Size of atoms: a periodic property. It was recognized in Chapter 3 that an atom consists of a central nucleus with electrons moving about it. Since the nucleus has a diameter which is about one one-hundred-thousandth that of the atom, most of the volume of an atom is attributable to the complex motion of the electrons. By their motion and their negative charge, the electrons effectively occupy the space around the nucleus by forming a spherical electron cloud which gives the atom its volume and excludes other atoms.

The volume of an atom is not a completely definite quantity because the boundary of an atom's electron cloud is not a distinct surface, but is somewhat fuzzy and indefinite. An atom may be rather easily distorted when it combines with other atoms, but very great force

PERIODIC TABLE OF ATOMIC RADII

I	II											III	IV	V	VI	VII	VIII
0.30 **H** 1																	0.93 **He** 2
1.23 **Li** 3	0.89 **Be** 4											0.80 **B** 5	0.77 **C** 6	0.70 **N** 7	0.66 **O** 8	0.64 **F** 9	1.12 **Ne** 10
1.57 **Na** 11	1.36 **Mg** 12											1.25 **Al** 13	1.17 **Si** 14	1.10 **P** 15	1.04 **S** 16	0.99 **Cl** 17	1.54 **Ar** 18
2.02 **K** 19	1.74 **Ca** 20	1.44 **Sc** 21	1.32 **Ti** 22	1.22 **V** 23	1.19 **Cr** 24	1.18 **Mn** 25	1.17 **Fe** 26	1.16 **Co** 27	1.15 **Ni** 28	1.18 **Cu** 29	1.21 **Zn** 30	1.25 **Ga** 31	1.24 **Ge** 32	1.21 **As** 33	1.17 **Se** 34	1.14 **Br** 35	1.69 **Kr** 36
2.16 **Rb** 37	1.91 **Sr** 38	1.62 **Y** 39	1.45 **Zr** 40	1.34 **Nb** 41	1.30 **Mo** 42	1.27 **Tc** 43	1.25 **Ru** 44	1.25 **Rh** 45	1.28 **Pd** 46	1.34 **Ag** 47	1.38 **Cd** 48	1.42 **In** 49	1.42 **Sn** 50	1.39 **Sb** 51	1.37 **Te** 52	1.33 **I** 53	1.90 **Xe** 54
2.35 **Cs** 55	1.98 **Ba** 56	1.56 **Lu** 71	1.44 **Hf** 72	1.34 **Ta** 73	1.30 **W** 74	1.28 **Re** 75	1.26 **Os** 76	1.26 **Ir** 77	1.30 **Pt** 78	1.34 **Au** 79	1.39 **Hg** 80	1.44 **Tl** 81	1.50 **Pb** 82	1.51 **Bi** 83	1.65 **Po** 84	**At** 85	2.2 **Rn** 86
Fr 87	2.20 **Ra** 88	**Lw** 103															

1.69 **La** 57	1.65 **Ce** 58	1.64 **Pr** 59	1.64 **Nd** 60	1.63 **Pm** 61	1.62 **Sm** 62	1.85 **Eu** 63	1.62 **Gd** 64	1.61 **Tb** 65	1.60 **Dy** 66	1.58 **Ho** 67	1.58 **Er** 68	1.58 **Tm** 69	1.70 **Yb** 70
2.0 **Ac** 89	1.65 **Th** 90	**Pa** 91	1.43 **U** 92	**Np** 93	**Pu** 94	**Am** 95	**Cm** 96	**Bk** 97	**Cf** 98	**Es** 99	**Fm** 100	**Md** 101	102

5-2 Periodic Table showing radii of the atoms of the elements in Ångström units.

must be used if it is to be compressed appreciably.

The apparent size of an atom varies somewhat with the method used to measure it. Scientists however have measured the distance between adjacent nuclei in the crystalline forms of elements and in the molecules of gaseous elements. These distances have been taken, with some slight corrections, as indicating the diameter of identical atoms. The diameter of an atom, and thus its radius and volume, does not increase regularly with atomic number as might be expected from the regular addition of an electron in successive elements. Atomic size varies in a periodic fashion as shown in Fig. 5-2, which is a miniature Periodic Table with element symbols and atomic numbers in black. Atomic radii are shown in color. The radii of atoms of the elements are given in Ångströms. Figure 5-3 shows the atomic radius plotted as a function of the atomic number.

From this chart and graph two conclusions about the relationship between atomic radius and the Periodic Table may be drawn:

1. The atomic radius increases with atomic number in a particular group or family of elements. Each element in a group has one more shell or energy level than the element above it. Even though the nuclear charge increases and tends to decrease the radii of the electron shells by drawing them closer, the addition of a shell more than counteracts this effect.

2. In a series or period, the atomic ra-

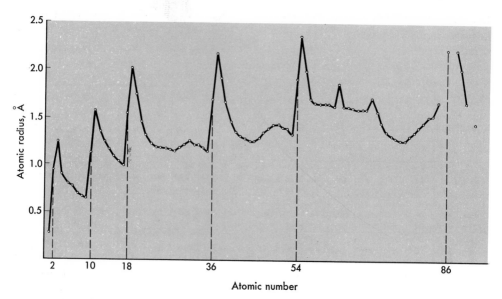

5-3   Graph showing atomic radius plotted as a function of atomic number.

dius *generally* decreases from Group I to Group VII. The noble gas in Group VIII has a larger radius, but not as great a one as that of the elements of Groups I and II of the same period. The decrease in atomic radius across a period is due to the greater attraction of the increasing nuclear charge for electrons entering the same shell, thus pulling them closer to the nucleus. The irregularities may be due to the shell-enlarging effect of the mutual repulsion of electrons entering the same subshell. The greater size of the noble gas atoms is due to the structural stability of an outer shell consisting of an octet.

8.   Ionization energy.   An electron is held in an atom essentially by the electrostatic attraction of the positively charged protons in the nucleus and the negative charge of the electron. By supplying energy, it is possible to remove an electron from an atom. Using **A** as a symbol for an atom of any element and → to mean "yields," this electron removal may be shown in equation form:

$$\mathbf{A} + \mathbf{energy} \rightarrow \mathbf{A^+} + e^-$$

The particle **A⁺** remaining after the removal of an electron, e^-, is a singly charged *ion. An ion is an atom* (or sometimes a group of atoms) *with an unbalanced electrostatic charge* resulting from an unequal number of positively charged protons and negatively charged electrons. *The energy required to remove an electron from an atom is its **ionization energy**.* It is usually expressed in electron-volts (an electron-volt is the energy acquired by an electron in falling through a potential difference of one volt). The chart, Fig. 5-4, shows the ionization energy required to remove the first electron from an atom of each element. Figure 5-5 is a graph showing ionization energy plotted as a function of atomic number. From these data the following conclusions may be drawn:

1. Low ionization energy is characteristic of a metal, while high ionization energy is characteristic of a nonmetal. An intermediate ionization energy is characteristic of a metalloid. The noble gases have unusually high ionization energies because of the stability of the outer shell octet.

2. Within a group of elements, the ionization energy generally decreases with increasing atomic number. In a group, increasing atomic number is accompanied by increasing atomic radius. Thus the outer-shell electrons of the elements of higher atomic number within a group are farther from the nucleus and will be attracted less by it. The ionization energy for removal of one such electron will therefore be less as the atomic number of the atom is greater.

3. Ionization energy does not vary uniformly from element to element within a series, but is a periodic property. In each series or period, the ionization energy increases from Group I to Group VIII, but the increase is not regular. There is a decrease between Group II and III in Periods 2 and 3 as the *s* sublevel is filled and the *p* sublevel is started. In these periods there is also a decrease between Groups V and VI as the *p* sublevel becomes half-filled. In Periods 4, 5, and 6, there is a sharp decrease in the ionization energy between the last transition element and Group III, where the *d* sublevel has become filled and the *p* sublevel is started. These apparent irregularities are due to the extra stability of completed and half-completed sublevels.

9. **Ionization energy to remove successive electrons.** It is, of course, possi-

PERIODIC TABLE OF IONIZATION ENERGIES

																	VIII
13.6 **H** 1																	
													III	IV	V	VI	VII	24.6 **He** 2
5.4 **Li** 3	9.3 **Be** 4												8.3 **B** 5	11.3 **C** 6	14.5 **N** 7	13.6 **O** 8	17.4 **F** 9	21.6 **Ne** 10
5.1 **Na** 11	7.6 **Mg** 12												6.0 **Al** 13	8.1 **Si** 14	11.0 **P** 15	10.4 **S** 16	13.0 **Cl** 17	15.8 **Ar** 18
4.4 **K** 19	6.1 **Ca** 20	6.6 **Sc** 21	6.8 **Ti** 22	6.7 **V** 23	6.8 **Cr** 24	7.4 **Mn** 25	7.9 **Fe** 26	7.9 **Co** 27	7.6 **Ni** 28	7.7 **Cu** 29	9.4 **Zn** 30	6.0 **Ga** 31	8.1 **Ge** 32	10.5 **As** 33	9.7 **Se** 34	11.8 **Br** 35	14.0 **Kr** 36
4.2 **Rb** 37	5.7 **Sr** 38	6.6 **Y** 39	7.0 **Zr** 40	6.8 **Nb** 41	7.2 **Mo** 42	7.5 **Tc** 43	7.5 **Ru** 44	7.7 **Rh** 45	8.3 **Pd** 46	7.6 **Ag** 47	9.0 **Cd** 48	5.8 **In** 49	7.3 **Sn** 50	8.6 **Sb** 51	9.0 **Te** 52	10.4 **I** 53	12.1 **Xe** 54
3.9 **Cs** 55	5.2 **Ba** 56	5.0 **Lu** 71	5.5 **Hf** 72	6 **Ta** 73	8.0 **W** 74	7.9 **Re** 75	8.7 **Os** 76	9.2 **Ir** 77	9.0 **Pt** 78	9.2 **Au** 79	10.4 **Hg** 80	6.1 **Tl** 81	7.4 **Pb** 82	8.0 **Bi** 83	**Po** 84	**At** 85	10.7 **Rn** 86
Fr 87	5.3 **Ra** 88	**Lw** 103															

	5.6 **La** 57	6.9 **Ce** 58	5.8 **Pr** 59	6.3 **Nd** 60	**Pm** 61	5.6 **Sm** 62	5.7 **Eu** 63	6.2 **Gd** 64	6.7 **Tb** 65	6.8 **Dy** 66	**Ho** 67	**Er** 68	**Tm** 69	6.2 **Yb** 70
	Ac 89	**Th** 90	**Pa** 91	4 **U** 92	**Np** 93	**Pu** 94	**Am** 95	**Cm** 96	**Bk** 97	**Cf** 98	**Es**	**Fm** 100	**Md** 101	102

5-4   Periodic Table showing ionization energies of the elements in electron volts.

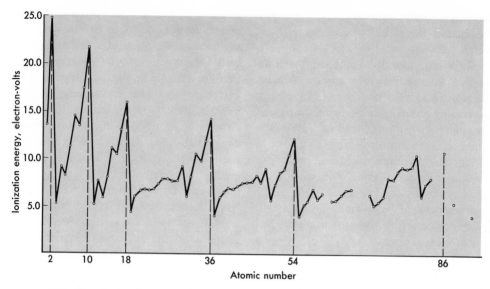

5-5   Graph showing ionization energy plotted as a function of atomic number.

ble to remove more than one electron from many-electron atoms.

Na + ionization energy
            1st electron → Na$^+$ + e^-

Na$^+$ + ionization energy
            2nd electron → Na^{++} + e^-

Na^{++} + ionization energy
            3rd electron → Na^{+++} + e^-

The ionization energy to remove successive electrons from atoms of sodium, magnesium, and aluminum is shown in the table below.

It is not surprising that the ionization energy increases with each electron removed from an atom, because each successive electron must be removed from a particle with an increasingly greater net positive charge. However, we need to examine the variation in ionization energies still more closely.

For sodium, there is a great increase between the first and second ionization energies. The first electron, a $3s$ electron, is rather easily removed; but to remove the second electron, almost ten times as much energy must be expended. This is because the second electron is a $2p$ elec-

ELECTRON CONFIGURATIONS AND IONIZATION ENERGIES OF SODIUM, MAGNESIUM, AND ALUMINUM

		Ionization Energy (electron-volts)			
		1st electron	2nd electron	3rd electron	4th electron
Na	$1s^2 2s^2 2p^6 3s^1$	5.138	47.06	70.72	
Mg	$1s^2 2s^2 2p^6 3s^2$	7.644	14.97	79.72	108.9
Al	$1s^2 2s^2 2p^6 3s^2 3p^1$	5.984	18.74	28.31	119.37

tron in a much lower energy level. See Fig. 5-6.

The removal of electrons from a magnesium atom proceeds at low ionization energy for the first two electrons, since both of these are $3s$ electrons. More energy is required to remove the first $3s$ magnesium electron than the first $3s$ sodium electron because of the magnesium atom's greater nuclear charge. But to remove the third magnesium electron, a $2p$ electron, between five and six times as much energy is needed as to remove the second. The great increase in ionization energy is again due to the fact that the third electron is in a much lower energy level than were the first two.

It is easy to remove the first three electrons from aluminum. It is, in fact, easier to remove the first aluminum electron than it is to remove the first magnesium electron. A look at the electron configuration indicates that the first aluminum electron is a $3p$ electron which is in a slightly higher energy sublevel than the first magnesium electron which is a $3s$ electron. The great increase in ionization energy between the third and fourth aluminum electrons is explained by the fact that the fourth electron is a $2p$ electron which is in a much lower energy level than the first three electrons, which were all 3rd energy level electrons.

10. Electron affinity. Some neutral atoms have a tendency to acquire additional electrons. The measure of this tendency is the *electron affinity, the energy released when an electron is added to a neutral atom.* When an electron is added to a neutral atom a singly negatively charged ion is formed, and an amount of energy, the electron affinity, is released. In equation form this electron transfer may be expressed as follows:

$$A + e^- \rightarrow A^- + \text{energy}$$

Like ionization energy, electron affinity may be measured in electron-volts. The electron affinity indicates how tightly an additional electron is bound to an atom. If the electron affinity is low, the electron is weakly bound; if the electron affinity is high, the electron is strongly bound. The table below gives the electron affinities for four members of the Halogen Family.

ELECTRON AFFINITIES OF THE HALOGENS

Element	Electron Affinity (electron-volts)
fluorine	3.62
chlorine	3.82
bromine	3.54
iodine	3.24

The Halogens would be expected to have high electron affinities, since the addition of one electron to these atoms gives them a stable outer shell consisting of an octet. It would also be expected that the elec-

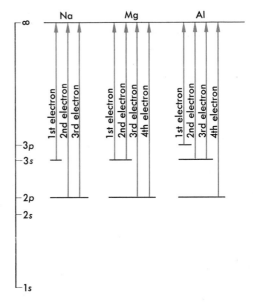

5-6 Energy-level transitions for the removal of successive electrons from sodium, magnesium, and aluminum atoms.

tron affinities would decrease with increasing atomic number, because the added electron enters shells which are increasingly farther from the nucleus. There is no simple explanation for the low electron affinity of fluorine, but because of their relatively small size many second-period elements show irregularities in properties from those of the rest of their group. Unfortunately, too, the determination of electron affinity is complex, and data are available for only a few elements.

The concepts of ionization energy and electron affinity are helpful in understanding the methods by which compounds are formed from atoms of metallic and non-metallic elements. This topic is discussed in greater detail in parts of Chapter 6.

11. Value of the Periodic Table. In former years the Periodic Table served as a check on atomic weight determinations and for the prediction of new elements. These uses are now outdated. For the present, however, the Periodic Table serves as a useful and systematic, though not perfect, classification of elements according to their properties. The periodicity of certain properties such as atomic size, ionization energy, and electron affinity have already been described. This information is valuable in determining the types of compounds which certain elements form, and makes the study of chemistry easier.

REVIEW OUTLINE

Classification of elements
     Triads (2)
     Law of Octaves (2)
     Periodic Table—Mendeleyev (3)
     Atomic numbers (4)
     Periodic law (5)

Modern Periodic Table
     Period or series (6)
     Group or family (6)
     Transition elements (6)
     Rare earth elements (6)
     Metalloids (6)

Periodic properties
     Atomic radius (7)
     Ionization energy: ion (8,9)
     Electron affinity (10)

QUESTIONS

Group A

1. (*a*) On what basis did Mendeleyev arrange the elements in his Periodic Table?
   (*b*) On what basis are they arranged today?
2. What use did Mendeleyev make of his Periodic Table?

3. How are X rays used to determine the atomic number of an element?
4. What is the Periodic Law?
5. (*a*) What information is given in each block of the Periodic Table? (*b*) How are these data arranged in each block?
6. (*a*) What is a group or family of elements? (*b*) What position does a family occupy in the Periodic Table?
7. (*a*) What is a series or period of elements? (*b*) What position does a period occupy in the Periodic Table?
8. (*a*) Name the elements in the second period. (*b*) How does the number of electrons in the outer shell vary in these elements? (*c*) How do their properties compare?
9. What is similar about the electron configurations of elements with similar properties?
10. How do the elements at the left of the Periodic Table vary in activity?
11. How do the elements in Group VII vary in activity?
12. What name is given to the elements which border the line dividing the metals from the nonmetals?
13. Why is the radius of an atom not a definitely fixed quantity?
14. (*a*) How do the atomic radii of the Group I elements compare with the radii of other elements of their period? (*b*) Why?
15. (*a*) Write an equation to represent the removal of the single outer shell electron from a potassium atom. (*b*) Write an equation to represent the addition of an electron to a neutral bromine atom. (*c*) What particles are produced from the neutral atoms by these reactions?
16. (*a*) Why do metals have low ionization energies? (*b*) Why are the ionization energies of nonmetals high?

Group B

17. How are the elements in Döbereiner's triads related? Illustrate your answer with a computation.
18. What was the basis for Newlands' *law of octaves?*
19. What family of elements was missing from Mendeleyev's Periodic Table?
20. (*a*) What are X rays? (*b*) How are they produced?
21. (*a*) How did Mendeleyev know where to leave gaps for undiscovered elements in his Periodic Table? (*b*) How did Moseley know where to leave gaps for undiscovered elements?
22. (*a*) Why is hydrogen placed separately in the Periodic Table? (*b*) Why is it placed above Group I?
23. (*a*) What are transition elements? (*b*) In which periods of elements do they appear?
24. (*a*) What are rare earth elements? (*b*) In which periods of elements do they appear?
25. (*a*) How does atomic size vary with atomic number within a family of elements? (*b*) Why does it vary this way?
26. (*a*) How does atomic size generally vary with atomic number within a period of elements? (*b*) Why does it vary this way?

27. (*a*) How would you expect the ionization energies of two atoms of about equal size but different atomic number to compare? (*b*) Why?

28. (*a*) If energy must be supplied to remove an outer shell electron from an atom, which is more stable, the atom or the resulting ion? (*b*) If energy is released during the addition of an electron to a neutral atom, which is more stable, the atom or the resulting ion?

29. What determines the number of elements in each period of the Periodic Table?

30. On a separate sheet of paper copy and complete the following table. *Do not write in this book.*

Chemical Element	Electron Configuration Notation	Ionization Energy			
		1st electron	2nd electron	3rd electron	4th electron
K		4.339	31.66	46.5	——
Ca		6.111	11.82	50.96	69.7
Ga		6.00	18.9	30.58	63.9

On the basis of the electron configuration, explain the variation in ionization energies for successive electrons for the atoms given.

31. How many 5th energy level orbitals would be filled theoretically in element 118?

32. What is the present value of the Periodic Table?

Chapter Six

CHEMICAL BONDS

1. Elements combine to form compounds. In Chapter 2 it was stated that elements *could* combine during a chemical change to form compounds. Now that the structure of the atoms of the elements has been described, we are ready to learn *how* atoms combine.

The following series of formulas shows that different numbers of hydrogen and chlorine atoms combine with single atoms of other elements.

HCl	NaCl
H_2O	$CaCl_2$
NH_3	$AlCl_3$
CH_4	CCl_4

One atom of hydrogen combines with one atom of chlorine. One atom of sodium also combines with one atom of chlorine. To form one compound of hydrogen and oxygen, two atoms of hydrogen are needed for each oxygen atom. Likewise, two chlorine atoms are required for each calcium atom when a compound of calcium and chlorine is formed. One atom of nitrogen combines with three hydrogen atoms, while one atom of aluminum combines with three chlorine atoms. One atom of carbon combines with either four hydrogen atoms or four chlorine atoms. Why is there this difference in the number of hydrogen and chlorine atoms which will combine with a single atom of another element? Is there any relation between the structure of an atom and the number of other atoms with which it will combine?

2. Valence electrons and chemical bonds. The electrons in the outermost shell of an atom play a very active part in the formation of compounds. The electrons in an *incomplete* outer shell are called *valence electrons*. The remainder of the atom, excluding the valence electrons, is called the *kernel* of the atom. In the formation of chemical compounds from the elements, *valence electrons are usually either transferred from the outer shell of one atom to the outer shell of another atom, or shared among the outer shells of the combining atoms.* This transfer or sharing of electrons produces *chemical bonds.* (The formation of some chemical bonds involves not only outer shell electrons but also those of the next inner shell as well.)

Electron transfer results in **ionic bonding** *while electron sharing produces* **covalent bonding.** When an atom of one element enters into chemical combination with an atom of another element, both atoms usually attain a stable outer shell consisting of an octet. (Hydrogen either shares its single 1s electron or attains a stable outer shell of two 1s electrons. Lithium loses its single 2s electron to attain a stable outer shell of two electrons.) *This particular kind of electronic structure, resembling that of the noble gases, has chemical stability.*

Energy changes are always involved in the process of electron transfer or electron sharing. In *most* cases when compounds are formed from the elements, energy is liberated—the process of electron transfer is always exothermic and that of electron sharing is usually exothermic. In a *few* cases of compound formation by electron sharing, energy is absorbed—the process of electron sharing may sometimes be endothermic.

3. Ionic bonding (electrovalence). In the formation of a compound by ionic bonding, electrons are actually transferred from the outer shell of one atom to the outer shell of a second atom. By this process both atoms usually attain outer shells containing eight electrons. For example, when sodium reacts with chlorine to form sodium chloride, the single 3s electron of the sodium atom is transferred to the singly occupied 3p orbital of the chlorine atom.

	1s	2s	2p	3s	3p
Na	⊗	⊗	⊗⊗⊗	⊗	○○○
Cl	⊗	⊗	⊗⊗⊗	⊗	⊗⊗⊘

The sodium atom, now deficient in one electron, has the stable electronic configuration of neon. The chlorine atom, now with one excess electron, has the stable electronic configuration of argon. Since only 1 atom of each element is required for the electron transfer which produces these stable electronic configurations, the *formula* of the compound is **NaCl.** *A* **chemical formula** *is a shorthand method of using chemical symbols to represent the composition of a compound.*

The particles which are produced by this transfer of an electron are no longer electrically neutral atoms of sodium and chlorine. They are an electrostatically charged *sodium ion* with a single excess positive charge and an electrostatically charged *chloride ion* with a single excess negative charge.

	1s	2s	2p	3s	3p
Na⁺	⊗	⊗	⊗⊗⊗	○	○○○
Cl⁻	⊗	⊗	⊗⊗⊗	⊗	⊗⊗⊗

These ions are arranged systematically in crystals of sodium chloride in the ratio of 1 sodium ion to 1 chloride ion. See Fig. 6-1.

The formula NaCl which represents the composition of sodium chloride is an **empirical formula,** since it merely indi-

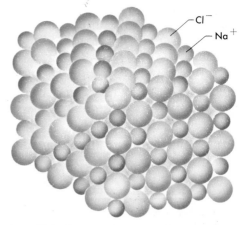

6-1 This diagram shows the arrangement of the sodium and chloride ions in sodium chloride.

cates the kind and simplest whole number ratio of the constituent atoms in the compound.

The table below shows the number of protons and electrons in the atoms and ions of sodium and chlorine, their resultant electrostatic charges, their electrovalent symbols, and their radii in Ångströms.

Using only the 3rd energy level electrons, the electron-dot symbol for an atom of sodium is

$$Na \cdot$$

while that for an atom of chlorine is

$$\cdot \overset{..}{\underset{..}{Cl}} :$$

After reaction, the formula for sodium chloride may be represented by an electron-dot formula as

$$Na^{+\circ}\overset{..}{\underset{..}{Cl}}:^{-}$$

or by a simpler ionic formula as Na^+Cl^-. (The symbols for electrons, ∘ and ·, which are used here and in other electron-dot formulas in this chapter, are only to show the origin of the electrons in the completed shells. They *do not mean* that electrons from different atoms are different from each other. All electrons, regardless of the atom from which they originate, are identical.)

4. Energy change in ionic bonding. The formation of sodium ions and chloride ions in a common salt crystal from separate sodium and chlorine atoms may

be assumed, for a study of the energy change involved, to consist of three separate reactions. The first, the removal of an electron from a sodium atom forming a sodium ion, is endothermic. The amount of energy required is the *ionization energy* of sodium.

$$Na^0 + energy \rightarrow Na^+ + e^-$$

Only one electron may be readily removed from a sodium atom because of the great increase in ionization energy between the first and second electrons. (See Chapter 5, Section 9).

The second reaction is the addition of an electron to a neutral chlorine atom. This reaction is exothermic, the energy evolved being the *electron affinity* of chlorine.

$$Cl^0 + e^- \rightarrow Cl^- + energy$$

The third reaction is the movement of the oppositely charged sodium ion and chloride ion into their equilibrium positions in the sodium chloride crystal. This reaction is also exothermic.

$$Na^+ + Cl^- \rightarrow Na^+Cl^- + energy$$

Since the energy required for the first of these three reactions is less than that evolved in the second and third, the overall effect is the evolution of energy. This is true of all ionic compound formation. The net process of electron transfer is exothermic.

DATA ON ATOMS AND IONS OF SODIUM AND CHLORINE

	Sodium Atom	Sodium Ion	Chlorine Atom	Chloride Ion
Number of Protons	11	11	17	17
Number of Electrons	11	10	17	18
Net Charge	0	+1	0	−1
Symbol	Na^0	Na^+	Cl^0	Cl^-
Radius, Å	1.57	0.95	0.99	1.81

5. Oxidation and reduction. Let us now consider still another aspect of the reactions by which sodium ions and chloride ions are produced. We may consider the formation of a sodium ion from a sodium atom to involve the loss of an electron:

$$Na^0 - e^- \rightarrow Na^+ \text{ (Loss of electron: Oxidation)}$$

Any chemical reaction which involves the loss of one or more electrons by an atom or ion is an **oxidation.** The particle which loses the electron(s) is said to be *oxidized.* In the reaction above, the sodium atom is oxidized to sodium ion since it undergoes a loss of one electron; the reaction is an *oxidation.*

The *oxidation state* of an element is represented by a signed number, called an **oxidation number,** which somewhat arbitrarily indicates the number of electrons which may be assumed to be lost, gained, or shared by an atom in compound formation. Oxidation numbers are assigned according to a set of seven rules, each of which will be introduced as needed in this chapter.

Rule 1. *The oxidation number of an atom of a free element is zero.*

Rule 2. *The oxidation number of a monatomic (one-atomed) ion is equal to its charge.*

From these rules we see that the oxidation number of elementary sodium is zero: Na^0; while the oxidation number of sodium ion is plus one: Na^{+1}.

The formation of a chloride ion from a chlorine atom involves the gain of an electron:

$$Cl^0 + e^- \rightarrow Cl^- \text{ (Gain of electron: Reduction)}$$

A chemical reaction which involves the gain of one or more electrons by an atom or ion is a **reduction.** The particle which gains the electron(s) is said to be *reduced.* Thus the chlorine atom is reduced to a chloride ion since it gains an electron; the reaction is a *reduction.* The oxidation number of elementary chlorine is zero: Cl^0 (Rule 1); the oxidation number of chloride ion is minus one: Cl^{-1} (Rule 2).

In the reaction

$$Na^0 + Cl^0 \rightarrow Na^{+1}Cl^{-1}$$

we recognize that elementary sodium is oxidized and elementary chlorine is reduced. *The substance which is reduced* has received electrons from the oxidized substance and is called the **oxidizing agent.** Conversely *the substance which is oxidized* has transferred electrons to the reduced substance and is called the **reducing agent.** NaCl is the correct empirical formula for sodium chloride. Note that the algebraic sum of the oxidation numbers is zero.

Rule 3. *The algebraic sum of the oxidation numbers of all the atoms in the formula of a compound is zero.*

6. Formation of magnesium bromide. In the formation of magnesium bromide, the two 3s electrons of the magnesium are transferred. *Both* 3s electrons must be transferred in order for the magnesium atom to acquire the stability of the electronic configuration of the noble gas neon. Recall that the ionization energies of the two 3s electrons in magnesium are low, but that there is a great increase in ionization energy between the second and third electron. Hence only two electrons may be removed chemically. The 4th energy level of the bromine atom already contains seven electrons, and eight is the number needed for an octet. So a single bromine atom has place for only one of the two electrons which the magnesium atom transfers. This means that two bromine atoms are needed to react with one mag-

	1s	2s	2p	3s	3p	3d	4s	4p
Br	⊗	⊗	⊗⊗⊗	⊗	⊗⊗⊗	⊗⊗⊗⊗⊗	⊗	⊗⊗⊗
Mg	⊗	⊗	⊗⊗⊗	⊗	○○○	○○○○○	○	○○○
Br	⊗	⊗	⊗⊗⊗	⊗	⊗⊗⊗	⊗⊗⊗⊗⊗	⊗	⊗⊗⊗

nesium atom. Each bromine atom gains one electron. See the schematic diagram above. The empirical formula for magnesium bromide is **MgBr₂**. The particles which compose this compound are magnesium ions, each with two excess positive charges, and bromide ions, each with a single excess negative charge. These particles are arranged in orderly fashion in crystals of magnesium bromide in the ratio of 2 bromide ions to 1 magnesium ion (see the data table below and also Fig. 6-2). The subscript ₂ following Br in the formula indicates that there are two bromide ions to each magnesium ion in the compound. When no subscript is used, as with the Mg, one atom or monatomic ion is understood.

The electron-dot symbol for an atom of bromine is

$$\cdot \ddot{\underset{\cdot\cdot}{\text{Br}}} :$$

The electron-dot formula for magnesium bromide is then

$$: \ddot{\underset{\cdot\cdot}{\text{Br}}} :^- \quad \text{Mg}^{++} \quad : \ddot{\underset{\cdot\cdot}{\text{Br}}} :^-$$

and the ionic formula is **Mg⁺⁺Br₂⁻**.

The energy required to remove two electrons from one magnesium atom is less than the electron affinity of two bromine atoms plus the energy released when one magnesium ion and two bromide ions move into their equilibrium positions in a magnesium bromide crystal. Thus the formation of magnesium bromide from separate magnesium and bromine atoms is another example of the exothermic nature of electron transfer.

In forming magnesium bromide from the elements magnesium and bromine, the magnesium atom is oxidized from Mg^0 to Mg^{+2},

$$Mg^0 - 2e^- \rightarrow Mg^{+2}$$

while two bromine atoms are reduced from Br^0 to Br^{-1}.

$$2Br^0 + 2e^- \rightarrow 2Br^{-1}$$

Bromine is the oxidizing agent; magnesium is the reducing agent.

In the formula $Mg^{+2}Br_2^{-1}$, the algebraic sum of $+2$ and $2(-1)$ equals zero. Note that in determining the algebraic sum of the oxidation numbers of the atoms in a formula, the oxidation number must be multiplied by the number of atoms or monatomic ions having that oxidation

DATA ON ATOMS AND IONS OF MAGNESIUM AND BROMINE

	Magnesium Atom	Magnesium Ion	Bromine Atom	Bromide Ion
Number of Protons	12	12	35	35
Number of Electrons	12	10	35	36
Net Charge	0	+2	0	−1
Symbol	Mg^0	Mg^{++}	Br^0	Br^-
Radius, Å	1.36	0.65	1.14	1.95

RADII OF REPRESENTATIVE ATOMS AND IONS

Ångströms

	Group I		Group II		Group III		Group VI		Group VII	
Period 2	Li⁰	1.23	Be⁰	0.89	B⁰	0.80	O⁰	0.66	F⁰	0.64
	Li⁺	0.60	Be⁺⁺	0.31	B⁺⁺⁺	0.20	O⁼	1.40	F⁻	1.36
Period 3	Na⁰	1.57	Mg⁰	1.36	Al⁰	1.25	S⁰	1.04	Cl⁰	0.99
	Na⁺	0.95	Mg⁺⁺	0.65	Al⁺⁺⁺	0.50	S⁼	1.84	Cl⁻	1.81
Period 4	K⁰	2.02	Ca⁰	1.74	Ga⁰	1.25	Se⁰	1.17	Br⁰	1.14
	K⁺	1.33	Ca⁺⁺	0.99	Ga⁺⁺⁺	0.62	Se⁼	1.98	Br⁻	1.95
Period 5	Rb⁰	2.16	Sr⁰	1.91	In⁰	1.42	Te⁰	1.37	I⁰	1.33
	Rb⁺	1.48	Sr⁺⁺	1.13	In⁺⁺⁺	0.81	Te⁼	2.21	I⁻	2.16
Period 6	Cs⁰	2.35	Ba⁰	1.98	Tl⁰	1.44				
	Cs⁺	1.69	Ba⁺⁺	1.35	Tl⁺⁺⁺	0.95				

number. Since the formulas of ionic compounds merely indicate the relative number of positive and negative ions which combine, *all formulas for ionic compounds are empirical.*

7. Elements with several oxidation numbers. Many elements exhibit more than one oxidation state. Some differences in the oxidation number of an element depend on the kind of bond which it forms with other elements. However, another factor is important. Transition elements, with four or five electronic sublevels, can readily transfer the electrons in the outermost sublevel. Many of them, with very little additional energy, can also transfer one or two electrons from the next-to-outermost sublevel. The electrons in excess of an octet in the next-to-outermost sublevel are those available for transfer. Iron is such a transition element. In forming compounds, it can transfer two 4s electrons. Sometimes, in more energetic reactions, a 3d electron can also be transferred. Thus its oxidation number can be +2 or +3. This accounts for the variable oxidation state which is characteristic of many of the transition metals.

8. Relative sizes of atoms and ions. In the tables accompanying Sections 3 and 6, the radii of the atoms and ions of sodium, magnesium, chlorine, and bromine are given. Notice the great difference in radius between an atom and the ion formed from it.

It is characteristic of metals to form positive ions. *Positive ions are called cations.* It is to be expected that metallic ions would be smaller than the corresponding metallic atoms since the outer shell electrons are no longer present. The remaining electrons are thus attracted more strongly to the nucleus by the unbalanced positive charge.

Nonmetallic elements form negative

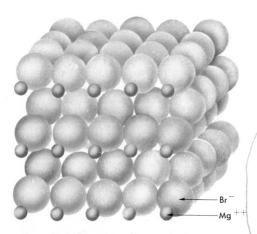

6-2 This diagram shows the arrangement of the magnesium and bromide ions in magnesium bromide.

ions. *Negative ions are called* **anions.** Nonmetallic ions are larger than the corresponding nonmetallic atoms since electrons have been added to make the outer shell an octet. Thus the excess negative charge weakens the attraction of the nucleus for the surrounding electrons.

The table opposite shows the sizes of representative atoms and ions. From these data, in addition to the generalizations given above, it will be seen that:

1. Within a group or family of elements, the ion size increases with atomic number.

2. Within a period of elements, greater positive charge produces markedly smaller cations while greater negative charge produces only slightly larger anions. This is because greater positive ionic charge is accompanied by greater nuclear charge, while greater negative ionic charge is accompanied by a lower nuclear charge.

Figures 6-1 and 6-2 show the arrangement of ions in crystals of sodium chloride and magnesium bromide. It is apparent that the arrangement of ions in a crystal depends on the relative numbers of each kind of ion present (which depends on their charge) and on the relative sizes of the ions. Crystals are described in more detail in Chapter 11.

9. Covalent bonding (covalence). In covalent bonding, electrons are not transferred from one atom to another, but are shared by the bonded atoms. In forming a single covalent bond, two atoms each share one of their electrons with the other. These two shared electrons effectively fill an orbital in each element and thus form a covalent electron pair. This constitutes the bond between these two atoms.

The atoms of the common elementary gases, hydrogen, oxygen, nitrogen, fluorine, and chlorine, form stable diatomic (two-atomed) *molecules* by covalent bonding. *A* **molecule** *is the smallest chemical unit of a substance which is capable of stable independent existence.* For the common elementary gases, the smallest chemical units capable of stable independent existence are diatomic units. (Single atoms of these gases are chemically unstable.) Hence these diatomic units constitute molecules of these gases.

In the diatomic hydrogen molecule, each hydrogen atom shares its single $1s$ valence electron with the other. These electrons revolve about both nuclei, so that each atom has two electrons revolving about it. Each atom, in effect, has its $1s$ orbital filled. This means that each hydrogen atom has, in effect, the stable electron configuration of a helium atom.

$$\begin{array}{cc} & \textbf{1s} \\ \textbf{H} & \boxed{\oslash} \\ \textbf{H} & \boxed{\oslash} \end{array}$$

The greater stability of hydrogen molecules over hydrogen atoms is shown by the fact that energy is evolved in the reaction

2 moles H → 1 mole H_2 + 103 kcal

Thus one mole of H_2 molecules has lower energy and is therefore more stable than two moles of uncombined H atoms. Energy is required to separate hydrogen molecules into their constituent atoms.

1 mole H_2 + 103 kcal → 2 moles H

The *electron-dot formula* for a molecule of hydrogen is

H : H

The *molecular formula* for hydrogen is **H_2.** The numerical subscript indicates the number of atoms per molecule. *A formula which indicates the actual composition of a*

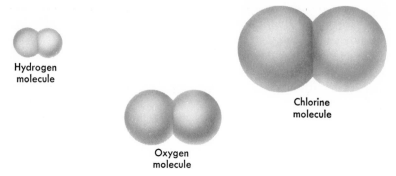

6-3 The molecules of the common gases, such as those of hydrogen, oxygen, and chlorine represented here, consist of two atoms joined by covalent bonding.

molecule is called a **molecular formula.**

Diatomic chlorine molecules are formed in the same way. Each atom shares one electron with the other, filling, in effect, an incomplete $3p$ orbital in each. This gives both atoms the stable electron arrangement of the inert gas argon, with an octet in the 3rd energy level.

	1s	2s	2p	3s	3p
Cl	⊗	⊗	⊗⊗⊗	⊗	⊗⊗ ◯
Cl	⊗	⊗	⊗⊗⊗	⊗	⊗⊗ ⊘

The electron-dot formula for a molecule of chlorine is

$$:\!\overset{\circ\,\circ}{\underset{\circ\,\circ}{Cl}} : \overset{\cdot\,\cdot}{\underset{\cdot\,\cdot}{Cl}} : $$

and its molecular formula is Cl_2.

Oxygen also exists as diatomic molecules. The reaction for the formation of one mole of O_2 molecules from oxygen atoms

$$\textbf{2 moles O} \rightarrow \textbf{1 mole } O_2 + \textbf{117 kcal}$$

is exothermic, showing that oxygen molecules have lower energy and are more stable than oxygen atoms. To separate oxygen molecules into their constituent atoms requires energy as shown in the following equation.

$$\textbf{1 mole } O_2 + \textbf{117 kcal} \rightarrow \textbf{2 moles O}$$

The orbital representation of an oxygen molecule is

	1s	2s	2p
O	⊗	⊗	⊗ ◯ ◯
O	⊗	⊗	⊗ ⊘ ◯

its electron-dot formula is

$$:\!\overset{\circ\,\circ}{\underset{\circ}{O}} : \overset{\cdot\,\cdot}{O} : $$

and its molecular formula is O_2.

Notice the unpaired electrons in the oxygen molecule. Liquid oxygen is attracted slightly by a magnet. The property of magnetism shown by the elements is due to unpaired electrons, and this evidence for oxygen leads us to believe that the structure given above is a reasonable one for an oxygen molecule.

Diatomic molecules of elements are considered to be free elements and each atom in the molecule may be assigned a zero oxidation number. (Rule 1).

10. Unlike atoms combine by covalent bonding. A hydrogen atom and a chlorine atom combine by covalent bonding to form a hydrogen chloride molecule. In this molecule the $1s$ hydrogen electron and a $3p$ chlorine electron complete a space orbital, as shown below.

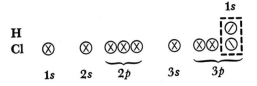

The electron-dot formula for hydrogen chloride is

$$H \overset{..}{\underset{..}{Cl}} :$$

and its molecular formula is HCl. Frequently chemists indicate a shared pair of electrons—a covalent bond—by a dash (—) instead of the symbol ($\overset{.}{.}$). Thus the formula for hydrogen chloride may be written

$$H \overset{..}{\underset{..}{Cl}} : \quad or \quad H \overset{..}{\underset{..}{—Cl}} :$$

or omitting the electrons which are not involved in the bonding, simply

H—Cl

This type of formula is called a structural formula.

Rule 4: *The oxidation number of hydrogen is +1.* By applying Rule 4, and then Rule 3, we observe that the oxidation number of hydrogen in hydrogen chloride is +1, while that of chlorine is −1.

The common compound, water, consists of molecules formed by covalent bonding of two hydrogen atoms with one oxygen atom. The orbital representation of this bonding is

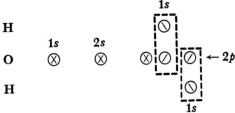

while the electron-dot formula for water is

$$H \overset{..}{\underset{\overset{.}{.}}{O}} : \\ H$$

its structural formula is

$$\overset{O}{\diagup \diagdown} \\ H \qquad H$$

and its molecular formula is **H₂O.**

The formation of water from hydrogen and oxygen molecules may be considered to occur in three sequential steps:

1 mole H₂ + 104 kcal → 2 moles H
(**Reaction 1**)

½ mole O₂ + 59 kcal → 1 mole O
(**Reaction 2**)

(This reaction is expressed for only ½ mole of O₂)

2 moles H + 1 mole O →
1 mole H₂O + 231 kcal   (**Reaction 3**)

Hydrogen chloride
molecule

Water
molecule

Hydrogen peroxide
molecule

6-4 Hydrogen chloride, water, and hydrogen peroxide are compounds whose simplest particles are molecules composed of covalently bonded atoms.

The combining of separate hydrogen and oxygen atoms into water molecules is highly exothermic.

Since more energy is evolved in Reaction 3 than is required for Reactions 1 and 2, [231 kcal − (104 kcal + 59 kcal) = 68 kcal], the overall process is exothermic.

1 mole H_2 + $\frac{1}{2}$ mole O_2 →
1 mole H_2O + 68 kcal

Thus water molecules have lower energy and are more stable than the hydrogen and oxygen molecules from which they are formed.

It is possible for more than one kind of molecule to be formed from the same kinds of atoms. A second compound which may be formed from hydrogen and oxygen is hydrogen peroxide, a well-known bleaching and oxidizing agent. The orbital notation of hydrogen peroxide is

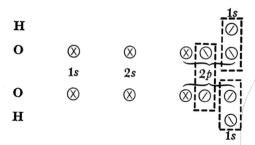

its electron-dot formula is

$$H \overset{\bullet}{\underset{\times}{\text{:}}} \overset{\bullet\bullet}{\underset{}{\text{O:}}}$$
$$\overset{\times\bullet}{\underset{\times\times}{\text{O}}} \overset{\times}{\underset{}{\text{H}}}$$

its structural formula is

$$H—O$$
$$\overset{|}{O—H}$$

and its molecular formula is H_2O_2.

Rule 5: *The oxidation number of oxygen is −2.* One exception to this rule is that in

peroxides, the oxidation number of oxygen is −1. Thus we see that in water, the oxidation number of hydrogen is +1 and of oxygen is −2; while in hydrogen peroxide, the oxidation number of hydrogen is +1, and of oxygen is −1. (Use Rule 3 as a check to verify this.)

Other examples of covalent bonding between hydrogen and nitrogen, and between hydrogen and carbon to form molecules are given in the table on the facing page.

In all of the examples of covalent bonding illustrated, except hydrazine, the bonded atoms are more stable due to filled orbitals. They have lower energy than the unbonded atoms. Thus these molecules are formed from the atoms by exothermic processes. Hydrazine is formed from nitrogen and hydrogen only by an endothermic process.

The covalent compound carbon disulfide, CS_2,

$$:\overset{\bullet\bullet}{S}::C::\overset{\bullet\bullet}{S}:$$

is another example of a compound which is less stable than the uncombined atoms. It can be made only by an endothermic process. Its instability may be due to the two double carbon-sulfur bonds in the molecule. (Two pairs of electrons shared by two atoms constitute a double bond between the atoms. Similarly three pairs of electrons shared by two atoms constitute a triple bond between the atoms. Double and triple bonds are usually less stable than single bonds.)

The neutral particle which results from covalent bonding of atoms is a molecule. Its composition is represented by a molecular formula.

11. More about particles of matter. Free and isolated atoms are rarely found in nature. Instead, atoms of most elements are combined with one another at

DATA ON SOME REPRESENTATIVE MOLECULES

	Ammonia	Hydrazine	Methane	Ethane
Molecular formula	NH_3	N_2H_4	CH_4	C_2H_6
Structural formula	H H \ / N | H	H H \ / N—N / \ H H	H | H—C—H | H	H H | | H—C—C—H | | H H
Electron-dot formula	H ° ° ° N ° H • ° H	H H ° • × • ° N ° N × • ° • × H H	H ° ° H ° C ° H • ° H	H H ° • × • H ° C × C × H • ° • × H H
Oxidation numbers	H = +1 N = −3	H = +1 N = −2	H = +1 C = −4	H = +1 C = −3
Model of molecule				

ordinary temperatures to form larger structural particles. Notable exceptions are the noble elements: helium, neon, argon, krypton, zenon, and radon. The atoms of these noble gases do not combine with each other to form larger particles. There is no distinction, therefore, between the atoms and molecules of these gases. We may say that a molecule of helium is monatomic, and is written as **He**.

As we have already mentioned, the atoms of some elements combine naturally to form pairs and exist as simple diatomic molecules. Atmospheric oxygen and nitrogen are two examples, their molecules being represented respectively as O_2 and N_2. Observe the O_2 means two atoms of oxygen bonded together to form one oxygen molecule, while **2O** means two separate unbonded oxygen atoms; $3O_2$ means three molecules of oxygen, each of which consists of two oxygen atoms bonded together. The other elementary gases, hydrogen, fluorine, and chlorine also exist as diatomic molecules, H_2, F_2, and Cl_2 respectively. The nonmetal bromine, a liquid at ordinary temperatures, exists as diatomic molecules, Br_2. Its sister element, iodine, forms molecular crystals in which each molecular particle is diatomic, I_2.

Other elements may form larger atom groups. Phosphorus has a molecular particle organization consisting of four atoms, and is written P_4. Sulfur molecules may be eight-atom particles or S_8. The metallic elements generally exhibit crystalline structures in which the atoms are closely packed in regular patterns that show no simple molecular units. In these instances, each individual crystal can be considered to be a single giant molecule.

Some compounds have distinct unit structures composed of simple molecules. Water is a familiar example; the molecules consist of two hydrogen atoms and one oxygen atom represented as H_2O.

PERIODIC TABLE OF ELECTRONEGATIVITIES

2.1
H
1

																	VIII
																	He 2
I	II											III	IV	V	VI	VII	
1.0 **Li** 3	1.5 **Be** 4											2.0 **B** 5	2.5 **C** 6	3.0 **N** 7	3.5 **O** 8	4.0 **F** 9	**Ne** 10
0.9 **Na** 11	1.2 **Mg** 12											1.5 **Al** 13	1.8 **Si** 14	2.1 **P** 15	2.5 **S** 16	3.0 **Cl** 17	**Ar** 18
0.8 **K** 19	1.0 **Ca** 20	1.3 **Sc** 21	1.5 **Ti** 22	1.6 **V** 23	1.6 **Cr** 24	1.5 **Mn** 25	1.8 **Fe** 26	1.8 **Co** 27	1.8 **Ni** 28	1.9 **Cu** 29	1.6 **Zn** 30	1.6 **Ga** 31	1.8 **Ge** 32	2.0 **As** 33	2.4 **Se** 34	2.8 **Br** 35	**Kr** 36
0.8 **Rb** 37	1.0 **Sr** 38	1.2 **Y** 39	1.4 **Zr** 40	1.6 **Nb** 41	1.8 **Mo** 42	1.9 **Tc** 43	2.2 **Ru** 44	2.2 **Rh** 45	2.2 **Pd** 46	1.9 **Ag** 47	1.7 **Cd** 48	1.7 **In** 49	1.8 **Sn** 50	1.9 **Sb** 51	2.1 **Te** 52	2.5 **I** 53	**Xe** 54
0.7 **Cs** 55	0.9 **Ba** 56	1.2 **Lu** 71	1.3 **Hf** 72	1.5 **Ta** 73	1.7 **W** 74	1.9 **Re** 75	2.2 **Os** 76	2.2 **Ir** 77	2.2 **Pt** 78	2.4 **Au** 79	1.9 **Hg** 80	1.8 **Tl** 81	1.8 **Pb** 82	1.9 **Bi** 83	2.0 **Po** 84	2.2 **At** 85	**Rn** 86
0.7 **Fr** 87	0.9 **Ra** 88	**Lw** 103															

1.1 **La** 57	1.1 **Ce** 58	1.1 **Pr** 59	1.1 **Nd** 60	1.1 **Pm** 61	1.1 **Sm** 62	1.1 **Eu** 63	1.1 **Gd** 64	1.1 **Tb** 65	1.1 **Dy** 66	1.1 **Ho** 67	1.1 **Er** 68	1.1 **Tm** 69	1.1 **Yb** 70
1.1 **Ac** 89	1.3 **Th** 90	1.5 **Pa** 91	1.7 **U** 92	1.3 **Np** 93	1.3 **Pu** 94	1.3 **Am** 95	1.3 **Cm** 96	1.3 **Bk** 97	1.3 **Cf** 98	1.3 **Es** 99	1.3 **Fm** 100	1.3 **Md** 101	102

6-5 Periodic Table showing the electronegativities of the elements on an arbitrary scale.

The expression $2H_2O$ represents two molecules of water, each containing two atoms of hydrogen and one atom of oxygen. Similarly, $5H_2O$ signifies five molecules of water. When no other coefficient is used ahead of a formula, it is understood that the coefficient is 1. Molecules of compounds range from a minimum of two atoms to large numbers of atoms.

Other substances may show complex unit structures formed by groups of molecules or molecular aggregates. Still others may have no molecular organization at all. Ordinary table salt, sodium chloride, has already been described as consisting of sodium and chloride ions distributed in a regular crystalline lattice pattern that is continuous to each crystal face. Simple molecules of sodium chloride do not exist except in the vapor state at very high temperatures.

12. Size of molecules. Molecules vary greatly in size. It has been estimated that if a drop of water could be magnified until it became as large as the earth, the molecules composing it would be about one meter in diameter. The simple molecules of gases, consisting of one, two, or three atoms, have diameters of approximately 3×10^{-8} cm. Some virus protein molecules consist of approximately 7.5×10^5 atoms and have diameters of about 2.3×10^{-6} cm. These have been photographed with an electron microscope. On the Ångström scale, this range of molecular diameters is from 3 Å to 230 Å.

13. Electronegativity. In ionic bonding, electrons are completely transferred from the outer shells of metallic atoms to the outer shells of nonmetallic atoms. In covalent bonding, electrons are shared in the outer shells of the bonded atoms. If two covalently bonded atoms are alike, their attractions for the shared electrons are equal, and the electrons are distributed equally about both atoms. Each atom remains electrically neutral even though they are bonded together. If two covalently bonded atoms are unlike, the attraction of one of the atoms for the shared electron pair may be stronger than the attraction of the other atom for them. Then, the electrons will not be equally shared, but will be more closely held by the atom with stronger attraction. This atom will not be electrically neutral, but will be slightly negative, though not as negative as a singly charged anion. The other atom will then be left slightly positive, though not as positive as a singly charged cation. *A covalent bond in which there is an unequal attraction for the shared electrons and a resulting unbalanced distribution of charge is called a **polar covalent bond**.* Polar covalent bonds thus are intermediate in nature between ionic bonds in which electron transfer is complete and pure covalent bonds in which electron sharing is equal.

Ionization energy is a measure of the strength with which an outer shell electron is held by a neutral atom. Electron affinity indicates the strength of the attraction between a neutral atom and an additional electron. By considering these two values, together with certain properties of molecules, chemists have derived an arbitrary scale to indicate *the attraction of an atom for the shared electrons forming a bond between it and another atom. This property is called* **electronegativity**. Atoms with high electronegativity have a strong attraction for shared electrons. Atoms with low electronegativity have a weak attraction for shared electrons. The relative electronegativities of two atoms give an indication of the type of bonding which may exist between them.

The chart, Fig. 6-5, gives values of the electronegativity for the elements. A study of this chart leads to the following conclusions:

1. Low electronegativity is characteristic of metals. The lower the electronegativity, the more active the metal. Thus the lowest electronegativities are found at the lower left of the Periodic Table.

2. High electronegativity is characteristic of nonmetals. Thus the highest electronegativities are found at the upper right of the Periodic Table. Fluorine is the most electronegative element. Oxygen is second.

3. The noble gases are not assigned electronegativity values.

4. Electronegativity generally decreases within the numbered groups or families with increasing atomic number. In the transition element groups there is usually only a slight variation in electronegativity.

5. Electronegativity increases within a period or series through the middle of the Periodic Table, decreases slightly in the remaining metals, and then increases to usually a maximum in Group VII.

14. Electronegativity difference and chemical bonding. The table (page 92) gives values for a useful approximate relationship between the difference of electronegativity of two elements and the percentage of ionic character of a single bond between the two atoms.

Bonds with more than 50% ionic character are considered to be essentially ionic. Thus it is evident that the bonds between metallic elements and the distinctly nonmetallic elements are largely ionic. Sodium chloride, NaCl, electro-

RELATIONSHIP BETWEEN ELECTRONEGATIVITY DIFFERENCE AND IONIC CHARACTER

Electronegativity Difference	Percentage of Ionic Character
0.2	1
0.4	4
0.6	9
0.8	15
1.0	22
1.2	30
1.4	39
1.6	47
1.8	55
2.0	63
2.2	70
2.4	76
2.6	82
2.8	86
3.0	89
3.2	92

negativity difference $3.0 - 0.9 = 2.1$, is a compound with ionic bonds. Similarly $CaBr_2$ and BaO are examples of compounds with ionic bonds.

Since the nonmetallic elements have rather similar electronegativity values, the bonding between nonmetallic elements is predominantly covalent. The hydrogen-oxygen bonds in water, electronegativity difference $3.5 - 2.1 = 1.4$, are 39% ionic. Thus these are polar covalent bonds, with the oxygen being somewhat negative and the hydrogen being somewhat positive. Since the water molecule contains two such bonds unsymmetrically arranged, *the water molecule as a whole shows regions of positive and negative charge and is a **polar molecule**.* Likewise the nitrogen-hydrogen bonds in ammonia are polar. Since the molecule is geometrically unsymmetrical, it, too, is a polar molecule. While the carbon-hydrogen bonds in methane are slightly polar, the symmetry of the molecule causes the methane molecule as a whole to be nonpolar.

Bonds between like atoms, such as are found in the oxygen or the chlorine molecule, have no ionic character since the electronegativity difference is zero.

While we have classed chemical bonds as ionic bonds or covalent bonds, it is now apparent that these are not clear, distinct classifications. On the Periodic Table, the type of bonding gradually changes from essentially ionic, as between the active metals of Groups I and II and oxygen or the halogens, to covalent bonding in the metalloids and between nonmetals. A third type of bonding, metallic bonding, occurs between atoms of metals. It will be described in Chapter 11.

The noble gases have electronic configurations which are chemically very stable. It has been found possible, however, to produce several stable compounds of krypton, xenon, and radon with fluorine.

We are now ready to introduce the sixth rule for assigning oxidation numbers.

Rule 6: *In combinations involving nonmetals, the oxidation number of the less electronegative element is positive and of the more electronegative element is negative.*

Rule 6 leads us to two further exceptions to the rules as already stated. First, hydrogen forms some ionic compounds with very active metals such as lithium and sodium, in which the hydrogen atom gains an electron from the metal and forms a hydride ion, H^{-1}. In hydrides, the oxidation number of hydrogen is -1. Second, in compounds with fluorine, oxygen is the less electronegative element and must have a positive oxidation number, $+2$.

15. Radicals. Some covalently bonded groups of atoms act like single atoms in forming ions. *These charged groups of covalently bonded atoms are called **radicals**.* Some of the common radicals are the sulfate ion, $SO_4^=$, the nitrate ion, NO_3^-, and the phosphate ion, $PO_4^=$. The bonds within these radicals are predominantly covalent, but the groups of atoms have an excess of electrons when combined, and thus are negative ions. There is only one common positive radical, the ammonium ion, NH_4^+, produced when a molecule of ammonia, NH_3, acquires a proton. Electron-dot representations of these radicals are:

$$\left[\begin{array}{c} \text{H} \\ \text{H} \overset{\bullet\bullet}{\underset{\circ\circ}{\text{N}}} \text{H} \\ \text{H} \end{array}\right]^+ \qquad \left[\begin{array}{c} \overset{\circ\,\bullet}{\underset{\circ\,\circ}{\text{O}}}\overset{\circ}{\bullet} \\ \text{N} \overset{\circ\circ}{\circ\circ}\text{O} \\ \overset{\bullet\,\circ}{\underset{\circ}{\text{O}}} \\ {\times\,\circ} \end{array}\right]^-$$

Ammonium ion **Nitrate ion**

$$\left[\begin{array}{c} \overset{\bullet\,\circ}{\text{O}}\overset{\circ}{\circ} \\ \times\overset{\circ}{\text{O}}\overset{\circ}{\underset{\bullet\bullet}{\text{S}}}\overset{\circ}{\text{O}}\times \\ \overset{\circ}{\text{O}}\overset{\circ}{\circ} \\ {\circ\,\circ} \end{array}\right]^= \qquad \left[\begin{array}{c} \overset{\circ\,\circ}{\text{O}}\overset{\circ}{\circ} \\ \times\text{O}\overset{\circ}{\underset{\circ\circ}{\text{P}}}\text{O}\times \\ \overset{\circ}{\text{O}} \\ {\times\,\circ} \end{array}\right]^{\equiv}$$

Sulfate ion **Phosphate ion**

There are some covalent bonds in which both electrons which form the bond between two atoms come from only one of the bonded atoms. Each of the electron-dot formulas shown here has at least one such bond. Let us use the ammonium ion as an example. In this ion three of the covalent nitrogen-hydrogen bonds consist of one shared nitrogen electron and one shared hydrogen electron. The other covalent nitrogen-hydrogen bond consists of two electrons, both of which are supplied by the nitrogen atom. A hydrogen ion (proton) can thus bond at this position and produce the single net positive charge of the ion. Or, going at it differently, there are eleven protons (seven in the nitrogen nucleus and one in each of four hydrogen nuclei) in the ammonium ion. There are only ten electrons (two $1s$ electrons of the nitrogen atom, and eight valence electrons shown). With eleven protons and only ten electrons, the ammonium radical has a net charge of +1.

Rule 7: *The algebraic sum of the oxidation numbers of the atoms in the formula of a radical is equal to its charge.*

In the ammonium radical, the oxidation number of hydrogen is +1 (Rules 4 and 6), and the algebraic sum of the oxidation numbers must equal +1 (Rule 7). Using x as the oxidation number of nitrogen:

$$\left[\overset{x\;+1\;+1}{\text{NH}_4}\right]^{+1}$$

$$x + 4(+1) = +1 \quad \text{and} \quad x = -3.$$

The bonding, charges, and oxidation numbers of the elements in the other radicals may be examined in similar fashion. The electrons represented by small crosses are acquired by the radical from other elements through electron transfer.

16. Summary of oxidation number rules.

1. The oxidation number of an atom of a free element is zero.

2. The oxidation number of a monatomic ion is equal to its charge.

3. The algebraic sum of the oxidation numbers of the atoms in the formula of a compound is zero.

4. The oxidation number of hydrogen is +1, *except* in metallic hydrides where its oxidation number is −1.

5. The oxidation number of oxygen is −2, *except* in peroxides, where its oxidation number is −1. In compounds with fluorine, oxygen is the less electronegative element and has a positive oxidation number, +2.

6. In combinations involving nonmetals, the oxidation number of the less electronegative element is positive and of the more electronegative element is negative.

7. The algebraic sum of the oxidation numbers of the atoms in the formula of a radical is equal to its charge.

REVIEW OUTLINE

Chemical bonding
    Valence electrons, kernel, noble gas structure (2)
    Ionic bonding—electrovalence (3)
        Electron transfer (3)
        Ion: cation, anion (8)
        Empirical formula (3)
        Energy changes (4)
        Relative sizes of atoms and ions (8)

    Covalent bonding—covalence (9)
        Electron sharing (9)
        Molecule (9)
        Molecular formula (9)
        Energy changes (9)

Oxidation and reduction
    Oxidation state (5)
    Oxidation number (5, 7, 16)
    Oxidizing agent (5)
    Reducing agent (5)

Particles of matter
    Elements
        Free atoms—monatomic molecules (11)
        Diatomic and polyatomic molecules (11)
        Giant molecules (11, 12)

    Compounds
        Simple molecules (11)
        Molecular aggregates (11)
        Ions in crystal lattice (11)

Electronegativity
    Ionic bond: ions (13)
    Polar covalent bond: polar molecule (13, 14)
    Covalent bond: nonpolar molecule (13, 14)
    Radicals (15)

QUESTIONS

Group A

1. (*a*) What part of the atom is involved in the production of a chemical bond? (*b*) How are such bonds formed?
2. (*a*) What are the types of chemical bonding? (*b*) What particles result from each type of bonding?

3. (*a*) What kind of outer electronic shell does an atom usually attain when it combines with other atoms? (*b*) Why is this electronic structure chemically stable?

4. Describe the types of energy changes which may occur: (*a*) in electron transfer; (*b*) in electron sharing.

5. (*a*) What is a chemical formula? (*b*) Distinguish between an empirical formula and a molecular formula.

6. (*a*) Which type of formula is used to represent the composition of an ionic compound? (*b*) A covalent compound?

7. Draw an electron-dot symbol for (*a*) a potassium atom; (*b*) a potassium ion.

8. Draw an electron-dot symbol for (*a*) a sulfur atom; (*b*) a sulfide ion.

9. Using electron-dot symbols show how an ionic compound of potassium and sulfur is formed.

10. (*a*) State the general definition for oxidation. (*b*) For reduction.

11. (*a*) Why is a substance which undergoes oxidation a reducing agent? (*b*) Why may a substance which undergoes reduction be considered an oxidizing agent?

12. Assuming chemical union between the following pairs, indicate in each case which element would have the positive oxidation number: (*a*) Hydrogen-sodium; (*b*) Chlorine-fluorine; (*c*) Chlorine-oxygen; (*d*) Hydrogen-lithium; (*e*) Bromine-hydrogen.

13. What is the oxidation number of each element in the following compounds: (*a*) MnO_2; (*b*) H_3PO_4; (*c*) HNO_3; (*d*) P_4O_{10}; (*e*) $NaOH$?

14. Explain why a barium atom is larger than a calcium atom.

15. Explain why a bromide ion is larger than a chloride ion.

16. For a fluorine molecule draw: (*a*) its orbital notation; (*b*) its electron-dot formula; (*c*) its molecular formula.

17. Distinguish between an atom and a molecule.

18. What is the difference between a symbol and a formula?

19. (*a*) What gaseous elements have diatomic molecules? (*b*) How is each represented?

20. (*a*) What gaseous elements have monatomic molecules? (*b*) How is each represented?

21. How many atoms of each element are represented by the following formulas: sugar, $C_{12}H_{22}O_{11}$; sand, SiO_2; salt, $NaCl$; hydrogen peroxide, H_2O_2; soap $C_{17}H_{35}COONa$?

22. What does each of the following represent? (*a*) Ar; (*b*) $4N_2$; (*c*) HI; (*d*) $6H_2SO_4$; (*e*) $3Cu$; (*f*) $2K^+Br^-$; (*g*) CO; (*h*) Co.

23. What is electronegativity?

24. What electronegativity difference is there between atoms which form (*a*) ionic bonds; (*b*) polar covalent bonds; (*c*) bonds with no ionic character?

Group B

25. Draw the orbital notation for (*a*) a calcium atom; (*b*) a calcium ion.

26. Draw the orbital notation for (*a*) a fluorine atom; (*b*) a fluoride ion.

27. Using orbital notation show how an ionic compound of calcium and fluorine is formed.

28. What is the oxidation state of manganese in: (*a*) potassium permanganate, $KMnO_4$; (*b*) manganese(II) sulfate, $MnSO_4$? (*c*) If manganese(II) sulfate is one of the products of a reaction in which potassium permanganate was one of the reactants, what kind of change has manganese undergone? (*d*) What could you call manganese under such circumstances?

29. The four oxygen acids of chlorine are: hypochlorous acid, $HClO$; chlorous acid, $HClO_2$; chloric acid, $HClO_3$; and perchloric acid, $HClO_4$. What is the oxidation number of the chlorine atom in each acid of the series?

30. Verify your conclusions in Question 29 by writing the electron-dot formula for each acid. Use small circles for hydrogen electrons, dots for oxygen electrons, and small crosses for chlorine electrons.

31. Explain why a calcium atom is smaller than a potassium atom.

32. Explain why a sulfide ion is larger than a chloride ion.

33. For a hydrogen bromide molecule, HBr, draw: (*a*) its orbital notation; (*b*) its electron-dot formula.

34. Hydrogen and sulfur form a simple molecular compound. Using both orbital notation and electron-dot notation, show how such a compound may be formed, and determine its probable molecular formula.

35. From the following data determine whether the reaction

$$\tfrac{1}{2} \text{ mole } H_2 + \tfrac{1}{2} \text{ mole } Cl_2 \rightarrow 1 \text{ mole } HCl$$

is exothermic or endothermic, and what the magnitude of the energy change is.

$$\tfrac{1}{2} \text{ mole } H_2 + 52 \text{ kcal} \rightarrow 1 \text{ mole } H$$
$$\tfrac{1}{2} \text{ mole } Cl_2 + 29 \text{ kcal} \rightarrow 1 \text{ mole } Cl$$
$$1 \text{ mole } H + 1 \text{ mole } Cl \rightarrow 1 \text{ mole } HCl + 103 \text{ kcal}$$

36. For each of the following bonds give the percent ionic character and indicate whether the bond is essentially ionic, polar covalent, or pure covalent. (*a*) K—Br; (*b*) C—O; (*c*) Na—O; (*d*) C—H; (*e*) Br—Br.

37. Classify each of the following as ionic crystal, polar covalent molecule, or nonpolar covalent molecule. (*a*) $MgCl_2$; (*b*) CCl_4, consisting of a central carbon atom and four symmetrically arranged chlorine atoms; (*c*) HCl; (*d*) CO_2, consisting of an oxygen atom, a carbon atom, and a second oxygen atom arranged linearly; (*e*) P_4.

38. What is the oxidation number of each element in the following radicals? (*a*) SO_4^-; (*b*) SO_3^-; (*c*) NO_2^-; (*d*) CO_3^-; (*e*) CrO_4^-.

Chapter Seven

CHEMICAL COMPOSITION

1. Table of Ions and their Charges.
A knowledge of the charges of common ions is very important in chemistry. They are given in a table on page 98. Cations other than ammonium have names which are the same as the elements from which they are formed. If a metallic atom forms more than one ion, the name of the ion includes its oxidation number in Roman numerals in parentheses. Many students will find it helpful to *memorize* this table before proceeding further.

Since an older system of naming metallic ions is still frequently used, the accompanying table of name equivalents will be helpful if you have to convert the name of a compound in the older system to the newer system used in this book.

2. Writing chemical formulas. The formulas for many ionic compounds can be easily derived by means of the table of ions and their charges without becoming involved with the details of atomic structure and chemical bonding. First let us try sodium chloride. Sodium ion is Na^+, while chloride ion is Cl^-. When formulas for ionic compounds are written, *the total*

METALLIC ION NAME EQUIVALENTS

Old System	New System
cuprous, Cu^+	copper(I), Cu^+
mercurous, Hg^+	mercury(I), Hg_2^{++}
cupric, Cu^{++}	copper(II), Cu^{++}
ferrous, Fe^{++}	iron(II), Fe^{++}
mercuric, Hg^{++}	mercury(II), Hg^{++}
chromic, Cr^{+++}	chromium(III), Cr^{+++}
ferric, Fe^{+++}	iron(III), Fe^{+++}

charge of the first (positive) part of the compound must be equal but opposite to the total charge of the second (negative) part of the compound. The total charge of an ion is found by multiplying the charge of the ion by the number of that ion taken. Since the charge of one sodium ion is equal but opposite to the charge of one chloride ion, the formula for sodium chloride, NaCl, indicates one of each ion.

Next we shall try calcium chloride. Calcium ion is Ca^{++}. Chloride ion is Cl^-. In order that the total charge of the positive part of the compound be equal but opposite to that of the negative part of the compound, two chloride ions will be needed. One calcium ion has a charge of $+2$, while

TABLE OF COMMON IONS AND THEIR CHARGES

+1	+2	+3
ammonium, NH_4^+	barium, Ba^{++}	aluminum, Al^{+++}
copper(I), Cu^+	calcium, Ca^{++}	chromium(III), Cr^{+++}
mercury(I), Hg_2^{++}	copper(II), Cu^{++}	iron(III), Fe^{+++}
potassium, K^+	iron(II), Fe^{++}	
silver, Ag^+	lead(II), Pb^{++}	
sodium, Na^+	magnesium, Mg^{++}	
	mercury(II), Hg^{++}	
	nickel(II), Ni^{++}	
	zinc, Zn^{++}	

−1	−2	−3
acetate, $C_2H_3O_2^-$	carbonate, $CO_3^=$	phosphate, $PO_4^=$
bromide, Br^-	chromate, $CrO_4^=$	
chlorate, ClO_3^-	oxide, $O^=$	
chloride, Cl^-	peroxide, $O_2^=$	
fluoride, F^-	sulfate, $SO_4^=$	
hydrogen carbonate, HCO_3^-	sulfide, $S^=$	
hydrogen sulfate, HSO_4^-	sulfite, $SO_3^=$	
hydroxide, OH^-		
iodide, I^-		
nitrate, NO_3^-		
nitrite, NO_2^-		

the total charge of two chloride ions is −2; thus the formula is $CaCl_2$. The subscript $_2$ indicates that two chloride ions combine with one calcium ion in forming calcium chloride.

What is the formula for aluminum bromide? Aluminum ion is Al^{+++}. Bromide ion is Br^-. To make the total charge of each part of the compound equal but opposite to the other, three bromide ions will be needed. They will have a total charge of −3, which will balance the +3 of the aluminum ion. The formula is $AlBr_3$.

Observe that this method of formula writing yields only an empirical formula which shows the simplest whole-number ratio of atoms in the compound.

3. Writing the formulas for other compounds. In the case of lead(II) sulfate, the work is easy. Lead(II) ion is Pb^{++}. Sulfate ion is $SO_4^=$. Since the charges are already equal but opposite, only one lead ion and one sulfate ion are needed to form the compound whose formula is $PbSO_4$.

In writing the formula for magnesium hydroxide, a radical must be used more than once in a formula. Magnesium ion is Mg^{++}. Hydroxide ion, a radical, is written OH^-. Two hydroxide ions are needed in order to have a negative charge which is equal but opposite to the positive charge of the magnesium ion. In writing this formula parentheses are used to enclose the hydroxide radical, (OH). Then, the subscript $_2$ is written outside the parentheses, $(OH)_2$. This shows that it is the *entire* OH^- ion which is taken twice. The complete formula for magnesium hydroxide is $Mg(OH)_2$. This formula must *not* be written $MgOH_2$. If the formula were written this way, it would indicate that there are two hydrogen atoms and one oxygen atom, not two hydroxide ions. Chemists put the subscript number outside the parentheses to indicate that the radical inside the parentheses is taken that number of times in the formula. *Parentheses are not used when a radical is taken only once in a formula.*

Let us try another similar formula, that for lead(II) acetate. Lead(II) ion is Pb^{++}. The acetate ion is $C_2H_3O_2^-$. One lead ion and two acetate ions are needed for the formula. Following the same system used for writing the formula for magnesium hydroxide, the formula for lead(II) acetate becomes $Pb(C_2H_3O_2)_2$. Note that in order to show that there are two acetate radicals in the formula, the $C_2H_3O_2$ is enclosed in parentheses, and the subscript $_2$ is placed outside.

Ammonium sulfate has two radicals in its formula. The ammonium ion is NH_4^+ and the sulfate ion is $SO_4^=$. In order to make the total charges equal but opposite, two ammonium radicals must be used. To represent these in the formula, the NH_4 is enclosed in parentheses, with the subscript $_2$ outside. The formula is then written $(NH_4)_2SO_4$.

Finally, let us write the formula for iron(III) carbonate. Iron(III) ion is Fe^{+++} and the carbonate ion is $CO_3^=$. In order to make the total charge of the positive part of the formula equal but opposite to that of the negative part of the formula, two Fe^{+++} ions and three $CO_3^=$ ions must be used. A total of six electrons is involved —three from each of two iron atoms are transferred, two going to each of three carbonate ions. The formula is $Fe_2(CO_3)_3$.

As a beginner in chemistry you must be warned against expecting too much from the ion-charge method. A formula can give no more information than that required to write it. It is possible to write the formula for a compound and then learn that such a compound just does not exist! Furthermore, there are many formulas for covalent compounds which do exist but which cannot be written using the ion-charge method.

4. Naming compounds from their formulas. For many compounds all that is necessary is to give the name of the first part of the formula and then follow it with the name of the second part. $BaSO_4$ is called barium sulfate (Ba^{++} is the barium ion; $SO_4^=$ is the sulfate radical). $FeCl_3$ is iron(III) chloride. Notice that there are two possible oxidation states for iron. One is iron(II) with an oxidation number of $+2$; the other is iron(III), with an oxidation number of $+3$. Since there are 3 chloride ions associated with the iron ion in this formula, the iron ion has a charge of $+3$, and the compound is *iron(III) chloride*. $FeCl_2$ is *iron(II) chloride*.

The use of Roman numerals to indicate oxidation states does not always provide simple and useful names for all known or possible compounds. Hence, another system using Greek numerical prefixes is sometimes used for certain binary covalent compounds. **Binary compounds** are those which consist of only two elements. They are named by the following steps.

1. The first word of the name is made up of: *a.* a prefix to indicate the number of atoms of the first element appearing in the formula, if more than one; and *b.* the name of the first element in the formula.

2. The second word of the name is made up of: *a.* a prefix to indicate the number of atoms of the second element appearing in the formula, if there exists more than one compound of these two elements; *b.* the root of the name of the second element; and *c.* the suffix *–ide,* which means that *only* the two elements named are present.

Carbon monoxide is written CO. Only one atom of the first element appears in the formula, so no prefix is used with the first word; it consists only of the name of the first element, *carbon.* The prefix *mon–* is used in the second word of the name because there is only one atom of oxygen in this formula, but there is more than one compound of carbon and oxygen. *Ox–* is the root of the name of the element oxygen. Then comes the suffix *–ide*.

In like manner, CO_2 is carbon dioxide. The prefix denoting three is *tri–*; for four it is *tetra–*; and for five it is *pent–* or *penta–*. These prefixes are used with both the first and second words in the name. Examples are $SbCl_3$, antimony trichloride; CCl_4, carbon tetrachloride; and As_2S_5, diarsenic pentasulfide.

5. Significance of chemical formulas. We have learned to write formulas for many chemical compounds using our knowledge of the charges of the ions composing them. When it is known that a substance exists as simple molecules, its formula represents one molecule of the substance. Thus it is known as a *molecular formula*. In instances where the molecular structure is not known, or where it is known that the substance does not exist as simple molecules, the formula represents the simplest whole-number ratio of the atoms of the constituent elements. This is called an *empirical*, or *simplest, formula*.

Let us examine some chemical formulas to learn their full significance. The compound water has the molecular formula H_2O. This molecular formula represents *one molecule* of water. It shows that each molecule of water is made up of *two atoms of hydrogen* and *one atom of oxygen*. Since the atomic weight of hydrogen is 1.0 and the atomic weight of oxygen is 16.0, this molecular formula signifies that the *formula weight of water* is 18.0 [(1.0, the atomic weight of hydrogen, $\times$ 2 atoms of hydrogen) + (16.0, the atomic weight of oxygen, $\times$ 1 atom of oxygen)].

The *formula weight* of any compound is *the sum of the atomic weights of all of the atoms present in the formula*.

The compound sodium chloride, table salt, has the empirical formula $NaCl$. It is a crystalline solid which has no simple molecular structure, since it is composed of an orderly arrangement of sodium and chloride ions. This empirical formula tells us the relative number of atoms of each element present in the compound sodium chloride. It shows that for each sodium atom there is one chlorine atom. Since the atomic weight of sodium is 23.0 and of chlorine is 35.5, this empirical formula signifies that the formula weight of sodium chloride is 23.0 + 35.5 or 58.5.

6. Molecular Weight. We have seen that a molecular formula represents one molecule of a substance. Since H_2O is a molecular formula and indicates one molecule of water, the formula weight, 18.0, is the relative weight of *one molecule* of water. *The formula weight of a molecular substance is its* **molecular weight**.

In the strictest sense it is not correct to speak of the molecular weight of a nonmolecular substance, such as sodium chloride, which is represented by an empirical formula. The term *formula weight* is more generally applicable than the term *molecular weight* and therefore is preferred by chemists. However, both terms are used; in elementary chemical calculations the distinction is not significant.

7. Formula weight of a compound. If you wish to know the total weight of your chemistry class, you must add the weights of all the individuals in the class. Similarly, if you wish to find the formula weight of any substance for which the formula is given, you must add the atomic weights of all the atoms present, as represented by the formula. Let us use the formula of cane sugar, $C_{12}H_{22}O_{11}$, as an example.

Number of atoms	Atomic weight	Total weight
12 of C	12	$12 \times 12 = 144$
22 of H	1	$22 \times 1 = 22$
11 of O	16	$11 \times 16 = 176$

formula weight (molecular weight) = 342

The formula for calcium hydroxide is $Ca(OH)_2$. The subscript $_2$ following the parentheses indicates that there are two hydroxide radicals, **OH**, combined with each calcium atom in the compound calcium hydroxide.

Number of atoms	Atomic weight	Total weight
1 of Ca	40.	$1 \times 40. = 40.$
2 of O	16	$2 \times 16 = 32$
2 of H	1	$2 \times 1 = 2$
		formula weight = 74

It may be easier in determining formula weights of substances containing such simple radical groups to consider the *combined atomic weights* of the radical group as we would the atomic weight of a single atom of any element present. Thus we may proceed in an alternate computation as follows:

1 atom of Ca, at. wt. 40. $1 \times 40. = 40.$
2 OH radicals, com-
  bined at. wt. 17 $2 \times 17 = 34$
           formula weight = 74

The atomic weights of the elements are relative weights based on an atom of carbon-12 having the assigned value of exactly 12. In the quantitative study of chemical reactions, the atomic weights and formula weights are exceedingly practical to use. They tell us the relative weights of elements or compounds that combine or react. We may convert these relative weights to any desired units. Thus formulas play a very important part in chemical calculations.

8. Percentage composition of a compound. Frequently it is important to know the composition of a compound in terms of the *mass percentage* of each constituent element. We may want to know the percentage of iron in the compound iron(III) oxide. Knowledge of the percentage of oxygen in potassium chlorate will enable us to determine the amount of this compound needed to furnish enough oxygen for a laboratory experiment.

The chemical formula of a compound enables us to determine directly its formula weight simply by adding the atomic weights of all the atoms present. The formula weight represents *all*, or 100%, of the composition of the substance as indicated by the formula. The total atomic weight (atomic weight $\times$ number of atoms) of each element present represents the *part* of the substance due to that element. The *fractional* part due to each element present is:

$$\frac{\text{total atomic weight of the element}}{\text{formula weight of the compound}}$$

The percentage of each element present in the compound is therefore a fractional part of 100 percent of the compound.

Bear in mind that atomic weights and formula weights are relative weights. They are expressed by numbers without dimensions, that is, numbers without units of measure. This relationship is dimensionally correct when expressed as follows:

$$\frac{(\text{at. wt.} \times \text{no. atoms}) \text{ element}}{\text{formula wt. compound}} \times 100\% \text{ compound} = \% \text{ element}$$

Let us consider the compound iron(III) oxide mentioned earlier. The formula is Fe_2O_3. What is the percentage of each of the elements in this compound?

1. Formula weight of Fe_2O_3

total at. wt. of Fe = $2 \times 55.8 = 111.6$
total at. wt. of O = $3 \times 16.0 = 48.0$
    formula weight of Fe_2O_3 = 159.6

2. Percentage of Fe

$$\frac{\text{total at. wt. Fe}}{\text{formula wt. } Fe_2O_3} \times 100\% \, Fe_2O_3 = \% \, Fe$$

Using three significant figures,

$$\frac{112 \text{ Fe}}{160. \text{ Fe}_2\text{O}_3} \times 100\% \text{ Fe}_2\text{O}_3 = 70.0\% \text{ Fe}$$

3. Percentage of O

$$\frac{\text{total at. wt. O}}{\text{formula wt. Fe}_2\text{O}_3} \times 100\% \text{ Fe}_2\text{O}_3 = \% \text{ O}$$

$$\frac{48.0 \text{ O}}{160. \text{ Fe}_2\text{O}_3} \times 100\% \text{ Fe}_2\text{O}_3 = 30.0\% \text{ O}$$

Of course, since there is no third element present, the percentage of oxygen is $100.0\% - 70.0\% = 30.0\%$.

Observe the dimensional character of the results of these simple computations. Many errors in the solutions to problems in chemistry can be avoided by consistently labeling each quantity properly and then solving the expression for both the numerical value and the label of the result.

As a second example, let us use crystallized sodium carbonate. From its formula, $Na_2CO_3 \cdot 10H_2O$, we see that ten molecules of water have combined with sodium carbonate to form the crystallized compound. (The raised period indicates a bond between the ions of the compound and the water molecules.) To find the percentage composition (to 3 significant figures) we proceed in the same manner as before:

1. Formula weight $Na_2CO_3 \cdot 10H_2O$

2 Na	$2 \times 23.0 =$	46.0
1 C	$1 \times 12.0 =$	12.0
3 O	$3 \times 16.0 =$	48.0
10 H₂O	$10 \times 18.0 =$	180.

formula weight = 286

2. Percentage of Na

$$\frac{46.0 \text{ Na}}{286 \text{ Na}_2\text{CO}_3 \cdot 10\text{H}_2\text{O}} \times$$
$$100\% \text{ Na}_2\text{CO}_3 \cdot 10\text{H}_2\text{O} = 16.1\% \text{ Na}$$

3. Percentage of C

$$\frac{12.0 \text{ C}}{286 \text{ Na}_2\text{CO}_3 \cdot 10\text{H}_2\text{O}} \times$$
$$100\% \text{ Na}_2\text{CO}_3 \cdot 10\text{H}_2\text{O} = 4.2\% \text{ C}$$

4. Percentage of O (in $CO_3^=$ ion)

$$\frac{48.0 \text{ O}}{286 \text{ Na}_2\text{CO}_3 \cdot 10\text{H}_2\text{O}} \times$$
$$100\% \text{ Na}_2\text{CO}_3 \cdot 10\text{H}_2\text{O} = 16.8\% \text{ O}$$

5. Percentage of H_2O

$$\frac{180. \text{ H}_2\text{O}}{286 \text{ Na}_2\text{CO}_3 \cdot 10\text{H}_2\text{O}} \times$$
$$100\% \text{ Na}_2\text{CO}_3 \cdot 10\text{H}_2\text{O} = 62.9\% \text{ H}_2\text{O}$$

Approximate atomic weights usually have no more than two or three significant figures. Your accuracy cannot be improved by carrying out your computations beyond the accuracy limits of the data used. The sum of the mass percentages, therefore, may only approximate 100 percent. Such results do not detract from the validity of the chemistry involved but properly reflect the approximations employed in the computations.

9. **Law of Definite Composition and the Atomic Theory.** The Law of Definite Composition (Chapter 2, Section 9) states, in effect, that the percentage composition of a chemical compound is always the same, regardless of the source of the compound. Since we have just learned how to calculate the percentage composition of chemical compounds, we are now ready to understand how this law may be explained in terms of the atomic theory.

From the method of calculating percentage composition, we can see that its constancy depends on two things: the constant mass of atoms of an element, and the constant proportion in which atoms combine to form a compound. Under normal conditions, the nearly exact constancy of atomic masses is a basic concept of the atomic theory. For practical purposes, the naturally occurring atoms of an element have a definite average mass characteristic of the element. For example, from their atomic weights, the average mass of a hydrogen atom is 1.00797 and of a chlorine atom is 35.453. The constancy of the proportion in which atoms combine is explained by the atomic theory in terms of the ability of individual atoms to lose, gain, or share definite numbers of electrons in forming bonds. In forming hydrogen chloride, for example, only one hydrogen atom can combine with one chlorine atom. The hydrogen atom can share only 1 electron and the chlorine atom needs only 1 electron to complete its octet of 3rd energy level electrons. The ratio of the two atoms which combine can be only 1 to 1. It cannot be 1 to 2, or 3 to 2, or some other ratio. Consequently, a molecule of hydrogen chloride always consists of one atom of hydrogen, atomic weight 1.00797, and one atom of chlorine, atomic weight 35.453, and has a molecular weight of 36.461. Furthermore, hydrogen chloride always contains $\frac{1.00797}{36.461}$ parts by weight of hydrogen, or 2.764% hydrogen, and $\frac{35.453}{36.461}$ parts by weight of chlorine, or 97.236% chlorine.

10. Law of Multiple Proportions. Hydrogen and oxygen unite in unvarying proportions, approximately 1 to 8, *by mass* to form water. There is also another compound of hydrogen and oxygen, hydrogen peroxide. The composition of hydrogen peroxide is 1 part of hydrogen to 16 parts of oxygen by mass. Note that for the same mass of hydrogen in the two compounds, 8 compares with 16 just as 1 is to 2, a ratio of small whole numbers. It is not uncommon in chemistry for two elements to form more than one compound, as shown above, right.

H_2O	1 g of H	and	8 g of O
H_2O_2	1 g of H	and	16 g of O
$FeCl_2$	56 g of Fe	and	71 g of Cl
$FeCl_3$	56 g of Fe	and	106.5 g of Cl

From these data it is observed that: *1.* if the mass of the hydrogen in the first pair of compounds is fixed, or constant, and the mass of iron in the second pair of compounds is also constant; then *2.* the masses of oxygen, 8 and 16, in the first case are in the simple ratio of 1 to 2; and the masses of chlorine, 71 and 106.5, in the second case are in the simple ratio of 2 to 3. It would be possible to give other examples, but in every case the *Law of Multiple Proportions* is found to be true: *When the same two elements unite to form two or more different compounds, if the mass of one element is constant, the masses of the other element in the series of compounds will be in the ratio of small whole numbers.* ~~to each other~~

This law was first proposed by John Dalton, as a direct consequence of his atomic theory. He recognized the possibility that two kinds of atoms could combine in more than one way and in more than one proportion. But since only whole atoms could be involved in such combinations, the ratios of the masses of the second atom joining with fixed masses of the first atom would have to be in the ratio of small whole numbers. This ratio would be the same as the ratio of the actual numbers of atoms of the second element joining with a fixed number of atoms of the first element. This explanation of the Law of Multiple Proportions is one of the strongest justifications of the atomic theory.

Today it is recognized that the Law of Multiple Proportions is true because some elements may exist in more than one oxidation state or can combine in more than one way with another element. Iron can exist in compounds as iron(II) ions with an oxidation number of +2 or iron(III) ions with an oxidation number of $+3$. When these forms of iron combine with chloride ions, for example, there are two possible compounds, $FeCl_2$, iron(II) chloride, and $FeCl_3$, iron(III) chloride. The ratio of the numbers of atoms of chlorine combining with a single atom of iron is 2 to 3. And since the numbers of atoms which combine is proportional to the masses which combine, the ratio of the masses of chlorine combining with a fixed mass of iron in these two compounds is also 2 to 3.

When the electron-dot formula for water

$$H \overset{..}{\underset{\circ\circ}{:}} \overset{..}{O} :$$
$$\overset{\circ}{\underset{\circ}{H}}$$

is compared with that for hydrogen peroxide,

$$H$$
$$: \overset{..}{O} \overset{\circ}{:} \overset{..}{O} :$$
$$\overset{\circ}{\underset{..}{H}}$$

it is obvious that there are two different ways in which these two kinds of atoms can combine. In water, 2 hydrogen atoms combine with only 1 oxygen atom. In hydrogen peroxide, 2 hydrogen atoms combine with 2 oxygen atoms. Since the numbers of atoms which combine is proportional to the masses which combine, the ratio of the masses of oxygen which combine with the same mass of hydrogen in these two compounds is 1 to 2, a ratio of small whole numbers.

11. Mole concept. Imagine that all the people on the earth were assigned the task of counting the molecules in a tablespoon of water at the rate of one molecule each second. Under these conditions approximately 8×10^6 years would be required to complete the project. However impractical this may seem, we can realize that the number of molecules involved is so large that it staggers the imagination!

Fortunately, chemists are not ordinarily faced with the problem of weighing out a certain number of molecules of a compound or atoms of an element. They do frequently need to weigh out equal numbers of atoms or molecules of different substances. A knowledge of the atomic weights of the elements allows this to be done very simply.

In Chapter 3, Sections 12 and 13, we recognized four important quantitative definitions.

1. The number of carbon-12 atoms in the defined quantity of exactly 12 grams of this isotope is the *Avogadro number*, approximately 6.02×10^{23}.

2. The amount of substance containing the Avogadro number of any kind of chemical unit is called a *mole* of that substance.

3. The mass in grams of one mole of naturally occurring atoms of an element is the *gram-atomic weight* of the element.

4. The numerical portion of the gram-atomic weight of an element is the *atomic weight* of the element.

From these definitions we see that if we wish to weigh out an Avogadro number (one mole) of carbon atoms, we must take one gram-atomic weight of carbon, 12 g. If we wish to weigh out an Avogadro number (one mole) of hydrogen atoms, we must take one gram-atomic weight of hydrogen, 1.0 g. These two quantities, 12 g of carbon and 1.0 g of hydrogen contain an equal number of atoms. Thus any given masses of carbon and hydrogen which are in the ratio of 12:1 (the ratio of their atomic weights) must have the same number of atoms.

If we wish to have 5.0 moles of oxygen atoms, we must weigh out 5.0×16 g $=$ 80. g of oxygen. To have 5.0 moles of sulfur atoms, we must take 5.0×32 g $= 160$ g of sulfur. The 80. g of oxygen and 160 g of sulfur contain an equal number of atoms.

Note that the ratio of these masses equals the ratio of the atomic weights of the elements:

$$\frac{80. \text{ g}}{160 \text{ g}} = \frac{16}{32} = \frac{1}{2}$$

By similar reasoning, using the atomic weights of other elements, we may recognize the following important generalization: *If the quantities of two elements are in the same ratio as their atomic weights, they contain the same number of atoms.*

Chemists measure quantities of substances in gram (mass) units and sometimes refer to their masses as their weights since they use "weighing" methods. However, it should be recognized that quantities measured in gram units are, in fact, mass quantities. It is evident that atomic weights are most useful when expressed in gram units. *The gram-atomic weight of an element is one mole of atoms of the element.* Thus one mole of O atoms is 16 g of oxygen, one mole of S atoms is 32 g of sulfur, and one mole of Fe atoms is 56 g of iron.

Let us extend our concept of a mole of atoms of an element to a mole of diatomic molecules of an element. One mole of O_2 molecules will contain two moles of O atoms. We know that two moles of O atoms has a mass of 2×16 g $= 32$ g. Hence a mole of O_2 molecules must have this same mass, 32 g. But we recognize that this is the molecular weight of O_2, 32, expressed in gram units. *The mass of a molecular substance in grams equal to its molecular weight is its* **gram-molecular weight.** Similar reasoning leads us to see that a mole of H_2 molecules has a mass of 2.0 g, and a mole of Cl_2 molecules has a mass of 71.0 g. Thus *the gram-molecular weight of a diatomic molecular element is one mole of molecules of the element.* Note that one mole of O atoms is 16 g, but one mole of O_2 molecules is 32 g, and so on. Also note that 16 g of O atoms, 32 g of O_2 molecules, 1.0 g of

H atoms, 2.0 g of H_2 molecules, 35.5 g of Cl atoms, and 71.0 g of Cl_2 molecules all contain the same number of *particles*.

One mole of H_2O molecules contains two moles of H atoms and one mole of O atoms. Two moles of H atoms has a mass of 2.0 g; one mole of O atoms has a mass of 16 g. Thus, by addition, one mole of H_2O molecules must have a mass of 18 g. This is the gram-molecular weight of water. One mole of methane, CH_4, contains one mole of C atoms and four moles of H atoms. One mole of C atoms has a mass of 12 g; four moles of H atoms has a mass of 4 g. One mole of CH_4 molecules must have a mass, then, of 16 g, its gram-molecular weight. From these examples we see that *the gram-molecular weight of a molecular substance is one mole of molecules of the substance.* There are the same number of molecules in 32 g of O_2, 18 g of H_2O, and 16 g of CH_4. Moles of all molecular substances contain the same number of molecules, the Avogadro number, 6.02×10^{23} molecules per mole. We may conclude further that masses of oxygen, water, and methane which are in the ratio of 32:18:16 contain the same number of molecules.

The concept of the mole may also be extended to include those substances which do not have molecules and are expressed by empirical formulas. Thus the **gram-formula weight** (the formula weight in grams) of sodium chloride, 58.5 g of sodium chloride, is one mole of this compound.

Not only does the symbol of an element stand for one atom of that element, but in quantitative relationships, it stands for one mole of atoms of that element. A formula for a diatomic molecule may represent one molecule of the element as well as one mole of such molecules. Similarly, the formula of a compound may represent the composition of the compound as well as one mole of that compound.

12. Determining the empirical formula of a compound. When given the formula of a compound we may determine the percentage composition of the constituent elements. So if the percent of each element composing a compound is known, we may calculate the ratio of the number of atoms of the elements combined. The elements of a compound written in their smallest whole-number ratio constitute the empirical, or simplest, formula of the compound.

This is the way in which most formulas are originally determined. A compound is analyzed to identify the elements present and determine their mass ratios or percentage composition. The empirical formula is then calculated from this information using the gram-atomic weight (mass per mole of atoms) of each element in order to reduce the mass ratios to atom ratios.

Dr. Morley of Western Reserve University found that 1.0000 part by weight of hydrogen combined with 7.9396 parts by weight of oxygen to form 8.9396 parts by weight of water vapor. Every 8.9396 parts of water formed required 1.0000 part of hydrogen and 7.9396 parts of oxygen. Thus water consists of

$$\frac{1.0000 \text{ part H}}{8.9396 \text{ parts water}} \times 100\% \text{ water} =$$
$$11.186\% \text{ hydrogen}$$

and

$$\frac{7.9396 \text{ parts O}}{8.9396 \text{ parts water}} \times 100\% \text{ water} =$$
$$88.814\% \text{ oxygen}$$

The relative number of atoms of hydrogen and oxygen in water may be determined by comparing the mass percentages of the elements, or their actual masses by analysis, to their respective gram-atomic weights (masses per mole of atoms).

$$\text{No. of moles of atoms of an element} = \frac{\text{mass of the element}}{\text{mass of 1 mole of atoms of the element}}$$

1. From percentage composition data. The simplest way to think of percentage composition is in terms of *parts per hundred.* Dr. Morley's experiments show that (rounding to 3 significant figures) 11.2% of water is hydrogen and 88.8% is oxygen; that is, 100.0 parts of water consist of 11.2 parts hydrogen and 88.8 parts oxygen. Similarly, they show that there are 11.2 g of hydrogen and 88.8 g of oxygen per 100.0 g of water. How many moles of hydrogen and oxygen atoms are present in 100.0 g of water?

H: $\quad \dfrac{11.2 \text{ g H}}{1 \text{ g/mole}} = 11.2 \text{ moles H}$

O: $\quad \dfrac{88.8 \text{ g O}}{16 \text{ g/mole}} = 5.56 \text{ moles O}$

Remembering that 1 mole of atoms of one element is the same number of atoms as 1 mole of atoms of any other element (the Avogadro number), the relative number of atoms is

$$\text{H : O} = 11.2 : 5.56$$

2. From relative mass data. Since the table of approximate atomic weights is used we may round off the relative masses given to 1 part hydrogen and 8 parts oxygen in 9 parts of water. Accordingly, each 9-g quantity of water produced required 1 g of hydrogen and 8 g of oxygen. We can determine the number of moles of hydrogen and oxygen atoms in 9 g of water and reduce this to the relative number of atoms of each in water as before.

H: $\quad \dfrac{1 \text{ g H}}{1 \text{ g/mole}} = 1 \text{ mole H}$

O: $\quad \dfrac{8 \text{ g O}}{16 \text{ g/mole}} = \frac{1}{2} \text{ mole O}$

The relative number of atoms is

$$H : O = 1 : \tfrac{1}{2}$$

H	:	O
$\tfrac{1}{2}$ | 1	:	$\tfrac{1}{2}$
2	:	1

From these calculations we may write the empirical formula of water as

$$H_{11.2}O_{5.56} \text{ or } HO_{\frac{1}{2}}.$$

Both formulas show the correct ratio of hydrogen atoms to oxygen atoms in the compound water. However, according to the Atomic Theory, only whole atoms combine chemically. We need to convert these atom ratios to their simplest whole-number values. This is accomplished by dividing each ratio by its lowest term.

	H	:	O
5.56 |	11.2	:	5.56
	2	:	1

and

The empirical formula of water is therefore H_2O.

Sometimes the operation just performed does not yield a simple whole-number ratio. In such instances the simplest whole-number ratio may be found by expressing the result as fractions and clearing. **CAUTION:** In some problems dividing by the lowest term may result in such ratios as 1 : 2.01, 1 : 2.98, or 1 : 3.99. Remember that results obtained by using approximate atomic weights can be no more accurate than these values. You should not attempt to clear the fractions in such instances; simply round off to 2, 3, or 4 respectively. These operations are illustrated further in the sample problems which follow.

Sample Problem

A compound is found by analysis to contain 75.0% carbon and 25.0% hydrogen. What is the empirical formula?

Solution

Since the compound is 75.0% carbon (75.0 parts per 100.0), 75.0 g per 100.0 g is carbon. Similarly 25.0 g per 100.0 g of the compound is hydrogen. The number of moles of atoms of each element in 100.0 g of the compound is determined by the following relation:

$$\text{No. of moles of atoms of an element} = \frac{\text{mass of the element}}{\text{mass of 1 mole of atoms of the element}}$$

C: $\dfrac{75.0 \text{ g C}}{12.0 \text{ g/mole}} = 6.25$ moles C

H: $\dfrac{25.0 \text{ g H}}{1.01 \text{ g/mole}} = 24.8$ moles H

Relative number of atoms, C : H = 6.25 : 24.8

Smallest ratio of atoms $= \dfrac{6.25}{6.25} : \dfrac{24.8}{6.25} = 1 : 4$

Empirical formula $= CH_4$

Sample Problem

A compound contains carbon, 81.7%, and hydrogen, 18.3%. Find the empirical formula.

Solution

Each 100.0-g quantity of the compound contains 81.7 g of carbon and 18.3 g of hydrogen as shown by the percentage composition.

$$\text{No. of moles of atoms of an element} = \frac{\text{mass of the element}}{\text{mass of 1 mole of atoms of the element}}$$

$$\text{C:} \quad \frac{81.7 \text{ g C}}{12.0 \text{ g/mole}} = 6.81 \text{ moles C}$$

$$\text{H:} \quad \frac{18.3 \text{ g H}}{1.01 \text{ g/mole}} = 18.1 \text{ moles H}$$

Relative number of atoms, C : H = 6.81 : 18.1

$$\text{Smallest ratio of atoms} = \frac{6.81}{6.81} : \frac{18.1}{6.81} = 1 : 2.66$$

Simplest whole number ratio = 1 : 2.66 = 1 : $2\frac{2}{3}$ = 3 : 8

Empirical formula = C_3H_8

Sample Problem

The reduction of 11.47 g of copper(II) oxide yields 9.16 g of copper. What is the empirical formula of the copper(II) oxide?

Solution

Since copper(II) oxide is composed of copper and oxygen, the mass of oxygen removed in the reduction process must be

$$11.47 \text{ g} - 9.16 \text{ g} = 2.31 \text{ g oxygen}$$

$$\text{No. of moles of atoms of an element} = \frac{\text{mass of the element}}{\text{mass of 1 mole of atoms of the element}}$$

$$\text{Cu:} \quad \frac{9.16 \text{ g Cu}}{63.5 \text{ g/mole}} = 0.144 \text{ mole Cu}$$

$$\text{O:} \quad \frac{2.31 \text{ g O}}{16.0 \text{ g/mole}} = 0.144 \text{ mole O}$$

Relative no. of atoms, Cu : O = 0.144 : 0.144

Smallest ratio of atoms = 1 : 1

Empirical formula = CuO

13. Finding the molecular formula. The analysis of a substance enables us to determine its empirical formula. This simplest formula may or may not be the molecular formula. We calculated the empirical formula of the gas, methane, and found it to be CH_4. Any multiple of CH_4, as C_2H_8, C_3H_{12}, or C_nH_{4n}, represents the same ratio of carbon and hydrogen atoms. How then may we know which is the correct molecular formula?

It is not possible to decide which is the true formula unless the molecular weight of the substance has been determined. Some substances lend themselves to known methods of determining molecular weights and some do not. These methods will be discussed in Chapters 10 and 12. If the molecular weight is known, it is a simple matter to decide which multiple of the empirical formula is the molecular formula.

Let us represent the correct multiple of the empirical formula by the subscript x. Then

$$(\text{empirical formula})_x = \text{molecular formula}$$

and $(\text{empirical formula weight})_x$ may then be equated to the known molecular weight.

$$(\text{empirical formula weight})_x = \text{molecular weight}$$

In the case of methane the molecular weight is known to be 16. Our equation is

$$(CH_4 \text{ weight})_x = 16$$
$$(12 + 4)_x = 16$$
$$x = 1$$
$$\text{molecular formula} = (CH_4)_1 \text{ or } CH_4$$

Hence the empirical formula of methane is also the molecular formula. We have seen that this is true also in the case of water. For another example, see the Sample Problem which follows.

Sample Problem

Hydrogen peroxide is found by analysis to consist of 5.9% hydrogen and 94.1% oxygen. Its molecular weight is determined to be 34. What is the correct formula?

Solution

1. The empirical formula determined from the analysis by the method described in Section 12, is

$$HO$$

2. The molecular formula determined from the empirical formula and molecular weight is

$$(HO \text{ weight})_x = 34$$
$$(1 + 16)_x = 34$$
$$x = 2$$
$$\text{molecular formula} = (HO)_2 \text{ or } H_2O_2$$

REVIEW OUTLINE

Ionic charge
    Table of ions and their charges (1)

Formula writing
    Total positive and negative charge agreement (2)
    Use of subscripts and parentheses (2)

Compound naming
    Ion names (3)
    Binary compound names (4)

Significance of a chemical formula
    Composition of compound (5)
    Formula weight—molecular weight (5)
    Percentage composition (8)
    Empirical formula determination (12)
    Molecular formula determination (13)

Law of Definite Composition and Atomic Theory (9)

Law of Multiple Proportions and Atomic Theory (10)

The mole and mass quantities
    Gram-atomic weight (11)
    Gram-molecular weight (11)
    Gram-formula weight (11)

QUESTIONS

Group A

1. What is the full significance of the molecular formula for ammonia, NH_3?
2. Why is the term *formula weight* more generally applicable than the term *molecular weight?*
3. What is the symbol and charge of (*a*) sodium ion; (*b*) copper(I) ion; (*c*) iron(III) ion; (*d*) nickel(II) ion; (*e*) lead(II) ion?
4. What are the names and charges of these radicals: (*a*) NH_4; (*b*) SO_4; (*c*) NO_3; (*d*) CO_3; (*e*) $C_2H_3O_2$?
5. What is the symbol or formula and charge of (*a*) hydrogen carbonate ion; (*b*) bromide ion; (*c*) chromate ion; (*d*) sulfite ion; (*e*) phosphate ion?
6. Write formulas for these compounds: (*a*) barium chloride; (*b*) calcium oxide; (*c*) magnesium sulfate; (*d*) silver bromide; (*e*) zinc carbonate.
7. Name these compounds: (*a*) $NaHCO_3$; (*b*) K_2O_2; (*c*) $HgCl_2$; (*d*) $Fe(OH)_3$; (*e*) $Ni(C_2H_3O_2)_2$.
8. Write the formulas for these compounds: (*a*) ammonium nitrate; (*b*) aluminum sulfide; (*c*) copper(II) hydroxide; (*d*) lead(II) phosphate; (*e*) iron(III) sulfate.
9. Name these compounds: (*a*) $CuCl_2$; (*b*) CaS; (*c*) $KHSO_4$; (*d*) $NaNO_2$; (*e*) $Ni_3(PO_4)_2$.

10. Write the formulas for these compounds: (*a*) chromium(III) fluoride; (*b*) nickel(II) chlorate; (*c*) potassium hydrogen carbonate; (*d*) calcium chromate; (*e*) mercury(II) iodide.

11. Name these compounds: (*a*) Na_2O_2; (*b*) NH_4NO_2; (*c*) $Mg_3(PO_4)_2$; (*d*) $FeSO_4$.

12. Write the formulas for (*a*) sodium hydrogen sulfate; (*b*) lead(II) chromate; (*c*) copper(I) chloride; (*d*) mercury(I) nitrate; (*e*) iron(II) oxide.

13. Name the following: (*a*) K_2SO_4; (*b*) $BaCrO_4$; (*c*) $Cr(OH)_3$; (*d*) $PbBr_2$.

14. What is the formula for: (*a*) aluminum hydroxide; (*b*) copper(I) oxide; (*c*) ammonium sulfide; (*d*) lead(II) acetate; (*e*) iron(III) bromide?

15. Write the formulas for: (*a*) magnesium hydrogen carbonate; (*b*) silver sulfide; (*c*) potassium sulfite; (*d*) chromium(III) sulfate; (*e*) sodium phosphate.

Group B

16. How are percentage composition, the Law of Definite Composition, and the Atomic Theory related?

17. Why is the Law of Multiple Proportions a consequence of the Atomic Theory?

18. Write the names for these compounds according to the system for naming binary compounds: (*a*) SO_3; (*b*) $SiCl_4$; (*c*) PBr_3; (*d*) As_2O_5; (*e*) PbO.

19. Write the formulas for these compounds: (*a*) sulfur dioxide; (*b*) bismuth trichloride; (*c*) manganese dioxide; (*d*) arsenic pentiodide.

20. Name these compounds: (*a*) CO; (*b*) CO_2; (*c*) CBr_4; (*d*) N_2O_3; (*e*) N_2O_5.

PROBLEMS

Group A

1. What is the formula weight of hydrazine, N_2H_4?

2. Find the formula weight of sulfuric acid, H_2SO_4.

3. Dextrose, or grape sugar, has the formula $C_6H_{12}O_6$. Determine its formula weight.

4. Find the formula weight of ethyl alcohol, C_2H_5OH.

5. Calcium phosphate has the formula $Ca_3(PO_4)_2$. Determine the formula weight.

6. Crystallized magnesium sulfate, or Epsom salts, has the formula $MgSO_4 \cdot 7H_2O$. What is its formula weight?

7. Determine the formula weight for each of these compounds: (*a*) HNO_3; (*b*) NaOH; (*c*) HgO; (*d*) $CuSO_4 \cdot 5H_2O$; (*e*) $HC_2H_3O_2$; (*f*) $MgBr_2$; (*g*) Al_2S_3; (*h*) $Ca(NO_3)_2$; (*i*) $Fe_2(Cr_2O_7)_3$; (*j*) $KMnO_4$.

8. Vinegar contains acetic acid, $HC_2H_3O_2$. Find its percentage composition.

9. All baking powders contain sodium hydrogen carbonate, $NaHCO_3$. Calculate its percentage composition.

10. What is the percentage composition of a soap having the formula $C_{17}H_{35}COONa$?

11. What is the percentage composition of each of these compounds: (*a*) SO_2; (*b*) $Ca(OH)_2$; (*c*) $Ca(H_2PO_4)_2 \cdot H_2O$; (*d*) $MgSO_4 \cdot 7H_2O$?

12. Which of these compounds contains the highest percentage of nitrogen: (*a*) $Ca(NO_3)_2$; (*b*) $CaCN_2$; or (*c*) $(NH_4)_2SO_4$?

13. A strip of pure copper, mass 6.356 g, is heated with oxygen until it is completely converted to an oxide, mass 7.956 g. What is the percentage composition of the copper(II) oxide?

14. Calculate the mass of (*a*) 1.00 mole of chlorine atoms; (*b*) 5.00 moles of nitrogen atoms; (*c*) 3.00 moles of bromine molecules; (*d*) 6.00 moles of hydrogen chloride; (*e*) 10.00 moles of magnesium sulfate.

15. You are given 25.00 g of each of these compounds: (*a*) CaO; (*b*) $Na_2CO_3 \cdot 10H_2O$; (*c*) $BaCl_2 \cdot 2H_2O$; (*d*) $(NH_4)_2SO_4$; (*e*) $Fe(NO_3)_3 \cdot 6H_2O$. How many moles of each do you have?

16. How many moles of iron may be recovered from 1.000 metric ton (1000. kg) of Fe_3O_4?

17. Cinnabar, an ore of mercury, has the formula HgS. Calculate the number of moles of mercury recovered from 1.00 kg of cinnabar.

18. Calculate the percentage of copper in each of these minerals: cuprite, Cu_2O; malachite, $CuCO_3 \cdot Cu(OH)_2$; and cubanite, $CuFe_2S_4$.

19. Calculate the percentage of CaO in $CaCO_3$.

20. Calculate the percentage of H_2O in $CuSO_4 \cdot 5H_2O$.

Group B

21. One compound of platinum and chlorine is known to consist of 42.1% chlorine. Another consists of 26.7% chlorine. What are the two empirical formulas?

22. What is the empirical formula of silver fluoride, which is 85% silver?

23. What is the percentage composition of the drug Chloromycetin, $C_{11}H_{12}N_2O_5Cl_2$?

24. Analysis: phosphorus, 43.67%; oxygen, 56.33%. What is the empirical formula?

25. Analysis: potassium, 24.58%; manganese, 34.81%; oxygen, 40.50%. What is the empirical formula?

26. Calculate the empirical formula for a compound having 37.70% sodium, 22.95% silicon, and 39.34% oxygen.

27. A compound has the composition: sodium, 28.05%; carbon, 29.26%; hydrogen, 3.66%; oxygen, 39.02%. What is the empirical formula?

28. The analysis of a compound shows: nitrogen, 21.21%; hydrogen, 6.06%; sulfur, 24.24%; oxygen, 48.48%. Find the simplest formula.

29. A compound has the composition: potassium, 44.82%; sulfur, 18.39%; oxygen, 36.79%. Determine its empirical formula.

30. A compound has the composition: calcium, 24.7%; hydrogen, 1.2%; carbon 14.8%; oxygen, 59.3%. What is its empirical formula?

31. An oxide of iron has the composition: Fe = 72.4%, O = 27.6%. Determine its empirical formula.

32. The analysis of a gas reveals this composition: carbon, 92.3%; hydrogen, 7.7%. Its molecular weight is 26. What is the molecular formula?

33. Analysis of a compound reveals this composition: 80.% carbon and 20.% hydrogen. Its molecular weight is 30. What is its molecular formula?

34. The percentages by weight of carbon in its two oxides are 42.8% and 27.3%. Use these data to illustrate the Law of Multiple Proportions.

Chapter Eight

CHEMICAL EQUATIONS

1. Formula equations. The simplest way to illustrate chemical action is by the use of *word equations*. Such equations are useful because they enable us to state briefly what substances enter into chemical actions and what substances are produced. Word equations have *qualitative* significance.

Water is formed by the combustion of hydrogen in the oxygen of the air. The word equation for this action is:

hydrogen + oxygen → water

We read, hydrogen *plus* oxygen *yields* water. Such an equation signifies that when hydrogen and oxygen react as indicated, water is the only product. Thus it briefly states an experimental fact. It does not tell us the circumstances under which the reaction occurs, or the quantities involved.

In our discussion of the Law of Conservation of Matter and Energy (Chapter 1, Section 11), we recognized a most useful generalization: *In ordinary chemical changes, the total mass of the reacting substances is equal to the total mass of the products.* This may be thought of in terms of the *Law of Conservation of Atoms*.

Suppose we replace the names of the *reactants*, hydrogen and oxygen, and the name of the *product*, water, with their respective formulas. The equation can now be written as a *balanced formula equation* which conforms with the Law of Conservation of Atoms.

$$2H_2 + O_2 \rightarrow 2H_2O$$

This agreement is verified by comparing the total number of atoms of hydrogen and oxygen on the left side of the reaction sign ($\rightarrow$) to their respective totals on the right. Two molecules of hydrogen contain 4 atoms of hydrogen; two molecules of water also contain 4 hydrogen atoms. One molecule of oxygen contains 2 atoms of oxygen; two molecules of water also contain 2 oxygen atoms. Thus the chemical equation, just as any algebraic equation, *expresses an equality. Until it is balanced it cannot express an equality and is not a true equation.* The yield sign ($\rightarrow$) has the meaning of an equals sign (=), and in addition, indicates the direction in which the reaction proceeds.

Our formula equation now signifies much more than the word equation.

1. It tells us the relative proportions of the reactants, hydrogen and oxygen, and the product, water.

2. It tells us that *2 molecules* of hydrogen react with *1 molecule* of oxygen to form *2 molecules* of water.

And since there is an Avogadro number of molecules in each mole of a molecular substance, most importantly,

3. It tells us that 2 moles of hydrogen react with 1 mole of oxygen to form 2 moles of water.

The mass of a mole of a molecular substance is its gram-molecular weight. So,

4. It tells us that *4 g* of hydrogen reacts with *32 g* of oxygen to form *36 g* of water.

Furthermore, these masses are only relative masses. Hence,

5. It tells us that any masses of hydrogen and oxygen which are in the ratio of 1 : 8 respectively will react to yield a mass of water which is related to the masses of hydrogen and oxygen as 1 : 8 : 9.

Finally, in any equation, the equality exists in both directions. If $x + y = z$, then $z = x + y$. So our chemical equation:

6. Tells us that *2 moles* of water, if decomposed, would yield *2 moles* of hydrogen and *1 mole* of oxygen.

From the foregoing, it is evident that formula equations have *quantitative* significance. They represent facts concerning reactions which have been established by experiments or other means. Equations indicate the nature and relative masses of reactants and products, but reveal nothing about the mechanism by which the reactants are converted into the products.

It is possible to write an equation for a reaction which does not occur. For example, hydrogen and oxygen may be shown by an equation to yield hydrogen peroxide. Such an equation can be balanced to conform to the Law of Conservation of Atoms. However, it would be a false equation and therefore useless. It would be contrary to known facts, since hydrogen and oxygen do not combine directly to form hydrogen peroxide.

2. Factors in equation writing. A chemical equation has no value unless it is correct in every detail. Three factors must be considered in writing a balanced equation.

1. The equation must represent the facts. If we are to write the equation for a reaction, we must know the facts concerning the reaction. We must know all the reactants and all the products. The chemist relies upon analysis for facts and writes equations only for those reactions that are known to occur.

2. The equation must include the symbols and formulas of all elements and compounds which are used as reactants or formed as products. We must know these symbols and formulas and must be sure that they are correctly written. The elements which exist as diatomic molecules are oxygen, hydrogen, nitrogen, fluorine, chlorine, bromine, and iodine. Others are usually considered to be monatomic in equation writing. In most instances our knowledge of the oxidation states of the elements and the ion-charge method of writing correct formulas will enable us to satisfy this requirement without extensive experience with experiments or analyses.

3. The Law of Conservation of Atoms must be satisfied. There must be the same number of atoms of each kind on each side of the equation. A new atom cannot appear on the product side and none can disappear from the reactant side. This is the *balancing requirement.* It is met by adjusting the *coefficients* of the formulas of reactants and products to the smallest possible whole numbers which satisfy the Law of Conservation of Atoms.

3. Procedure in writing equations. Let us consider some elementary chemical reactions and write the chemical equations which represent them. We must proceed in steps which satisfy the three factors in equation writing in their proper order. This order is as follows: *represent the facts; balance formulas of compounds as to oxidation number or ion charge* (formulas for elementary gases with diatomic molecules must be correctly written); and *balance the equation as to atoms.*

You may have already prepared hydrogen and oxygen in the laboratory by the electrolysis of water. As an equation does not tell the rate or conditions under which a reaction proceeds, we do not concern ourselves with these matters in writing the equation.

Step 1: What are the facts? The only reactant is water and the only products are hydrogen and oxygen. We may represent these facts by the word equation:

water → hydrogen + oxygen

Now let us substitute the formulas for these substances as accurately as we know them to be.

$H_2O → H_2 + O_2$ (not balanced)

Step 2: Are the formulas correctly written? The oxidation number of hydrogen is +1 and of oxygen −2, so the formula for water is correctly written as H_2O. Both hydrogen and oxygen exist in the free state as diatomic molecules, so the formulas of molecular hydrogen and molecular oxygen are correctly written as H_2 and O_2.

Step 3: Is the equation balanced as to atoms? Starting on the left we have one molecule of water consisting of 2 hydrogen atoms and 1 oxygen atom. On the right of the reaction sign (→) we have one molecule

of hydrogen consisting of 2 atoms and one molecule of oxygen made up of 2 atoms. *But we had only 1 atom of oxygen on the left.* How may we adjust this difference? We cannot add a subscript $_2$ to the oxygen of the water formula for this would alter a formula which we have already established as correctly written. We can, however, increase the number of water molecules to two by placing the coefficient 2 ahead of the formula H_2O, making it $2H_2O$. Thus we have two molecules of water each with 1 oxygen giving us our necessary 2 atoms of oxygen on the left.

$2H_2O → H_2 + O_2$ (not balanced)

Two molecules of water have a total of 4 atoms of hydrogen. We must now move to the right side of the equation and adjust the number of hydrogen atoms to 4. This may be done by placing the coefficient 2 ahead of the hydrogen molecule, making it $2H_2$. We now have a total of 4 atoms of hydrogen on the right and our equation reads:

$2H_2O → 2H_2 ↑ + O_2 ↑$

We have achieved the same number of atoms of each element on both sides of the equation with the lowest whole-number ratio of coefficients possible. Thus the equation is balanced (the arrows pointing upward are used to indicate gaseous products).

Oxygen is one of the most active elements as would be expected from its high electronegativity. It combines with other elements forming compounds called *oxides*. *An oxide is a compound consisting of oxygen and (at least) one other element.* All oxides are formed by exothermic reactions and are usually very stable compounds. Nonmetals like hydrogen, carbon, and sulfur burn in oxygen. Because the electronegativity difference between these nonmetals and oxygen is small, the oxides which are formed are covalent bonded and exist as molecules.

In the burning of sulfur, oxygen combines with the sulfur to form sulfur dioxide gas. These are the facts, so we may write:

$$\text{sulfur} + \text{oxygen} \rightarrow \text{sulfur dioxide}$$
$$\text{S} + \text{O}_2 \rightarrow \text{SO}_2 \uparrow$$

Molecular oxygen is diatomic, O_2, and the binary name "sulfur dioxide" indicates that its formula must be SO_2. All formulas are correctly written. The numbers of atoms of sulfur and oxygen are the same on both sides of the equation. No further adjustments are required; the equation is balanced.

Oxygen may be prepared in the laboratory by heating mercury(II) oxide. The facts are: heating mercury(II) oxide yields metallic mercury and oxygen gas.

$$\textbf{mercury(II) oxide} \rightarrow \textbf{mercury} + \textbf{oxygen}$$

Substituting the proper symbols and formulas, we write:

$$\textbf{HgO} \rightarrow \textbf{Hg} + \textbf{O}_2 \textbf{ (not balanced)}$$

Our oxidation-number check tells us that the formula of mercury(II) oxide is correctly written. The equation is not balanced with respect to oxygen. We can see that two molecules of HgO must decompose to yield the 2 atoms making up the diatomic molecule of oxygen. This will, however, produce 2 atoms of mercury. The balanced equation is:

$$\textbf{2HgO} \rightarrow \textbf{2Hg} + \textbf{O}_2 \uparrow$$

In your laboratory work you may have learned that zinc reacts with hydrochloric acid to produce hydrogen gas and zinc chloride. These facts may be represented by the word equation:

$$\textbf{zinc} + \textbf{hydrochloric acid} \rightarrow$$
$$\textbf{zinc chloride} + \textbf{hydrogen}$$

With proper consideration for oxidation numbers and ion charges we may write:

$$\textbf{Zn} + \textbf{HCl} \rightarrow \textbf{ZnCl}_2 + \textbf{H}_2 \textbf{ (not balanced)}$$

In balancing atoms we see that two molecules of HCl are required to furnish the 2 chlorine atoms of $ZnCl_2$ and the 2 hydrogen atoms of the diatomic hydrogen molecule. Thus our balanced equation is:

$$\textbf{Zn} + \textbf{2HCl} \rightarrow \textbf{ZnCl}_2 + \textbf{H}_2 \uparrow$$

One of the most common mistakes that beginners make in balancing equations is that of destroying the ion charge or oxidation number balance of a formula in order to get the required number of atoms. Do not become discouraged at this time if equations offer considerable difficulty. The trouble lies not in the method of balancing but in the large number of facts that must be known. As you continue to make progress in class and gain experience in the laboratory, the equations that now seem difficult will prove to be simple.

Let us try an equation for a reaction encountered in a process of water purification. Aluminum sulfate and calcium hydroxide are added to water containing objectionable suspended matter. These two substances react in water to produce two insoluble products, aluminum hydroxide and calcium sulfate. These facts may be represented by the word equation:

$$\underset{\text{sulfate}}{\text{aluminum}} + \underset{\text{hydroxide}}{\text{calcium}} \rightarrow$$
$$\underset{\text{hydroxide}}{\text{aluminum}} + \underset{\text{sulfate}}{\text{calcium}}$$

By ion-charge balancing to assure correct formulas we may write:

$$\textbf{Al}_2(\textbf{SO}_4)_3 + \textbf{Ca(OH)}_2 \rightarrow$$
$$\textbf{Al(OH)}_3 + \textbf{CaSO}_4 \textbf{ (not balanced)}$$

We now begin at the left with $Al_2(SO_4)_3$ to balance for atoms. Two Al atoms are indicated. To provide 2 Al atoms on the right we place the coefficient 2 ahead of $Al(OH)_3$. Three SO_4 radicals are indicated, so we place the coefficient 3 in front of $CaSO_4$. Our equation now reads:

$$Al_2(SO_4)_3 + Ca(OH)_2 \rightarrow$$
$$2Al(OH)_3 + 3CaSO_4 \text{ (not balanced)}$$

Next we observe that there must be 3 Ca atoms on the left to equal the 3 Ca atoms now on the right. We place the coefficient 3 in front of $Ca(OH)_2$. This gives us 6 OH radicals on the left and we observe that there are 6 OH radicals on the right. We now have a balanced equation:

$$Al_2(SO_4)_3 + 3Ca(OH)_2 \rightarrow$$
$$2Al(OH)_3 \downarrow + 3CaSO_4 \downarrow$$

(The downward arrows indicate those products which are insoluble and leave the reaction environment as *precipitates*.)

To be successful in writing chemical equations: *1. you must know the symbols of the common elements; 2. you must know the usual oxidation number or ionic charges of the common elements and radicals; 3. you must know the facts* relating to the reaction for which an equation is to be written; *4. you must insure that all formulas are correctly written* prior to any attempt to balance atoms; and *5. you must balance the equation as to atoms* of all elements present, so as to have the lowest ratio of whole-number coefficients possible.

4. Stoichiometric relations. The determination of empirical formulas of compounds is always the result of experimentation. Empirical formulas are derived from the relative numbers of moles of atoms of the elements composing compounds. Therefore, they indicate the relative numbers of atoms present. Nothing can be inferred from the empirical for-

mula about the nature of the association of the atoms, the make-up of the molecular structure, or whether the substance even exists in simple molecular units. Nevertheless, empirical formulas are very useful in calculations involving the combining and reacting relationships among substances.

The branch of chemistry which deals with the numerical relationships of elements and compounds and the mathematical proportions of reactants and products in chemical transformations is known as stoichiometry *(stoy-key-om-eh-tree).* The determination of the percentage composition of compounds and of empirical formulas discussed in Chapter 7 are examples of *stoichiometric relations.* An understanding of the mole concept together with some skill in writing and balancing chemical equations will enable you to solve stoichiometric problems involving the mass relations of reactants and products in chemical reactions. The introduction of the concept of mole volumes of gases in Chapter 10 will enable you to solve a great number of problems involving mass and volume relations of gaseous reactants and products by means of very simple computations.

5. Mole relations of reactants and products. When carbon is burned in the oxygen of the air, carbon dioxide, a covalent molecular gas, is produced.

$$C + O_2 \rightarrow CO_2 \uparrow$$

We stated in Section 1 of this chapter that the balanced equation signifies the mole proportions of the reactants and products, as well as the composition of each substance in terms of the kinds of elements and the relative number of each kind of atom present. Thus the equation signifies that 1 mole of carbon combines with 1 mole of oxygen to yield 1 mole of carbon dioxide. This may be indicated as follows:

$$C \quad + \quad O_2 \quad \rightarrow \quad CO_2 \uparrow$$

1 mole	1 mole	1 mole
= 12.0 g	= 32.0 g	= 44.0 g

The mole proportions of reacting substances and products are readily convertible to equivalent mass quantities as shown above. Thus the equation is used when we wish to determine the mass of one substance that reacts with, or is produced from, a definite mass of another. This is one of the common problems chemists are called upon to solve.

6. Methods of solving mass-mass problems. Two general methods are employed in solving problems which involve mass relations of reactants and products. These are *the mole method* and *the proportion method.* Each method is explained in the following problem illustrations. Your instructor may prefer that you use a particular method regularly in your problem work. If not, it is suggested that you study each explanation carefully and use the method which seems most logical to you. The mole concept is quite important in advanced work in chemistry so, other considerations being equal, it is best to work with mole quantities wherever possible.

It is always desirable to make a preliminary mental estimate to determine the *order of magnitude* of the answer to a problem before undertaking the indicated computations. Thus you may avoid accepting an answer as correct which actually is quite absurd due to errors in computation or in operations with units.

7. Solving by moles. Let us assume that we must determine how much calcium oxide will be produced by heating 50.0 g of calcium carbonate. Observe that the mass of the reactant is given and the mass of a product is required. From the data in the problem and the facts known concerning the reaction, we can proceed

to *set up the problem.* This may be accomplished in four steps.

Step 1. Write the balanced equation.

Step 2. Show the problem specifications: what is given and what is required. To do this we write the mass of calcium carbonate, 50.0 g, above the formula $CaCO_3$. Letting X represent the unknown mass of calcium oxide produced, we write X above the formula CaO.

Step 3. Show the mole proportions established by the balanced equation. This is accomplished by writing under each substance involved in the problem the number of *moles* indicated by the equation.

Step 4. Determine the mass of 1 mole of each substance involved in the problem. These should be written below the equation set up. The problem is now ready to be solved.

Step 2:   50.0 g X

Step 1: $CaCO_3 \rightarrow CaO + CO_2 \uparrow$

Step 3.   1 mole   1 mole

Step 4.   1 mole $CaCO_3$ = 100.1 g
           1 mole CaO   = 56.1 g

The number of moles of $CaCO_3$ *given in the problem* is found by dividing the given mass of $CaCO_3$, 50.0 g, by the mass of 1 mole of $CaCO_3$, 100.1 g, or

$$\frac{50.0 \text{ g } CaCO_3}{100.1 \text{ g/mole}} = \text{no. moles } CaCO_3$$

The balanced equation indicates that for each mole of $CaCO_3$ decomposed, 1 mole of CaO is produced. So from the given mass of $CaCO_3$ we may produce

$$\frac{50.0 \text{ g } CaCO_3}{100.1 \text{ g/mole}} \times \frac{1 \text{ mole CaO}}{1 \text{ mole } CaCO_3} =$$
$$\text{no. moles CaO}$$

To determine the mass of CaO produced, we next multiply by the mass of 1 mole of CaO:

$$\frac{50.0 \text{ g CaCO}_3}{100.1 \text{ g/mole}} \times \frac{1 \text{ mole CaO}}{1 \text{ mole CaCO}_3} \times$$

$$\frac{56.1 \text{ g}}{\text{mole}} = \text{g CaO}$$

A check of the units indicates that they are correct. We are now ready to perform the arithmetic calculations.

$$\frac{50.0 \text{ g } \cancel{\text{CaCO}_3}}{100.1 \text{ g/} \cancel{\text{mole}}} \times \frac{1 \cancel{\text{ mole}} \text{ CaO}}{1 \cancel{\text{ mole CaCO}_3}} \times$$

$$\frac{56.1 \text{ g}}{\cancel{\text{mole}}} = 28.0 \text{ g CaO}$$

By estimating the answer from the quantities involved, we see that 28.0 g of CaO is reasonable.

Note that solving a mass-mass problem according to the mole method involves four operations following the problem set-up.

1. Determine the number of moles of the substance whose mass is given in the problem by dividing its mass by the mass per mole of the substance.

2. Determine the number of moles of substance whose mass is required by multiplying the expression from operation 1 by the ratio of the number of moles of substance whose mass is required and the number of moles of substance whose mass is given as indicated by the balanced equation.

3. Determine the mass of the substance required by multiplying the expression from operation 2 by the number of grams per mole of the substance required.

4. Check the units assigned to make sure they yield the proper units for the answer, and estimate the answer. Perform the arithmetic operations, and compare the calculated result with your estimated one.

See the following Sample Problem.

Sample Problem

How many grams of potassium chlorate must be decomposed to yield 30.0 g of oxygen?

Solution   (Mole Method)

We set up the problem by *first,* writing the balanced equation; *second,* writing the specifications of the problem above the equation; *third,* writing the number of moles of each specified substance under its formula; and *fourth,* calculating the mass/mole of each of the specified substances. We will let X represent the mass of potassium chlorate decomposed.

Step 2: X 30.0 g
Step 1: $2KClO_3 \longrightarrow 2KCl + 3O_2 \uparrow$
Step 3:   2 moles   3 moles

Step 4:   1 mole $KClO_3$ = 122.6 g
            1 mole O_2 = 32.0 g

Operation 1: $\dfrac{30.0 \text{ g O}_2}{32.0 \text{ g/mole}}$ = no. moles O_2

Operation 2: $\dfrac{30.0 \text{ g O}_2}{32.0 \text{ g/mole}} \times \dfrac{2 \text{ moles KClO}_3}{3 \text{ moles O}_2}$ = no. moles $KClO_3$

Operation 3: $\dfrac{30.0 \text{ g } O_2}{32.0 \text{ g/mole}} \times \dfrac{2 \text{ moles } KClO_3}{3 \text{ moles } O_2} \times \dfrac{122.6 \text{ g}}{\text{mole}} = \text{g } KClO_3$

Operation 4: $\dfrac{30.0 \text{ g } O_2}{32.0 \text{ g/mole}} \times \dfrac{2 \text{ moles } KClO_3}{3 \text{ moles } O_2} \times \dfrac{122.6 \text{ g}}{\text{mole}} = 76.6 \text{ } KClO_3$

▶**8. Solving by proportion.** We wish to determine the mass of sodium hydroxide produced by the reaction of 5.00 g of metallic sodium and water. In the proportion method the first three steps in the problem set-up are the same as those for the mole method. The *fourth step* consists of converting the molar quantities shown by the equation into corresponding equation masses.

Step 2: 5.00 g X
Step 1: $2Na + 2H_2O \rightarrow 2NaOH + H_2 \uparrow$
Step 3: 2 moles =   2 moles =
Step 4: 46.0 g   80.0 g

The balanced equation indicates that 46.0 g of Na yields 80.0 g of NaOH. We may reason that any other mass of Na used and NaOH produced must be in the same ratio as that of the equation masses of Na and NaOH. This is an equality of ratios and is expressed by the *proportion:*

$$\frac{5.00 \text{ g Na}}{X} = \frac{46.0 \text{ g Na}}{80.0 \text{ g NaOH}}$$

Solving $X = \dfrac{5.00 \text{ g Na} \times 80.0 \text{ g NaOH}}{46.0 \text{ g Na}}$

$X = 8.70 \text{ g NaOH}$

See the Sample Problem which follows.

Sample Problem

a. How many grams of oxygen are required to oxidize 140. g of iron to iron(III) oxide? *b.* How many moles of iron(III) oxide will be produced?

Solution   (Proportion Method)

The problem set-up for Parts *a* and *b* is:

Step 2:   140. g X Y
Step 1:   4Fe   + $3O_2$ → $2Fe_2O_3$
Step 3: 4 moles =   3 moles =   2 moles =
Step 4:   223.2 g   96.0 g   319.2 g

The solution set-up for Part *a* is:

$$\frac{223.2 \text{ g Fe}}{96.0 \text{ g } O_2} = \frac{140. \text{ g Fe}}{X}$$

$$X = \frac{140. \text{ g Fe} \times 96.0 \text{ g } O_2}{223.2 \text{ g Fe}} = 60.3 \text{ g } O_2$$

The solution set-up for Part *b* is:

$$\frac{223.2 \text{ g Fe}}{319.2 \text{ g } Fe_2O_3} = \frac{140. \text{ g Fe}}{Y}$$

$$Y = \frac{140. \text{ g Fe} \times 319.2 \text{ g } Fe_2O_3}{223.2 \text{ g Fe}} = 200. \text{ g } Fe_2O_3$$

But 1 mole Fe_2O_3 = 159.6 g, so

$$\frac{200. \text{ g } Fe_2O_3}{159.6 \text{ g/mole}} = 1.25 \text{ moles } Fe_2O_3$$

REVIEW OUTLINE

Chemical equations

>Word equation: qualitative significance (1)

>Formula equation: quantitative significance (1)

>Written equations
>Represent facts (2)
>Include all symbols and formulas of reactants and products (2)
>Satisfy the Law of Conservation of Atoms (2)

>Balanced equations show
>Formula proportions (3)
>Mole proportions (3)
>Mass proportions (3)

Stoichiometry: chemical arithmetic (4, 5)

>Mass-mass problems (6)
>Mole method (7)
>Proportion method (8)

EQUATIONS

Group A

Write balanced formula equations for these reactions. *Do not write in this book.*

1. iron + sulfur $\rightarrow$ iron(II) sulfide.
2. sodium chloride + silver nitrate $\rightarrow$ silver chloride $\downarrow$ + sodium nitrate.
3. calcium oxide + water $\rightarrow$ calcium hydroxide.
4. calcium hydroxide + carbon dioxide $\rightarrow$ calcium carbonate $\downarrow$ + water.
5. sodium chloride + sulfuric acid (H_2SO_4) $\rightarrow$ sodium hydrogen sulfate hydrogen chloride $\uparrow$.
6. zinc + copper(II) sulfate $\rightarrow$ zinc sulfate + copper.
7. magnesium bromide + chlorine $\rightarrow$ magnesium chloride + bromine.
8. hydrogen + chlorine $\rightarrow$ hydrogen chloride $\uparrow$.
9. aluminum + iron(III) oxide $\rightarrow$ aluminum oxide + iron.
10. silver nitrate + copper $\rightarrow$ copper(II) nitrate + silver $\downarrow$.
11. hydrogen + nitrogen $\rightarrow$ ammonia (NH_3) $\uparrow$.
12. sodium hydroxide + carbon dioxide $\rightarrow$ sodium carbonate + water.
13. ammonium nitrite $\rightarrow$ nitrogen $\uparrow$ + water.
14. barium chloride + sodium sulfate $\rightarrow$ sodium chloride + barium sulfate $\downarrow$.
15. calcium + hydrochloric acid (HCl) $\rightarrow$ calcium chloride + hydrogen $\uparrow$.
16. iron(II) sulfide + hydrochloric acid $\rightarrow$ hydrogen sulfide $\uparrow$ + iron(II) chloride.
17. lead(II) nitrate + sulfuric acid $\rightarrow$ lead(II) sulfate + nitric acid (HNO_3).

18. zinc chloride + ammonium sulfide → zinc sulfide ↓ + ammonium chloride.
19. ammonia + oxygen → nitric acid + water.
20. magnesium + nitric acid → magnesium nitrate + hydrogen ↑.
21. mercury(I) chloride → mercury + mercury(II) chloride.
22. nickel + hydrochloric acid → nickel(II) chloride + hydrogen ↑.
23. sodium iodide + bromine → sodium bromide + iodine.
24. carbon + steam (H_2O) → carbon monoxide ↑ + hydrogen ↑.
25. zinc + lead(II) acetate → lead ↓ + zinc acetate.
26. calcium carbonate → calcium oxide + carbon dioxide ↑.
27. iron(III) oxide + carbon monoxide → iron + carbon dioxide ↑.
28. lead(II) acetate + hydrogen sulfide → lead(II) sulfide ↓ + acetic acid ($HC_2H_3O_2$).
29. calcium phosphate + sulfuric acid → calcium sulfate + phosphoric acid (H_3PO_4).
30. iron(III) chloride + sodium carbonate → sodium chloride + iron(III) carbonate ↓.
31. calcium oxide + diphosphorus pentoxide → calcium phosphate.
32. copper + chlorine → copper(I) chloride.
33. iron(III) chloride + sodium hydroxide → iron(III) hydroxide ↓ + sodium chloride.
34. calcium carbonate + hydrochloric acid → calcium chloride + water + carbon dioxide ↑.
35. sodium hydrogen carbonate + sulfuric acid → sodium sulfate + water + carbon dioxide ↑.
36. calcium hydroxide + phosphoric acid → calcium phosphate + water.
37. aluminum hydroxide + sulfuric acid → aluminum sulfate + water.
38. copper + sulfuric acid → copper(II) sulfate + water + sulfur dioxide ↑.
39. sodium sulfite + sulfuric acid → sodium sulfate + water + sulfur dioxide ↑.
40. calcium hydroxide + ammonium sulfate → calcium sulfate + ammonia ↑ + water.

Group B

Complete the following word equations and write and balance the formula equations for these reactions. From experiments already performed in the laboratory, you should know the identities of the products. *Do not write in this book.*

41. copper + oxygen →
42. magnesium + oxygen →
43. zinc + sulfuric acid →
44. copper(II) oxide + hydrogen →
45. magnesium + hydrochloric acid →
46. silver nitrate + hydrochloric acid →
47. iron + sulfuric acid →
48. potassium + water →
49. magnesium + sulfuric acid →
50. sodium peroxide + water →

PROBLEMS

Group A

1. Mercury(II) oxide (25.0 g) is to be decomposed by heating. (*a*) How many moles of mercury(II) oxide are given? (*b*) How many moles of oxygen can be prepared? (*c*) How many grams of oxygen can be prepared?
2. Potassium chlorate (25.0 g) is to be decomposed by heating. (*a*) How many moles of potassium chlorate are given? (*b*) How many moles of oxygen can be prepared? (*c*) How many grams of oxygen can be prepared?
3. A quantity of zinc reacts with sulfuric acid to produce 0.10 g of hydrogen. (*a*) How many moles of hydrogen are produced? (*b*) How many moles of zinc were required? (*c*) How many grams of zinc were required?
4. Sodium chloride reacts with 10.0 g of silver nitrate in water solution. (*a*) How many moles of silver nitrate react? (*b*) How many moles of sodium chloride are required? (*c*) How many grams of sodium chloride are required?
5. (*a*) How many moles of silver chloride are precipitated in the reaction of Problem 4? (*b*) How many grams of silver chloride is this?
6. In a reaction between sulfur and oxygen, 80.0 g of sulfur dioxide is formed. How many grams of sulfur were burned?
7. How many grams of hydrogen are required to completely convert 25 g of hot magnetic iron oxide (Fe_3O_4) to metallic iron? Steam is the other product of the reaction.
8. What mass of copper(II) oxide is formed by oxidizing 1.00 kg of copper?
9. What mass of silver is precipitated when 40.0 g of copper reacts with silver nitrate in solution?
10. Suppose 10.0 g of iron(II) sulfide is treated with enough hydrochloric acid to complete the reaction. How many grams of hydrogen sulfide gas could be collected?

Group B

11. An excess of sulfuric acid reacts with 150. g of barium peroxide. (*a*) How many moles of hydrogen peroxide are produced? (*b*) How many moles of barium sulfate are formed?
12. Approximately 130 g of zinc was dropped into a solution containing 100. g of HCl. After the action ceased, 41 g of zinc remained. How many moles of hydrogen were produced?
13. A mixture of 10.0 g of powdered iron and 10.0 g of sulfur is heated to its reaction temperature in an open crucible. (*a*) How many grams of iron(II) sulfide are formed? (*b*) The reactant in excess is oxidized. How many grams of its oxide are formed?
14. What mass of calcium hydroxide can be produced from 1.00 kg of limestone, calcium carbonate? (Decomposition of calcium carbonate by heating produces calcium oxide and carbon dioxide. Calcium hydroxide is formed by the reaction of calcium oxide and water.)

15. How many grams of air are required to complete the combustion of 93 g of phosphorus to diphosphorus pentoxide, assuming the air to be 23% oxygen by weight?

16. How many metric tons of carbon dioxide may be produced from the combustion of 1.000 metric ton (1000. kg) of coke which is 90.% carbon?

17. (*a*) What mass of H_2SO_4 is required in a reaction with an excess of aluminum to produce 0.50 mole of aluminum sulfate? (*b*) How many moles of hydrogen are also produced?

18. A certain rocket uses butane, C_4H_{10}, as fuel. How many kilograms of liquid oxygen should be carried for the complete combustion of each 1.00 kg of butane to carbon dioxide and water vapor?

19. When 45 g of ethane gas, C_2H_6, is burned completely in air, carbon dioxide and water vapor are formed. (*a*) How many moles of carbon dioxide are produced? (*b*) How many moles of water are produced?

20. (*a*) How many grams of sodium sulfate are produced in the reaction between 150. g of sulfuric acid and an excess of sodium chloride? (*b*) How many grams of sodium chloride are used? (*c*) How many grams of hydrogen chloride are also produced?

Chapter Nine

THE GAS LAWS

1. Kinetic theory. In Chapter 1 we recognized that matter exists in three physical states—gas, liquid, and solid. Then we found that particles composing various substances are atoms, molecules, or ions. The *kinetic theory* helps explain the properties of gases, liquids, and solids in terms of the forces between the particles of matter and the energy they possess.

Most of the data that support the kinetic theory come from indirect observation. It is almost impossible to observe the behavior of individual particles of matter. Even if such observations could be made easily, they would be hard to interpret. Scientists, however, can observe the behavior of large groups of particles. From the results of these observations, they can then describe their average behavior.

The three basic assumptions of the *kinetic theory* are:

1. Matter is composed of very tiny particles. The chemical properties of the particles of matter depend on their composition. Their physical properties depend on the forces they exert on each other and the distance separating them.

2. The particles of matter are in constant motion. Their average kinetic energy (energy of motion) depends on the temperature.

3. The particles of matter do not lose energy in collisions. When particles collide with each other or with the walls of their container, there is no loss of energy. Collisions of this type are said to be perfectly *elastic*.

2. Observed properties of gases. A study of gases reveals four characteristic properties:

1. Expansion. A gas does not have a definite shape or a definite volume. It completely fills any container into which it is introduced.

2. Pressure. When we inflate a toy balloon, it becomes larger because we increase the pressure on its inside surface. If we let air escape, the balloon becomes smaller due to decreased pressure. If we raise the temperature of the air in the balloon by warming it carefully, the balloon becomes larger, indicating that pressure increases with an increase in temperature. Conversely, if we cool the balloon, its size decreases as the pressure decreases.

3. Low density. The density of a gas is about 10^{-3} times that of the same substance in the liquid or solid state. Oxygen gas has a density of 1.429 g/l (0.001429 g/ml) at 0° C and 1 atmosphere pressure, while liquid oxygen has a density of 1.14 g/ml at −183° C, and solid oxygen has a density of 1.426 g/ml at −252.5° C. Hydrogen gas has a density of 0.0899 g/l (0.0000899 g/ml) at 0° C and 1 atmosphere pressure, while liquid hydrogen has a density of 0.0708 g/ml at −253° C, and solid hydrogen has a density of 0.0807 g/ml at −262° C.

4. Diffusion. If the stopper is removed from a container of ammonia, its irritating properties soon become evident throughout the room. When the chemistry class makes the foul-odored hydrogen sulfide gas in the laboratory, objections frequently come from other students and teachers in all parts of the building. The gases are said to *diffuse* (or scatter) throughout the laboratory and throughout the building.

3. Kinetic theory description of a gas. According to the kinetic theory, a gas consists of infinitely small independent particles, moving randomly in space and experiencing perfectly elastic collisions. This theoretical description is of an imaginary gas called an ***ideal gas.***

The particles of substances which are gases at room temperature are molecules. Some of these molecules consist of a single atom (He, Ne, Ar), many consist of two atoms (O_2, H_2, HCl, etc.), while others consist of several atoms (NH_3, CH_4, C_2H_2, etc.). Matter in the gaseous state occupies a volume of the order of 10^3 times that which it does in the liquid or solid states. Thus molecules of gases are much farther apart than those of liquids or solids. This accounts for the much lower density of gases as compared to liquids or solids. Even so, 1 ml of a gas contains about

3×10^{19} molecules. Many ordinary molecules have diameters of the order of 4 Å or 4×10^{-10} m. In gases, these molecules are widely separated. They are, on an average, about 4×10^{-9} m or about 10 diameters apart. The kinetic energy of the molecules of a gas (except near its condensing temperature) overcomes the attractive forces between them. The molecules are on the average essentially independent particles, traveling in random directions at high speed, of the order of 10^3 m/sec. At this speed, they travel about 10^{-7} m before colliding with other molecules or with the walls of the container, and undergo about 5×10^9 collisions per second.

The expansion and diffusion of gases are both explained by the fact that gas molecules are essentially independent particles. They move through space until they strike another gas molecule or the walls of the container. Gas pressure is due to the constant bombardment of the walls of the container by many billions of moving molecules. If we increase the number of molecules within the container, the number of collisions against the inside surface, and therefore the pressure on the inside surface, increases. If the temperature of the gas is raised, the molecules have more kinetic energy. They move more rapidly, and collide more energetically with the walls of the container, thus in-

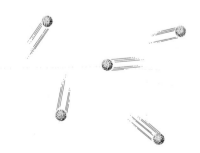

9-1 Molecules of a gas are widely separated and move rapidly.

creasing the pressure. The pressure drops when the number of molecules is decreased or the temperature is lowered.

All molecules of a gas do not have the same kinetic energy. However, in any given volume most of them at any time may be expected to have an energy value near the average kinetic energy of all the molecules. *An increase in the temperature increases the rate at which the molecules move.* Thus the temperature of a gas provides an indication of the average kinetic energy of the molecules.

4. Attractive forces between gas molecules. The lowest temperature at which a substance may exist as a gas at atmospheric pressure is the *condensation temperature* of the gas. At this temperature the kinetic energy of the gas particles is not sufficient to overcome the forces of attraction between them, and the gas condenses to a liquid. The kinetic theory tells us that the temperature of a substance is a measure of the kinetic energy of its particles. Thus a study of condensation temperatures of various substances should give us an idea of the magnitude of the forces of attraction between particles of matter. The table to the right of this column gives condensation temperatures for a variety of substances.

Substances such as H_2, O_2, and CH_4 (methane) consist of low-molecular-weight nonpolar covalent molecules. They may exist as gases to very low temperatures. Evidently the attractive forces between such molecules in the gaseous state is very small. More complex, higher-molecular-weight nonpolar covalent molecular substances such as CCl_4 and C_6H_6 (benzene) have condensation temperatures somewhat above room temperature. The forces of attraction between such molecules must be higher than those between similar molecules of lesser complexity.

Ammonia (NH_3) and H_2O consist of

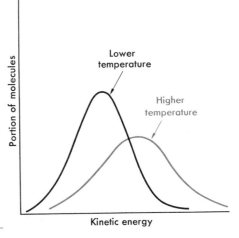

9-2   Energy distribution in a gas at different temperatures.

CONDENSATION TEMPERATURES OF VARIOUS SUBSTANCES

Type of Substance	Substance	Condensation Temperature (1 atm, °C)
Nonpolar covalent molecular	H_2	−253
	O_2	−183
	CH_4	−162
	CCl_4	77
	C_6H_6	80
Polar covalent molecular	NH_3	−33
	H_2O	100
Ionic	NaCl	1413
	MgF_2	2227
Macro-molecular	SiO_2	2230
	C_x (diamond)	4200
Metallic	Fe	3000
	Cu	2336

polar covalent molecules. Notice that while their molecular weight and molecular complexity are small, their condensation temperatures are considerably above those of nonpolar molecules of the same molecular weight.

The condensation temperatures of ionic compounds, macromolecular substances, and metals are all very high. Evidently the forces between particles of such substances are very strong. The nature of the forces of attraction in these types of substances will be described in Chapter 11.

The attractive forces between gaseous nonpolar covalent molecules are van der Waals forces. These forces become significant only when molecules are very close together. Hence they are not effective unless the molecules of a gas are under very high pressure or are at temperatures near their condensation temperatures. The strength of the van der Waals forces depends on the number of electrons in a molecule and the tightness with which they are held. The greater the number of electrons and the less tightly they are bound, the greater are the attractive forces between nonpolar molecules. Thus, generally, the higher the molecular weight of a nonpolar molecule, the higher its condensation temperature will be. We can observe this from the table by comparing the condensation temperatures of oxygen, hydrogen, and methane, with those of carbon tetrachloride and benzene.

In addition to the van der Waals forces, polar molecules have forces of attraction between the oppositely charged portions of neighboring molecules. This explains the much higher condensation temperatures of polar molecules as compared to nonpolar molecules of similar complexity. For example, methane, ammonia, and water have comparable molecular weights. Yet the condensation temperature of ammonia is about 130 C° higher than that of methane; that of water is over 250 C° higher.

5. Diffusion of gases. Suppose the air is pumped out of a container and a gas is then allowed to enter it. We observe that the container is instantly filled with the gas. We would expect this to occur because of the great speed of the molecules and the almost complete lack of collisions.

Molecules of a gas escaping into a room already occupied by other gases do, of course, experience frequent collisions, perhaps as many as 5 billion per second. The resulting random directions of motion delay the scattering of the molecules of the new gas throughout the other gases. Eventually, random motion of all of the gas molecules results in their uniform distribution throughout the room. *This process of spreading out spontaneously to fill a space uniformly is characteristic of all gases and is known as* **diffusion.** Gaseous diffusion is slowed down, but not prevented, by the presence of other gases.

All gases existing at the same temperature have the same average kinetic energy. Should we then expect their molecules to have the same average velocities? The kinetic energy of a particle is dependent on both its mass and velocity.

$$\textbf{K.E.} = \tfrac{1}{2}\,mv^2$$

where K.E. is kinetic energy, m is the mass of the particle, and v is its velocity. Thus molecules of different gases having the same kinetic energy move at different rates if their masses are different. The lighter molecules move more rapidly, the heavier molecules more slowly.

For two molecules having the same kinetic energy,

$$\tfrac{1}{2}\,m_1v_1{}^2 = \tfrac{1}{2}\,m_2v_2{}^2$$

where m_1 and v_1 are the mass and velocity of the first molecule and m_2 and v_2 are the mass and velocity of the second molecule respectively. Multiplying by 2 and transposing terms,

$$\frac{v_2{}^2}{v_1{}^2} = \frac{m_1}{m_2}$$

Taking the square root of both sides,

$$\frac{v_2}{v_1} = \frac{\sqrt{m_1}}{\sqrt{m_2}}$$

The mass of a molecule and its molecular weight are proportional, so m_1 and m_2 may also represent the molecular weights of the two molecules. The rates of diffusion of the two molecules, r_1 and r_2, are proportional to their molecular velocities and may be substituted for them.

$$\frac{r_2}{r_1} = \frac{\sqrt{m_1}}{\sqrt{m_2}}$$

This relationship is the mathematical expression for *Graham's Law of Diffusion: The rate of diffusion of a gas is inversely proportional to the square root of its molecular weight.* Hydrogen, which has the lowest molecular weight of any gas, diffuses more rapidly than other gases under similar conditions. At room temperature the velocity of hydrogen molecules is about one mile per second. See the Sample Problem below.

6. Dependence of gas volume on temperature and pressure. A given number of gas molecules can occupy widely different volumes. The expression "a cubic foot of air" means little unless the temperature and pressure at which it is measured are also known. A cubic foot of air can be compressed to a few cubic inches in volume. It can also expand to fill a high school auditorium. Steel cylinders containing oxygen and hydrogen with an internal volume of two cubic feet are widely used in industry. When such cylinders are returned "empty" they still contain two cubic feet of gas, although when they were delivered "full" they may have had 100 times as many molecules of the gas compressed within the cylinder.

We have already stated that the temperature of a gas is an indication of the average kinetic energy of the gas molecules. The higher the temperature of a gas, the more kinetic energy its molecules possess, and the more rapidly they move about. As gas molecules strike the walls of a container they exert a pressure against it. If the volume which an Avogadro number of gas molecules occupies remains constant, we should expect the pressure exerted by the gas to increase if its tem-

Sample Problem

How does the rate of diffusion of oxygen gas compare with that of hydrogen gas under similar conditions?

Solution

$$\frac{r_2}{r_1} = \frac{\sqrt{m_1}}{\sqrt{m_2}}$$

Substituting 2, the molecular weight of hydrogen, for m_1 and 32, the molecular weight of oxygen, for m_2,

$$\frac{r_2}{r_1} = \frac{\sqrt{2}}{\sqrt{32}} = \sqrt{\frac{2}{32}} = \sqrt{\frac{1}{16}} = \frac{1}{4}$$

The rate of diffusion of oxygen is $\frac{1}{4}$ that of hydrogen.

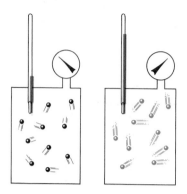

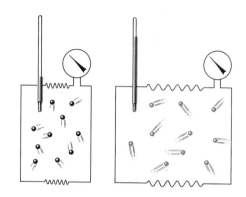

9-3 At constant volume, as the temperature of a gas increases, the pressure it exerts increases.

9-4 At constant pressure, as the temperature of a gas increases, the volume it occupies increases.

perature is raised. We should also expect the pressure exerted by an Avogadro number of gas molecules to decrease if the temperature is lowered (Fig. 9-3).

Furthermore, if the pressure exerted by an Avogadro number of gas molecules is to remain the same as the temperature is increased, the volume which the gas occupies must increase. Since the molecules move faster at higher temperatures they strike the walls of the container more frequently and with more force. Only if the area which they strike becomes greater will the force of the molecules striking a unit area remain the same, and the pressure remain the same. The area which they strike can become larger if the volume of the container is larger. In a similar fashion, with pressure remaining constant, and the temperature decreased, the volume which an Avogadro number of gas molecules occupies must become less (Fig. 9-4).

Finally, if the temperature of an Avogadro number of gas molecules remains constant, we should expect the pressure exerted by the gas to be greater if the volume which the gas occupies becomes smaller. And similarly, the pressure exerted by an Avogadro number of gas molecules would be less if the volume

available to the gas were larger (Fig. 9-5). As a result of these consequences of the Kinetic Theory, it can readily be seen that gas volumes are related to the temperature and pressure of the gas. Accordingly, both temperature and pressure must be considered when measuring the volume of a gas.

7. Standard temperature and pressure. Variations in gas volumes make it necessary to select some standard temperature and pressure for use when measuring or comparing gas volumes. *Standard temperature is exactly zero degrees Celsius.* It is the temperature of melting ice. This temperature was selected because it

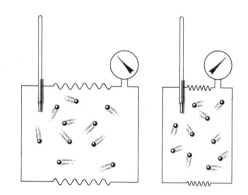

9-5 At constant temperature, as the volume of a gas decreases, the pressure it exerts increases.

is convenient and precise. *Standard pressure is the pressure exerted by a column of mercury exactly 760 millimeters high.* We use 760 millimeters of mercury as the standard pressure because that is the average atmospheric pressure at sea level. Temperatures are easily measured with an accurate thermometer. The pressure of a gas is measured by means of a barometer. *Standard temperature and pressure is commonly abbreviated as S.T.P.*

8. Pressure of a gas collected over mercury. Suppose some hydrogen is delivered into a gas measuring tube called a eudiometer (you-dee-*om*-eh-ter), which was previously filled with mercury. As hydrogen enters the tube, it bubbles to the top, and pushes the mercury down. Suppose enough hydrogen is added to make the level of the mercury inside the tube just the same as that of the mercury in the bowl, as in (*1*), Fig. 9-7. *When these two levels are equal, the pressure of the hydrogen is the same as that of the atmosphere.* This pressure can be determined by reading the barometer.

Suppose, however, that not enough hydrogen is delivered into the eudiometer to make the levels equal. Then the level inside the tube is above the level outside the tube, as in (*2*), Fig. 9-7. The pressure of

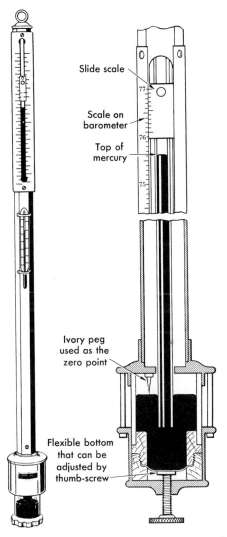

Slide scale

Scale on barometer

Top of mercury

Ivory peg used as the zero point

Flexible bottom that can be adjusted by thumb-screw

9-6 A barometer is used to measure air pressure.

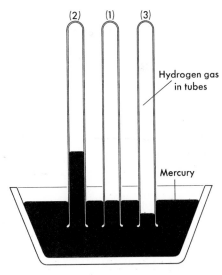

Hydrogen gas in tubes

Mercury

9-7 In (1) the pressure of the hydrogen is the same as that of the atmosphere. In (2) the pressure of the hydrogen is less than that of the atmosphere. In (3) the pressure of the hydrogen is greater than that of the atmosphere.

the gas inside the tube is less than the pressure of the air outside; otherwise, the enclosed gas would push the mercury down to the same level. To determine the pressure of the hydrogen, the difference between the level of the mercury inside the tube and outside the tube, must be *subtracted* from the barometer reading.

Suppose enough hydrogen is delivered into the eudiometer to drop the mercury level inside the tube below the outside level. Then the gas inside the tube will be under a greater pressure than the air outside, as in (*3*), Fig. 9-7. To determine the pressure of the gas in this case, the difference between the level of the mercury inside the tube and outside the tube must be *added* to the barometer reading.

These corrections are often inconvenient to make. We usually try to adjust the mercury levels inside and outside the tube to the same level by moving the eudiometer up or down in the bowl of mercury. Then the gas pressure inside will be the same as that read on the barometer. If the bowl of mercury is not deep enough to make this possible, the corrections just noted must be applied. See the Sample Problem at the bottom of the page.

9. Pressure of a gas collected over water. In elementary work, gases are usually collected over water rather than over mercury. Since mercury is 13.6 times as dense as water, a given pressure will support a column of water 13.6 times as

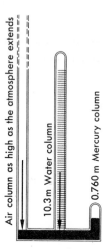

9-8   The pressure of the atmosphere supports a column of water 13.6 times as high as the column of mercury it supports.

high as an equivalent column of mercury (Fig. 9-8). When a gas is collected over water, pressure corrections similar to those just noted for differences in mercury level must be applied. *But a difference in water levels must be divided by 13.6 to convert it to its equivalent length in terms of a column of mercury.*

The advantage of collecting a gas over mercury is that mercury does not evaporate appreciably at room temperatures. When a gas is bubbled through water, however, the collected gas always has some water vapor mixed with it. Water vapor, like other gases, exerts pressure. Since the gas pressure is due to the collision of the various gas molecules with the

Sample Problem

What is the pressure of the gas in a eudiometer tube when the mercury level in the tube is 18 mm higher than that outside. The barometer reads 735 mm.

Solution

Since the mercury level inside is higher than that outside, the pressure on the gas in the eudiometer tube must be less than atmospheric pressure. Accordingly, the difference in levels is subtracted from the barometric pressure to obtain the pressure of the gas. 735 mm − 18 mm = 717 mm, the pressure of the gas.

walls of the container, *the total pressure of the mixture of gases* (the collected gas and the water vapor) *is the sum of their partial pressures.* This is a statement of **Dalton's Law of Partial Pressures.** The partial pressure is the pressure each gas would exert if it alone were present. In Chapter 11 we shall see that the partial pressure of the water vapor, called water vapor pressure, depends only on the temperature of the water. Table 7 in the Appendix gives the pressure of water vapor at different water temperatures. *To determine the pressure of the dry gas* (unmixed with water vapor), *the vapor pressure of water at the given temperature is subtracted from the total pressure of the gas within the tube.* See the Sample Problem below.

10. Variation of gas volume with pressure: Boyle's Law. If a rubber ball filled with air is squeezed, the volume of the gas inside is decreased. But it expands again when the pressure is released. Robert Boyle (1627–1691) first made careful measurements to show the relationship between pressures and volumes of gases. He found that doubling the pressure on a gas would reduce its volume by one half. Boyle formulated the results of his experiments in a law that bears his name. We

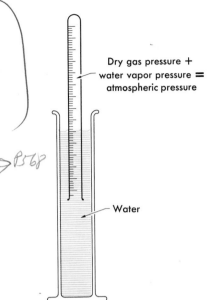

Dry gas pressure + water vapor pressure = atmospheric pressure

Water

9-9 Because the liquid levels inside and outside this eudiometer are the same, the sum of the pressures of the confined gas and water vapor equals atmospheric pressure. To determine the dry gas pressure, the water vapor pressure must be subtracted from the atmospheric pressure.

may state **Boyle's Law:** *The volume of a certain amount of dry gas is inversely proportional to the pressure, provided the temperature remains constant.*

Sample Problem

Oxygen is collected in a eudiometer tube over water. The water level inside the tube is 27.2 mm higher than that outside. The temperature is 20.° C. The barometric pressure is 740.0 mm. What is the pressure of the dry oxygen?

Solution

To convert the difference in water levels to an equivalent difference in mercury levels, the difference in water levels is divided by 13.6. 27.2 mm ÷ 13.6 = 2.0 mm, the equivalent difference in mercury levels. Since the level inside the tube is higher than that outside, the difference in levels must be subtracted from the barometric pressure. 740.0 mm − 2.0 mm = 738.0 mm. To correct for the water vapor pressure, Table 7 in the Appendix indicates that the water vapor pressure at 20.° C is 17.5 mm. This must be subtracted from the pressure corrected for difference in levels. 738.0 mm − 17.5 mm = 720.5 mm, the pressure of the dry oxygen.

This law may be stated mathematically as

$$\frac{V}{V'} = \frac{p'}{p}$$

where V is the original volume, V' the new volume, p the original pressure, and p' the new pressure. Solving the expression for V', we obtain this frequently more useful mathematical statement of Boyle's Law,

$$V' = V\frac{p}{p'},$$

11. Using Boyle's Law. Suppose 200. ml of a gas such as hydrogen is collected over mercury when the barometer reads 740. mm. The mercury level inside the tube is adjusted so that it is the same as that outside. The pressure on the confined gas is thus the same as atmospheric pressure, 740. mm. If the tube is permitted to stand until the next day, we may find that the temperature of the gas is unchanged, but that the pressure has risen to 750. mm. When the tube is lowered into the bowl of mercury to make the mercury level inside the tube the same as that outside, we find that the volume of gas has decreased. The new volume V' is

$\frac{p}{p'}$ or $\frac{740.\ \text{mm}}{750.\ \text{mm}}$ of its volume V, 200. ml,

on the first day. Substituting in the Boyle's

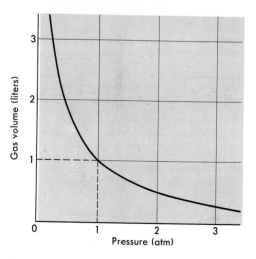

9-10 The variation of volume with pressure at constant temperature of 1 liter of an ideal gas measured at 1 atmospheric pressure.

Law formula, and solving, we obtain

$V' = V\,p/p'$
$V' = 200.\ \text{ml} \times 740.\ \text{mm}/750.\ \text{mm}$
$V' = 197\ \text{ml}$

It is possible that by the third day the pressure may have fallen to 720. mm. When the mercury levels are adjusted so that they are the same inside the tube and out, we find that the gas volume V' is

$V' = 200.\ \text{ml} \times 740.\ \text{mm}/720.\ \text{mm}$
$V' = 205\ \text{ml}$

The Sample Problems which follow give other examples of the use of Boyle's Law.

Sample Problem

A 500. ml sample of hydrogen is collected when the pressure is 800. mm of mercury. What volume will the gas occupy when the pressure is 760. mm of mercury?

Solution

$V' = V\,p/p'$
$V' = 500.\ \text{ml} \times 800.\ \text{mm}/760.\ \text{mm}$
$V' = 526\ \text{ml}$, the new volume

Sample Problem

The volume of oxygen in a eudiometer tube is 40.0 ml. The water level inside the tube is 20.4 mm higher inside than outside. The barometer reading is 730.0 mm. The temperature is 22° C. What will be the volume of the dry oxygen at 760.0 mm pressure, if the temperature remains unchanged?

Solution

1. Correction for difference in levels.

$$730.0 \text{ mm} - (20.4 \text{ mm} \div 13.6) = 728.5 \text{ mm}.$$

2. Correction for water vapor pressure. Water vapor pressure at 22° C is 19.8 mm.

$$728.5 \text{ mm} - 19.8 \text{ mm} = 708.7 \text{ mm}.$$

3. Correction for change in pressure.

$$V' = V p/p'$$
$$V' = 40.0 \text{ ml} \times 708.7 \text{ mm}/760.0 \text{ mm}$$
$$V' = 37.3 \text{ ml, volume at } 760.0 \text{ mm and } 22° \text{ C}$$

12. Variation of gas volume with temperature. Bread dough rises when put in a hot oven. The increase in temperature causes the bubbles of carbon dioxide gas within the dough to expand. The rather large increase in the volume of the dough as it is baked into bread shows that the gas must expand considerably as the temperature is increased. In fact this gas, as well as other gases, expands many times as much per degree rise in temperature as do liquids and solids.

Jacques Charles (1746–1823), a French scientist, first made careful measurements of the changes in volume of gases with changes in temperature. His experiments revealed that:

1. All gases expand or contract at the same rate with changes in temperature, provided the pressure is unchanged.

2. The change in volume amounts to $\frac{1}{273}$ of the original volume at 0° C for each Celsius degree the temperature is changed.

We may start with a definite volume of a gas at 0° C and experiment by heating it. Just as the whole of anything may be considered as made up of two halves, $\frac{2}{2}$, or three thirds, $\frac{3}{3}$, so we can consider this volume as $\frac{273}{273}$. If we warm the gas one Celsius degree, it expands $\frac{1}{273}$ of its original volume. Its new volume is $\frac{274}{273}$. In the same manner, the gas expands $\frac{100}{273}$ when it is heated 100. C°. Such expansion, added to the original volume, makes the new volume $\frac{373}{273}$. Any gas warmed 273 Celsius degrees expands $\frac{273}{273}$, or its volume is just doubled, as represented by the fraction $\frac{546}{273}$.

A gas whose volume is measured at 0° C contracts by $\frac{1}{273}$ of its volume if it is cooled 1 C°. Its new volume is $\frac{272}{273}$ of its former volume. Cooling this gas to −100.° C reduces the volume $\frac{100}{273}$. In other words the gas shrinks to $\frac{173}{273}$ of its former volume. At this rate, if we cooled the gas to −273° C, it would lose $\frac{273}{273}$ of its volume, and its volume would become zero. Such a situa-

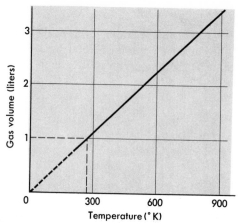

9-11 The variation of volume with Kelvin temperature at constant pressure of 1 liter of an ideal gas measured at 273° K.

tion cannot occur, however, because all gases become liquids before such a low temperature is reached. This rate of contraction with cooling applies only to gases.

13. Kelvin temperature scale. Scientists believe that −273.15° C is the lowest possible temperature. At this temperature a body would have lost all the heat that it is possible for it to lose. Scientists have come very close to this lowest possible temperature, but theoretically it is impossible to reach.

The physicist Sir William Thomson (1824–1907), better known by his title, Lord Kelvin, invented the Kelvin temperature scale which measures absolute temperature or the average kinetic energy of the particles of a substance.

A Kelvin degree is the same temperature interval as a Celsius degree. Physicists have learned that the interval between the lowest possible temperature and the triple point temperature of water is 273.16 C°. So, if the temperature of the triple point is defined as 273.16 °K, <u>0° K is the lowest possible temperature</u>, frequently called *absolute zero.* Since the triple point temperature is 0.01° above the

normal freezing point of water, 0.00° C = 273.15° K. In most calculations this temperature is rounded off to 273° K. The table below will help you in comparing Kelvin and Celsius temperatures.

COMPARISON OF KELVIN AND CELSIUS SCALES

Celsius	Kelvin
100.°	373°
50.°	323°
20.°	293°
0.°	273°
− 100.°	173°
− 273°	0.°

If you observe corresponding temperatures on the Celsius and Kelvin scales, you will note that Kelvin temperatures are just 273 degrees higher than Celsius temperatures.

Kelvin temperature =

   Celsius temperature + 273°

14. Charles' Law. Thermometers are not graduated to give Kelvin scale readings, but the scale makes it easy to solve problems dealing with the changes in gas volumes as temperatures vary. It eliminates the use of zero and of negative numbers. Using the Kelvin temperature scale, *Charles' Law* can be stated: *The volume of a certain amount of dry gas varies directly with the Kelvin temperature, provided the pressure remains constant.*

Charles' Law may be stated mathematically:

$$\frac{V}{V'} = \frac{T}{T'}$$

where V is the original volume, V' the new volume, T the original *Kelvin* temperature, and T' the new *Kelvin* temperature. Solving the expression for V'

$$V' = V\frac{T'}{T}$$

Sample Problem

A 500. ml volume of gas is measured at 20.° C. If the pressure remains unchanged, what will be the volume of the gas at 0.° C?

Solution

Change the Celsius temperatures to Kelvin temperatures:

$$20.° C + 273° = 293° K. \qquad 0.° C + 273° = 273° K.$$
$$V' = V\, T'/T$$
$$V' = 500.\ ml \times 273°\ K/293°\ K$$
$$V' = 466\ ml, \text{ the new volume}$$

The Sample Problem above illustrates the use of this formula in the solution of problems that involve Charles' Law.

15. Combined use of Boyle's and Charles' Laws. The calculation of the new volume of a gas when both temperature and pressure are changed involves no new principles. We merely multiply the original volume first by a ratio of the pressures to determine the new volume corrected for pressure alone. Then we multiply this answer by a ratio of the Kelvin temperatures to calculate the new volume corrected for both pressure and temperature.

Expressed mathematically,

$$V' = V \times \frac{p}{p'} \times \frac{T'}{T}$$

The Sample Problems below illustrate the use of this formula. You will find it much easier to solve Gas-Law problems if you use logarithms or a slide rule in making your calculations.

Sample Problem

A gas measures 200. ml at 20.° C and 750. mm pressure. What will be its volume at 15° C and 735 mm pressure?

Solution

$$20.° C = 293° K; 15° C = 288° K.$$
$$V' = V \times p/p' \times T'/T$$
$$V' = 200.\ ml \times 750.\ mm/735\ mm \times 288°\ K/293°\ K$$
$$V' = 201\ ml, \text{ the new volume}$$

Sample Problem

A gas-measuring tube holds 25.0 ml of air, collected over water at a temperature of 20.° C. The water level inside the eudiometer is 68.0 mm higher than that outside. The barometer reading is 740.0 mm. Calculate the volume of dry air at S.T.P.

Solution

1. Correction for difference in levels. 68.0 mm ÷ 13.6 = 5.0 mm. Since the water level inside is higher than that outside, the air is under pressure less than atmospheric, and the correction is subtracted. 740.0 mm − 5.0 mm = 735.0 mm.

2. Correction for water vapor pressure. Table 7 in the Appendix indicates that the water vapor pressure at 20.° C is 17.5 mm. This correction is subtracted. 735.0 mm − 17.5 mm = 717.5 mm.

3. Correction for pressure and temperature changes.

$$V' = V \times p/p' \times T'/T$$
$$V' = 25.0 \text{ ml} \times 717.5 \text{ mm}/760.0 \text{ mm} \times 273° \text{ K}/293° \text{ K}$$
$$V' = 22.0 \text{ ml, volume of dry air at S.T.P.}$$

16. Behavior of real gases. Boyle's and Charles' Laws describe the behavior of the *ideal gas.*

Real gases within the normal ranges of temperatures and pressures conform closely to the behavior of an ideal gas, even though they consist of molecules of finite size which do exert forces on each other. Under normal temperatures and pressures, the spaces separating the molecules are large enough so that the actual size of the molecules and forces between them have little effect.

Boyle's Law applies to real gases with a fairly high degree of accuracy. But it does not apply to gases under such high pressure that the molecules are close enough together to attract each other. Under this condition the gas is almost at the condensation point.

Charles' Law holds for real gases with considerable accuracy, except at low temperature. Under this condition, gas molecules move more slowly and molecular attraction exerts a greater influence. Thus, at temperature conditions near the point where the gas condenses into a liquid, Charles' Law does not apply.

REVIEW OUTLINE

Kinetic theory
>   Matter is composed of tiny particles (1)
>   Particles of matter are in constant motion (1)
>   Particles of matter undergo elastic collisions (1)

>   Properties of gases
>   Expansion (2)
>   Pressure (2)
>   Low density (2)
>   Diffusion (2)

Kinetic theory description of a gas: the ideal gas (3)

Attractive forces between gas molecules
>   Strength indicated by condensation temperatures (4)
>   van der Waals forces (4)
>   Attraction between polar molecules (4)

Diffusion: Graham's Law (5)

P–V–T relations of gases (6)

S.T.P. (7)

Measuring gas volume and pressure: eudiometer; barometer (8)

    Over mercury: difference in levels (8)

    Over water: difference in levels; water vapor pressure (9)

Boyle's Law (10)

Kelvin temperature scale (13)

Charles' Law (14)

Combined Gas-Law formula (15)

Real gas behavior (16)

QUESTIONS

Group A

1. What are the three basic assumptions of the kinetic theory? $P / 2 5$
2. Why does the pressure of a gas in a closed vessel remain constant indefinitely under constant conditions?
3. (*a*) What is the relationship between the temperature of a gas and the kinetic energy of its molecules? (*b*) Do all gas molecules have exactly the same kinetic energy at the same temperature? Explain.
4. (*a*) What is the condensation temperature of a gas? (*b*) What occurs at this temperature? (*c*) Explain in terms of the kinetic theory.
5. What two types of attractive forces may exist between the molecules of molecular substances? Explain each.
6. Why is the term "a cubic foot of air" unsatisfactory?
7. (*a*) What is standard temperature? (*b*) What is standard pressure?
8. If some hydrogen gas is enclosed in a eudiometer, what are three possibilities concerning its pressure compared with that of the air in the room?
9. State Boyle's Law (*a*) in words; (*b*) mathematically.
10. (*a*) What is the Celsius temperature corresponding to 0° K? (*b*) How does any Celsius temperature compare with the corresponding Kelvin temperature?
11. State Charles' Law (*a*) in words; (*b*) mathematically.

Group B

12. In terms of the kinetic theory explain (*a*) expansion of a gas; (*b*) pressure of a gas; (*c*) low density of a gas; (*d*) diffusion of a gas.
13. Compare the strength of the attractive forces between the particles of nonpolar covalent molecular substances and polar covalent molecular substances as indicated by their condensation temperatures.
14. Compare the strength of the attractive forces between the particles of molecular substances and the particles of ionic, macromolecular, and metallic substances, as indicated by their condensation temperatures.
15. Ammonia, NH_3, and chlorine, Cl_2, have distinct but different odors. If equal quantities of the two gases are released in the laboratory under exactly similar conditions, which gas will first be detected by students on the far side of the laboratory? Explain.

16. At constant volume, how is the pressure exerted by a gas related to the temperature?

17. At constant pressure, how is the volume occupied by a gas related to the temperature?

18. At constant temperature, how is the volume occupied by a gas related to its pressure?

19. (*a*) What is meant by the vapor pressure of water? (*b*) What effect does it have on the observed pressure of a gas collected over water? (*c*) How is the observed pressure corrected to obtain the pressure of the dry gas?

20. What corrections are applied to the barometer reading: (*a*) gas measured over mercury, level inside the eudiometer the same as that outside; (*b*) gas measured over mercury, level inside eudiometer higher than that outside; (*c*) gas measured over water, level inside eudiometer same as that outside; (*d*) gas measured over water, level inside eudiometer higher than that outside?

21. If we assume that the molecules of a solid or a liquid are in contact with each other, but those of a gas are about 10 diameters apart, why is the volume occupied by a gas about 1000 times that of the solid or liquid?

22. Boyle's and Charles' Laws describe the behavior of the ideal gas. Under what conditions do they describe the behavior of real gases?   *High T Low P*

PROBLEMS

Group A (Use cancellation whenever possible)

1. Calculate the ratio of the rates of diffusion of carbon monoxide, CO, and nitrogen, N_2.

2. What is the ratio of the rates of diffusion of methane, CH_4, and sulfur dioxide, SO_2?

3. Some oxygen occupies 250. ml when the barometer reads 720. mm. What will be its volume when the barometer reads 750. mm?

4. A gas collected when the pressure is 800. mm has a volume of 380. ml. What volume will the gas occupy at standard pressure?

5. A gas has a volume of 100. ml when the pressure is 735 mm. What volume will the gas occupy at 700. mm pressure?

6. A gas has a volume of 240.0 ml at 70.0 cm pressure. What pressure is needed to reduce the volume to 60.0 ml?

7. Change the following temperatures to Kelvin scale: (*a*) 20.° C; (*b*) 85° C; (*c*) −15° C; (*d*) −190.° C.

8. Given 90.0 ml of hydrogen gas collected when the temperature is 27° C. What volume will the hydrogen occupy at 42° C?

9. A gas has a volume of 180. ml when its temperature is 43° C. To what temperature must the gas be lowered to reduce its volume to 135 ml?

10. A gas measures 500. ml at a temperature of −23° C. Find its volume at 23° C.

11. A sample of gas occupies 50.0 l at 27° C. What is the volume of the gas at standard temperature?

12. Convert to standard conditions: 2280. ml of gas measured at 30.° C and 808 mm pressure.

X 13. Convert to standard conditions: 1000. ml of gas at $-23°$ C and 700. mm pressure.

X 14. Convert to standard conditions: 1520. ml of gas at $-33°$ C and 720. mm pressure.

X 15. A gas collected when the temperature is $27°$ C and the pressure is 80.0 cm measures 500. ml. Find the volume at $-3°$ C and 75.0 cm.

X 16. Given 100. ml of gas measured at $17°$ C and 380. mm pressure. What volume will the gas occupy at $307°$ C and 500. mm pressure?

Group B (Use logarithms or a slide rule)

17. What is the ratio of the rates of diffusion of ammonia and chlorine in the experiment of Question 15?

18. In an experiment 35.0 ml of hydrogen was collected in a eudiometer over mercury. The mercury level inside the eudiometer was 40. mm higher than that outside. The temperature was $25°$ C and the barometric pressure was 740.0 mm. Correct the volume of hydrogen to S.T.P.

19. A gas collected over mercury in an inverted graduated cylinder occupies 60.0 ml. The mercury level inside the cylinder is 25 mm higher than that outside. Temperature: $20.°$ C; barometer reading: 715 mm. Correct the volume of gas to S.T.P.

20. Hydrogen is collected by water displacement in a eudiometer. Gas volume, 25.0 ml; liquid levels inside and outside the eudiometer are the same; temperature, $17°$ C; barometer reading, 720.0 mm. Correct the volume to that of dry gas at S.T.P.

21. Some nitrogen is collected over water in a gas-measuring tube. Gas volume, 45.0 ml; liquid levels inside and outside the gas-measuring tube are the same; temperature, $23°$ C; barometer reading, 732.0 mm. Correct the volume to that of dry gas at S.T.P.

22. A volume of 50.0 ml of oxygen is collected over water. The water level inside the eudiometer is 65 mm higher than that outside. Temperature, $25°$ C; barometer reading, 727.0 mm. Correct the volume to that of dry gas at S.T.P.

23. At $18°$ C and 745.0 mm pressure, 12.0 ml of hydrogen is collected over water. The liquid level inside the gas-measuring tube is 95 mm higher than that outside. Correct the volume to that of dry gas at S.T.P.

24. The density of carbon dioxide at S.T.P. is 1.98 g/l. What is the mass of exactly one liter of the gas, if the pressure increases by 40. mm of mercury?

25. The density of oxygen at S.T.P. is 1.43 g/l. Find the mass of exactly one liter of oxygen at a temperature of $39°$ C, if the pressure remains unchanged.

26. The density of nitrogen is 1.25 g/l at S.T.P. Find the mass of exactly one liter of nitrogen at a temperature of $27°$ C and 90.0 cm of mercury pressure.

27. A gas measures 400. ml at a temperature of $25°$ C, and under a pressure of 800. mm. To what temperature must the gas be cooled if its volume is to be reduced to 350. ml when the pressure falls to 740. mm?

Chapter Ten

MOLECULAR COMPOSITION OF GASES

1. Law of Combining Volumes of Gases. The Law of Definite Composition, formulated by Proust, served as a basis for Dalton's Atomic Theory. While Dalton investigated the masses of combining substances, his contemporary, the Swedish chemist Berzelius, was developing methods of chemical analysis. During this same period another contemporary of Dalton, the French chemist Joseph Louis Gay-Lussac (1778–1850), became interested in the combining volumes of gaseous substances.

Gay-Lussac investigated the reaction between hydrogen and oxygen. He noticed that under similar conditions of temperature and pressure 2 liters of hydrogen was required for each liter of oxygen consumed and that 2 liters of water vapor was formed.

hydrogen + oxygen → water vapor
2 vol. 1 vol. 2 vol.

He found that 1 liter of hydrogen combined with 1 liter of chlorine to form 2 liters of hydrogen chloride gas. Also 1 liter of hydrogen chloride combined with 1 liter of ammonia to produce a white powder with no residue of either gas remaining.

hydrogen + chlorine → hydrogen chloride
1 vol. 1 vol. 2 vol.

hydrogen chloride + ammonia → ammonium chloride
1 vol. 1 vol. (a solid)

His friend, Berthollet, recognized a similar relationship in experiments with hydrogen and nitrogen. He found that 3 liters of hydrogen always combined with 1 liter of nitrogen to form 2 liters of ammonia.

hydrogen + nitrogen → ammonia
3 vol. 1 vol. 2 vol.

In 1808 Gay-Lussac summarized the results of these experiments and set forth the principle which bears his name, *Gay-*

Lussac's Law of Combining Volumes of Gases: *Under similar conditions of temperature and pressure, the volumes of reacting gases and of their gaseous products are expressed in ratios of small whole numbers.*

Proust had demonstrated the definite proportion of elements in a compound. Dalton's Atomic Theory had explained this regularity in the composition of substances. However, Dalton pictured the atoms of two elements combining to form *a compound atom* of the product. He could not explain why one volume of hydrogen united with one volume of chlorine to form *two* volumes of hydrogen chloride gas. To do so would require that his atoms be subdivided. He had described the atoms of elements as "ultimate particles" and not capable of subdivision. Here was an inconsistency between Dalton's theory and Gay-Lussac's observations. Was there no possible explanation to resolve the difficulty?

2. Avogadro's Principle. Avogadro proposed a possible explanation for Gay-Lussac's simple ratios of combining gases in 1811. This *hypothesis* was to become one of the important laws of chemistry, although it was not until after his death that its implications were fully recognized. *Avogadro's hypothesis was that equal volumes of all gases, under the same conditions of temperature and pressure, contained the same number of molecules.* He arrived at this plausible theory after studying the behavior of gases and immediately recognized its application to Gay-Lussac's volume ratios.

Avogadro reasoned that the molecules of all gases, as reactants and products, must be in the same ratio as their respective gas volumes. Thus the composition of water vapor could be represented as 2 molecules of hydrogen combining with 1 molecule of oxygen to produce 2 molecules of water vapor.

hydrogen	+	oxygen	→	water vapor
2 volumes		1 volume		2 volumes
2 molecules		1 molecule		2 molecules

Thus each molecule of oxygen must consist of **at least** *two identical parts (atoms)* which are equally divided between the two molecules of water vapor formed. Avogadro did not repudiate the atoms of Dalton. He merely postulated that they did not exist as independent ultimate particles but were grouped into molecules which were divisible by two. The simplest such molecule would, of course, contain two atoms.

Avogadro's reasoning applied equally well to the combining volumes in the composition of hydrogen chloride gas.

hydrogen	+	chlorine	→	hydrogen chloride
1 volume		1 volume		2 volumes
1 molecule		1 molecule		2 molecules

Each molecule of hydrogen must be divisible by two, with identical parts in each of the two molecules of hydrogen chloride. Likewise, each chlorine molecule must be divisible by two, with identical parts in each of the two molecules of hydrogen chloride.

By Avogadro's hypothesis, the simplest molecules of hydrogen, oxygen, and chlorine each contain two atoms. The simplest possible molecule of water contains two atoms of hydrogen and one atom of oxygen. The simplest molecule of hydrogen chloride contains one atom of hydrogen and one atom of chlorine.

The correctness of Avogadro's hypothesis is so widely recognized today that it has become known as *Avogadro's Principle.* It is supported by the Kinetic Theory of gases, and is employed extensively in the determination of molecular weights and molecular formulas.

3. Molecules of active gaseous elements are diatomic. The application of

Avogadro's Principle to Gay-Lussac's Law of Combining Volumes of Gases enables us to recognize the simplest possible makeup of elementary gases. How may we determine whether this simplest structure is the correct one?

Chemists have analyzed hydrogen chloride gas and, with the aid of atomic weights, have determined the empirical formula to be HCl. By finding the molecular weight of the compound, HCl is established as the correct or molecular formula (see Chapter 7, Section 13). Thus a molecule of the compound contains *only* one atom of hydrogen and *only* one atom of chlorine. Since two molecules of HCl are formed from one molecule of hydrogen and one molecule of chlorine, each contains *only* two atoms. *Thus the hydrogen and chlorine molecules must be diatomic.* We may write the equation as follows:

$$H_2 + Cl_2 \rightarrow 2HCl$$

Similarly, the oxygen molecule may be proved to be diatomic since H_2O is known to be the molecular formula of water vapor.

$$2H_2 + O_2 \rightarrow 2H_2O$$

Let us examine one additional gaseous reaction. Berthollet found that *3 volumes* of hydrogen combined with *1 volume* of nitrogen to form *2 volumes* of ammonia. By Avogadro's Principle we conclude that *3 molecules* of hydrogen combine with *1 molecule* of nitrogen to form *2 molecules* of ammonia. Analysis of ammonia reveals that it is composed of 82% nitrogen and 18% hydrogen. The atomic weights of nitrogen and hydrogen are 14 and 1.0 respectively. The molecular weight of ammonia is known to be 17.0. Therefore the molecular formula is:

N: $\dfrac{82 \text{ gN}}{14 \text{ g/mole}} = 5.9$ moles N

H: $\dfrac{18 \text{ g H}}{1.0 \text{ g/mole}} = 18$ moles H

N : H $= \dfrac{5.9}{5.9} : \dfrac{18}{5.9} = 1.0 : 3.0$

Empirical formula = NH_3
Molecular formula = $(NH_3)_x$
and $(NH_3 \text{ weight})_x = 17$
thus $x = 1$
Molecular formula $= NH_3$

Two. molecules of NH_3 produced must contain a total of 2 nitrogen atoms which must therefore compose the 1 molecule of nitrogen reactant. Again the 2 molecules of NH_3 produced must contain a total of 6 hydrogen atoms which therefore compose the 3 molecules of hydrogen reactant. We may summarize these relations as follows:

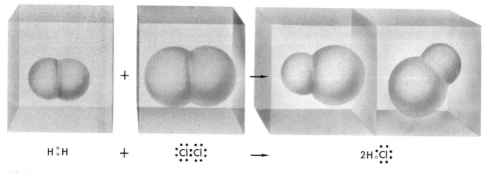

H °H   +   :Cl:Cl: →   2H °Cl:

10-1 As HCl is known to be the correct formula for hydrogen chloride gas, the molecules of hydrogen and chlorine are proved to be diatomic.

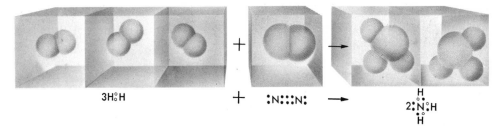

3H°H   +   :N:::N: ⟶   2:N°H with H above and H below

10-2 Application of Avogadro's Law to Gay-Lussac's Combining Volumes can show molecules of elementary gas reactants to be diatomic.

hydrogen	+	nitrogen	→	ammonia
3 volumes		1 volume		2 volumes
3 molecules		1 molecule		2 molecules
$3H_2$	+	N_2	→	$2NH_3$

Both nitrogen and hydrogen molecules are diatomic.

4. Molecules of the noble gases are monatomic. By using the methods described in the preceding sections, we are able to show that the molecules of all ordinary gaseous elements contain two atoms. Other methods have been used to show that the noble gaseous elements, such as helium and neon, have only one atom to each molecule. The rule does not apply to solids, and it may not even apply to the vapors of certain elements which are liquid or solid at room temperature. For example, at high temperatures the molecules of mercury and iodine are known to consist of only one atom each.

5. Specific gravity of gases. It is frequently convenient to compare the density of a substance with that of a suitable standard. As this is a comparison of the masses of *equal* volumes of the two, it tells us how much more (or less) dense the one is than the standard of reference. The density of water is the standard of reference for solids and liquids; air is the most commonly used standard of reference for gases. *The ratio of the density of a substance to the density of the standard of reference* is called its *specific gravity.*

$$\text{sp gr (gas)} = \frac{\text{density of gas}}{\text{density of standard (air)}}$$

The density of oxygen is 1.43 grams per liter. Thus the mass of 1 liter of oxygen is 1.43 g at S.T.P. The density of air is 1.29 g/l; one liter of air has a mass of 1.29 g at S.T.P. The specific gravity of oxygen may be expressed:

$$\text{sp gr } O_2 = \frac{\text{density of } O_2}{\text{density of air}}$$

$$\text{sp gr } O_2 = \frac{1.43 \text{ g/l}}{1.29 \text{ g/l}} = 1.11$$

Observe that specific gravity is a dimensionless numerical ratio which tells us that oxygen is 1.11 times denser than air. Table 8, in the Appendix, lists the density and specific gravity of gases.

6. Molar volume of a gas. Oxygen gas consists of diatomic molecules. One mole of O_2 contains the Avogadro number of molecules (6.02×10^{23}) and has a mass of 31.9988 g. One mole of H_2 contains the same number of molecules and has a mass of 2.016 g. Helium is a monatomic gas. One mole of He contains the Avogadro number of monatomic molecules and has a mass of 4.003 g. One-mole quantities of all molecular substances contain the Avogadro number of molecules.

The volume occupied by 1 mole (1 g-mol wt) of a gas at S.T.P. is called its **molar volume.** Since moles of gases have equal numbers of molecules, Avogadro's Principle tells us that they must occupy equal volumes under similar conditions of temperature and pressure. *The molar volumes of all gases are equal under similar conditions.* This has great practical significance in chemistry. Let us see how the molar volume of gases may be determined.

The densities of gases represent the masses of equal numbers of molecules measured under standard conditions of temperature and pressure. The differences in densities are due, therefore, to differences in the masses of the molecules of the different gases.

The density of hydrogen is 0.0899 g/l, measured at S.T.P. A mole of hydrogen, 1 g-mol wt, has a mass of 2.016 g. Now 0.0899 g of H_2 occupies 1 liter volume at S.T.P. What volume will 2.016 g of H_2 occupy under similar conditions? Obviously the molar volume will be as much greater than 1 liter as 2.016 g is greater than 0.0899 g. This proportionality may be expressed as follows:

$$\frac{\text{molar volume of } H_2}{1 \text{ liter}} = \frac{2.016 \text{ g}}{0.899 \text{ g}}$$

Solving for molar volume:

$$\text{molar volume of } H_2 = \frac{2.016 \text{ g} \times 1 \text{ liter}}{0.0899 \text{ g}}$$

$$\text{molar volume of } H_2 = 22.4 \text{ liters}$$

The density of oxygen is 1.43 g/l. A mole of oxygen has a mass of 31.9988 g. Following our reasoning in the case of hydrogen, we may compute the molar volume of O_2.

$$\frac{\text{molar volume of } O_2}{1 \text{ liter}} = \frac{32.0 \text{ g}}{1.43 \text{ g}}$$

$$\text{molar volume of } O_2 = \frac{32.0 \text{ g} \times 1 \text{ liter}}{1.43 \text{ g}}$$

$$\text{molar volume of } O_2 = 22.4 \text{ liters}$$

Computations with other gases would yield similar results. However, it is clear from Avogadro's Principle that this is unnecessary. We may generalize the proportion used above to read as follows:

$$\frac{1 \text{ molar volume (l)}}{1 \text{ liter (l)}} = \frac{\text{g-mol wt (g)}}{\text{mass of 1 liter (g)}}$$

Transposing terms,

$$\frac{\text{mass of 1 liter (g)}}{1 \text{ liter (l)}} = \frac{\text{g-mol wt (g)}}{1 \text{ molar volume (l)}}$$

But

$$\frac{\text{mass of 1 liter (g)}}{1 \text{ liter (l)}} = \text{density } (D) \text{ of a gas}$$

and

$$1 \text{ molar volume (l)} = 22.4 \text{ l}$$

So

$$D \text{ (of a gas)} = \frac{\text{g-mol wt (g)}}{22.4 \text{ l}}$$

and

$$\text{g-mol wt (g)} = D \times 22.4 \text{ l}$$

Thus we see that the *gram-molecular weight* (mass in grams of one mole) *of a gaseous substance is the mass, in grams, of 22.4 liters of the gas measured at S.T.P.;* it is simply the density of the gas multiplied by the constant, 22.4 liters. Similarly, the density of a gas may be found by dividing its g-mol wt by the constant, 22.4 liters.

If the molecular formula of a gas is known, its density may be determined directly from the formula. Let us use sulfur dioxide, SO_2, as an example. The mass of one mole of SO_2 is 64 g. Thus

$$D_{SO_2} = \frac{64 \text{ g}}{22.4 \text{ l}} = 2.9 \text{ g/l}$$

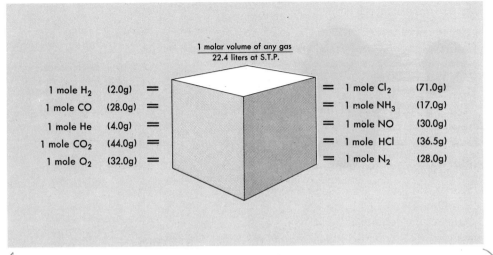

10-3   At S.T.P., 22.4 liters of all gases have the same number of molecules, and the mass of each volume in grams is numerically equal to its molecular weight.

7. Molecular weight of gases determined experimentally. The molecular weights of substances which are gaseous, or which may be vaporized without decomposition, may be determined by use of the *molar-volume method.*

It would be impractical in the laboratory to weigh directly a molar volume

10-4   A type of glass bulb used in determining density of gases.

(22.4 l) of a gas or vapor at standard conditions of temperature and pressure. Indeed, some substances, otherwise suitable for this method, are liquids or even solids under S.T.P. conditions. Consequently, any quantity of a gas or vapor which can be weighed to determine its mass precisely may be employed in the molecular-weight determination. Its volume is measured under any suitable conditions of temperature and pressure. This volume may be converted to S.T.P. and then the mass of 22.4 liters may be calculated. The Sample Problem (page 148) shows how this experimental method is used to determine molecular weight.

It follows naturally that the volume occupied by a known mass of a gas under any conditions of temperature and pressure can be calculated if the molecular formula of the gas is known. The molecular formula provides the mass of 1 mole of the gas which is known to occupy the molar volume, 22.4 liters, at S.T.P. By proportion, the volume of the known mass of the gas at S.T.P. can be determined. Then

Sample Problem

A gas sample, mass 0.350 g, is measured over water at 20.° C and 750. mm pressure. Its volume is 150. ml. What is its molecular weight?

Solution

The partial pressure of the gas is the difference between the indicated pressure and the partial pressure due to water vapor, 750. mm − 17.5 mm, or (750. − 17.5) mm. As the temperature is lowered the volume will decrease in the ratio $\dfrac{273° \text{ K}}{293° \text{ K}}$. As the pressure is raised the volume will decrease in the ratio $\dfrac{(750. - 17.5) \text{ mm}}{760 \text{ mm}}$.

Therefore, the volume at S.T.P. is:

$$V = 150. \text{ ml} \times \frac{273° \text{ K}}{293° \text{ K}} \times \frac{(750. - 17.5) \text{ mm}}{750 \text{ mm}}$$

$$V = 135 \text{ ml, or } 0.135 \text{ l at S.T.P.}$$

The quantity 0.350 g per 0.135 liter at S.T.P. is an expression of the density of the gas and may be substituted for it. Thus

$$\text{g-mol wt} = \frac{0.350 \text{ g}}{0.135 \text{ l}} \times 22.4 \text{ l}$$

$$\text{g-mol wt} = 58.1 \text{ g}$$
$$\text{mol wt} = 58.1$$

by application of the Gas Laws, the volume at any temperature and pressure can be computed. This is illustrated in the Sample Problem opposite.

8. Chemical problems involving gases. As illustrated in Chapter 8, the equation for a chemical reaction expresses quantities of reactants and products in *moles*. The numerical coefficients in the balanced equation tell us the number of moles of each substance.

Frequently a reactant or a product of a reaction is a gas. Indeed, all reactants and products may be gaseous in certain reactions. By applying Avogadro's Principle we recognize that single moles of all such gases have the same volume under similar conditions of temperature and pressure. At S.T.P. a mole of any gas occupies 1 molar volume, 22.4 liters. *Consequently,* the relation in moles in the equation is also the relation of volumes of gases.

It should be remembered that real gases deviate slightly from the behavior of an ideal gas. Calculations which involve the molar volume as 22.4 liters can give only approximately correct answers.

There are two general types of problems which involve chemical equations and the volumes of gases. These are: *gas volume-gas volume problems*, in which a certain *volume of a gas* reactant or product is given and the *volume of another gas* reactant or product is required; and *mass-gas volume problems*, in which a certain *mass* of a reactant or product is given and the *volume of a gas* reactant or product is required, or vice versa.

9. Gas volume-gas volume problems. In this type of problem, the *volume* of one *gaseous substance* is given and we are asked

Sample Problem

What is the volume of 10. g of carbon dioxide gas, CO_2, at 20.° C and 740 mm?

Solution

The formula CO_2 indicates that the molecular weight is 44. Now 44 g (1 mole) of CO_2 occupies 22.4 l (1 molar volume) at S.T.P. The volume occupied by 10. g will be represented as X.

$$\frac{44 \text{ g}}{22.4 \text{ l}} = \frac{10. \text{ g}}{X}$$

Solving for X:

$$X = 10. \text{ g} \times \frac{22.4 \text{ l}}{44 \text{ g}} = 5.1 \text{ l, at S.T.P.}$$

As the temperature rises the volume will increase in the ratio $\frac{293° \text{ K}}{273° \text{ K}}$. As the pressure decreases the volume will increase in the ratio $\frac{760 \text{ mm}}{740 \text{ mm}}$.

Thus the volume at 20.° C and 740 mm is:

$$V = 5.1 \text{ l} \times \frac{293° \text{ K}}{273° \text{ K}} \times \frac{760 \text{ mm}}{740 \text{ mm}}$$

$$V = 5.6 \text{ liters, at } 20.° \text{ C and 740 mm}$$

to determine the *volume* of another *gaseous substance* involved in the chemical action. We recall that single moles of all gases at the same temperature and pressure occupy the same volume. Thus in a correctly balanced equation the volumes of gases are proportional to the number of moles indicated by the numerical coefficients. To illustrate:

(gas)		(gas)		(gas)
2CO	+	O_2	→	$2CO_2$
2 moles		1 mole		2 moles
2 vol		1 vol		2 vol

The balanced equation signifies that 2 moles of CO reacts with 1 mole of O_2 to produce 2 moles of CO_2. From Avogadro's Principle, 2 volumes (liters, cubic feet, etc.) of carbon monoxide reacts with 1 volume (liter, cubic foot, etc.) of oxygen to produce 2 volumes (liters, cubic feet, etc.) of carbon dioxide, the temperature and pressure of all three gases being the same. Thus 10 liters of CO would require 5 liters of O_2 for complete combustion and would produce 10 liters of CO_2. The volume relationship is 2 : 1 : 2 under similar conditions of temperature and pressure.

Obviously, since the above reaction is exothermic, the resultant gas expands due to the rise in temperature. The volume relations apply only after the temperature of the gaseous product has been reduced to that of the reactants at the beginning of the reaction.

The conditions of temperature and pressure must be known in order to determine which substances exist as gases. Whenever the conditions are not stated they are assumed to be standard. Let us consider the complete combustion of methane.

(gas)   (gas)   (gas)
$CH_4 + 2O_2 \rightarrow CO_2 + 2H_2O$
1 mole   2 moles   1 mole   2 moles
1 vol   2 vol   1 vol

At temperatures under 100° C water is a liquid. Thus, if the volumes of the gaseous reactants are measured under ordinary conditions, water could not be included in the volume ratio. The reactants, methane and oxygen, and the product, carbon dioxide, are gases, and their volume relationship is seen to be 1 : 2 : 1.

Gas volume-gas volume problems are very simple to solve. The problem set-up is similar to that of mass-mass problems (see Chapter 8, Section 8), except that it is not necessary to use atomic weights to convert moles of the specified gases to their respective equation masses. Once set up, most gas volume-gas volume problems may be solved by inspection. The following example shows how these problems are commonly solved.

Suppose we wish to know the volume of hydrogen which will combine with 4.0 liters of nitrogen to form ammonia gas. We set up the problem in the following manner:

$$X \qquad 4.0\,l$$
$$3H_2 + N_2 \rightarrow 2NH_3$$
3 moles   1 mole

The equation shows that H_2 and N_2 combine in the ratio of 3 moles to 1 mole. From Avogadro's Principle, these gases must combine in the ratio of 3 volumes to 1 volume. Thus, simply by inspection, it is evident that 4.0 liters of nitrogen requires 12 liters of hydrogen for complete reaction. Since 2 moles of NH_2 is shown, it is equally plain that 8.0 liters of this gas is produced. This is, in reality, a solution by the proportion method:

$$\frac{X}{4.0\,l\ N_2} = \frac{3\ moles\ H_2}{1\ mole\ N_2}$$

Solving for X:

$$X = \frac{3\ moles\ H_2 \times 4.0\,l\ N_2}{1\ mole\ N_2}$$
$$= 12\ liters\ of\ H_2$$

See the Sample Problem on page 151.

10. Mass-gas volume problems. In this type of problem, we are concerned with the relation between the *volume of gas* and the *mass* of another substance in a reaction. Either the mass of the substance is given and the volume of the gas is required, or the volume of the gas is given and the mass of the substance is required.

As an illustration let us determine the number of grams of calcium carbonate, $CaCO_3$, which must be decomposed to produce 4.00 liters of carbon dioxide, CO_2, at S.T.P. The problem set-up is as follows:

$$X \qquad\qquad 4.00\,l$$
$$CaCO_3 \rightarrow CaO + CO_2 \uparrow$$
1 mole   1 mole

1 mole $CaCO_3$ = 100. g
1 mole CO_2 = 22.4 liters

Observe that the molar volume (22.4 liters) is used in place of the mass/mole (44 g/mole) of CO_2. This is possible since each mole of gas occupies 22.4 liters at S.T.P. (*and only at S.T.P.*). The problem may now be solved by any of the methods used previously with mass-mass relations.

1. Solution by moles. The volume of CO_2 divided by the molar volume will indicate the number of moles of CO_2 given (operation 1):

$$\frac{4.00\,l\ CO_2}{22.4\,l/mole} = no.\ moles\ CO_2$$

Then, following operations 2, 3, and 4 of the solution of a mass-mass problem,

$$\frac{4.00 \text{ l } CO_2}{22.4 \text{ l /mole}} \times \frac{1 \text{ mole } CaCO_3}{1 \text{ mole } CO_2} \times \frac{100. \text{ g}}{\text{mole}} =$$

17.9 g CaCO₃

equation mass of $CaCO_3$ to the equation volume occupied by CO_2 at S.T.P.

$$\frac{X}{4.00 \text{ l } CO_2} = \frac{100. \text{ g } CaCO_3}{22.4 \text{ l } CO_2}$$

2. Solution by proportion. We reason that the ratio of the mass of $CaCO_2$ to the volume of CO_2 is equal to the ratio of the

$$X = \frac{100. \text{ g } CaCO_3 \times 4.00 \text{ l } CO_2}{22.4 \text{ l } CO_2}$$

$$= 17.9 \text{ g } CaCO_3$$

Sample Problem

Assuming air to be 21% oxygen by volume: *a.* How many liters of air must enter the carburetor to complete the combustion of 60.0 liters of octane vapor? *b.* How many liters of carbon dioxide are formed? (All gases are measured at the same temperature and pressure.)

Solution

Octane has the formula C_8H_{18}, and its complete oxidation produces carbon dioxide and water. Since it is the oxygen of the air which combines with octane, we must determine first the volume of oxygen required. Let X be this volume, and Y the volume of CO_2 formed. The problem set-up is:

$$\begin{array}{ccc} 60.0 \text{ liters} & X & Y \\ 2C_8H_{18} & + \quad 25O_2 & \rightarrow \quad 16CO_2 \quad + \quad 18H_2O \\ 2 \text{ moles} & 25 \text{ moles} & 16 \text{ moles} \end{array}$$

a. Solving by proportion:

$$\frac{60.0 \text{ liters}}{X} = \frac{2 \text{ moles}}{25 \text{ moles}}$$

$$X = \frac{60.0 \text{ liters} \times 25 \text{ moles}}{2 \text{ moles}} = 750. \text{ liters of } O_2$$

Now 750. liters of O_2 is 21.0% of the air required. So

$$\text{Air required} = 750. \text{ l} \times \frac{100\%}{21.0\%} = 3570 \text{ liters}$$

b. Solving as before:

$$\frac{60.0 \text{ liters}}{Y} = \frac{2 \text{ moles}}{16 \text{ moles}}$$

$$Y = \frac{60.0 \text{ liters} \times 16 \text{ moles}}{2 \text{ moles}} = 480. \text{ liters of } CO_2$$

Reminder: The volumes of air and CO_2 computed are those which would be measured at the temperature and pressure of the octane vapor prior to its combustion. Under such conditions, the water, formed as water vapor at the reaction temperature, would have condensed and could not enter the problem as a gas. The quantity of water can, of course, be computed in moles or grams using the methods presented in Section 10.

11. Gases not measured at S.T.P.
Gases are seldom measured under standard conditions of temperature and pressure. Only gas volumes under standard conditions can be placed in a proportion with the molar volume of 22.4 liters. Therefore, *gas reactants measured under conditions other than S.T.P. must first be corrected to S.T.P.* in accordance with the Gas Laws in Chapter 9 before proceeding with mass-gas volume calculations.

If the gas in question is a *product*, and its volume is to be measured under conditions other than S.T.P., *the volume at S.T.P. is first calculated from the chemical equation.* This volume at S.T.P. is then converted to the required conditions of temperature and pressure by proper application of the Gas Laws.

Gas volume-gas volume calculations do not require S.T.P. corrections since volumes of gases are related to moles rather than to mole volumes. Thus it is only necessary that measurements of gas volumes be carried out at a constant temperature and pressure in gas volume-gas volume problems.

12. Gases collected over water. The volume of a gaseous product in a mass-gas volume problem is calculated under S.T.P. conditions and must be corrected for any other specified conditions of temperature and pressure. If this gas is collected over water, the equilibrium vapor pressure of the water must be taken into account. At the specified temperature, the partial pressure of the gas is the difference between the measured pressure and the partial pressure which is exerted by the water vapor.

Let us suppose that the volume of a gaseous product collected over water is to be determined at 29° C and 752 mm pressure by a mass-gas volume calculation. The volume at S.T.P. is computed from the chemical equation. The vapor pressure of water at 29° C is found in the tables to be 30. mm. Thus

$$V_{29°,\ 752\ \text{mm}} =$$
$$V_{\text{S.T.P.}} \times \frac{302°\text{K}}{273°\text{K}} \times \frac{760\ \text{mm}}{(752 - 30.)\ \text{mm}}$$

See the Sample Problem on page 153.

▶ **13. The gas constant.** Gases are commonly measured under conditions far removed from the standard and then calculated back to standard conditions using the familiar gas laws. The behavior of a real gas differs from that of the ideal gas (which conforms strictly to the gas laws) in that its molecules have a definite volume and exert an attraction for each other. The ideal gas behavior can be approximated by making measurements at reduced pressures and high temperatures.

From Avogadro's Principle, it follows that the volume of a mole is the same for all gases under similar conditions of temperature and pressure. Therefore, the volume of any gas is directly proportional to the number of moles (n) of the gas, if pressure and temperature are constant.

$$V \propto n\ (p\ \textbf{and}\ T\ \textbf{constant})$$

From Boyle's Law we know that the volume of a gas is inversely proportional to the pressure applied to it if the quantity of gas (moles of gas) and temperature are constant.

$$V \propto \frac{1}{p}\ (n\ \textbf{and}\ T\ \textbf{constant})$$

Similarly, from Charles' Law we know that the volume is directly proportional to the Kelvin temperature if the pressure and quantity of gas remain constant.

$$V \propto T\ (p\ \textbf{and}\ n\ \textbf{constant})$$

Thus,

$$V \propto n \times \frac{1}{p} \times T$$

Sample Problem

What volume of oxygen, collected over water at 20.° C and 750.0 mm pressure, can be obtained by the decomposition of 175 g of potassium chlorate?

Solution

A mass is given and a gas volume is required. The volume of the gas at S.T.P. may first be found from the chemical equation. The problem set-up is as follows:

$$
\begin{array}{cc}
175 \text{ g} & X \\
2KClO_3 \rightarrow & 2KCl + 3O_2\uparrow \\
2 \text{ moles} & 3 \text{ moles}
\end{array}
$$

$$1 \text{ mole } KClO_3 = 122.6 \text{ g}$$
$$1 \text{ mole } O_2 \quad = \; 22.4 \text{ l}$$

Solution by moles

$$\frac{175 \text{ g } KClO_3}{122.6 \text{ g/mole}} \times \frac{3 \text{ moles } O_2}{2 \text{ moles } KClO_3} \times \frac{22.4 \text{ l}}{\text{mole}} = 48.0 \text{ l } O_2 \text{ at S.T.P.}$$

As the temperature is increased to 20.° C, the volume will increase in the ratio $\frac{293° \text{ K}}{273° \text{ K}}$. The vapor pressure of water at 20.° C is found to be 17.5 mm. As the pressure is decreased to 750.0 mm, the volume will increase in the ratio $\frac{760. \text{ mm}}{750.0 \text{ mm} - 17.5 \text{ mm}}$. Thus the volume of O_2 at 20.° C and 750.0 mm pressure is:

$$V = 48.0 \text{ l} \times \frac{293° \text{ K}}{273° \text{ K}} \times \frac{760. \text{ mm}}{(750.0 - 17.5) \text{ mm}}$$

$$V = 53.5 \text{ l } O_2 \text{ at } 20.° \text{ C and } 750.0 \text{ mm}$$

By the insertion of a proportionality constant R of suitable dimensions, this proportion may be restated as an equation.

$$V = Rn\left(\frac{1}{p}\right)T$$

or $$pV = nRT$$

R is the proportionality constant known as the *gas constant*. When the quantity of gas is expressed in moles, R has the same value for all gases. Conventionally the gas volume V is expressed in *liters*, the quantity n in *moles*, the temperature T in *degrees Kelvin*, and the pressure p in *atmospheres*. Of course, the standard pressure of 760 mm is *1 atmosphere*. So

$$\frac{\text{pressure in mm of Hg}}{760 \text{ mm of Hg/atm}} = \text{pressure in atm}$$

With the convention of units stated, let us determine the dimensional units of the gas constant R from the ideal gas equation.

$$pV = nRT$$

Then, $$R = \frac{pV}{nT}$$

$$R = \frac{\text{atm} \times \text{liters}}{\text{moles} \times °\text{K}}$$

Thus, R must have the dimensions *liter-atm per mole-°K*.

Careful measurements of the density of oxygen at low pressures yields the volume of 22.414 liters accepted as the accurate molar volume of an ideal gas, that is, the volume occupied by 1 mole of ideal gas under conditions of 1 atm and 273.15° K. Substituting in the ideal gas equation and solving the expression for R,

$$R = \frac{pV}{nT} = \frac{1 \text{ atm} \times 22.414 \text{ l}}{1 \text{ mole} \times 273.15° \text{ K}}$$

$$R = 0.082057 \text{ l-atm/mole-°K}$$

Suppose the properties of an unknown gas are being examined at a temperature of 28° C and 740. mm pressure and it is found that the mass of 1 liter is 4.62 g under these conditions. By an application of the gas constant R, 0.0821 l-atm per mole-°K, and the ideal gas equation, $pV = nRT$, the molecular weight of the gas can be determined directly. Its use in the ideal gas equation enables moles per liter of the gas to be computed.

$$T = 273° + 28° = 301° \text{ K}$$
$$V = 1 \text{ liter}$$
$$p = \frac{740. \text{ mm}}{760 \text{ mm/atm}} = 0.974 \text{ atm}$$
$$pV = nRT$$

Solving for n moles:

$$n = \frac{pV}{RT}$$

$$n = \frac{0.974 \text{ atm} \times 1 \text{ l}}{\dfrac{0.0821 \text{ l-atm}}{\text{mole-°K}} \times 301° \text{ K}}$$

$$n = \frac{0.974 \text{ mole}}{0.0821 \times 301} = 0.0395 \text{ mole}$$

This shows that the experimental mass of 1 liter of the gas, 4.62 g, constitutes 0.0395 mole.

Since 0.0395 mole has a mass of 4.62 g, the mass of 1 mole is

$$1 \text{ mole} \times \frac{4.62 \text{ g}}{0.0395 \text{ mole}} = 117 \text{ g}$$

Therefore, the molecular weight of the gas is 117.

The ideal gas equation simplifies the solution of mass to gas volume problems under non-standard conditions. The number of moles of gas required is calculated by the mole method. This may then be substituted in the ideal gas equation, together with the pressure and temperature conditions, and the gas volume calculated directly. Conversely, the ideal gas equation can be used to calculate the number of moles of a gas from its volume under known non-standard pressure and temperature conditions. This quantity may then be used to complete the solution of a gas volume to mass problem by the mole method.

14. Real gases and the ideal gas. Precise experimental determinations of molar volumes of gases reveal that all gases deviate slightly from the perfect-gas characteristics assigned to them by the Gas Laws and Avogadro's Principle. This does not mean that the laws are only approximately true. Rather, it indicates that real gases do not behave as ideal gases over wide ranges of temperature and pressure.

Two factors contribute to the deviation of real gases from the perfect behavior of an ideal gas. Compression of a gas is *limited* by the fact that the molecules themselves occupy space even though their volumes are extremely small. Compression is *aided* by the fact that van der Waals (attractive) forces, however weak, do exist between the molecules.

Only when these two opposing forces within the gas exactly balance will it respond as an ideal gas. Such gases as ammonia and chlorine, which at ordinary temperatures are not far above their condensation points, show rather marked deviations from 22.4 liters as the molar volume. Such gases as oxygen and nitrogen, having low condensation points, behave more nearly as ideal gases under ordinary conditions.

When expressed to five significant figures, the molar volume of an ideal gas is 22.414 liters. The molar volumes of ammonia and chlorine, measured under normal conditions, are 22.09 l and 22.06 l respectively; those of oxygen and nitrogen are 22.394 l and 22.404 l respectively. For most gases, deviations from ideal gas performance through ordinary ranges of temperature and pressure do not exceed two percent.

REVIEW OUTLINE

Law of Combining Volumes of Gases—Gay-Lussac's Law (1)

Avogadro's Principle (2)
        Common gases—diatomic molecules (3)
        Noble gases—monatomic molecules (4)

Specific gravity (5)

Molar volume (6)

Density of a gas = gram-molecular weight ÷ molar volume (6)

Experimental determination of molecular weight (7)

Gas volume-gas volume problems (9, 11)

Mass-gas volume problems (10, 11)
        Solution by moles (10)
        Solution by proportion (10)

Gases collected over water (12)

Ideal gas equation—gas constant (13)

Real gases and the ideal gas (14)

PROBLEMS

(In the absence of stated conditions of temperature and pressure, they are assumed to be S.T.P.)

Group A

1. Calculate the density of hydrogen chloride gas, HCl, at S.T.P. to three significant figures.
2. What is the density of hydrogen sulfide, H_2S, at S.T.P., calculated to three significant figures?
3. What is the mass in grams of 1.00 liter of methane gas, CH_4, at S.T.P.?
4. The mass of 1.00 liter of gas at S.T.P. is 2.5 g. What is its molecular weight?
5. The mass of 1.00 liter of nitrogen at S.T.P. is 1.25 g. (*a*) Calculate the molecular weight of nitrogen from these data. (*b*) From this calculated molecular weight, determine the number of atoms in a molecule of nitrogen.

6. Hydrogen is the gas of lowest density. What is the mass in grams of 300. ml of hydrogen at S.T.P.?

7. At standard conditions, 225 ml of sulfur dioxide gas has a mass of 0.6428 g. Calculate the molecular weight of sulfur dioxide from these data.

8. What is the mass in grams of 750. ml of CO_2 at S.T.P.?

9. If the mass of 250. ml of methane is 0.179 g at S.T.P., what is its molecular weight?

10. The compounds HBr, PH_3, and N_2O are all gaseous at room temperature. (*a*) Calculate their molecular weights to 3 significant figures. (*b*) What is the density of each?

11. Find the mass in grams of 4.00 liters of: N_2, NH_3, and C_2H_2.

12. Calculate the specific gravity of carbon monoxide, CO, air standard, to three significant figures.

13. The specific gravity of argon, air standard, is 1.3796. What is its density?

14. The specific gravity of a gas, air standard, is 2.695. What is its molecular weight?

15. Find the molecular weight of a gas whose specific gravity, air standard, is 1.554.

16. What is the specific gravity, air standard, of the gas arsine, AsH_3, to three significant figures?

17. Carbon monoxide burns in oxygen to form carbon dioxide. (*a*) How many liters of carbon dioxide are produced when 15 liters of carbon monoxide burns? (*b*) How many liters of oxygen are required?

18. Acetylene gas, C_2H_2, burns in oxygen to form carbon dioxide and water vapor. (*a*) How many liters of oxygen are needed to burn 25.0 liters of acetylene? (*b*) How many liters of carbon dioxide are formed?

19. Ethane gas, C_2H_6, burns in air to produce carbon dioxide and water vapor. (*a*) How many liters of carbon dioxide are formed when 12 liters of ethane is burned? (*b*) How many moles of water are formed?

20. How many liters of air are required to furnish the oxygen to complete the reaction in Problem 19? (Assume the air to be 21% oxygen by volume.)

21. How many grams of sodium are needed to liberate 4.0 liters of hydrogen from water?

22. What volumes of hydrogen and nitrogen are required to produce 20. liters of ammonia gas?

23. (*a*) How many liters of hydrogen are required to convert 25.0 g of hot copper(II) oxide to metallic copper? (*b*) How many moles of water are formed?

24. When 130. g of zinc reacts with 150. g of HCl, how many liters of hydrogen are formed? (Note: first determine which reactant is in excess.)

25. (*a*) How many liters of oxygen can be produced by the decomposition of 90.0 g of water? (*b*) How many liters of hydrogen are produced in the same reaction?

26. If 400. ml of hydrogen and 400. ml of oxygen are mixed and ignited, (*a*) what volume of oxygen remains uncombined? (*b*) What volume of water vapor is formed if all gases are measured at 100° C?

27. (*a*) How many grams of copper will be produced when hydrogen is passed over 39.75 g of hot copper(II) oxide? (*b*) How many liters of hydrogen are required?

28. How many liters of hydrogen will be produced by the action of 25 g of calcium metal and an excess of hydrochloric acid? Calcium chloride is the other product of the reaction.

Group B

29. A compound contains: nitrogen, 30.51%; oxygen, 69.49%. The density of the gas is 4.085 g/l. Find: (*a*) its empirical formula. (*b*) its molecular weight. (*c*) its molecular formula.

30. It is found that 1.00 liter of a certain gas collected at a pressure of 720. mm of mercury, and at a temperature of 27° C has a mass of 1.30 g. Calculate its molecular weight.

31. It is found that 1.00 l of nitrogen combines with 1.00 l of oxygen in an electric arc to form 2.00 l of a gas which, by analysis, contains 46.7% nitrogen and 53.3% oxygen. Its density is determined to be 1.34 g/l. (*a*) Find the empirical formula of the product. (*b*) What is the molecular formula? (*c*) Using the information of this problem and the arguments of Avogadro, determine the number of atoms per molecule of nitrogen and oxygen.

32. How many liters will 2.0 g of CS_2 vapor occupy at 756 mm pressure and 50.° C?

33. A 1.00-liter flask filled with a gas at S.T.P. is attached to a high vacuum pump and evacuated until the pressure is only 1.00×10^{-4} mm. Assuming no temperature change, how many molecules remain in the flask?

34. A sample of a vapor having a mass of 0.865 g measures 174 ml at 100° C and 745 mm. What is the molecular weight?

35. (*a*) How many liters of sulfur dioxide gas at S.T.P. are formed when 50. g of sulfur burns? (*b*) What volume will this gas occupy at 25° C and 745 mm pressure?

36. What mass in grams of magnesium reacting with hydrochloric acid will be required to produce 400. ml of hydrogen at 20.° C and 740. mm pressure?

37. How many liters of hydrogen, collected over water at 25° C and 755.0 mm pressure, can be obtained from 6.0 g of magnesium and an excess of sulfuric acid?

38. How many grams of oxygen are contained in 12.0 liters of the gas measured over water at 23° C and 745.0 mm pressure?

39. A reaction between 5.0 g of aluminum and an excess of dilute sulfuric acid is used as a source of hydrogen gas. What volume of hydrogen is collected over water at 20.° C and 765 mm pressure? Aluminum sulfate is the other product of the reaction.

40. How many liters of dry air, measured at 29° C and 744 mm pressure, are required to complete the combustion of 1.00 mole of carbon disulfide, CS_2, to carbon dioxide, CO_2, and sulfur dioxide, SO_2?

41. What is the volume of the mixture of CO_2 and SO_2 produced in the reaction of Problem 40, if measured under the same conditions as the air used in the reaction?

42. Chlorine gas may be generated in the laboratory by a reaction between manganese dioxide and hydrogen chloride. The equation is:

$$MnO_2 + 4HCl \rightarrow MnCl_2 + 2H_2O + Cl_2\uparrow$$

(*a*) How many grams of MnO_2 are required to produce 1.00 liter of Cl_2 gas at S.T.P.? (*b*) How many grams of HCl are required?

43. In Problem 42, the HCl is available as a water solution which is 37.4% hydrogen chloride by mass, and the solution has a specific gravity (water standard) of 1.189. What volume of HCl solution (hydrochloric acid) must be furnished to the reaction?

44. How many grams of charcoal, 90.0% carbon, must be burned to produce 100. liters of CO_2 measured at 20.° C and 747 mm pressure?

45. How many grams of chlorine gas would be contained in a 5.00-liter flask at 20.° C and 600. mm pressure?

▶46. What temperature must be maintained to insure that a 2.50-liter flask containing 0.100 mole of a certain gas will show a continuous pressure of 745 mm?

▶47. From the ideal gas equation, $pV = nRT$, and the density of a gas defined as the mass per unit volume, $D = m/V$, prove that the density of a gas at S.T.P. is directly proportional to its molecular weight.

▶48. At 12.0° C and 740. mm, 1.07 liters of a gas has a mass of 1.98 g. Calculate the molecular weight of the gas from the ideal gas equation.

Chapter Eleven

LIQUIDS—SOLIDS—WATER

LIQUIDS

1. Properties of liquids. All liquids have several readily observable properties in common.

1. Definite volume. A liquid occupies a definite volume; it does not expand and completely fill its container as does a gas. A liquid has one free surface; its other surfaces must be supported by the container walls.

2. Fluidity. A liquid may be made to flow or may be poured from one container to another. It takes the shape of its container.

3. Noncompressibility. If water at 20° C is subjected to a pressure of 1000 atmospheres, its volume decreases to the extent of only 4%. This very slight compressibility of water under very high pressure is typical of the behavior of liquids.

4. Diffusion. If some ethanol (ethyl alcohol) is slowly poured down the side of a graduated cylinder already half full of water, the alcohol can be made to float on the water with a fairly definite boundary between the liquids. However, as this system stands, the boundary becomes less and less distinct as the water diffuses into the alcohol and the alcohol diffuses into the water. If the cylinder is allowed to stand undisturbed for some time, the alcohol and water completely mix.

5. Evaporation. If a liquid is left in an open container, it may gradually disappear. Many liquids will gradually, yet spontaneously, change into the vapor state at room temperature.

2. Kinetic theory description of a liquid. The particles of a liquid are much closer together than those of a gas; in fact, they are almost as close together as it is possible for them to be. Hence a liquid is practically noncompressible. Because the liquid particles are closer, the attractive forces between them are much stronger than those between the particles of a gas. The forces of attraction between the particles of a liquid are strong enough to cause it to have one free surface, and thus a definite volume. But the kinetic energy of the particles is sufficient to enable

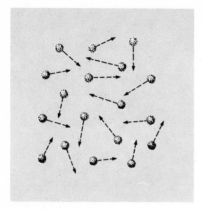

11-1 The attractive forces between the particles of a liquid are strong enough so that a liquid has a definite volume, but are weak enough so that the particles can move with respect to one another.

LIQUID STATE TEMPERATURE RANGES OF REPRESENTATIVE SUBSTANCES

Type of Substance	Substance	Temperature Range of Liquid State, °C (1 atm pressure)	
Nonpolar covalent molecular	H_2	−259 -	−253
	O_2	−219 -	−183
	CH_4	−182 -	−162
	CCl_4	−23 -	77
	C_6H_6	6 -	80
Polar covalent molecular	NH_3	−78 -	−33
	H_2O	0 -	100
Ionic	NaCl	800 -	1413
	MgF_2	1396 -	2227
Macromolecular	SiO_2	1710 -	2230
	C_x (diamond)	3500 -	4200
Metallic	Fe	1535 -	3000
	Cu	1083 -	2336

single particles or groups of particles to move with respect to one another. This indicates why a liquid is fluid and takes the shape of its container.

The forces of attraction between non-polar molecules are the relatively weak van der Waals attractions. Hence substances composed of such molecules are liquids only at temperatures below room temperature. Only high-molecular-weight, nonpolar molecular substances are liquids at room temperature.

The attractions between polar molecules are van der Waals forces plus the attraction of oppositely charged regions of neighboring molecules. Substances composed of such particles are usually liquids at room temperature.

The attractive forces between the particles of metals, ionic compounds, and macromolecular substances are much stronger. Usually these are liquids only at temperatures well above room temperature. The table at the top of this page gives the range of temperatures over which examples of each of these kinds of substances exist as a liquid.

There is abundant evidence that the par-

ticles of a liquid are in motion. Finely divided particles of a solid suspended in water or other liquids can be viewed through a microscope. They are observed to move about in a random manner. The motion is increased by using lighter or smaller molecules and higher temperatures. This is in agreement with the kinetic theory. Thus we may conclude that the observed random motion is caused by collisions with molecules of the liquid.

The diffusion of liquid molecules is readily explained by the kinetic theory as being due to the intermingling of liquid molecules through the agency of their motion. The diffusion of liquids is slower than that of gases because the molecules move more slowly and are closer together. Their movement in a given direction is hindered.

Water and other liquids, such as per-

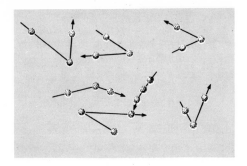

11-2 This enlarged diagram shows the movement of particles of paint as they are bombarded by invisible molecules of the liquid in which they are suspended.

fume, evaporate because some molecules continually acquire sufficient kinetic energy to escape from the surface. The vapor molecules of liquids in closed containers exert pressure as do all confined gases. This vapor pressure reaches some maximum value depending on the temperature of the substance.

The molecules of the vapors of liquids and solids have properties similar to those which we have attributed to gases. As stated previously, there is no distinction between a vapor and a gas other than the temperatures at which they normally exist. On cooling, gases may become liquids, and with further cooling, may become solids.

3. Specific gravity. The standard of reference for specific gravity of liquids and solids is water, which has a density of 1 g/cm^3. So

Specific gravity =
(liquids and solids)
$$\frac{\text{density of liquid or solid}}{\text{density of water}}$$

and

Specific gravity =
(liquids and solids)
$$\frac{\text{density of liquid or solid}}{1 \text{ g/cm}^3}$$

4. Dynamic equilibrium. When a cover is placed over a container partially filled with a liquid it appears that evaporation of the liquid continues for a while and then ceases. Let us examine this apparent situation in light of the Kinetic Theory. The temperature of the liquid is proportional to the average kinetic energy of all the molecules of the liquid. Most of these molecules have energies very close to the average. However, some have very high energies and a few have very low energies at any particular time. The motions of all are random.

High energy molecules near the surface and moving toward the surface may overcome the attractive forces of the surface molecules completely and escape or evaporate. Some of these may collide with molecules of gases in the air or other vapor molecules and rebound into the liquid. As the evaporation continues, the concentration of vapor molecules continues to increase. Consequently, the chance of collisions of escaping molecules with vapor molecules increases and the number rebounding into the liquid increases.

Eventually the number of vapor molecules returning to the liquid equals the

11-3 Water evaporates because some molecules acquire sufficient kinetic energy to escape continually from the surface. Some rebound into the surface after colliding with molecules of gases in the air or with other water vapor molecules.

number of liquid molecules evaporating. Beyond this point there will be no *net* increase in the *concentration* of vapor molecules, that is, in the number of vapor molecules per unit volume of air above the liquid. The motions of the molecules do not cease and so the two actions, evaporation and condensation, do not cease; both merely continue at equal rates. We may conclude that an *equilibrium* is attained between the rate of liquid molecules evaporating and the rate of vapor molecules condensing. It is obvious that this is a dynamic condition in which *opposing* processes are proceeding at *equal* rates. Since this dynamic equilibrium involves purely physical activity, it is referred to as *physical equilibrium: a dynamic state in which two opposing physical processes in the same system proceed at equal rates.*

We might represent the evaporation process in the following manner:

liquid + energy → vapor

The condensation process would be, accordingly,

vapor → liquid + energy

We could then represent this state of dynamic equilibrium occurring in a confined space as

liquid + energy ⇌ vapor

5. Equilibrium vapor pressure. The vapor molecules of liquids in closed containers exert pressure as do all confined gases. When equilibrium is reached there is no net change in the system. The concentration of vapor molecules in the space above the liquid surface remains constant. Thus, at equilibrium, there is a vapor pressure characteristic of the liquid present in the system. It is known as the *equilibrium vapor pressure* of the liquid. **Equilibrium vapor pressure** *is the pressure exerted by a vapor in equilibrium with its liquid.*

What is the effect on a liquid-vapor equilibrium system if the temperature of the liquid is raised? Again, let us examine this situation in terms of the kinetic theory. The rise in temperature means that the average kinetic energy of the

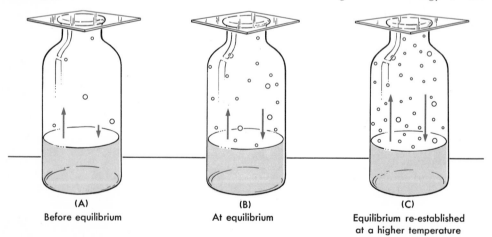

(A)	(B)	(C)
Before equilibrium	At equilibrium	Equilibrium re-established
		at a higher temperature

11-4 An example of physical equilibrium and the influence of temperature. The different sizes of the arrows indicate the relative rates of evaporation (up) and condensation (down). The pressure exerted by the vapor molecules at equilibrium is known as the equilibrium vapor pressure of that particular liquid.

liquid molecules has been raised. A relatively larger number of liquid molecules now possess sufficient energy to escape through the liquid surface; the rate of evaporation is increased.

liquid + energy ⇄ vapor

Thus, the liquid-vapor equilibrium is *disturbed* and the concentration of vapor molecules above the liquid surface is increased. This, in turn, increases the chances of collisions with escaping molecules, causing an increase in the rate of condensation. Soon the equilibrium is reestablished, but at a *higher equilibrium vapor pressure.*

All liquids have characteristic forces of attraction between their molecules. If the attractive forces are strong, there is less tendency for the liquid to evaporate. The equilibrium vapor pressure of such a liquid is correspondingly low. Glycerol is an example of a liquid with a low equilibrium vapor pressure. Conversely, if the attractive forces between liquid molecules are weak, the liquid tends to evaporate readily with a resulting high equilibrium vapor pressure. Ether is such a liquid. The magnitude of the equilibrium vapor pressure of a liquid depends on the *nature of the liquid and its temperature.*

6. Le Chatelier's principle. In systems that have attained equilibrium, opposing actions occur at equal speeds. Any change which alters the speed of either the forward or the reverse action disturbs the equilibrium. It is frequently possible to displace an equilibrium in a desired direction by altering the equilibrium conditions.

In 1888 the French chemist Henri Louis Le Chatelier (luh-*shah*-teh-lee-ay) (1850–1936) published an important principle which is the basis for much of our knowledge of equilibrium. *Le Chatelier's principle* may be stated as follows: *If a system at equilibrium is subjected to a stress, the equilibrium will be displaced in such direction as to relieve the stress.* This is a general law that applies to all kinds of dynamic equilibria. Let us see how it applies to the

liquid + energy ⇄ vapor

system we have been considering.

We have already learned from Kinetic Theory considerations that if the system is at equilibrium at a given temperature, and the temperature is then raised, equilibrium can be reestablished, but at a greater vapor concentration. The rise in temperature is a stress on the system. According to Le Chatelier's principle, the equilibrium will be displaced in the direction which relieves the stress. In this case the equilibrium will be displaced to the right, since the forward reaction is endothermic, and will tend to absorb the applied heat. This means that the vapor concentration must be higher when equilibrium is reestablished. By similar reasoning, we can apply Le Chatelier's principle to the lowering of the temperature of the system at equilibrium. Here the reverse reaction is favored and equilibrium will be reestablished at the lower temperature with a reduced vapor concentration. We can thus see that Le Chatelier's principle enables us to predict the dependence of equilibrium vapor pressure on the temperature.

Suppose next we keep the temperature of the system constant, but alter the volume which the system occupies. This means that the vapor pressure must remain constant. It also means that the concentration of vapor molecules (density of the vapor) must remain constant.

First let us increase the volume which the system occupies. The volume of the liquid cannot change appreciably, but the volume of the vapor can. When the volume of the vapor is increased, its pressure necessarily drops (Boyle's law). In order to restore the vapor to its equilibrium concentration at the constant temperature, more vapor molecules must be produced. Le Chatelier's principle indicates that the equilibrium must shift to the right, and more liquid must evaporate. Equilibrium is then restored with the same vapor pressure and the same concentration of vapor molecules as before. But with a larger volume of vapor, the actual number of vapor molecules must be greater. The number of liquid molecules is therefore necessarily reduced.

If we reduce the volume which the system occupies, the pressure of the vapor increases. To reduce this pressure to the equilibrium vapor pressure at the constant temperature, Le Chatelier's principle indicates that vapor molecules must condense to liquid molecules. The reverse reaction is favored. Equilibrium is once again established, this time with fewer vapor molecules and a greater number of liquid molecules.

7. Boiling of liquids. An understanding of the nature of equilibrium phenomena, and in particular the manner in which equilibrium vapor pressures are established, leads naturally to an understanding of the phenomenon of *boiling*. From physics we know that pressure exerted anywhere on the surface of a confined liquid is transmitted undiminished in every direction throughout the liquid (Pascal's law).

Consider a beaker of water being heated over a Bunsen flame (Fig. 11-5). Vapor bubbles first appear at the bottom of the beaker where the water is hottest. They diminish in size and disappear completely as they rise into the cooler layers of the water. Atmospheric pressure acts on the surface of the vapor bubble, according to Pascal's law, to collapse it. Only when the equilibrium vapor pressure exerted by the vapor molecules on the liquid at the sur-

face of the bubble is equal to the atmospheric pressure can the vapor bubble be maintained.

As the temperature of the water rises with its attendant rise in vapor pressure, *a temperature is reached where the equilibrium vapor pressure becomes equal to the pressure of the atmosphere acting on the surface of the liquid.* At this temperature the vapor bubbles maintain themselves in the liquid and present to the liquid a greatly increased liquid-vapor surface allowing evaporation (a surface phenomenon) to occur at a greatly increased rate. We say that the liquid *boils. The boiling point of a liquid is the temperature at which the equilibrium vapor pressure of the liquid is equal to the prevailing atmospheric pressure.* If the pressure on the surface of a liquid is increased, the boiling point of the liquid is raised. If the pressure is decreased, the boiling point of the liquid is lowered.

The boiling point of water is exactly 100° C at *standard pressure.* This is known

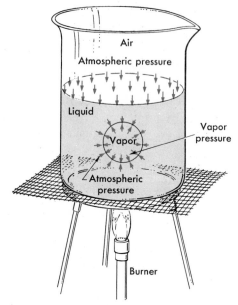

11-5 A liquid boils when its equilibrium vapor pressure becomes equal to the prevailing atmospheric pressure.

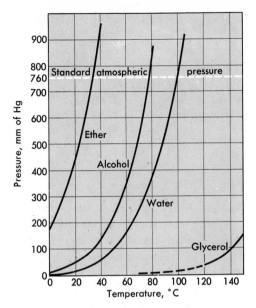

11-6 The equilibrium vapor pressures of some common liquids as a function of temperature.

as the *standard* (or *normal*) *boiling point of water*. When the boiling points of liquids are given, standard pressure conditions are understood. Ether, which has a high equilibrium vapor pressure, boils at 34.6° C. The boiling point of glycerol, mentioned earlier (Section 5) for its low equilibrium vapor pressure, is 290° C. See Fig. 11-6.

During boiling the temperature of a liquid remains constant. The temperature of the vapor is the same as that of the liquid. Hence the kinetic energies of liquid and vapor molecules must be the same. But energy must be supplied for boiling to be continuous and this energy is absorbed by the liquid in becoming a vapor. This energy does work in separating the liquid molecules to the spacing of gas molecules —it increases their potential energy. The heat energy required to vaporize one mole of liquid at its standard boiling point is its *standard molar heat of vaporization*. Its magnitude is a measure of the degree of attraction between liquid molecules.

▶**8. Liquefaction of gases.** Michael Faraday (1791–1867) discovered that it is possible to liquefy certain gases by cooling them and compressing them at the same time. He used a thick-walled sealed tube of the type shown in Fig. 11-7 to liquefy chlorine, sulfur dioxide, and some other gases. One end of the glass tube containing the chlorine gas was strongly heated. That caused the gas in the heated end of the tube to expand and exert pressure on the gas in the other end of the tube, which was cooled in a freezing mixture. Cooling and compression in this manner converted the gaseous chlorine into liquid chlorine.

In order to liquefy a gas, it is necessary first to compress the gas and then to absorb the heat of compression. The second step is to permit the cool, compressed gas to expand rapidly. If the expansion is sufficiently rapid, it will cool the remaining part of the gas to a temperature at which some of it will liquefy.

Compressing a gas always raises its temperature since energy is acquired by the molecules of a gas when work is done to push them closer together. In liquefying gases this heat of compression is absorbed by a suitable refrigerant. The gas molecules thereby lose the energy acquired during compression. Thus the compressed

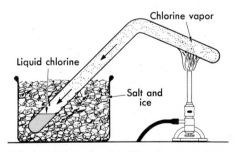

11-7 By using a tube like the one above, Faraday succeeded in liquefying chlorine, sulfur dioxide, and several other gases which have high critical temperatures.

gas is reduced to the same temperature that it had before compression. The molecules possess the same energy they had prior to compression but are now closer together.

When a compressed gas is permitted to expand, the molecules lose energy as they do work in spreading apart against the force of molecular attraction. This energy loss by the molecules is observed as a decrease in the temperature of the gas. Since the temperature of the compressed gas was that which it had before compression, the expanded gas is now at a much lower temperature than originally. By repetition of this compression, cooling, and expansion cycle the temperature of the gas is reduced still further.

The liquefaction of gases is accomplished by the combined efforts of lowered temperature and increased pressure. The increased pressure crowds the gas molecules together. The lowered temperature slows their movement. Ultimately, they are slowed down and crowded together so closely that the attractive forces between the molecules cause them to condense to a liquid.

Scientists have found that above a certain temperature it is impossible to liquefy a gas by pressure alone because the kinetic energy of the molecules is great enough to overcome the attracting forces between them. Thus the gas will not liquefy however great the pressure applied. *The highest temperature at which it is possible to liquefy a gas with any amount of pressure is called its* **critical temperature.** *The pressure required to liquefy a gas at its critical temperature is called its* **critical pressure.** *The volume occupied by one mole of a gas under these conditions is called its* **critical volume.** The critical temperature and critical pressure of several common gases are given in the table shown at the top of the next column.

CRITICAL TEMPERATURES AND PRESSURES

Gas	Critical Temperature (°C)	Critical Pressure (atm)
water	374.0	217.7
sulfur dioxide	157.2	77.7
chlorine	144.0	76.1
carbon dioxide	31.1	73.0
oxygen	− 118.8	49.7
nitrogen	− 147.1	33.5
hydrogen	− 239.9	12.8

From these data it is easy to see that two conditions are necessary to liquefy a gas. Its temperature must be lowered below its critical temperature, and simultaneously its pressure must be raised above the vapor pressure of the liquefied gas at this temperature.

▶ **9.   Critical temperature and molecular attraction.** Since the critical temperature of a gas is the temperature above which it cannot be liquefied no matter how great the pressure, the magnitude of the critical temperature serves as a measure of the attractive forces between molecules. The higher the critical temperature of a gas, the greater is the attractive force between its molecules. The lower the critical temperature of a gas, the less is the attractive force between its molecules.

The high critical temperature of water shown in the table indicates that the forces of attraction between polar water molecules are so great that they can cause the liquefaction of water vapor even at 374° C. The critical temperature of sulfur dioxide is less than that of water. Thus the attractive forces between sulfur dioxide molecules must be less than those between water molecules. This we would expect because sulfur dioxide molecules are less polar than water molecules. Consequently, sulfur dioxide can be condensed to a liquid only below 157° C.

The attractive forces between non-polar covalent molecules such as chlorine, carbon dioxide, oxygen, nitrogen, and hydrogen are van der Waals forces. Since these generally increase with an increase in the complexity of a nonpolar molecule, the higher the molecular weight of such a molecule, the higher its critical temperature will be. This is borne out by the order of the critical temperatures of chlorine, carbon dioxide, oxygen, nitrogen, and hydrogen shown in the table.

SOLIDS

10.   Properties of solids.   Some of the more readily observed general properties of solids are:

1. Definite shape. A solid maintains its shape. Unlike liquids and gases, it does not flow under ordinary circumstances. The shape of a solid is independent of its container.

2. Definite volume. All of the surfaces of a solid are free surfaces. Hence the volume of a solid is also independent of its container.

3. Noncompressibility. The pressures required to decrease the volumes of solids are even greater than those required for liquids. Hence, for all practical purposes, solids are noncompressible. Remember that solids such as wood, cork, sponge, etc., which are apparently compressible are very porous. Compression does not reduce the volume of the solid portion of such substances significantly. It merely reduces the volume of the pores of the solid.

4. Very slow diffusion. If a lead plate and a gold plate are in close contact for several months, particles of gold may be detected in the lead and vice versa. This observation is evidence that diffusion occurs even in solids although at a *very* slow rate.

5. Crystal formation. Solids may be described as either *crystalline* or *amorphous.*

Crystalline solids have a regular arrangement of particles while amorphous solids have a completely random particle arrangement.

11.   Kinetic theory description of a solid.   Particles of a solid are held close together in fixed positions by forces which are stronger than those between particles of a liquid. This accounts for the definite shape and volume of a solid as well as its noncompressibility. The type of particle arrangement determines whether the solid is crystalline or amorphous. The particles of a solid are in weak vibratory motion back and forth about their fixed positions. Their kinetic energy, related to the amplitude of this vibratory motion, is proportional to the temperature of the solid. At low temperatures the kinetic energy is small; at higher temperatures it is larger. This vibratory motion explains why there is relatively little diffusion of solids.

12.   Changes of state involving solids.   The physical change of a liquid to a solid is called *freezing*, and involves a loss of energy by the liquid.

$$\text{liquid} \rightarrow \text{solid} + \text{energy}$$

Since this change occurs at constant temperature, the liquid and solid particles

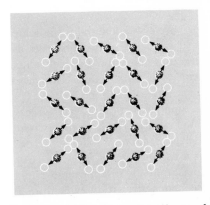

11-8   The particles of a solid vibrate about fixed positions.

11-9 X-ray diffraction photograph of ice. Chemists use X-ray diffraction in their study of crystal structure. (Polytechnic Institute of Brooklyn)

both must have the same kinetic energy. The energy loss is a loss of potential energy by the particles as the forces of attraction do work on them.

The converse physical change, *melting*, also occurs at constant temperature.

$$\text{solid} + \text{energy} \rightarrow \text{liquid}$$

It involves a gain of potential energy by the particles of the solid as they do work against the attractive forces in becoming liquid particles.

For pure crystalline solids the temperatures at which these two processes occur, the freezing point and the melting point, coincide. For pure water, both processes occur at 0° C, that is, ice melts at 0° C to form liquid water and water freezes at 0° C to form ice. The heat energy required to melt one mole of solid at its melting point is its *molar heat of fusion*.

If ice gradually disappears in a mixture of ice and water, it is evident that the melting process is proceeding at a rate faster than the freezing process. If, how-

ever, the relative amounts of ice and water remain unchanged in the mixture, both processes must be proceeding at equal rates and a state of physical equilibrium is indicated.

$$\text{solid} + \text{energy} \rightleftarrows \text{liquid}$$

Not all particles of a solid have the same energy. If a surface particle of a solid acquires sufficient energy to overcome the attractive forces holding it to the body of the solid, the particle may escape from the solid and become a vapor particle.

$$\text{solid} + \text{energy} \rightarrow \text{vapor}$$

If a solid is placed in a closed container, vapor particles cannot escape from the system. Eventually they come in contact with the solid, and are held by its attractive forces.

$$\text{vapor} \rightarrow \text{solid} + \text{energy}$$

Thus a solid in contact with its vapor can reach an equilibrium

$$\text{solid} + \text{energy} \rightleftarrows \text{vapor}$$

and exhibits a characteristic equilibrium vapor pressure. Like that of a liquid, it depends only on the temperature and the substance involved. Some solids like camphor and naphthalene (moth crystals) have fairly high equilibrium vapor pressures. They evaporate noticeably when exposed to air. Certain solids like carbon dioxide (Dry Ice) and iodine have equilibrium vapor pressures which rise so rapidly with temperature increases that they equal atmospheric pressure before the solid melts. In such cases the solid vaporizes directly, without passing through the liquid state. The change of state from a solid to a vapor is known as *sublimation*.

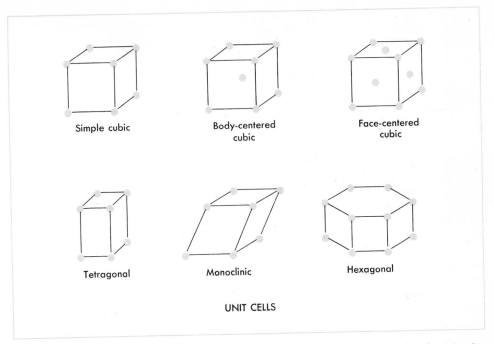

Simple cubic   Body-centered cubic   Face-centered cubic

Tetragonal   Monoclinic   Hexagonal

UNIT CELLS

11-10   The kind of symmetry found throughout a crystalline substance is determined by the type of unit cell which generates the lattice structure.

13.   Amorphous solids. Amorphous solids are those which appear to have random particle arrangement. Truly amorphous solids are rare. Many solids which scientists once thought were amorphous have been found to have a minute crystalline structure. Charcoal is such a solid. However, materials like glass and paraffin may be considered to be amorphous. These materials have the properties of solids in that they have definite shape and volume and diffuse slowly. But they do not have the orderly arrangement of particles characteristic of crystals. They also lack sharply defined melting points. In many respects they resemble liquids which flow very slowly at room temperature.

14.   Nature of crystals. Most substances exist as solids in some characteristic crystalline form. *A crystal is a homogeneous portion of a substance bounded by plane surfaces making definite angles with each other, giving a regular geometric form.*

The arrangement of particles composing a crystal is determined by a mathematical analysis of photographs of the diffraction patterns produced when the crystal is illuminated by X rays. The pattern of points which describe the arrangement of particles in a crystal structure is known as the *crystal lattice.* The smallest portion of the crystal lattice which determines the pattern of the lattice structure is called the *unit cell.* The unit cell defines the kind of symmetry to be found throughout a crystalline substance. The kinds of unit cells are shown in Fig. 11-10.

▶ The classification of crystals by shape, a part of the science of *crystallography,* helps chemists to identify crystals. Any crystal can be placed in one of six crystalline systems:

1. Isometric (or *cubic*), in which the three axes are at right angles as in a cube, and of equal length;

2. Tetragonal, in which the three axes are at right angles to each other, but only the two lateral axes are equal;

3. Triclinic, in which there are three unequal axes and oblique intersections;

4. Hexagonal, in which three equilateral axes intersect at angles of 60° and with a vertical axis of variable length at right angles to the equilateral axes;

5. Orthorhombic, in which there are three unequal axes at right angles to each other;

6. Monoclinic, in which there are three unequal axes, with one oblique intersection. (See Fig. 11-11)

▶ Crystals of common salt, NaCl, are isometric (cubic). This can be seen by sprinkling a little table salt on a black surface and examining with a magnifying lens. Alum crystals, $K_2SO_4 \cdot Al_2(SO_4)_3 \cdot 24H_2O$, are also isometric, being formed as *octahedrons*. Copper(II) sulfate pentahydrate forms blue triclinic crystals.

Crystals of many chemical compounds are commonly formed by the evaporation of their solutions, or by the cooling of their hot saturated solutions. Crystals are also formed when some substances change from the liquid to the solid state and when others change from the gaseous to the solid state. Most of us are familiar with snowflake crystals which are formed when water vapor changes to the solid state. Molten sugar, sulfur, and iron form crystals in a similar manner when they change from the liquid to the solid state. In some cases crystals grow from the solid state.

15. Binding forces in crystals. The regularity of crystal structures is their most fascinating feature. All crystalline structure is the result of the universal tendency in nature for the symmetrical distribution of force. Where the opportunity occurs, ions or atoms or molecules arrange themselves in positions of least energy. The more opportunity there is for these particles to orient themselves during the formation of crystals, the more

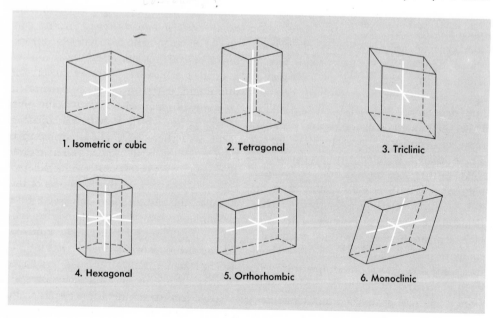

1. Isometric or cubic   2. Tetragonal   3. Triclinic

4. Hexagonal   5. Orthorhombic   6. Monoclinic

11-11 Schematic diagram of the six basic crystal systems.

11-12 A garnet crystal, left, and a group of quartz crystals, right, show how crystal structure follows a characteristic pattern. (B. M. Shaub)

symmetrical and regular they will be. Thus, crystals that form slowly will be more nearly perfect.

The classification of crystals into the six crystalline systems is based on considerations of symmetry. It is frequently more useful to classify crystals according to the types of lattice structure, that is, whether the particles that compose the crystal lattice are *ionic, covalent, metallic,* or *molecular.* Of these, the ionic and molecular crystals represent the two extremes, whereas the covalent and metallic crystals are of the intermediate types.

1. Ionic crystals. The ionic crystal lattice consists of an array of positive and negative ions arranged in a characteristic pattern with such regularity that no molecular units are evident within the crystal. The binding forces are the strong electrostatic bonds of positive and negative charges. Consequently, ionic crystals are hard and brittle, have rather high melting points, and are good insulators. Generally speaking, compounds of Group I and Group II metals combined with the Group VI and Group VII nonmetals and the nonmetallic radicals form crystals of this type.

2. Covalent crystals. The covalent crystal lattice consists of an array of atoms that share electrons with their neighboring atoms. The binding forces are strong covalent bonds which extend in fixed directions. The resulting crystals are giant, compact, interlocking structures called *macromolecules.* They are very hard and brittle, have rather high melting points, and are nonconductors. Diamond, silicon carbide, silicon dioxide, and oxides of transition metals are of this type.

3. Metallic crystals. The metallic crystal lattice consists of positive ions permeated by a cloud of valence electrons, commonly referred to as the *electron gas.* The binding force is the attraction between the positive ions of the metal and the electron cloud. The valence electrons may be considered to have been donated by the atoms of the metal and to belong to the crystal as a whole. These electrons are free to migrate throughout the crystal lattice giving rise to the high electric conductivity associated with metals. The hardness characteristics and melting points of metallic crystals vary over wide ranges for different metals. Sodium, iron, tungsten, copper, and silver are typical examples of metallic crystals that have good electric conductivity but quite different characteristics such as hardness and melting point.

4. Molecular crystals. The molecular crystal lattice consists of symmetrical aggregates of discrete molecules. The binding force is the relatively weak van der Waals forces between the molecules. If the molecules are polar, there is the additional attraction between the oppositely charged parts of neighboring molecules. The covalent chemical bonds which bind the atoms within the molecules are much stronger than the forces which form the crystal lattice. Thus, molecular crystals have low melting points, are relatively soft, volatile, and good insulators. Iodine, carbon dioxide, water, and hydrogen form crystals of this type. (See chart on p. 173.)

WATER

16. Physical properties of water. Pure water is a transparent, odorless, tasteless, and almost colorless liquid. The faint blue or blue-green color of water is apparent only in deep layers.

Any odor or taste in water is due to impurities such as dissolved mineral matter, dissolved liquids, or dissolved gases. The pronounced odor and taste of the water from some mineral springs is due to the presence of such substances in considerable quantity.

Water may exist as a vapor, liquid, or solid. Liquid water changes to ice at 0° C under standard pressure, 760 mm of mercury. As water solidifies, it gives off heat and expands one ninth in volume. Consequently, ice has a density of about 0.9 g/cm³. The density of ice increases slightly as ice is cooled below 0° C. The molar heat of fusion of ice at 0° C is 1.44 kcal.

When water at 0° C is warmed, it contracts until its temperature reaches 4° C. Then water gradually expands as its temperature is raised further. *At its temperature of maximum density, 4° C, one milliliter of water has a mass of one gram.*

When the pressure on the surface of water is *one atmosphere* (760 mm of mercury), water boils at a temperature of

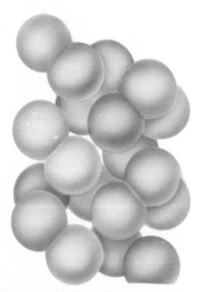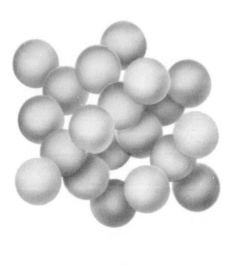

11-13 Solid iodine (left) forms molecular crystals. Compare its molecular structure with that of the diamond (right) which forms covalent crystals called macromolecules.

MELTING POINTS AND BOILING POINTS OF REPRESENTATIVE TYPES OF SUBSTANCES

Type of Substance	Substance	Melting Point °C	Boiling Point, °C (1 atm pressure)
Nonpolar covalent molecular	H_2	−259	−253
	O_2	−219	−183
	CH_4	−182	−162
	CCl_4	−23	77
	C_6H_6	6	80
Polar covalent molecular	NH_3	−78	−33
	H_2O	0	100
Ionic	NaCl	800	1413
	MgF_2	1396	2227
Macromolecular	SiO_2	1710	2230
	C_x (diamond)	3500	4200
Metallic	Fe	1535	3000
	Cu	1083	2336

100° C. The molar heat of vaporization of water at 100° C is 9.70 kcal. The steam that is formed by heating water at its boiling point occupies a much greater volume than the water from which it was formed. When one liter of water evaporates, the steam occupies about 1700 liters at normal atmospheric pressure.

When water is heated in a closed vessel so that the steam cannot escape, the boiling temperature of the water is raised above 100° C. Conversely, if the air and water vapor above the liquid in a closed vessel are partially removed by means of a vacuum pump, the water boils at a lower temperature than 100° C. Pressure cookers are used for cooking food because the higher temperature of the water cooks the food in a shorter time, thus saving fuel. Vacuum evaporators are used to concentrate milk and sugar solutions. Under reduced pressure the liquid boils away at a temperature low enough so that the sugar or milk is not scorched.

17. Structure and properties of water molecules. Water molecules are composed of two atoms of hydrogen and one atom of oxygen joined by polar covalent bonds. Studies of the crystal structure of ice indicate that these atoms are not joined in a straight line, but that the molecule is unsymmetrical with a structure which may be represented as

The angle between the two hydrogen-oxygen bonds is about 105°. Since oxygen is more strongly electronegative than hydrogen, the bonds are polar, the electronegativity difference indicating about 39% ionic character. Thus the electrons are not uniformly distributed about the molecule, but are on the average slightly clustered about the oxygen nucleus. This has the effect of giving the oxygen part of the molecule a partial negative charge, and leaves the hydrogen parts with a partial positive charge. Since the polar covalent bonds in this molecule are unsymmetrically arranged, the molecule as a whole is polar.

We may represent the bond formation in a water molecule as

	1s	2s	$2p_x$	$2p_y$	$2p_z$
H					
O	⊗	⊗	⊗		
H					

A model of the water molecule, assuming the spatial orientation of the oxygen $2p$ orbitals is not altered by the bonding of the hydrogen atoms, is shown in Fig. 11-14. From this model we would expect the bond angle to be 90°. Mutual repulsion of the somewhat positively charged hydrogen atoms accounts for some of the increase in the bond angle. A more adequate explanation is deferred until Chapter 16.

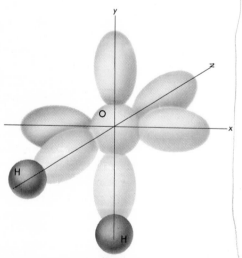

11-14 A representation of the structure of the water molecule assuming the spatial orientation of the oxygen $2p$ orbitals is not altered by the bonding of the hydrogen atoms.

The polarity of water molecules enables them to join together, or associate, into groups of molecules. One somewhat positive hydrogen atom of a water molecule may be weakly, but effectively, attracted to the somewhat negative oxygen of a second water molecule. Such a bond is called a *hydrogen bond*. A hydrogen of the second water molecule may be attracted to the oxygen of a third water molecule, and so on. While the number of molecules in a group decreases with an increase in temperature, the number usually ranges from eight to four in liquid water. The formation of molecular groups by hydrogen bonding causes water to be liquid at room temperature while other substances with nonpolar molecules of similar size and mass such as methane, CH_4, are gases.

Ice consists of water molecules arranged in a definite hexagonal structure. They are held together by hydrogen bonds in a rather open hexagonal pattern (Fig. 11-15). As heat is applied to ice, the increased energy of the atoms and molecules causes them to vibrate more vigorously. This stretches the hydrogen bonds, and the ice expands as it is heated.

When the melting point of ice is reached, the energy of the atoms and molecules is so great that the rigid open lattice structure of the ice crystals breaks down—the ice turns into water. Despite the fact that the hydrogen bonds in water at 0° C are longer than those in ice, they are more flexible and the groups of liquid molecules can crowd together more compactly than those in ice. As a result, H_2O molecules occupy less volume as water than they do as ice. Thus water is denser than ice.

As water is warmed from 0° C, two phenomena having opposite effects occur: *1.* the breaking down of some hydrogen bonds enables water molecules to crowd more closely together; and *2.* the in-

11-15 Model of the crystal structure of ice. (Chemical Bond Approach)

creased energy of the water molecules causes them to overcome molecular attractions more effectively and spread apart. Up to 4° C, the first effect predominates and water increases in density. Above 4° C, while the first phenomenon continues to occur, the effect of the second is so much greater that the density of water decreases.

DENSITY OF WATER

°C	g/ml	°C	g/ml
0	0.99987	10	0.99973
1	0.99993	20	0.99823
2	0.99997	30	0.99567
3	0.99999	40	0.99224
4	1.00000	50	0.98807
5	0.99999	60	0.98324
6	0.99997	70	0.97781
7	0.99993	80	0.97183
8	0.99988	90	0.96534
9	0.99981	100	0.95838

Groups of molecules in water must absorb enough energy to be broken up into single molecules before water boils. This is what makes the boiling point of water high, and makes it necessary to use a large amount of heat to vaporize it at its normal boiling point.

▶ **18. Water as a standard.** It is easy to obtain water in *fairly pure* condition. For this reason it is used as a *scientific standard*:

1. For defining the relationship between vol-ume and mass in the metric system. We have already mentioned that one milliliter of water at its temperature of maximum density, 4° C, has a mass of one gram.

2. For establishing a temperature scale and graduating thermometers. The temperature at which water freezes is called 0° C and fixes the *ice-point* on the Celsius thermometer scale. The boiling point of water under a pressure of 760 mm of mercury is called 100° C and determines the steam-point on the Celsius thermometer scale.

3. For measuring heat. In defining the units used for measuring heat, water is used as a standard. For example *the calorie is traditionally the amount of heat needed to warm one gram of water one Celsius degree.*

4. For a standard of specific gravity. Water is the standard for the specific gravity of solids and liquids. One cubic centimeter of iron has 7.6 times the mass of one cubic centimeter of water. Thus the *specific gravity* of iron is 7.6.

19. Chemical behavior of water.

1. The stability of water. Water is a very **stable compound;** that is, *a compound which does not break up, or decompose, easily.* Mercury(II) oxide, on the other hand, is a rather **unstable compound** because *it does not require much energy to decompose it into its elements.* Water is so stable that it does not decompose appreciably until its temperature reaches about 2700° C. The stability of water is evidence of the strength of the covalent bonds between the oxygen and hydrogen atoms.

2. Behavior with metals. Very active metals such as sodium and potassium react with cold water, setting free hydrogen and forming metallic hydroxide solutions.

$$2Na + 2HOH \rightarrow 2NaOH + H_2 \uparrow$$

Magnesium reacts with boiling water to form magnesium hydroxide and hydrogen. When heated red hot, iron reacts with steam forming iron oxide and hydrogen. Aluminum and zinc also react with water at high temperatures.

3. Behavior with metallic oxides. The oxides of many metals are insoluble and water has little or no effect upon them. But water does react with the ionic oxides of the very active metals. The oxides of sodium, potassium, calcium, and barium unite with water and form soluble hydroxides. Soluble metallic hydroxides are compounds whose water solutions contain a *base.* This term will be defined later in Chapter 14. Calcium hydroxide is formed when water is added to calcium oxide, CaO.

$$CaO + H_2O \rightarrow Ca(OH)_2$$

Compounds such as calcium oxide, CaO, are known as *anhydrides.* The word anhydride means "without water." Since it forms a solution containing a base when water is added to it, calcium oxide is called a *basic anhydride.* We may define a **basic anhydride** *as the oxide of a metal which will unite with water to form a solution containing a base.*

4. Behavior with oxides of nonmetals. The oxides of such nonmetals as carbon, sulfur, and phosphorus are molecular compounds, containing polar covalent bonds. They unite with water to form a solution containing an *acid.* For example, water unites with carbon dioxide to form carbonic acid, H_2CO_3.

$$CO_2 + H_2O \rightarrow H_2CO_3$$

Carbon dioxide is an anhydride, and since it forms a solution containing an acid with water, it is called an *acid anhydride.* In general, *the oxides of nonmetals unite with water to form solutions which contain an acid, and consequently are known as* **acid anhydrides.**

5. Water of crystallization. Many positive ions, and a few negative ions, are sur-

rounded by a definite number of water molecules in crystals formed by evaporating the water from their solutions. This water is called *water of crystallization* or *water of hydration. A crystallized substance that contains water of crystallization is a* **hydrate.** Each hydrate holds a definite proportion of water because it is necessary for the formation of its crystal structure. For example, blue crystals of copper(II) sulfate consist of copper(II) ions, each surrounded by four water molecules, and sulfate ions, each with one water molecule. The formula of this substance is written as

$$CuSO_4 \cdot 5H_2O$$

The water molecules are totaled, and their loose attachment to the copper(II) and sulfate ions (shown empirically as $CuSO_4$) is indicated by the raised dot. If $CuSO_4 \cdot 5H_2O$ is heated to a temperature slightly above the boiling point of water, the water of crystallization is driven off.

$$CuSO_4 \cdot 5H_2O \rightarrow CuSO_4 + 5H_2O$$

The substance which then remains is called an **anhydrous compound.** Anhydrous copper(II) sulfate, $CuSO_4$, is a white powder that may be prepared by heating the blue crystals gently in a test tube. The fact that water turns anhydrous copper(II) sulfate blue may be used as a *test for water.*

Other examples of hydrates are the compounds $ZnSO_4 \cdot 7H_2O$, $CoCl_2 \cdot 6H_2O$, and $Na_2CO_3 \cdot 10H_2O$. Some hydrates have two or more forms which are stable over different temperature ranges. Many other compounds form crystals which do not require water of crystallization. Examples are: NaCl, KNO_3, and $KClO_3$.

6. Water promotes many chemical changes. A good example of one of these changes is the reaction of baking powder, which is a mixture of dry chemicals. As long as bak-

11-16   Water acts to promote some reactions, as shown when water is added to dry baking powder. (Fundamental Photographs)

ing powder is kept dry, no chemical action occurs. When water is added to the baking powder, the chemicals in the mixture react immediately, and bubbles of gas are liberated (see Fig. 11-16).   Mixtures of many other dry substances do not react until water is added. The role of water in promoting chemical changes will be more fully explained in Unit 5.

▶ **20. Efflorescence.** Suppose we put ten grams of sodium sulfate crystals, $Na_2SO_4·10H_2O$, on a watch glass and counterpoise it on a balance. In a few minutes the crystals begin to show a loss of mass. By the end of the laboratory period the loss in mass may amount to a gram or more.

Some hydrated crystals hold water of crystallization very loosely. Water is given off from them when they are exposed to relatively dry air. The crystals lose their glassy luster and become powdery. *This loss of water when such crystals are exposed to the air is called* **efflorescence.** Efflorescence occurs much more rapidly in a warm, dry atmosphere than in one that is cool and moist. Hydrates which effloresce have higher vapor pressures than that of the

water vapor in the air about them. Sodium carbonate decahydrate, $Na_2CO_3·10H_2O$, has a high aqueous vapor pressure. When exposed to the atmosphere, it effloresces forming the monohydrate, $Na_2CO_3·H_2O$. Thus a pound of freshly packaged "washing soda" may weigh considerably less when purchased.

▶ **21. Deliquescence.** Suppose we put ten grams of calcium chloride granules on a watch glass and counterpoise it on a balance. After the calcium chloride has been exposed to the air for half an hour, we find that it shows a decided gain in mass. The granules have become moist, or perhaps have even formed a solution with water from the air. *Deliquescence is the property of certain substances to take up water from the air to form a solution.* Such substances are very soluble in water. Their crystals have aqueous vapor pressures that are low compared to the normal range of partial pressures of water vapor in the air.

Many materials such as silk, wool, hair, and tobacco take up water vapor from the air. The water molecules may be held in pores and imperfections of the solid. All

11-17   Calcium chloride removes water vapor from the air to control the dust on an unpaved road. (Allied Chemical Corporation)

such materials, along with deliquescent substances, are classed as *hygroscopic*. Common table salt is hygroscopic only because it contains a small amount of magnesium chloride, a very deliquescent substance. This impurity causes table salt to "cake" and clog the holes of a salt shaker.

22. Deuterium oxide. While most water molecules are composed of hydrogen atoms with mass number 1 and oxygen atoms with mass number 16, there are other possible types of water molecules. This is because there are three isotopes of hydrogen with mass numbers 1, 2, and 3, and three isotopes of oxygen with mass numbers 16, 17, and 18. The possible combinations of these six isotopes give 18 types of water molecules which in the liquid state are associated most commonly in chains of from four to eight units. In water there is also a very small proportion of hydronium (H_3O^+) ions, hydroxide ions, and oxide ions which are formed from the various isotopes of hydrogen and oxygen. Water is a complex mixture of many kinds of molecules and ions.

While particles other than ordinary water molecules exist in only small traces in a water sample, one type of water molecule has been studied rather extensively. This is the *deuterium oxide* molecule, D_2O, in which the symbol D is used to represent an atom of the isotope of hydrogen with mass number 2. Professor G. N. Lewis (1875–1946), while doing research at the University of California, first separated deuterium oxide, sometimes called "heavy water," in 1932. Professor Hugh S. Taylor (1890–   ) and his co-workers at Princeton University subjected 2300 liters of water to electrolysis and finally succeeded in isolating 83 ml of deuterium oxide from this large volume of water. It is possible to separate D_2O from H_2O by electrolysis because D_2O molecules are not as readily decomposed by the passage of electric current as are H_2O molecules. Thus the concentration of D_2O molecules increases as H_2O molecules are decomposed by electrolysis.

Deuterium oxide is about 10% denser than ordinary water. It boils at 101.42° C, freezes at 3.82° C, and has its maximum density at 11.6° C. Delicate tests have been devised for detecting deuterium oxide. It has been used as a "tracer" in research work in physiology. By tracing the course of deuterium oxide molecules through living organisms, new information has been obtained concerning certain life processes. Deuterium oxide usually produces harmful effects on living things, particularly when present in high concentrations. The most important use of deuterium oxide is as a moderator in nuclear reactors (see Chapter 31).

REVIEW OUTLINE

Effervescence gives up gas soda pop

Liquids
    General properties
        Definite volume (1)
        Fluidity (1)
        Noncompressibility (1)
        Diffusion (1)
        Evaporation (1)
    Kinetic theory description of a liquid (2)
    Specific gravity (3)
    Equilibrium—physical equilibrium (4)

QUESTIONS

Group A

1. In terms of the kinetic theory explain these properties of liquids: (*a*) definite volume; (*b*) fluidity; (*c*) noncompressibility; (*d*) diffusion; (*e*) evaporation.
2. What evidence is there that the particles of a liquid are in constant motion?
3. What are the necessary conditions for a system in equilibrium?
4. Would you expect an equilibrium vapor pressure to be reached in the space above a liquid in an open container? Why?
5. Water standing in a covered flask experiences a drop in temperature of 10. C°. How is the liquid-vapor equilibrium disturbed? Explain.
6. What effect does the pressure on a water surface have on the boiling temperature of the water?
▶ 7. Define (*a*) critical temperature; (*b*) critical pressure; (*c*) critical volume.
▶ 8. What conditions must be met in order for a gas to be liquefied?
9. In terms of the kinetic theory, explain these properties of solids: (*a*) definite shape; (*b*) definite volume; (*c*) noncompressibility; (*d*) very slow diffusion; (*e*) crystal formation.
10. What are the general properties of solids composed of (*a*) ions; (*b*) molecules; (*c*) macromolecules; (*d*) metal ions in an "electron gas"?
11. List six physical properties of water.
12. How does the volume of steam compare with the volume of water from which it was produced?
13. Describe the structure of the water molecule and tell why it is a polar molecule.
14. (*a*) What is a hydrogen bond? (*b*) What effect do the hydrogen bonds in water have on its boiling point?
▶15. In what ways is water used as a scientific standard?
16. (*a*) What is a stable compound? Give an example. (*b*) What is an unstable compound? Give an example.
17. (*a*) List five metals which react with water. (*b*) Give the conditions under which they react.
18. (*a*) What is an anhydride? (*b*) Distinguish between a basic anhydride and an acid anhydride. (*c*) What type of compound may be an acid anhydride? (*d*) What type of compound may be a basic anhydride?
19. What is the significance of the raised dot in $BaCl_2 \cdot 2H_2O$?
20. Give an example of a chemical change which is promoted by the presence of water.
▶21. A package of washing soda, $Na_2CO_3 \cdot 10H_2O$, labeled "one pound" was found to weigh only 14 ounces. Was the packer necessarily dishonest? Explain.
▶22. (*a*) Explain why anhydrous calcium chloride may be used to keep the air in a basement dry. (*b*) Suggest a suitable method of accomplishing this.
23. How is deuterium oxide separated from ordinary water?
24. Give some uses for deuterium oxide.

Group B

25. What kind of particles compose substances which are liquids (*a*) well below room temperature; (*b*) at room temperature; (*c*) well above room temperature?

26. (*a*) Using the curves of Fig. 11-6, determine the temperature at which water in an open vessel will boil when the atmospheric pressure is reduced to 600. mm. (*b*) What is the boiling point of alcohol at this pressure? (*c*) of ether?

27. The system alcohol liquid + energy ⇌ alcohol vapor is at equilibrium in a closed container at 50° C. What will be the effect of each of the following stresses on the equilibrium? (*a*) Temperature is raised to 60° C. (*b*) Volume of container is doubled. (*c*) Barometer rises from 720. mm to 740. mm.

▶28. (*a*) Why does compressing a gas raise its temperature? (*b*) Why does a gas become colder when it is allowed to expand?

▶29. (*a*) Can carbon dioxide be liquefied at 100.° C? (*b*) Can chlorine be liquefied at 100.° C? Explain.

▶30. A bottle of alum crystals was erroneously labeled "sodium chloride." How could the error be detected at once by an alert chemistry student?

31. Camphor crystals are soft and volatile. Explain.

32. Explain why ice occupies a greater volume than the water from which it is formed.

33. The system ice + energy ⇌ water is at equilibrium at 0° C in an open vessel. What will be the effect on the system if (*a*) heat is supplied to the system? (*b*) heat is removed from the system? (*c*) the pressure on the system is increased?

34. Explain why water has a point of maximum density at 4° C.

35. What does the extreme stability of H_2O molecules indicate about the strength of the covalent bonds between the oxygen and hydrogen atoms?

▶36. Tobacco growers prefer to handle dried tobacco leaves during damp weather. Explain.

37. What particles are present in water besides ordinary H_2O molecules?

38. (*a*) How does the addition of the molar heat of vaporization affect the energy of the particles of one mole of liquid at its standard boiling point? (*b*) How does the addition of the molar heat of fusion affect the energy of the particles of one mole of a solid at its standard melting point?

PROBLEMS

Group A

1. A mixture of 50.0 ml of hydrogen and 30.0 ml of oxygen is ignited by an electric spark. What gas remains? What is its volume?

2. A mixture of 40.0 ml of oxygen and 120.0 ml of hydrogen is ignited. What gas remains and what is its volume?

3. (*a*) What volume of hydrogen is needed for complete reaction with 37.5 ml of oxygen? (*b*) What fraction of a mole of water is produced?

4. A mixture of equal volumes of oxygen and hydrogen has a volume of 100.0 ml. (*a*) After the mixture is ignited, what gas remains, and what is its volume? (*b*) How many millimoles of water are formed?

5. How many grams of hydrogen and oxygen will be required to produce 15.0 moles of water?

Group B

6. What mass of anhydrous sodium carbonate may be obtained by heating 100. g of $Na_2CO_3 \cdot 10H_2O$?

7. Calculate the percentage of cobalt, chlorine, and water in $CoCl_2 \cdot 6H_2O$.

8. What is the empirical formula of certain hydrated crystals having a composition of 56.14% $ZnSO_4$ and 43.86% water?

9. If 124.8 g of copper(II) sulfate crystals is heated to drive off the water of crystallization, the loss of mass is 45.0 g. What is the percentage of water in hydrated copper(II) sulfate?

10. The anhydrous copper(II) sulfate in Problem 9 was found to contain copper, 31.8 g; sulfur, 16.0 g; and oxygen, 32.0 g. Determine the empirical formula of the hydrated copper(II) sulfate crystals.

▶11. The specific gravity of carbon tetrachloride at 0° C is 1.600. (*a*) Calculate the volume occupied by a single molecule of CCl_4. (*b*) Assuming the molecules to be spherical, calculate the approximate diameter in Ångströms of a CCl_4 molecule.

▶12. Obtain from Fig. 5-2 the radius of an atom of mercury. (*a*) If we assume an atom of mercury to be spherical, what is its volume in Å? (*b*) If we assume that in liquid mercury the atoms are packed in a cubic array with six nearest neighbors, what is the volume in milliliters of 1.00 mole of liquid mercury?

Chapter Twelve

THE SOLUTION PROCESS

1. Nature of solutions. If a lump of sugar is dropped into a beaker of water, it disappears gradually. The sugar is said to dissolve in the water. Careful examination of the water with a microscope does not reveal the dissolved sugar. More sugar may be added and it, too, will dissolve. But if this process of adding sugar is continued, finally a point is reached where the sugar no longer dissolves.

By tasting the liquid, we can tell that the sugar is present in the water. The molecules of sugar have become mixed with the molecules of water so that the same degree of sweetness is detected in all parts of the water. Such a mixture of sugar and water is known as a *solution*.

In general terms, *a* **solution** *is a homogeneous mixture of two or more substances, the composition of which may be varied within definite limits.* The *dissolving medium* is called the **solvent.** The *substance dissolved* is called the **solute.** The simplest solution consists of molecules of a single solute diffused throughout a single solvent.

Not all substances form true solutions in water. If clay is mixed with water, for example, very little actually dissolves. The particles of clay are huge when compared to molecules, and a turbid, heterogeneous mixture, called a *suspension*, results. Because the components of the mixture have different densities, they readily separate into two distinct phases. However, some very small particles, larger than molecules, are kept permanently suspended by the bombardment of the water molecules. Such mixtures may appear to be homogeneous, but careful examination shows that they are not true solutions. Mixtures of this type are called *colloidal suspensions* and are discussed more fully in Chapter 15.

It was stated in Chapter 6, Section 3, that electrovalent solids do not exist as molecules. Each has a crystal lattice composed of ions bound together by electrostatic forces. Such substances form water solutions that conduct electricity, and are called **electrolytes.** In general, covalent substances form molecular solutions with water which do not conduct electricity. Such substances are called **nonelectrolytes.** Acids are exceptions. When they are undissolved they are molecular, but their solutions conduct electricity. Thus, acids are electrolytes. Solutions of electrolytes have physical properties which are different from solutions of nonelectrolytes. They will be considered in detail in Chapters 13 and 14. The remainder of our present discussion of the properties of solutions will deal with solutions of nonelectrolytes.

2. Types of solutions. Matter may exist in three states: solid, liquid, and gas. Therefore, we may expect to have nine different types of solutions.

TYPES OF SOLUTIONS

Solute	Solvent	Example
gas	gas	air
gas	liquid	soda water
gas	solid	hydrogen in palladium
liquid	gas	water vapor in air
liquid	liquid	alcohol in water
liquid	solid	mercury in copper
solid	gas	sulfur vapor in air
solid	liquid	sugar in water
solid	solid	copper in nickel

All mixtures of gases are solutions since they consist of homogeneous mixtures of molecules. Solutions of solids in liquids are by far the most common. Since water is a liquid at ordinary temperatures, we may think of water vapor in air as a liquid-in-gas solution. Solutions of gases in solids are rare. The *adsorption* of hydrogen by palladium and platinum is, in a sense, the condensation of a gas on the surface of a solid, and approaches the nature of a solution.

In general, substances of similar composition such as silver and gold, or alcohol and water, are apt to form solutions. *Two liquids which are mutually soluble in each other are said to be* **miscible.** Ethanol (ethyl alcohol) and water are miscible in all proportions. Similarly, ether and ethanol are completely miscible. Ether and water, on the other hand, are practically **immiscible.** Chemists frequently dry the inside surface of freshly washed glassware by rinsing first with distilled water, then with ethanol, and finally with ether. The ether has a high vapor pressure and quickly evaporates, leaving a dry glass surface.

3. Solution equilibrium. We may think of the solution process as being *reversible.* Suppose we again consider the lump of sugar dropped into a beaker of water. The sugar molecules which break away from the crystals and enter the water have completely random motions. Some of these molecules which have broken away come in contact with the undissolved sugar. Here they are attracted by

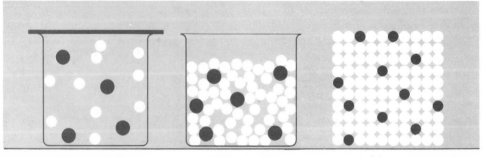

Gaseous solution   Liquid solution   Solid solution

12-1 Models of solutions.

the sugar molecules in the crystal and become a part of the crystal structure once more. Thus, the solution process includes both the act of dissolving and the act of crystallizing.

At first, since there are no sugar molecules in solution, the solution process occurs in the direction of dissolving. Molecules leave the crystal structure and diffuse throughout the water. As the *solution concentration or number of sugar molecules per unit volume of solution increases, the reverse process begins.* The rate at which the sugar crystals rebuild increases as the concentration of the sugar solution increases. Eventually, if undissolved sugar remains, sugar crystals rebuild as fast as they dissolve. The concentration of the solution reaches the maximum possible under existing conditions and the solution is said to be *saturated.* An *equilibrium* is reached between undissolved sugar and sugar dissolved in water. **Solution equilibrium** *is the physical state in which the opposing processes of dissolving and crystallizing of a solute occur at equal rates. A* **saturated solution** *is one in which the dissolved and undissolved solutes are in equilibrium.* (In Fig. 12-2, what visible evidence is there, apart from the labeling, that this solution is saturated?)

If more water is added to the sugar solution, it is no longer saturated; the concentration of solute molecules has been decreased. In terms of the Le Chatelier Principle, this decrease in concentration of solute particles places a stress on the equilibrium which is relieved by an increase in the dissolving rate. More sugar dissolves to restore the same *equilibrium concentration* of solute molecules. Solution equilibrium thus acts to limit the quantity of a solute which can dissolve in a given quantity of solvent. *The* **solubility** *of a solute is defined as the amount of that solute dissolved in a given amount of a certain solvent at equilibrium, under specified conditions.*

4. Influence of pressure on solubility. Ordinary changes in pressure affect the solubility of solids and liquids so slightly that they may be neglected altogether. Of course, the "solubility" of one gas in another is independent of pressure. All mixtures of gases are homogeneous and obey the Gas Laws in the same manner as individual gases. The solubility of gases

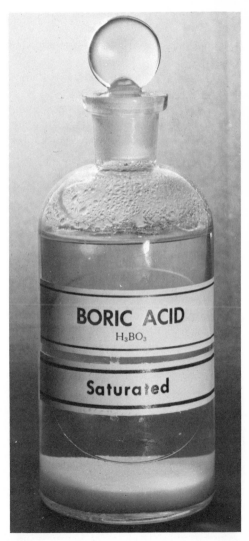

12-2 A saturated solution contains the equilibrium concentration of solute, under existing conditions. (Fundamental Photographs)

in liquids and solids, on the other hand, is appreciably affected by changes in pressure.

Carbonated beverages *fizz* or *effervesce* when poured into an open glass tumbler. At the bottling plant carbon dioxide gas is forced into solution in the flavored water under a pressure of from 5 to 10 atmospheres. While under such pressure the gas-in-liquid solution is sealed in the bottles. When the cap is removed, the pressure is reduced to 1 atmosphere and much of the carbon dioxide escapes from solution as gas bubbles. *This rapid evolution of a gas from a liquid in which it is dissolved* is known as **effervescence.**

Solutions of gases in liquids reach equilibrium in about the same way that solids in liquids do. The attractive forces between gas molecules are negligible on the average and their motions are relatively great. If a gas is in contact with the surface of a liquid, gas molecules may easily enter the liquid surface. As the concentration of dissolved gas molecules increases, some begin to escape from the liquid and re-enter the gaseous phase above the liquid. An equilibrium is eventually reached between the rates at which gas molecules are dissolving and escaping from solution. After the equilibrium is attained, there is no increase in the concentration of the gaseous solute. Thus the solubility of the gas is limited to its equilibrium concentration in the liquid, under existing conditions.

If the pressure of the gas above the liquid is increased, the equilibrium is disturbed in accordance with Le Chatelier's Principle and more gas dissolves. This action, of course, increases the concentration of the dissolved gas. This, in turn, causes gas molecules to escape from the liquid surface at a faster rate. When equilibrium is reestablished there will be a higher concentration of solute at the higher external pressure. The increase in gas pressure has the effect of increasing the concentration of the undissolved solute in contact with the solvent. Thus the solubility of the gas in the liquid is increased. *The solubility of gases in liquids is directly proportional to the pressure of the gas above the liquid.* This is **Henry's Law,** named after William Henry, an English chemist (1775–1836).

Gases that react chemically with their liquid solvents are generally more soluble than those which do not form compounds with the solvent molecules. Oxygen, hydrogen, and nitrogen are only slightly soluble in water. Ammonia, carbon dioxide, and sulfur dioxide are more soluble, probably due to the formation of unstable compounds with the water solvent. Such gases deviate from Henry's Law.

If different gases are mixed in a confined space, each gas exerts the same pressure it would if it alone occupied the space. The pressure of the mixture is the *total* of the individual, or *partial*, pressures of the gases composing the mixture according to *Dalton's Law of Partial Pressures.* (See Chapter 9, Section 9.) The partial pressure of each gas in the mixture is proportional to the number of molecules of that gas, at a definite temperature and for a constant volume.

If a mixture of gases is in contact with a liquid, the solubility of each gas is proportional to its partial pressure. Assuming that the gases present in the mixture do not react in any way when in solution, each will dissolve to the same extent it would if the other gases were not present.

Air is about 20 percent oxygen. When air is bubbled through water, only about 20 percent as much oxygen dissolves as would dissolve if pure oxygen were used, at the same pressure. Oxygen remains dissolved in the water only because it is in equilibrium with the oxygen in the air above the water. If the oxygen were removed from the atmosphere above the surface of the water this equilibrium would be disturbed. By Le Chatelier's Principle, much of the dissolved oxygen would eventually escape from the water. This fact has great significance when we consider the abundance of life that exists in water.

5. Temperature and solubility.

1. Gases in liquids. A glass of water drawn from the hot water tap often appears milky because tiny bubbles of air are suspended throughout the water. Part of the air which was dissolved in the cold water has been driven out of solution as the water was heated.

Raising the temperature of a solution increases the average speed of its molecules. Molecules of dissolved gas leave the solvent at a faster rate than gas molecules enter the solvent. This lowers the equilibrium concentration of the solute. The solubility of a gas decreases as the temperature of the solvent is increased. Table 9 of the Appendix shows that the solubility of gases varies with the kind of gas, and that it decreases as the temperature of the gas is increased.

2. Solids in liquids. An excess of sugar added to water results in an equilibrium between the sugar solute and the undissolved crystals characteristic of a saturated solution.

If the solution is warmed, the equilibrium is disturbed and solid sugar dissolves as the temperature of the solution rises. It is evident that the solubility of the sugar in water has increased with the rise in temperature. A new solution equilibrium will be established at the higher solution temperature with a higher equilibrium concentration of solute sugar.

Cooling the solution causes solid sugar to separate, indicating that the solubility diminishes as the temperature falls. No more than the equilibrium concentration of solute may normally remain in solution. Thus with the lowering of the temperature, the equilibrium is shifted and sugar crystallizes from solution faster than solid crystals dissolve.

It is possible, however, to cool a hot saturated solution very carefully so that the excess solute does not separate. Such a solution is said to be *supersaturated*. There is a strong tendency, in a supersaturated solution, to reestablish normal equilibrium. By a slight disturbance, or by seeding the solution with a small crystal, the excess solute will separate and the equilibrium concentration of solute will be established.

Increasing the temperature usually increases the solubility of solids in liquids. Sometimes, however, the reverse effect is observed. A certain rise in temperature may result in a large increase in solubility in one case, a slight increase in another, and a decrease in still another. For example, the solubility of potassium nitrate in 100. g of water changes from 13 g to nearly 140 g with a temperature change from 0.° C to

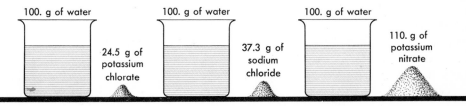

12-3 A comparison of the masses of three common solutes that can be dissolved in 100. g of water at 60° C. Convert these quantities to moles of solute per 100. g of water and compare them.

70.° C. Under similar circumstances the solubility of sodium chloride increases only about 2 g. The solubility of cerium sulfate, on the other hand, decreases nearly 14 g. Typical solubility curves are shown in Fig. 12-4. If the solubility curve for cane sugar in water were included, the graph would have to be extended considerably. At 0.° C, 179 g of sugar dissolves in 100. g of water. This increases to 487 g at 100.° C. The solubility of solids depends upon the nature of the solid, the nature of the solvent used, and the temperature. Solubility data for various substances in water are given in the table below.

When a solid dissolves in a liquid we may think of the solid as having changed in physical state to a liquid. Such a change is endothermic and heat is absorbed. Thus we should expect the temperature of the solution to be lowered as the solid dissolves, and the solubility of the solid to increase as temperature is raised. Deviations from this normal pattern may indicate that some kind of chemical activity occurs between solute and solvent.

3. Liquids in liquids. Similar logic may be applied to solutions of liquids in liquids. As no change in physical state occurs when such solutions are prepared, we might expect little change in temperature.

If large changes in temperature are observed, as in the case of sulfuric acid in water, some type of chemical activity between solute and solvent is suggested. When water is the solvent this chemical activity may be a form of *hydration*. The process of hydration will be discussed in Chapter 13.

6. Dissolving mechanisms. Let us examine possible mechanisms by which a solid dissolves in a liquid to see why this process is spontaneous, or self-acting. We may assume that at least three important actions occur in the dissolving process:

1. Solute particles must be separated from the solid mass (as a solid changing physical state to a liquid); *this action takes up energy.*

2. Solvent particles must be moved apart to allow solute particles to enter the liquid environment; *this action also takes up energy.*

3. Solute particles are attracted to solvent particles; *this action gives up energy.*

The first two of these actions are endothermic and the last one is exothermic. Unless this exothermic action exceeds the combined effect of the first two, the net change is endothermic and the temperature of the solution will *decrease* as the solid dissolves. This is the usual pattern for solid-in-liquid solutions. In such cases,

SOLUBILITY OF SOLUTES AS A FUNCTION OF TEMPERATURE
(Grams of solute per 100. grams of H_2O)

Substance	0°	20°	40°	60°	80°	100°
$AgNO_3$	122	222	376	525	669	952
$C_{12}H_{22}O_{11}$ (sugar)	179	204	238	287	362	487
$Ce_2(SO_4)_3$	20.8	10.1	—	3.87	—	—
KCl	27.6	34.0	40.0	45.5	51.1	56.7
KNO_3	13.3	31.6	63.9	110.	169	246
KI	128	144	160.	176	192	208
Li_2CO_3	1.54	1.33	1.17	1.01	0.85	0.72
NaCl	35.7	36.0	36.6	37.3	38.4	39.8
$NaNO_3$	73	88	104	124	148	180.
CO_2 (gas at S.P.)	0.335	0.169	0.097	0.058	—	—
O_2 (gas at S.P.)	0.0069	0.0043	0.0031	0.0023	0.0014	0.0000

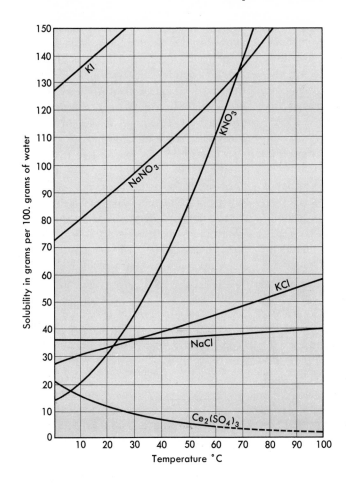

12-4 Solubility curves. The solubility of a solute is expressed in grams per 100. grams of solvent, at a stated temperature.

heating the solution results in an increase in the solubility of the solid. Where the net change is exothermic, the temperature of the solution will *increase* as the solid dissolves. Heating such solutions results in a decrease in the solubility of the solid. The reasons for these effects will be discussed in Section 7.

We have seen that natural processes generally lead to lower energy states (see Chapter 2, Section 14). Thus, an endothermic energy change cannot account for the spontaneity of the dissolving process. Perhaps the entropy change in such instances can account for it.

The mixture of solute and solvent particles in a solution represents a more disordered state (higher entropy) than that of the unmixed solid and liquid. Thus, the mixture is more probable than the unmixed state because of this higher entropy. The favorable entropy change of the dissolving process may cause solution to occur even though the energy change is not toward a lower state.

How well is this logic sustained when it is applied to solutions of gases in liquids? The solute is in a more random state as a gas than when dissolved in the liquid. Thus, the higher entropy of the gaseous state opposes the dissolving process. For dissolving to occur, the energy change must be favorable (to a lower state) and of sufficient magnitude to overcome the unfavorable entropy change.

Accordingly, the dissolving process for a gas-in-liquid solution should be exothermic. If the temperature of the solution is raised, the solubility of the gas should be lowered. Experiments show that heat is evolved when a gas dissolves in water, and that the solubility of the gas decreases as the temperature of the solution is raised.

7. Heat of Solution. From the foregoing discussions it is clear that no single rule can be stated for changes of solubility with increasing temperature. Gases generally become less soluble in water as temperature is raised. The brief solubility table in Section 5 shows that some solids become more soluble in water as temperature is raised. Other solids become less soluble, and still others experience practically no change in solubility.

In Section 6 we recognized that heat may be evolved or absorbed when a solute dissolves in a solvent. Thus, the total heat content of a solution may not be the same as that of its separate components. *The difference between the heat content of a solution and the heat contents of its components is called the heat of solution.*

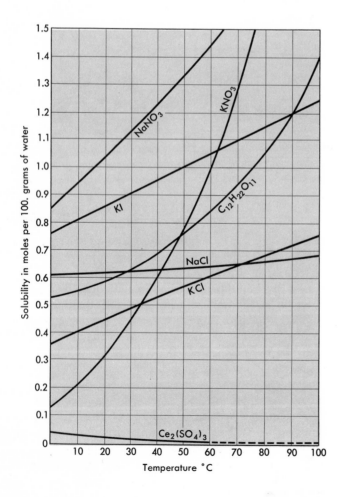

12-5 Solubility plotted in moles of solute per 100. grams of water as a function of temperature. Compare the relative positions of the curves with those of Fig. 12-4.

solute + solvent → solution + heat

or   *solute + solvent + heat → solution*

The heat of solution of any system depends on the concentration of the final solution. This is revealed by the fact that the dilution of a concentrated solution may cause the evolution or absorption of heat. For this reason heat of solution is measured in kilocalories per mole of solute dissolved in a specific number of moles of solvent.

When the dissolving process is exothermic, the total heat content of the solution is *less* than that of its separate components. The solution usually warms as dissolving proceeds. The heat of solution is said to be *negative*. When the process is endothermic, the heat content of the solution is *greater* than that of its components. The solution usually cools as dissolving proceeds and the heat of solution is said to be *positive*. Heats of solution for some common substances are given in the table below. How are these data related to those in the Solubility Table of Section 5?

HEATS OF SOLUTION

(kcal/mole solute in 200 moles H_2O)
[(s) = solid, (l) = liquid, (g) = gas at S.P.]

Substance	Heat of Solution
$AgNO_3$(s)	+5.47
CH_3COOH(l)	−0.32
CO_2(g)	−4.76
$CuSO_4$(s)	−16.20
HCl(g)	−17.74
HI(g)	−7.02
KCl(s)	+4.20
KI(s)	+5.11
KNO_3(s)	+8.46
KOH(s)	−13.04
Li_2CO_3(s)	−3.06
$NaCl$(s)	+1.02
$NaNO_3$(s)	+5.02
$NaOH$(s)	−10.11
NH_3(g)	−8.28
NH_4NO_3(s)	+6.08

Observe that the change in solubility of a substance with temperature is closely related to its heat of solution. The heat of solution of sodium chloride, for example, is nearly zero. The solubility change with temperature is very small.

In a saturated solution with undissolved solute we have an equilibrium between the two processes, dissolving and crystallizing. Let us consider such a solution of KCl. The symbols (s) and (l) indicate solid and liquid, respectively.

KCl(s) + H_2O(l) + heat $\rightleftarrows$ solution

The heat of solution is +4.20 kcal/mole so the dissolving process is endothermic. The crystallizing process is, therefore, exothermic. Since the two processes are in equilibrium, the entropy change and the energy change are equal and there is no net driving force in the system.

Suppose we now add heat to the solution. The rise in temperature will produce a stress on the equilibrium system. From Le Chatelier's Principle, the system will relieve this stress by increasing the rate of the *endothermic* process. Thus, dissolving proceeds faster than crystallizing until the stress is relieved and the concentration of KCl in solution is increased. Solutes with positive heats of solution become more soluble as the temperature of their solution is raised.

For the same reasons, the effect of temperature on saturated solutions of solutes having negative heats of solution is the reverse of the foregoing. In such cases the dissolving process is exothermic and the crystallizing process is endothermic. A rise in solution temperature favors the endothermic process and solute separates from the solution.

8. Increasing the rate of dissolving. The rate at which a solid dissolves in a liquid depends on the solid and liquid involved. In general, the more nearly the solute and solvent are alike in structure the more rapidly will solution occur. However, we may increase the rate of solution of a solid in a liquid in three ways.

1. By stirring. The diffusion of solute molecules throughout the solvent occurs rather slowly. Stirring or shaking the mixture aids in the dispersion of the solute particles by bringing fresh portions of the solvent in contact with the undissolved solid.

2. By powdering the solid. Solution action occurs only at the surface of the solid. By grinding the solid into a fine powder we greatly increase the surface area. Hence, finely powdered solids will dissolve much more rapidly than large lumps or crystals of the same substance.

3. By heating the solvent. The rate of dissolving rises with temperature. If we apply heat to a solvent the molecular activity increases and the dissolving action is speeded. At the same time the solubility of the substance is increased if the dissolving process is endothermic.

These actions influence the rate of dissolving either by increasing the effective contact area between solid and liquid, or by producing a more favorable energy distribution among the particles of the solid. As temperature is raised, a larger portion of the solute particles have sufficient kinetic energy to overcome the binding forces and leave the surface of the solid.

Figure 12-6 shows the change in distribution of kinetic energy among the particles of substance when the temperature is raised from T_1 to T_2.

9. Solutions: dilute or concentrated. The more solute that is dissolved in a solvent, the more *concentrated* the solution becomes. Conversely, the more solvent that is added, the more *dilute* the solution becomes. In the first instance *the concentration of solute particles was increased.* In the second, *the concentration of solute was decreased.* We may increase the concentration of solutions by adding solute or by removing solvent by evaporation.

The terms *dilute* and *concentrated* are qualitative and are useful in a general sense. However, they lack the definiteness, or quantitative significance, which chemists require in describing the precise concentration of solutions.

10. Concentration of solutions. The properties of solutions depend upon the

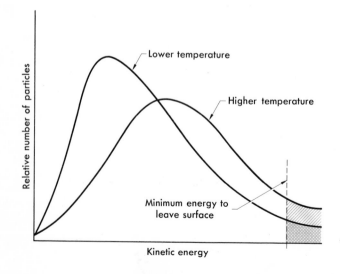

12-6 Effect of temperature on the kinetic energy distribution of the particles of a substance.

relative proportions of solute and solvent. Chemists use several different methods for expressing the concentration of solutions quantitatively. These include expressions for the quantity of solute in (1) a given *volume of solution*, (2) a given *quantity of solvent*, and (3) a given *quantity of solution*. The various methods will be explained as they are introduced into the discussion.

When it is important to know the quantity of solvent in a solution as well as the quantity of solute, the concentration is stated in terms of *molality*. The **molality** of *a solution is an expression of the number of moles of solute per kilogram of solvent.* The symbol for molality is the small letter *m*.

A one-molal (1-*m*) solution is one containing *1 mole of solute per kilogram of solvent.*

A *half-molal* (0.5-*m*) solution contains *one half mole* of solute per kilogram of solvent. A *two-molal* (2-*m*) solution has *two moles* of solute in 1 kilogram of solvent. Of course, 0.5 mole of solute dissolved in 0.5 kg of solvent, or 0.25 mole of solute in 0.25 kg of solvent gives a 1-*m* solution.

Molal solutions are important to the chemist because (for a given solvent) *two solutions of equal molality have the same ratio of solute to solvent molecules.* Molality is preferred when portions are to be weighed. The use of the molality method is illustrated in the following sample problems.

Sample Problem

How would one prepare a 0.125-*m* solution of $AgNO_3$ in 250. ml of H_2O?

Solution

0.125-*m* solution = 0.125 mole solute/kg H_2O.
250. ml H_2O = 250. g H_2O = 0.250 kg H_2O.
The gram-formula weight of $AgNO_3$ = 170. g = mass of 1 mole $AgNO_3$.
A 1.00-*m* solution would contain 170. g $AgNO_3$ dissolved in 1.00 kg H_2O. Thus, a 0.125-*m* solution in 0.250 kg of water would require

$$\frac{170.\ g\ AgNO_3}{mole} \times \frac{0.125\ mole}{kg\ H_2O} \times 0.250\ kg\ H_2O = 5.30\ g\ AgNO_3$$

Sample Problem

A solution contains 17.1 g of sugar, $C_{12}H_{22}O_{11}$, dissolved in 125 g of water. Determine the molal concentration.

Solution

The formula weight of $C_{12}H_{22}O_{11}$ = 342.
Thus, 1 mole has a mass of 342 g.
The concentration is 17.1 g sugar/125 g H_2O. To express in terms of molality, we must convert this to moles sugar/125 g H_2O, then to moles sugar/g H_2O, then to moles sugar/kg H_2O. This is accomplished as follows:

$$\frac{17.1\ g\ sugar}{125\ g\ H_2O} \times \frac{mole}{342\ g} \times \frac{1000\ g}{kg} = \frac{0.400\ mole\ sugar}{kg\ H_2O} \quad or \quad 0.400\ m$$

11. Solvents are selective. In general, the more nearly solutes and solvents are alike structurally the more rapidly solution will occur. It is also true, in a very general sense, that the *possibility* of solvent action is increased by a similarity in the composition and structure of substances. Chemists believe that the distribution of electronic forces helps to explain why solvents are selective; that is, why they will dissolve some substances readily, and others only to a negligible extent.

The water molecule has been described as a polar structure with a distinct negative region (the oxygen atom) and a distinct positive region (the hydrogen atoms). The water molecule is frequently referred to as the *water dipole*. When a molecule contains *unsymmetrically distributed* polar covalent bonds, it has dipole characteristics (a negative region and a positive region) and is said to be polar.

The carbon tetrachloride molecule, CCl_4, contains four polar covalent bonds. However, these are *symmetrically* distributed. Due to the regular tetrahedral structure, the molecule is nonpolar. Gasoline-type hydrocarbons, while unsymmetrical in bond distribution, are practically nonpolar since the electronegativity difference between the hydrogen and carbon atoms is small.

If we apply the rough rule that *like dissolves like* to these typical solvents we would expect water to dissolve polar-type substances and carbon tetrachloride to dissolve nonpolar-type substances. Polar solute molecules and charged ions of crystals are held together by strong attractive forces. They are more likely to be attracted away from the solid structure by polar water molecules than by nonpolar solvents. Thus many ionic crystalline salts and molecular solids like table salt and sugar are readily dissolved by water. Many organic compounds, such as oils and greases, which are insoluble in water, are readily dissolved by nonpolar carbon tetrachloride.

Ethyl alcohol, C_2H_5OH, is typical of a group of solvents which dissolve both polar and nonpolar substances.

$$\begin{array}{c} \mathbf{H}\quad \mathbf{H} \\ \overset{\cdot\times}{}\;\overset{\cdot\times}{}\;\overset{\circ\circ}{} \\ \mathbf{H}\overset{\times}{.}\mathbf{C}:\mathbf{C}\overset{\circ}{.}\mathbf{O}\overset{\circ}{\times}\mathbf{H} \\ \overset{\times\cdot}{}\;\overset{\times\cdot}{}\;\overset{\circ\circ}{} \\ \mathbf{H}\quad \mathbf{H} \end{array}$$

There are five essentially nonpolar carbon-hydrogen bonds and one carbon-carbon bond which is completely nonpolar. The carbon-oxygen bond and the hydrogen-oxygen bond are polar. The

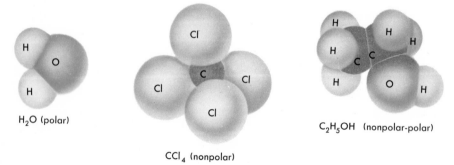

H_2O (polar) CCl_4 (nonpolar) C_2H_5OH (nonpolar-polar)

12-7   Molecular diagrams of three common solvents. Differences in molecular structure may help to explain why they are selective.

12-8 A possible mechanism of the solution process.

presence of distinct polar and nonpolar regions may account for the fact that alcohol is a good solvent for some polar and some nonpolar substances.

12. Solvation. The actual manner in which substances enter into solution is not fully understood by chemists. However, some of the aspects of the solution process are fairly well understood. They may be examined by referring again to a sugar crystal placed in a beaker of water.

The crystal of sugar is a regular lattice structure of sugar molecules held together by the attractive forces acting between the molecules themselves. These are van der Waals attractions. Energy is required to remove a sugar molecule from the crystal in order for it to go into solution. Similarly, there is some attraction between the water molecules due to the existence of hydrogen bonds. (See Section 13.) Energy is required to overcome these attractive forces to make room for the sugar molecule among the water molecules.

An attractive force also exists between unlike molecules, its magnitude depend-ing on the nature of the molecules them-selves. Water molecules are attracted to the surface molecules of the sugar crystal and energy is released. Thus, both energy-acquiring and energy-yielding activities occur in the solution process. If the net re-sult is exothermic, the temperature of the solution is raised. If the net result is endo-thermic, as in the case of the sugar-water solution, the temperature of the solution is lowered. In either case, with a solid dis-solving, the entropy of the system increases.

We may think of solution being aided by the attraction between solute and sol-vent. The movements of solvent molecules are random. As they cluster about the sur-face molecules of the solute crystal, enough energy may be released to enable them to carry off solute molecules. This process, arising from the attraction between un-like molecules of solute and solvent, is known as *solvation*. Where water is the sol-vent, the solvation process is known more specifically as *hydration*. The solute mole-cule which leaves the crystal, associated with its cluster of solvent molecules, is said to be *solvated*. Where water molecules compose the solvent cluster, the solute molecule is said to be *hydrated*.

13. Hydrogen bonds and the prop-erties of solvents. An electronegative atom is one which has a great tendency to attract electrons. Hydrogen forms dis-tinctly polar covalent bonds with highly electronegative elements such as fluorine, oxygen, chlorine, and nitrogen. The hy-drogen end of such a bond is unique in that it consists essentially of an exposed proton. In all other elements (except hy-drogen) which tend to lose electrons, the atom kernel has an electronic field that tends to repel the highly electronegative regions of other particles. The hydrogen end of a polar bond, however, attracts the relatively negative atoms of other mole-cules with enough force to be recognized as a loose chemical bond. This is known as the **hydrogen bond.** By far the most common hydrogen bonds involve oxygen, although those with fluorine are generally stronger.

Such properties of water as the abnormally high boiling and melting points may be attributed in part to the presence of hydrogen bonds between molecules. The formation of hydrogen bonds between solvent and solute increases the solubility of the solute. Hydrogen bond formation between water and ethyl alcohol may partially explain their complete miscibility.

14. Freezing and boiling points of solutions. In the preceding sections we have examined in some detail the nature of the solution process. Now let us see some of the ways the addition of solute affects the properties of the solvent.

Vapor pressure experiments show that, at any temperature, the vapor pressure of a pure solvent is higher than that of the solvent which contains dissolved solute. The vapor pressure of a liquid can be

looked upon as a measure of the *escaping tendency* of the liquid molecules. Thus, the presence of solute particles in solution lowers the escaping tendency of the solvent molecules. This seems to be a reasonable effect if we think of the solute particles in solution as reducing the concentration of solvent molecules.

Figure 12-10 shows plots of vapor pressure of solvent as a function of temperature for a pure solvent, a dilute solution of molal concentration X, and a dilute solution of molal concentration 2X. Observe that, at any given temperature, the *reduction* in vapor pressure of solvent is proportional to the concentration of solute particles. This reduction in solvent vapor pressure has the effect of extending the liquid range of the solution to both higher and lower temperatures than that of the pure solvent. What can we infer from this concerning the boiling points and freezing points of solution?

Salt water freezes at a lower temperature than fresh water. Sea water is a dilute

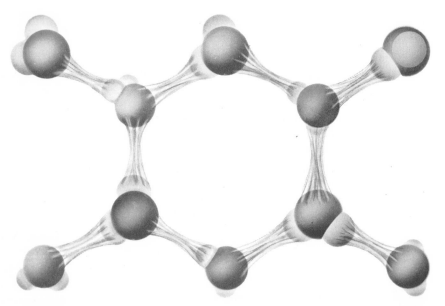

12-9   Hydrogen bond formations in an ice crystal.

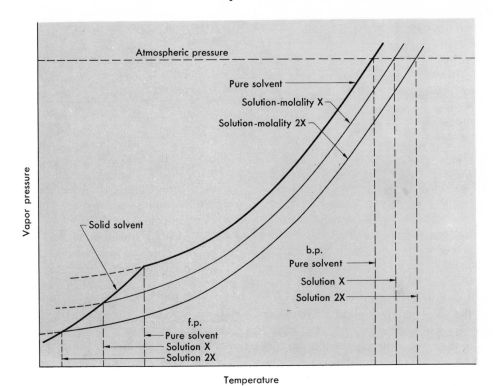

12-10 Vapor pressure of solvent as a function of temperature plotted for a pure solvent and dilute solutions of molalities X and 2X. Freezing-point depressions and boiling-point elevations are shown to be proportional to the molal concentrations of the solutions.

solution of common salt, NaCl, and many other minerals. When a dilute solution is cooled enough for freezing to occur, the crystals produced are those of the *pure solvent* itself, not of the solution. In general, *solutes lower the freezing point of the solvent in which they are dissolved.* We make use of this fact when we add alcohol, ethylene glycol, or other soluble compounds to the water of an automobile radiator during the winter months.

Francois Râoult (rah-*oo*) (1830–1901), a French chemist, found that a one-molal (1-*m*) solution of alcohol in water has a freezing point of −1.86° C. Later investigations revealed that 1-molal solutions of all nonelectrolytes in water freeze at this same temperature. The difference between this temperature and the normal freezing

point of water, 0° C, is 1.86 C°; this temperature interval is called the *molal freezing-point depression of water.*

Experiments with different molalities proved that *the lowering of the freezing point is proportional to the molecular concentration of the solute.* Solvents other than water have their own characteristic molal-freezing point depressions.

The boiling point of a solution is higher than that of the pure solvent, provided the solute is not a volatile substance. Experiments have shown that, in dilute solutions of nonvolatile nonelectrolytes, *the elevation of the boiling point is proportional to the molecular concentration of the solute.* Molal solutions of nonelectrolytes in water raise the boiling point 0.52 C°. That is, the solution boils at 100.52° C at 760 mm pres-

MOLAL BOILING–POINT ELEVATIONS AND FREEZING–POINT DEPRESSIONS

Solvent	Normal b.p. °C	Molal b.p. elevation C°	Normal f.p. °C	Molal f.p. depression C°
water	100	0.52	0	1.86
benzene	80.2	2.53	5.4	4.90
ethanol	78.3	1.22	—	—
ether	34.4	2.02	—	—
phenol	182	3.56	41	7.4

sure. Thus 0.52 C° (100.52° C − 100° C) is the *molal boiling-point elevation of water.*

The freezing points and boiling points of solutions of electrolytes are altered in an abnormal manner. Such solutes are not molecular and do not conform to the generalization about molecular substances just described.

15. Molecular weights of solutes. We have applied Avogadro's Principle to determine the molecular weights of gases and volatile liquids by the molar-volume method. Now we shall see how molecular weights can be determined for those substances which cannot be vaporized without decomposition, *but which are soluble in water or some other common solvent.* Of course such solutes must form molecular solutions and must not react with the solvent.

In the previous section it was stated that the freezing-point depression and the boiling-point elevation depend on the relative number of solute molecules mixed with a definite number of solvent molecules, rather than upon the nature of the solute. One-molal solutions of all non-electrolytes in water freeze at −1.86° C and, if the solute is nonvolatile, boil at 100.52° C at standard pressure. Knowing this we have a method of determining the molecular weights of such substances. The freezing point depression is more frequently used in determining molecular weights.

Suppose a known mass of nonelectrolyte is dissolved in a known mass of water and the freezing point of this solution is deter-

mined experimentally. Knowing the concentration of the solution and observing its freezing-point depression, we may readily calculate the mass of this solute (its g-mol wt) which must be dissolved in a kilogram of water to give the molal freezing-point depression, 1.86 C°.

$$\frac{\text{g solute/kg } H_2O}{\text{obs. depr., } C°} = \frac{\text{g-mol wt solute/kg } H_2O}{1.86 \; C°}$$

Solving for g-mol wt solute:

$$\frac{1 \text{ g-mol wt solute} \times \text{obs. depr., } C°}{\text{kg } H_2O} = \frac{\text{g solute} \times 1.86 \; C°}{\text{kg } H_2O}$$

$$\text{g-mol wt solute} = \frac{\text{g solute} \times 1.86 \; C°}{\text{obs. depr., } C°}$$

Suppose 5.00 g of a substance dissolved in 100.0 g of water lowers the freezing point of the water 0.370 C°. *Remember that the mass of solute dissolved in 1 kg of water, which lowers the freezing point 1.86 C°, is a mole of the solute and is numerically equal to the molecular weight.* Then 50.0 g of this solute dissolved in 1 kg of water will lower the freezing point 0.370 C°. From the above expression, on substituting the problem data,

$$\text{g-mol wt solute} = 50.0 \text{ g} \times \frac{1.86 \; C°}{0.370 \; C°}$$

$$\text{g-mol wt solute} = 250. \text{ g}$$

Therefore,

mol wt solute = 250.

Molecular weights may be calculated from the boiling-point elevation in the same manner, remembering that the molal boiling-point elevation of water is

0.52 C°. Solvents other than water may be used in molecular weight determinations for substances not soluble in water. Each solvent has its own characteristic molal freezing-point depression and molal boiling-point elevation which would be used instead of the values used for water.

REVIEW OUTLINE

Nature of solutions
    Solute (1)
    Solvent (1)
    Nonelectrolyte (1)
    Types of solutions (2)

Solution equilibrium
    Saturated solution (3)
    Pressure and solubility (4)
    Henry's Law (4)
    Temperature and solubility (5)

Dissolving mechanisms
    Dissolving actions that require energy (6)
    Dissolving actions that yield energy (6)
    Net actions that are exothermic (6)
    The role of entropy (6)

Heat of solution
    Meaning of positive values (7)
    Meaning of negative values (7)
    Heat of solution—change in solubility with temperature relationship (7)
    Le Chatelier Principle explanation (7)
    Increasing the rate of dissolving (8)
    Dilute and concentrated solutions (9)

Concentration of solution
    Molality (10)
    Selectivity of solvents (11)
    Solvation and hydration (12)
    The hydrogen bond (13)
    Molal freezing-point depression (14)
    Molal boiling-point elevation (14)
    Determination of molecular weights (15)

QUESTIONS

Group A

1. List, by name, five common solvents.
2. Why are the terms *dilute* and *concentrated* not entirely satisfactory as applied to solutions?
3. (*a*) Name the nine different types of solutions possible. (*b*) Which type is the most common?
4. Why does carbonated water effervesce when it is drawn from the soda fountain?
5. What action limits the amount of a solute which can dissolve in a given quantity of solvent under fixed conditions?
6. Explain the difference between *dissolve* and *melt*.
7. What is the influence of pressure on the solubility of: (*a*) a gas in a liquid; (*b*) a solid in a liquid?
8. What is the influence of temperature on the solubility of: (*a*) a gas in a liquid; (*b*) a solid in a liquid?
9. (*a*) What is the difference between *miscible* and *immiscible*? (*b*) Give an example of each.
10. What is the distinguishing characteristic of *polar* molecules?
11. Alcohol is a nonelectrolyte and is soluble in water, yet a molal solution of alcohol in water does not give the molal boiling-point elevation of water. Explain.
12. Explain the expression *saturated solution* in terms of solution equilibrium.

Group B

13. (*a*) What determines the amount of oxygen which remains dissolved in water which is at constant temperature and in contact with the atmosphere? (*b*) Explain what would happen if the oxygen were removed from the air above the water.
14. Suppose you wished to make a concentrated solution of copper(II) sulfate in water. How would you hasten the solution process?
15. The carbon tetrachloride molecule contains four polar covalent bonds yet the molecule as a whole is nonpolar. Explain.
16. How may we explain the fact that alcohol is a good solvent for both water and ether?
17. Why do caps sometimes blow off the tops of ginger ale bottles when they are exposed to direct sunlight for some time?
18. Why is cold water more appropriate than hot water for making a saturated solution of calcium hydroxide?
19. How are the solubility curves like those in Fig. 12-4 constructed?
20. Liquid methanol, CH_3OH, and water are miscible in all proportions. When 1 mole of CH_3OH (solute) is mixed with 10 moles of H_2O (solvent), the heat of solution is found to be -1.43 kcal. (*a*) Is the formation of solution accompanied by an increase or decrease in entropy? (State the argument upon which your answer is based.) (*b*) Does the change in entropy favor the separate components or the solution? (*c*) Is the dissolving process endothermic or exo-

thermic? Justify your answer. (*d*) Does the energy change as indicated by the sign of the heat of solution favor the separate components or the solution? (*e*) Are your previous answers consistent with the fact that methanol and water are freely miscible? Explain.

PROBLEMS

1. A solution consists of 60.0 g of cane sugar, $C_{12}H_{22}O_{11}$, in 150.0 g of water. What is the freezing point of the water?
2. What is the boiling point of the solution described in Problem 1?
3. What is the freezing point of 250 g of water containing 11.25 g of a non-electrolyte which has a molecular weight of 180?
4. Calculate: (*a*) the freezing point, (*b*) the boiling point of water in which 50.0 g of $C_{12}H_{22}O_{11}$ is dissolved per 100.0 g of water.
5. The analysis of a compound shows: carbon, 32.0%; hydrogen, 4.0%; oxygen, 64.0%. Fifteen grams of the compound added to 1000. g of water lowered the freezing point of the water 0.186 C°. (*a*) Find its empirical formula. (*b*) What is its molecular weight? (*c*) What is its molecular formula?
6. A compound contains: carbon, 40.00%; hydrogen, 6.67%; oxygen, 53.33%. Nine grams of the compound dissolved in 500. g of water raised the boiling point of the water 0.052 C°. (*a*) Find its empirical formula. (*b*) Find its molecular weight. (*c*) What is its molecular formula?
7. The analysis of a compound shows: carbon, 30.4%; hydrogen, 1.69%; bromine, 68%. The substance is soluble in benzene and 10.0 g of it lowers the freezing point of 100. g of benzene 2.17 C°. The normal freezing point of benzene is 5.48° C, and the molal freezing-point depression is 5.12 C°. (*a*) Find its empirical formula. (*b*) Determine its molecular weight. (*c*) What is its molecular formula?

Chapter Thirteen

IONIZATION

1. Conductivity of solutions. We have observed that solutions of electrovalent and covalent compounds may have different properties, due to differences in the chemical nature of electrovalent and covalent solutes. Electrovalent compounds are ionic, and their water solutions conduct electricity.

The conductivity of a solution may be tested by the use of the apparatus shown in Fig. 13-1. An incandescent lamp is connected in series with a switch and a pair of platinum electrodes which can be dipped into the test solution. A battery, or some other power supply, having a voltage rating similar to that of the lamp serves as the source of current. If the liquid under test is a *conductor of electricity*, the lamp filament glows when the switch is closed.

If pure water is used in the beaker, the filament does not glow. Pure water is (for all practical purposes) a *nonconductor*. Water solutions of such covalent substances as sugar, alcohol, and glycerin do not conduct electricity. These solutes are *nonelectrolytes*.

Solutions of electrovalent substances, such as sodium chloride, copper(II) sulfate, and potassium nitrate, are *conductors*. These solutes are *electrolytes*. Hydrogen chloride is an example of a covalent compound which, in water solution, conducts an electric current. Such substances are also called electrolytes.

2. The effect of electrolytes on the freezing point. One mole of a *nonelectrolyte* dissolved in 1 kg of water lowers the freezing point of the water 1.86 C°. One-molal solutions of *electrolytes* have a somewhat greater influence on the freezing point. For example, a one-molal solution of sodium chloride in water lowers the freezing point *nearly twice* as much as a one-molal solution of sugar. A one-molal solution of potassium sulfate in water lowers the freezing point *nearly three times* as much as a one-molal solution of sugar. In general, *electrolytes in water solutions lower the freezing point nearly 2, or 3, or more times*

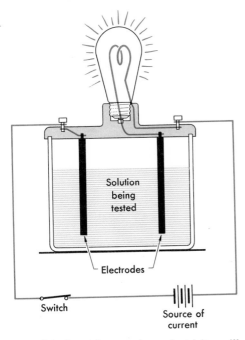

13-1 Solutions that conduct electricity will enable the lamp to glow when the switch is closed.

as much as nonelectrolytes in water solutions of the same molality.

3. The effect of electrolytes on the boiling point. One mole of sugar dissolved in 1 kg of water raises the boiling point of the water 0.52 C°. One-molal solutions of electrolytes have a greater effect on the boiling point of the solvent than do nonelectrolytes. Sodium chloride solutions have boiling-point elevations *almost twice* those of sugar solutions of equal molality. A one-molal solution of potassium sulfate shows *almost three times* the rise in boiling point as a one-molal solution of sugar. In general, *electrolytes in water solutions raise the boiling point nearly 2, or 3, or more times as much as nonelectrolytes in water solutions of the same molality.*

4. Behavior of electrolytes explained. Michael Faraday, an English chemist and physicist (1791–1867), first used the terms

electrolyte and *nonelectrolyte* in his experiments on the conductivity of solutions. He concluded that conducting solutions contained particles which carried electricity from one electrode to the other. Faraday called these particles *ions.* He assumed that they were produced from molecules by the electric potential difference between the electrodes. As other properties of electrolytic solutions were revealed, it became apparent that they contained ions regardless of the presence of the charged electrodes.

In 1887 the Swedish chemist Svante Arrhenius (1859–1927) published a report of his study of the behavior of solutions of electrolytes, known as the *Theory of Ionization.* Arrhenius believed that ions were produced by the *ionization* of molecules of electrolytes in water solution. He considered the ions to be electrically charged. When molecules ionized, they produced both positive ions and negative ions. The solution as a whole contained equal numbers of positive and negative charges. He considered the ionization to be complete only in very dilute solutions. In more concentrated solutions the ions were in equilibrium with *un-ionized* molecules of the solute.

For many years these assumptions formed the basis of the theory of solutions. Recently, however, some of the concepts of Arrhenius have been modified or replaced by new concepts concerning the structure of crystals and of the water molecule.

It is a great tribute to Arrhenius that his original theory of ionization served so long as the guide for the study of the properties of solutions. Present-day knowledge that the chemist has concerning the crystalline structure of electrovalent compounds was not available to him when, at the age of 28, he published his thesis on ionization.

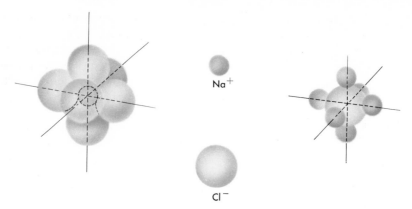

13-2   The packing of Na^+ and Cl^- ions in the NaCl crystal.

5. Modern theory of ionization. In the modern theory of ionization the solvent plays an important part in the solution process. Water is by far the most important solvent. The nature of the polar water molecule is of great importance in understanding the solution process. The theory of ionization assumes:

1. That electrolytes in solution exist in the form of ions.

2. That an ion is an atom or a group of atoms which carries an electric charge.

3. That the water solution of an electrolyte contains an equal number of positive and negative charges.

6. Structure of electrovalent compounds. Electrovalent compounds result from the actual transfer of electrons from one kind of atom to another. Consequently, electrovalent compounds are not made up of neutral atoms; they consist of atoms which have lost or gained electrons. Atoms which *gained* electrons in forming the compound have a *negative charge*. Those which *lost* electrons carry a *positive charge*. Such atoms or groups of atoms which carry an electric charge are called *ions*. In forming ions, atoms lose electric neutrality and gain chemical stability.

Ions have quite different properties from the atoms from which they were produced. This is reasonable because of the difference in structure and electronic stability resulting from the formation of ions. A neutral sodium atom with a single $3s$ electron in the third energy level is different from a sodium ion. The sodium ion does not have the $3s$ electron and thus has one excess positive charge of electricity and an octet in the second energy level. We must remember that chemical properties are determined chiefly by the outer electron arrangement of an atom or an ion. If the outer electronic structure is different, the properties will be different. The loss of the $3s$ electron gives sodium the stable electronic configuration of neon. *The charge of a simple ion is the same as its oxidation number.* In fact, the charge on the ion determines its oxidation number.

Electrovalent compounds usually exist as crystals made up in a very orderly fashion. For example, the cubic structure of crystalline sodium chloride is shown in Fig. 13-2 and Fig. 13-3. By X-ray analysis, the crystals are known to be composed of ions. Other electrovalent compounds crystallize in different patterns, each having a lattice structure which depends on the relative size and charge of the ions.

7. Hydration of ions. Suppose a few crystals of sodium chloride are dropped into a beaker of water. The water dipoles exert an attractive force on the ions forming the surfaces of the crystals. The negative oxygen end of several water dipoles exerts an attractive force on a positive sodium ion. Likewise, the positive hydrogen end of other water dipoles exerts an attractive force on a negative chloride ion. This weakens the bond by which the sodium and chloride ions are held together in the crystal lattice. They are then torn away to diffuse throughout the solution, loosely bonded to these solvent molecules. Other sodium and chloride ions are similarly attracted by solvent molecules and diffuse in the solution. In this way the salt crystal is gradually dissolved and the ions spread throughout the solution. *The separation of ions from the crystals of electrovalent compounds during the solution process is called **dissociation**.* We may represent the dissociation of sodium chloride crystals in water by use of an ionic equation:

$$Na^+Cl^- \text{ (solid)} \rightarrow$$
$$Na^+ \text{ (in water)} + Cl^- \text{ (in water)}$$

Sodium chloride is said to *dissociate* when it is dissolved in water.

We have already used the symbol (s) for (solid). Solutions in water are commonly referred to as "aqueous solutions" and (aq) is used in this sense for (in water). Thus the dissociation of the ionic salt in water is usually written in the form:

$$Na^+Cl^-(s) \rightarrow Na^+(aq) + Cl^-(aq)$$

The number of water dipoles which attach themselves to the ions of the crystal depends largely upon the size and charge of the ion. *This attachment of water molecules to ions of the solute is called **hydration**.* The ions are said to be *hydrated*. The degree of hydration of these ions is somewhat indefinite, water molecules being interchanged continuously from ion to ion and between ions and solvent. In certain cases the water dipoles are not involved in reforming the crystal structure during the evaporation of the solvent. This is true of sodium chloride whose crystals do not contain water of crystallization. On the other hand, a characteristic number of water molecules is retained by the ions in forming the crys-

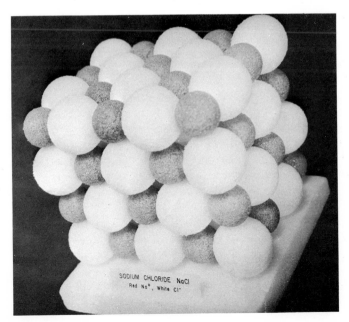

SODIUM CHLORIDE NaCl
Red Na⁺, White Cl⁻

13-3 Model of a portion of a cubic sodium chloride crystal. The lattice structure is composed of sodium ions and chloride ions. Each ion has six neighbors of opposite charge, the arrangement being repeated in each direction to the edge of the crystal. (H. Bassow, Fieldston School)

tal lattice of a salt in the hydrated form.

Extensive hydration of the solute ions ties up a substantial portion of the solvent molecules. This reduces the number of *free* water molecules in the spaces separating hydrated ions of opposite charge. Attraction between ions then becomes stronger and the crystal begins to form again. A practical limit of solubility is reached as the tendency for hydrated ions to reform the crystal lattice reaches an *equilibrium* with the tendency of ions to be hydrated.

$$Na^+Cl^-(s) \rightleftarrows Na^+(aq) + Cl^-(aq)$$

Here the tendency toward minimum energy (crystallizing) equals the tendency toward maximum entropy (dissolving).

Many ionic compounds as crystalline solids are quite soluble in water. They dissolve to give solutions with high concentrations of hydrated ions. The following examples are typical.

$$Ca^{++}Cl_2^-(s) \rightarrow Ca^{++}(aq) + 2Cl^-(aq)$$
$$K^+Cl^-(s) \rightarrow K^+(aq) + Cl^-(aq)$$
$$K^+ClO_3^-(s) \rightarrow K^+(aq) + ClO_3^-(aq)$$
$$Ag^+NO_3^-(s) \rightarrow Ag^+(aq) + NO_3^-(aq)$$

Ionic compounds of very slight solubility in water do show measurable dissociation tendencies. Low concentrations of aqueous ions are present in their water solutions. Silver chloride, AgCl, is such a substance. Its dissociation equation is

$$Ag^+Cl^-(s) \rightarrow Ag^+(aq) + Cl^-(aq)$$

Observe that both KCl and AgNO₃ have been described as very soluble ionic compounds. Their aqueous solutions consist of hydrated ions which can be quite concentrated, $K^+(aq)$ and $Cl^-(aq)$ ions in one case and $Ag^+(aq)$ and $NO_3^-(aq)$ ions in the other. Yet AgCl is only very slightly soluble in water. This means that only very low concentrations of $Ag^+(aq)$ and $Cl^-(aq)$ ions can be present in the water solution.

Suppose we mix fairly concentrated solutions of KCl and AgNO₃. In a single solution environment we will have the four ionic species: $K^+(aq)$, $Cl^-(aq)$, $Ag^+(aq)$, and $NO_3^-(aq)$. The concentrations of $Ag^+(aq)$ and $Cl^-(aq)$ ions will greatly exceed the solubility of AgCl. Those ions in

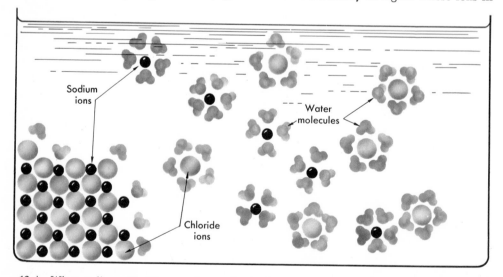

13-4   When sodium chloride crystals are dissolved in water, the polar water molecules exert attracting forces which weaken the ionic bonds. The process of solution occurs as the ions of sodium and chloride become hydrated.

excess will separate from the solution as a *precipitate* of solid AgCl. *The separation of a solid from a solution is called **precipitation**.*

The empirical equation for this reaction can be written as follows:

KCl + AgNO₃ → KNO₃ + AgCl ↓

Since KCl, AgNO₃, and KNO₃ are all quite soluble in water, only their aqueous ions are present in the solution environment. A more useful form of the equation would thus be

$$K^+(aq)+Cl^-(aq)+Ag^+(aq)+NO_3^-(aq)$$
$$\rightarrow K^+(aq)+NO_3^-(aq)+AgCl(s)$$

In this form, the equation shows clearly that the $K^+(aq)$ and $NO_3^-(aq)$ ions take no part in the action. Thus they are called *spectator ions.* By eliminating these spectator ions and retaining only the reacting species, the chemical action is shown more simply by the following net ionic equation:

$$Ag^+(aq) + Cl^-(aq) \rightarrow AgCl(s)$$

Unless there is some reason to write the complete empirical equation or the complete ionic equation, the balanced chemical equation may show only the species actually participating in a reaction.

Ionic compounds can act as conductors of electricity in another way. Since they consist of ions, any effect which reduces sufficiently the mutual attraction between the ions enables them to conduct electricity. We have seen how water does this. Heating produces the same effect. If an electrovalent compound is heated until it melts, or *fuses*, the ions become mobile and conduct an electric current through the molten material. Some solids, silver nitrate and potassium chlorate for example, melt at fairly low temperatures. The electric conductivity of such fused salts can be easily demonstrated in the

laboratory. Ionic compounds such as sodium chloride must be heated to a high temperature before they melt, but when melted will conduct electricity.

8. Some covalent compounds ionize. Covalent bonds are formed by the sharing of electrons by two atoms. The shared electrons revolve about both atoms joined by the covalent bond. If one of the atoms is highly electronegative, the valence electrons may be thought of as spending more time revolving about this atom. In this way, one end of the covalent molecule tends to be more negative and the other end more positive. This type of molecule is said to be a polar molecule. How strongly polar it is depends on the electronegativity difference between the two atoms forming the covalent linkage.

The covalent bond is generally a strong chemical bond. However, when polar molecules are dissolved in water, the water dipoles may weaken the bonds enough to pull the molecule apart. *Thus the portions of the polar solute molecule become hydrated as ions.* The ions *did not exist* in the undissolved solute, but were formed by the action of the solvent. This process is *ionization.*

Hydrogen chloride, in the liquid state, does not conduct electricity. The hydrogen and chlorine atoms are joined by a covalent bond, but the more highly electronegative chlorine attracts the electrons forming the covalent bond. Hence, the chlorine end of the molecule tends to be negative, while the hydrogen end tends to be positive. The result is a polar molecule.

Hydrogen chloride dissolved in water does, however, conduct an electric current indicating that ions have been formed in the solution. Because a solution of hydrogen chloride in a nonpolar solvent does not conduct electricity, we may conclude that the water dipoles play a part in this ionization process.

Arrhenius believed that the ionization

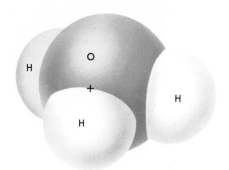

13-5 A model of the hydronium ion, H_3O^+.

of HCl involved simply the separation of the solute molecule into hydrogen ions and chloride ions on entering the solution. Today, chemists recognize that single hydrogen ions, actually protons, do not exist *free* in a water solution. They do, however, show a strong tendency to become hydrated. Thus the solvent plays a definite part in the separation of protons from the solute molecules, as shown in the equation

$$HCl(g) + H_2O(l) \rightarrow H_3O^+(aq) + Cl^-(aq)$$

If the physical states of the reactants and products are of no concern, the equation may be written more simply as

$$HCl + H_2O \rightarrow H_3O^+ + Cl^-$$

The H_3O^+ ion is a hydrated proton ($H^+ \cdot H_2O$) *and is known as the* **hydronium ion.** Because of the ionization, a solution of hydrogen chloride in water has decidedly different properties from hydrogen chloride gas. As a consequence, the solution is given the name *hydrochloric acid.*

Aluminum chloride, Al_2Cl_6 (usually represented by the empirical formula $AlCl_3$), is a nonconductor in the liquid state. In water solution, however, it is a good conductor. It must, therefore, ionize during the solution process. We may represent the ionization as in the case of hydrogen chloride:

$$Al_2Cl_6 + 12H_2O \rightarrow 2Al(H_2O)_6^{+++} + 6Cl^-$$

or more simply using the empirical formula

$$AlCl_3 + 6H_2O \rightarrow Al(H_2O)_6^{+++} + 3Cl^-$$

Other hydrated aluminum ions are probably formed at the same time.

9. Strength of electrolytes. The strength of an electrolyte is determined by the concentration of its ions in solution. Electrovalent compounds are ionic as crystalline solids. Their solutions are therefore completely ionized. Hydrogen chloride has a strong tendency to ionize in water solution. Even at ordinary dilutions, it is considered to be completely ionized. Such substances are said to be *strong electrolytes.* Their water solutions conduct electricity exceedingly well.

A water solution of acetic acid, $HC_2H_3O_2$, is a poor conductor. The fact that the solution conducts at all tells us that some ionization has occurred. This is shown in the reversible reaction

$$HC_2H_3O_2 + H_2O \rightleftharpoons H_3O^+ + C_2H_3O_2^-$$

We must assume that the ion concentration is low. Acetic acid molecules show only a slight tendency to hydrate as ions. Such substances are said to be *weak electrolytes.* Solutions of weak electrolytes are largely molecular.

We must be careful to avoid confusing the terms strong and weak with the terms dilute and concentrated. *Strong* and *weak* refer to the *degree of ionization. Dilute* and *concentrated* refer to the *amount of solute dissolved in a solvent.*

10. Ionization of water. Water is a polar covalent compound. Probably because of the influence of these polar molecules on each other, water ionizes to the extent of about two molecules in a billion. This low concentration of ions, however,

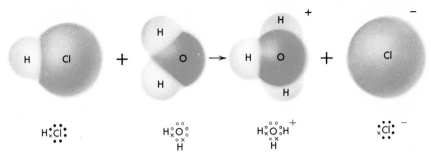

13-6 The polar hydrogen chloride molecule ionizes in water solution to form the hydronium ion and the chloride ion.

is very important in chemistry as will be shown in Chapter 15. Such slight ionization may be neglected when dealing with substances such as hydrogen chloride which ionize completely, but must be taken into consideration when dealing with very weak electrolytes.

The ionization of water probably begins with the formation of a hydrogen bond between two water molecules. Under the right conditions this bond may be stronger than the normal covalent bond of the molecule. The result of such a chance situation would be the formation of a hydrated proton and a hydroxide ion according to the reaction:

$$H_2O + H_2O \rightleftarrows H_3O^+ + OH^-$$

Chemically the *hydronium ion*, H_3O^+, acts just like a hydrogen ion H^+ or proton. In any reaction involving the hydronium ion the water of hydration is always left behind. Thus, whenever the hydrogen ion H^+ is indicated in connection with its water solution, *it is understood that this ion exists in the hydrated form,* H_3O^+.

11. Substances that do not ionize. We have seen that some substances do not conduct an electric current either as a pure substance, or in water solution. Many covalent compounds do not show the polar nature that characterizes the hydrogen chloride molecule. The attractive force of each of the atoms for the electrons forming the covalent bond may be about the same. The valence electrons are thus almost equally shared, and little separation of electric charge occurs. Such molecules with *symmetrical electronic fields* are not acted on by water dipoles to produce ions. Consequently, these substances are nonelectrolytes.

13-7 The formation of a hydrogen bond between two water dipoles may be an intermediate step in the ionization of water.

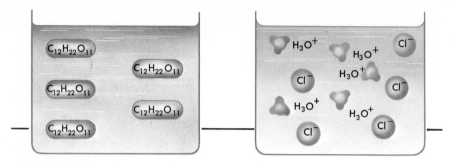

13-8 Five sugar molecules produce only five particles in solution. Five hydrogen chloride molecules, on the other hand, produce ten particles when dissolved in water.

Carbon tetrachloride is a covalent compound with four polar bonds symmetrically distributed. The structure as a whole is nonpolar, and it is a nonelectrolyte. Furthermore, it is not acted on by water molecules because of the dissimilar nature of their electronic fields.

12. Effects of electrolytes on the freezing and boiling points. Molal solutions have a definite solute particle-to-solvent molecule ratio. The lowering of the freezing point of a solvent by a solute is directly proportional to the number of particles of solute present. The same reasoning applies to the elevation of the boiling point of a solvent by a solute. How, then, do we explain why one mole of hydrogen chloride dissolved in 1 kg of water lowers the freezing point more than one mole of sugar does? The abnormal lowering is caused by the separation of each molecule of hydrogen chloride which ionizes into two particles.

Suppose that in a concentrated solution, 90 out of every 100 molecules ionize. Then, for every 100 molecules in solution, there are formed 190 particles (180 ions and 10 un-ionized molecules). Such a solution would therefore have its freezing point lowered 1.9 (190 ÷ 100) times as much as that of the solution of a solute which does not ionize.

Suppose 100% of the hydrogen chloride molecules were ionized, as in a more dilute solution. We would then expect the lowering of the freezing point to be double that caused by the solute in a solution of a nonelectrolyte having the same molality.

The following equation shows the complete ionization of sulfuric acid in very dilute solutions.

$$H_2SO_4 + 2H_2O \rightarrow 2H_3O^+ + SO_4^=$$

Every molecule of sulfuric acid which ionizes completely forms *three ions*. Two are hydronium ions which have one positive charge each; one is a sulfate ion with two negative charges. A solution of sulfuric acid of a given molality should, therefore, lower the freezing point of its solvent *three times* as much as a solution of a nonelectrolyte of the same molality.

Careful experiments show this supposition to be true for very dilute solutions, in which the apparent degree of ionization reaches 100%. Under these circumstances the ionization theory is in accord with the facts. Of course, the reason for the different rise in the boiling point caused by electrolytes in solution is that ionization increases the number of particles present in the solution.

Now let us consider a solution of an ionic substance such as calcium chloride in water. The dissociation equation is

$$Ca^{++}Cl_2^-(s) \rightarrow Ca^{++}(aq) + 2Cl^-(aq)$$

We have seen that a mole of a nonelectrolyte such as sugar provides one mole, the Avogadro number, of solute particles when dissolved in water. However, one mole of $CaCl_2$ dissociates to provide, altogether, three times the Avogadro number of solute particles in solution. We might expect a $CaCl_2$ solution of a given molality to produce three times the freezing-point lowering as that of a nonelectrolyte having the same molality. Experiments do not bear this out except for very dilute solutions.

13. The degree of ionization. The larger the number of ions in a given volume of a solution, the better it conducts electricity. This suggests one way of determining the concentration of ions in a solution. It is also possible to find the degree of ionization by measuring the lowering of the freezing point by an ionized solute in a measured amount of solvent. If a one-molal solution of an electrolyte such as sodium chloride were to freeze at $-3.72°$ C $[0° - (2 \times 1.86$ C$°)]$, we could assume the solute to be 100% ionized.

Actual measurements, however, give only an *apparent degree of ionization*. We have seen that electrovalent compounds, by the nature of their structure, must be 100% ionized in solution. Experimental results give a degree of ionization somewhat less than 100%. We may explain this discrepancy by the attraction between ions of opposite charge, especially in concentrated solutions.

Charged ions, when close together in solution, tend to interfere with each other's activities. They may tend to act as a group rather than as individual hydrated ions. In this way the *apparent* number of ions may be less than the actual number. The freezing and boiling points will be influenced accordingly.

It may be that there are not enough water molecules to hydrate all the ions present. By diluting such a solution we may reduce the influence of the ions on each other and increase the apparent degree of ionization.

Water solutions of various concentrations of sodium chloride, for example, are observed to give the molal freezing-point lowerings shown in the table (page 212).

14. Ionization explains electrolysis. Electrolysis is an important method of producing chemical reactions. We have seen one example of electrolysis in the preparation of oxygen and hydrogen by

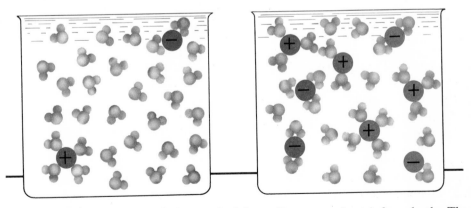

13-9 The ions in the dilute solution on the left are far apart and act independently. The activity of the ions in the solution on the right is somewhat restricted because of the concentration. Thus the apparent number of ions present may be less than the actual number.

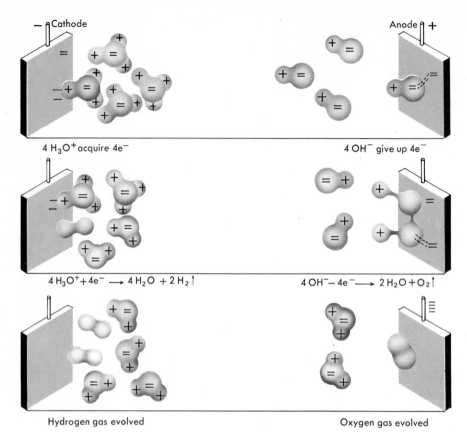

−ıCathode

Anode ı+

4 H₃O⁺ acquire 4e⁻

4 OH⁻ give up 4e⁻

$4 H_3O^+ + 4e^- \longrightarrow 4 H_2O + 2 H_2\uparrow$

$4 OH^- - 4e^- \longrightarrow 2 H_2O + O_2\uparrow$

Hydrogen gas evolved

Oxygen gas evolved

13-10   The electrolysis of water.

INFLUENCE OF CONCENTRATION ON FREEZING–POINT LOWERING

Concentration of NaCl in water solution	Freezing-point lowering/mole NaCl, in C°
0.10 *m*	3.48
0.010 *m*	3.60
0.0010 *m*	3.66
0.00010 *m*	3.72

decomposing water. Now an explanation of the chemical action during electrolysis is possible. Since water ionizes only slightly, additional ions must be supplied in order that an adequate electric current may be conducted between the electrodes.

These may come from an ionic compound such as sodium hydroxide. However, sulfuric acid is most commonly used to supply the necessary ions.

When the electrodes are connected to a source of direct current, certain changes take place on their surfaces. In the electrolysis of water containing a dilute solution of sulfuric acid, three types of ions are present. There are *hydronium ions* from the sulfuric acid, and also a few hydronium ions from the ionization of water. There are *sulfate ions* from the acid, and a few *hydroxide ions* from the ionization of water. The hydronium ions carry a single positive charge and are attracted to the negative electrode, called the **cathode.** (Ions attracted to the cathode of an electrolytic cell are commonly referred to as *cations.*) At the cathode, each hydronium ion is discharged by gaining an electron, e⁻, and forms a hydrogen atom. Two atoms combine to form a hydrogen molecule, and groups of these molecules bubble from the solution as hydrogen gas.

$$2H_3O^+ + 2e^- \rightarrow 2H_2O + H_2^0 \uparrow$$

The reaction at the positive electrode, called the **anode,** is not as simple. There are two types of negative ions in the solution, hydroxide ions and sulfate ions. Both of these are attracted to the anode. (Ions attracted to the anode of an electrolytic cell are commonly referred to as *anions.*) There are a great many more sulfate ions than hydroxide ions. Even so, the hydroxide ions give up electrons to the anode more easily than the sulfate ions; they are the ions discharged. Four hydroxide ions are required to produce a molecule of oxygen.

$$4OH^- - 4e^- \rightarrow 2H_2O + O_2^0 \uparrow$$

Observe that *twice* as many electrons are involved in liberating a molecule of oxygen as are needed to liberate a molecule of hydrogen. Consequently, twice as many hydrogen molecules are liberated as oxygen molecules. The relative volumes of the two gases liberated are *two and one, two volumes of hydrogen and one of oxygen.*

$$4H_3O^+ + 4OH^- \xrightarrow[\text{of } 4e^-]{\text{transfer}}$$
$$2H_2 \uparrow + O_2 \uparrow + 6H_2O$$

If ions other than those of sulfuric acid are used to conduct the current between the electrodes, the same electrode reactions take place in most cases, *providing very dilute solutions are used.* Under this condition, hydronium ions take electrons more readily than many other positive ions. Therefore, they are liberated at the cathode in preference to those positive ions. Even if dilute solutions of sodium hydroxide or sodium chloride are used, hydrogen is liberated directly from the water. No metallic sodium is ever liberated from such solutions. Hydroxide ions in dilute solutions of electrolytes give up electrons more readily than many other negative ions. Therefore, in accordance with the reaction described above, oxygen is liberated at the anode in preference to other negative ions, which remain in the solution.

REVIEW OUTLINE

Electrolytes (1)
    Method of testing (1)
    Comparisons with nonelectrolytes (2, 3)

Theory of Ionization (4)
    Modern concepts (5)
    Structure of electrolytes (6)

Hydration of ions (7)
    Dissociation process (7)
    Ionization process (8)
    Weak electrolytes (9)
    Ionization in water (10)
    Substances that do not ionize (11)

Behavior of electrolytes
    Effect on freezing and boiling points (2, 3, 12)
    Measuring degree of ionization (13)
    Electrolysis of water (14)

QUESTIONS

Group A

1. What is the distinction between an electrolyte and a nonelectrolyte?
2. What effect does the addition of electrolytes have on the boiling points and freezing points of solvents such as water?
3. What theory helps to explain the behavior of electrolytes?
4. What are the important assumptions of this theory?
5. What is an ion?
6. Write the equation for the ionization of water.
7. Explain why the water molecule is a polar molecule.
8. Why is it impossible to have a molecule of an electrovalent compound?
9. What is the nature of the crystal structure of an electrovalent compound?
10. How does an atom differ from an ion?
11. How may we account for the stability of an ion?
12. (*a*) How do water molecules cause an electrovalent compound to dissociate? (*b*) How may the process be reversed?
13. Why is the dissociation of electrovalent compounds 100%?
14. Melted potassium chloride conducts an electric current. Explain.

Group B

15. (*a*) Explain how the action of water on a polar compound like hydrogen chloride produces ionization. (*b*) Write the equation for the ionization of hydrogen chloride in water solution showing the part played by the water.
16. What is the distinction between dissociation and ionization?
17. Describe the solution equilibrium in a saturated solution of sodium nitrate containing an excess of the crystals.
18. (*a*) What are symmetrical covalent molecules? (*b*) Why don't they ionize?
19. Explain the abnormal freezing point lowering and boiling point elevation of solvents produced by electrolytes in terms of the theory of ionization.
20. (*a*) Write an equation for the dissociation of calcium chloride. (*b*) What will be the theoretical freezing point of a one-molal solution of calcium chloride in water?
21. What are two ways of measuring the apparent degree of ionization?
22. Why does the measurement of the apparent degree of ionization not coincide with the theory that electrovalent compounds are 100% dissociated in solution?
23. How does a concentrated solution of a weak electrolyte differ from a dilute solution of a strong electrolyte?
24. (*a*) Write equations for the electrode reactions during the electrolysis of water. (*b*) Why must two volumes of hydrogen be liberated for each volume of oxygen liberated?

25. When potassium nitrate is dissolved in water, the dissolving process is endothermic. (*a*) What temperature change does the solution undergo? (*b*) Which
is greater, the hydration energy or the lattice energy? (*c*) To what do you
attribute the driving force that causes the dissolving process to proceed?
26. (*a*) How is the solubility of potassium nitrate affected by warming the solution
of Question 25? (*b*) Apply the Principle of Le Chatelier to account for this
change in solubility.
27. One mole of a substance dissolved in 1 kg of water lowers the freezing point
of the water 3.60 C°. (*a*) What can you predict about the nature of the solution?
(*b*) What can you infer about the oxidation numbers of the particles of solute?

Chapter Fourteen

ACIDS, BASES, AND SALTS

ACIDS

1. Importance of acids. Compounds whose water solutions contain ions are traditionally classed as *acids*, *bases*, or *salts*. Even in ancient times acids were recognized as a separate class of chemicals. Today we encounter them, directly or indirectly, in practically all of our normal activities.

Nearly all fruits contain acids and so do many common foods. Lemons, oranges, and grapefruit contain citric acid. Apples contain malic acid. The souring of milk produces lactic acid. Rancid butter contains butyric acid. The fermentation of hard cider forms the acetic acid of vinegar. These, because of their origin and nature, are called *organic* acids. Chemists prepare large quantities of important industrial acids synthetically. Some are made by combination reactions directly from the elements. They are often manufactured from minerals and are known as *inorganic* acids, or more commonly as *mineral acids*. These substances are the *traditional acids* although the modern concept of acids (Section 4, pages 217–219) includes many substances not considered to be acids in the traditional sense.

2. Industrial acids. If a manufacturing chemist were asked to name the most important acid, he would probably say *sulfuric acid*. This is a very versatile mineral acid. The consumption of sulfuric acid is an index to the state of civilization and prosperity of a country. If a dye chemist, or one engaged in making explosives, were asked, he would tell you that *nitric acid* is important. A third important industrial acid is *hydrochloric acid*. It is used for cleaning metals before they are plated. It composes about 0.4 percent of the human gastric juice and aids in digestion of foods.

1. Sulfuric acid. This acid, which has the formula H_2SO_4, is a dense, oily liquid with a high boiling point. *Concentrated sulfuric acid* contains 95%–98% sulfuric acid, the balance being water. Its specific gravity is 1.84. Ordinary *dilute sulfuric acid* is made by adding 1 part of concentrated sulfuric acid into 6 parts of water. Other dilutions are sometimes used.

CAUTION: *The acid should be added to water slowly with stirring, but water must never be added to concentrated sulfuric acid. This causes a very violent reaction which produces steam, and spatters the concentrated acid.*

2. *Nitric acid.* This acid is a volatile liquid which has the formula HNO_3. The 100% nitric acid is too unstable for marketing, but the *concentrated nitric acid* of commerce is fairly stable. It contains 68% nitric acid dissolved in water and has a specific gravity of 1.42. A solution of pure nitric acid is colorless. It may turn brown on standing due to slight decomposition. Nitric acid may be mixed with water in any proportion. Ordinary *dilute nitric acid* is usually made by adding 1 part of nitric acid to 5 parts of water. It contains about 10% nitric acid.

3. *Hydrochloric acid.* Hydrogen chloride, HCl, is a gas which is extremely soluble in water, forming a colorless solution known as hydrochloric acid. *Concentrated hydrochloric acid* contains in water solution about 38% hydrogen chloride. Its specific gravity is nearly 1.20. Ordinary dilute hydrochloric acid is made by adding 1 part of concentrated hydrochloric acid to 4 parts of water. Such a solution contains from 6% to 8% hydrogen chloride. Hydrochloric acid may be diluted to any concentration desired.

3. Nature of acids. Arrhenius first gave the clue to the chemical nature of acids in his Theory of Ionization. He concluded that all acids ionize in water solutions to form hydrogen ions.

The three acids we have just described are essentially covalently bonded structures and have one element in common, *hydrogen.* Sulfuric and nitric acids in pure form are exceedingly poor conductors, being only very slightly ionized. Liquid hydrogen chloride, as has been stated already, is considered to be a nonconductor

of electricity. In water solution, however, each of these substances becomes strongly ionized due to the hydrating action of the water dipoles. We may represent their ionization in water solutions by the equations:

$$H_2SO_4 + H_2O \rightarrow H_3O^+ + HSO_4^-$$
$$HNO_3 + H_2O \rightarrow H_3O^+ + NO_3^-$$
$$HCl + H_2O \rightarrow H_3O^+ + Cl^-$$

The hydronium ion, H_3O^+, is common to all of these solutions. It is reasonable to assume that the acidic properties they have in common are the properties of this ion.

When sulfuric acid solutions are very dilute, the HSO_4^- ions may contribute additional H_3O^+ ions by ionizing to some degree:

$$HSO_4^- + H_2O \rightarrow H_3O^+ + SO_4^=$$

The HSO_4^- is a moderately weak acid and does not contribute much to the total hydronium ion concentration in solutions of ordinary dilution. If the ionization of H_2SO_4 were complete, the equation could be written:

$$H_2SO_4 + 2H_2O \rightarrow 2H_3O^+ + SO_4^=$$

Acids which ionize completely, or nearly so, in water solution provide a high concentration of hydronium ions. They are called *strong acids.* Sulfuric, nitric, and hydrochloric acids are strong mineral acids. Acids which furnish few hydronium ions in water solution, such as acetic and carbonic acids, are known as *weak* acids. They are only slightly ionized in water, even in solutions that are quite dilute.

4. Modern definition of acids. The hydronium ion is in reality a hydrated proton. In water solution it is considered to be in the hydrated form $H^+ \cdot H_2O$ or H_3O^+, protons combined with polar water molecules.

Chemists have found conclusive evidence of the existence of the H_3O^+ ion in hydrated crystals of perchloric acid (a very strong acid) and in concentrated solutions of strong acids. In dilute aqueous solutions of acids, however, the proton hydration may be more complete. Physical evidence such as electric and thermal conductivities suggests the formula $H^+ \cdot 4H_2O$ corresponding to the ionic species $H_9O_4^+$. A model of the $H_9O_4^+$ ion having the spatial structure of a triagonal pyramid is shown in Fig. 14-1.

Other species of the hydrated proton that have been suggested for dilute aqueous acid solutions are $H^+ \cdot 2H_2O$ and $H^+ \cdot 3H_2O$ corresponding respectively to the species $H_5O_2^+$ and $H_7O_3^+$. Chemists write formulas of this kind only when the degree of hydration is itself the subject of discussion. Otherwise, in the interest of simplicity, the hydrated proton in aqueous solutions is written in the form of the hydronium ion, H_3O^+.

We may consider that protons (hydrogen ions) will not be released by such molecules as HCl unless there are molecules or ions present which can accept them. This explains why hydrogen chloride, dissolved in a nonpolar solvent such as toluene, remains a nonconductor.

Hydrogen chloride dissolved in ammonia reacts the same way as in water.

$$HCl + H_2O \rightarrow H_3O^+ + Cl^-$$
$$HCl + NH_3 \rightarrow NH_4^+ + Cl^-$$

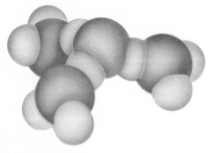

14-1 A model of the $H_9O_4^+$ ion which suggests an H_3O^+ ion with $3H_2O$ molecules attached.

The manner in which the reactions occur may be seen by using electron-dot formulas.

The proton is transferred to the ammonia structure forming the *ammonium ion* just as it transferred to the water structure forming the hydronium ion. The proton is given up by the hydrogen chloride molecule, which is said to be a *proton donor*. In the modern concept advanced by J. N. Brønsted, a Danish chemist, *an acid is simply a proton donor—a substance which gives up protons to another substance.* Thus hydrogen chloride is an acid, according to Brønsted's theory, even though it doesn't contain hydrogen ions when pure.

According to this general definition, water is an acid when gaseous ammonia is dissolved in it. Some water molecules donate protons to ammonia molecules according to the reaction:

$$NH_3 + H_2O \rightleftharpoons NH_4^+ + OH^-$$

Furthermore, in water solutions of the strong mineral acids described in Section 3, the hydronium ion, H_3O^+, becomes the acid since it is the actual proton donor in reactions involving the solutions.

This modern definition of acids is very broad. It describes the behavior of substances as a source of protons for combination with the molecules or ions of other substances. It is very useful in advanced

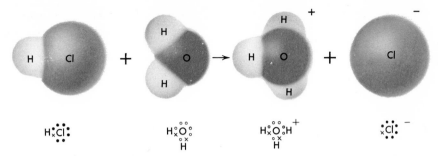

14-2 When HCl is dissolved in water, a proton is donated by the polar HCl molecule to form the hydronium ion, H_3O^+, and the chloride ion, Cl^-.

chemistry as well as in elementary chemistry. Definitions do not alter the facts of chemistry; they are useful if they help one organize the facts of chemistry. In our discussions, this broad concept of acids will be used extensively.

5. Properties of traditional acids. Most traditional acids are quite soluble in water. Other physical properties differ so widely that it is not possible to mention many general similarities. However, they have many chemical properties in common.

1. Acids contain ionizable hydrogen in covalent combination with a nonmetallic element or radical. The strength of an acid depends upon the *degree* of ionization in water solution, not upon the *amount* of hydrogen in the molecule. Perchloric acid, $HClO_4$, hydrochloric acid, HCl, and nitric acid, HNO_3, are strong acids by this rule. Each contributes one proton per molecule.

Acetic acid, $HC_2H_3O_2$, is a weak acid, ionizing slightly in water and yielding one proton per ionized molecule.

Sulfuric acid ionizes in two stages, depending on the amount of dilution, according to the ionic equations:

$$H_2SO_4 + H_2O \rightarrow H_3O^+ + HSO_4^-$$
$$HSO_4^- + H_2O \rightarrow H_3O^+ + SO_4^=$$

The first stage is completed in fairly concentrated solutions. In this form sulfuric acid can produce *acid salts*, in which the HSO_4^- ion is present. Sodium *hydrogen* sulfate, $NaHSO_4$, is an example. The second stage may be completed in sufficiently dilute solutions. Here the $SO_4^=$ ion is present. Under such conditions *normal salts* are formed. Sodium sulfate, Na_2SO_4, is an example.

The rather weak phosphoric acid ionizes in three stages.

14-3 When hydrogen chloride is dissolved in ammonia, a proton is donated by the polar HCl molecule to the NH_3 molecule to form the ammonium ion, NH_4^+, and the chloride ion, Cl^-.

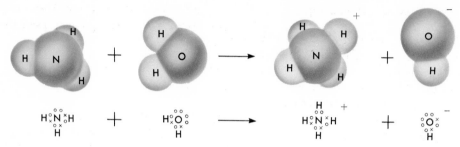

14-4 When ammonia is dissolved in water, water molecules are the proton donors and ammonia molecules are the proton acceptors.

$$H_3PO_4 + H_2O \rightarrow H_3O^+ + H_2PO_4^-$$
$$H_2PO_4^- + H_2O \rightarrow H_3O^+ + HPO_4^=$$
$$HPO_4^= + H_2O \rightarrow H_3O^+ + PO_4^\equiv$$

Only the first stage occurs in solutions of moderate concentrations producing the *dihydrogen phosphate ion*, $H_2PO_4^-$. In more dilute solutions the *monohydrogen phosphate ion*, $HPO_4^=$, is formed. In very dilute solutions appreciable concentrations of the normal *phosphate ion*, $PO_4^\equiv$, may be formed.

2. Acids furnish protons when they react with bases. Their many common properties depend on this characteristic behavior. Acids which furnish only one proton per molecule are called *monoprotic acids*. Examples are HCl, HNO_3, and $HC_2H_3O_2$. Sulfuric acid, H_2SO_4, and carbonic acid, H_2CO_3, are *diprotic*, being capable of giving two protons per molecule. Phosphoric acid, H_3PO_4, is *triprotic*.

3. Acids have a sour taste. Lemons, grapefruit, and limes are sour. These contain weak acids in solution. A solid acid tastes sour as it dissolves in the saliva forming a water solution. Most laboratory acids are very corrosive and powerful poisons. **The "taste test" should never be used in the laboratory.**

4. Acids affect indicators. If a drop of an acid solution is placed on a test strip of blue *litmus*, the *blue* color changes to *red*. Litmus is a dye extracted from certain lichens. Some other substances may be used as indicators. *Phenolphthalein* is colorless in the presence of acids. *Methyl orange* turns red in acid solutions.

5. Acids neutralize hydroxides. If solutions of an acid and a metallic hydroxide are mixed in chemically equivalent quantities, each cancels the properties of the other. This process is called *neutralization* and is an example of an ionic reaction. The products are a salt and water, the salt being recovered in crystalline form by the evaporation of water. The acid is said to neutralize the hydroxide, but it is just as accurate to say that the hydroxide neutralizes the acid.

When one mole of sodium hydroxide is treated with one mole of hydrochloric acid the empirical equation may be written:

$$HCl + NaOH \rightarrow NaCl + H_2O$$

Since both reactants and the salt product are in completely ionized form the ionic equation is more appropriate.

$$H_3O^+ + Cl^- + Na^+ + OH^- \rightarrow$$
$$Na^+ + Cl^- + 2H_2O$$

Observe that sodium ions and chloride ions remain in solution and actually play no part in the reaction. By writing the simplest ionic equation, these spectator ions are eliminated. Only those which actually participate in the primary action are shown in the net ionic equation.

$$H_3O^+ + OH^- \rightarrow 2H_2O$$

This shows that the neutralization reaction is entirely between the hydronium ion and the hydroxide ion of the soluble metallic hydroxide. In all neutralizations of very soluble hydroxides by strong acids the reaction is the same. The nonmetallic ions of the acid and the metallic ions of the hydroxide undergo no chemical change. We may prefer to write the complete equation because it shows what salt could be recovered by evaporation of the water solvent.

6. *Acids react with many metals.* They release hydrogen and form a salt. The equation for the action of sulfuric acid on zinc is typical.

$$Zn + H_2SO_4 \rightarrow ZnSO_4 + H_2 \uparrow$$

Written ionically, the equation is

$$Zn + 2H_3O^+ + SO_4^= \rightarrow$$
$$Zn^{++} + SO_4^= + H_2 \uparrow + 2H_2O$$

or simply

$$Zn + 2H_3O^+ \rightarrow Zn^{++} + H_2 \uparrow + 2H_2O$$

The salt separates as crystals of $ZnSO_4$ on evaporation of the water. Remember that in solution, such *salts* are simply solutions of hydrated ions.

7. *Acids react with oxides of metals.* They form salts and water. As an example, consider the reaction of copper(II) oxide and sulfuric acid.

$$CuO + H_2SO_4 \rightarrow CuSO_4 + H_2O$$

Written ionically,

$$CuO + 2H_3O^+ + SO_4^= \rightarrow$$
$$Cu^{++} + SO_4^= + 3H_2O$$

The net reaction is

$$CuO + 2H_3O^+ \rightarrow Cu^{++} + 3H_2O$$

8. *Acids react with carbonates.* They liberate carbon dioxide and produce a salt and water.

$$CaCO_3 + 2HCl \rightarrow CaCl_2 + H_2O + CO_2 \uparrow$$

Ionically:

$$Ca^{++}CO_3^= + 2H_3O^+ + 2Cl^- \rightarrow$$
$$Ca^{++} + 2Cl^- + 3H_2O + CO_2 \uparrow$$

Net:

$$Ca^{++}CO_3^= + 2H_3O^+ \rightarrow$$
$$Ca^{++} + 3H_2O + CO_2 \uparrow$$

6. Naming the traditional acids. Some acids are *binary* compounds, containing only *two* elements; others are *ternary* compounds, containing three elements.

1. Binary acids. Hydrogen chloride in water solution is called *hydrochloric* acid. The prefix *hydro–* shows it is a binary acid. The root *–chlor–* is derived from the element chlorine. Binary acids always have the ending *–ic*. A water solution of HBr is called *hydro-brom-ic* acid. A water solution of hydrogen sulfide, H_2S, is known as *hydro-sulfur-ic* acid.

2. Ternary acids. The formulas and names of the various oxygen acids of chlorine may be used to illustrate the general method of naming acids which contain hydrogen, oxygen, and a third element.

$HClO_4$ . . . . **per-chlor-ic acid**
$HClO_3$ . . . . **chlor-ic acid**
$HClO_2$ . . . . **chlor-ous acid**
$HClO$ . . . . **hypo-chlor-ous acid**

In all of these acids chlorine is the central element. For this reason the root *–chlor–* is used in each case. $HClO_3$ is named *chlor-ic acid*. It contains the chlorate radical and no prefix is used. The acid of chlorine which contains *more* oxygen than chloric acid is called *per-chlor-ic* acid. The chlorine acid containing *one less* oxygen atom per molecule than chloric acid is called *chlorous* acid. The acid of chlorine which contains *still less* oxygen than chlorous acid has the prefix *hypo–*, the root *–chlor–*, and the suffix *–ous*.

To use these rules for naming acids it is necessary to know the formula for one ternary oxygen acid in any series. Chloric acid is $HClO_3$, nitric acid is HNO_3, bromic acid is $HBrO_3$, sulfuric acid is H_2SO_4, and phosphoric acid is H_3PO_4.

7. Acid anhydrides. Only fluorine is more highly electronegative than oxygen. Its compounds with oxygen are fluorides rather than oxides. All other elements, except the noble gases, form oxides with oxygen. The most common oxidation state of oxygen in these compounds is -2. Oxides range structurally from ionic to covalent. The more ionic oxides involve the highly electropositive metals on the

H:O:Cl:

Hypochlorous acid

H:O:Cl:O:

Chlorous acid

H:O:Cl:O:
:O:

Chloric acid

:O:
H:O:Cl:O:
:O:

Perchloric acid

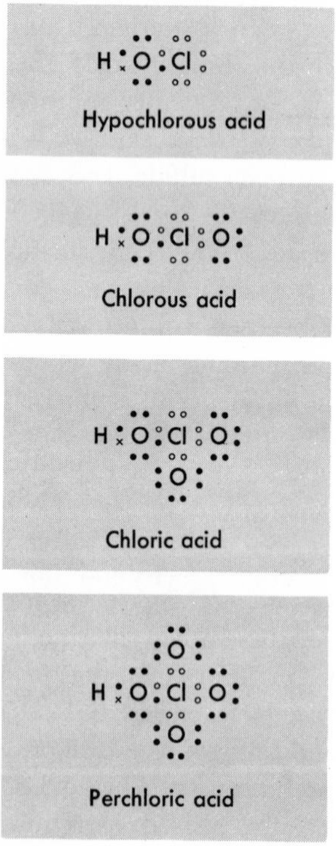

14-5 Electron-dot formulas of the four oxyacids of chlorine.

left side of the periodic table. The oxides formed with nonmetals on the right side of the periodic table are, in general, covalent molecular structures.

Many of the molecular (nonmetallic) oxides are gases at ordinary temperatures. Examples are carbon monoxide, CO, carbon dioxide, CO_2, and sulfur dioxide, SO_2. Diphosphorus pentoxide, P_4O_{10}, on the other hand, is a solid. Most nonmetallic oxides, but not all, react with water to form oxygen-containing acids called *oxyacids*.

Oxyacids are distinguished by the presence of one or more oxygen-hydrogen (OH) groups in the covalent structure. These are called *hydroxyl* groups to distinguish them from oxygen-hydrogen groups existing as OH⁻ ions, whose compounds are called *hydroxides*. The hydroxyl group is arranged in the molecule in such a manner that it may donate a proton, thus giving the molecule its acid character.

When carbon dioxide dissolves in water carbonic acid is formed in the reversible reaction

$$CO_2 + H_2O \rightleftharpoons H_2CO_3$$

Nearly all of the carbonic acid decomposes again into water and carbon dioxide as it is formed and the molecular concentration of the solute CO_2 remains high. A small portion of the H_2CO_3 molecules ionize to give the aqueous solution a very low concentration of H_3O^+ ions according to the reaction

$$H_2CO_3 + H_2O \rightleftharpoons H_3O^+ + HCO_3^-$$

The net reaction which shows the acid-producing behavior of CO_2 in aqueous solution is

$$CO_2 + 2H_2O \rightleftharpoons H_3O^+ + HCO_3^-$$

Because the carbonic acid has in reality

been *dehydrated*, carbon dioxide is called the *acid anhydride* of carbonic acid. *Oxides that react with water to form acids, or that are formed by the removal of water from acids, are known as **acid anhydrides**.*

Binary acids do not contain oxygen and do not have an anhydride form. Thus, the reaction between an acid anhydride and water cannot be considered a general method of preparing acids. However, it is an important method of preparing some oxyacids.

Sulfur dioxide is the acid anhydride of sulfurous acid.

$$SO_2 + H_2O \rightleftarrows H_2SO_3$$

Sulfur trioxide is the acid anhydride of sulfuric acid.

$$SO_3 + H_2O \rightleftarrows H_2SO_4$$

These anhydrides are important in the manufacture of sulfuric acid. Sulfuric acid, because it is cheap and has a high boiling point, is used in the production of several other acids. Hydrochloric acid is an example, although important quantities of hydrochloric acid are now being produced by direct composition from the elements hydrogen and chlorine.

Nitric acid can also be produced by the reaction of sulfuric acid with a nitrate. However, this process is not generally used commercially because it is more expensive than other processes.

BASES

8. Nature of bases. There are several substances found in almost every home that have long been called bases. Household ammonia, an ammonia-water solution, is a common cleaning agent. Lye is a commercial grade of sodium hydroxide, NaOH, used for cleaning clogged sink drains. Limewater is a solution of calcium hydroxide, $Ca(OH)_2$. Milk of magnesia is a suspension of magnesium hydroxide, $Mg(OH)_2$, in water. It is used as an antacid, a laxative, and an antidote for strong acids.

Arrhenius considered a base to be any soluble hydroxide which destroyed the properties of an acid when their solutions were mixed. We now know that the only reaction occurring in the neutralization is between hydronium ions and hydroxide ions. The nonmetal of the acid and the metal of the hydroxide remain in solution as hydrated ions.

Bases are now defined as substances which acquire protons from another substance. The hydroxide ion is the most common base. It reacts with the hydronium ion to form water. The soluble metallic hydroxides which yield hydroxide ions when dissolved in water, together with ammonia water, are still frequently referred to as bases. However, *it is the hydroxide ion which reacts as the base in the neutralization process.* Ammonia-water solutions are traditionally referred to as ammonium hydroxide. However, ammonium hydroxide as an actual molecular species probably does not exist in these solutions except through the possibility of the formation of hydrogen bonds between some NH_4^+ ions and OH^- ions. These solutions are more appropriately called ammonia-water solutions, or simply NH_3-Aq (ammonia-aqua). The most common basic solutions used in the laboratory, those of NaOH, KOH, $Ca(OH)_2$, and NH_3-Aq, are said to be *alkaline* in their behavior.

In the modern concept of Brønsted, an acid is simply a proton donor. Accordingly, *a base is a proton acceptor.* Since the OH^- ion is not the only particle that combines with protons, our general use of the term base includes other substances which accept protons.

We have stated that hydrogen chloride ionizes in water solution as a result of the hydrating action of the solvent dipoles.

$$\text{HCl} + \text{H}_2\text{O} \rightarrow \text{H}_3\text{O}^+ + \text{Cl}^-$$
$$\text{acid} \quad \text{base} \quad \text{acid} \quad \text{base}$$

Here the water molecule is the strong base, accepting protons to form the hydronium ion H_3O^+ which is a strong acid. (The relative strengths of acids and bases is discussed further in Section 12.)

In the neutralization reaction between HCl and NaOH described earlier, the H_3O^+ ion may be considered to be the acid, since it, and not the HCl molecule, is the proton donor. The OH^- ion is, of course, the proton acceptor or base.

When HCl is dissolved in liquid ammonia, the NH_3 molecule acts as the base.

$$\text{HCl} + \text{NH}_3 \rightarrow \text{NH}_4^+ + \text{Cl}^-$$
$$\text{acid} \quad \text{base} \quad \text{acid} \quad \text{base}$$

When NH_3 is dissolved in water, protons are donated by the water which, therefore, acts as an acid. Ammonia accepts protons and, therefore, is the base. A low concentration of NH_4^+ ions and OH^- ions is produced in the reversible action.

$$\text{NH}_3 + \text{H}_2\text{O} \rightleftharpoons \text{NH}_4^+ + \text{OH}^-$$
$$\text{base} \quad \text{acid} \quad \text{acid} \quad \text{base}$$

This general concept of acids and bases is quite broad, but is very useful in more advanced studies of nonaqueous solutions. In elementary chemistry, the bases we deal with most frequently are the soluble metallic hydroxides and their water solutions containing the basic hydroxide ion, OH^-.

9. Characteristics of hydroxides.

1. Hydroxides of the active metals furnish OH^- *ions in solution.* Sodium and potassium hydroxides are very soluble in water. They are electrovalent (ionic) compounds and are completely ionized in water solution.

Their solutions are *strongly basic* due to the high concentration of OH^- ions.

$$\text{Na}^+\text{OH}^- \rightarrow \text{Na}^+ + \text{OH}^-$$
$$\text{K}^+\text{OH}^- \rightarrow \text{K}^+ + \text{OH}^-$$

Calcium and strontium hydroxides are not very soluble in water. However, they too are ionic compounds. Their water solutions are completely ionized and, because of their low solubility, are *moderately basic*.

$$\text{Ca}^{++}(\text{OH}^-)_2 \rightarrow \text{Ca}^{++} + 2\text{OH}^-$$
$$\text{Sr}^{++}(\text{OH}^-)_2 \rightarrow \text{Sr}^{++} + 2\text{OH}^-$$

We can see that the strength of the base depends on the concentration of OH^- ions in solution and not on the number of hydroxide ions per formula weight of the compound.

Ammonia-water solutions are *weakly* basic due to a low concentration of OH^- ions. Ammonia, NH_3, is not a strong base and so does not acquire very many protons from water molecules when in solution. Relatively few NH_4^+ ions and OH^- ions are formed.

2. Soluble hydroxides have a bitter taste. Possibly you have tasted limewater and know that it is bitter. Soapsuds also taste bitter because of the presence of hydroxide ions. **The taste test should never be used in the laboratory.** Strongly basic solutions are very *caustic* and the accompanying metallic ions are sometimes poisonous.

3. Solutions of hydroxides feel slippery. The very soluble hydroxides, such as sodium hydroxide, attack the skin and may produce severe caustic burns. Their solutions have a soapy, slippery feeling when rubbed between the thumb and fingers.

4. Soluble hydroxides affect indicators. The basic OH^- ions in solutions of the soluble hydroxides cause *litmus* to turn from *red* to *blue*. This is just the opposite color change to that caused by H_3O^+ ions of acid solutions. In a basic solution, *phenolphthalein* turns *red*, and *methyl orange* changes to *yellow.* The insoluble hydroxides, on the other hand, seldom produce enough OH^- ions to cause these changes; they do not affect indicators.

5. *Hydroxides neutralize acids.* The neutralization of HNO_3 by KOH may be represented empirically by the equation:

$$KOH + HNO_3 \rightarrow KNO_3 + H_2O$$

Of course, ionic KOH is dissociated in water solution and exists as hydrated K^+ ions and OH^- ions.

$$K^+OH^- \rightarrow K^+ + OH^-$$

In water solution, the covalent HNO_3 is ionized and exists as hydrated protons and nitrate ions.

$$HNO_3 + H_2O \rightarrow H_3O^+ + NO_3^-$$

The complete ionic equation for this neutralization reaction may be written:

$$H_3O^+ + NO_3^- + K^+ + OH^- \rightarrow$$
$$K^+ + NO_3^- + 2H_2O$$

Removing the spectator ions, we have:

$$H_3O^+ + OH^- \rightarrow 2H_2O$$

This is the only change that takes place in the neutralization reaction. The hydrated K^+ and NO_3^- ions are joined in the form of ionic crystals of the salt, KNO_3, only upon removal of water by evaporation.

6. *Hydroxides react with the oxides of nonmetals.* They form salts and water. For example, the reactions of carbon dioxide and sodium hydroxide give the carbonate or the hydrogen carbonate ions depending on the relative quantities of reactants. Two moles of $NaOH$ per mole of CO_2 forms sodium carbonate, Na_2CO_3. One mole of $NaOH$ per mole of CO_2 forms sodium hydrogen carbonate, $NaHCO_3$.

$$CO_2 + 2NaOH \rightarrow Na_2CO_3 + H_2O$$

and

$$CO_2 + NaOH \rightarrow NaHCO_3 + H_2O$$

The net reactions are

$$CO_2 + 2OH^- \rightarrow CO_3^= + H_2O$$

and

$$CO_2 + OH^- \rightarrow HCO_3^-$$

Observe that these are essentially neutralization reactions between carbonic acid and sodium hydroxide since carbon dioxide is the acid anhydride of carbonic acid.

7. *Certain hydroxides may have either acidic or basic properties.* Hydroxide substances which are weakly basic in the presence of acids may also behave as acids in the presence of strong bases. Zinc hydroxide, $Zn(OH)_2$, reacts with hydrochloric acid to produce zinc chloride and water.

$$Zn(OH)_2 + 2HCl \rightarrow ZnCl_2 + 2H_2O$$

In the presence of a solution of sodium hydroxide it acts as an acid forming the *zincate* ion, $ZnO_2^=$.

$$Zn(OH)_2 + 2NaOH \rightarrow Na_2ZnO_2 + 2H_2O$$

We may more readily understand this behavior of $Zn(OH)_2$ if we rewrite its formula as H_2ZnO_2. Thus,

$$H_2ZnO_2 + 2NaOH \rightarrow Na_2ZnO_2 + 2H_2O$$

Such substances which may have either acidic or basic properties under certain conditions are said to be **amphiprotic.** The hydroxides of aluminum, chromium, tin, and lead are also amphiprotic.

In the modern concept of acids and bases, water is an amphiprotic substance.

When a water molecule accepts a proton from hydrogen chloride it acts as a base. On the other hand, when a water molecule donates a proton to ammonia it acts as an acid. Indeed, in the slight ionization of water, one water molecule donates a proton to another water molecule. Thus, some of the water molecules behave as an acid while others behave as a base.

$$H_2O + H_2O \rightleftarrows H_3O^+ + OH^-$$

Ammonia undergoes a similar self-ionization but to a lesser extent than water. (NH_2^- is called the amide ion.)

$$NH_3 + NH_3 \rightleftarrows NH_4^+ + NH_2^-$$

Ammonia is therefore amphiprotic.

10. Basic anhydrides. The active metals react with water to produce hydrogen gas and the corresponding hydroxide. These metallic hydroxides are ionic in structure and exist in solution as hydrated metallic and hydroxide ions.

The more dense metals form hydroxides which are practically insoluble in water. These are produced more conveniently by indirect methods using a salt and a soluble hydroxide. See Fig. 14-6.

$$Fe^{+++} + 3Cl^- + 3Na^+ + 3OH^- \rightarrow$$
$$Fe(OH)_3 \downarrow + 3Na^+ + 3Cl^-$$

As the reaction involves only the Fe^{+++} and OH^- ions, we may write the simpler net equation:

$$Fe^{+++} + 3OH^- \rightarrow Fe(OH)_3 \downarrow$$

Such precipitates vary somewhat in composition, depending on the conditions under which they are formed. The actual composition is that of a *hydrated oxide*. In the case above the precipitate is more correctly represented in the following manner:

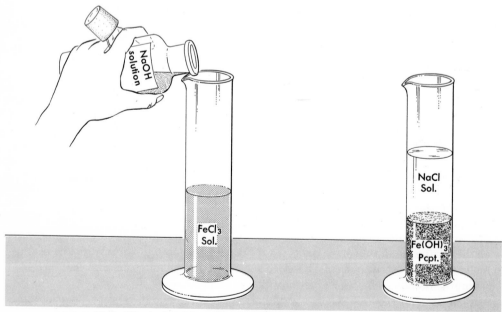

14-6   The hydroxides of heavy metals are practically insoluble.

$$Fe_2O_3 \cdot (H_2O)_n$$

where n is some small integer which varies with conditions. It is convenient in equation writing to represent such precipitates as hydroxides. Aluminum, chromium, tin, and lead also form hydrated oxides.

We stated in Section 7 that the oxides of the active metals are ionic in structure. Like other ionic substances, they are solid at room temperature. They contain the $O^=$ ion. When they are placed in water, the $O^=$ ion reacts with the water to form the basic OH^- ion.

$$O^= + H_2O \rightarrow 2OH^-$$

If the metallic hydroxide is soluble in water, the solution is basic due to the presence of OH^- ions.

Oxides of sodium, potassium, calcium, strontium, and barium react vigorously with water. You may have seen a plasterer *slaking* quicklime, CaO, by adding water to it. He was forming *slaked lime*, $Ca(OH)_2$.

$$CaO + H_2O \rightarrow Ca(OH)_2$$

Oxides which react with water to produce solutions containing the basic OH^- ions are called **basic anhydrides.** The oxides of the active metals are basic anhydrides. In contrast, acid anhydrides are oxides of nonmetals (see Section 7). They are covalent compounds which, in the solid state, have molecular crystalline structures.

11. Formulas of acids and bases. It may not be apparent from the formula of a substance whether it has either acidic or basic properties. We have observed that oxides which react with water form oxygen-hydrogen groups. In general, the oxygen-hydrogen groups formed by ionic oxides (metal oxides) are OH^- ions, their compounds are hydroxides and their solutions are basic.

Oxygen-hydrogen groups formed by molecular oxides (nonmetal oxides) are not ionic but are bonded covalently to another atom in the product molecule. These were identified as hydroxyl groups in Section 7. In aqueous solution such hydroxyl groups donate protons to give the solution acid properties, these compounds being the oxyacids.

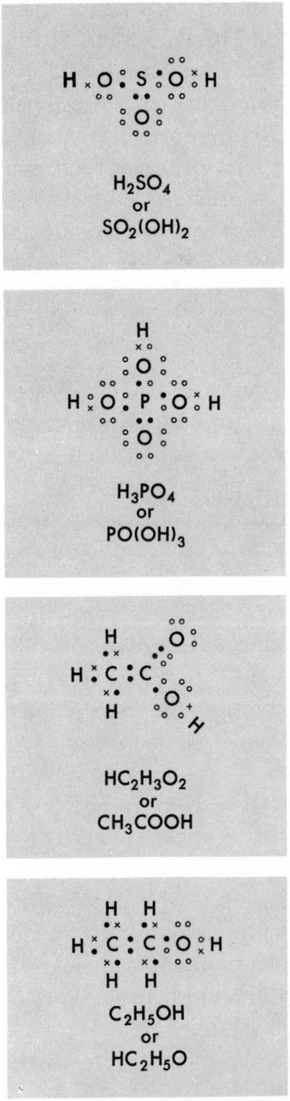

H_2SO_4
or
$SO_2(OH)_2$

H_3PO_4
or
$PO(OH)_3$

$HC_2H_3O_2$
or
CH_3COOH

C_2H_5OH
or
HC_2H_5O

14-7 Molecular formulas alone will not identify acidic or basic properties.

The electron-dot formulas of several molecular substances containing hydroxyl groups are shown in Fig. 14-7. From structural considerations their molecular formulas could be written $SO_2(OH)_2$, CH_3COOH, $PO(OH)_3$, and C_2H_5OH. However, none has basic properties characteristic of the OH^- ion in water solution. Three are oxyacids and this acidic character is shown by writing their formulas as H_2SO_4, $HC_2H_3O_2$, and H_3PO_4. Experimental evidence must establish the acidic or basic character of a substance.

12. Relative strengths of acids and bases. The Brønsted concept of acids and bases provides a broad basis for the study of *protolysis*, or proton-transfer, reactions. Any molecule or ion capable of donating a proton is considered to be an acid. Any molecule or ion that can accept the proton is a base.

When an acid (in the Brønsted sense) gives up a proton, the remainder of the acid particle becomes itself capable of accepting a proton. Therefore, it may be considered to be a base; it is called a *conjugate base*. *A conjugate base is the structure that remains after an acid has given up a proton.*

An aqueous solution of sulfuric acid contains H_3O^+ ions and HSO_4^- ions. With further dilution, the HSO_4^- ions may give up protons:

$$HSO_4^- + H_2O \rightarrow H_3O^+ + SO_4^=$$
$$\text{acid} \qquad \text{base} \qquad \text{acid} \qquad \text{base}$$

The $SO_4^=$ ion is what is left of the HSO_4^- after its proton has been removed. It is the conjugate base of the acid HSO_4^-.

The $SO_4^=$ ion, being a base, can accept a proton. When this occurs, the acid HSO_4^- ion is formed (the reaction to the left). The HSO_4^- ion can be called the *conjugate acid* of the base $SO_4^=$. *A conjugate acid is what is formed when a base takes on a*

proton. Thus, in the example given, the HSO_4^- ion and the $SO_4^=$ ion become a *conjugate acid-base pair.*

Observe that these same considerations can be applied equally well to the remaining participants in the above reaction, the H_2O molecule and the H_3O^+ ion. The H_2O molecule is a base because it receives the proton given up by the HSO_4^- ion. When this base acquires a proton it forms the H_3O^+ ion. The H_3O^+ ion is the conjugate acid of the base H_2O.

Similarly, when the acidic H_3O^+ ion gives up a proton to the basic $SO_4^=$ ion it forms the H_2O molecule. The H_2O molecule is the conjugate base of the acid H_3O^+. The H_2O molecule and the H_3O^+ ion become the second conjugate acid-base pair in the reaction.

We know that HCl is highly ionized even in concentrated aqueous solutions. The hydrogen chloride molecule tends to give up protons readily and is, therefore, a strong acid. It follows that the Cl^- ion, the conjugate base of this acid, has little tendency to retain the proton. It is, consequently, a weak base.

This suggests an important corollary of the Brønsted Theory of acids and bases: *the stronger an acid, the weaker its conjugate base; and the stronger a base, the weaker its conjugate acid.*

An aqueous solution of the strong acid $HClO_4$ is highly ionized. The reaction to the right is practically complete even in concentrated solutions.

$$\underset{\text{acid}}{\overset{\text{stronger}}{HClO_4}} + \underset{\text{base}}{\overset{\text{stronger}}{H_2O}} \rightleftharpoons \underset{\text{acid}}{\overset{\text{weaker}}{H_3O^+}} + \underset{\text{base}}{\overset{\text{weaker}}{ClO_4^-}}$$

The ClO_4^- ion, the conjugate base of $HClO_4$, is too weak a base to compete successfully with the base H_2O in acquiring protons. The H_3O^+ ion, the conjugate acid of H_2O, is too weak an acid to compete successfully with the acid $HClO_4$ in donating protons. Thus, there is little tendency for the reaction to proceed to the left in re-forming the $HClO_4$ and H_2O molecules.

Now let us examine the situation in an aqueous solution of acetic acid.

weaker **weaker** **stronger** **stronger**
$$HC_2H_3O_2 + H_2O \underset{\longleftarrow}{\overset{\longrightarrow}{}} H_3O^+ + C_2H_3O_2^-$$
acid **base** **acid** **base**

The H_3O^+ ion concentration is quite low even in dilute solutions indicating that $HC_2H_3O_2$ is indeed a weak acid. It does not compete very successfully with H_3O^+ ions to donate protons to a base. The H_2O molecules do not compete very successfully with $C_2H_3O_2^-$ ions to accept protons. Thus the reaction tendency back to the left predominates; the H_3O^+ ion is the stronger acid and the $C_2H_3O_2^-$ ion is the stronger base.

Observe that in each illustration the stronger acid had the weaker conjugate base and the stronger base had the weaker conjugate acid. Of the two reaction tendencies in each reversible situation cited, the reaction toward the weaker acid and base predominated.

These observations suggest a second important corollary to the Brønsted Theory: *protolysis reactions favor the production of the weaker acid and the weaker base.*

When a proton donor and a proton acceptor are brought together in a common solution environment, the extent of the protolysis will depend on the relative strengths of the acids and bases involved. For the proton transfer reaction to approach completeness, the acid and base reactants must be much stronger than the products.

The table below shows the relative strengths of several Brønsted acids and of their conjugate bases. Observe that the strongest acid listed, $HClO_4$, has the weakest conjugate base listed, ClO_4^-. The weakest acid listed has the strongest base, the H^- ion. A violent and dangerous protolysis could result from bringing together the strongest acid and the strongest base in the proper proportions.

TITRATION

13. Molar solutions. In our studies of the effects of solutes on the freezing and boiling points of solvents (Chapter 12) we

RELATIVE STRENGTHS OF ACIDS AND BASES

	Acid	Formula	Conjugate base	Formula	
Decreasing Acid Strength	perchloric	$HClO_4$	perchlorate ion	ClO_4^-	Decreasing Base Strength
	hydrogen chloride	HCl	chloride ion	Cl^-	
	nitric	HNO_3	nitrate ion	NO_3^-	
	sulfuric	H_2SO_4	hydrogen sulfate ion	HSO_4^-	
	hydronium ion	H_3O^+	water	H_2O	
	hydrogen sulfate ion	HSO_4^-	sulfate ion	$SO_4^=$	
	phosphoric	H_3PO_4	dihydrogen phosphate ion	$H_2PO_4^-$	
	acetic	$HC_2H_3O_2$	acetate ion	$C_2H_3O_2^-$	
	carbonic	H_2CO_3	hydrogen carbonate ion	HCO_3^-	
	hydrogen sulfide	H_2S	hydrosulfide ion	HS^-	
	ammonium ion	NH_4^+	ammonia	NH_3	
	hydrogen carbonate ion	HCO_3^-	carbonate ion	$CO_3^=$	
	water	H_2O	hydroxide ion	OH^-	
	ammonia	NH_3	amide ion	NH_2^-	
	hydrogen	H_2	hydride ion	H^-	

found that the significant consideration was the ratio of solute to solvent molecules. Solution concentrations were stated in terms of molality. Recall that molal concentration expresses the quantity of solute in moles per kilogram of solvent. For a given solvent, two solutions of equal molality have the same ratio of solute to solvent molecules.

In our present studies of the solutions of acids, bases, and salts it will be advantageous for us to deal with solution concentrations in terms of *a known quantity of solute in a given volume of solution.*

Perhaps the most generally used expression gives the quantity of solute in *moles* and the volume of solution in *liters*. This is called *molarity* and the symbol for molarity is the capital letter *M*. *The **molarity** of a solution is an expression of the number of moles of solute per liter of solution.*

A *one-molar* (1–*M*) solution is one containing 1 *mole* of solute per *liter of solution.* Molecular solutions of the same molarity have the same concentration of solute molecules. A one-molar solution may contain 1 gram-molecular weight of a molecular solute per liter of solution, or 1 gram-formula weight of an ionic solute per liter of solution. Sometimes the terms *formality* and *formal solution* are used to distinguish the latter type of solute.

A mole of sodium chloride, NaCl, its gram-formula weight, has a mass of 58.5 g. This quantity of NaCl dissolved in enough water to make exactly 1 liter of solution gives a 1–*M* solution. Half this quantity of NaCl in 1 liter of solution gives a 0.5–*M* solution, and twice this quantity of NaCl per liter of solution gives a 2–*M* solution.

A volumetric flask similar to the one shown in Fig. 14-8 is commonly used in preparing solutions of known molarity. A measured quantity of solute is dissolved in a portion of solvent in the flask. Then ad-

ditional solvent is added to fill the flask to the mark on the neck. Thus, the quantity of solute and the volume of solution are known and the concentration can be expressed in terms of its molarity.

As another example, the molecular weight of H_2SO_4 is 98. Thus, a mole of H_2SO_4 has a mass of 98 g. To make 1 liter of a 1–*M* solution of H_2SO_4 requires 98 g of the solute. A 0.5–*M* solution needs only one-half mole, or 49 g of H_2SO_4 per liter of solution. Observe that molar solutions are based on the *volume of solution.* Molal solutions, on the other hand, are based on the *mass of solvent. Equal volumes of molecular solutions of equal molarity have the same number of molecules.* Molarity is preferred when volumes of solution are to be measured.

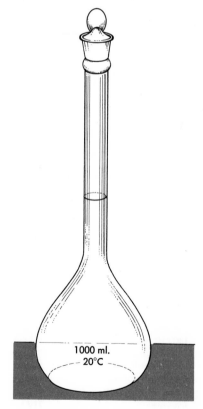

14-8   A volumetric flask. When filled to the mark at 20° C it contains 1000 ml ± 0.3 ml.

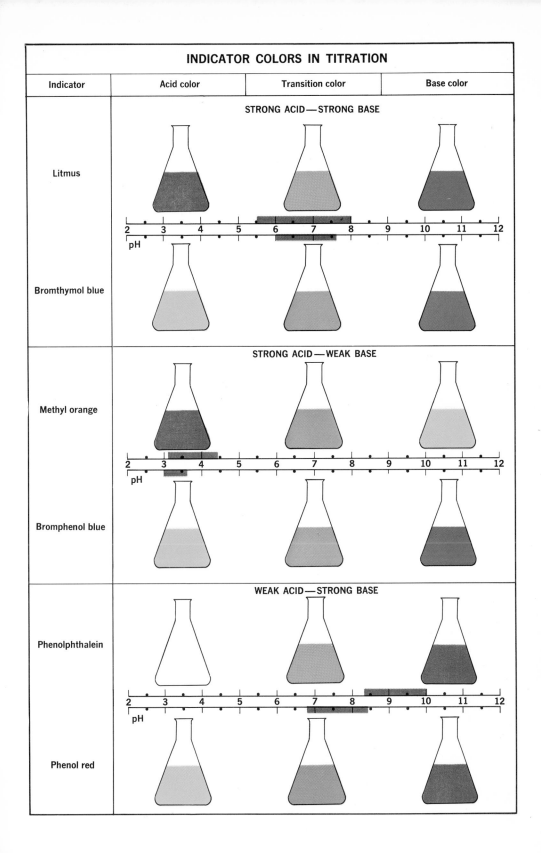

INDICATOR COLORS IN TITRATION

Indicator	Acid color	Transition color	Base color

EMISSION SPECTRA

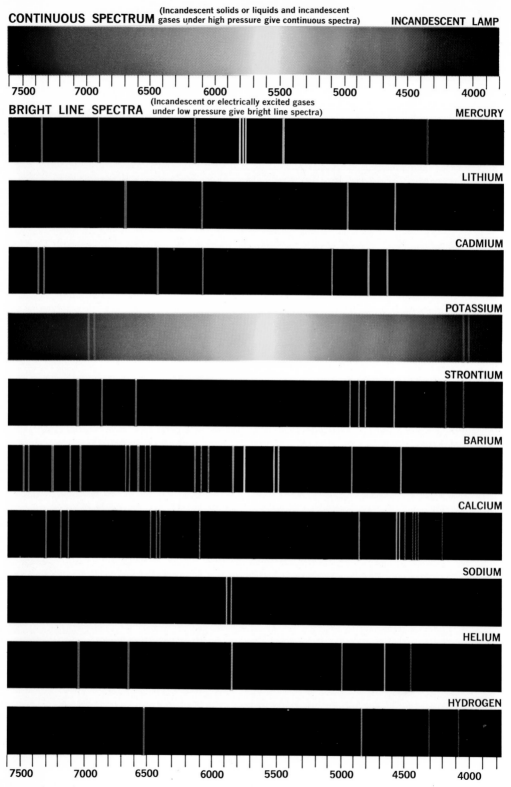

CONTINUOUS SPECTRUM (Incandescent solids or liquids and incandescent gases under high pressure give continuous spectra) INCANDESCENT LAMP

BRIGHT LINE SPECTRA (Incandescent or electrically excited gases under low pressure give bright line spectra)

MERCURY

LITHIUM

CADMIUM

POTASSIUM

STRONTIUM

BARIUM

CALCIUM

SODIUM

HELIUM

HYDROGEN

Adapted from the SPECTRUM CHART, Welch Scientific Company

FLAME TESTS FOR CERTAIN METALS

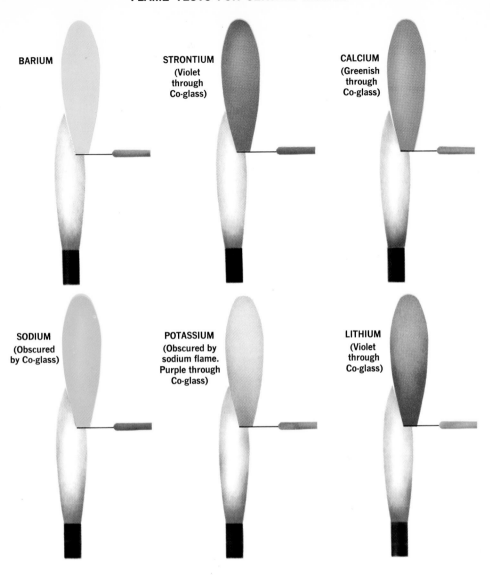

BARIUM

STRONTIUM
(Violet
through
Co-glass)

CALCIUM
(Greenish
through
Co-glass)

SODIUM
(Obscured
by Co-glass)

POTASSIUM
(Obscured by
sodium flame.
Purple through
Co-glass)

LITHIUM
(Violet
through
Co-glass)

BORAX BEAD TESTS FOR CERTAIN METALS
(All beads formed in the oxidizing flame)

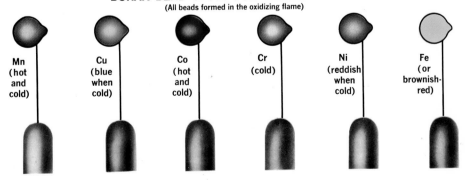

Mn
(hot
and
cold)

Cu
(blue
when
cold)

Co
(hot
and
cold)

Cr
(cold)

Ni
(reddish
when
cold)

Fe
(or
brownish-
red)

THE BEHAVIOR OF SOME NEGATIVE IONS IN THE PRESENCE OF CERTAIN METALLIC IONS

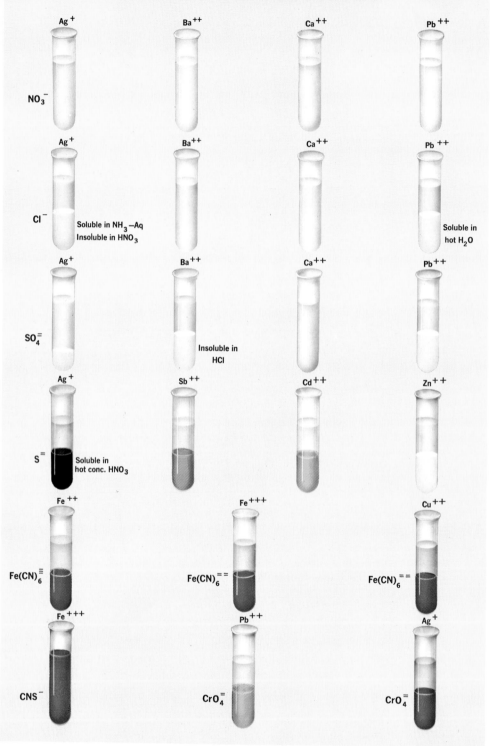

14. The gram-equivalent. Solution concentrations can be expressed in a way which permit chemically equivalent quantities of different solutes to be measured very simply. This makes use of quantities of solutes measured in *gram-equivalents* (g-eq). *One* **gram-equivalent** *of a substance is usually defined as the mass in grams which contains, replaces, or reacts with (directly or indirectly) the Avogadro number of hydrogen atoms.* The Avogadro number of hydrogen atoms is one mole of hydrogen atoms, or one-half mole of hydrogen molecules, or 1.0079 g of hydrogen (1 gram-atomic weight of hydrogen).

An atom of hydrogen, as a reacting particle, may release or acquire one electron. A mole of hydrogen atoms exchanges the Avogadro number of electrons (also called a mole of electrons) in a reaction with another substance. Thus, the gram-equivalent of a reactant may be thought of as *the mass of the substance that acquires or furnishes the Avogadro number of electrons.*

The gram-equivalent of an element is determined ordinarily by dividing its gram-atomic weight by its oxidation number. Special consideration must be given to oxidizing and reducing agents in this connection. Oxidation-reduction reactions will be discussed in Chapter 23.

The gram-equivalent of oxygen is 8 g (16 g ÷ 2). Eight grams of oxygen combines with 1 gram of hydrogen. Sodium has a gram-equivalent of 23 g (23 g ÷ 1). Twenty-three grams of sodium will replace 1 g of hydrogen, and will combine with 8 g of oxygen. Thus 23 g of Na, 8 g of O_2, and 1 g of H_2 are *chemically equivalent.*

The gram-equivalent of a compound is ordinarily determined by dividing the mass of a mole of the compound (1 g-formula wt) by its total positive (or negative) charge. A mole of H_2SO_4 has a mass of 98 g and the total charge (positive or negative) is 2. One gram-equivalent of

sulfuric acid is 49 g, one-half mole. One mole of $Ca_3(PO_4)_2$ has a mass of 310 g. The total charge is 6. One gram-equivalent of $Ca_3(PO_4)_2$ is 51.7 g, one-sixth mole.

Gram-equivalents are very convenient to use in acid-base neutralizations since these reactions require equal numbers of hydronium and hydroxide ions. One mole of hydronium ions, 19 g of H_3O^+, combines with 1 mole of hydroxide ions, 17 g of OH^-, to form 2 moles of water, 36 g of H_2O in a neutralization reaction. *Thus, 1 gram-equivalent of any acid furnishes 1 mole of protons and 1 gram-equivalent of any base accepts 1 mole of protons.*

15. Normal solutions. We can now express solution concentration based on the volume of solution in a second way by stating the quantity of solute in gram-equivalents. This method is called *normality* and the symbol for normality is the capital letter N. *The normality of solution is an expression of the number of gram-equivalents of solute per liter of solution.*

A one-normal $(1-N)$ solution is one containing 1 gram-equivalent of solute per *liter of solution.* Equal volumes of solutions of the same normality are chemically equivalent.

The advantage of having solution concentrations expressed in molarity or normality is that any desired mass of solute may be taken in the form of its solution simply by measuring out a certain volume. The disadvantage is that the mass or volume of solvent present is not known precisely.

A mole of the monoprotic acid HCl has a mass of 36.5 g and can furnish 1 mole of hydrogen as protons. Thus, 1 mole of HCl in 1 liter of aqueous solution provides 1 mole of protons to form 1 mole of H_3O^+ ions and has a $1-N$ concentration.

Suppose we require a solution of HCl which furnishes 0.1 mole of H_3O^+ ion per liter, a $0.1-N$ HCl solution. It is evident that 3.65 g of HCl must be used diluted to 1 liter volume. *However, this is 3.65 g of anhydrous hydrogen chloride in one liter of solution,* not 3.65 g of the concentrated hydrochloric acid found in the laboratory. How may we determine the volume of concentrated hydrochloric acid which will contain 3.65 g of hydrogen chloride? This may be found very simply from the *assay* information printed on the manufacturer's label on the bottle of concentrated hydrochloric acid. See Fig. 14-9.

Suppose the concentrated HCl is 37.23% HCl by weight and has a specific gravity of 1.19. One ml of the solution has a mass of 1.19 g of which 37.23% is HCl. One ml then contains

0.3723 × 1.19 g = 0.443 g of HCl

and the volume of solution needed to provide 3.65 g of HCl is

3.65 g ÷ 0.443 g/ml = 8.24 ml con. HCl

We have already seen that 1 mole of H_2SO_4 contains 2 g-eq of that substance. A 1–*M* solution contains 98 g of H_2SO_4 per liter of solution. However, a 1–*N* solution contains 49 g (98 g ÷ 2) of H_2SO_4 per liter of solution. A 5–*N* solution contains 245 g (49 g × 5) of H_2SO_4 per liter, and 0.01–*N* H_2SO_4 contains 0.49 g (49 g ÷ 100) H_2SO_4 per liter of solution. Concentrated sulfuric acid is usually 95%–98% H_2SO_4 and has a specific gravity of about 1.84. Dilutions to specific normalities are calculated as shown above for HCl.

Crystalline salts containing water of hydration must be given special consideration in making up solutions. For example, crystalline copper(II) sulfate has the empirical formula

$CuSO_4 \cdot 5H_2O$

A 1–*M* $CuSO_4$ solution would contain

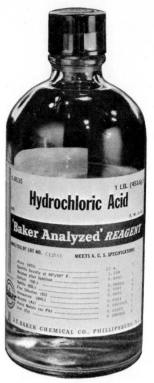

14-9 The manufacturer's label on a reagent bottle carries information that is important to the chemist. Look at the bottle of hydrochloric acid on the reagent shelf in your laboratory and check the assay and specific gravity values given on the label. (Baker Chemical Works)

159.5 g of $CuSO_4$ per liter of solution. Because $CuSO_4$ contains 2 g-eq, this is a 2–*N* solution. A 1–*N* solution would contain 79.75 g of $CuSO_4$ per liter. Of course, this solution would be 0.5*M*. However, the formula weight of this hydrate is 249.5; crystalline copper(II) sulfate is 64% $CuSO_4$. This fact must be recognized when weighing out moles or gram-equivalents of such crystalline hydrates.

If a mole of a solute contains one gram-equivalent, the molarity and normality of the solution *are the same.* Thus a 1–*M* HCl solution is also a 1–*N* solution. If a mole of solute has two gram-equivalents, a 1–*M* solution is 2*N*. A 1–*M* H_2SO_4 solution is therefore 2N. Similarly a 1–M H_3PO_4 solution is 3N. *The advantage of normality is that solutions of equal normality are chemically equivalent, volume for volume.*

16. Ion concentration in water. Water becomes very weakly ionized by self-ionization, a process sometimes referred to as *autoprotolysis*. We stated in Chapter 13, Section 10, that this self-ionizing mechanism probably started with hydrogen bond formation. The feeble conductivity of very pure water is due to the slight ionization of the water itself and not to traces of dissolved impurities. This can be demonstrated by testing highly purified water.

Very precise measurements of electric conductivity of the purest water obtainable have shown that it is ionized to the extent of one molecule in 5.54×10^8 at room temperature, 25° C. This means that the water is about 0.0000002% ionized at this temperature. You will recall that each water molecule which ionizes contributes one proton to form the H_3O^+ ion and one OH^- ion.

From the foregoing, it becomes apparent that 5.54×10^8 *moles* of water will contain 1 mole of H_3O^+ ions. We can express this as a ratio:

$$\frac{1 \text{ mole } H_3O^+}{5.54 \times 10^8 \text{ moles } H_2O} \text{ (at 25° C)}$$

One mole of H_2O has a mass of 18.0 g and there are 997 g of water in 1 liter of 25° C (1 liter = 1000 g at 4° C). So 1 liter contains 55.4 moles of water.

$$\frac{997 \text{ g/liter}}{18.0 \text{ g/mole}} = 55.4 \text{ moles/liter}$$

Now the volume occupied by 5.54×10^8 moles of water can be obtained as follows:

$$\frac{5.54 \times 10^8 \text{ moles } H_2O}{55.4 \text{ moles/liter}} =$$
$$1.00 \times 10^7 \text{ liters } H_2O$$

Therefore, the concentration of H_3O^+ ions (and also of OH^- ions) in water at 25° C is

$$\frac{1 \text{ mole } H_3O^+}{10^7 \text{ liters } H_2O}$$

An expression of ion concentration in terms of moles per liter rather than moles per 10,000,000 liters would be more meaningful here. This can be accomplished by dividing both terms in the last expression by 10^7. We can now state the concentration of H_3O^+ ions in water at 25° C as follows:

$$\frac{10^{-7} \text{ mole } H_3O^+}{\text{liter } H_2O}$$

In chemistry a standard notation is used to represent concentration in terms of *moles/liter*. The symbol or formula of the particular ion or molecule is enclosed in brackets, [ ]. For example, $[H_3O^+]$ means *hydronium ion concentration in moles per liter.* For the ionic concentrations in water at 25° C, we may write

$$[H_3O^+] = 10^{-7} \text{ mole/liter}$$

and $[OH^-] = 10^{-7} \text{ mole/liter}$

or $[H_3O^+] = [OH^-] = 10^{-7} \text{ mole/liter}$

Because the H_3O^+ ion concentration and the OH^- ion concentration are equal, water is neutral, that is, neither acidic nor basic. This is true of any solution in which $[H_3O^+] = [OH^-]$. If the H_3O^+ ion concentration in a solution exceeds 10^{-7} mole/liter, the solution is acidic. If the OH^- ion concentration exceeds 10^{-7} mole per liter, the solution is basic or *alkaline*.

It is also true that the *product* of the $[H_3O^+]$ and $[OH^-]$ remains constant in water and dilute aqueous solutions as long as temperature does not change. Recall that Le Chatelier's principle tells us that an increase in the concentration of either of these ionic species in an aqueous mixture at equilibrium will cause a decrease in the concentration of the other species. In water and dilute aqueous solutions at 25° C,

$$[H_3O^+] \times [OH^-] = \text{a constant}$$

$$[H_3O^+][OH^-] = (1 \times 10^{-7} \text{ mole/liter})^2$$

$$[H_3O^+][OH^-] = 1 \times 10^{-14} \text{ mole}^2/\text{liter}^2$$

The ionization of water increases as its temperature rises. At 0° C the product $[H_3O^+][OH^-]$ is 0.11×10^{-14} mole^2 per liter^2. At 60° C it is 9.6×10^{-14} mole^2 per liter^2.

17. The pH of a solution. The range of solution concentrations encountered by chemists is quite extensive, varying from about 10 molar to perhaps 10^{-15} molar. However, most solutions have concentrations less than 1 molar. Chemists work almost entirely with dilute solutions.

In Section 16 it was stated that the H_3O^+ ion concentration, $[H_3O^+]$, in water is 0.0000001 or 10^{-7} mole/liter at 25° C. In a 0.01–M aqueous solution of HCl (assuming complete ionization) the $[H_3O^+]$ is 0.01 or 10^{-2} mole/liter.

On the other hand, the OH^- ion concentration of a 0.01–M NaOH solution is 0.01 or 10^{-2} mole/liter. The H_3O^+ ion concentration of this solution is calculated as follows:

$$[H_3O^+][OH^-] = 1 \times 10^{-14} \text{ mole}^2/\text{liter}^2$$

$$[H_3O^+] = \frac{1 \times 10^{-14} \text{ mole}^2/\text{liter}^2}{[OH^-]}$$

$$[H_3O^+] = \frac{1 \times 10^{-14} \text{ mole}^2/\text{liter}^2}{1 \times 10^{-2} \text{ mole/liter}}$$

$$[H_3O^+] = 1 \times 10^{-12} \text{ mole/liter}$$

If either the H_3O^+ ion or OH^- ion concentration of a solution is known, the other can be determined from the above relationship.

We can express the acidity or alkalinity of a solution in terms of its hydronium ion concentration. A value *larger* than 10^{-7} mole/liter (a *smaller* negative exponent) indicates an acid solution. A value for the H_3O^+ ion concentration *smaller* than 10^{-7} mole/liter (a *larger* negative exponent) indicates an alkaline solution.

The expression of acidity or alkalinity in terms of hydronium ion concentration becomes cumbersome especially in dilute solutions whether decimal or exponential notations are used. It is more convenient to use logarithmic functions of concentration to indicate this character of solutions. That is, it is simpler to state that the pH of water is 7 than that the hydronium ion concentration of water is 10^{-7} mole/liter.

The pH scale has been devised to express the H_3O^+ ion concentration in dilute

METHODS OF EXPRESSING CONCENTRATION OF SOLUTIONS

Name	Symbol	Solute unit	Solvent unit	Dimensions
Molality	m	mole	kilogram solvent	$\dfrac{\text{mole solute}}{\text{kg solvent}}$
Molarity	M	mole	liter solution	$\dfrac{\text{mole solute}}{\text{liter solution}}$
Normality	N	gram-equivalent	liter solution	$\dfrac{\text{g-eq solute}}{\text{liter solution}}$

solutions conveniently. Numerically, the pH of a solution is the common logarithm of the number of liters of solution that contains 1 mole of hydronium ions, 19 g of H_3O^+ ions.

The number of liters of solution required to furnish 1 mole of H_3O^+ is equal to the *reciprocal* of the H_2O^+ ion concentration given in moles of H_3O^+ per liter. This is

$$\frac{1}{[H_3O^+]}$$

Thus, the pH of a solution is defined as the common logarithm of the reciprocal of the hydronium ion concentration and is expressed by the equation:

$$pH = \log \frac{1}{[H_3O^+]}$$

Pure water is slightly ionized, and at 25° C contains 0.0000001 or 10^{-7} mole of H_3O^+ per liter. The pH of water is therefore:

$$pH = \log \frac{1}{0.0000001}$$

$$pH = \log \frac{1}{10^{-7}}$$

$$pH = \log 10^7$$

$$pH = 7$$

The common logarithm of a number is the power to which 10 must be raised to give the number. Thus 0.0000001 is 10^{-7} and its reciprocal is 10,000,000, or 10^7. The logarithm of 10^7 is 7.

If the H_3O^+ ion concentration is *greater* than that in pure water, the number of liters required to provide 1 mole of H_3O^+ ions is *smaller*. Consequently, the pH is a *smaller* number than 7. Such a solution is *acidic*. Conversely, if the H_3O^+ ion concentration is *less than* that in pure water, the pH is a *larger* number than 7. Such a solution is *basic*.

APPROXIMATE pH OF SOME COMMON SUBSTANCES

Substance	pH
1.0–*N* HCl	0.1
1.0–*N* H_2SO_4	0.3
0.1–*N* HCl	1.1
0.1–*N* H_2SO_4	1.2
gastric juice	2.0
0.01–*N* H_2SO_4	2.1
lemons	2.3
vinegar	2.8
0.1–*N* $HC_2H_3O_2$	2.9
soft drinks	3.0
apples	3.1
grapefruit	3.1
oranges	3.5
cherries	3.6
tomatoes	4.2
bananas	4.6
bread	5.5
potatoes	5.8
rainwater	6.2
milk	6.5
pure water	7.0
eggs	7.8
0.1–*N* $NaHCO_3$	8.4
seawater	8.5
milk of magnesia	10.5
0.1–*N* NH_3	11.1
0.1–*N* Na_2CO_3	11.6
0.1–*N* NaOH	13.0
1.0–*N* NaOH	14.0
1.0–*N* KOH	14.0

The range of pH values usually falls between 0 and 14. The pH system is particularly useful in describing the acidity or alkalinity of solutions that are not far from neutral. This includes many food substances and fluids encountered in physiology.

Special indicators, such as Hydrion paper, show varying shades of color which correspond to the whole range of pH values. To measure the *acidity* or *alkalinity* of a solution, a drop of solution is placed on the paper and the color is compared to the Hydrion color chart furnished with the test papers.

Gramercy Universal Indicator is a

14-10   Approximate pH values over a wide range may be determined by the use of special indicators. (Welch Scientific Co.)

mixture of solutions of dyes that can be used to measure the pH of a solution. To 10 ml of solution, 1 ml of the indicator solution is added. By comparing the color produced with those of an indicator color chart, a reliable determination of the pH is obtained. A color system is also used in the titration method of determining pH, and is described in Section 19.

▶ **18. pH calculations.** The two basic types of pH problems with which we are concerned are:

(*1*) the calculation of pH when $[H_3O^+]$ of a solution is known, and

(*2*) the calculation of $[H_3O^+]$ when pH of a solution is known.

In their most simple form these problems can be solved *by inspection*. The pH equation based on the definition stated in Section 17 is

$$pH = \log \frac{1}{[H_3O^+]}$$

Since $\log \dfrac{1}{[H_3O^+]} = -\log [H_3O^+]$

we can write the equation in this more generally useful form:

$$pH = -\log [H_3O^+]$$

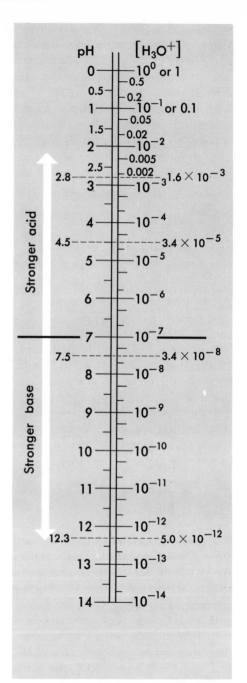

14-11   The relationship between the numerical expression for the pH of a solution and its corresponding hydronium ion concentration, $[H_3O^+]$, may be easily compared in this chart.

Remembering that the base of common logarithms is 10, this equation can be restated in terms of $[H_3O^+]$ as follows:

$$\log [H_3O^+] = -pH$$
and
$$[H_3O^+] = 10^{-pH}$$

For a solution having a $[H_3O^+] = 10^{-6}$ mole/liter, the pH = 6. For one in which the pH = 2, $[H_3O^+] = 10^{-2}$ mole/liter. If the pH = 0, $[H_3O^+] = 1$ mole/liter since 10^0 (ten to the zero power) = 1.

The above examples have hydronium ion concentrations which are integral powers of ten and pH values which are positive integers and are readily solved by inspection. Problems related to solutions not so simply described require some basic knowledge of logarithms and exponents for their solution.

Suppose the $[H_3O^+]$ of a solution is found to be 3.4×10^{-5} mole/liter. Observe that 3.4×10^{-5} lies between 1×10^{-4} and 1×10^{-5}. Thus, the pH of the solution must be between 4 and 5. While calculations are required to determine the pH value, a simple qualitative estimate such as this will prevent errors that are otherwise quite common.

The relationship between the pH and $[H_3O^+]$ is shown in the scale of Fig. 14-11. This scale can be used to make the qualitative estimate of a pH value described in the preceding paragraph. The calculation for this pH value and the calculation for $[H_3O^+]$ from a known pH value are shown in the sample problems on page 238.

The table below shows the relationship between the hydronium ion and hydroxide ion concentrations, the product of these concentrations, and the pH for several solutions of typical molarities. Since KOH is a soluble ionic compound, its aqueous solutions are completely ionized. The molarity of each KOH solution indicates directly the $[OH^-]$. Since the product $[H_3O^+][OH^-]$ is constant, 10^{-14} mole² per liter² at 25° C, the $[H_3O^+]$ can be calculated. Knowing the $[H_3O^+]$, the pH can then be determined as $-\log [H_3O^+]$.

Any aqueous solution of HCl below 1–M concentration can be considered to be completely ionized. Thus, the molarity of the 0.001–M HCl solution indicates directly the $[H_3O^+]$.

The weakly ionized $HC_2H_3O_2$ solution presents a different problem. In the absence of information about the concentration of $HC_2H_3O_2$ molecules, H_3O^+ ions, and $C_2H_3O_2^-$ ions in the equilibrium mixture which exists in the aqueous solution, we could determine the pH of the solution experimentally. Knowing the pH, the $[H_3O^+]$ can be determined as antilog $(-pH)$.

19. Acid-base titration. In a neutralization reaction the basic OH^- ion acquires a proton from the H_3O^+ ion to form a molecule of water.

$$H_3O^+ + OH^- \rightarrow 2H_2O$$

One mole of H_3O^+ ions (19 g) and 1 mole of OH^- ions (17 g) are chemically equivalent. Neutralization occurs when H_3O^+ ions and OH^- ions are supplied in equal numbers. We have recognized that a liter

RELATIONSHIP OF $[H_3O^+]$ TO $[OH^-]$ AND pH

Solution	$[H_3O^+]$	$[OH^-]$	$[H_3O^+][OH^-]$	pH
0.02–M KOH	5.0×10^{-13}	2.0×10^{-2}	1.0×10^{-14}	12.3
0.01–M KOH	1.0×10^{-12}	1.0×10^{-2}	1.0×10^{-14}	12.0
Pure H_2O	1.0×10^{-7}	1.0×10^{-7}	1.0×10^{-14}	7.0
0.001–M HCl	1.0×10^{-3}	1.0×10^{-11}	1.0×10^{-14}	3.0
0.1–M $HC_2H_3O_2$	1.3×10^{-3}	7.7×10^{-12}	1.0×10^{-14}	2.9

of water at room temperature has residual $[H_3O^+]$ and $[OH^-]$ of 10^{-7} M each and that the product $[H_3O^+][OH^-]$ of 10^{-14} mole^2/liter^2 is a constant for water and all dilute aqueous solutions.

If 0.1 mole of gaseous HCl is dissolved in the liter of water, the H_3O^+ ion concentration will rise to 0.1 or 10^{-1} M. Since the product $[H_3O^+][OH^-]$ remains at 10^{-14}, the $[OH^-]$ obviously must decrease from 10^{-7} to 10^{-13} M.

Of course, the removal of OH^- ions is

Sample Problem

What is the pH of a solution if the hydronium ion concentration is 3.4×10^{-5} mole/liter?

Solution

$$pH = -\log [H_3O^+]$$
$$pH = -\log (3.4 \times 10^{-5})$$

The logarithm of a product is equal to the sum of the logarithms of each of the factors. Thus,

$$pH = -(\log 3.4 + \log 10^{-5})$$

The log of $10^{-5} = -5$ and, from the table of logarithms, the log of 3.4 is found to be 0.53.

$$pH = -(0.53 - 5)$$

Therefore, $pH = 4.47$

Sample Problem

The pH of a solution is found to be 7.52. What is the hydronium ion concentration?

Solution

The magnitude of $[H_3O^+]$ is the number whose logarithm is -7.52, that is, the antilog of -7.52.

$$pH = -\log [H_3O^+]$$

Solving for $[H_3O^+]$

$$\log [H_3O^+] = -pH$$
$$[H_3O^+] = \text{antilog } (-pH)$$
$$[H_3O^+] = \text{antilog } (-7.52)$$

But,   antilog $(-7.52) = $ antilog $(0.48 - 8)$
Thus $[H_3O^+] = $ antilog $(0.48 - 8)$
$$[H_3O^+] = \text{antilog } (0.48) \times \text{antilog } (-8)$$

The antilog of $(-8) = 10^{-8}$ and the antilog of (0.48) is found from the table of logarithms to be 3.0. Therefore,

$$[H_3O^+] = 3.0 \times 10^{-8} \text{ mole/liter}$$

accomplished by their combining with H_3O^+ ions according to the above reaction. Thus 10^{-6} mole of H_3O^+ ions is also removed, but this is a negligible portion (0.001%) of the 0.1 mole of H_3O^+ ions present in the liter of solution.

Now suppose we add 0.1 mole (4 g) of solid NaOH to the liter of 0.1–M HCl solution. The NaOH dissolves furnishing altogether 0.1 mole of OH^- ions to the solution. Both $[H_3O^+]$ and $[OH^-]$ are high and their product is greatly in excess of the constant value 10^{-14} for the dilute aqueous solution.

The ion-removal reaction will be as before except that this time there are as many OH^- ions as H_3O^+ ions to be removed. H_3O^+ and OH^- ions combine until the product $[H_3O^+][OH^-]$ is returned to the constant value 10^{-14} and

$$[H_3O^+] = [OH^-] = 10^{-7} \ M$$

The solution is now neither acidic nor basic, but is said to be neutral. The process was one in which chemically equivalent quantities of H_3O^+ ions and OH^- ions combined, a neutralization process.

These considerations should indicate clearly the nature of the chemical activity between acids and bases when the solution of one is progressively added to the other in order to compare their concentrations. This progressive addition of an acid to a base or a base to an acid is called *titration.* *Titration* *may be defined as the process by which the capacity of a solution of unknown concentration to combine with one of known concentration is quantitatively measured.*

An acid-base titration provides a sensitive means of determining the relative volumes of acidic and basic solutions that are chemically equivalent. By knowing the concentration of one, the concentration of the other can be calculated. Titration is an important laboratory procedure and is much used in analytical chemistry.

If successive additions of a base to a measured volume of an acid are continued until the acid has been neutralized and the solution has become distinctly basic, the pH will have changed from a low to a high value. The change in pH occurs slowly at first, then rapidly through the neutral point, and slowly again as the solution becomes basic. Typical pH curves for strong acid-strong base and weak acid-strong base titrations are shown in Fig. 14-12.

The very rapid change in pH occurs in the region where chemically equivalent quantities of H_3O^+ and OH^- ions are present. Any method which shows this

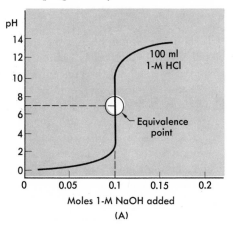

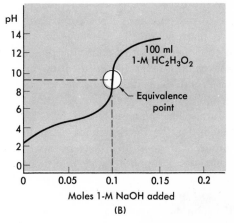

14-12 Acid-base titration curves: (A) strong acid-strong base, (B) weak acid-strong base.

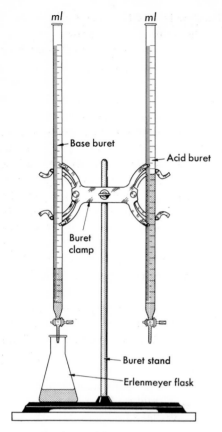

14-13   An acid-base titration stand.

abrupt change in pH can be used to detect the *equivalence point* or *end point* of a titration.

Many dyes have colors that are sensitive to pH changes. If a color transition takes place within the pH range in which an equivalence point occurs, the dye may serve as an *indicator* in the titration process. A table of indicators accompanies Section 20.

Burets like those shown in Fig. 14-13 provide for the measurement of solution volumes with good precision and are used in titration. Suppose small additions of NaOH solutions of unknown concentration are titrated into 10.0 ml of 0.01–*M* HCl solution, containing a few drops of a suitable indicator, until the equivalence

point is reached. Careful readings of the base buret show that 20.0 ml of the basic solution has been used. How can these titration data indicate the molarity of the basic solution?

The empirical equation for the neutralization reaction is

$$HCl + NaOH \rightarrow NaCl + H_2O$$

From the volumes of the known solution of HCl used and its molarity, we can determine the quantity, in moles, of HCl used:

$$\frac{10.0 \text{ ml}}{1000 \text{ ml/liter}} \times \frac{0.01 \text{ mole HCl}}{\text{liter}} =$$
$$0.0001 \text{ mole HCl used}$$

The balanced equation shows that *1 mole* of NaOH is used for *1 mole* of HCl; NaOH and HCl are chemically equivalent, mole for mole. Therefore the quantity of NaOH used in the titration is also 0.0001 mole. But this was furnished by 20.0 ml of NaOH solution. Therefore, the molarity of the NaOH solution is obtained as follows:

$$\frac{0.0001 \text{ mole NaOH}}{20.0 \text{ ml}} \times \frac{1000 \text{ ml}}{\text{liter}} =$$
$$0.005 \text{ mole NaOH/liter}$$

or   **0.005-*M* NaOH**

It should be apparent that the accuracy of the titration method is limited by the accuracy with which the concentration of the "known" solution is actually known. For this reason, much care is exercised in establishing the concentration of the known solutions used in titration.

When this solution is prepared and adjusted volumetrically to the desired concentration, its concentration is established with maximum precision by titrating it against a carefully measured quantity of a highly purified compound known as a *primary standard.* The process is called a *standardization* and the solution is referred to as a *standard solution.*

Let us return to the titration example and assume that the diprotic acid H_2SO_4 was used as the standard solution instead of HCl. The same titration data will now yield a different answer for the molarity of the NaOH solution. The equation is:

$$H_2SO_4 + 2NaOH \rightarrow Na_2SO_4 + H_2O$$

$$\frac{10.0 \text{ ml}}{1000 \text{ ml/liter}} \times \frac{0.01 \text{ mole } H_2SO_4}{\text{liter}} =$$
$$0.0001 \text{ mole } H_2SO_4 \text{ used}$$

The equation shows that *2 moles* of NaOH are required for *1 mole* of H_2SO_4. Therefore, 0.0002 mole NaOH is used in the titration as the chemical equivalent of 0.0001 mole H_2SO_4. The molarity of the NaOH solution is obtained as follows:

$$\frac{0.0002 \text{ mole NaOH}}{20.0 \text{ ml}} \times \frac{1000 \text{ ml}}{\text{liter}} =$$
$$0.01 \text{ mole NaOH/liter}$$

or   **0.01-*M* NaOH**

The sample problem below will further illustrate the titration process.

Solution concentrations in terms of normality are sometimes preferred in analytical chemistry since concentrations are expressed directly in terms of gram-equivalents of solute. Solutions of the same normality are always chemically equivalent, milliliter for milliliter. We have seen that molar quantities may or may not contain chemical equivalents of reactants, depending on the substances involved.

A very simple relationship exists between volumes and normalities of solutions used in titration. For example, 50. ml

Sample Problem

In a titration, 27.4 ml of a standard solution of $Ba(OH)_2$ was added to 20.0 ml sample of an HCl solution. The concentration of the standard solution was 0.0154 *M*. What is the molarity of the acid solution?

Solution

The equation for this reaction is:

$$2HCl + Ba(OH)_2 \rightarrow BaCl_2 + 2H_2O$$

The quantity, in moles, of $Ba(OH)_2$ used in the reaction can be found from the molarity of the standard solution and the volume used.

$$\frac{27.4 \text{ ml}}{1000 \text{ ml/liter}} \times \frac{0.0154 \text{ mole } Ba(OH)_2}{\text{liter}} = 0.000422 \text{ mole } Ba(OH)_2 \text{ used}$$

The balanced equation shows that *2 moles* of HCl are used for *1 mole* of $Ba(OH)_2$. Therefore, 0.000844 mole of HCl is used since this is the chemical equivalent of 0.000422 mole of $Ba(OH)_2$.

20.0 ml of the unknown solution contained 0.000844 mole of HCl. The concentration is

$$\frac{0.000844 \text{ mole HCl}}{20.0 \text{ ml}} \times \frac{1000 \text{ ml}}{\text{liter}} = 0.0422 \text{ mole/liter}$$

or   0.0422–*M* HCl

of a standard solution of 0.10–N NaOH was required to reach an equivalence point with 10. ml of ordinary vinegar. Since 5.0 times as much of the standard base solution was used in the titration as acid, the vinegar is obviously 5.0 times more concentrated than the base. Therefore the vinegar is 0.50 N.

The relationship between volumes and normalities in titration can be expressed in equation form as follows:

$$V_1 N_1 = V_2 N_2$$

V_1 and N_1 are the volume and normality respectively of the standard solution and V_2 and N_2 are those of the unknown solution.

The acidity of vinegar is due to the presence of acetic acid. A 1.0–N acetic acid solution contains 1 g-equivalent (in this case, 1 mole) or 60. g of $HC_2H_3O_2$ per liter of solution. The 0.50–N solution must contain 30. g of $HC_2H_3O_2$ per liter. Since a liter of vinegar has a mass of approximately 1000 g, the sample of vinegar used was 3% acetic acid.

NaOH is a strong base and $HC_2H_3O_2$ is a weak acid. The pH curve for this titration, Fig. 14-12(B), is not similar to the curve for a strong acid-strong base titration. The equivalence point occurs at a higher pH because the sodium acetate solution formed in the titration is basic in character. This property of some salts, called *hydrolysis*, is described in Chapter 22.

20. Indicators in titration. Chemists have a wide choice of indicators for use in titrations. They are able to choose one which changes color over the right pH range for any particular reaction. Let us see why it is not always suitable to have our indicator change color at a pH of 7.

Solutions of soluble hydroxides and acids mixed in chemically equivalent quantities may not be exactly neutral.

They will be neutral only if both solutes are ionized to the same degree. The purpose of the indicator is to show that the end-point has been reached—that is, when equivalent quantities of the two solutes are together. The accompanying Table of Indicator Colors shows the color changes of several common indicators used in acid-hydroxide titrations. Notice the variations in the transition interval column for the different indicators. These variations enable a chemist to choose the best indicator for a given reaction.

The combinations of acidic and basic solutions involved in titration, which have end-points occurring in different pH ranges, are as follows:

1. Strong acid—strong hydroxide: pH is about 7. Litmus may be a suitable indicator. However, the color change is not sharply defined. Bromthymol blue performs more satisfactorily.

2. Strong acid—weak hydroxide: pH is less than 7. Methyl orange may be a suitable indicator.

3. Weak acid—strong hydroxide: pH is greater than 7. Phenolphthalein may be a suitable indicator.

4. Weak acid—weak hydroxide: pH may be either greater than or less than 7, depending on which solution is stronger. None of the indicators performs very well.

21. pH measurements. Indicators used to detect the end points in neutralization reactions are organic compounds possessing weak acidic or basic characteristics. When added to a solution in suitable form and concentration, an indicator imparts a characteristic color to the solution. If the pH of the solution is changed, as in titration, the color of the indicator changes over a definite range of pH values, called the *transition interval*.

The difference in color of an indicator at pH values above and below its transition interval may be attributed to the fact

TABLE OF INDICATOR COLORS

INDICATOR	COLOR			TRANSITION INTERVAL (pH)
	Acid	Transition	Alkaline	
methyl violet	yellow	aqua	violet	0.2– 2.0
methyl yellow	red	orange	yellow	2.9– 4.0
bromphenol blue	yellow	green	blue	3.0– 3.6
methyl orange	red	orange	yellow	3.1– 4.4
methyl red	red	buff	yellow	4.4– 6.0
litmus	red	pink	blue	5.5– 8.0
bromthymol blue	yellow	green	blue	6.0– 7.6
phenol red	yellow	orange	red	6.8– 8.4
phenolphthalein	colorless	pink	red	8.3–10.0
thymolphthalein	colorless	pale	blue	9.3–10.5
alizarine yellow	yellow	green	violet	10.1–12.1

that the un-ionized indicator molecule possesses a color different from that of the indicator ions. The ratio of the indicator-ion concentration to that of indicator molecules is a function of the pH of the solution. Therefore, the indicator color is dependent on the pH and changes as a function of the pH of the solution.

If an indicator added to different solutions assumes the same *transition color*, the solutions may be considered to have the same pH. This is the basis for the common *colorimetric* determination of pH. A measured volume of a suitable indicator is added to each solution whose pH is to be determined. The color is then compared with that of the same indicator in solutions of known pH. By careful color comparison, the pH of a solution can be estimated to the nearest 0.1 pH unit.

The use of indicators for determining end-points in titrations and the pH of solutions involves simple and common techniques in chemistry. However, it is by no means the only way these procedures may be performed. Modern instruments enable the chemist to make rapid titrations and pH determinations with higher precision than is possible using color-comparison methods.

Laboratory pH meters may be divided into two general groups, *potentiometric* and *conductometric* instruments. Their theory of operation is entirely different and quite complicated. Briefly, the potentiometric method is similar to common indicator methods in that a change of the electric potential of a special electrode is a function of the pH of the solution. A large change in potential at the end-point of a

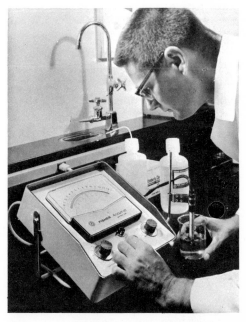

14-14   A modern laboratory pH meter in use in the laboratory. (Fisher Scientific Company)

titration, for example, is equivalent to the color change of an indicator. Modern *glass-electrode* pH meters are now available which cover the entire pH range. They are very convenient to use and give more accurate readings than are obtainable by using color indicators.

Conductometric methods rely on the fact that ions present in an electrolytic solution contribute to the electric conductivity of the solution. If ions of one electrolyte unite with ions of another to form a slightly ionized or slightly soluble product, the conductivity of the solution undergoes an appreciable change. Conductometric instruments are designed to detect this change in electric conductivity.

SALTS

22. Nature of salts. Common table salt, NaCl, is only one of a large class of compounds which the chemist calls by the name *salt*.

An acid in water solution ionizes forming H_3O^+ ions and negatively charged nonmetallic ions. A soluble metallic hydroxide is an ionic solid. When dissolved in water, it dissociates releasing OH^- ions and positively charged metallic ions. The hydronium and hydroxide ions are almost entirely removed in neutralization. They form water, which is only very slightly ionized. The negative ions of the acid and positive ions of the hydroxide have no part in the neutralization reaction; they are simply spectator ions. For example:

$$HCl + H_2O \rightarrow H_3O^+ + Cl^-$$

$$K^+OH^- \rightarrow K^+ + OH^-$$

$$H_3O^+ + Cl^- + K^+ + OH^- \rightarrow$$
$$K^+ + Cl^- + 2H_2O$$

Or simply,

$$H_3O^+ + OH^- \rightarrow 2H_2O$$

After the water is evaporated, the oppositely charged ions are no longer isolated from each other by water dipoles. They form a characteristic ionic crystalline structure and separate from solution as a salt. *A salt may be defined as a compound made up of positive metallic ions or radicals bonded to negative ions.* It is the result of proton transfer from certain acids to a base. All true salts, by this definition, are electrovalent substances. They vary in solubility in water, but aqueous solutions of salts are simply solutions of their hydrated ions.

23. Salt-producing reactions. There are several ways in which salts are formed, but not all of them are applicable to the formation of every salt.

1. Direct union of the elements. Sodium may be burned in chlorine to produce the salt, sodium chloride.

$$2Na + Cl_2 \rightarrow 2NaCl$$

2. Salts are formed by the replacement of the hydrogen of an acid by a metal. Zinc reacts with hydrochloric acid to form zinc chloride and hydrogen.

$$Zn + 2HCl \rightarrow ZnCl_2 + H_2 \uparrow$$

3. The oxide of a metal may react with an acid to form a salt. Magnesium oxide, MgO, can be treated with hydrochloric acid to form magnesium chloride and water.

$$MgO + 2HCl \rightarrow MgCl_2 + H_2O$$

4. The oxide of a nonmetal may react with a soluble hydroxide to form a salt. Carbon dioxide, in reacting with limewater, $Ca(OH)_2$, forms calcium carbonate and water.

$$CO_2 + Ca(OH)_2 \rightarrow CaCO_3 \downarrow + H_2O$$

5. Acids neutralize soluble hydroxides and form salts. Sodium hydroxide and hydrochloric acid are mixed in chemically equivalent quantities. The solvent is

RECAST

SOLUBILITY OF SALTS

1. Common sodium, potassium, and ammonium compounds are soluble in water.
2. Common nitrates, acetates, and chlorates are soluble.
3. Common chlorides are soluble except silver, mercury(I), and lead. (Lead(II) chloride is soluble in hot water.)
4. Common sulfates are soluble except calcium, barium, strontium, and lead.
5. Common carbonates, phosphates, and silicates are insoluble except sodium, potassium, and ammonium.
6. Common sulfides are insoluble except calcium, barium, strontium, magnesium, sodium, potassium, and ammonium.

evaporated and sodium chloride remains. Many different salts can be prepared by neutralization.

$$NaOH + HCl \rightarrow NaCl + H_2O$$

6. Two salts may be prepared at one time by ionic reactions. A solution of sodium sulfate, Na_2SO_4, added to a solution of barium chloride, $BaCl_2$, reacts according to the equation:

$$Ba^{++} + 2Cl^- + 2Na^+ + SO_4^= \rightarrow$$
$$2Na^+ + 2Cl^- + Ba^{++}SO_4^= \downarrow$$

It is not usually possible to separate two salts unless one of them is practically insoluble. In this case barium sulfate is only very slightly soluble. It readily precipitates and can be filtered from the solution. The water may then be evaporated to obtain the sodium chloride, which of course would not be in pure form. It will contain some barium sulfate, since the $BaSO_4$ was precipitated from its saturated solution.

7. Salts may be formed by the action of an acid on a carbonate. If we add hydrochloric acid, HCl, to a solution of sodium carbonate, Na_2CO_3, the following reaction occurs:

$$2HCl + Na_2CO_3 \rightarrow$$
$$2NaCl + H_2O + CO_2 \uparrow$$

Carbon dioxide bubbles out of the mixture as a gas. The sodium chloride may be recovered by evaporation.

8. Salts may be formed by the reaction between a metal oxide and a nonmetal oxide. Metallic carbonates and silicates are formed this way.

$$MgO + CO_2 \rightarrow MgCO_3$$
$$CaO + SiO_2 \rightarrow CaSiO_3$$

24. Naming salts. Salts are generally named by combining the names of the ions of which they are composed. For example, the name of $Ba(NO_3)_2$ is barium nitrate. Conventionally the more metallic ion, in this case the barium ion, Ba^{++}, is named first. The name of the negative ion, in this case the nitrate ion, NO_3^-, follows.

SALT NOMENCLATURE

Formula	Stock Name
Binary salts	
CuCl	copper(I) chloride
$CuCl_2$	copper(II) chloride
FeO	iron(II) oxide
Fe_2O_3	iron(III) oxide
Fe_3O_4	iron(II, III) oxide
$MnCl_2$	manganese(II) chloride
$MnCl_4$	manganese(IV) chloride
Ternary salts	
$Fe_3(PO_4)_2$	iron(II) phosphate
$Hg(NO_3)_2$	mercury(II) nitrate
Cu_2SO_4	copper(I) sulfate
$CuSO_4$	copper(II) sulfate
Mixed salts	
$KCaPO_4$	potassium calcium phosphate
$NaHCO_3$	sodium hydrogen carbonate

COMMON ACIDS

Formula	Name of Acid	Name of Negative Ion of Salt
HF	hydrofluoric	fluoride
HBr	hydrobromic	bromide
HI	hydriodic	iodide
HCl	hydrochloric	chloride
HClO	hypochlorous	hypochlorite
$HClO_2$	chlorous	chlorite
$HClO_3$	chloric	chlorate
$HClO_4$	perchloric	perchlorate
H_2S	hydrosulfuric	sulfide
H_2SO_3	sulfurous	sulfite
H_2SO_4	sulfuric	sulfate
HNO_2	nitrous	nitrite
HNO_3	nitric	nitrate
H_2CO_3	carbonic	carbonate
H_3PO_3	phosphorous	phosphite
H_3PO_4	phosphoric	phosphate

Over the years many inconsistencies have been encountered among the names of salts. These inconsistencies have been carried into our present nomenclature in spite of the fact that they do not provide for a simple translation from name to formula or from formula to name. In 1940 the International Union of Pure and Applied Chemistry recommended a comprehensive system for naming inorganic compounds. This is known as the *Stock system,* which provides the uniformity and simplicity needed to improve our system of chemical nomenclature.

The part of the Stock system that applies to the naming of salts containing metals with variable oxidation states is used throughout this text. Several examples of Stock nomenclature for binary, ternary, and mixed salts are given in the table on page 245. Observe that the more electropositive cation is named first in mixed salts.

The names of negative ions take the same root and prefix as the acid in which they occur. But the ending *–ic* is changed to *–ate,* and the ending *–ous* is changed to *–ite.* Salts derived from binary acids take the ending *–ide.* The table above shows the formulas for many common acids. It also gives the names of the acids, and the names of the negative ions of the salts which are produced by the reactions of these acids.

REVIEW OUTLINE

Nature of acids
Ionization of strong mineral acids (2)
Arrhenius' explanation of an acid (3)
Brønsted acid (4)
Proton donor in nonaqueous solution (4)
Properties of acids (5)
Monoprotic, diprotic, triprotic acids (5)
Naming traditional acids (6)
Acid anhydride reactions (7)

Nature of bases
- Brønsted base (8)
- Properties of hydroxide compounds (9)
- Amphiprotism (9)
- Basic anhydride reactions (10)
- Formulas of acids and bases (11)
- Relative strengths of acids and bases (12)
- Conjugate acid-base pair (12)

Concentration of solutions
- Molar solutions (13)
- Gram-equivalent (14)
- Normal solutions (15)
- Autoprotolysis (16)
- Ion concentrations in water (16)
- Meaning of pH (17)
- Calculations of pH from $[H_3O^+]$ (18)
- Calculations of $[H_3O^+]$ from pH (18)
- Acid-base titration (19)
- Titration calculations (19)
- Indicators in titration (20)
- Indicators for pH measurement (21)

Salts as a class of compounds
- Nature of salts (22)
- Examples of salt-producing reactions (23)
- Naming salts by Stock system (24)

QUESTIONS

Group A

1. Name the three most important industrial acids and tell why each is important.
2. What ion is responsible for the acidic properties of acid solutions?
3. Why is an acid thought of as a proton donor?
4. (*a*) What is an acid anhydride? (*b*) A basic anhydride? (*c*) Give an example of each.
5. (*a*) State the rules for naming binary acids. (*b*) For naming ternary acids.
6. Why may a base be defined as a proton acceptor?
7. Write the net ionic equation of the neutralization reaction.
8. Aluminum hydroxide has basic properties in the presence of a strong acid, and acidic properties in the presence of a solution which is strongly basic. (*a*) Write the formula of aluminum hydroxide to show its basic properties. (*b*) Rewrite the formula to show its acidic properties. (*c*) What term is used to describe such substances?
9. What is the nature of true salts?
10. How are salts named?

11. What method would you use to prepare a small quantity of calcium sulfate quickly and safely in the laboratory? Justify the method used and write the equation.
12. Would barium sulfate be a suitable source of the sulfate ion for an ionic reaction with another salt? Explain.

Group B

13. Explain why a water solution of hydrogen chloride has acidic properties but pure hydrogen chloride does not, in the usual sense.
14. Hydrogen chloride, HCl, has 1 gram-equivalent of hydrogen per mole and hydrogen carbonate, H_2CO_3, has 2 gram-equivalents of hydrogen per mole. Yet hydrochloric acid is described as a *strong* acid and carbonic acid as a *weak* acid. Explain.
15. (*a*) How can you justify calling hydrogen chloride an acid when it is dissolved in ammonia? (*b*) Write the equation.
16. (*a*) Explain the manner in which water may be considered to be an acid. (*b*) Write an equation which illustrates this behavior using electron-dot formulas.
17. (*a*) How would you test the soil in your lawn or garden to find out whether it is acidic or basic? (*b*) If you find it to be acidic, what can be added to it to remedy the condition?
18. (*a*) What basic solution would you use for cleaning a greasy sink? Explain. (*b*) For removing grease spots from clothing? Explain.
19. What basic solutions would you use for neutralizing acid stains on clothing? Explain.
20. Test your saliva with litmus paper. (*a*) Is the saliva acidic or alkaline? (*b*) Do you think that a tooth paste is likely to be acidic or basic? Test some of them.
21. Which of the following salts are soluble, and which are considered to be insoluble in water: NaCl, $CaCO_3$, $BaSO_4$, $(NH_4)_2S$, $Al(C_2H_3O_2)_3$, Ag_2SO_4, $Pb(NO_3)_2$, Hg_2Cl_2, $Mg_3(PO_4)_2$, CuS?
22. In a neutralization reaction between hydrochloric acid and potassium hydroxide, the K^+ ion and the Cl^- ion are called *spectator ions*. (*a*) Explain. (*b*) How could the potassium chloride be recovered?
23. What indicator would you use to show the end-point of the neutralization reaction described in Question 22? Justify your selection.
24. (*a*) Explain the meaning of pH. (*b*) What is the usual range of the pH scale?
25. How many moles of sodium hydroxide are needed to neutralize: (*a*) 1 mole of hydrochloric acid; (*b*) 1 mole of sulfuric acid; and (*c*) 1 mole of phosphoric acid? (*d*) Write the equation for each reaction.
26. (*a*) What mass of calcium hydroxide is required to make up 1.0 liter of 0.010–N solution? (*b*) To make up 1.0 liter of 0.010–M solution?
27. (*a*) What volume of water contains a mole of H_3O^+ ions? (*b*) How many gram-equivalents of hydronium ions is this? (*c*) How many grams of H_3O^+ ion? (*d*) What is the mole-concentration of OH^- ion in this volume of water? (*e*) How many gram-equivalents of hydroxide ions is this? (*f*) How many grams of OH^- ion?

28. What is the normality of (*a*) a 0.0040–*M* solution of phosphoric acid? (*b*) a 0.15–*M* solution of potassium hydroxide? (*c*) a 2–*M* solution of sulfuric acid?
29. What is the molarity of (*a*) a 0.006–*N* solution of phosphoric acid? (*b*) a 0.0036–*N* solution of aluminum sulfate? (*c*) a 0.030–*N* solution of barium hydroxide?
30. Name the following compounds: (*a*) H_2Se, (*b*) HIO_3, (*c*) $Ga(OH)_3$, (*d*) $CsOH$, (*e*) $RaBr_2$.
31. (*a*) When the H_2O molecule acts as a base, what is its conjugate acid? (*b*) When the H_2O molecule acts as an acid, what is its conjugate base?
32. (*a*) When the NH_3 molecule acts as a base, what is its conjugate acid? (*b*) When the NH_3 molecule acts as an acid, what is its conjugate base?

PROBLEMS

Group A

1. (*a*) How many grams of sodium hydroxide are required to neutralize 54.75 g of hydrogen chloride in water solution? (*b*) How many moles of each reactant are involved in the reaction?
2. Nitric acid can be prepared in the laboratory by the reaction of sodium nitrate with sulfuric acid. Sodium hydrogen sulfate is also formed. (*a*) How many grams of sulfuric acid are required to produce 50.0 g of nitric acid? (*b*) How many grams of sodium hydrogen sulfate are formed?
3. How many liters of carbon dioxide can be collected at 20.° C and 745 mm pressure from a reaction between 25 g of calcium carbonate and an excess of hydrochloric acid?
4. What quantity of potassium nitrate would you add to 500. g of water to prepare a 0.250-*m* solution?
5. How many grams of sugar, $C_{12}H_{22}O_{11}$, are contained in 50.0 ml of an 0.800–*M* solution?

Group B

6. How many solute molecules are contained in each milliliter of a 0.1–*M* solution?
7. What is the molality of a solution that contains 2.0 g of sodium chloride in 100.0 g of water?
8. (*a*) What is the pH of a 0.01–*M* solution of HCl, assuming complete ionization? (*b*) What is the OH^- ion concentration of a 0.01–*M* solution of sodium hydroxide? (*c*) What is the pH of this solution?
9. How many milliliters of a 0.150–*N* solution of a metallic hydroxide are required to neutralize 30.0 ml of a 0.500–*N* solution of an acid?
10. A chemistry student finds that it takes 34 ml of a 0.50–*N* acid solution to neutralize 10. ml of a sample of household ammonia. What is the normality of the ammonia-water solution?
11. The stockroom supply of concentrated sulfuric acid is 98% H_2SO_4 by weight and has a specific gravity of 1.84. (*a*) How many milliliters are needed to make 1.0 liter of 1.0–*N* H_2SO_4 solution? (*b*) To make 100. ml of 0.20–*N* solution?

12. An excess of zinc reacts with 400. ml of hydrochloric acid and 2.55 liters of H_2 gas is collected over water at 20.° C and 745.0 mm. What was the molarity of the acid?

13. Suppose 10.0 ml of vinegar is diluted to 100. ml with distilled water and titrated against 0.100–M sodium hydroxide solution. From the burets, 30.0 ml of the diluted vinegar and 25.0 ml of the solution of the base were withdrawn. What percentage of acetic acid, $HC_2H_3O_2$, did the vinegar contain?

▶14. What is the pH of a 0.054–M solution of HCl?

▶15. 25.0 ml of 0.150–M NaOH and 50.0 ml of 0.100–M HCl solutions are mixed. What is the pH of the resulting solution?

▶16. Find the pH of a 0.02–M LiOH solution.

▶17. A solution is determined experimentally to have a pH of 2.9. (*a*) Find the H_3O^+ ion concentration. (*b*) What is the OH^- ion concentration?

Chapter Fifteen

SUSPENSIONS

THE COLLOIDAL STATE

1. Colloidal suspensions. In 1861 a Scottish scientist, Thomas Graham (1805–1869), performed a series of experiments with starch, glue, and sugar in water. He enclosed these materials in parchment bags which he suspended in water, as in Fig. 15-1. He observed that substances that are easily crystallized passed through the parchment readily. He called these materials *crystalloids*. Sticky substances, on the other hand (starch and glue in water), passed through the membrane hardly at all. He called these materials *colloids*, from the Greek word for glue. Sugar and salt form *true solutions* when added to water, because they are dispersed through the liquid as molecules or ions. Colloids only *appear* to go into solution when added to water. Actually, they are dispersed as particles larger than ordinary molecules. These are too large to pass through the parchment. Since Graham's time *the word colloid has been broadened to include any dispersion of very small particles that are larger*

than simple molecules. We still call such mixtures colloids, although they may not have anything to do with sticky substances such as those which Graham investigated.

Later investigations showed that some materials, under certain conditions, were nondiffusing and colloidal in behavior. Yet under different conditions, they were crystalline in nature. We now know that *the state of subdivision, rather than the chemical nature of a material, determines whether it forms a suspension or a true solution when dispersed in a second medium.* Sodium chloride may form a colloidal suspension if the sodium ions and chloride ions are brought together in a medium in which sodium chloride is not soluble.

A true solution is formed when a solute, as molecules or ions, diffuses throughout the solvent to form a homogeneous mixture. It consists of a *single phase*. The solute is said to be soluble in the solvent. *A colloidal suspension, on the other hand, is a two-phase system having dispersed particles*

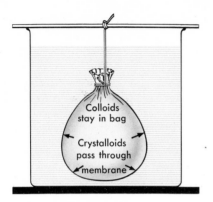

15-1 A colloidal dispersion is held back by the parchment membrane, permitting it to be separated from substances in solution. This process is called dialysis.

rather than a solute, and a dispersing medium rather than a solvent. The dispersed substance (*internal phase*) is not soluble in the dispersing medium (*external phase*). It consists of finely divided particles which remain suspended in the medium.

2. Range of colloidal size. The colloidal state has been called *the world of neglected dimensions.* It lies between true solutions which are homogeneous, and coarse mixtures which separate on standing. Colloidal size has no fixed limits. However, particles between molecular size and a size great enough to be seen in the optical microscope are said to be colloidal. This includes particles with diameters ranging from approximately 10 Å to 1000 Å. Some chemists prefer to extend the colloidal range to 10,000 Å. (Recall that 1 Å = 10^{-8} cm.) Ordinary simple molecules are only a few Ångstroms in diameter. The diameter of protein macromolecules may approach 100 Å and their molecular weights may be several hundred thousand. Viruses, known to be large protein molecules, may have molecular weights between one million and one billion. These macromolecular substances are well within the colloidal range.

If the size of the dispersed particles is at the lower limit of the colloidal range, a dispersion may begin to have the characteristics of a solution. As the size of the dispersed particles approaches the upper limit of the colloidal range, a dispersion may begin to show the properties of an ordinary suspension. Thus, we see that there is no definite division between the true solution and the colloidal state on one hand, and the colloidal state and the ordinary suspension on the other.

3. Types of colloidal suspensions. Since there are three (physical) states of matter—gas, liquid, and solid—we might assume that there are nine possible types of dispersion. However, all gases consist of simple molecules, and molecules of one gas mix completely in any proportion with the molecules of another gas. Therefore, dispersed systems of *gas-in-gas* cannot occur. The eight possible types of colloidal systems are listed in the accompanying table together with typical examples of each.

TYPES OF SUSPENSIONS

Colloidal Dispersion	Example
Liquid in gas	Fog, clouds
Solid in gas	Smoke
Gas in liquid	Whipped cream, foam
Liquid in liquid	Cream, mayonnaise
Solid in liquid	Glue, India ink
Gas in solid	Floating soap
Liquid in solid	Opal, jelly
Solid in solid	Ruby glass

The properties of most colloidal systems fall into two general patterns of behavior. These depend primarily on the relationship which exists between the internal and external phases.

1. Lyophobic (lie-oh-*foh*-bik) *systems.* Suppose we prepare a dispersion of diarsenic trisulfide, As_2S_3, in water. Since water can disperse only a small amount of diarsenic trisulfide, *the concentration of the internal phase (the diarsenic trisulfide) is low.* The dispersed particles have negligible attraction for the water. Consequently this dispersion *has the same fluidity (viscosity) as pure water.* The particles of diarsenic trisulfide become negatively charged due to adsorption of hydroxide ions. If a solution of an electrolyte such as hydrochloric acid is added, *the dispersion coagulates and precipitates due to the loss of the charge.* The behavior of this diarsenic trisulfide dispersion is typical of *lyophobic colloids,* called **suspensoids.**

2. Lyophilic (lie-oh-*fill*-ik) *systems.* If a relatively large amount of powdered gelatin is mixed in water and the dispersion is allowed to stand, it *sets* to form a firm *gel or jelly.* The dispersed particles of gelatin have a strong attraction for the dispersing medium (the water) and become thoroughly hydrated. This traps the water in such a way that *the viscosity of the system increases.* The relative concentration of gelatin is high and *small additions of solutions of electrolytes have little effect on the jelly.* The behavior of gelatin in water is typical of *lyophilic colloids,* which are called **emulsoids.**

Because of this significant difference between lyophobic colloids and lyophilic colloids, their characteristics and properties will be considered separately later in this chapter.

Since the dispersed phase of colloidal

Hydrogen atom   Average molecule   Colloidal particle   Visible particle

(not drawn to scale)

15-2 The colloidal range of particle size lies between that of simple molecules and visible particles.

systems consists of extremely finely divided particles, the surface area of this phase is enormous. Under such circumstances actions peculiar to *surface* are most important. Therefore some of the characteristics of surface behavior should be examined before specific colloidal suspensions are considered. *This study of surface properties is called* **surface chemistry.**

SURFACE CHEMISTRY

4. Effects of subdivision. Colloidal particles have a tremendous *specific surface.* **Specific surface** *is the ratio of the surface area of the particles to their volume.* If a one-inch cube of soft clay is divided across the middle of each face, eight smaller cubes are formed (see Fig. 15-3). The surface area of the one-inch cube was 6 in², but the total surface area of the eight smaller cubes is 12 in². The total surface area has been doubled by this division, but the total volume of material has remained the same. *Thus the specific surface has been doubled.* If each of the half-inch cubes is divided as before, the specific surface is again doubled. If we proceed in this manner until the original volume of material has been reduced to colloidal dimensions, the surface area will be more than 200 acres!

This great increase in surface results in a corresponding increase in the number of surface molecules, or ions, or atoms, as the case may be. Surface molecules are those which are not surrounded on all sides by molecules similar to themselves. This increase in the number of surface molecules is always accompanied by changes in physical properties and the appearance of new properties.

The appearance of these new properties with the subdivision of matter characterizes the colloidal state. Changes may occur in solubility, melting point, heat of solution, and

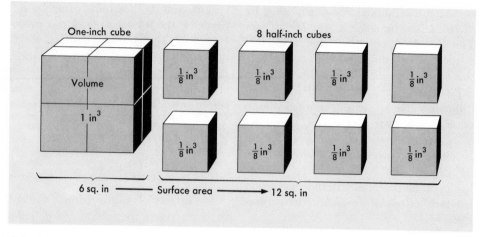

15-3 The specific surface of a substance is increased when the surface area is increased and the volume remains constant.

color of the subdivided material. With this vast increase in surface there appears a peculiar phenomenon called *adsorption*.

5. Nature of adsorption. *Adsorption is defined as the concentration of a gas, liquid, or solid on the surface of a liquid or solid with which it is in contact.* The adsorption of a gas on a solid is sometimes referred to as *occlusion*. The material providing the surface upon which adsorption occurs is known as the **adsorbent.** The material adsorbed is called the **adsorbate.** Because of the tremendous surface of particles of colloidal dimensions, a remarkable amount of adsorption may occur. One volume of palladium black (finely divided palladium metal) adsorbs nearly 1000 volumes of hydrogen. A gas cylinder, first filled with activated charcoal and then with nitrogen under pressure, discharges over 65% more nitrogen than it would without the charcoal. An adsorbent is *activated* by heating it to free its surface of adsorbed gases.

Adsorption is selective. This means that a given adsorbent shows a preference for one adsorbate over another. Activated

coconut charcoal used in gas mask canisters selectively adsorbs most toxic gases in preference to oxygen and nitrogen even though the poisons may be present in the atmosphere in relatively minor proportions. In general, *gases of low volatility are adsorbed more readily than those of higher volatility.*

Adsorption is specific. The extent to which any substance is adsorbed under any given set of conditions depends on the physical and chemical natures of the adsorbent and adsorbate. We may, however, list two general rules which apply to adsorption of gases on solids.

1. Effect of pressure. The adsorption of a gas on a solid *increases* with *increase* in pressure.

2. Effect of temperature. Adsorption is *increased* as the temperature of a system is *decreased*.

6. Some practical applications of adsorption. The use of activated charcoal in gas cylinders to store nitrogen and in gas masks has been mentioned. Several different *ad*sorbents may be used together with selected *ab*sorbents in gas mask canisters to provide protection against various combinations of gases which may be irritating or toxic.

Activated charcoal is used in liquefying gases, to obtain extremely high vacuums, and in the separation of gases. Helium is the least readily adsorbed of any known substance. It may be separated from the other noble gases by permitting them to be adsorbed on cold activated charcoal. Activated alumina, Al_2O_3, made by moderately heating aluminum hydroxide, is an effective adsorbent for water vapor. It is useful for removing water vapor from various gases. Activated alumina is often used in the chemistry laboratory as a desiccant.

A liquid adsorbed on the surface of a solid is said to *wet* the solid. Water will wet clean glass but mercury will not. It is possible to float powders on water because of the slowness with which the particles adsorb water. This is the basis for *flotation processes* used in the concentration of ores. Diamonds are separated from the *blue earth* in which they naturally occur by passing it over greased tables.

Exhausted oil sands have been made productive again by the addition of water or sodium carbonate solution. These are strongly adsorbed on the surface of the sand and displace more oil. Formations of glazes on pottery and of baked enamels on metals depend on the molten *frit* or glazing compound being adsorbed on the surface and remaining there after it cools.

The relative sizes of the particles of two solids seems to determine which is adsorbed on the other. If one is much finer than the other, the finer will be adsorbed on the coarser. If the two solids are of different colors, the mixture will have the color of the one adsorbed. This fact is taken into account in the manufacture of paints.

Slow-setting cement consists of finely powdered gypsum which is adsorbed on the coarser cement particles. Manufacturers of chewing gum have made use of the fact that the first taste of a mixture of sugar and paprika is very sweet if the sugar in the mixture is very finely powdered.

A hydrogen electrode may be used as a reference electrode in an electrochemical cell. A layer of finely divided platinum is deposited on a platinum wire or foil by electrolysis. The electrode is then placed in the solution and hydrogen gas is passed over it. Hydrogen is adsorbed on the relatively great surface of the platinum. Thus, in effect, the electrode presents a surface of hydrogen to the solution and acts as a "metallic" hydrogen electrode. The hydrogen electrode provides chemists with a direct method of determining the pH of solutions. An electrochemical series is compiled using the hydrogen electrode as a reference electrode.

7. Contact catalysts. The rates of many slow reactions can be increased to practical levels by placing the reactants in contact with the surfaces of certain solids. As these solids are not permanently altered by the reactions in which they are involved we may consider them to be

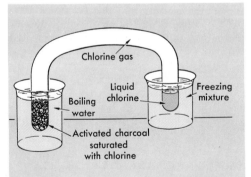

15-4 Liquefaction of chlorine. Adsorbed chlorine is released as the temperature of the charcoal is raised; the pressure of the chlorine gas increases and liquid chlorine forms in the cold end of the tube.

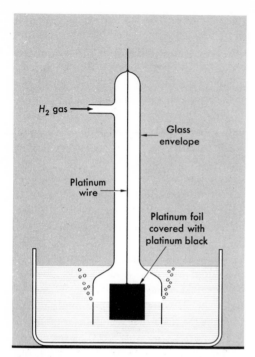

15-5 Hydrogen electrode, the standard reference electrode for the electrochemical series.

catalytic agents. Due to the nature of the catalytic action they are known as *contact catalysts* or simply **contact agents.**

If even a minute quantity of the catalyst is subdivided to colloidal size, it presents a very great surface area to the reacting substances. The reactants are then adsorbed on the surface of the contact agent, bringing about an increase in the concentration of the reacting substances. This produces a corresponding increase in the reaction rate. Many chemical industries are vitally interested in catalytic research. Consequently, catalytic agents, and the way in which they are used are sometimes closely guarded secrets.

In the Haber process for the synthesis of ammonia, a contact agent (usually iron with the oxides of aluminum and potassium) is necessary to make the process economically feasible. Platinum gauze is employed as a contact agent in the synthesis of nitric acid by the Ostwald process. Finely divided divanadium pentoxide, or platinum, is similarly used in the contact process for manufacturing sulfuric acid.

The hydrogenation of vegetable oils to form solid fats is accomplished by using colloidal nickel as a contact catalyst. Semisolid vegetable shortenings are partially hydrogenated products from such liquid fats as cottonseed oil. Complete hydrogenation forms hard, brittle fats.

Methanol is sometimes referred to as wood alcohol because it was originally produced by the destructive distillation of wood. Methanol is now made synthetically from carbon monoxide and hydrogen in the presence of zinc chromite.

8. Catalytic poisoning. Chemical reactions that employ contact catalysts must be very carefully controlled. The presence of even slight amounts of certain foreign substances may seriously retard, or even stop, the chemical action. Chemists believe that these materials are preferentially adsorbed on the surface of the contact agent. Thus, the molecules or ions of the reactants are prevented from reaching the surface of the catalyst. Such substances are known as *catalytic poisons.* Partial poisoning of a catalyst may be deliberately induced as a means of controlling the activity of a contact agent.

SUSPENSOIDS AND EMULSOIDS

9. The characteristics of suspensoids. *Lyophobic colloidal* systems, or suspensoids, were described in Section 3. Several different media are used for suspending the colloidal particles. When water is the suspending medium the term **hydrosol** is used. Thus a colloidal dispersion of metallic gold in water is called a gold hydrosol. In **organosols** an organic liquid makes up the external phase. *Aerosols* are suspensoids in which a gas is the dispersing medium. This type of suspensoid is produced when an insecticide is released from a spray bomb.

10. Properties of suspensoids. The size of colloidal particles, together with the resulting vast specific surface, is responsible for the unusual properties of colloidal dispersions. Some of these properties are:

1. Brownian movement. In 1827 Robert Brown, an English botanist, observed the haphazard motion of particles from pollen grains in water while viewing the suspension through his microscope. He suspected that the motion was in some way associated with the life process. However, when he examined other suspended materials, which could in no way be related to living matter, he observed similar motion.

With the invention of the *ultramicroscope* about 1900 by the German chemist Richard Zsigmondy (1865–1929), the colloidal range could be studied directly. Brownian movement was rediscovered by

15-6 When an aerosol bomb is used, a suspensoid is produced in which air is the dispersing medium. The propellent is usually "Freon." (duPont)

Zsigmondy in a gold hydrosol. He described the astonishing motion of the tiny gold particles as "a swarm of dancing gnats in a sunbeam." Careful investigations have eliminated all possible outside factors as the cause of these random motions. *Thus we may conclude that the forces which act upon the dispersed particles are the result of collisions between these particles and the molecules of the dispersing medium.* This offers excellent support to the kinetic theory of matter.

We see here the *first* of three general reasons why colloidal suspensions do not settle. *The influence of gravity is not great enough to overcome the collision forces of the dispersing medium on particles which show Brownian movement.* Consequently they do not settle. A gold hydrosol prepared by Michael Faraday over one hundred years ago still exists as a colloidal suspension. The two remaining reasons for the stabilization of colloidal suspensions will appear later in this chapter.

2. Tyndall effect. If a beam of light is directed into a darkened room, a surprising amount of dust is observed suspended in the air of the room. Rays of light are deflected sidewise, or *scattered*, from the surfaces of the dust particles. If the particles responsible for the scattering are extremely small, the scattered light will be somewhat bluish since only the shortest wavelengths of light are affected. Smoke suspended in air sometimes appears blue, and distant haze usually has a bluish tint. The blue sky and the redness of the sun at sunset are due to the scattering of light.

Suppose a strong beam of light is directed through a true solution, or through pure water, in a darkened room. There is little evidence of scattering; the beam is practically invisible. When light is passed through a colloidal dispersion, however, the beam is plainly visible. This diffusion of light by colloidal particles is known as

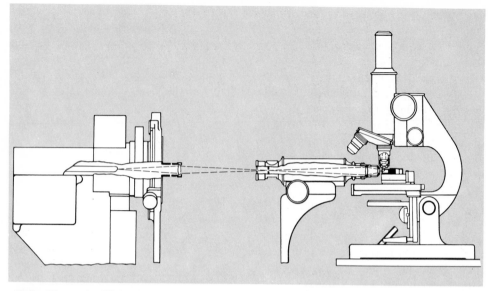

15-7 The path of light through a slit ultramicroscope. The ultramicroscope makes it possible to observe the light scattered by colloidal particles too small to be seen with an ordinary microscope. (Bausch and Lomb)

the **Tyndall effect,** after the English physicist John Tyndall (1820–1893). It may be used to detect suspended particles.

3. Structural colors. A physical chemist might classify all colors under two headings: *pigment* colors and *structural* colors. Pigment colors are due to the absorption by the pigment of some portions of the white light illuminating a substance. The color observed is the complement of that absorbed. Colored inorganic substances generally contain elements found in the central region of the Periodic Table. The halogenides of the Sodium and Calcium Families are colorless. Anhydrous copper(II) sulfate is not colored, but water solutions prepared from anhydrous copper(II) sulfate or from the crystalline hydrate, $CuSO_4 \cdot 5H_2O$, are blue. Observe that it is the $Cu(H_2O)_4^{++}$ ion that is colored. Scientists believe that pigment colors are associated with the electronic arrangement of particles.

Structural colors, on the other hand, are due to the physical structure of the mass.

They are not dependent upon the electronic configuration of the substance. The color of colloidal suspensions is usually structural. There is no blue pigment in the blue feathers of birds. Tiny air bubbles dispersed throughout the solid matter of the feathers are responsible for the scattering of light. There are no blue pigments in the irises of blue eyes. Green and gray eyes result from the combined effect of structural blue, and yellow and brown pigments. The eye of the albino lacks both structural and pigment colors.

A very dilute solution of $FeCl_3$ possesses a faint yellow pigment color due to the hydrated Fe^{+++} ion. If such a solution is boiled, colloidal $Fe(OH)_3$ is formed, resulting in a rich, deep-red structural color. The quantity of iron present remains the same.

4. Electric charge. Scientists have learned that the dispersed particles of lyophobic colloids are electrically charged in a stable system. Some types possess positive charge and others negative charge. However,

15-8 The Tyndall effect. The jar at the left contains a suspension of gelatin in water. The jar at the right contains a water solution of sodium chloride. (*Fundamental Photographs*)

within a system all suspended particles of the same substance have the same kind of electric charge. Since particles with like charge repel each other, their mutual repulsion prevents them from joining together and settling out. Thus the system tends to remain stable. Here we have the *second* reason why colloidal suspensions do not settle: *The accumulation of similar charges on the suspended particles holds them apart, thus stabilizing the system.*

The charge is generally acquired by adsorbing positive or negative ions from the dispersing medium. The external phase has the charge opposite to that on the dispersed particles and the system as a whole is neutral. Most colloidal metals, sulfides, and acid dyestuffs acquire a *negative* charge. Most colloidal oxides and hydroxides of metals and basic dyestuffs become *positively* charged. Proteins appear to gain either a positive or a negative charge with equal ease.

We should expect such colloidal dispersions to be *precipitated* by the addition

of solutions having a high concentration of ions of charge opposite to those which are adsorbed. An interesting result of this action is the formation of deltas at the mouths of large rivers. Colloidal sediment suspended in the river water flowing into the sea is precipitated by ions of the salt water. Fresh water is less dense than sea water. Thus, when fresh water first encounters the sea water, it fans out over the sea water in a surface layer. The deposition of the precipitated silt and clay even-

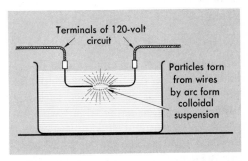

Terminals of 120-volt circuit

Particles torn from wires by arc form colloidal suspension

15-9 A Bredig arc. Less active metals may be used to form hydrosols. More active metals form organosols.

tually produces a fan-shaped delta. The large delta at the mouth of the Mississippi River is the result, in part at least, of this precipitating action.

11. The preparation of suspensoids. The colloidal state is dependent on the size of the suspended particles. There are two general methods by which particles may be brought to colloidal size.

1. The size of solute particles, which is below the colloidal range, may be increased. This is known as *condensation.* Condensation of solute particles to colloidal size may be accomplished by hydrolysis, oxidation, or reduction reactions. Very rapid precipitation or crystallization may produce colloidally suspended microcrystals of the solute. Colloidal iron(III) hydroxide is prepared by the hydrolysis of iron(III) chloride in hot water.

$$Fe^{+++} + 6H_2O \rightarrow Fe(OH)_3 + 3H_3O^+$$

Colloidal gold may be prepared by adding a reducing agent such as tin(II) chloride or iron(II) sulfate to a dilute solution of gold chloride.

$$2Au^{+++} + 3Sn^{++} \rightarrow 2Au^0 + 3Sn^{++++}$$

The color of the gold hydrosol which results depends on the size of the gold particles but is usually purple.

If hydrogen peroxide, an oxidizing agent, is added to a water solution of hydrogen sulfide, sulfur is precipitated according to the following reaction:

$$H_2S + H_2O_2 \rightarrow S + 2H_2O$$

The particles of sulfur are found to be colloidal when an attempt is made to filter the suspension. The sulfur particles pass through the filter paper along with the water. Frequently, colloidal suspensions formed by condensation methods interfere with analytic procedures since ordinary filtration does not remove the precipitated material.

2. The size of visible particles, which is above the colloidal range, may be reduced. This is known as **dispersion.** The dispersion method of producing colloidal particles may involve the use of an electric arc, mechanical methods such as grinding, shaking, or homogenizing, or the addition of a third substance. An electric arc may be produced under water by momentarily placing two energized conductors together and then separating them slightly so as to maintain the arc. If the conductors are made of gold, a purple gold dispersion will result from the disintegration of the ends of the electrodes within the arc. In a similar manner platinum electrodes will yield a brownish-black dispersion, and silver a brownish-green dispersion.

Many grinding and powdering operations are carried out in the chemistry laboratory with a mortar and pestle. Coarse particles may be so reduced in size that some colloidal suspensions are prepared in this way. In commercial operations, large grinding and shearing machines, called *colloid mills,* are used to break down coarse particles to the desired colloidal size.

Cement manufacturers use colloid mills to reduce cement particles to colloidal size because the final hardness of concrete depends largely on the fineness of the cement particles used. Colloidal dispersions may be produced by putting the coarse particles and the dispersing medium into the colloid mill together.

Suppose a few drops of oil are added to water in a test tube and the mixture is shaken vigorously. The oil is broken down into tiny droplets which remain suspended for a short time in the water before coalescing and rising to the surface. If these oil droplets are made much smaller, their separation from the water can be delayed considerably. Milk is *homogenized* by breaking down the fat globules into particles

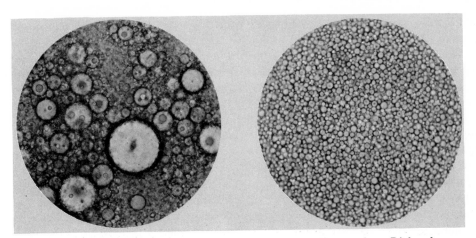

15-10 Left, an emulsion of oil in water produced by an ordinary mixer. Right, the same emulsion after passing through a colloid mill. (Premier Mill)

of such small dimensions that they do not readily join together. Thus they do not rise to the surface as cream.

Colloidal dispersions are sometimes prepared by adding a third substance to the system. This substance acts upon the particles and reduces them to colloidal dimensions. Such a substance is called a *peptizing agent* and the process is known as **peptization**. Certain of the digestive processes of animals involve peptization.

12. Precipitation of suspensoids. The formation of river deltas by the introduction of an opposite electric charge into a colloidal dispersion has already been mentioned. In the manufacture of soap, the product is formed in the colloidal state. The soap is precipitated, or *salted out*, by adding sodium chloride to the suspension. The salting-out process is frequently used in the precipitation of proteins. The opposite charge of iron(III) hydroxide and diarsenic trisulfide suspensions results in the precipitation of both when they are mixed.

Acids are sometimes used as coagulating agents. The milky colloid called *latex*, obtained from the rubber tree, is coagulated by the addition of acetic acid. Ammonia water, on the other hand, prevents coagulation of the latex.

Heat coagulates some colloids. If the colloidal dispersions produced during chemical analysis are boiled, the internal phase may coagulate. Then it can be removed by ordinary filtration. Egg albumen, a lyophilic colloid, is coagulated by hot water or hot grease in the poaching or frying of eggs.

13. Protective colloids. In some colloidal systems the precipitation of the internal phase may be prevented by the addition of a second colloid known as a *protective agent*. When a pharmacist prepares an emulsion he makes an intimate mixture of the oil and the dispersing medium with gum arabic or gum tragacanth. The protective agent is adsorbed on the surface of the dispersed particles, coating them and thus preventing actual contact and subsequent coagulation. Here we have the *third* reason why colloidal suspensions do not settle: *a protective layer of adsorbed material stabilizes the suspended particles.*

Gelatin added to milk tends to prevent curdling. When added to an ice cream mix, it prevents the formation of objectionable ice crystals, producing a smoother product. A protective colloid such as glue is added to electroplating baths to secure a smoother surface. Glue or starch added to boiler water acts to prevent the deposition of scale.

Detergents (cleaning agents) are used to stabilize grease and water emulsions. A detergent molecule has a long hydrocarbon portion and an ionic portion. The hydrocarbon part of the molecule is insoluble in water but is soluble in oils. The ionic part is insoluble in oils but is soluble in water. A small amount of soap or detergent added to water forms a colloidal suspension. The hydrocarbon ends of groups of detergent molecules cluster together leaving the ionic ends in contact with the water. If grease or oil is introduced, and the system is agitated, the oil droplets are stabilized by the detergent as a colloidal suspension of oil in water. In this condition the grease or oil is easily floated away.

Mayonnaise is salad oil colloidally dispersed in vinegar, using egg as an emulsifying agent. The egg stabilizes the oil droplets by forming a protective coating around them to prevent their coalescence.

14. Flotation process. *Foam* is a colloidal dispersion of a gas in a liquid. A very small quantity of an oil may act as a foam stabilizer, particularly in the presence of finely divided solids. Many metallic ores are found in nature in low concentrations. These are usually sulfides mixed with worthless earthy materials known as *gangue*. Before the metal in such an ore may be extracted profitably the ore must be concentrated.

This concentration is often accomplished by a process called *flotation.* Flotation depends on the fact that the gangue is preferentially wetted by water while the unwetted ore particles become attached to the oil-covered air bubbles. The low grade

ore is ground very fine, then mixed with water, oil, and air to form a foamy, frothy mixture. The water-wetted particles of gangue settle to the bottom. The unwetted ore particles are carried to the surface in the frothy suspension of air bubbles and are skimmed off.

In our modern economy the demand for minerals and metals steadily increases. Consequently the reserve of high grade minerals and ores steadily declines. This situation has stimulated the development of new flotation techniques. Chemists are able to change the composition of the flotation mixture so that various substances are made floatable. Specific chemical additives, called *collectors,* may be introduced. These are selectively adsorbed by the particles to be floated. The collec-

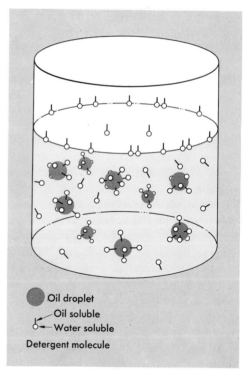

● Oil droplet

Oil soluble

Water soluble

Detergent molecule

15-11 A detergent will stabilize an oil-in-water emulsion.

15-12 A froth flotation cell. The particles of ore are carried to the surface by air bubbles in the froth. (Denver Equipment Company)

the air bubbles. They float to the surface and are skimmed off.

The gangue and pyrite, both water wetted, are pumped to a second cell. Here the mixture is treated with another collector chemical. This displaces the water from the pyrite surfaces and makes them water-repellent. The frothing action is repeated and the pyrite particles are separated from the gangue.

Chemists have found flotation procedures for concentrating all solid mineral substances. Flotation techniques are also employed in sewage disposal and in many areas in the chemical industry. The rapid strides made recently in flotation chemistry are largely the result of radioactive tracer studies of the behavior of the chemicals used as collectors.

15. Characteristics of emulsoids. The internal phase of *emulsoids* shows a marked attraction for the external phase.

tor provides the proper kind of surface for these particles and enables them to adhere to air bubbles in the froth.

It is even possible to control the surface wetting of mixtures of desirable minerals. The minerals may be floated, one at a time, and thus concentrated and separated in the same operation. A low grade copper ore, *chalcopyrite*, containing copper, iron, and sulfur, is often found mixed with *pyrite*, a sulfide of iron. Suppose we wish to separate the two ores and recover them in concentrated form.

The raw ore is first pulverized with water in colloid mills to make a thick *slurry* which is pumped into a flotation cell along with water and very small quantities of certain chemicals. One chemical substance acts as a collector for the chalcopyrite, another causes the pyrite to be wetted. As air is blown through the cell only the copper ore particles stick to

15-13 Photomicrograph of particle-bubble attachment in flotation. Tiny particles of galena are clinging to air bubbles and are being rafted to the surface. View is horizontal through the side of a glass flotation cell. (H. R. Spedden)

The intermingling of internal and external phases makes the viscosity of the system greater than that of the external phase alone. The system *sets* to form a gelatinous mass called a **gel**.

In general, this class includes those substances which naturally form colloidal suspensions. They are usually organic materials, while most suspensoids are inorganic. Some emulsoids are reversible. That is, they will redisperse in a liquid after having been separated from it. Brownian movement and the Tyndall effect are much less noticeable in emulsoids. The dispersed particles of emulsoid systems carry an electric charge, usually negative. However, they are not easily precipitated by electrolytes, as are suspensoids.

A second factor, *solvation*, contributes to the stability of emulsoids. The internal phase becomes *solvated* in the presence of the dispersing liquid. The dispersed particles adsorb molecules of the dispersing liquid and thus become surrounded by a protective layer. If the liquid is water, this process is called *hydration.*

Solvation accounts for the change in viscosity of emulsoids. It is the basic distinction between lyophilic and lyophobic colloidal systems. The setting, or formation of gels, is due to proper conditions of concentration, temperature, and hydronium-ion concentration.

16. Some common gels. Gelatin desserts are gels consisting of hydrated suspensions of gelatin, a protein, to which certain flavors have been added.

Fruit jellies consist of fruit acids, sugar, and *pectin.* Pectin, in the presence of fruit acids, produces the gel. During setting, the colloidal particles are thought to link together. This forms a network of fibrils that entrap the liquid medium in which they are suspended (see Fig. 15-14). Enough pectin is present in some fruits, such as apples and grapes, to cause a jelly to set. However, the pectin content of berry juices is usually insufficient, so apple juice or a commercial pectin product is generally added in the preparation of berry jellies.

When 15 ml of a saturated solution of calcium acetate is added to 85 ml of denatured alcohol, a jelly-like mass forms which is known as *solid alcohol.* Unless stabilized, however, the gel breaks down on standing. For this reason it is sometimes referred to as a *false gel.* Solid alcohol ("canned heat") is sold in small cans as a fuel for outdoor fires.

Gelatin dynamite and photographic film are gels. Silica gel is formed by dehydrating gelatinous silicic acid. It has a remarkable capacity for the adsorption of many gases and vapors.

17. Biocolloids. Lyophilic colloidal systems are of great importance in physiology and biology. Life processes depend on natural colloidal substances, called **biocolloids,** which compose the protoplasm of living cells.

The biocolloids include nearly all of the energy foods: starches (insoluble carbohydrates), proteins, and fats. Together with water they are the chief constituents of

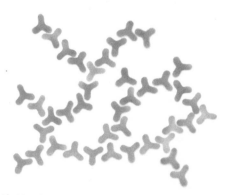

15-14 A gel forms a network of fibrils that entrap the liquid.

living matter. Included also are the bio-catalysts: enzymes, hormones, and vitamins. These stimulate and control the various chemical reactions involving the biocolloids. Thus the reactions within living organisms take place in matter that is colloidal in nature.

The biocolloids are the stable parts of the body, while the soluble substances are the migrating parts. The colloidal starches, proteins, and fats cannot pass through the tissue membranes but their soluble components do so freely.

Sugar circulates in the vein system of the plant. However, on entering the cells it is either utilized or converted, by catalytic action, to starch for storing. Similarly, in the animal body the blood sugar is con-verted to *glycogen* (animal starch) in the liver and muscles. The process is reversed, again by catalytic action, whenever this stored food is required.

The digestive process prepares food substances for passage through the membranous walls of the intestine into the blood stream. Colloidal starches are acted upon by enzymes to produce water-soluble simple sugar. Colloidal proteins, during digestion, are broken down to soluble *amino acids*. Colloidal fat substances are converted to soluble *fatty acids* and *glycerin*. Upon entering the blood stream these soluble food substances are distributed to the body tissues. Within the living cells they may be changed back into the colloidal state.

REVIEW OUTLINE

QUESTIONS

Group A

1. What distinction did Graham make between crystalloids and colloids?
2. What is the colloidal range of particle size?
3. Name eight possible types of colloidal suspensions.
4. Why is it not possible to have a colloidal suspension of a gas in a gas?
5. List three characteristics which are typical of lyophobic colloids.
6. List three characteristics typical of lyophilic colloids.
7. Distinguish between a true solution and a colloidal suspension.
8. Distinguish between the *internal* phase and the *external* phase of a colloidal system.
9. (*a*) What is the meaning of specific surface? (*b*) What is the relationship between the specific surface and the extent of subdivision of a substance?
10. Distinguish between *adsorption* and *absorption*.
11. How is an adsorbent activated?
12. What is meant by Brownian movement?
13. Describe the Tyndall effect.
14. Distinguish between pigment colors and structural colors.
15. State three general reasons why colloidal suspensions do not settle on standing.
16. (*a*) What dispersions acquire a negative electric charge? (*b*) A positive charge?
17. What are four common properties of suspensoids?
18. What are the two general methods by which suspensoids may be prepared?
19. What are three different methods by which suspensoids may be precipitated?
20. What kind of colloidal suspensions are usually formed by organic materials?

Group B

21. Explain why we now consider the colloidal state to depend on the subdivision rather than the chemical nature of a substance.
22. How can you account for the changes in physical properties and the appearance of new properties which accompany the subdivision of a substance to colloidal dimensions?
23. What conditions of temperature and pressure would you maintain if you were interested in causing a large volume of gas to be adsorbed on a solid?
24. How would you treat a lump of charcoal in preparing it to act as an adsorbent for a gas?
25. Explain why a gas mask is effective in removing poison gases from the air.
26. A solid which is more dense than water may be floated on the surface of the water if it is first reduced to a fine powder. Explain.
27. Given two solids each capable of adsorbing the other, what determines which will be adsorbed on the surface of the other when they are mixed?
28. Explain how a contact catalyst may bring about or speed up a chemical reaction.
29. Explain how a hydrogen electrode is formed.
30. Explain why the viscosity of a suspensoid is quite similar to that of the dispersing medium alone.

31. A suspensoid is formed with pure water acting as the dispersing medium. The particles of the internal phase are found to have acquired a negative charge. What possible source of this negative charge can you suggest?
32. It is found that the addition of a very small quantity of an electrolyte such as hydrochloric acid to the negatively charged suspensoid of Question 31 causes the dispersion to precipitate. What does this reveal about the concentration of the internal phase of the suspensoid?
33. (a) Explain how a colloidal suspension of diarsenic trisulfide in water may acquire a negative charge. (b) What would be the result of adding hydrochloric acid to the suspensoid?
34. (a) Define peptization. (b) A peptizing agent is involved in certain predigestive processes. What does this suggest about the nature of these processes?
35. Explain how soap can act as a protective colloid to stabilize oil in water.
36. Explain the function of collectors in the flotation process.
37. Suggest a possible reason why Brownian movement is less noticeable in emulsoids than in suspensoids.
38. Why do colloidal suspensions sometimes cause difficulties in chemical analysis?
39. Account for the formation of deltas at the mouths of large rivers.
40. What result would you expect when colloidal suspensions of iron(III) hydroxide and diarsenic trisulfide are mixed? Explain.

Chapter Sixteen

CARBON AND ITS OXIDES

CARBON

1. Carbon: abundance and importance. Carbon has been known from earliest times in the forms of charcoal and soot. In abundance, carbon ranks eleventh by weight among the elements in the earth's crust. In importance, it ranks far higher than this. It is present in the tissues of our bodies and in the foods we eat. It is found in coal, petroleum, natural gas, limestone, and in all living things. In addition, hundreds of thousands of carbon compounds have been synthesized in laboratories. The study of carbon compounds is so important that it is a separate branch of chemistry called *organic chemistry*. Originally, organic chemistry was defined as the study of materials derived only from living organisms. Inorganic chemistry was the study of materials derived from mineral sources. We have known for over a century that this is not a clear distinction. Many substances identical with those produced in living things can be made also from mineral materials. As a result, *organic chemistry today includes the study of carbon compounds whether or not they are produced by living organisms.*

In most substances containing carbon, the carbon is present in the *combined* form. It is usually united with hydrogen, or with hydrogen and oxygen. In this chapter we shall first describe the solid element carbon in its *free* or *uncombined* forms. Then we shall consider the two oxides of carbon, carbon dioxide and carbon monoxide.

2. Structure and properties of carbon atoms. Carbon is the element with atomic number 6. On the Periodic Table it is in the second period midway between the active metal lithium and the active nonmetal fluorine. Two of its six electrons are in the K shell, and are tightly bound to the nucleus. The remaining four L-shell electrons are the valence electrons. In order to attain a stable outer electronic shell, we might think that carbon atoms would either lose four electrons or gain four electrons. But carbon atoms usually

16-1 The four covalent bonds of a carbon atom are directed in space toward the four vertices of a regular tetrahedron if the center of the atom is at the center of the tetrahedron.

do neither under ordinary conditions. They show a very strong tendency to share electrons and form covalent bonds. The four valence electrons make it possible for a carbon atom to form four covalent bonds. These bonds are directed in space toward the four vertices of a regular tetrahedron. We assume the center of the atom is at the center of the tetrahedron (see Fig. 16-1).

The electron configuration of a carbon atom indicates that the valence electrons should be two $2s$ and two $2p$ electrons. However, when carbon atoms combine, it is believed that one of the $2s$ electrons acquires sufficient energy to occupy a $2p$ orbital. Thus the bonding electrons of a carbon atom are one $2s$ electron and three $2p$ electrons. A carbon atom therefore can form four covalent bonds with other carbon atoms. It can also form bonds with atoms of other elements, especially the nonmetals. Figure 16-2 represents a methane molecule, CH_4, in which a carbon atom is covalently bonded to four hydrogen atoms. Observe that the hydrogen atoms are symmetrically located as if at the vertices of a regular tetrahedron with the carbon atom at the center. The bond angles are all 109.5°. Since one of the valence electrons is a $2s$ electron and the

other three are $2p$ electrons, it might be expected that one of the carbon-hydrogen bonds in methane would be different from the other three. This, however, is found experimentally not to be the case; all the bonds are equivalent. This can be explained by assuming that *hybridization* of the $2s$ and three $2p$ orbitals occurs, producing four equivalent orbitals.

3. Hybridization in carbon compounds and water molecules. *Hybridization is the combining of two or more orbitals of the same energy level but different sublevels into new orbitals of equal energy.* The hybrid orbitals of the carbon atom are called sp^3 (read *sp*-three) orbitals since they result from the combination of one s orbital and three p orbitals. They are in tetrahedral orientation because this arrangement permits the farthest separation of four orbitals grouped about a given point.

The property of forming covalent bonds is so strong in carbon atoms that they join readily with other elements. They also link together with other carbon atoms in chains, rings, plates, and even in macromolecules, such as diamond. These varieties of ways in which carbon atoms can be linked indicate why there are several times as many more carbon compounds than there are noncarbon compounds.

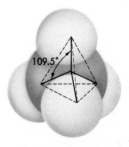

16-2 In the methane molecule, CH_4, a carbon atom is covalently and symmetrically bonded to four hydrogen atoms. Similar molecules may be formed by bonding with other elements such as chlorine and bromine.

In Chapter 11, Section 17, we pictured the space orbitals of the oxygen atom at right angles to each other along the three axes in space. If this spatial orientation were not disturbed during bonding with hydrogen atoms to form a water molecule, the hydrogen-oxygen-hydrogen bond angle should be 90°. Instead it is found experimentally to be about 105°. Apparently, even though a pair of 2s electrons and a pair of 2p electrons of the oxygen are *not* involved in bonding in the water molecule, there is considerable *sp*³ hybridization with a resultant change in the orientation of the oxygen space orbitals. This helps account for the observed bond angle of 105°, which is much closer to the tetrahedral bond angle of 109° than to a 90° angle.

4. Allotropic forms of carbon. Carbon and some other nonmetallic elements such as oxygen, sulfur, and phosphorus, exhibit *allotropy*. *Allotropy is the existence of an element in two or more forms in the same physical state.* Allotropy is due to the existence of two or more kinds of molecules, each with different numbers of atoms. Or it may result from two or more different arrangements of atoms or molecules in a crystal. Carbon occurs in two solid allotropic forms. *Diamond* is a beautiful crystalline form, and *graphite* is a grayish-black crystalline form.

When substances which contain combined carbon are heated, they produce black residues. These are sometimes collectively called *amorphous carbon* because they seem to have no definite crystalline shape. Examples of amorphous carbon are charcoal, coke, boneblack, and lampblack. Studies of their structure by X-ray scattering, however, reveal that the various forms of so-called amorphous carbon consist of extremely tiny graphite crystals. Thus there are really only two allotropic forms of carbon.

5. Diamond. The most famous diamond mines in the world are located in South Africa. Diamonds from this region usually occur in the shafts of extinct volcanoes. It is believed they were formed slowly under extreme heat and pressure. Diamonds as they are mined do not have the shape or luster of gem stones. They must be cut and polished to give their brilliant appearance.

Synthetic diamonds may be prepared by subjecting carbon-containing compounds to extremely high pressure and temperature for nearly a day.

Diamond is one of the hardest materials. It is the densest form of carbon, about 3.5 times as dense as water. This hardness and density can both be explained by its structure. Figure 16-3 shows that carbon atoms in diamond are covalently bonded in a strong, compact fashion, with internuclear distances of 1.54 Å. Note that each carbon atom is tetrahedrally oriented to its four nearest neighbors. This type of structure is strong in all three dimensions. The rigidity of the structure gives diamond its hardness. The compactness resulting from the small distances between nuclei gives it its high density. A diamond is a macromolecule, which accounts for its extremely high melting point, above 3500° C. Since all the valence electrons are used in forming covalent

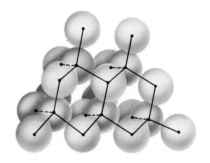

16-3   The crystal structure of diamond.

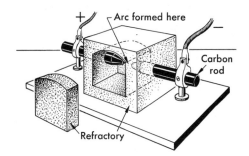

16-4 The electric arc, conducted from one carbon rod to the other by carbon vapor, produces a temperature of about 3500° C.

bonds, none is free to migrate. Diamond is thus a nonconductor of electricity. Aside from its use as a gem, diamond is used for cutting and drilling because of its extreme hardness.

Diamond is insoluble in ordinary reagents. The French chemist Antoine Laurent Lavoisier (1743–1794) burned a clear diamond in pure oxygen and obtained carbon dioxide as a product. This proved to him that diamond contains carbon. The English chemist Sir Humphry Davy (1778–1829) and other scientists repeated the experiment. They found that the mass of carbon dioxide produced by burning diamond in pure oxygen corresponds to the mass of carbon dioxide that should be produced if diamond were pure carbon.

6. Some carbon reactions occurring in electric furnaces. There are several types of electric furnaces. One of the simplest forms has two carbon rods as elec-

trodes. The rods are mounted in a block of *refractory material*—a material which has a *very high melting point*. To start the furnace, the rods are brought together momentarily, and then separated slightly. The intense heat produced by the electric current vaporizes some of the carbon, forming carbon vapor. This vapor continues to conduct the electric current as an electric arc, producing a temperature of about 3500° C. Electric furnaces of this type are called *arc-type electric furnaces.* At the high temperature of this furnace, some endothermic chemical reactions take place that cannot readily be brought about in any other way. Carbon disulfide, CS_2, and elementary phosphorus are produced in arc-type electric furnaces.

Another type of electric furnace has a central core of loose pieces of coke. The core is heated because of the high resistance which coke offers to the passage of an electric current. The core is surrounded by a thick bed of material which retains the heat. Accumulation of heat within the central mass results finally in a high temperature. Such furnaces are called *resistance furnaces.*

7. Graphite: Resonance. Natural graphite is found in New York and Pennsylvania; but Ceylon, Madagascar, and the Soviet Union are more important sources.

Artificial graphite is made in a resistance furnace by surrounding the central

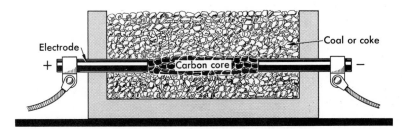

16-5 The carbon core offers resistance to the passage of an electric current and becomes heated by it. This type of resistance furnace is used for making graphite.

core with anthracite or coke. Iron(III) oxide is used as a catalyst. A temperature of 3000° C converts the anthracite to graphite.

Graphite is nearly as remarkable for its softness as diamond is for its hardness. It is easily crumbled and has a greasy feel. Graphite crystals are hexagonal in shape, with specific gravity of about 2.25. Although graphite is a nonmetal, it is a fairly good conductor of electricity.

The structure of graphite readily explains these properties. The carbon atoms in graphite are arranged in layers of thin hexagonal plates (Fig. 16-6). The distance between the centers of adjacent carbon atoms in a layer is 1.42 Å, less than the distance between adjacent carbon atoms in diamond. However, the distance between the centers of atoms in adjacent layers is 3.40 Å. Each carbon atom in a layer is bonded to only three other carbon atoms in that layer. Figure 16-6 shows that bonding within a layer consists of single and double covalent bonds between carbon atoms. When represented in this fashion, three different equivalent patterns can be drawn. In each of these, some carbon-carbon bonds are single and others are double. There is, however, no experimental evidence that the bonds in a layer of graphite are of these two distinct types. On the contrary, the evidence indicates that the bonds are all the same. This is explained by the phenomenon of *resonance.* It is sometimes possible to write two or more valence bond structures which differ only in the arrangement of electrons. But even when this is done, none of these structures has an independent existence, and no one valence bond structure properly represents the structure of the substance. The actual structure is a combination or resonance hybrid of the written structures. ***Resonance*** *designates the nature of the bonding in substances when combination of two or more valence bond structures is required.* The layers of graphite have a resonating structure in which the carbon-carbon bonds are intermediate in character between single and double bonds.

The layers of carbon atoms in graphite are too far apart for the formation of covalent bonds between them. They are held together by weak van der Waals attractive forces resulting from electronic motion within the layers. Thus each layer in graphite is a strongly-bonded macromolecule, accounting for its extremely high melting point, about 3500° C. The weak attraction between layers accounts for the softness of graphite and its greasy feel as one layer slides over another. On the average the carbon atoms in graphite are farther apart than they are in diamond, and so graphite has a lower specific gravity. The mobile electrons in a carbon atom layer make it an electrical conductor.

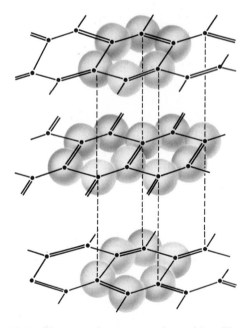

16-6 The crystal structure of graphite. The distance between the layers has been exaggerated in order to show the structure of each layer more clearly.

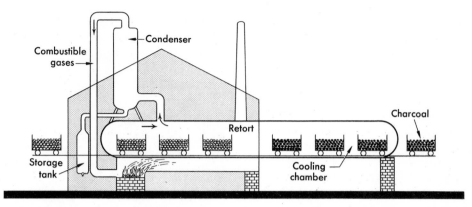

16-7 Charcoal is made by the destructive distillation of wood in large closed retorts. Liquid by-products collect in the storage tank. The combustible gases are used as fuel.

Like diamond, graphite does not dissolve in any ordinary solvent. It forms carbon dioxide when burned in oxygen.

8. Uses of graphite. Graphite is a very good lubricant, particularly when mixed with petroleum jelly to form a graphite grease. It may be used for lubricating machine parts that operate at temperatures too high for the usual oil lubricants.

Graphite has a very high melting point, about 3500° C. Hence, it is an excellent refractory. Mixed with a binder to hold the particles together, graphite is made into crucibles which are used for melting steel and other metals. Graphite is also used for the electrodes of electric furnaces. Powdered graphite is dusted over a wax impression of printer's type to make the surface a conductor of electricity. When immersed in a copper-plating bath, metallic copper is deposited on the graphite and takes the outline of the type. These plates are then nickel or chrome plated to insure longer wear. Books are printed from such plates, which are called electrotypes.

Graphite leaves a gray streak or mark when it is drawn across a sheet of paper. In making "lead" pencils, graphite is powdered, mixed with clay, and then formed into sticks. The hardness of a pencil depends upon the relative amount of clay that is used.

Graphite is also used as a moderator in nuclear reactors (see Chapter 31).

9. Destructive distillation. When a complex material containing compounds of carbon, such as wood or bituminous coal, is *heated in a closed container without access to air or oxygen, it decomposes into simpler substances.* This process is known as *destructive distillation.* Charcoal, coke, and boneblack are prepared by destructive distillation from wood, coal, and bones, respectively.

10. Charcoal. Destructive distillation of wood yields combustible gases, methanol (wood alcohol), acetic acid, and other volatile products. The solid residue is charcoal. Charcoal is prepared commercially by heating wood in closed retorts. The resulting combustible gases provide supplementary fuel. The other volatile products are condensed and sold as by-products.

Charcoal is a porous, black, brittle solid that is odorless and tasteless. It is denser than water, but it often adsorbs enough gas to make it float on water. The ability to adsorb a large quantity of gas is the most remarkable physical property of charcoal. One cubic inch of freshly prepared willow charcoal adsorbs about 90 cubic inches of ammonia gas. Because of its ability to adsorb gases, charcoal is a good deodorizer. A layer of wood charcoal is often used between layers of sand and gravel in water purification for this purpose. Charcoal also removes the color from certain liquids. Gas masks depend upon some form of carbon to adsorb the harmful gases from the air.

Charcoal is **activated,** increasing its ability to adsorb gases, by treating it with steam in retorts. It may also be impregnated with certain chemicals, which serve as catalysts, to make it more effective.

At ordinary temperatures, charcoal is inactive and insoluble in all ordinary solvents. It is a good reducing agent because it unites with oxygen at a high temperature. Charcoal is also a good fuel, but it is more expensive than other common fuels and is not widely used for this purpose.

11. Coke. When bituminous coal is heated in a hard-glass test tube, a flammable gas escapes, and a tarlike liquid condenses on the upper walls of the tube. If the heating is continued until all the volatile matter is driven off, coke is left as a residue.

Commercially, coke is prepared by the destructive distillation of bituminous coal in by-product coke ovens. The volatile products are separated into *coal gas*, which may be used as a fuel; *ammonia*, which is used in making fertilizers; and *coal tar*. The coal tar can be separated by distillation into many materials which are used to make drugs, dyes, and explosives. The black pitch that remains after distillation is used to surface roads.

About 50,000,000 tons of coke are produced each year in the United States. Coke is a gray solid that is harder and denser than charcoal. It burns with little flame, has a high heat content, and is a valuable fuel.

16-8   Coke is produced by the destructive distillation of bituminous coal in by-product coke ovens. Here the red-hot coke is being discharged from an oven into a waiting railroad car. (American Iron and Steel Institute)

Coke is an excellent reducing agent. It is widely used in the smelting of metals since many of the ores of iron, tin, copper, and zinc are oxides, or are converted into oxides.

12. Boneblack. Animal charcoal, or *boneblack*, is produced by the destructive distillation of bones. The by-products of the process include bone oil and pyridine, which are used for denaturing alcohol (making it unfit for human consumption). Boneblack usually contains calcium phosphate as an impurity. This can be removed by treating the boneblack with an acid.

Boneblack is used as an adsorbent to decolorize liquids. In sugar refineries crude sugar solutions are decolorized by passing them through large tanks partially filled with boneblack.

▶**13. Lampblack.** Finely divided particles of carbon, or soot, are set free when kerosene or light oil burns in an insufficient supply of air. The carbon, called *lampblack*, forms a velvety black powder on cool surfaces near the flame. Lampblack is used in printer's ink, shoe polish, India ink, carbon paper, and black varnish and paint.

▶ **14. Carbon black.** *Carbon black* is made by burning natural gas in an insufficient supply of air. It is not so greasy or tarlike as lampblack, and for many purposes it is more desirable. Carbon black is especially useful in making automobile tires. It helps to preserve the rubber and makes the tires wear longer.

▶ **15. Gas carbon and petroleum coke.** Carbon scraped from the walls of retorts in a coal gas plant is called *gas carbon*. A somewhat similar product, *petroleum coke*, is scraped from the walls of retorts in which petroleum has been distilled. Rods of gas carbon and petroleum coke are used as electrodes because they are fairly good conductors of electricity. Gas carbon rods are used for the positive electrodes of dry cells. Petroleum coke electrodes are used in the production of aluminum by electrolysis.

CARBON DIOXIDE

16. Carbon dioxide is a common, widely distributed gas. Carbon dioxide comprises only about 0.04% of the atmosphere by volume, yet it is a very important component of air. The water of rivers, lakes, and oceans contains between twenty and thirty times as much dissolved carbon dioxide as the atmosphere. The decay of organic matter, the burning of fossil fuels, and respiration all produce carbon dioxide. Sometimes it accumulates in considerable amounts in low-lying areas such as bogs, swamps, and marshes. It may also collect in appreciable quantities in mines, caves, and caverns.

17. Preparation of carbon dioxide.

1. By burning carbonaceous material. Carbon dioxide is one of the products of the complete combustion in oxygen or air of any material which contains carbon. Carbon dioxide prepared in this way is mixed with other gases from the air. If these gases do not interfere with the uses for which the carbon dioxide has been prepared, this method is by far the cheapest and easiest.

$$C \text{ (combined)} + O_2 \rightarrow CO_2 \uparrow$$

2. By heating a carbonate. When calcium carbonate (as limestone, marble, or shells) is heated strongly, calcium oxide and carbon dioxide are the products.

$$CaCO_3 \rightarrow CaO + CO_2 \uparrow$$

Calcium oxide, known as *quicklime*, is used for making plaster and mortar. The carbon dioxide is a by-product. It is piped from the kiln in which the carbonate is heated, and compressed into steel cylinders.

3. By fermentation of molasses. The enzymes of *zymase* are produced by yeast. They catalyze the fermentation of the sugar, $C_6H_{12}O_6$, in molasses to produce ethanol (ethyl alcohol) and carbon dioxide. While the process is complex, the over-all reaction is:

$$C_6H_{12}O_6 \rightarrow 2C_2H_5OH + 2CO_2 \uparrow$$

This is a method by which industrial alcohol is produced, and is an important source of carbon dioxide.

4. By the action of an acid on a carbonate. This is the usual laboratory method for preparing carbon dioxide. The gas-generating bottle in Fig. 16-9 contains a few pieces of marble, $CaCO_3$. If dilute hydrochloric acid is poured through the funnel tube, carbon dioxide is evolved rapidly. Calcium chloride may be recovered from the solution in the bottle.

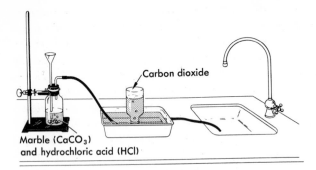

Marble (CaCO₃)
and hydrochloric acid (HCl)

16-9   The laboratory preparation of carbon dioxide.

This reaction proceeds in two stages. *First*, the marble and hydrochloric acid undergo an exchange reaction:

$$CaCO_3 + 2HCl \rightarrow CaCl_2 + H_2CO_3$$

Second, carbonic acid is unstable and decomposes:

$$H_2CO_3 \rightarrow H_2O + CO_2 \uparrow$$

The equation which summarizes these two reactions is

$$CaCO_3 + 2HCl \rightarrow CaCl_2 + H_2O + CO_2 \uparrow$$

Even though carbon dioxide is soluble in water, it may be collected by water displacement if it is generated rapidly. It may also be collected by displacement of air. In this case, the receiver must be kept *mouth upward* because the gas is more dense than air.

This is a general type reaction for an acid and carbonate. Almost any acid may be used, even a weak one such as the acetic acid in vinegar. Almost any carbonate, too, may be used. The equation for the reaction between sodium carbonate and sulfuric acid is:

$$Na_2CO_3 + H_2SO_4 \rightarrow$$
$$Na_2SO_4 + H_2O + CO_2 \uparrow$$

5. *By respiration and decay.* This is a natural method of preparation of carbon dioxide. The foods we eat contain compounds of carbon. Oxygen from the air we inhale is used in oxidizing our food. This supplies us with energy to maintain body temperature, activate muscles, synthesize new compounds in the body, and transmit nerve impulses. Carbon dioxide, which we exhale into the air, is one of the products of this oxidation. All living things give off carbon dioxide during respiration.

When plants and animals die, decay begins and carbon dioxide is produced. This gas eventually finds its way into the surrounding air, or becomes dissolved in surface or underground streams.

18. Structure of the carbon dioxide molecule. Carbon dioxide molecules are linear with the two oxygen atoms symmetrically bonded on opposite sides of the carbon atom. See Fig. 16-10. The carbon-oxygen bonds in the molecule are somewhat polar due to the electronegativity difference between carbon and oxygen. However, the symmetry of the molecule causes it to be nonpolar.

From a consideration of the electron-dot symbols for carbon and oxygen, we might assign the carbon dioxide molecule the electron dot formula

$$\ddot{\overset{..}{O}} :: C :: \ddot{\overset{..}{O}}$$

However, the carbon-oxygen bond distance predicted by this structure is larger than that actually found in the carbon dioxide molecule. Apparently this structure is not an accurate representation. Carbon dioxide molecules are believed to be resonance hybrids of four electronic structures, each of which contributes about equally to the actual structure.

$$\left\{ \begin{array}{ll} :\overset{..}{O}::C::\overset{..}{O}:, & ^{-}:\overset{..}{O}:C:::O:^{+} \\ :\overset{..}{O}::C::\overset{..}{O}:, & ^{+}:O:::C:\overset{..}{O}:^{-} \end{array} \right\}$$

Such a resonance hybrid has the carbon-oxygen bond distance and energy actually observed for the carbon dioxide molecule.

19. Physical properties of carbon dioxide. Because of its simple nonpolar molecular structure, carbon dioxide is a gas at room temperature. It is colorless with a very faint pungent odor and a slightly pungent taste. The molecular weight of carbon dioxide is 44 and its density is thus about 1.5 times that of air. The large, heavy molecules of carbon dioxide move more slowly than the smaller, lighter molecules of oxygen or hydrogen. Because of its higher density and slower rate of diffusion, carbon dioxide can be poured from one vessel to another, and sometimes collects at the bottom of caves, mines, or dry wells.

At room temperature, under a pressure of about 70 atmospheres, carbon dioxide

molecules are pushed very close together. They then attract each other sufficiently to condense to a liquid. If this liquid is permitted to evaporate rapidly under atmospheric pressure, part of it changes into a gas. This process absorbs heat from the remaining liquid, which is thus cooled until it solidifies in the form called *Dry Ice*.

Solid carbon dioxide has a high vapor pressure. Many molecules of carbon dioxide, even in the solid state, possess sufficient energy to escape from the surface of the solid into the air. The vapor pressure of solid carbon dioxide equals atmospheric pressure at −78.5° C. As a result, solid carbon dioxide under atmospheric pressure sublimes at this temperature. Liquid carbon dioxide does not exist at atmospheric pressure. At low temperatures, with pressures higher than 5 atmospheres, carbon dioxide may be liquefied.

20. Chemical properties of carbon dioxide. Carbon dioxide is a stable gas which neither burns nor supports combustion. However, burning magnesium is hot enough to decompose carbon dioxide. Thus a piece of burning magnesium ribbon continues to burn in a bottle of the gas. The magnesium unites vigorously with the oxygen set free by the decomposition, and carbon is produced, as shown by a coating of soot on the inside of the bottle.

$$\mathbf{2Mg + CO_2 \rightarrow 2MgO + C}$$

Carbon dioxide dissolves readily in *cold water*. Some of the dissolved molecules also unite with the water forming a weak acid, carbonic acid (carbon dioxide is the anhydride of carbonic acid).

$$\mathbf{H_2O + CO_2 \rightleftarrows H_2CO_3}$$

This acid exists only in water solution.

$$\mathbf{H_2O + H_2CO_3 \rightleftarrows H_3O^+ + HCO_3^-}$$
$$\mathbf{H_2O + HCO_3^- \rightleftarrows H_3O^+ + CO_3^=}$$

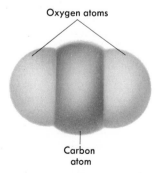

Oxygen atoms

Carbon atom

16-10 The carbon dioxide molecule is linear and consists of one carbon atom and two oxygen atoms.

It is easily decomposed by heat since CO_2 is less soluble at higher temperatures. The reduction of the concentration of CO_2 in the water causes all the equilibria to shift to the left, thus decreasing the H_2CO_3 and H_3O^+ concentrations.

When carbon dioxide is passed into a water solution of a hydroxide, it reacts to form a carbonate.

$$2NaOH + CO_2 \rightarrow Na_2CO_3 + H_2O$$

If the positive ion of the hydroxide forms an insoluble carbonate, it will be precipitated when carbon dioxide passes through the hydroxide solution.

A *test for carbon dioxide* is to bubble the gas through a saturated solution of $Ca(OH_2)$, called limewater. The precipitation of the white calcium carbonate indicates the presence of carbon dioxide.

$$Ca^{++} + 2OH^- + CO_2 \rightarrow CaCO_3 \downarrow + H_2O$$

If excess carbon dioxide gas is bubbled through the solution, the precipitate disappears due to the formation of soluble calcium hydrogen carbonate.

$$CaCO_3 + H_2O + CO_2 \rightarrow Ca^{++} + 2HCO_3^-$$

Carbon dioxide is not poisonous, but a person will suffocate in an atmosphere of carbon dioxide because of the lack of oxygen.

21. Uses of carbon dioxide.

1. It is necessary for photosynthesis. **Photosynthesis** means "*putting together by means of light.*" It is a complex process by which green plants manufacture carbohydrates with the aid of sunlight. *Chlorophyll*, the green coloring matter of plants, acts as a catalyst. Carbon dioxide from the air and water from the soil are the raw materials. Glucose, a simple sugar, $C_6H_{12}O_6$, is one of the products. The following simplified equation gives only the *reactants* and the *final products* of this synthesis.

$$6CO_2 + 12H_2O \rightarrow$$
$$C_6H_{12}O_6 + 6O_2 \uparrow + 6H_2O$$

The sugar may then be converted into a great variety of other plant products.

2. Carbon dioxide is used in most fire extinguishers. When the *soda-acid type* of fire extinguisher is inverted, the sulfuric acid pours out and reacts with the sodium hydrogen carbonate solution. See Fig. 16-11.

$$2NaHCO_3 + H_2SO_4 \rightarrow$$
$$Na_2SO_4 + 2H_2O + 2CO_2 \uparrow$$

The pressure of the gas forces a stream of liquid a considerable distance. The carbon dioxide dissolved in the liquid is of some benefit in putting out the fire, but water is the main extinguishing agent.

The *foam type* of fire extinguisher is similar in construction to the soda-acid type.

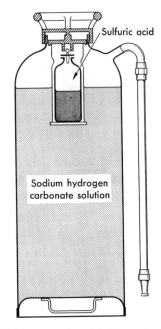

Sulfuric acid

Sodium hydrogen carbonate solution

16-11 When a soda-acid fire extinguisher is inverted, the acid spills and reacts with the sodium hydrogen carbonate to liberate carbon dioxide.

16-12 A liquid carbon dioxide fire extinguisher is effective in putting out oil fires. (Walter Kidde and Company, Inc.)

A solution of aluminum sulfate, $Al_2(SO_4)_3$, acts as an acid because of hydrolysis. It reacts with sodium hydrogen carbonate and liberates carbon dioxide. See the equations below.

A sticky substance dissolved in the sodium hydrogen carbonate solution prevents the escape of the gas by stabilizing the foam. The foam smothers the fire, shutting off the air. Foam fire extinguishers are particularly effective for putting out oil and gasoline fires.

Liquid carbon dioxide fire extinguishers are widely used and quite efficient. When the valve is opened, the nozzle directs a stream of carbon dioxide "snow" against the flame. Such an extinguisher is effective against oil fires and may be used around electric switchboards.

3. Carbonated beverages contain carbon dioxide in solution. Soft drinks are carbonated by forcing the gas into the beverages under pressure. When the bottles are opened, the excess pressure is released and bubbles of carbon dioxide rapidly escape from the liquid.

4. Leavening agents produce carbon dioxide. Yeast is mixed with the flour and other ingredients in making dough for bread. The living yeast plants produce an enzyme which ferments the starches and sugars, producing ethanol and carbon dioxide. The bubbles of carbon dioxide become entangled in the plastic dough, causing it to rise. The ethanol is vaporized and driven off during the baking process.

Baking powder differs from baking soda, sodium hydrogen carbonate. Baking powder is always a dry mixture, not just one compound. It contains baking soda, which can yield the carbon dioxide, and some powder that forms an acid when water is added. The acid compound varies with the kind of baking powder used. Cornstarch is used in baking powders to keep them dry until they are used.

5. Carbon dioxide is used as a refrigerant. While Dry Ice costs more than ice for refrigeration, it is superior to ice in two respects. It leaves no liquid because it changes directly from a solid to a gas. Also, because of its low temperature, one

$$2Al^{+++} + 3SO_4^= + 4H_2O \rightleftarrows 2Al(OH)^{++} + 2H_3O^+ + 3SO_4^=$$
$$Na^+ + HCO_3^- + H_3O^+ \rightleftarrows Na^+ + H_2CO_3 + H_2O$$
$$H_2CO_3 \rightarrow H_2O + CO_2 \uparrow$$

pound of Dry Ice produces a greater cooling effect than an equal weight of ice. The temperature of Dry Ice is so low that it *must never be handled with bare hands* because serious frostbite may result.

CARBON MONOXIDE

22. Carbon monoxide in the air. Air does not commonly contain carbon monoxide. But there are several ways by which this poisonous gas may get into the air. If a coal-burning furnace is not properly operated, carbon monoxide may escape and mix with the air in living or sleeping rooms. An unvented gas heater is also a potential source of carbon monoxide in a home. Carbon monoxide is a component of some fuel gases. Leaking gas lines are dangerous because of the poisonous nature of the gas as well as the fire hazard. Carbon monoxide is present in the exhaust from internal combustion engines. Therefore you should never leave the engine of an automobile running in a closed garage. Likewise, an automobile engine should not be kept running to provide heat to a car parked in cool weather with the windows closed. The smoke from burning tobacco also contains measurable quantities of carbon monoxide.

Because carbon monoxide has no odor and induces drowsiness before actual asphyxiation, it is very hazardous. The air in cities where automobile traffic is heavy may contain considerable amounts of this gas. The breathing of air containing as little as one part of carbon monoxide per thousand parts of air will produce nausea and headache in less than an hour. One part of carbon monoxide in one hundred parts of air may produce fatal results in ten minutes.

23. Preparation of carbon monoxide.
1. By reducing carbon dioxide. If carbon dioxide comes into contact with white-hot carbon or coke, it is reduced to carbon monoxide.

$$CO_2 + C \rightarrow 2CO \uparrow$$

2. By action of steam on hot coke. Passing steam over red-hot coke produces a mixture, called *water gas*, containing mainly carbon monoxide and hydrogen. This is an industrial method of producing both carbon monoxide and hydrogen for use as fuel gases.

$$C + H_2O \rightarrow CO \uparrow + H_2 \uparrow$$

The two gases may be separated by cooling and compression which liquefies the carbon monoxide but not the hydrogen.

3. By decomposing formic acid. This is the

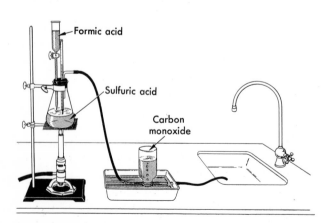

16-13 Carbon monoxide can be prepared in the laboratory by dehydrating formic acid with hot, concentrated sulfuric acid.

usual laboratory method for preparing carbon monoxide. Formic acid, HCOOH, is allowed to fall, a drop at a time, into hot, concentrated sulfuric acid. Carbon monoxide is produced as each drop strikes the hot acid (see Fig. 16-13). Concentrated sulfuric acid is an excellent dehydrating agent. It removes a molecule of water from each molecule of the formic acid, leaving only carbon monoxide, CO.

$$HCOOH \rightarrow H\ O + CO \uparrow$$

CAUTION: When using this method, always be sure the connections are tight so that the carbon monoxide does not escape into the room.

24. Structure of the carbon monoxide molecule. Carbon monoxide molecules consist of one carbon atom and one oxygen atom covalently bonded. See Fig. 16-14. The distance between the nuclei is 1.13 Å. The molecule is slightly polar, with *the carbon atom somewhat negative*. In order to account for these properties, the carbon monoxide molecule is believed to be a resonance hybrid of four structures:

$$\left\{ \begin{array}{ll} {}^+\!:C\!:\!\overset{..}{O}\!:^-, & :C\!:\!:\!\overset{..}{O}\!: \\ :C\!:\!:\!\overset{..}{O}\!:, & {}^-\!:C\!:\!:\!:O\!:^+ \end{array} \right\}$$

Unlike carbon dioxide, however, these four structures do not contribute equally. The hybrid is estimated to be 10 percent ${}^+\!:C\!:\!\overset{..}{O}\!:^-$, 20 percent each $:C\!:\!:\!\overset{..}{O}\!:$ and $:C\!:\!:\!\overset{..}{O}\!:$, and 50 percent ${}^-\!:C\!:\!:\!:O\!:^+$. The electronegativity difference discussed in Chapter 6 would indicate that the oxygen in carbon monoxide would be negative. However, you must remember that those data apply only to *single* bonds between elements. The structure of carbon monoxide is more complicated. The high proportional effect of the triple bonded structure, ${}^-\!:C\!:\!:\!:O\!:^+$, makes carbon

Oxygen atom

Carbon atom

16-14   The carbon monoxide molecule is a slightly polar molecule consisting of one carbon atom and one oxygen atom.

monoxide molecules quite stable at ordinary temperatures, and gives the carbon atom the slight negative charge in the polar molecule.

25. Physical properties of carbon monoxide. Carbon monoxide is a colorless, odorless, tasteless gas. It is slightly less dense than air and is only slightly soluble in water. It is difficult to liquefy, since its critical temperature is $-138.7°$ C and its critical pressure is 34.6 atm. Carbon monoxide is not readily adsorbed by charcoal. However, charcoal can be treated with certain oxides that oxidize the monoxide to the dioxide. Gas masks containing this treated charcoal protect wearers against carbon monoxide.

26. Chemical properties and uses of carbon monoxide.

1. As a reducing agent. Carbon monoxide is a very good reducing agent. It is used in the extraction of iron, copper, and some other metals from their oxides.

$$Fe_2O_3 + 3CO \rightarrow 2Fe + 3CO_2 \uparrow$$

2. As a fuel. Carbon monoxide burns with a blue flame. Many fuel gases contain this gas mixed with other combustible gases. Coal gas and water gas always contain carbon monoxide.

3. For synthesizing organic compounds. Methanol, CH_3OH, is made by synthesis from carbon monoxide and hydrogen, under pressure. A mixture of zinc oxide and copper is used as a catalyst.

$$CO + 2H_2 \rightarrow CH_3OH$$

Carbon monoxide is also used in the synthesis of many other organic compounds.

27. Physiological action of carbon monoxide. This gas is poisonous because it unites very readily with *hemoglobin*, the red substance in blood that serves as an oxygen carrier. If hemoglobin unites with carbon monoxide, it is not available for carrying oxygen. When sufficient carbon monoxide has been breathed, the person collapses because of oxygen starvation. The compound formed by carbon monoxide and hemoglobin is so stable that artificial respiration is not usually successful. Blood transfusions, which supply fresh hemoglobin, may help to revive victims of carbon monoxide poisoning. Autopsies performed on the bodies of those who have been killed by carbon monoxide reveal a peculiar red color in the blood of the victims. This color aids physicians in determining the cause of death.

REVIEW OUTLINE

Carbon—abundance and occurrence (1)

Organic chemistry (1)

Carbon atom structure—hybridization (2, 3)

Forms of carbon—allotropy (4)
    Diamond (5)
    Graphite—electric furnace; resonance (6, 7, 8)
    Charcoal—destructive distillation; activation (9, 10)
    Coke (11)
    Boneblack and lampblack (12, 13)
    Carbon black, gas carbon, petroleum coke (14, 15)

Carbon dioxide
    Occurrence (16)
    Preparations (17)
        Industrial (17)
        Laboratory (17)
        Natural (17)
    Molecular structure (18)
    Properties
        Physical (19)
        Chemical (20)
    Uses (21)

Carbon monoxide
    Occurrence (22)
    Preparations
        Industrial (23)
        Laboratory (23)
    Molecular structure (24)

Properties
    Physical (25)
    Chemical (26)
Uses (26)
Physiological action (27)

QUESTIONS

Group A

1. (*a*) Why does the study of carbon compounds constitute a separate branch of chemistry? (*b*) What name is given to this branch of chemistry?
2. What is the orientation of the four covalent bonds of a carbon atom?
3. What property of carbon atoms makes possible the large number of carbon compounds?
4. (*a*) What is *allotropy*? (*b*) What are the allotropic forms of carbon? (*c*) Why is amorphous carbon no longer classified as a third allotropic form of carbon?
5. Why are diamonds useful in industry?
6. (*a*) What are the two types of electric furnaces? (*b*) How is the heat produced in each furnace?
7. (*a*) What is *resonance*? (*b*) Using valence bond structures for graphite layers, show how the structure of graphite illustrates resonance.
8. Give several reasons why graphite is used as a lubricant.
9. (*a*) What is *destructive distillation*? (*b*) Is it really destructive? Explain.
10. Why does a form of carbon such as charcoal or coke remain after the destructive distillation of wood or bituminous coal?
11. What is *activated* charcoal?
12. Why is boneblack a relatively impure form of carbon?
▶13. Distinguish between lampblack and carbon black.
▶14. What use is made of petroleum coke?
15. Why is carbon dioxide an important component of the atmosphere even though it occurs to only 0.04% by volume?
16. (*a*) Name the three commercial methods for preparing carbon dioxide. (*b*) What is the usual laboratory method? (*c*) Write balanced chemical equations for these methods.
17. What difficulties are experienced when collecting carbon dioxide: (*a*) by water displacement; (*b*) by air displacement?
18. By comparing their molecular weights, arrange oxygen, hydrogen, carbon dioxide, and carbon monoxide in order of increasing density.
19. What are the chemical properties of carbon dioxide?
20. (*a*) How is carbonic acid produced? (*b*) Is it a strong or a weak acid? Explain.
21. What is the test for carbon dioxide?
22. How does a liquid carbon dioxide fire extinguisher put out fires?

23. Write a balanced equation for the reaction which occurs in the discharging of a soda-acid fire extinguisher.
24. (*a*) What is the source of carbon dioxide in most leavening agents? (*b*) How is it released?
25. What are the sources of carbon monoxide contamination in the atmosphere?
26. What is the function of sulfuric acid in the preparation of carbon monoxide from formic acid?
27. Why are both carbon dioxide and carbon monoxide gases at room temperature when water, with a lower molecular weight, is a liquid?
28. What are three uses of carbon monoxide?

Group B

29. Explain why carbon atoms usually do not form ionic bonds with other elements.
30. (*a*) What is *hybridization?* (*b*) Show how the carbon atom illustrates hybridization in the formation of sp^3 orbitals.
31. Summarize the explanations for the 105° angle between the hydrogen-oxygen bonds in the water molecule.
32. Diamond is very hard and is a nonconductor of electricity. Graphite is soft and is a conductor of electricity. Diamond is more dense than graphite. Both diamond and graphite withstand very high temperatures without melting. Explain these properties in terms of the similarities and differences in the structures of diamond and graphite.
33. Why is charcoal a good adsorbent?
34. When coke is used as a reducing agent, what is oxidized?
35. What proof is there that diamond is pure carbon?
36. Why is it so difficult to remove stains made by printer's ink?
37. Powdered charcoal, copper(II) oxide, and manganese dioxide are all black substances. How could you identify each?
38. What property of a solid determines whether it will sublime or melt when heated?
39. What is the function of an enzyme?
40. Write an ionic equation to represent the overall reaction between calcium carbonate and hydrochloric acid to produce carbon dioxide.
41. Write an ionic equation to represent the overall reaction between sodium carbonate and sulfuric acid.
42. Show by means of ionic equations that the reaction between aqueous sodium hydroxide and carbon dioxide may be considered to be a hydronium ion-hydroxide ion neutralization reaction.
43. Show by means of ionic equations that the reaction which serves as a test for carbon dioxide may be considered to be a neutralization reaction combined with a precipitation.
44. Does magnesium ribbon actually burn in carbon dioxide? Explain.
45. Distinguish between baking soda and baking powder.
46. Both carbon dioxide and carbon monoxide will produce asphyxiation. Explain the differences in their action on the body.

47. When a bottle of limewater is left unstoppered, a white ring is formed on the inside of the bottle at the surface of the liquid. Explain its cause, and tell how it can be removed.

48. Explain why carbon dioxide molecules are nonpolar, while carbon monoxide molecules are polar.

PROBLEMS

Group A

1. (*a*) How many moles of iron(III) oxide can be reduced by the carbon in 2.00 moles of carbon monoxide, according to the equation: $Fe_2O_3 + 3CO \rightarrow 2Fe + 3CO_2 \uparrow$? (*b*) How many moles of iron are produced? (*c*) How many moles of carbon dioxide are produced?

2. How many grams of carbon monoxide are needed to react with 12.21 g of zinc oxide to produce elementary zinc? $ZnO + CO \rightarrow Zn + CO_2 \uparrow$

3. In Problem 2 (*a*) how many grams of zinc are produced? (*b*) What is the volume in liters at S.T.P. of the carbon dioxide produced?

4. How many grams of H_2SO_4 are required for the reaction with 1.00 kg of sodium hydrogen carbonate in a soda-acid fire extinguisher? $2NaHCO_3 + H_2SO_4 \rightarrow Na_2SO_4 + 2H_2O + 2CO_2 \uparrow$

5. Calculate the number of liters of carbon dioxide at S.T.P. liberated during the discharge of the fire extinguisher of Problem 4.

Group B

6. How many grams of carbon monoxide can be obtained by the dehydration of 230. g of formic acid by sulfuric acid?

7. How many liters of dry carbon monoxide will be produced in Problem 6 if the temperature is 27° C and the barometer reading is 750. mm?

8. How many liters of carbon dioxide will be produced by the combustion of the carbon monoxide of Problem 7 if the product is restored to 27° C and 750. mm pressure?

9. Compare the rates of diffusion of hydrogen and carbon monoxide.

10. How much faster does oxygen diffuse than carbon dioxide?

11. A pupil wishes to prepare 2.50 liters of dry carbon dioxide at 17° C and 740. mm pressure by the reaction between calcium carbonate and hydrochloric acid. How many grams of calcium carbonate will be required?

12. How many milliliters of concentrated hydrochloric acid must be diluted with water to provide the HCl needed for the reaction of Problem 11? Concentrated hydrochloric acid is 38.0% HCl by weight and has a specific gravity of 1.20.

Chapter Seventeen

HYDROCARBONS

HYDROCARBON SERIES

1. Abundance of carbon compounds. The number of possible carbon compounds seems to be almost unlimited. More than 1,000,000 are known and about 100,000 new ones are isolated or synthesized each year. In this chapter we shall describe only a few compounds which are basic to an understanding of organic chemistry. In Chapters 18 and 19, other organic compounds important in everyday life will be discussed.

There are two reasons for the existence of so many carbon compounds.

Carbon atoms link together with covalent bonds. In Chapter 16, we described how carbon atoms readily form covalent bonds with other carbon atoms. This makes possible the existence of molecules in which as many as 70 carbon atoms are bonded together to form a long chain. The molecules of some organic compounds are principally long carbon-atom chains with carbon-atom groups attached. Other carbon compound molecules have carbon atoms linked together to form rings. Still others may consist of several such rings joined together. Not only are carbon atoms linked by single covalent bonds, but they are sometimes linked by double or triple covalent bonds.

The same atoms may be arranged in several different ways. One of the substances in petroleum is a compound called *octane*. Its molecular formula is C_8H_{18}, so a molecule of octane consists of 8 carbon atoms and 18 hydrogen atoms. Remembering that a carbon atom may form four single covalent bonds while a hydrogen atom forms only one single covalent bond, the straight-chain electron-dot structure for an octane molecule may be written:

$$
\begin{array}{c}
\text{H} \quad \text{H} \quad \text{H} \quad \text{H} \quad \text{H} \quad \text{H} \quad \text{H} \quad \text{H} \\
\text{H}:\text{C}:\text{C}:\text{C}:\text{C}:\text{C}:\text{C}:\text{C}:\text{C}:\text{H} \\
\text{H} \quad \text{H} \quad \text{H} \quad \text{H} \quad \text{H} \quad \text{H} \quad \text{H} \quad \text{H}
\end{array}
$$

But there are other ways in which these same atoms can be arranged. For instance, here are three branched-chain formulas:

```
    H     H     H H H H
 H:C  :  C  :  C:C:C:C:H
    H   H:C:H  H H H H
        H:C:H
          H

            H
    H    H H:C:H H H H
 H:C  :  C  :  C  :  C:C:C:H
    H   H:C:H H     H H H
          H

          H        H
    H  H:C:H H  H:C:H H
 H:C  :  C  :  C  :  C  :  C:H
    H  H:C:H H     H     H
          H
```

These are all arrangements of 8 carbon atoms and 18 hydrogen atoms in which each carbon atom shares four electrons and each hydrogen atom shares one electron. In addition to these four structures for octane, there are 14 others, making a total of 18 possible structures for octane. While they each have the same molecular formula, the different arrangements of the atoms in the molecules give each molecule slightly different properties. Thus each of these molecular arrangements represents a separate chemical compound. *These different compounds, all with the same molecular formula but with different structures, are called* **isomers.**

2. Structural formulas for organic compounds. The formula H_2SO_4 for sulfuric acid is satisfactory for most purposes in inorganic chemistry. But a molecular formula such as C_8H_{18} is not at all satisfactory in organic chemistry. We have already noted that there are 18 different isomers of this compound. In order to indicate clearly the particular isomer with

which the organic chemist is dealing, he uses a **structural formula.** *Such a formula not only indicates what kinds of atoms and how many of each, but also indicates how they are arranged in the molecule.* Electron-dot formulas have been used to illustrate the isomers of octane. However, such formulas are tedious to draw for routine equation work. Thus the organic chemist frequently substitutes a dash (—) for the pair of shared electrons forming a covalent bond. Using the dash, he can represent the straight-chain structural formula for octane as:

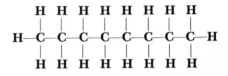

When structural formulas are written, there must be no dangling bonds. Each dash must represent an electron pair which forms the covalent bond linking two atoms.

3. Determination of an organic structural formula. There are two different organic compounds which consist of carbon, 52.2%, hydrogen, 13.0%, and oxygen, 34.8%. They have the same molecular weight, 46, and thus are isomers. One compound is a colorless liquid which boils at 78° C, while the other is a colorless gas which condenses to a liquid at −25° C under one atmosphere pressure. Each has its own distinctive odor. How may we determine their structural formulas?

From the percentage composition, the empirical formula may be calculated, according to the method of Chapter 7, Section 12, to be C_2H_6O. Since this formula has a formula weight of 46, this must also be the molecular formula of each compound. From what we have already learned about bonding, there are only two ways in which two carbon atoms, six hydrogen atoms, and a single oxygen atom may be combined:

H—C—C—O—H   Structure A

H—C—O—C—H   Structure B

Now our problem is to match these structures to the two compounds. If we investigate the reaction of each compound with metallic sodium, only the liquid reacts. In the reaction an amount of hydrogen is liberated which corresponds to one-sixth that which the compound contains. From this, we might assume that in the molecules of the liquid one of the six hydrogen atoms is bonded differently from the others. Hence, Structure A is indicated.

Next we discover that the liquid reacts with phosphorus trichloride to give a product with the molecular formula C_2H_5Cl. In this reaction we see that chlorine has replaced both a hydrogen atom and an oxygen atom. We can write only one structural formula for C_2H_5Cl:

H—C—C—Cl

Now we may assume that the oxygen and hydrogen atoms which were replaced by the chlorine occupied the same position in the molecule as the chlorine does in the reaction product. Structure A is again indicated. We might continue further, because a great deal more evidence can be cited to indicate that the liquid does indeed have Structure A. This liquid substance is ethanol or ethyl alcohol. The gaseous substance has the other structural formula and is called dimethyl ether.

The methods of deducing the structural formulas of other simple organic compounds follow much the same techniques as we have described. More complicated molecules are generally broken down into simpler molecules. The structure of these simpler molecules is then used to deduce the structure of the complex molecule. Sometimes simpler molecules of known structure are combined to produce the larger molecule. Its structure is then worked out in this fashion. Occasionally a comparison of chemical and physical properties of compounds of unknown structure with those of known structures is very helpful.

4.   Differences between organic and inorganic compounds. The basic laws of chemistry hold true equally for organic and inorganic chemistry. The behavior of organic compounds, and the reactions between them, however, show some differences from those of inorganic compounds. Some of the important differences are:

1. Most organic compounds do not dissolve in water. The majority of inorganic compounds do dissolve more or less readily in water. Organic compounds generally dissolve in such organic liquids as alcohol, chloroform, ether, carbon disulfide, or carbon tetrachloride.

2. Organic compounds are decomposed by heat more easily than most inorganic compounds. The decomposition (charring) of sugar when it is heated moderately is familiar. Such charring on heating is often a test for organic substances. But an inorganic compound, such as common salt (sodium chloride), can be vaporized at a red heat without decomposition.

3. Organic reactions generally proceed at much slower rates. Such reactions often require hours or even days for completion. Organic reactions in living cells take place with great speed. Most inorganic reactions occur almost as soon as solutions of the reactants are brought together.

4. Organic compounds exist as molecules consisting of atoms joined by covalent bonds. Many inorganic compounds have ionic bonds.

CAUTION: Many organic compounds are flammable and toxic, and some organic reactions are rapid and highly exothermic. A student should not perform any experiments with organic compounds without detailed laboratory directions, and then only under the supervision of an experienced instructor.

5. Series of hydrocarbons. *Hydrocarbons are compounds composed of only two elements—hydrogen and carbon.* Any study of organic compounds logically begins with a study of the hydrocarbons, because they have the basic structures from which other organic compounds are derived. Hydrocarbons may be grouped into several different series of compounds based mainly on the type of bonding between carbon atoms.

1. The *alkanes* (al-*kaynes*), sometimes called the paraffin series, are straight-chain or branched-chain hydrocarbons, in which the carbon atoms are connected by only *single* covalent bonds.

2. The *alkenes* (al-*keens*), sometimes called the olefin series, are straight- or branched-*chain* hydrocarbons in which

two carbon atoms in their molecules are connected by a *double* covalent bond.

3. The *alkynes* (al-*kynes*), sometimes called the acetylene series, are also straight- or branched-*chain* hydrocarbons in which two carbon atoms in their molecules are connected by a *triple* covalent bond.

4. The *alkadienes* (al-kah-*dy*-eens) are also straight- or branched-*chain* hydrocarbons which have *two double* bonds between carbon atoms in the molecule.

5. The *aromatic hydrocarbons* have resonating structures usually represented by alternate single and double covalent bonds in six-membered carbon *rings*.

6. The alkane series. This series is sometimes called the *paraffin series* because paraffin wax is a mixture of hydrocarbons of this series. The word "paraffin" means little affinity, or little attraction. The members of this series have low chemical reactivity compared with the other hydrocarbon series because of the very stable single covalent bonds in their molecules. Because they have only single covalent bonds in their molecules, the alkanes are known as *saturated hydrocarbons.*

The table below lists a few of the straight-chain members of the alkane series. The names of the first four mem-

ALKANE SERIES

Name	Formula	Melting Point °C	Boiling Point °C
methane	CH_4	−183	−162
ethane	C_2H_6	−172	−89
propane	C_3H_8	−187	−42
n-butane	C_4H_{10}	−135	0
n-pentane	C_5H_{12}	−130	36
n-hexane	C_6H_{14}	−94	69
n-heptane	C_7H_{16}	−90	98
n-octane	C_8H_{18}	−57	126
n-nonane	C_9H_{20}	−54	151
n-decane	$C_{10}H_{22}$	−30	174
* * *			
n-eicosane	$C_{20}H_{42}$	36	
* * *			
n-hexacontane	$C_{60}H_{122}$	99	

bers of this series are unsystematic. However, beginning with pentane, the first part of the name is the Greek or Latin numerical prefix for the number of carbon atoms. The name of each member ends in *-ane*, the same as the name of the series. The letter prefix "*n*" for "normal" indicates the straight-chain isomer.

If you examine the formulas for successive alkanes, you see that each member of the series differs from the preceding one by the group CH_2,

$$
\begin{array}{c}
H \\
| \\
-C- \\
| \\
H
\end{array}
$$

Compounds which differ in this fashion belong to a *homologous series*. It is not necessary to remember the formulas of each member of a homologous series. A general formula, such as C_nH_{2n+2} for the alkanes, can be derived. Suppose a member of this series has 30 carbon atoms in its molecule. The number of hydrogen atoms is found by multiplying 30 by 2, then adding 2. The formula becomes $C_{30}H_{62}$.

7. Structures of the lower alkanes. There is only one possible molecular structure for the first three alkanes.

$$
\begin{array}{c}
H \\
| \\
H-C-H \\
| \\
H \\
\text{methane}
\end{array}
\qquad
\begin{array}{c}
H \ \ H \\
| \ \ \ | \\
H-C-C-H \\
| \ \ \ | \\
H \ \ H \\
\text{ethane}
\end{array}
$$

$$
\begin{array}{c}
H \ \ H \ \ H \\
| \ \ \ | \ \ \ | \\
H-C-C-C-H \\
| \ \ \ | \ \ \ | \\
H \ \ H \ \ H \\
\text{propane}
\end{array}
$$

However, there are two ways in which the four carbon atoms and ten hydrogen atoms of C_4H_{10} may be arranged in a molecule having single covalent bonds:

$$
\begin{array}{c}
H \quad\ \ H \quad\ \ H \\
| \qquad | \qquad | \\
H-C\quad\ C\quad\ C-H \\
| \quad H-C-H \quad | \\
H \quad | \quad H \\
H \\
\text{isobutane}
\end{array}
$$

$$
\begin{array}{c}
H \ \ H \ \ H \ \ H \\
| \ \ \ | \ \ \ | \ \ \ | \\
H-C-C-C-C-H \\
| \ \ \ | \ \ \ | \ \ \ | \\
H \ \ H \ \ H \ \ H \\
\textit{n}\text{-butane}
\end{array}
$$

The straight-chain molecule is *n*-butane. The branched-chain molecule is called isobutane.

The structure of isobutane is that of propane in which a CH_3— group is substituted for one of the hydrogen atoms attached to the middle, or second, carbon atom. Methane is CH_4. The CH_3— group (methane without one hydrogen atom) is called the *methyl group*. Isobutane may also

methane

ethane

propane

17-1 Models of molecules of the first three members of the alkane series of hydrocarbons.

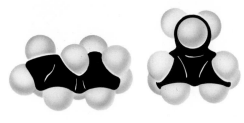

n-butane   isobutane

17-2 Models of molecules of the two isomers of butane.

be called 2-methylpropane since it is basically propane with a methyl group instead of a hydrogen atom attached to the second carbon atom (counting from the end).

There are three possible pentanes (C_5H_{12}). See the formulas below.

$$
\begin{array}{ccccc}
\text{H} & \text{H} & \text{H} & \text{H} & \text{H} \\
| & | & | & | & | \\
\text{H—C—C—C—C—C—H} \\
| & | & | & | & | \\
\text{H} & \text{H} & \text{H} & \text{H} & \text{H}
\end{array}
$$

n-pentane

isopentane

neopentane

Isopentane might also be called 2-methylbutane. It would not be called 3-methylbutane, because the numbering of the carbon chain is done from the end of the molecule which results in the lowest number(s) as prefix(es). Neopentane might also be called tetramethylmethane, since its structure is four methyl groups substituted for the hydrogen atoms in methane. Another name for neopentane is 2,2-dimethylpropane.

Just as the CH_3— group derived from methane is the methyl group, C_2H_5— derived from ethane is the ethyl group. C_3H_7— derived from propane is the propyl group, and C_4H_7— derived from butane is the butyl group. C_5H_9— is usually called the amyl group rather than the pentyl group. Other groups are given names following the general rule of dropping the *-ane* suffix and adding *-yl*. Any such group derived from an *alkane* is an *alkyl* group. The symbol R— is frequently used to represent an alkyl group in a formula.

▶**8. Bonding in the alkanes.** Hydrocarbon molecules contain carbon-hydrogen and carbon-carbon bonds. The electronegativity difference between carbon and hydrogen is slight ($2.5 - 2.1 = 0.4$). Thus carbon-hydrogen bonds have about 4 percent ionic character and may be considered essentially nonpolar bonds. Carbon-carbon bonds, since they are between like atoms, are of course nonpolar bonds.

In ethane we have one carbon-carbon bond and six carbon-hydrogen bonds. The carbon-carbon bond is an sp^3-sp^3 bond. It is formed by electron sharing between two sp^3 hybrid orbitals, one from each of the bonded carbon atoms. The carbon-hydrogen bonds are sp^3-s bonds formed by electron sharing between a carbon sp^3 orbital and a hydrogen s orbital. Remember that sp^3 bonds are oriented tetrahedrally. Rotation can occur about

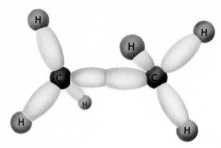

17-3 Bonding in ethane. Each carbon atom has four *sp³* hybrid orbitals. Each hydrogen atom has one *s* orbital. The carbon-carbon bond is an *sp³-sp³* bond. The carbon-hydrogen bonds are *sp³-s* bonds.

the *sp³-sp³* bond. This rotation is somewhat restricted, however, by the interaction of the tetrahedrally oriented groups of carbon-hydrogen bonds at the ends of the molecule.

9. Preparation of the alkanes. The alkanes are generally found in petroleum and natural gas. They are separated from these mixtures by the process of *fractional distillation.* *Fractional distillation is a method of separating the components of a mixture which have different boiling points.* It is possible to separate effectively the lower members of the alkane series from petroleum and natural gas by fractional distillation. However, it is usually only practicable to separate the higher boiling substances into mixtures containing compounds having similar boiling points.

Methane is a colorless, nearly odorless gas which forms about 90% of natural gas. If pure methane is required, it may be separated from the other components of natural gas. Small amounts of methane may be prepared in the laboratory by heating soda lime (which contains sodium hydroxide) with sodium acetate:

$$NaC_2H_3O_2 + NaOH \rightarrow CH_4 \uparrow + Na_2CO_3$$

Ethane is a colorless gas which occurs in natural gas and is also a product of

petroleum refining. It has a higher melting point and boiling point than methane. These properties would be expected because of its higher molecular weight.

10.   Reactions of the alkanes.

1. Combustion. The most important reaction of the alkanes is combustion, since they constitute a large proportion of our gaseous and liquid fuels. Methane burns with a bluish flame.

$$CH_4 + 2O_2 \rightarrow CO_2 \uparrow + 2H_2O \uparrow$$

Ethane and other alkanes also burn in air to form carbon dioxide and water vapor.

$$2C_2H_6 + 7O_2 \rightarrow 4CO_2 \uparrow + 6H_2O \uparrow$$

2. Substitution. The alkanes react with halogens such as chlorine or bromine. The products are called *substitution products* because one or more atoms of a halogen are substituted for one or more atoms of hydrogen:

$$\overset{\displaystyle H}{\underset{\displaystyle H}{H-C-H}} + Br_2 \rightarrow \overset{\displaystyle H}{\underset{\displaystyle H}{H-C-Br}} + HBr$$

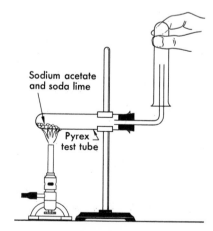

17-4 A small quantity of methane can be prepared in the laboratory by heating a mixture of sodium acetate and soda lime.

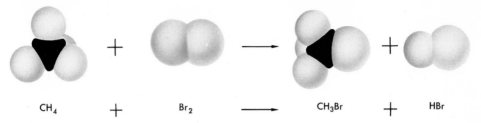

$$CH_4 \quad + \quad Br_2 \quad \longrightarrow \quad CH_3Br \quad + \quad HBr$$

17-5   Methane and bromine undergo a substitution reaction.

By supplying additional molecules of the halogen, a halogen atom may be substituted for each of the hydrogen atoms.

3. Preparation of hydrogen. Propane reacts with steam in the presence of a nickel catalyst at a temperature of about 850° C:

$$\mathbf{C_3H_8 + 6H_2O \rightarrow 3CO_2 \uparrow + 10H_2 \uparrow}$$

The carbon dioxide may be separated from the hydrogen by dissolving it in water under pressure.

Hydrogen may also be prepared by heating hydrocarbons in the absence of air. The decomposition of methane is shown as:

$$\mathbf{CH_4 \rightarrow C + 2H_2 \uparrow}$$

The carbon produced is in the form of lampblack.

11. Alkene series. The alkenes are characterized by a double covalent bond between two carbon atoms. Consequently the simplest alkene must have two carbon atoms. Its structural formula is:

$$\overset{\displaystyle H}{\diagdown}\ \ \overset{\displaystyle H}{\diagup}$$
$$C = C$$
$$\overset{\displaystyle \diagup}{H}\ \ \overset{\displaystyle \diagdown}{H}$$

and its name is ethene. The names of the alkenes are derived from the names of the alkanes with the same number of carbon

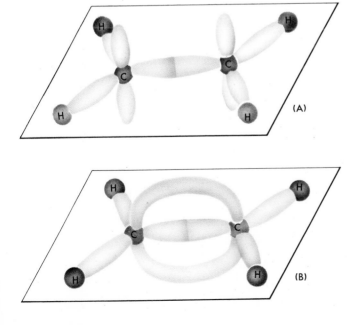

(A)

(B)

17-6   Bonding in ethene. (*A*) Each carbon atom has three sp^2 hybrid orbitals in the plane and a *2p* orbital perpendicular to the plane. Each hydrogen atom has one *s* orbital. (*B*) The carbon-carbon double bond is a combination of an sp^2-sp^2 bond with a *p-p* overlap bond having lobes above and below the plane. The carbon-hydrogen bonds are sp^2-*s* bonds.

atoms by merely substituting the suffix -*ene* for the suffix -*ane*. Since eth*ane* is the alk*ane* with two carbon atoms, the alk*ene* with two carbon atoms will be named eth*ene*. (This substance is also commonly called *ethylene*.) The general formula for the alkenes is C_nH_{2n}.

▶ In ethene the bonding mechanism is more complex than in the alkanes. It is believed that the carbon atoms form three sp^2 hybrid orbitals which produce bonds that are 120° apart in a plane. The three sp^2 orbitals are formed by promotion of a $2s$ electron to the vacant $2p$ orbital and hybridization of one $2s$ and *two* $2p$ orbitals. This leaves one $2p$ orbital, with one electron, oriented perpendicular to the plane. See Fig. 17–6(A). These $2p$ orbitals can overlap and form a new orbital consisting of two lobes, one above and one below the plane. See Fig. 17–6(B). This combination of an sp^2-sp^2 bond and the p-p overlap bond constitutes the double bond in the ethene molecule. No rotation occurs about a carbon-carbon double bond. Hence in an ethene molecule all six atoms, the sp^2-sp^2 bond, and the four sp^2-s bonds all lie in the same plane. The carbon to carbon internuclear distance is shorter in ethene than in ethane. In ethane it is 1.53 Å, almost the same as that found in diamond, while in ethene, it is 1.33 Å.

12.   Preparations of alkenes.

1. Cracking alkanes. Alkenes are made from petroleum by *cracking*. **Cracking** *is a process by which complex organic molecules are broken up into simpler molecules by the action of heat and usually a catalyst.* The cracking of ethane at about 600° C produces ethene and hydrogen.

$$C_2H_6 \xrightarrow{\text{600° C}} C_2H_4 \uparrow + H_2 \uparrow$$

2. Dehydration of alcohols. Ethene may be prepared in the laboratory by dehydrating ethyl alcohol. Hot concentrated sulfuric acid is used as the dehydrating agent.

$$C_2H_5OH \rightarrow C_2H_4 \uparrow + H_2O$$

13.   Reactions of alkenes.

1. Addition. An organic compound which has a double covalent bond between two carbon atoms is said to be *unsaturated*. It is chemically possible to add other atoms directly to its molecule to form a new compound. Hydrogen atoms may be added to an alkene, in the presence of a finely divided nickel catalyst, to produce the corresponding alkane.

$$\begin{array}{c} H \\ \diagdown \\ \end{array} C = C \begin{array}{c} H \\ \diagup \\ \end{array} + H_2 \xrightarrow{\text{Ni}} H - \overset{\displaystyle H}{\underset{\displaystyle H}{C}} - \overset{\displaystyle H}{\underset{\displaystyle H}{C}} - H$$

Halogen atoms may be readily added to alkene molecules. For example, two bromine atoms may be added directly to ethene to form 1,2-dibromoethane.

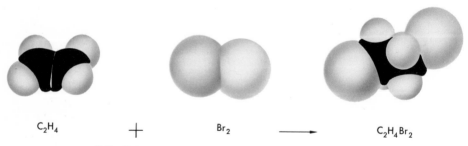

C_2H_4 + Br_2 $\longrightarrow$ $C_2H_4Br_2$

17-7   Ethene and bromine undergo an addition reaction.

$$
\begin{array}{c}
\text{H}\qquad\text{H} \\
\diagdown\qquad\diagup \\
\text{C}=\text{C} \quad + \text{Br}_2 \rightarrow \text{H—C—C—H} \\
\diagup\qquad\diagdown \\
\text{H}\qquad\text{H}
\end{array}
\qquad
\begin{array}{c}
\text{Br}\;\;\text{Br} \\
|\;\;\;| \\
\text{H—C—C—H} \\
|\;\;\;| \\
\text{H}\;\;\text{H}
\end{array}
$$

As the double bond between the carbon atoms breaks, there is one bond position available for each bromine atom.

The name of the product, 1,2-dibromoethane, is easily derived. The basic part of the name, ethane, is that of the related alkane with two carbon atoms. Dibromomeans two bromine atoms have been substituted for hydrogen atoms in ethane. 1,2- means that one bromine atom is bonded to the first carbon atom and the other is bonded to the second carbon atom. An isomer, 1,1-dibromoethane has the formula

$$
\begin{array}{c}
\text{Br}\;\;\text{H} \\
|\;\;\;| \\
\text{Br—C—C—H} \\
|\;\;\;| \\
\text{H}\;\;\text{H}
\end{array}
$$

A molecule of a hydrogen halogenide, such as hydrogen bromide, may be added to an alkene molecule.

$$
\begin{array}{c}
\text{H}\qquad\text{H} \\
\diagdown\qquad\diagup \\
\text{C}=\text{C} \quad + \text{HBr} \rightarrow \text{H—C—C—H} \\
\diagup\qquad\diagdown \\
\text{H}\qquad\text{H}
\end{array}
\qquad
\begin{array}{c}
\text{H}\;\;\text{Br} \\
|\;\;\;| \\
\text{H—C—C—H} \\
|\;\;\;| \\
\text{H}\;\;\text{H}
\end{array}
$$

2. Polymerization. Molecules of ethene will join together, or polymerize, at 250° C and 1000 atmospheres pressure. The resulting large molecules have molecular weights of about 30,000. This polymerized material is called *polyethylene*. It is made up of many **monomers** (single units)

$$
\begin{array}{c}
\text{H}\;\;\text{H} \\
|\;\;\;| \\
\text{—C—C—} \\
|\;\;\;| \\
\text{H}\;\;\text{H}
\end{array}
$$

joined together to make the **polymer** (many units). Polyethylene is used in making electric insulation, transparent wrappings, and a variety of containers.

3. Combustion. The alkenes burn in oxygen:

$$C_2H_4 + 3O_2 \rightarrow 2CO_2 \uparrow + 2H_2O \uparrow$$

14. Alkyne series. The alkynes have a triple covalent bond between two carbon atoms. The simplest alkyne must therefore have two carbon atoms, with the formula

$$\text{H—C}\equiv\text{C—H}$$

The names of the alk*ynes* are derived from the names of the alk*anes* with the same number of carbon atoms by substituting the suffix *-yne* for *-ane*. Hence the name of the simplest alkyne is *ethyne*. (This compound is more commonly known as *acetylene*.) The general formula for the alkynes is C_nH_{2n-2}.

▶ In ethyne the carbon atoms form two *sp* hybrid orbitals, oriented 180° apart. One is to the other carbon atom and one to a hydrogen atom. Hence the ethyne molecule is linear. The *sp* hybrid orbitals are formed by promotion of a *2s* electron to the vacant *2p* orbital and hybridization of one *2s* and *one 2p* orbital. This leaves two *2p* orbitals, with one electron each. They are oriented perpendicularly to each other and to the line joining the nuclei of the carbon and hydrogen atoms. The two *2p* orbitals may overlap and form two merging orbitals surrounding the carbon atoms in a form resembling a thick-walled cylinder. See Fig. 17-8. The internuclear distance between the carbon atoms in ethyne is 1.20 Å, less than in ethane or ethene.

15. Preparations of ethyne.

1. From calcium carbide. Ethyne, a colorless gas, may be prepared by the action of water on calcium carbide. Calcium car-

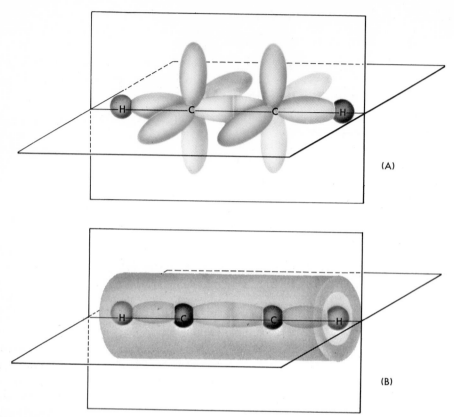

17-8 Bonding in ethyne. (*A*) Each carbon atom has two *sp* hybrid orbitals in the line of intersection of the planes and two *2p* orbitals perpendicular to each other in the planes. Each hydrogen atom has one *s* orbital. (*B*) The carbon-carbon triple bond is a combination of an *sp-sp* bond with two *p-p* overlap bonds which surround the carbon atoms like a thick-walled cylinder. The carbon-hydrogen bonds are *sp-s* bonds.

bide is made from limestone, $CaCO_3$, by first producing CaO in a lime kiln.

$$CaCO_3 \rightarrow CaO + CO_2 \uparrow$$

The calcium oxide is then heated with coke at 2000° C in an electric resistance furnace.

$$CaO + 3C \rightarrow CaC_2 + CO \uparrow$$

Calcium carbide is an ionic compound with the electron-dot structure

$$Ca^{++}$$
$$^{-x}_{\cdot}C \vdots\vdots_{\circ}^{\circ} C^{\circ}_{x}-$$

When it reacts with water, two hydrogen atoms replace the calcium in the calcium carbide structure:

$$CaC_2 + 2H_2O \rightarrow C_2H_2 \uparrow + Ca(OH)_2$$

2. By cracking alkanes. Ethyne may be produced by passing methane through an electric arc.

$$2CH_4 \rightarrow C_2H_2 \uparrow + 3H_2 \uparrow$$

16.   Reactions of ethyne.

1. Combustion. Ethyne burns in air with a very smoky flame. Carbon, carbon dioxide, and water vapor are the products of combustion. With special burners, the combustion to carbon dioxide and water vapor is complete.

$$2C_2H_2 + 5O_2 \rightarrow 4CO_2 + 2H_2O$$

The oxyacetylene welding torch is an application of the combustion of ethyne.

2. Halogen addition. Ethyne is more unsaturated than ethene because of the triple bond. It is possible chemically to add to an ethyne molecule two molecules of bromine to form 1,1,2,2,-tetrabromoethane.

$$H-C\equiv C-H + 2Br_2 \rightarrow H-\overset{\overset{\displaystyle Br}{|}}{C}-\overset{\overset{\displaystyle Br}{|}}{C}-H$$
$$\underset{Br}{|}\quad\underset{Br}{|}$$

3. Water addition. Ethyne will react with water from dilute sulfuric acid in the presence of mercury(I) sulfate to yield an important compound, acetaldehyde.

$$H-C\equiv C-H + H_2O \xrightarrow[Hg_2SO_4]{H_2SO_4}$$

4. Dimerization. Two molecules of ethyne may combine to form the *dimer* (two units), vinylacetylene. This is done by passing ethyne through a water solution of copper(I) chloride and ammonium chloride which acts as a catalyst.

$$2H-C\equiv C-H \xrightarrow[NH_4Cl]{Cu_2Cl_2}$$

vinylacetylene

The $CH_2=CH-$ group is the vinyl group. Vinylacetylene is the basic raw material for producing Neoprene, a synthetic rubber.

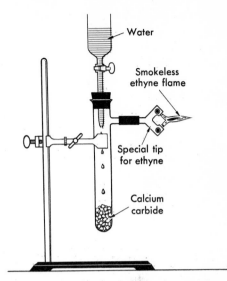

17-9 A convenient method of preparing a small quantity of ethyne (acetylene) in the laboratory by the action of water on calcium carbide.

17. Butadiene: an important alkadiene. Alkadienes have two double covalent bonds in each molecule. The *-ene* suffix indicates a double bond. The *-diene* suffix indicates two double bonds. The names of the alkadienes are derived in a manner similar to those of the other hydrocarbon series. Butadiene must, therefore, have four carbon atoms and contain two double bonds in its molecule:

Actually, this is 1,3-butadiene, since the double bonds follow the first and third carbon atoms. However, 1,2-butadiene, its isomer, is so uncommon that 1,3-butadiene is commonly called simply butadiene.

Butadiene is prepared by cracking petroleum fractions containing butane. It is used in the manufacture of SBR rubber, the most common type of synthetic rubber.

18. The aromatic hydrocarbons. The aromatic hydrocarbons are generally obtained from coal tar and petroleum. Benzene, the best known aromatic hydrocarbon, has the molecular formula C_6H_6. It is represented by the following resonance formula in which the two structures contribute equally.

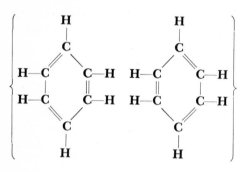

The bonds in benzene are neither single bonds nor double bonds, but each bond is a resonance hybrid bond. All the carbon-carbon bonds in the molecule are equivalent. As a result benzene and other aromatic hydrocarbons do not show the property of unsaturation to the extent that the alkenes do.

▶ The carbon-carbon bonding in the benzene molecule is believed to be sp^2-sp^2 bonding similar to that in the ethene structure. The carbon-hydrogen bonding is sp^2-s bonding. This results in 120° bond angles, and a planar molecule. The singly occupied p orbitals of each carbon atom are perpendicular to the plane of the molecule. These p orbitals above and below the plane overlap to form three orbitals. The principal one of these consists of two doughnut-shaped rings, one above and one below the plane of the molecule. See Fig. 17-10. The other two orbitals also encompass the entire molecule, but are difficult to represent diagrammatically.

Because of the resonance structure of benzene, the benzene ring is usually abbreviated:

The C_6H_5— group derived from benzene is called the *phenyl* group.

Benzene is obtained commercially by the distillation of coal tar. It is a flammable liquid that is used as a solvent. Benzene is the starting point in the manufacture of many other chemicals, principally dyes, drugs, and explosives. Benzene has a strong, yet fairly pleasant aromatic odor. It is less dense than water and only very slightly soluble in water. Benzene is poisonous. It should be used only where there is adequate ventilation, since the vapors are harmful to breathe and are very flammable.

19. Reactions of benzene.

1. Halogenation. Benzene reacts with bromine in the presence of ron to form the substitution product bromobenzene or phenyl bromide.

$$\bigcirc + Br_2 \xrightarrow{Fe} \bigcirc\!\!-Br + HBr$$

Further treatment causes the successive substitution of other bromine atoms for hydrogen atoms by bromine atoms until hexabromobenzene is produced.

$$\begin{array}{c} Br \\ Br-\bigcirc-Br \\ Br--Br \\ Br \end{array}$$

2. Nitration. Nitrobenzene is produced by treating benzene with concentrated nitric and sulfuric acids.

$$\bigcirc + HNO_3 \xrightarrow{H_2SO_4} \bigcirc\!\!-NO_2 + H_2O$$

3. Sulfonation. Benzenesulfonic acid is produced at room temperature by treating benzene with fuming sulfuric acid (sulfuric acid containing an excess of sulfur trioxide).

4. Friedel-Crafts reaction. An alkyl group may be introduced into the benzene ring by using an alkyl halogenide in the presence of anhydrous aluminum chloride.

20. Other aromatic hydrocarbons. Toluene, or methyl benzene, is obtained from coal tar or petroleum.

The xylenes or dimethylbenzenes, $C_6H_4(CH_3)_2$, are a mixture of three liquid

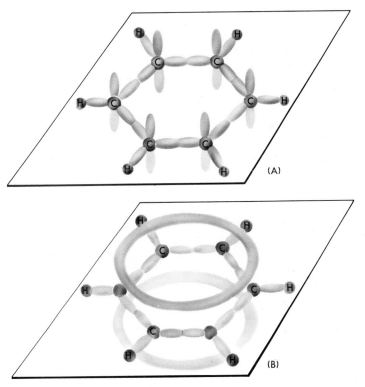

(A)

(B)

17-10 Bonding in benzene. (*A*) Each carbon atom has three sp^2 hybrid orbitals in the plane and a $2p$ orbital perpendicular to the plane. Each hydrogen atom has one s orbital. (*B*) The carbon-carbon bonds are combinations of sp^2-sp^2 bonds with p-p overlap bonds which may be partially represented by rings above and below the plane of the molecule. The carbon-hydrogen bonds are sp^2-s bonds.

isomers. The xylenes are used as starting materials for the production of certain synthetic fibers and films.

Ethylbenzene is produced by the Friedel-Crafts reaction of benzene and ethene in the presence of hydrogen chloride.

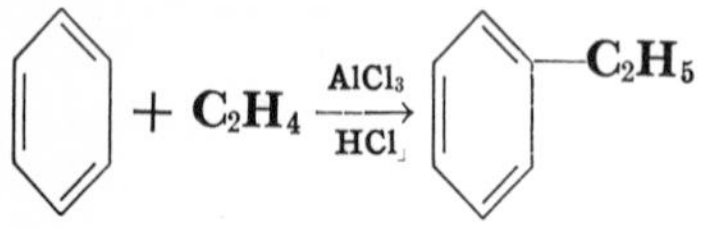

Ethylbenzene is treated with a catalyst of mixed metallic oxides to eliminate hydrogen and produce styrene, used along with butadiene in making SBR synthetic rubber.

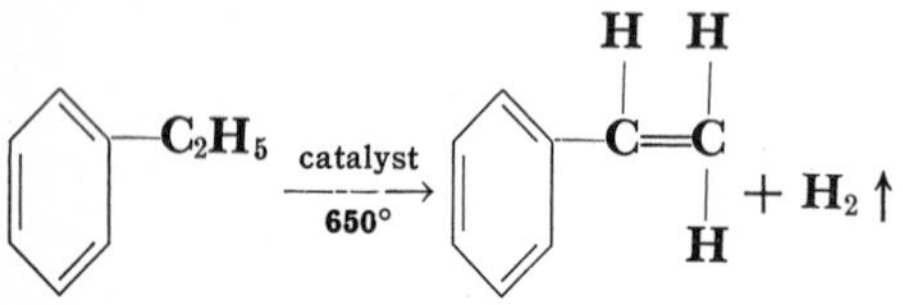

Styrene may be polymerized to polystyrene, a tough, transparent plastic. Polystyrene molecules have molecular weights of about 500,000. Styrofoam is a porous form of polystyrene used as a packaging and insulating material.

Naphthalene, $C_{10}H_8$, is a coal tar product which crystallizes in white shining scales. It is the largest single component of coal tar, sometimes occurring in quantities as high as 6%. The naphthalene molecule has a structure corresponding to two benzene rings joined by a common side.

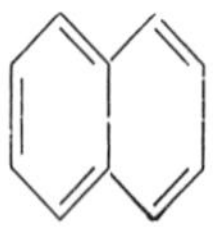

Naphthalene may be used, either as flakes or balls, to kill larvae of clothes moths that attack woolen garments. Naphthalene is also used as a raw material for the manufacture of some resins and dyes.

Anthracene, $C_{14}H_{10}$, has a structure like three benzene rings joined together.

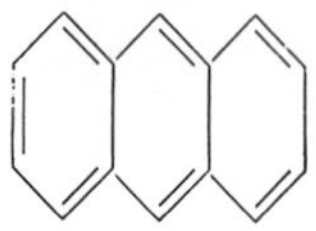

Like naphthalene, it forms a whole series of hydrocarbons. They differ from the compounds related to benzene in that there is more than one ring. Anthracene, like naphthalene, is obtained commercially from coal tar. It is used in the production of alizarin, a well-known red dye, and other synthetic dyes.

RUBBER

▶ **21. Nature of rubber.** *Rubber* is a plastic hydrocarbon obtained from rubber trees. Each tree yields, daily, about one ounce of a milky fluid called *latex.* Latex contains about 35% rubber in colloidal suspension. When acetic acid is added to latex, the rubber *coagulates.* After being washed and dried, it is shipped to market in large sheets of crude rubber.

The simplest formula for rubber is $(C_5H_8)_x$. The C_5H_8 unit is presumed to have the following structure:

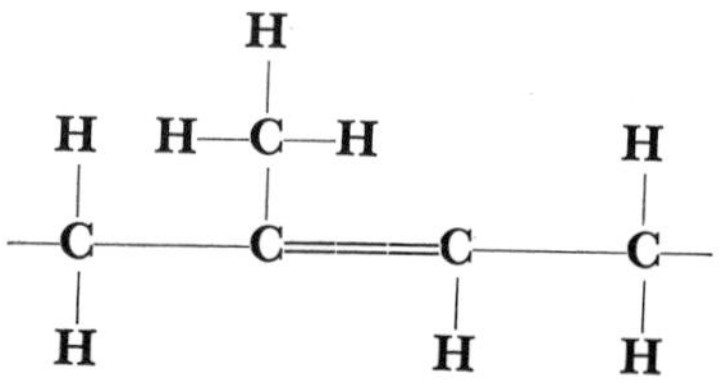

The "*x*" is believed to be a large number. Rubber is thus a polymer of C_5H_8. The monomers in rubber are joined in a zigzag chain that accounts for its elasticity.

▶ **22. Compounding of rubber.** For commercial processing, raw rubber is thoroughly mixed with a number of other

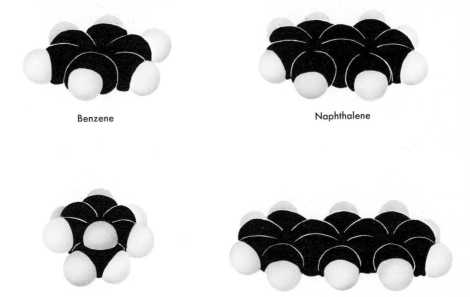

Benzene

Naphthalene

Toluene

Anthracene

17-11 Molecular models of common aromatic hydrocarbons.

materials in large batches. The ingredients in the batch vary according to the products to be made, but sulfur is always one of the ingredients. Automobile tires contain considerable amounts of carbon black. This increases the wearing qualities of the tires by forming bonds between the rubber molecules.

After mixing, the product is shaped either in a mold or from thin sheets. The whole mass is then vulcanized. *Vulcanization is the heating of the rubber mixture to a definite temperature for a definite time.* It gives the article a permanent shape, makes the rubber more elastic, and causes it to lose its sticky qualities. The changes which occur during vulcanization are many and complex. It is believed, however, that the sulfur atoms form cross-linkages between adjacent rubber molecules. Organic catalysts, known as *accelerators*, are added to speed the process. *Anti-oxidants* are also organic chemicals that prevent the rubber from becoming hard and brittle.

▶**23. Neoprene, a hydrocarbon synthetic rubber.** Scientists first produced hydrocarbon synthetic rubber about 1910 by polymerizing isoprene, C_5H_8. However, the cost was too high and its properties too inferior to compete with natural rubber from plantations in the East Indies. In 1931 *neoprene*, a successful hydrocarbon synthetic rubber, appeared on the market.

Hydrogen chloride will add to vinylacetylene to yield chloroprene:

$$\begin{array}{c} H\ \ H \\ |\ \ \ | \\ C{=}C{-}C{\equiv}C{-}H + HCl \rightarrow \\ | \\ H \end{array}$$

vinylacetylene

$$\begin{array}{c} H\ \ H\ \ \ \ \ \ H \\ |\ \ \ |\ \ \ \ \ \ \ | \\ C{=}C{-}C{=}C \\ |\ \ \ |\ \ \ \ \ | \\ H\ \ Cl\ \ H \end{array}$$

chloroprene

The catalytic polymerization of chloroprene yields the neoprene unit:

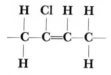

Oils and greases cause natural rubber to swell and rot. They have little effect on neoprene. Hence this synthetic material is used for gasoline delivery hoses.

▶**24. SBR, a synthetic rubber for tires.** *SBR*, Styrene Butadiene Rubber, is used for automobile tires. It is made by churning *butadiene* (Section 17) and *styrene* (Section 19) together in soapy water. The churning is carried out at 5° C, using cumene hydroperoxide as a catalyst. This causes the chemicals to polymerize to form *SBR* rubber. The addition of an acid causes the rubber to separate in curd-like masses, which are washed and dried. The structural unit is shown below.

SBR is a good all-purpose synthetic rubber, and can be used in place of natural rubber for most purposes. It is excellent for tire treads because it resists wear better than other synthetic rubbers. More than one million tons have been produced in one year in the United States.

▶**25. Other synthetic rubbers.** Butyl rubber is made from *isobutene* and *isoprene.* These materials react at −95° C with aluminum chloride as a catalyst. Butyl rubber holds air better than natural rubber and is used for inner tubes. It also resists the action of ozone and many other chemicals.

Nitrile rubber is produced from acrylonitrile and butadiene. It is important because it does not swell on contact with oils and greases.

A synthetic rubber of the same composition as natural rubber is now being made by polymerizing isoprene at 40° C, using finely divided lithium as a catalyst. This material, *polyisoprene*, is replacing natural rubber to an increasing degree.

SBR structural unit

REVIEW OUTLINE

Hydrocarbon series
- Reasons for existence of so many carbon compounds (1)
  - Carbon atoms bond covalently (1)
  - Isomers (1)
- Structural formula (2, 3)
- Organic and inorganic compounds differ (4)
  - Solubility in water (4)
  - Ease of decomposition (4)
  - Reaction rates (4)
  - Type of bonding (4)

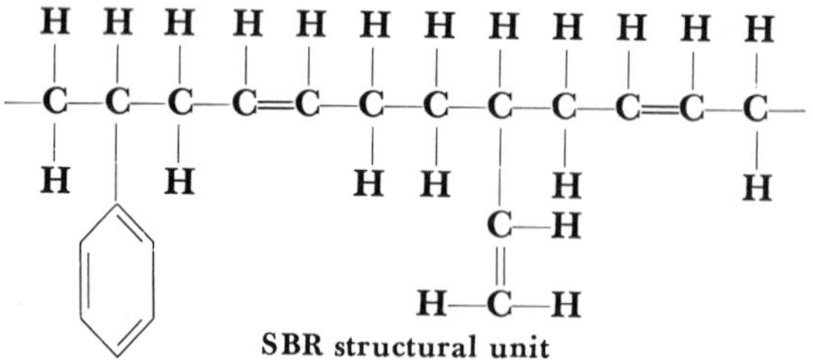

QUESTIONS

Group A

1. Give two reasons for the existence of so many carbon compounds.
2. What does a dash (—) represent in a structural formula?
3. What information do you obtain from a properly written structural formula?
4. Give four important differences between organic and inorganic compounds.
5. What are the general formulas for (*a*) the alkane series; (*b*) the alkene series; (*c*) the alkyne series?
6. A hydrocarbon contains 6 carbon atoms. Give its empirical formula if it is: (*a*) an alkane; (*b*) an alkene; (*c*) an alkyne.

7. Beyond the first four members of the alkane series, how are the hydrocarbons of this series named?

8. What does the formula RH represent?

9. (*a*) What is *fractional distillation?* (*b*) How effective is it in separating the alkanes?

10. (*a*) How is methane produced in nature? (*b*) In the laboratory?

11. Write a balanced formula equation for the complete combustion of: (*a*) methane; (*b*) ethene; (*c*) ethyne; (*d*) butadiene.

12. Write equations for the stepwise substitution of each of the hydrogen atoms in methane by bromine.

13. Butene reacts with hydrogen in the presence of a nickel catalyst. Write a structural-formula equation for the reaction.

14. (*a*) What is a monomer? (*b*) a dimer? (*c*) a polymer? (*d*) polymerization?

15. What are two uses for ethyne?

16. What do the terms *saturated* and *unsaturated* mean when applied to hydrocarbons?

17. Why is calcium carbide sold in air-tight metal cans?

18. How are naphthalene and anthracene related structurally to benzene?

▶ 19. How is rubber coagulated from latex?

▶ 20. What probably accounts for the elasticity of rubber?

▶ 21. How is rubber compounded?

▶ 22. Why are accelerators and anti-oxidants used in making rubber goods?

▶ 23. What is vulcanization?

▶ 24. What advantage does neoprene have over natural rubber?

Group B

25. A compound consists of 60.0% carbon, 26.7% oxygen, and 13.3% hydrogen. Its molecular weight is 60. What are the possible structures for molecules of this compound?

26. Why would you expect organic compounds with covalent bonds to be less stable to heat than inorganic compounds with ionic bonds?

27. Draw structural formulas for the five isomers of hexane.

28. When burned completely, decane, $C_{10}H_{22}$, forms carbon dioxide and water vapor. Write the chemical equation.

29. Draw the structural formula for 2,2-dichloropropane.

30. Draw structural formulas for three isomers of trichloropentane.

31. The element which appears in the greatest number of compounds is hydrogen. The element forming the second greatest number of compounds is carbon. Why are there more hydrogen compounds than carbon compounds?

32. Write structural formula equations for the preparation of (*a*) acetaldehyde from ethyne; (*b*) vinylacetylene from ethyne.

▶ 33. (*a*) Is it geometrically possible for the four hydrogen atoms attached to the end carbon atoms in the 1,3-butadiene molecule to lie in the same plane? (*b*) If carbon-hydrogen bonds on adjacent singly-bonded carbon atoms tend to repel each other, would it be likely that all six hydrogen atoms lie in the same plane? (*c*) If they do, what is their relation to the plane of the carbon atoms?

▶ 34. For the compound propadiene (*a*) draw the structural formula; (*b*) write the electron-dot formula; (*c*) using tetrahedral carbon atoms, draw the molecule, showing the orientation of the valence bonds; (*d*) from your drawing, decide whether all the hydrogen atoms lie in the same plane or not.

35. The formulas for the first four members of the benzene series are C_6H_6, C_7H_8, C_8H_{10}, C_9H_{12}. What is the general formula for the benzene series?

36. (*a*) What is *resonance?* (*b*) Using structural valence-bond formulas, explain resonance in the benzene molecule. (*c*) Is a double bond in a benzene molecule the same as a double bond in an ethene molecule?

▶ 37. Compare the carbon-carbon bonding in ethane, ethene, ethyne, and benzene according to the orbital theory.

38. Write equations for the stepwise substitution of each of the hydrogen atoms in benzene by bromine.

39. Write a structural formula equation for the preparation of methyl benzene from benzene and methyl chloride by the Friedel-Crafts reaction.

40. (*a*) Draw the three possible valence-bond structural formulas for naphthalene; (*b*) the four possible valence-bond structural formulas for anthracene.

▶ 41. (*a*) What materials are polymerized to produce *SBR* rubber? (*b*) What is an important use for *SBR* rubber? (*c*) Why is it used for this purpose?

▶ 42. (*a*) What is an important use for butyl rubber? (*b*) Why is it used for this purpose?

Chapter Eighteen

HYDROCARBON SUBSTITUTION PRODUCTS

HALOGEN SUBSTITUTION PRODUCTS

1. Preparations of alkyl halogenides. *An alkyl halogenide is an alkane in which one or more halogen atoms*—fluorine, chlorine, bromine, or iodine—*is substituted for a like number of hydrogen atoms.* Since **R** is frequently used to represent an alkyl group and **X** may be used to represent any halogen, a monosubstituted alkyl halogenide may be represented as **RX**.

1. Direct halogenation. In Chapter 17, Section 10, it was noted that the halogens react with alkanes to form substitution products. Under suitable conditions, for example, halogen atoms can be substituted for each of the four hydrogen atoms in methane. This reaction occurs in four steps:

$$CH_4 + X_2 \rightarrow CH_3X + HX$$
$$CH_3X + X_2 \rightarrow CH_2X_2 + HX$$
$$CH_2X_2 + X_2 \rightarrow CHX_3 + HX$$
$$CHX_3 + X_2 \rightarrow CX_4 + HX$$

2. From alkenes and alkynes. We have already recognized in Chapter 17, Sections 13 and 16, that alkenes and alkynes will react with halogens or hydrogen halogenides to form alkyl halogenides.

3. From alcohols. Alcohols are alkanes in which the hydroxyl group, —**OH,** has been substituted for hydrogen. Hence an alcohol has the type formula **ROH.** The reaction of an alcohol with a hydrogen halogenide, HCl, HBr, or HI, yields the corresponding alkyl halogenide.

$$ROH + HX \rightarrow RX + H_2O$$

2. Reactions of the alkyl halogenides.

▶ *1. Grignard reagent formation.* When an alkyl halogenide is slowly added to dry ether containing magnesium, a vigorous exothermic reaction occurs. One product of this reaction is a compound in which the alkyl group and a halogen atom are combined with an atom of magnesium.

$$RX + Mg \rightarrow RMgX$$

Compounds of the **RMgX** type are called *Grignard reagents* after the French chemist Victor Grignard (1871–1935).

2. With hydroxide ion. Alkyl halogenides react with aqueous solutions of strong hydroxides to yield alcohols and the halogenide ion.

$$\mathbf{RX + OH^- \rightarrow ROH + X^-}$$

3. Specific alkyl halogenides. Tetrachloromethane, CCl_4, more commonly called carbon tetrachloride, is a colorless, volatile, nonflammable liquid. It is an excellent solvent used for dry cleaning fabrics, degreasing metals, and extracting oils from seeds. Its vapors are toxic, however, and there must be good ventilation whenever carbon tetrachloride is used. Its most important use is in the preparation of Freon refrigerants and aerosol propellants. Carbon tetrachloride is prepared commercially by the reaction between carbon disulfide and chlorine, using iron as a catalyst.

$$\mathbf{CS_2 + 2Cl_2 \xrightarrow{Fe} CCl_4 + 2S}$$

Trichloromethane, $CHCl_3$, commonly called chloroform, is a sweet-smelling, colorless liquid used as a solvent and also in medicinal preparations. Chloroform is manufactured by reducing carbon tetrachloride with moist iron.

Dichlorodifluoromethane, CCl_2F_2, commonly called Freon, is used as a refrigerant in mechanical refrigerators and air conditioners. It is also used as the propellant in spray cans of various kinds. Freon is an odorless, nontoxic, nonflammable, easily liquefied gas. It is prepared from carbon tetrachloride and hydrofluoric acid with antimony compounds as catalysts.

$$\mathbf{CCl_4 + 2HF \xrightarrow{catalyst} CCl_2F_2 + 2HCl}$$

Tetrafluoroethene, C_2F_4, may be polymerized to give a product with

monomer units. This material is called Teflon. Teflon is a very inactive, flexible substance which is stable up to about 325° C. It is made into fibers for weaving chemical-resistant fabrics, or into rods from which small parts may be machined. Teflon has a very low coefficient of friction, and is used where heat-resistant, nonlubricated moving parts are needed. It is also used to coat frying pans for fat-free cooking.

ALCOHOLS

4. Preparations of alcohols. Alcohols are alkanes in which one or more hydroxyl groups, —OH, have been substituted for a like number of hydrogen atoms. (The covalent bonded hydroxyl group must not be confused with the ionic bonded hydroxide ion.)

1. Hydration of alkenes. Ethene reacts with concentrated sulfuric acid at room temperature exothermically. The sulfuric acid molecule adds to the double bond; one hydrogen atom adds to one carbon, and the remainder of the sulfuric acid molecule adds to the other carbon. See the equation below.

If this mixture is diluted with water, the ethene-sulfuric acid addition compound reacts to produce C_2H_5OH, called ethanol or ethyl alcohol. See the equation which follows.

$$\begin{array}{cccc} H & H & & O \\ | & | & & \| \\ H-C-C-O- & S & -O-H+H-O-H \rightarrow \\ | & | & & \| \\ H & H & & O \end{array}$$

$$\begin{array}{ccc} H & H & & H-O & O \\ | & | & & \diagdown \diagup \\ H-C-C-O-H + & & S \\ | & | & & \diagup \diagdown \\ H & H & & H-O & O \end{array}$$

The overall effect of these two reactions is the addition of water across the ethene double bond.

2. From alkyl halogenides. We have already mentioned in Section 2 the reaction of alkyl halogenides with aqueous solutions of strong hydroxides to yield alcohols.

3. Methanol. Methanol is prepared from carbon monoxide and hydrogen under pressure, using a catalyst. See Chapter 16, Section 28. Methanol is a colorless liquid with a rather pleasant odor. It has a low density, and boils at 64.7° C. It is very poisonous, even when used externally. If taken internally in small quantity, it causes blindness by destroying the cells of the optic nerve; larger quantities may cause death. Methanol is a good fuel, burning with a hot, smokeless flame. It is used as a solvent, an alcohol denaturant, and as a starting material for preparing other organic compounds.

4. Ethanol. Large quantities of ethanol are produced by hydrating ethene. Another method is by fermentation. If yeast is added to a dilute solution of sugar or molasses at room temperature, chemical action soon occurs. The yeast plants secrete the enzymes of sucrase and zymase,

which act as catalysts in changing the sugar into alcohol and carbon dioxide.

$$C_{12}H_{22}O_{11} + H_2O \rightarrow 4CO_2 \uparrow + 4C_2H_5OH$$

Both processes are widely used for the production of industrial ethanol. However, the hydration of ethene is a less expensive method and is gradually replacing the fermentation process.

Ethanol is a colorless liquid which has a characteristic odor and a sharp, biting taste. It boils at 78° C, freezes at −115° C, and burns with a nearly colorless blue flame. Ethanol is a good solvent for many organic compounds which are insoluble in water. Accordingly it is used for making tinctures, spirits, and fluid extracts for medicinal use. Ethanol is sometimes used as an antifreeze in automobiles, and for making ether and acetaldehyde.

Denatured alcohol is a mixture, composed principally of ethanol, to which poisonous and nauseating materials have been added to make it unfit for beverage purposes.

5. Ethylene glycol. The dihydric compound ethylene glycol, $C_2H_4(OH)_2$,

$$\begin{array}{cc} H & H \\ | & | \\ H-C-C-H \\ | & | \\ O & O \\ | & | \\ H & H \end{array}$$

is an alcohol containing two hydroxyl groups. It is used extensively as a "permanent type" antifreeze in automobile radiators. Its boiling point is so much higher than that of water that it does not readily evaporate or boil away. Ethylene glycol is very poisonous.

6. Glycerol. Glycerol, or glycerin, a trihydric alcohol, $C_3H_5(OH)_3$, is represented by the following formula:

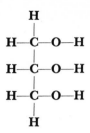

It is a colorless, odorless, viscous liquid with a sweet taste. It has a low vapor pressure and is hygroscopic. It is used in making synthetic resins for paints, in cigarettes to keep the tobacco moist, in the manufacture of cellophane, in making nitroglycerin, and in some toilet soaps. Glycerol is an important pharmaceutical ingredient, and is used in many foods and beverages. It is a by-product of soap manufacture. Important quantities of glycerol are synthesized from propene, a product of petroleum cracking.

5. Reactions of alcohols.

1. With sodium. Sodium reacts vigorously with ethanol, evolving hydrogen. A second product of the reaction, sodium ethoxide, C_2H_5ONa, may be recovered as a white solid after the excess ethanol is evaporated. This reaction is similar to the reaction of sodium with water.

$$2C_2H_5OH + 2Na \rightarrow 2C_2H_5ONa + H_2 \uparrow$$

2. With HX and PX$_3$. Alcohols react with concentrated water solutions of hydrogen halogenides, particularly hydrobromic and hydriodic acids, to form alkyl halogenides. Sulfuric acid is used as a dehydrating agent.

$$ROH + HBr \rightarrow RBr + H_2O$$

Alcohols also react with phosphorus trihalogenides to yield alkyl halogenides. Using phosphorus tribromide,

$$3ROH + PBr_3 \rightarrow 3RBr + H_3PO_3$$

H_3PO_3 is known as phosphorous acid.

3. Dehydration. Depending on the reaction conditions, ethanol may be dehydrated by hot concentrated sulfuric acid to yield either diethyl ether, $C_2H_5OC_2H_5$, or ethene.

$$2C_2H_5OH \rightarrow C_2H_5OC_2H_5 + H_2O$$
$$C_2H_5OH \rightarrow C_2H_4 \uparrow + H_2O$$

4. Oxidation. Alcohols which have the hydroxyl group attached to the end carbon may be oxidized by hot copper(II) oxide to produce an aldehyde, RCHO.

$$RCH_2OH + CuO \rightarrow RCHO + H_2O + Cu$$

Low molecular weight alcohols are flammable, and burn readily in air.

$$2CH_3OH + 3O_2 \rightarrow 2CO_2 \uparrow + 4H_2O \uparrow$$

5. Sulfation of long-chain alcohols. 1-dodecanol, $C_{12}H_{25}OH$, commonly called lauryl alcohol, is obtained from coconut oil by hydrogenation and partial decomposition. Sulfation of lauryl alcohol by treatment with sulfuric acid and subsequent neutralization with sodium hydroxide yields sodium lauryl sulfate, $C_{12}H_{25}OSO_2ONa$. This compound is a very effective detergent.

$$C_{12}H_{25}OH + H_2SO_4 \rightarrow$$
$$C_{12}H_{25}OSO_2OH + H_2O$$
$$C_{12}H_{25}OSO_2OH + NaOH \rightarrow$$
$$C_{12}H_{25}OSO_2ONa + H_2O$$

ETHERS

6. Ethers: organic oxides. Ethers have the general formula **ROR'** in which **R** and **R'** may be the same or different alkyl groups. Thus they are derivatives of water in which both hydrogen atoms have been replaced by alkyl groups. They may be prepared by the dehydration of alcohols as described in Section 5. Diethyl ether is commonly called ether. It is a volatile, very flammable, colorless liquid of characteristic odor. It may be made by heating ethanol and sulfuric acid to 140° C.

$$2C_2H_5OH \xrightarrow{H_2SO_4} C_2H_5OC_2H_5 + H_2O$$

Besides its use as an anesthetic, ether is employed as a solvent for fats and oils.

Ethers may be synthesized by the action of a sodium alkoxide, such as sodium ethoxide, on an alkyl halogenide, such as methyl bromide. The ether and a sodium halogenide are products.

$$RONa + R'X \to ROR' + NaX$$
$$C_2H_5ONa + CH_3Br \to$$
$$C_2H_5OCH_3 + NaBr$$

By properly choosing the alkyl group in the alkoxide and in the alkyl halogenide, ethers with different alkyl groups attached to the oxygen may be produced. The equation above shows the preparation of methyl ethyl ether. This method is known as the *Williamson synthesis*, after the English chemist Alexander W. Williamson (1824–1904).

ALDEHYDES

7. Preparations of aldehydes. An aldehyde is a compound which has a hydrocarbon group and one or more formyl,

$$-C\!\!\!\diagup^{\displaystyle O}_{\diagdown H}$$

, groups. The general formula for an aldehyde is **RCHO.**

1. From alcohols. This method of preparing aldehydes has already been mentioned in Section 5. If methanol vapor and a regulated amount of air are passed over heated copper, formaldehyde, HCHO, is produced.

$$2Cu + O_2 \to 2CuO$$
$$CH_3OH + CuO \to HCHO\uparrow + H_2O + Cu$$

At room temperature, formaldehyde is a gas with a suffocating odor. Dissolved in water, it makes an excellent disinfectant. It is used for preserving anatomical specimens. By far the largest use for formaldehyde is in the preparation of certain types of plastics.

2. Acetaldehyde from ethyne. Acetaldehyde is manufactured commercially by the addition of water to ethyne. See Chapter 17, Section 16. Acetaldehyde is a stable liquid used in preparing other organic compounds.

8. Reactions of aldehydes.

1. Oxidation. The mild oxidation of an aldehyde produces the organic acid having the same number of carbon atoms. The oxidation of acetaldehyde to acetic acid is typical.

CH$_3$CHO + O (from oxidizing agent) →
CH$_3$COOH

2. Fehling's test. Fehling's solution A is copper(II) sulfate solution. Fehling's solution B is sodium hydroxide and sodium tartrate solution. If these are mixed with an aldehyde and heated, the aldehyde is oxidized. The copper(II) ion is reduced to copper(I) and precipitated as brick-red copper(I) oxide.

RCHO + 2CuSO$_4$ + 5NaOH →
RCOONa + Cu$_2$O ↓ + 2Na$_2$SO$_4$+ 3H$_2$O

3. Hydrogen addition. Alcohols are produced by the addition of hydrogen to aldehydes in the presence of finely divided nickel or platinum.

$$RCHO + H_2 \xrightarrow{Ni} RCH_2OH$$

This is the reverse of the oxidation of alcohols to produce aldehydes.

► *4. Grignard reagent.* Grignard reagents add to aldehydes, and subsequent hydrolysis with dilute acid produces an alcohol.

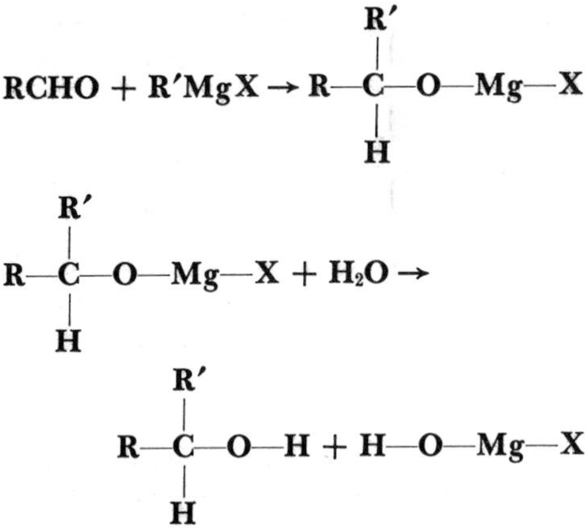

$$RCHO + R'MgX \rightarrow R{-}\underset{\underset{H}{|}}{\overset{\overset{R'}{|}}{C}}{-}O{-}Mg{-}X$$

$$R{-}\underset{\underset{H}{|}}{\overset{\overset{R'}{|}}{C}}{-}O{-}Mg{-}X + H_2O \rightarrow$$

$$R{-}\underset{\underset{H}{|}}{\overset{\overset{R'}{|}}{C}}{-}O{-}H + H{-}O{-}Mg{-}X$$

► *5. Aldol condensation.* Under certain conditions one molecule of an aldehyde will

add to the $\diagdown C{=}O$, carbonyl, group of a

second aldehyde molecule. For example, two molecules of acetaldehyde will combine to form *aldol*, from which the name of the reaction is derived. See the equation below.

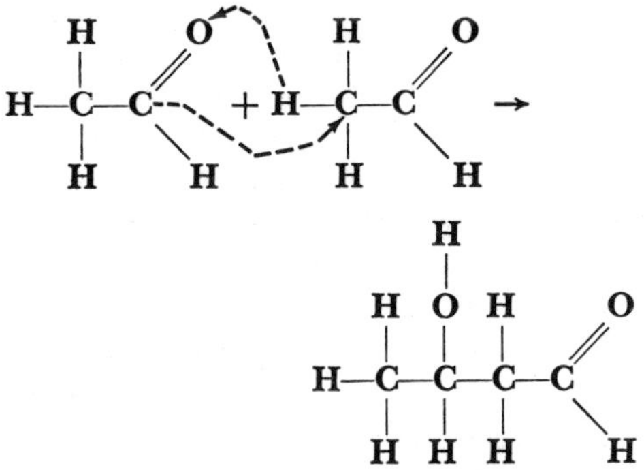

aldol

With higher aldehydes, it is only a hydrogen atom on the carbon atom next to the carbonyl group which adds to the other aldehyde molecule.

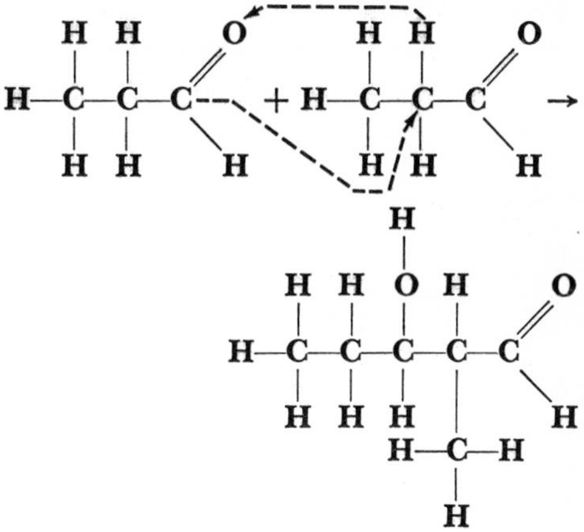

► *6. Phenylhydrazine.* Phenylhydrazine,

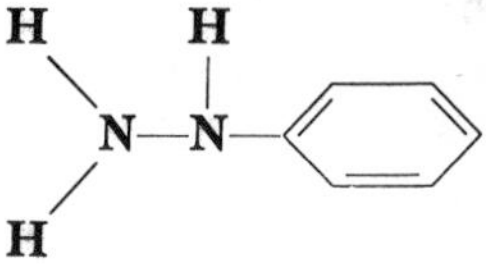

reacts with aldehydes to form phenylhydrazone derivatives. These are usually sharp-melting crystalline solids which may be used for identifying aldehydes. See the equation below.

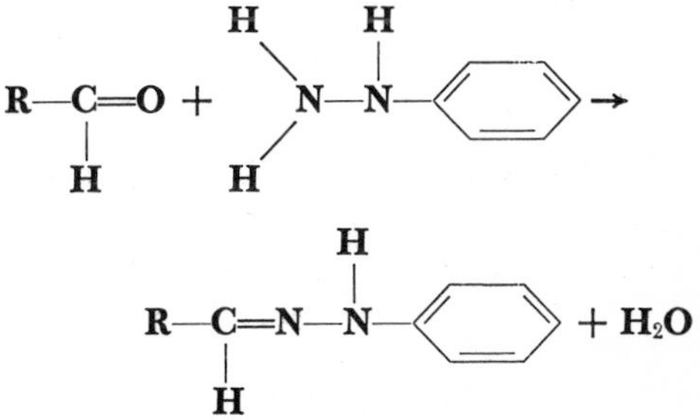

a phenylhydrazone

KETONES

9. Preparation of ketones. Ketones are organic compounds that contain the carbonyl group. The general formula for a ketone is **RCOR'.**

Ketones may be prepared from alcohols having the hydroxyl group *not* attached to an end carbon atom. For example, acetone, CH_3COCH_3, is prepared by the mild oxidation of 2-propanol, $CH_3CHOHCH_3$.

$$
\begin{array}{c}
H \\
| \\
H \quad O \quad H \\
| \quad | \quad | \\
H-C-C-C-H + O \ \text{(from oxidizing agent)} \rightarrow \\
| \quad | \quad | \\
H \quad H \quad H
\end{array}
$$

$$
\begin{array}{c}
H \quad O \quad H \\
| \quad \| \quad | \\
H-C-C-C-H + H_2O \\
| \quad\quad | \\
H \quad\quad H \\
\text{acetone}
\end{array}
$$

Acetone, a colorless, volatile liquid, is widely used as a solvent in the manufacture of acetate rayon. Tanks for the storage of ethyne gas are loosely filled with asbestos saturated with acetone. The ethyne dissolves in the acetone and thus increases the amount of ethyne which may safely be compressed into the tank. Acetone and other ketones are used for cleaning metals, removing stains, and for preparing synthetic organic chemicals. Acetone is a metabolic product which accumulates in the blood stream of diabetics.

10. Reactions of ketones.

1. Hydrogen addition. Hydrogen may be added to a ketone in the presence of finely divided metal catalysts. This reaction produces an alcohol with the hydroxyl group attached to the carbonyl carbon of the original ketone.

▶ *2. Grignard reagent.* A Grignard reagent adds to the oxygen of the carbonyl group of a ketone. Hydrolysis produces an alcohol in which the hydroxyl group is attached to a carbon atom to which three different alkyl groups may also be bonded. This makes possible the preparation of a large variety of alcohols.

▶ *3. Aldol condensation.* Two molecules of acetone will react in an aldol condensation in the presence of barium hydroxide as a catalyst. The product, called diacetone alcohol, is used as a solvent and for the preparation of other compounds. See equation at the bottom of this page.

▶ *4. Phenylhydrazine.* Phenylhydrazine reacts with ketones in much the same manner as with aldehydes. The reactions produce crystalline solids useful in melting point determinations for identification.

CARBOXYLIC ACIDS AND ESTERS

11. Preparations of carboxylic acids. Many organic acids and their salts occur naturally in sour milk, in unripe fruits, in rhubarb and sorrel, as well as in other plants. All organic acids contain

$$
\begin{array}{c}
\quad\quad O \\
\quad\quad \| \\
-C \\
\quad\quad \backslash \\
\quad\quad O-H
\end{array}
$$

or the carboxyl group; hence the general

$$
\begin{array}{c}
H \quad O \quad H \quad\quad H-C-H \quad\quad\quad\quad\quad H \\
| \quad \| \quad | \quad\quad\quad\quad\quad\quad\quad\quad\quad\quad | \\
H-C-C-C-H + \quad C=O \rightarrow \quad H-C-H \\
| \quad\quad | \quad\quad\quad\quad | \\
H \quad\quad H \quad\quad H-C-H \quad\quad H \quad O \quad H \\
\quad\quad\quad\quad\quad\quad | \quad\quad\quad\quad | \quad \| \quad | \\
\quad\quad\quad\quad\quad\quad H \quad\quad H-C-C-C-C-O-H \\
\quad\quad\quad\quad\quad\quad\quad\quad\quad\quad\quad | \quad\quad | \quad\quad | \\
\quad\quad\quad\quad\quad\quad\quad\quad\quad\quad\quad H \quad\quad H \quad H-C-H \\
\quad\quad\quad\quad\quad\quad\quad\quad\quad\quad\quad\quad\quad\quad\quad\quad\quad\quad | \\
\quad\quad\quad\quad\quad\quad\quad\quad\quad\quad\quad\quad\quad\quad\quad\quad\quad\quad H
\end{array}
$$

diacetone alcohol

formula is represented as RCOOH.

1. Oxidation of alcohols or aldehydes. The oxidation of alcohols to aldehydes and of aldehydes to carboxylic acids has been described in Sections 5 and 8. Pure acetic acid is produced by the catalytic oxidation of acetaldehyde. Concentrated acetic acid is a colorless liquid that is a good solvent for some organic chemicals. It is used for making cellulose acetate, which is processed into fibers and films.

Cider vinegar is made from apple cider which has fermented to hard cider. The ethanol in hard cider is slowly oxidized by the oxygen of the air to acetic acid. This reaction is catalyzed by enzymes from certain bacteria.

$$C_2H_5OH + O_2 \rightarrow CH_3COOH + H_2O$$

Good vinegar contains from 4% to 6% acetic acid. Malt vinegar and wine vinegar are made by a similar process of fermentation and oxidation.

2. Formic acid. Formic acid, HCOOH, is prepared from sodium hydroxide solution and carbon monoxide under pressure. This reaction yields sodium formate, HCOONa.

$$NaOH + CO \rightarrow HCOONa$$

If sodium formate is carefully heated with sulfuric acid, formic acid distills off.

$$HCOONa + H_2SO_4 \rightarrow$$
$$HCOOH \uparrow + NaHSO_4$$

Formic acid is found in nature in stinging nettles, in the sting of bees, wasps, and hornets, and in red ants. Formic acid is used commercially in the textile industry.

12. Reactions of carboxylic acids.

1. Ionization. The one hydrogen atom bonded to an oxygen atom in the carboxyl group becomes ionized in water solution, giving carboxylic acids their acid properties. The hydrogen atoms bonded to carbon atoms in these acids are *never* ionized in water solution.

$$HCOOH + H_2O \rightleftarrows H_3O^+ + HCOO^-$$
$$CH_3COOH + H_2O \rightleftarrows H_3O^+ + CH_3COO^-$$

Since these equilibria yield low H_3O^+ ion concentrations, carboxylic acids are generally weak acids.

2. Neutralization. Organic acids may be neutralized by hydroxides forming salts just as inorganic acids are.

$$CH_3COOH + NaOH \rightarrow$$
$$CH_3COONa + H_2O$$

*3. Esterification. An **ester** is produced when an acid reacts with an alcohol.* For example, ethyl acetate is the ester formed when ethanol and acetic acid react. See the equation shown at the bottom of this page. Such reactions, which result in the formation of esters are *esterification reactions.* Reactions between acids and alcohols are reversible. Achievement of equilibrium is slow and sulfuric acid is used as a catalyst. Experiments with alcohols containing oxygen-18 have shown that the oxygen of the water product comes from the acid.

$$CH_3COOH + C_2H_5OH \xrightarrow{H_2SO_4} CH_3COOC_2H_5 + H_2O$$

13. Esters. It is also possible to prepare esters by the reaction of alcohols with inorganic acids. Glyceryl trinitrate, known as nitroglycerin, is an example.

$$C_3H_5(OH)_3 + 3HNO_3 \xrightarrow{H_2SO_4} C_3H_5(NO_3)_3 + 3H_2O$$

Esters give fruits their characteristic flavors and odors. Amyl acetate has an odor somewhat resembling bananas. As "banana oil" this ester is used as the vehicle for some aluminum paints. Ethyl butyrate has an odor and flavor that resembles pineapples. Ripe pineapples contain some of this ester, together with smaller amounts of other esters.

The elementary chemistry of esters is concerned with their hydrolysis into the alcohol and acid from which they were derived. This hydrolysis may be carried out in the presence of dilute acid or metallic hydroxide solutions. The alkaline hydrolysis is known as *saponification*, since it is the process involved in making soap. See Chapter 19, Section 4.

AMINES

▶ **14. Classes of amines.** Amines are derivatives of ammonia in which one, two, or all three hydrogen atoms have been replaced by alkyl groups. In primary amines, one alkyl group has been substituted for one hydrogen atom, RNH_2. In secondary amines, two alkyl groups have been substituted, R_2NH; and in tertiary amines, three alkyl groups have been substituted for the three hydrogen atoms in the ammonia molecule, R_3N.

▶ **15. Preparation of amines.** Ammonia reacts with alkyl halogenides.

$$RX + NH_3 \rightarrow RNH_3^+ + X^-$$

Then treatment of RNH_3^+ with a strong metallic hydroxide produces the amine.

$$RNH_3^+ + Na^+ + OH^- \rightarrow RNH_2 + H_2O + Na^+$$

Some secondary amines may be produced by subsequent reaction of RNH_2 with more alkyl halogenide. Tertiary amines may be produced by the further reaction of the secondary amine R_2NH with more alkyl halogenide.

▶ **16. Reactions of amines.** Amines show much the same basic properties as ammonia. Consequently amines react with acids to produce salts.

$$RNH_2 + HCl \rightarrow RNH_3Cl$$

Nitrous acid reacts with primary amines to yield nitrogen. It reacts with secondary amines to produce an oily compound, and with tertiary amines only to form salts. Since these three effects are readily visible, nitrous acid reactions give a useful method for distinguishing between the three types of amines. The equations for the reaction with ethylamine, diethylamine, and triethylamine are as follows:

$$C_2H_5NH_2 + HNO_2 \rightarrow$$
ethyl-   nitrous
amine   acid
$$C_2H_5OH + N_2 + H_2O$$

$$(C_2H_5)_2NH + HNO_2 \rightarrow$$
diethyl-
amine
$$(C_2H_5)_2N{-}N{=}O + H_2O$$
nitrosodiethyl-
amine

$$(C_2H_5)_3N + HNO_2 \rightarrow (C_2H_5)_3NHNO_2$$
triethyl-   triethylammonium
amine   nitrite

AMIDES

▶ **17. Preparation of amides.** Amides are derivatives of ammonia in which one of the hydrogen atoms has been replaced by an RCO— group. The other two hydrogen atoms have been possibly replaced by alkyl groups. Hence they may have the structures $RCONH_2$, $RCONHR'$, and $RCONR'R''$.

Carboxylic acids react with ammonia to yield ammonium salts. If these ammonium salts are heated gently, they lose water and form amides. Acetamide, for example, may be produced by heating ammonium acetate in solution with acetic acid.

$$CH_3COONH_4 \rightarrow CH_3CONH_2 + H_2O$$
acetamide

▶ **18. Reactions of amides.** Amides are easily hydrolyzed to carboxylic acids and ammonia in the presence of mineral acids or strong metallic hydroxides.

$$RCONH_2 + H_2O \rightarrow RCOOH + NH_3$$

Simple amides react with nitrous acid to evolve nitrogen quantitatively and form carboxylic acids.

$$RCONH_2 + HNO_2 \rightarrow$$
$$RCOOH + N_2 \uparrow + H_2O$$

▶ **19. Nylon.** Nylon is the name given to fibers made from any long chain synthetic polyamide having recurring

$$-\overset{\displaystyle \overset{}{C}}{\underset{\displaystyle O}{\|}}-\overset{\displaystyle \overset{H}{|}}{N}-$$

groups as an integral part of the polymer chain. The chains may have the construction shown at the bottom of this page, with hydrogen bonds between chains connecting $C{=}O$ with $N{-}H$ of different chains. Since nylon has no bulky side chains, the molecules can pack closely together and the resulting fiber has the characteristics of silk.

Nylon is made from the six-carbon dicarboxylic acid, adipic acid,

and hexamethylenediamine,

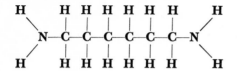

This acid and amine react to form nylon salt (see Section 16) which is polymerized with the evolution of water into giant molecules or polyamides which may have the structure shown at the bottom of page 315. The polyamide is melted, extruded, and hardened by cooling.

Nylon fibers are strong and elastic. These fibers, made extra strong by stretching, are used for tire cord and other industrial uses. Regular nylon filament yarns are used for lightweight, dense, wind resistant apparel. Special filament nylon yarns with extra bulk are prepared for knit goods and carpet pile, while nylon monofilaments are used in sheer hosiery.

NITRILES

▶**20. Nitriles.** Nitriles are alkyl derivatives of hydrogen cyanide, HCN. They have the general formula **RCN**. Acrylonitrile,

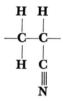

is the only nitrile in which we are presently interested. It is prepared by the addition of hydrogen cyanide to ethyne in the presence of copper(I) and ammonium salts as catalysts.

$$H—C\equiv C—H + H—C\equiv N \xrightarrow[\text{NH}_4\text{Cl}]{\text{Cu}_2\text{Cl}_2}$$

Acrylonitrile is used in vinyl-type polymerizations and copolymerizations to produce synthetic fibers such as Orlon, Acrilan, and Dynel.

▶**21. Acrylic fibers.** These were first introduced under the trademarks Orlon and Acrilan. Their fibers consist of long chain synthetic polymers composed of at least 85% by weight of acrylonitrile units,

Acrylonitrile is usually combined with small amounts of other chemicals to improve the fiber's ability to combine with dyestuffs.

Acrylic fibers produce warm, luxurious fabrics which have good shape retention and resistance to sunlight, weather, oils, and chemicals.

REVIEW OUTLINE

QUESTIONS

Group A

1. What are the type formulas for (*a*) alkyl halogenides; (*b*) alcohols; (*c*) ethers; (*d*) aldehydes; (*e*) ketones; (*f*) carboxylic acids; (*g*) esters?
▶ 2. What are the type formulas for (*a*) primary amines; (*b*) secondary amines; (*c*) tertiary amines; (*d*) amides; (*e*) nitriles?
3. (*a*) What are the uses of carbon tetrachloride? (*b*) What precautions must be exercised in its use?
4. How do alcohols differ from inorganic hydroxides?
5. What is the effect of methanol on the human body?
6. What property of glycerol makes it useful for keeping tobacco moist?
7. Compare the action of sodium with water and with methanol.
8. How many molecules of oxygen are required for the complete combustion of one molecule of butanol?
9. How is formaldehyde used in a biology laboratory?
10. (*a*) What is Fehling's test? (*b*) What organic group gives a positive Fehling's test?
▶ 11. What physical characteristic makes the phenylhydrazones useful?
12. For what purposes is acetone used?
13. (*a*) What is cider vinegar? (*b*) How may it be prepared?

14. (*a*) Oxalic acid is a dicarboxylic acid with the structural formula

$$\underset{\displaystyle \text{H—O—C—C—O—H.}}{\overset{\displaystyle \text{O O}}{\underset{\displaystyle \|\ \ \|}{}}}$$

Write equations for the stepwise complete ionization of oxalic acid. (*b*) How many moles of potassium hydroxide are required for the complete neutralization of four moles of oxalic acid?

15. What is the source of the hydrogen and oxygen atoms of the water eliminated during an esterification reaction?

16. In what types of reactions mentioned in this chapter is sulfuric acid used as a dehydrating agent?

▶ 17. What is the principal monomer in an acrylic fiber polymer?

Group B

18. Draw structural formulas for (*a*) dichloromethane; (*b*) 1,2,3,-trihydroxypropane; (*c*) diethyl ether; (*d*) formaldehyde; (*e*) diethylketone; (*f*) acetic acid; (*g*) methyl formate.

▶ 19. Draw structural formulas for (*a*) ethylamine; (*b*) dimethylamine; (*c*) dimethylethylamine; (*d*) acetamide; (*e*) acrylonitrile.

20. Write the equations for the preparation of ethyl chloride starting with (*a*) ethane; (*b*) ethene; (*c*) ethanol.

▶ 21. (*a*) How are Grignard reagents prepared? (*b*) What type of compound is prepared when a Grignard reagent reacts with an aldehyde and the intermediate product is hydrolyzed? (*c*) What type of compound is prepared when a Grignard reagent reacts with a ketone and the intermediate product is hydrolyzed?

22. Starting with carbon disulfide, chlorine, and hydrogen fluoride, show how Freon is prepared.

23. Using structural formula equations, show how ethanol may be prepared from (*a*) ethene; (*b*) ethyl chloride; (*c*) sugar ($C_{12}H_{22}O_{11}$).

24. On the basis of molecular weight and boiling point, what are the comparative advantages of methanol, ethanol, and ethylene glycol as automobile antifreezes?

25. Write equations for two different methods of preparing propyl iodide, starting with propyl alcohol.

26. Describe two methods by which dipropyl ether may be prepared.

27. Starting with ethyne, show how acetic acid may be prepared.

28. What ketone is prepared by the mild oxidation of 2-butanol?

29. Write a structural formula equation showing the reaction which occurs when hydrogen is catalytically added to diethyl ketone.

▶ 30. What shift in atomic arrangement occurs during an aldol condensation?

31. Write an equation showing the formation of the ester *n*-butyl acetate.

▶ 32. Write equations showing (*a*) the preparation of methylamine starting with methyl bromide; (*b*) the reaction of methylamine with nitrous acid.

▶33. (*a*) Write equations showing the preparation of propionamide, $C_2H_5CONH_2$, starting with propionic acid, C_2H_5COOH. (*b*) What are two methods by which propionamide may be reconverted to propionic acid?

▶34. By means of structural formulas show how a molecule of adipic acid and a molecule of hexamethylenediamine form a salt.

Chapter Nineteen

NATURAL ORGANIC COMPOUNDS

FATS

▶ **1. Importance of fats.** The three largest groups of naturally occurring organic compounds are the fats, carbohydrates, and proteins. These three types of materials make up most of the organic matter of living cells.

Protoplasm, the basic material of living things, contains 75–90% water plus substances either in solution or in colloidal suspension. Oxygen, hydrogen, nitrogen, and carbon constitute about 96% of the total weight of protoplasm. In addition to the hydrogen and oxygen in the water, these elements are combined mainly as fats, carbohydrates, and proteins. In this chapter we shall briefly describe some fundamental chemistry of each of these groups of compounds.

Fats provide energy for body processes. They are a more concentrated source of energy than proteins and carbohydrates. Fats provide about 9 kcal/g, compared to about 4 kcal/g for proteins and carbohydrates. On digestion, fats provide certain unsaturated carboxylic acids which appear to be necessary for the maintenance of good health. Fats occur chiefly in the fatty tissues of animals, in milk, and in seeds, nuts, and fruits.

▶ **2. Chemical nature of fats.** Fats belong to a class of organic compounds called *lipids*. Lipids are materials found in plant and animal tissue which are insoluble in water, but are soluble in such solvents as ether, chloroform, or benzene.

*Chemically **fats** are esters of glycerol and long carbon chain acids.* The carbon chains of the acids usually contain an even number of carbon atoms, ranging from about 12 to 20. The structure of a fat may be represented as

$$\text{RCOOCH}_2$$
$$|$$
$$\text{R'COOCH}$$
$$|$$
$$\text{R''COOCH}_2$$

in which R, R', and R'' are saturated or

unsaturated long chain hydrocarbon groups.

Molecules of fats and oils have the same structure. The only difference between a fat and an oil is its physical state at room temperature. Oils are liquids at room temperature, while fats are solids. Long carbon chain acids with double bonds produce esters having lower melting points. Hence oils usually contain hydrocarbon chains which are more unsaturated than those found in fats.

The table at the bottom of the page indicates the principal types of long carbon chain acids found as glyceryl esters in common fats and oils.

▶3. **Rule of even distribution.** In a fat, one might expect a given molecule to contain identical long carbon chains, or long carbon chains with the acids of the fat distributed randomly. Actually neither of these expected acid chain distributions is observed. Each carboxylic acid in the fat appears to be as evenly and widely distributed among the individual molecules as possible. Each fat molecule tends to have three different long chain acids, rather than having two or three of one

type and none of another. This condition has been called the *rule of even distribution.*

▶4. **Chemical reactions of fats.** Since fats are esters, they show the chemical reactions typical of esters.

1. Hydrolysis. The hydrolysis of a fat in the presence of an acid catalyst, or with superheated steam yields the alcohol, glycerol, and the long chain carboxylic acids.

RCOOCH$_2$
|
R'COOCH + 3HOH $\xrightarrow{\text{H}_2\text{SO}_4}$
|
R''COOCH$_2$
    RCOOH + R'COOH + R''COOH +
                    C$_3$H$_5$(OH)$_3$

2. Saponification. **Saponification** *is hydrolysis of a fat using a solution of a strong hydroxide.* In alkaline hydrolysis the sodium salt of the long chain carboxylic acid is formed instead of the acid itself.

RCOOCH$_2$
|
R'COOCH + 3NaOH →
|
R''COOCH$_2$
RCOONa + R'COONa + R''COONa +
                    C$_3$H$_5$(OH)$_3$

PRINCIPAL ACIDS OBTAINED BY HYDROLYSIS OF COMMON FATS AND OILS
(Weight Percent of Acids)

Fat or Oil	Lauric C$_{11}$H$_{23}$COOH	Myristic C$_{13}$H$_{27}$COOH	Palmitic C$_{15}$H$_{31}$COOH	Stearic C$_{17}$H$_{35}$COOH	Oleic *	Linoleic **
coconut	44–51	15–18	8–10	1–3	5–8	1–2
corn			8–10	3–6	46–50	34–42
cottonseed		1–3	20–23	1–2	23–30	45–54
olive			7–15		70–85	4–12
palm		1–3	35–40	3–6	40–50	5–11
peanut			6–9	3–5	52–66	17–27
soybean			7–10	3–6	22–33	50–66
beef fat (tallow)	0–1	2–3	25–33	15–28	42–50	2–3
hog fat (lard)		1	25–30	12–16	41–51	5–8

* C$_8$H$_{17}$CH=CHC$_7$H$_{14}$COOH
** C$_5$H$_{11}$CH=CHCH$_2$CH=CHC$_7$H$_{14}$COOH

Soaps are generally made by hydrolyzing fats and oils with superheated water at about 250° C under a pressure of about 50 atmospheres. The long chain carboxylic acids thus produced are neutralized with sodium hydroxide to yield a mixture of sodium salts which constitutes soap.

If the acid chains are unsaturated, a soft soap results. Soaps with hydrocarbon chains of 10 to 12 carbon atoms are soluble in water and produce a large-bubble lather. Soaps containing hydrocarbon chains of 16 to 18 carbon atoms are less soluble in water and give a longer-lasting small-bubble lather. Soap which is a mixture of potassium salts rather than of sodium salts, is generally more soluble in water. Liquid soap is a water solution of the potassium soaps produced from coconut oil.

3. Hydrogenation. Cottonseed oil containing unsaturated oleic acid and linoleic acid chains is converted from liquid oil to solid fat by hydrogenation, using finely divided nickel as catalyst. The equation for the complete hydrogenation of the glyceryl ester of oleic acid is shown below.

In practice, not all the unsaturated hydrocarbon chains in the liquid oil are permitted to add hydrogen. For example, perhaps only one oleic acid chain per molecule is converted into a stearic acid chain. We have already indicated that saturated hydrocarbon chains give a fat molecule a higher melting point. Hence, hydrogenation converts an oil into a fat. The hydrogenation is controlled so that the resulting product is not completely saturated. It retains sufficient unsaturation to be a fat at room temperature but

becomes liquid at body temperature. Most vegetable shortenings on the market today are hydrogenated oils.

Fats may also be hydrogenated under more severe conditions. Using copper(I) and chromium(III) oxides as catalysts, hydrogen at high temperature (250° C) and high pressure (2000 atm) will saturate all carbon-carbon double bonds in the hydrocarbon chains. This process simultaneously reduces the ester to a mixture of long chain alcohols and glycerol.

$$\begin{array}{l} RCOOCH_2 \\ | \\ R'COOCH \ + 6H_2 \xrightarrow[Cr_2O_3]{Cu_2O} \\ | \\ R''COOCH_2 \end{array}$$

$$RCH_2OH + R'CH_2OH + R''CH_2OH + \\ C_3H_5(OH)_3$$

This reaction is used to prepare the long chain alcohols like lauryl alcohol required for the production of synthetic detergents. (See Chap. 18, Sec. 5.)

CARBOHYDRATES

▶**5. The importance of carbohydrates.** The carbohydrates include a great variety of materials. Sugars, starches, and various forms of cellulose such as wood, paper, and cotton, are all carbohydrates. Carbohydrates are products of photosynthesis in plants. They are an important source of energy for both plants and animals, and in plants they also provide structural support. Both animals and man use certain carbohydrates as foods. Man uses many carbohydrates for clothing and shelter. Carbohydrates are starting materials for

$$\begin{array}{l} C_8H_{17}CH{=}CHC_7H_{14}COOCH_2 \\ | \\ C_8H_{17}CH{=}CHC_7H_{14}COOCH \ + 3H_2 \xrightarrow{Ni} \\ | \\ C_8H_{17}CH{=}CHC_7H_{14}COOCH_2 \end{array} \quad \begin{array}{l} C_{17}H_{35}COOCH_2 \\ | \\ C_{17}H_{35}COOCH \\ | \\ C_{17}H_{35}COOCH_2 \end{array}$$

some industrial processes, particularly those related to fermentation.

▶**6. Chemical nature of carbohydrates.** The name *carbohydrate* literally means "hydrate of carbon." This name was given to these compounds because the ones whose compositions were first worked out conformed to the general formula $C_x(H_2O)_y$. In this formula, x and y may have a variety of whole-number values. For example, ordinary sugar, sucrose, has the molecular formula, $C_{12}H_{22}O_{11}$. This can be written $C_{12}(H_2O)_{11}$. Another example is glucose, $C_6H_{12}O_6$. This formula may be written $C_6(H_2O)_6$. The more common carbohydrates conform to the general formula. There are many compounds which should be classed as carbohydrates which do not fit this general formula, however. It has no structural significance since carbohydrates are not composed of carbon and water in the sense that a hydrated ionic crystal is composed of ions and water molecules.

Most simple carbohydrates are polyhydroxyaldehydes or polyhydroxyketones. In one molecular form, the carbon atoms are in a chain. In other molecular forms, the carbon atoms and an oxygen linkage form a ring structure.

Carbohydrates may be classified as monosaccharides, disaccharides, or polysaccharides. Monosaccharides are carbohydrates which cannot be hydrolyzed by dilute acid into simpler substances. The disaccharides yield monosaccharides on acid hydrolysis. Each disaccharide molecule yields two monosaccharide units; hence the name, disaccharide. The polysaccharides, as their name suggests, hydrolyze to yield many monosaccharide units per molecule.

Monosaccharides and disaccharides are soluble in water. Polysaccharides are insoluble, though the simpler ones do form colloidal suspensions with water.

▶**7. Glucose: an important monosaccharide.** Glucose is a white, sweet-tasting, crystalline solid which is readily soluble in water. It is the most abundant monosaccharide, being found in ripe grapes, in honey, and in many fruit juices. Corn syrup is a familiar form of glucose. It is a normal component of blood.

Cornstarch is a polysaccharide composed of glucose units. Glucose is produced commercially by the hydrolysis of cornstarch, under pressure, using dilute hydrochloric acid as a catalyst.

Glucose assumes several structures each with characteristic properties. The open-chain form is the polyhydroxyaldehyde structure of the glucose molecule. By the addition of a water molecule to this structure and then subsequently eliminating it, the ring form of glucose is produced.

(open-chain form)   (ring form)

The ring form may be drawn in another fashion,

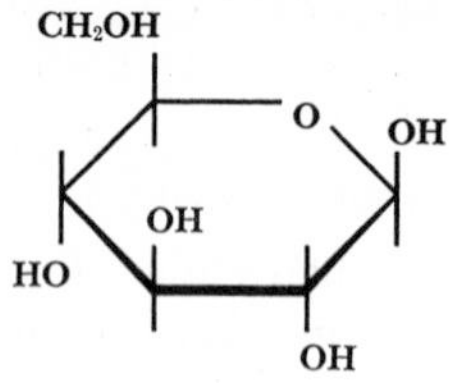

CH₂OH

in which the ring is considered to be flat, with the forward edges represented by the heavier lines. The different groups attached to the ring are represented at right angles above and below the plane of the ring. Note that carbon atoms in the ring and hydrogen atoms attached to these carbon atoms are omitted as in writing a benzene ring.

Because glucose molecules contain an aldehyde group, they can reduce copper(II) ion in Fehling's solution, and give a positive test. (See Chapter 18, Section 8.) Glucose also reacts with phenylhydrazine to give an osazone with a characteristic crystalline form and melting point, which is useful for identification purposes.

Glucose undergoes fermentation to produce ethanol, as described in Chapter 18, Section 4.

▶ **8. Some other important monosaccharides.** Fructose with the open chain and cyclic structures

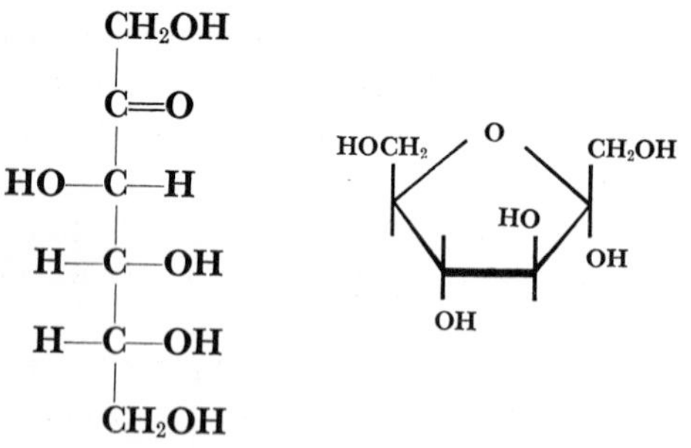

CH₂OH
C=O
HO—C—H
H—C—OH
H—C—OH
CH₂OH

occurs in sweet fruits and honey. It is one of the saccharide units in common table sugar, sucrose. It reduces Fehling's solu-

tion and forms an osazone with phenylhydrazine.

Galactose,

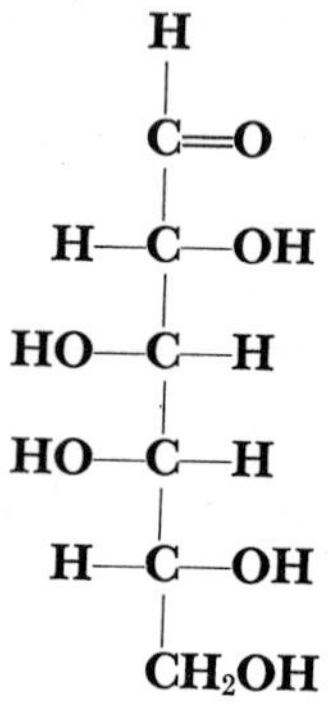

H
C=O
H—C—OH
HO—C—H
HO—C—H
H—C—OH
CH₂OH

is one of the saccharide units in lactose, and occurs in the body in certain proteins and in nerve tissue. As a constituent of polysaccharides, it is found in seaweeds, lichens, and mosses.

▶ **9. Disaccharides.** Ordinary sugar, sucrose, is the most common disaccharide. On hydrolysis, one molecule of sucrose yields a molecule of glucose and a molecule of fructose.

$$C_{12}H_{22}O_{11} + H_2O \rightarrow C_6H_{12}O_6 + C_6H_{12}O_6$$
sucrose   glucose   fructose

Since it is possible to obtain the same two molecules of monosaccharide from different disaccharides, there must be more than one way in which two different monosaccharide units may be combined in a disaccharide molecule.

1. Sucrose. Sucrose is the pure organic compound which is produced commercially in greatest quantity. In producing sucrose, the juice is squeezed from sugar cane or sugar beets. This raw juice is neutralized with lime, filtered, and then subjected to vacuum evaporation to remove the excess water. After vacuum evaporation, crystals of raw sugar remain mixed with the mother liquor. The mother liquor, blackstrap molasses, is removed by centrifuging. The raw sugar is dissolved in water and decolorized by filtration through boneblack. Recrystallization is accomplished by vacuum evaporation followed by centrifuging.

The structure of sucrose is given by the following formula.

You will note that its structure includes no formyl or carbonyl groups. Hence sucrose is not a reducing sugar, and forms no osazone with phenylhydrazine.

2. Maltose. Maltose does not often occur in the free state in nature. It is, however, produced by the action of certain enzymes on polysaccharides such as starch and glycogen. Maltose is a reducing sugar. On hydrolysis it yields two molecules of glucose.

3. Lactose. Lactose is found in the milk of mammals to the extent of about 2% to 6%. It is a reducing sugar which on hydrolysis yields a molecule of glucose and a molecule of galactose.

▶ **10.   Polysaccharides.**   These are high molecular weight carbohydrates made up of a large number of monosaccharide units linked together. Polysaccharides except cellulose produce colloidal suspensions in water. Cellulose shows no dispersing or solubility properties with water. Polysaccharides have no reducing properties and they do not taste sweet.

1. Starch. Starch occurs as distinct granules in most plants. It is the form in which carbohydrates are stored in the roots and seeds of plants. Starch is broken down into monosaccharide units when these more soluble and more reactive carbohydrates are needed. Important sources of starch are corn, wheat, rice, peas, beans, and potatoes. Starch is formed in leaves during photosynthesis. Green fruits contain starch, which is changed to sugars during ripening. Starch is the most important dietary source of carbohydrate.

Starch is usually a mixture of two polysaccharides, amylose and amylopectin, both of which yield glucose on hydrolysis. The iodine test for starch depends on the blue color exhibited by the amylose components when starch is treated with dilute iodine solution.

2. Glycogen. This is the form in which carbohydrates are stored in animals. Glycogen is found principally in the liver and muscles. It forms a colloidal suspension with water and when treated with iodine produces a reddish color. Glycogen may be hydrolyzed in the presence of enzyme or mineral acid catalysts to yield glucose.

3. Cellulose. Cellulose is the most abundant organic compound known. It occurs mainly in the cell walls of plants where it serves as a support for the plant tissues. Cellulose is an inactive compound. It is insoluble in water and gives no color with iodine. It consists of long chains of glucose units which are bonded side-by-side to each other by hydrogen bonds. This structure gives cellulose fibers their great strength.

▶ **11.   Modified cellulose.**

1. Viscose process. Rayon is regenerated cellulose. It consists of cellulose chains similar to those of cotton, except that they are shorter.

Most rayon is made by the viscose process. Raw cellulose is treated with sodium hydroxide to form alkali cellulose. This is converted into cellulose xanthate by treatment with carbon disulfide. Cellulose xanthate is then dissolved in sodium hydroxide solution to form "viscose" solution. After filtration, the viscose solution is forced through tiny openings into a bath of dilute sulfuric acid. This converts the viscose solution into a continuous, glossy, transparent filament of rayon. The extrusion of viscose solution through a narrow slit into the acid bath produces cellophane.

2. Cellulose acetate. Cellulose acetate is made by treating cellulose with acetic acid, acetic anhydride, and sulfuric acid. The cellulose acetate separates out in solid white flakes which are then dissolved in acetone. The solution is then passed through tiny openings. When the solvent is evaporated, a fiber of cellulose acetate results. Sheets of cellulose acetate form the base for photographic film; solutions of cellulose acetate are used as lacquers. Cellulose acetate is also an important plastic.

3. Cellulose nitrate. When cellulose is treated with a mixture of nitric and sulfuric acids, cellulose nitrate results. Partially nitrated cellulose is known as guncotton, and is an effective explosive from which smokeless powder is made.

PROTEINS

▶ **12. Importance of proteins.** Proteins on the average make up over two-thirds of the dry weight of all living cells. While fats and carbohydrates are used by living cells mainly as sources of energy, proteins are involved in the variety of chemical and physical changes which occur within living cells.

Proteins are the main component of skin, hair, nails, and muscle tissue of animals. They occur also in blood plasma and red corpuscles, and in egg white. Enzymes, hormones, antibodies, and viruses are mostly or entirely proteins. Proteins are required in animal diets and are the usual source of nitrogen and sulfur for body use. The number of proteins is very large because each type of animal synthesizes its own specific kinds. No two proteins seem to have exactly the same physiological action.

▶ **13. Chemical nature of proteins.** *Proteins are high molecular weight complex amides which contain carbon, hydrogen, oxygen, and nitrogen.* Some also contain sulfur, phosphorus, and other elements. The proteins have molecular weights ranging from about 6000 to many millions. They form colloidal dispersions in water and in neutral salt solutions. They are insoluble in organic solvents. On hydrolysis with strong acids or strong hydroxides, proteins yield a mixture of about 25 amino acids.

Amino acids link together in chainlike molecules. Since there are about 25 different amino acids, and the simplest proteins contain over one hundred amino acid units, it is obvious that a very large number of different proteins is possible.

▶ **14. Amino acids.** Amino acids are compounds with the properties of both amines and carboxylic acids, since their structure includes both $-NH_2$ and $-COOH$ groups. Specific examples are the nine amino acids which have been found essential for humans.

Amino acids are colorless crystalline solids. Their amino and carboxyl groups make them generally soluble in water, but they are insoluble in organic solvents. They form salts with both acids and hydroxides. Since they are organic acids, they will form esters with alcohols.

The amino group reacts with nitrous acid, evolving nitrogen.

$$R-\underset{\underset{\displaystyle H}{|}}{\overset{\overset{\displaystyle NH_2}{|}}{C}}-COOH + HNO_2 \rightarrow$$

$$R-\underset{\underset{\displaystyle H}{|}}{\overset{\overset{\displaystyle OH}{|}}{C}}-COOH + H_2O + N_2 \uparrow$$

AMINO ACIDS ESSENTIAL FOR HUMAN NUTRITION

valine

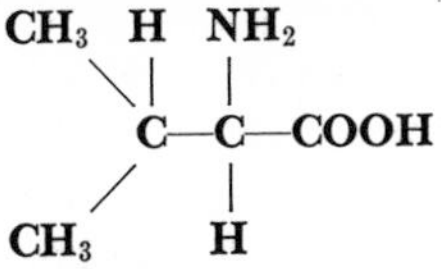

$$CH_3 \quad H \quad NH_2$$
$$CH_3\text{—}C\text{—}C\text{—COOH}$$
$$CH_3 \qquad H$$

leucine

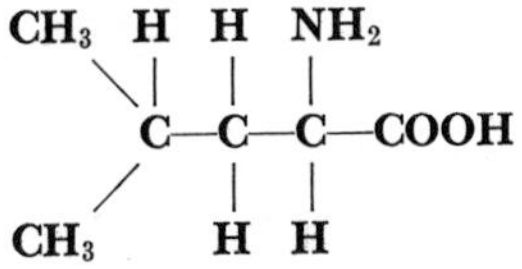

$$CH_3 \quad H \quad H \quad NH_2$$
$$CH_3\text{—}C\text{—}C\text{—}C\text{—COOH}$$
$$CH_3 \qquad H \quad H$$

isoleucine

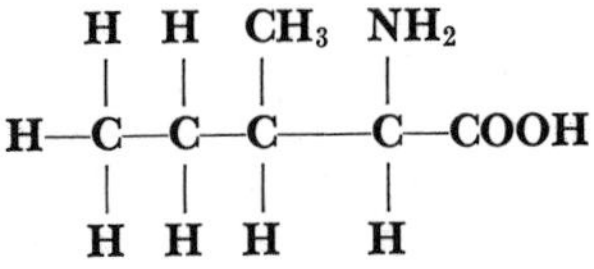

$$H \quad H \quad CH_3 \quad NH_2$$
$$H\text{—}C\text{—}C\text{—}C\text{—}C\text{—COOH}$$
$$H \quad H \quad H \qquad H$$

threonine

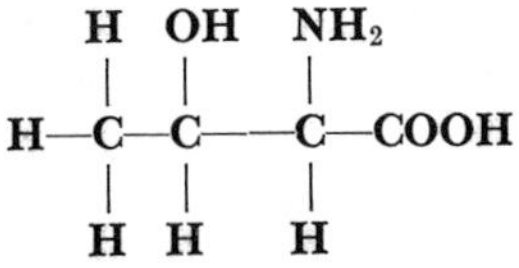

$$H \quad OH \quad NH_2$$
$$H\text{—}C\text{—}C\text{—}C\text{—COOH}$$
$$H \quad H \qquad H$$

methionine

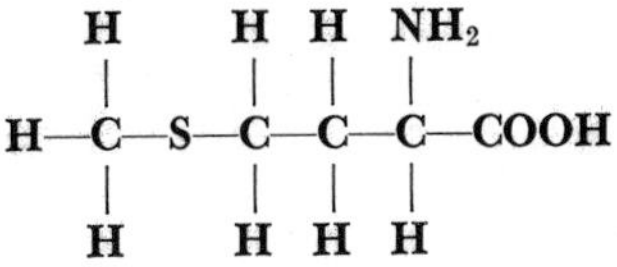

$$H \qquad H \quad H \quad NH_2$$
$$H\text{—}C\text{—}S\text{—}C\text{—}C\text{—}C\text{—COOH}$$
$$H \qquad H \quad H \quad H$$

lysine

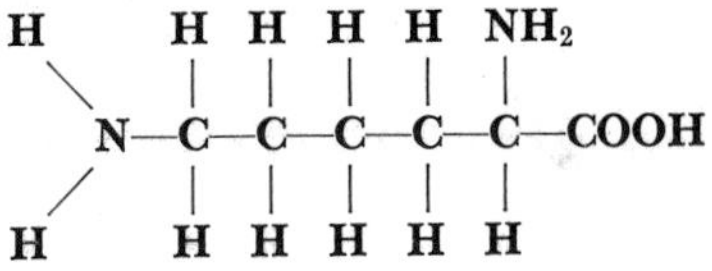

$$H \qquad H \quad H \quad H \quad H \quad NH_2$$
$$N\text{—}C\text{—}C\text{—}C\text{—}C\text{—}C\text{—COOH}$$
$$H \qquad H \quad H \quad H \quad H$$

arginine

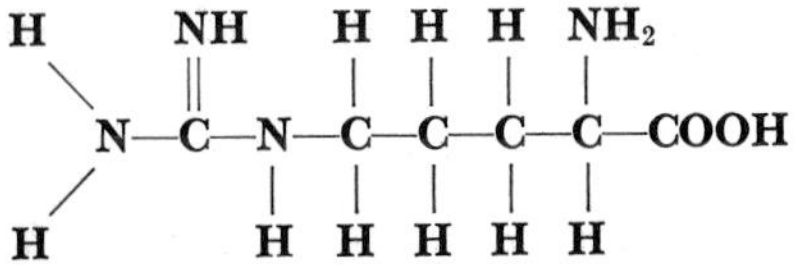

$$H \qquad NH \qquad H \quad H \quad H \quad NH_2$$
$$N\text{—}C\text{—}N\text{—}C\text{—}C\text{—}C\text{—}C\text{—COOH}$$
$$H \qquad \qquad H \quad H \quad H \quad H$$

phenylalanine

$$H \quad NH_2$$
$$\text{—}C\text{—}C\text{—COOH}$$
$$H \quad H$$

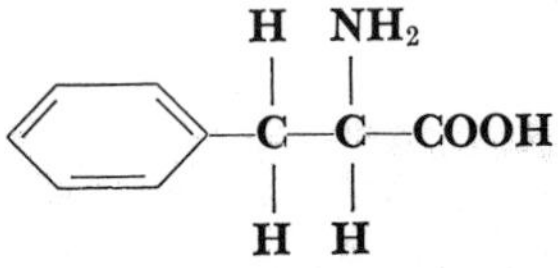

tryptophane

$$H \quad NH_2$$
$$\text{—}C\text{—}C\text{—COOH}$$
$$H \quad H$$

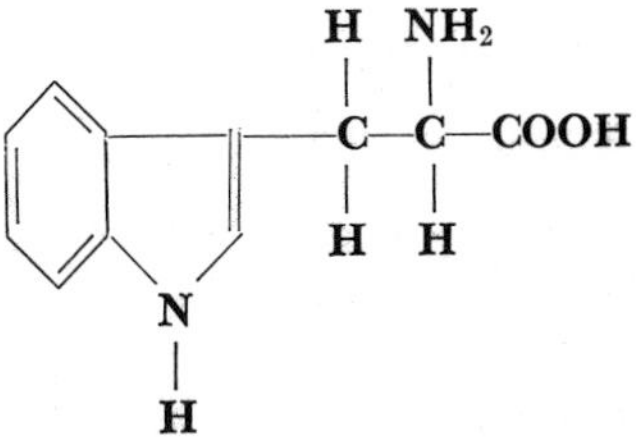

Since amino acids contain both acidic and basic groups, they act in water solution as both an acid and a base.

As acid
$$H_2N-\overset{\overset{R}{\mid}}{\underset{\underset{H}{\mid}}{C}}-COOH + H_2O \rightarrow$$

$$H_2N-\overset{\overset{R}{\mid}}{\underset{\underset{H}{\mid}}{C}}-COO^- + H_3O^+$$

As base
$$H_2N-\overset{\overset{R}{\mid}}{\underset{\underset{H}{\mid}}{C}}-COOH + H_2O \rightarrow$$

$$^+H_3N-\overset{\overset{R}{\mid}}{\underset{\underset{H}{\mid}}{C}}-COOH + OH^-$$

When both ionizations occur to the same extent, the amino acid has a positive charge at one end of the molecule and a negative charge at the other.

$$^+H_3N-\overset{\overset{R}{\mid}}{\underset{\underset{H}{\mid}}{C}}-COO^-$$

Such an ion is called a *dipolar ion* or *zwitterion*. Addition of acid or base to the solution favors a shift in equilibrium to the acid side or to the alkaline side, in accordance with LeChatelier's principle. See the equation on the opposite page.

▶ **15. Peptides.** Amino acids bond by joining the amino group of one acid to the carboxyl group of another acid. Water is eliminated. For example, glycine and alanine can react in one of two ways to produce two different products. (See bottom of page.) Such combinations are called dipeptides because they contain two amino acid groups joined by the

$$-\overset{\overset{O}{\|}}{C}-\overset{\overset{H}{\mid}}{N}-$$

linkage, called the *peptide linkage*. Three

glycine + alanine →
glycylalanine + H_2O

alanine + glycine →
alanylglycine + H_2O

$$H_2O + {}^+H_3N-\underset{\underset{H}{|}}{\overset{\overset{R}{|}}{C}}-COOH \underset{\longrightarrow}{\overset{+\ H_3O^+}{\longleftarrow}} {}^+H_3N-\underset{\underset{H}{|}}{\overset{\overset{R}{|}}{C}}-COO^- \underset{\longleftarrow}{\overset{+\ OH^-}{\longrightarrow}} H_2N-\underset{\underset{H}{|}}{\overset{\overset{R}{|}}{C}}-COO^- + H_2O$$

amino acids joined together in similar fashion form a tripeptide, while many amino acids similarly bonded form a polypeptide. Peptides have molecular weights up to about 6000.

▶ **16. Classification of proteins.** Proteins are classified as either *simple* or *conjugated proteins*. Simple proteins on hydrolysis yield only amino acids. Common examples of simple proteins are the *albumins* in blood and egg white, and cereal proteins such as *glutenin* of wheat. *Keratin* in hair, nails, and feathers, and *globin* in hemoglobin are also simple proteins.

Conjugated proteins yield amino acids plus other substances on hydrolysis. Conjugated proteins include the *mucin* of saliva (protein linked with a carbohydrate) and *casein* of milk (protein linked with phosphoric acid). *Virus proteins* (protein linked with nucleic acid), and the *lipoproteins* (protein linked with a lipid) are also conjugated proteins.

▶ **17. Chemical properties of proteins.**

1. Xanthoproteic reaction. Proteins which contain aromatic amino acids give a deep yellow color with concentrated nitric acid.

2. Biuret reaction. An alkaline suspension of a protein, treated with aqueous copper(II) sulfate, gives a violet color. Since the intensity of the color is an indication of the amount of protein, this is both a qualitative and a quantitative test.

3. Precipitation. Because proteins form colloidal suspensions in water, they may be precipitated by the usual methods for precipitating colloids. Strong mineral acids, solutions of lead or mercury salts, and organic acids such as tannic acid may be used as precipitating agents. High concentrations of ammonium sulfate or magnesium sulfate, and alcohol and acetone may also be used for precipitation.

4. Heat coagulation. Heating in neutral or slightly acid solutions will coagulate most proteins. The hardening of the white of an egg on heating is an example.

5. Hydrolysis. Proteins may be hydrolyzed by the action of strong mineral acids and strong hydroxides at boiling temperature. The first products are simpler peptides; continued hydrolysis yields amino acids. Enzymes will also catalyze the hydrolysis of proteins at lower temperatures.

▶ **18. Structure of proteins.** X-ray analysis makes it possible to unravel the structure of protein molecules. Two types have been discovered.

1. Fibrous proteins. These are long, rod-like molecules which are used in living organisms mainly for structural purposes. Examples are the keratin of the hair and the fibroin of the silkworm. Fibrous proteins consist of hundreds of polypeptide chains held together by hydrogen bonds and disulfide linkages. Sometimes they are coiled in the form of a helix, and sometimes they are nearly straight.

2. Globular proteins. The molecules of these proteins are compact and have a spherical shape. These are found dispersed in body fluids. Globular proteins can usually be crystallized; some can even be changed to the fibrous variety.

Scientists have worked out the sequence of amino acids in some of the biologically important proteins. Proteins are broken down into peptide fragments by hydrolysis and these are analyzed. By looking for overlapping sequences of peptide chains, and reassembling them, it is possible to reconstruct the original protein.

REVIEW OUTLINE

Fats—lipids (1, 2)
    Chemical nature—esters (2)
        Fats and oils (2)
        Rule of even distribution (3)
    Reactions (4)
        Hydrolysis (4)
        Saponification (4)
        Hydrogenation (4)

Carbohydrates (5)
    Chemical nature—polyhydroxyaldehydes or polyhydroxyketones (6)
    Monosaccharides (7)
        Glucose (7)
        Fructose (8)
        Galactose (8)
    Disaccharides (9)
        Sucrose (9)
        Maltose (9)
        Lactose (9)
    Polysaccharides (10)
        Starch (10)
        Glycogen (10)
        Cellulose (10)
        Modified cellulose (11)
           Viscose process (11)
           Cellulose acetate (11)
           Cellulose nitrate (11)

Proteins (12)
    Chemical nature—complex amides (13)
    Amino acids (14)
    Peptides—peptide linkage (15)
    Simple and conjugated proteins (16)
    Reactions (17)
        Xanthoproteic reaction (17)
        Biuret reaction (17)
        Precipitation (17)
        Heat coagulation (17)
        Hydrolysis (17)
    Structure (18)
        Fibrous (18)
        Globular (18)
        Amino acid sequence (18)

QUESTIONS

Group A

1. What is the chemical nature of (*a*) a fat; (*b*) a carbohydrate; (*c*) a protein?
2. Compare the functions of fats, carbohydrates, and proteins in plants and animals.
3. What is the chemical composition of protoplasm?
4. What are the important physical and chemical differences between fats and oils?
5. What uses, other than as food, does man make of carbohydrates?
6. Distinguish between monosaccharides, disaccharides, and polysaccharides.
7. Describe how sugar is produced from sugar cane or sugar beets.
8. In what form and where does starch occur?
9. What is the hydrolysis product of both starch and glycogen?
10. (*a*) What is the most abundant organic compound known? (*b*) What is the pure organic compound prepared commercially in largest quantity?
11. What is the function of sulfuric acid in the preparation of cellulose nitrate?
12. Using specific examples, distinguish between simple proteins and conjugated proteins.
13. Distinguish between fibrous and globular proteins.
14. What is the general method of determining the amino acid sequence in a protein?

Group B

15. What are (*a*) lipids; (*b*) amino acids; (*c*) peptide linkages?
16. Draw the structural formula for a fat molecule containing one palmitic acid chain, one stearic acid chain, and one oleic acid chain.
17. Explain what is meant by "the rule of even distribution."
18. Write formula equations for the following reactions on the fat molecule of Question 16: (*a*) acid hydrolysis; (*b*) saponification with sodium hydroxide; (*c*) mild hydrogenation; (*d*) severe hydrogenation.
19. Would you expect galactose and sucrose to give positive Fehling's solution tests and form osazones? Explain.
20. Compare starch and glycogen.
21. Draw a block diagram flow chart for (*a*) the viscose process; (*b*) the production of cellulose acetate.
22. Write structural formula equations for the reaction of (*a*) phenylalanine and nitrous acid; (*b*) ionization of isoleucine as an acid; (*c*) ionization of leucine as a base; (*d*) valine adding to methionone (two ways).
23. Draw the structural formula of the zwitterion of tryptophane.
24. What reaction occurs when egg albumin is subjected to (*a*) concentrated nitric acid; (*b*) mild heating; (*c*) sulfuric acid solution; (*d*) sodium hydroxide solution and copper(II) sulfate solution in succession; (*e*) boiling with sulfuric acid?

Chapter Twenty

CHEMICAL KINETICS

1. Energy changes in chemical reactions. Recent advances in chemistry, whether involving new analytical processes, new compounds, or new synthesis techniques, have a common basis, namely that problems in *chemical kinetics* had to be solved. This branch of chemistry is concerned with the sequence of steps by which chemical reactions occur and the rate at which they proceed. These are known respectively by the terms *reaction mechanism* and *reaction velocity*. Chemists who study chemical reactions and the forces that drive them must understand the role of energy in these processes.

Every substance has a characteristic internal energy as a consequence of its structure and its physical state. This is apparent from the fact that definite amounts of energy are released or absorbed when new substances are formed from reacting substances even though both products and reactants have the same temperature. The energy change is related directly to the change in number and strengths of bonds as the system transforms from reactants to products.

2. Heat of reaction. In most chemical actions the energy change can be measured in terms of the heat released or absorbed during the reaction. If a process is exothermic, we might say that the *heat content* of the atoms of the reactants is lowered as they are rearranged to form the products. The products of an endothermic reaction must have a higher heat content than the reactants.

Each mole of a substance has a characteristic heat content just as it has a characteristic mass. The heat content measures the internal energy stored in the substance during its formation. It cannot be measured directly, but the *change* in heat content that occurs during chemical action can be measured. This is the heat released during an exothermic change or the heat absorbed during an endothermic change. It is called *heat of reaction.* The **heat of reaction** *is the quantity of heat evolved or absorbed during a chemical reaction.*

The value of the heat of reaction is taken when the final state of the system is brought to the same temperature as that of the initial state. Unless otherwise stated, the reaction is assumed to be at room temperature (25° C) under standard atmospheric pressure with each substance present in its normal state under these conditions. For this reason the states of reactants and products should be shown along with their formulas when an equation is written to include heat of reaction information (thermochemical equation).

If a mixture of hydrogen and oxygen is ignited, water is formed and heat energy is released. By experiment we would find the quantity of heat given up to be proportional to the quantity of water produced. Since no heat was supplied externally, except to ignite the mixture, we must conclude that the heat content of the product water is less than that of the reactants before ignition.

The equation for this reaction is ordinarily written

$$2H_2 + O_2 \rightarrow 2H_2O$$

From this equation we may state that when 2 moles of hydrogen gas (at room temperature) are burned, 1 mole of oxygen gas is used, and 2 moles of water vapor are formed. After the product water is brought back to room temperature (the temperature of the initial state) the reaction heat given up by the system is found to be 136.64 kcal. The thermochemical equation is then written

$$2H_2(g) + O_2(g) \rightarrow 2H_2O(l) + 136.64\,kcal$$

where (g) and (l) indicate gas and liquid states respectively. When a solid state is to be indicated, (s) is used.

Heats of reaction are commonly expressed in terms of *kilocalories per mole* of substance. From the above equation the following equality is evident.

heat content of 1 mole of hydrogen gas + heat content of $\frac{1}{2}$ mole of oxygen gas = heat content of 1 mole of liquid water + 68.32 kcal

The thermochemical equation may now be written to indicate heat of reaction in kcal/mole of product as follows

$$H_2(g) + \tfrac{1}{2}O_2(g) \rightarrow H_2O(l) + 68.32\,kcal$$

The equation now tells us that the product water has a heat content *lower* by 68.32 kcal/mole than the elements composing it. If one mole of water is decomposed to produce hydrogen and oxygen, this much energy must be supplied to the reaction from an external source. In the electrolysis of water, an endothermic reaction, it is supplied as electric energy. The equation is

$$H_2O(l) + 68.32\,kcal \rightarrow H_2(g) + \tfrac{1}{2}O_2(g)$$

Here the products, 1 mole of hydrogen plus $\frac{1}{2}$ mole of oxygen, have a heat content *higher* by 68.32 kcal when 1 mole of water is decomposed. The two reactions may be shown by a reversible equation.

$$H_2(g) + \tfrac{1}{2}O_2(g) \rightleftarrows H_2O(l) + 68.32\,kcal$$

Careful measurements show that energy is conserved in these processes.

Chemists symbolize the heat content of a substance by the letter H. The change in heat content during a reaction, *the heat of reaction*, is the difference between the heat content of the products and the heat content of the reactants. The heat of reaction then becomes ΔH, the Greek letter Δ (delta) signifying "change in."

$$\Delta H = \frac{\text{heat content}}{\text{of products}} - \frac{\text{heat content}}{\text{of reactants}}$$

In this notation scheme, the ΔH for an exothermic reaction has a negative sign. Thus, in the synthesis of water

$$\Delta H = -68.32 \text{ kcal/mole}$$

and the thermochemical equation

$$H_2(g) + \tfrac{1}{2}O_2(g) \rightarrow H_2O(l)$$
$$\Delta H = -68.32 \text{ kcal}$$

is completely equivalent to

$$H_2(g) + \tfrac{1}{2}O_2(g) \rightarrow H_2O(l) + 68.32 \text{ kcal}$$

The ΔH for an endothermic reaction is signified by using a positive sign.

This sign convention is an arbitrary one, but it is logical since the heat of reaction is said to be *negative* when the heat content of the system is *decreasing* (exothermic reaction). It is said to be *positive* when the heat content of the system is *increasing* (endothermic reaction). See Fig. 20-1. Chemists generally prefer this sign convention over an older one in which the signs are reversed.

3. Heat of formation. Chemical action in which elements combine to form compounds are generally exothermic. In these composition reactions the product compounds have lower heat contents than their constituent elements and are more stable than these elements uncombined. Water synthesis from hydrogen and oxygen illustrates this change in stability.

Elementary hydrogen and oxygen exist as nonpolar diatomic molecules. Water molecules are covalent structures with polar characteristics because of the electronegativity difference between the hydrogen and oxygen atoms.

When the single covalent bonds of the hydrogen and oxygen molecules were formed originally, energy was given up. Energy is required to break these bonds if the hydrogen and oxygen atoms are to combine. However, a great deal of energy is released when the two polar bonds of the water molecule are formed and so heat is evolved during the composition reaction. The heat of reaction is quite high ($\Delta H = -68.3$ kcal/mole of water formed) suggesting that the water molecules are quite stable compared to the hydrogen and oxygen molecules.

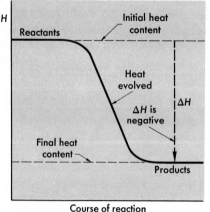

Course of reaction
(A) Exothermic change

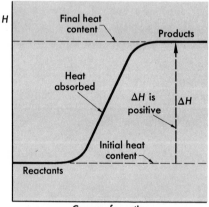

Course of reaction
(B) Endothermic change

20-1   Change in heat content during chemical action.

Indeed, the heat evolved or absorbed in a composition reaction is a useful indicator of product stability and is referred to as the *heat of formation* of the compound. *The heat of reaction evolved or absorbed when 1 mole of a compound is formed from its elements is called the* **heat of formation** *of the compound.* More specifically it is the *molar* heat of formation of the compound. The heats of formation of some common compounds are listed in Table 12 of the Appendix.

The sign convention and ΔH notation we adopted for heats of reaction in general apply to heats of formation also. The latter are merely one category of reaction heats. When it is desirable to distinguish a particular reaction heat as a heat of formation, we may use the more explicit notation ΔH_f. Thus, heats of formation have negative values for exothermic composition reactions and positive values for endothermic composition reactions.

Observe that most of the heats of formation given in Appendix Table 12 are negative. Only a few compounds such as hydrogen iodide and carbon disulfide have positive heats of formation.

4. Stability and heat of formation. A compound with a high negative heat of formation is formed with the release of considerable energy. In order to decompose such a compound into its constituent elements the same amount of energy must be supplied to the reaction from an external source. *Such compounds are very stable.* The reactions forming them proceed spontaneously, once they start, and are usually vigorous. Carbon dioxide has a high heat of formation, its ΔH_f being -94.05 kcal per mole of the gas produced.

Compounds with low heats of formation are generally unstable. Hydrogen sulfide, H_2S, has a heat of formation of -4.82 kcal per mole. It is not very stable and decomposes when heated. Hydrogen iodide, HI, has a low positive heat of formation, $+6.20$ kcal/mole. It is a colorless gas which undergoes some decomposition when stored at room temperatures, so that violet iodine vapor may be seen throughout the container of the gas.

A compound with a high positive heat of formation is likely to be explosive. Such a compound is formed only by expending a great deal of energy. Mercury fulminate, $HgC_2N_2O_2$, has a heat of formation of $+64$ kcal/mole. It is used extensively as a detonator for explosives because of its instability.

In general, the greater the difference in electronegativity of two elements, the greater is the strength of the bond between them when they combine chemically. It is not surprising, therefore, to observe a relationship between the separation of two elements on the electronegativity scale and the heat-of-formation measurements made when they react. In fact, observed heats of formation figure prominently in the calculations by which the electronegativity scale was formulated. Compounds formed between the metals of Groups I and II and the nonmetals of Groups VI and VII, which are far apart in electronegativity, are in general stable and have high heats of formation. Those formed between elements close together in electronegativity tend to be unstable and have low heats of formation.

5. The heat of combustion. Fuels, whether for the furnace, automobile, or rocket, are energy-rich substances and the products of their combustion are energy-poor substances. In these combustion reactions the energy yield may be very high and the products of the chemical action may be of little interest compared to the quantity of heat energy evolved.

The combustion of 1 mole of pure carbon (graphite) yields 94.05 kcal of heat energy.

$$C(s) + O_2(g) \rightarrow CO_2(g)$$
$$\Delta H = -94.05 \text{ kcal}$$

The heat of reaction evolved by the complete combustion of 1 mole of a substance is called the **heat of combustion** *of the substance.* Observe that we have defined the heat of combustion in terms of *1 mole of reactant*, whereas we defined the heat of formation in terms of *1 mole of product*. The general ΔH notation applies to heats of combustion, but when desirable, the more explicit ΔH_c notation may be used to distinguish a particular reaction heat as a heat of combustion.

When a substance cannot be formed in a rapid composition reaction directly from its constituent elements, its heat of formation may be calculated by using the heats of reaction of a series of related reactions. Heats of combustion of such substances are sometimes useful in this connection.

The complete combustion products of many organic compounds are CO_2 and H_2O. Since the heats of formation of these two substances are known, the heats of formation of the organic compounds can be calculated from the equality stated at the bottom of this page.

When carbon is burned in a limited supply of oxygen, carbon monoxide is produced. In this reaction carbon is probably oxidized to CO_2 which in turn may be reduced by hot carbon to CO giving an uncertain mixture of the two gases. Thus we could not successfully determine the heat of formation of CO by measuring the heat evolved during the reaction.

Both carbon and carbon monoxide can be burned completely to carbon dioxide. The heat of formation of CO_2 and the heat of combustion of CO are then known.

From these reaction heats, the heat of formation of CO can be found using the equality stated below. For the combustion of carbon:

$$C(s) + O_2(g) \rightarrow CO_2(g) + 94.05 \text{ kcal}$$

Thus

$$\Delta H_f \text{ of } CO_2 = -94.05 \text{ kcal/mole}$$

For the combustion of carbon monoxide:

$$2CO(g) + O_2(g) \rightarrow$$
$$2CO_2(g) + 135.28 \text{ kcal}$$

Rewriting this equation in the form which yields 1 mole of CO_2,

$$CO(g) + \tfrac{1}{2}O_2(g) \rightarrow CO_2(g) + 67.64 \text{ kcal}$$

Thus

$$\Delta H_c \text{ of } CO = -67.64 \text{ kcal/mole}$$

But

$$\Delta H_f(CO) = \Delta H_f(CO_2) - \Delta H_c(CO)$$

Then, by substitution,

$$\Delta H_f(CO) = -94.05 \text{ kcal/mole} - (-67.64 \text{ kcal/mole})$$

$$\Delta H_f(CO) = -26.41 \text{ kcal/mole}$$

Now that we know the heat of formation of CO, observe that it may be added to the heat of combustion of CO to yield the heat of formation of the CO_2. A thermochemical equation for the production of CO might be written as shown at the top of page 337.

Because the energy of a system is conserved during chemical activity, the heat absorbed in decomposing a compound must be equal to the heat evolved in its formation under the same conditions. *At*

| heat of formation of compound X | = | sum of heats of formation of products of combustion of compound X | − | heat of combustion of compound X |

$$C(s) + O_2(g) \rightarrow \cancel{CO_2(g)} \quad \text{(oxidation of C)}$$
$$C(s) + \cancel{CO_2(g)} \rightarrow 2CO(g) \quad \text{(reduction of CO)}$$
$$\overline{2C(s) + O_2(g) \rightarrow 2CO(g) \quad \text{(net reaction)}}$$

Thus,

$$C(s) + \tfrac{1}{2}O_2(g) \rightarrow \cancel{CO(g)} \quad \Delta H = -26.41 \text{ kcal}$$
$$\cancel{CO(g)} + \tfrac{1}{2}O_2(g) \rightarrow CO_2(g) \quad \Delta H = -67.64 \text{ kcal}$$
$$\overline{C(s) + O_2(g) \rightarrow CO_2(g) \quad \Delta H = -94.05 \text{ kcal}}$$

constant pressure the overall heat of reaction of a system is the same regardless of the intermediate steps involved. Thus, if there is a reason to write the equation for a reaction in reverse form, the sign of ΔH for the reaction must be reversed.

Let us apply these principles to the thermochemical equation for the combustion of carbon monoxide.

$$CO(g) + \tfrac{1}{2}O_2(g) \rightarrow CO_2(g)$$
$$\Delta H = -67.64 \text{ kcal}$$

Writing the reverse of this reaction

$$CO_2(g) \rightarrow CO(g) + \tfrac{1}{2}O_2(g)$$
$$\Delta H = +67.64 \text{ kcal}$$

This provides us with another way of illustrating the *additivity* of heats of reaction, as shown in the equations at the top of page 338.

In Chapter 2, Section 14, we referred to an endothermic reaction between carbon and steam that occurs spontaneously at the temperature of the white hot carbon. This is the "water-gas" reaction of the fuel industry which produces a mixture of CO and H_2 as a gaseous fuel.

The heat of formation of water is normally expressed in terms of the change in heat content between liquid water at 25° C and its constituent elements at the same temperature. Water vapor must give

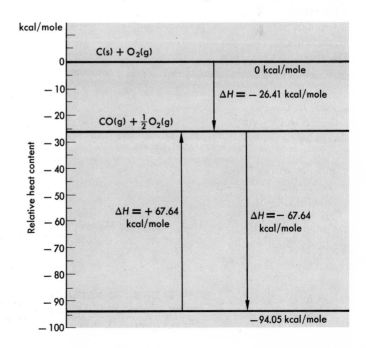

20-2 Heat of formation diagram for carbon monoxide and carbon dioxide.

$C(s)$	$+$	$O_2(g)$	$\rightarrow$	$CO_2(g)$			$\Delta H = -94.05$ kcal
		$CO_2(g)$	$\rightarrow$	$CO(g)$	$+$	$\frac{1}{2}O_2(g)$	$\Delta H = +67.64$ kcal
$C(s)$	$+$	$\frac{1}{2}O_2(g)$	$\rightarrow$	$CO(g)$			$\Delta H = -26.41$ kcal

up 10.52 kcal/mole in condensing to its normal liquid state at 25° C, a purely physical change.

$$H_2O(g) \rightarrow H_2O(l) + 10.52 \text{ kcal}$$

Thus, the steam entering into the water-gas reaction has a higher heat content (and a lower heat of formation) by 10.52 kcal than liquid water.

The heat of formation of the product water as a gas from its composition reaction may be shown by the following thermochemical equation.

$$H_2(g) + \frac{1}{2}O_2(g) \rightarrow H_2O(g) + 57.80 \text{ kcal}$$

The complete relationship is shown by an appropriate series of equations at the bottom of this page.

Experimental measurements of the quantity of heat absorbed in the water-gas reaction yield a value of 31.39 kcal per mole of carbon used. The thermochemical equation is

$$H_2O(g) + C(s) + 31.39 \text{ kcal} \rightarrow$$
$$CO(g) + H_2(g)$$

The heat of reaction is absorbed and the heat content of the products CO and H_2 has been increased, the ΔH for each being positive.

When the product gases are burned as fuel two combustion reactions occur, CO_2 being the product of one and water vapor the product of the other. Both are familiar reactions from earlier discussions in this section.

$$CO(g) + \frac{1}{2}O_2(g) \rightarrow CO_2(g) + 67.64 \text{ kcal}$$
$$H_2(g) + \frac{1}{2}O_2(g) \rightarrow H_2O(g) + 57.80 \text{ kcal}$$

These reactions are exothermic and the heats of combustion have negative values.

Suppose we now arrange the three thermochemical equations representing the formation of the water gas and its combustion as a fuel into a series and see what the net additive result will be, as in the equations shown at the top of the following page.

Observe that while the combined heat of combustion of CO and H_2 (-125.44 kcal) is higher than that of carbon (-94.05 kcal), it is higher only by the amount of heat energy put into the first reaction ($+31.39$ kcal). In the overall reaction system, energy is conserved.

6. Bond energy and reaction heat. In Section 1 we stated that the change in heat content of a reaction system is related to the change in the number and strength of bonds as the system transforms from reactants to products. The reaction for the formation of water gas can be used to test this relationship.

The two oxygen-to-hydrogen bonds of each molecule of steam and the carbon-to-carbon bonds of the graphite must be broken. Bonds between carbon and oxygen and hydrogen-to-hydrogen bonds must be formed. Energy is absorbed when bonds are broken and is liberated when bonds are formed.

We will assume a possible reaction mechanism in which there is an intermediate stage of free atoms. This is illus-

$H_2(g)$	$+$	$\frac{1}{2}O_2(g)$	$\rightarrow$	$H_2O(g)$	$\Delta H = -57.80$ kcal
		$H_2O(g)$	$\rightarrow$	$H_2O(l)$	$\Delta H = -10.52$ kcal
$H_2(g)$	$+$	$\frac{1}{2}O_2(g)$	$\rightarrow$	$H_2O(l)$	$\Delta H = -68.32$ kcal

~~H₂O(g)~~	+	C(s)	→	~~CO(g)~~	+ ~~H₂(g)~~	$\Delta H = +31.39$ kcal
~~CO(g)~~	+	$\frac{1}{2}$O₂(g)	→	CO₂(g)		$\Delta H = -67.64$ kcal
~~H₂(g)~~	+	$\frac{1}{2}$O₂(g)	→	~~H₂O(g)~~		$\Delta H = -57.80$ kcal
C(s)	+	O₂(g)	→	CO₂(g)		$\Delta H = -94.05$ kcal

trated in Fig. 20-3. Notice that a heat input of 390 kcal is required to break the bonds of 1 mole of graphite and 1 mole of steam. The formation of bonds in the final state releases 358 kcal of heat energy. The net effect is that 32 kcal of heat must be supplied to the system from an external source. This is in close agreement with the experimental value of 31.39 kcal of heat input per mole of carbon used in the reaction.

7. The driving force of reactions. "Whether a reaction will occur" and "why a reaction does go" are questions that have always concerned chemists. Complete answers to these questions can be achieved only through a thorough quantitative study of reaction mechanisms and reaction kinetics within the framework of the laws of thermodynamics. This is the realm of *physical chemistry*. What we can do here is examine qualitatively the concepts which

$$C(s) + H_2O(g) + 31.4 \text{ kcal} \longrightarrow CO(g) + H_2(g)$$

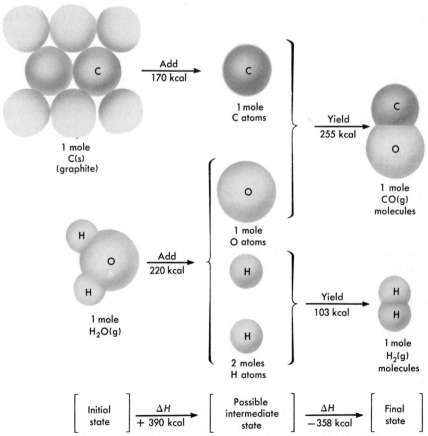

20-3 A possible mechanism for the water-gas reaction.

chemists label collectively as the "driving force" of chemical reactions. Some of these ideas were discussed briefly in Chapter 2, Section 14.

By observation we have come to recognize that most reactions which occur spontaneously in nature are exothermic. These exothermic processes evolve energy and lead to lower energy states and more stable configurations. Certainly a factor in the driving force of chemical reactions is this *tendency for processes to occur which lead to the lowest possible state of energy.*

If this were the only factor, we would predict that only exothermic reactions could take place and that no chemical reaction could, of itself, take place with absorption of energy. We have a great deal of qualitative evidence that seems to show not only that reactions evolve energy, but that the greater the quantity of energy given up, the more vigorous they are.

The disturbing fact is that chemical reactions do, of themselves, as a result of simply mixing reactants, take place with absorption of energy. The production of water gas utilizes such a reaction. Steam is passed into white-hot coke and the reaction proceeds by and of itself. It is not driven by any activity external to the reacting system. The absorption of heat has a cooling effect and more heat must be supplied by periodically blowing air into the coke to cause some combustion. We have seen from Section 5 that the product gases carbon monoxide and hydrogen have collectively a higher heat content than the reactants steam and carbon. The energy change is positive so this cannot be the driving force of the reaction.

To see how an endothermic reaction can occur spontaneously, let us observe a simple physical process that proceeds by and of itself *with no energy change.* In Fig. 20-4 we have two identical flasks connected by a valve. One flask is filled with

ideal gas *A* and the other with ideal gas *B*, the entire system being at room temperature.

When the valve is opened the two gases will mix until they are finally distributed evenly throughout the two containers. Since the temperature remains constant throughout the process, the total heat content cannot have changed to a lower level. The self-mixing process, which produced a more disordered system, must have been caused by a driving force other than the energy-change tendency. We can leave the intermixed system as it is indefinitely and we will observe no tendency for the two gases to separate or become "unmixed."

In our earlier discussion in Chapter 2, we identified a *tendency for processes to occur which leads to the highest possible state of disorder.* In general, a system that can go from one state to another without experiencing an energy change will adopt the state that is more disordered. The property which describes the state of disorder of a system is called *entropy.* We merely need to agree that the final intermixed system of gases represents a more disordered state than the initial pure-gas system to recognize that an entropy change has occurred. The driving force in this instance was the tendency for the entropy of the system to *increase.*

Thus, the property of a system that makes the reaction go consists of two driving forces, a tendency toward the *lowest* energy and a tendency toward the *highest* entropy. Where the energy change and the entropy change oppose each other, the

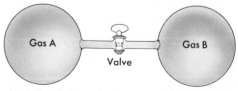

20-4   The mixing of the gases may occur without an energy change.

system will go in the direction of the larger change.

This net driving force is called the *free-energy change* of the system. For reactions carried out at atmospheric (constant) pressure and at a constant temperature, the free-energy change is

$$\Delta G = \Delta H - T\Delta S$$

where ΔG is the change in free energy of the system, ΔH is the change in heat content, T is the temperature in °K, and ΔS is the change in entropy. (ΔS is multiplied by T to give the term the same unit dimensions as ΔH.)

A chemical reaction will proceed if it is accompanied by a decrease in free energy, that is, if the free energy of the products is less than that of the reactants. In such a case the *free-energy change* ΔG in the system is said to be *negative*.

In exothermic reactions ΔH has a negative value and in endothermic reactions its value is positive. The entropy change ΔS is positive in any change accompanied by an increase in entropy and is negative for a decrease in entropy. Thus an endothermic reaction will proceed only if the action is accompanied by an increase in entropy such that $T\Delta S$ is positive and larger than ΔH. Then the expression for ΔG, which is $\Delta H - T\Delta S$, will have a negative value. This is the foremost fundamental principle of chemical spontaneity: *a chemical reaction tends to proceed spontaneously in the direction of diminished free energy content. This means that when the free energy change ΔG for the reaction is negative, free energy is released.*

In the water gas reaction,

$$\mathbf{H_2O(g) + C(s) \rightarrow CO(g) + H_2(g)}$$
$$\Delta H = +31.39 \text{ kcal}$$

we must find a reason for increased entropy which enables the reaction to go on.

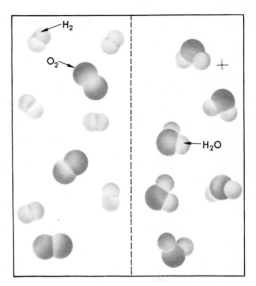

20-5   A mixture of hydrogen and oxygen molecules will form very stable water molecules when properly activated.

Recall that the solid state is well ordered and the gaseous state is random. One of the reactants, carbon, is a solid and the other, steam, is a gas. However, both products are gases. The change from the orderly solid state to the random gaseous state is accompanied by an *increase* in entropy.

In general, a change from a solid to a gas will proceed with an increase in entropy. If all reactants and products are gases, an increase in the number of product particles increases entropy.

Increases in temperature tend to favor increases in entropy. When ΔS is positive a high temperature gives $T\Delta S$ a large positive value. Thus, the water gas reaction proceeds *when the temperature of the system is high enough.*

When the temperature of a system is low, whether ΔS is positive or negative, the product $T\Delta S$ may be small compared to ΔH. In such cases the reaction may proceed as the energy change predicts. We may assume that a perfect crystal at absolute zero, 0° K, would have zero entropy.

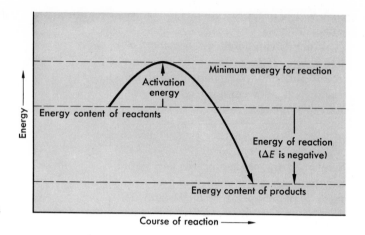

20-6 Pathway of an exothermic reaction.

8. Activation energy. The production of water from its elements is a vigorous exothermic reaction and the heat of formation is quite high; ΔH_f is -68.3 kcal/mole at $25°$ C. The free energy change is also large, ΔG_f being -56.7 kcal/mole. Why then, when hydrogen and oxygen are mixed at room temperature, do they not combine spontaneously to form water?

Hydrogen and oxygen gases exist as diatomic molecules. By some reaction mechanism, the bonds of these molecular species must be broken and new bonds between oxygen and hydrogen atoms must be formed. Bond breaking is an endothermic process and bond forming is exothermic. Even though the net process is exothermic, it appears that an initial energy "kick" is needed to start the action.

It might be helpful to think of the reactants as lying in an energy trough from which they must be lifted before they can react to form water, despite the fact that the energy content of the product is lower than that of the reactants. Once the reaction is started, the energy released is enough to sustain the action and activate other molecules. Thus the reaction rate keeps increasing, being finally limited only by the time required for the reactant molecules to acquire the energy and to make contact.

The energy needed to lift the reactants from the energy trough is called *activation energy*. This is the energy required to loosen bonds in molecules so they can become reactive. Energy from a flame, a spark discharge, or the energy associated with high temperatures or radiations may be sufficient to start reactants along the pathway of reaction. See Fig. 20-6.

The product water lies in an energy trough that is deeper than the one from which the reactants were lifted. In the reverse reaction, the decomposition of water, the water molecules must be lifted from this deeper energy trough before they can decompose to form hydrogen and oxygen.

The activation energy needed to initiate this endothermic reaction is greater than that required for the original exothermic change by the amount of energy of reaction ΔE released in the original reaction. See Fig. 20-7.

An analogous situation would exist where two mountain valleys are separated by a high mountain pass. One valley is lower than the other, but to get to it from the upper valley, one must climb over the

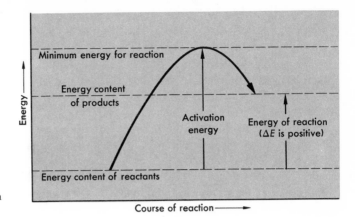

20-7 Pathway of an endothermic reaction.

high pass. It is apparent that the return trip to the upper valley can be made only by climbing over the same high pass again. However, for this trip, one must climb a greater distance since the starting point is lower.

In Fig. 20-8, the difference in height of the floors of the two valleys in our analogy can be compared with the energy of reaction ΔE. The heights of the pass above the high and low valleys can be compared with the activation energies E_a and E_a' of the forward and reverse reactions respectively.

9. Collision Theory. In order for reactions to occur between substances, it would seem that their particles (molecules, atoms, or ions) must collide and that these collisions must result in interactions. Chemists use this *collision theory* to interpret many facts they observe in connection with chemical reactions.

From Kinetic Theory we know that the molecules of gases are continuously in random motion. The molecules have kinetic energies ranging from very low to very high values, the energies of the greatest portion being near the average for all the

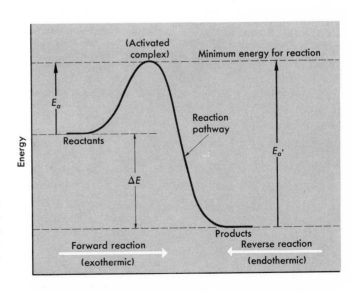

20-8 Activation energies for the forward reaction E_a and the reverse reaction E_a', and the change in internal energy ΔE in a reversible reaction.

molecules in the system. Such an energy distribution is shown in Chapter 12 as Fig. 12-6.

Suppose we consider what happens on a molecular scale in a simple *homogeneous* reaction system, one in which reactants and products are all in the same phase. The formation of hydrogen iodide from hydrogen and iodine is such a reaction.

$$\mathbf{H_2(g) + I_2(g) \rightleftarrows 2HI(g)}$$

According to the collision theory, for hydrogen to react with iodine vapor, hydrogen molecules must collide with iodine molecules. If the reactants collide with suitable orientation and with enough energy to disrupt the bonds of the molecules, a reshuffling of the bonds leads to the formation of the new molecular species of the product.

In a collision that is too gentle, the dis-

tance between hydrogen and iodine molecules is never small enough for a stable H-I bond to form. The two molecules simply rebound from each other unchanged. See Fig. 20-9(A).

Similarly, a collision in which the hydrogen and iodine molecules are poorly oriented does not produce a small enough HI distance for H-I bond formation. The molecules bounce off each other without change. This is illustrated in Fig. 20-9(B).

Only when the collision is violent enough to cause an interpenetration of the H_2 and I_2 electron clouds, does the HI distance become small enough for H-I bonds to form. See Fig. 20-9(C). The minimum energy required to produce this *effective collision* defines the activation energy needed for the $H_2 + I_2$ reaction.

Thus, from the collision theory we can

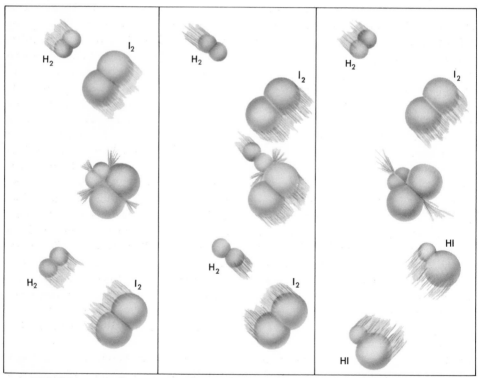

(A) Collision too gentle   (B) Collision with poor orientation   (C) Effective collision

20-9   Possible collision patterns for H_2 and I_2 molecules.

recognize two reasons why a collision between reactant molecules may be ineffective in producing new chemical species: *the collision is not energetic enough to supply the required activation energy,* and *the colliding molecules are not oriented in a way that enables them to react with each other.* What then is the reaction pathway of an effective collision which does result in the production of new chemical species?

10. The activated complex. The possession of high motion (kinetic) energy does not make molecules unstable. However, if enough of this energy is converted into internal (potential) energies of the parts of molecules in collision, the molecules may become activated.

When colliding molecules are pressed together with energy at least equal to the activation energy for the species involved, their interpenetration disrupts existing bonds and allows new bonds to form. In the fleeting interval of bond disruption and bond formation the collision complex is said to be in a *transition state* with some sort of partial bonding. *The transitional structure resulting from an effective collision and persisting while old bonds are breaking and new bonds are forming is called the* **activated complex.**

An activated complex is formed by an effective collision when the internal energies of the reactants are raised to their *minimum-energy-for-reaction level* as shown in Fig. 20-8. Observe that the activated complex configuration occurs at the maximum energy position along the reaction pathway. In this sense the activated complex defines the activation energy for the system. *Activation energy is the energy required to transform the reactants into the activated complex.*

In the brief interval of its existence with partial bonding of both reactants and product character, the activated complex may respond to either of two possibilities: it may re-form the original bonds and

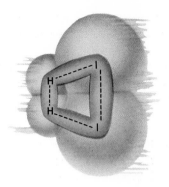

20-10 Possible configuration of the activated complex $H_2I_2{}^{\ddagger}$ showing, by dotted lines, some kind of partial bonding between the atoms.

separate into the reactant molecules, or it may form new bonds and separate into product molecules. Usually the formation of products is just as likely as the formation of reactants.

Let us now return to the $H_2 + I_2$ reaction previously discussed. In the pathway for this reaction, the two reactant molecules are believed to form an activated complex having the intermediate configuration $H_2I_2{}^{\ddagger}$ shown in Fig. 20-10. (The symbol $\ddagger$ is commonly used to designate the activated complex.) The dotted lines represent some sort of partial bonding thought to exist in the transient particle.

In the forward reaction, the bond between the hydrogen atoms and the bond between the iodine atoms break as the bonds in the two hydrogen iodide molecules form. The activation energy E_a is approximately 43.0 kcal/mole. The reaction is slightly exothermic. When one mole of H_2 and one mole of I_2 disappear, 2 moles of HI and 2.5 kcal of heat appear.

$$H_2(g) + I_2(g) \rightarrow 2HI(g) + 2.5 \text{ kcal}$$

The reverse reaction progresses back along the same reaction pathway forming an activated complex having the same energy and configuration as that of the forward reaction. Here the bond between the hydrogen atoms and the bond between the iodine atoms form as the bonds in the hydrogen iodide molecules break. The activation energy E_a' is approximately 45.5 kcal/mole (of $H_2 + I_2$), 2.5 kcal greater than E_a.

$$\mathbf{2HI(g) + 2.5\ kcal \rightarrow H_2(g) + I_2(g)}$$

The energy profile for this reversible reaction is shown in Fig. 20-11.

11. Rate of chemical reaction. Reaction rates range all the way from those which are practically instantaneous to those which may take months, or even years, to complete. *The rate of reaction is measured by the amount of reactants converted to products in a unit of time.* In order for reactions (other than simple decompositions) to occur at all, particles must come in contact, and this contact must result in interaction. Thus the rate of such reactions depends on the *collision frequency* of the reacting substances and the *collision efficiency.*

Any change in conditions that affects either the frequency of collisions or the collision efficiency will influence the re-action rate. Let us consider five important factors which influence the rate of chemical reaction.

1. Nature of the reactants. Hydrogen may combine vigorously with chlorine under certain conditions. Under the same conditions it may react only feebly with nitrogen. Sodium and oxygen combine much more rapidly than iron and oxygen under similar circumstances. Platinum and oxygen do not combine directly. Atoms, ions, and molecules are the particles of substances that react. Since bonds are broken and bonds are formed in chemical reactions, it seems reasonable that the rate of reaction should depend on the particular bonds involved.

2. Amount of surface. We discovered in the laboratory that the solution rate for a crystalline solid in water is increased if the crystals are first broken down into small pieces. A cube of solute measuring 1 cm on each edge presents only 6 cm² of contact area to the solvent. This same cube when ground to a fine powder might provide a contact area 10^4 times the original area and the solution rate would be greatly increased.

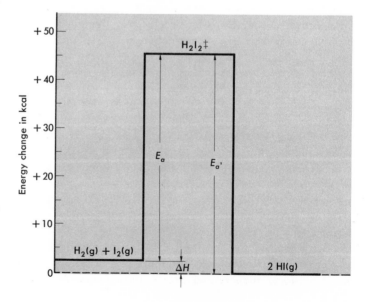

20-11 A comparison of the energy of 1 mole $H_2(g)$ plus 1 mole $I_2(g)$, 1 mole $H_2I_2^{\ddagger}$ (activated complex), and 2 moles $HI(g)$.

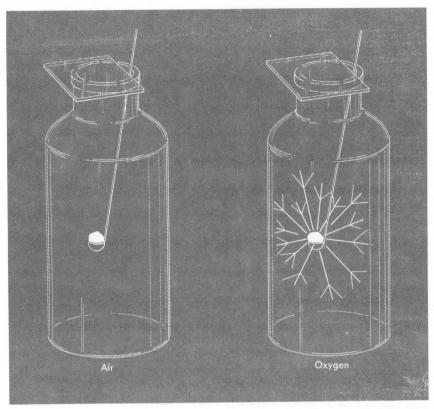

20-12   Carbon burns faster in oxygen than in air because of the higher concentration of oxygen molecules.

A lump of coal burns slowly when kindled in air. The rate of burning can be increased by breaking the lump into smaller pieces exposing new surfaces. If the piece of coal is powdered and ignited while suspended in air, it will burn explosively. Nickel in massive form shows no noticeable oxidation in air, but when finely pulverized the reaction is vigorous and spectacular.

These reactions between solids and gases are examples of *heterogeneous reactions* because they involve reactants in two different phases or states. Such reactions can occur only where the two phases are in contact. Thus, the amount of surface of a solid (or liquid) reactant is an important *rate* consideration. *Gases* and *dissolved* par-

ticles do not have surfaces in the sense just described. *In heterogeneous reactions the reaction rate is proportional to the area of contact.*

3. Effect of concentration. If a small lump of charcoal is heated in air until combustion begins and then lowered into a bottle of pure oxygen, the reaction proceeds at a much faster rate. A substance which oxidizes in air reacts more vigorously in pure oxygen. The partial pressure of oxygen in air is approximately one-fifth of the total pressure. In pure oxygen, at the same pressure as the air, we should expect to have five times the *concentration* of oxygen molecules.

This is a heterogeneous reaction system in which one reactant is a gas. Not only does the reaction rate depend on the amount of exposed charcoal surface, but *it depends on the concentration of the gas as well.*

In homogeneous reaction systems, those in which all components are in the same phase, reaction rates depend on the concentration of the reactants. From collision theory, we can expect a rate increase if the concentration of one or more of the reactants is increased. Lowering the concentration should have the opposite effect. However, the specific effect of concentration changes in a reaction system must be determined by experimental methods.

Homogeneous reactions may involve reactants in liquid or gaseous solutions. The concentration of gases changes with pressure according to Boyle's law. In liquid solutions, the concentration of reactants can be changed by altering either the quantity of solute or the quantity of solvent present. It is not possible to change, to any appreciable extent, the concentration of pure solids and pure liquids since they are practically incompressible.

The H_2(gas) + I_2(gas) reaction proceeds by a simple one-step mechanism in which the activated complex $H_2I_2{}^{\ddagger}$ is formed by one H_2 molecule and one I_2 molecule in an effective collision. The collision theory accounts for the reaction rate behavior observed when changes in concentration of these reactants are made.

$$H_2(g) + I_2(g) \rightleftarrows 2HI(g)$$

Under constant conditions, the forward reaction (to the right) proceeds at a rate proportional to the frequency of effective collisions between the two kinds of molecules. *Thus the reaction rate is proportional to the concentrations of both hydrogen and iodine molecules.*

If the concentration of hydrogen in the vessel is doubled, the chances of a collision between hydrogen and iodine molecules are doubled; the reaction speed is therefore *doubled.*

If the concentration of iodine is also doubled, the chances of a collision are *four times as great.* Of course, it must be understood that any other conditions which would affect the reaction rate must remain the same.

As stated earlier, the specific influence of reactant concentration on reaction rate must be determined by experiment. Generally an increase in concentration of reactant increases the reaction rate. In some reactions, however, it seems to have no effect; and in others it decreases the reaction rate.

Chemists account for these differences in behavior in terms of the reaction mechanisms. Complex chemical reactions may take place in a *series* of simple steps. Instead of a single activated complex, such as $H_2I_2{}^{\ddagger}$ for the hydrogen iodide reaction, there may be several activated complexes formed in sequence along the reaction pathway. Of these steps, the one which proceeds at the slowest rate will determine the overall reaction rate. When this slowest rate step can be identified, it is called the *rate-determining* step for the reaction.

4. Effect of temperature. The temperature of a substance is proportional to the average kinetic energy of its particles. Again the collision theory gives us the model that explains why a rise in temperature increases the rate of chemical reaction. A decrease in temperature, by this model, lowers the reaction rate. This is true for both exothermic and endothermic reactions.

At room temperature the rates of many reactions approximately double or triple with a 10 C° rise in temperature. Such large increases in reaction rate can be accounted for partially by the increase in collision frequency of reactant particles. However, particles which collide must also react if the chemical change is to move along. At higher temperatures more par-ticles possess enough energy to form the activated complex when collisions occur; they have the necessary activation energy. Thus a rise in temperature produces an increase in collision efficiency as well as collision frequency.

5. Action of catalysts. Some reactions pro-ceed quite slowly. Frequently, the rate of such reactions can be increased to a re-markable degree by the presence of *cata-lysts*. These are foreign substances, some-times in trace quantities, that do not them-selves appear in the final products of the reaction.

Catalysts introduced into a reaction system in the same phase as all the react-ants and products are called *homogeneous catalysts*. When their phase is different from

that of the reactants, they are called *hetero-geneous catalysts*. Metals are often used in this latter category. See Chapter 15, Sec-tion 7.

Catalytic action may be hindered by the presence of other agents called *inhibitors*. Trace quantities of other agents some-times increase the activity of catalysts. These substances are called *promoters*. A catalyst that promotes one reaction may be worthless in another reaction. Catalysis plays an important role in many modern chemical processes. Nonetheless the cata-lytic mechanism is little understood and remains one of the challenging problems in chemistry.

It is believed that a catalyst somehow provides an alternate pathway or reaction mechanism by which the potential energy

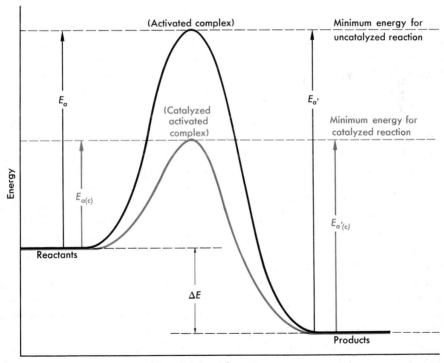

20-13 Possible difference in potential-energy change along alternate reaction pathways, one catalyzed and the other uncatalyzed.

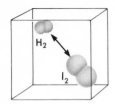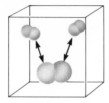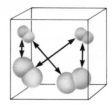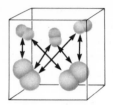

20-14   Under constant conditions, the collision frequency increases with the concentration of each reactant.

barrier between reactants and products is lowered. This could be accomplished by way of an alternate activated complex requiring a lower activation energy that somehow involved the catalyst. See Fig. 20-13.

12. Law of Mass Action. In 1867 two Norwegian scientists, Guldberg and Waage, stated the general principle known as the *Law of Mass Action: the rate of a chemical reaction is proportional to the product of the concentrations of the reacting substances.*

The Law of Mass Action as stated is directly applicable to an idealized homogeneous reaction occurring in one step. For many reactions the actual mechanism is more complex than that implied by the equation which gives only the initial reactants and final products. In such cases the mass-action principle cannot be applied without modification.

The development of the Law of Mass Action marked an important milestone in the study of chemical reactivity. We shall apply it to the simple mechanism of the $H_2 + I_2$ reaction, an example of a one-step homogeneous reaction system.

Concentration is expressed *in moles of a gas per liter of volume* or *moles of solute per liter of solution.* Let R_1 be the rate for the forward ($\rightarrow$) reaction forming hydrogen iodide. $[H_2]$ and $[I_2]$ represent the molecular concentrations of hydrogen and iodine in moles per liter. Then

$$R_1 \propto [H_2] \times [I_2]$$

where $\propto$ is a proportionality sign and is read "*is proportional to.*" If the concentrations of both hydrogen and iodine vapor are *1 mole per liter*, at a fixed temperature the reaction rate is a certain constant value called the *rate constant:*

$$R_1 = k_1$$

where k_1 is the rate constant for the forward reaction. For *any* concentration of hydrogen and iodine, the reaction rate is expressed as follows:

$$R_1 = k_1 \times [H_2] \times [I_2]$$

If $[H_2]$ is *2 moles per liter* and $[I_2]$ is *1 mole per liter*, the equation becomes

$$R_1 = k_1 \times 2 \times 1 = 2k_1$$

The reaction rate is *twice* the value for 1 mole per liter concentrations of both reactants. If now $[I_2]$ is also increased to *2 moles per liter:*

$$R_1 = k_1 \times 2 \times 2 = 4k_1$$

The reaction rate is *four times* the value for 1 mole per liter concentrations of both reactants. Similarly, if $[H_2]$ is *3 moles per liter* and $[I_2]$ is *2 moles per liter:*

$$R_1 = k_1 \times 3 \times 2 = 6k_1$$

The reaction rate is *six times* the value for 1 mole per liter concentrations of both reactants.

At the fixed temperature of the forward reaction, hydrogen iodide molecules decompose. Let this reaction rate in the reverse ($\leftarrow$) direction be R_2 for the formation of hydrogen and iodine. However, two molecules of HI must collide to form the activated complex $H_2I_2{}^{\ddagger}$ which decomposes to form a molecule of H_2 and a molecule of I_2. Thus the rate for the reverse reaction *is proportional to the molecular concentration of HI squared.*

$$R_2 \propto [HI] \times [HI]$$

and

$$R_2 \propto [HI]^2$$

or

$$R_2 = k_2 \times [HI]^2$$

where k_2 represents the rate constant for the decomposition of HI at the fixed temperature.

REVIEW OUTLINE

Energy changes in reactions (1)
    Heat of reaction (2)
    Heat of formation (3)
    Meaning of negative values for ΔH (3)
    Meaning of positive values for ΔH (3)
    Relationship of stability to heat of formation (4)
    Heat of combustion (5)
    Thermochemical equations (5)

Driving force of reactions (7)
    Energy change (7)
    Entropy change (7)
    Free-energy change (7)

Activation energy (8)
    Potential energy barrier (8)
    Collision theory (9)
    Activated complex (10)
    Reaction mechanisms (10)

Rate of reactions (11)
    Influencing factors (11)
    Rate determining step (11)
    Alternate path of reaction (11)
    Law of Mass Action (12)

QUESTIONS

Group A

1. What evidence can be cited to show that a substance has a characteristic internal energy?
2. How does the heat content of the products of a reaction system compare with the heat content of the reactants when the reaction is (*a*) exothermic, (*b*) endothermic?

3. Define the molar heat of formation of a compound.
4. Name two factors that can be identified in the driving force of chemical reactions.
5. What is the basis for assigning a negative value to the change in heat content ΔH in an exothermic system?
6. Changes of state in the direction of the solid state favor what kind of an entropy change?
7. What is the effect on the entropy of a system when temperature is raised?
8. Define activation energy in terms of the activated complex.
9. In a reversible reaction, how does the activation energy required for the exothermic change compare with the activation energy for the endothermic change?
10. Give two reasons why a collision between reactant molecules may not be effective in producing new chemical species.
11. (*a*) Distinguish between homogeneous and heterogeneous reaction systems. (*b*) Give an example of each using a balanced equation.
12. To what does the term "activated complex" refer?

Group B

13. Considering the structure and physical state of substances in a reacting system, to what is the energy change in the reaction related?
14. In an exothermic reaction, ΔH is said to have a negative value. Explain.
15. A compound is found to have a heat of formation H_f of -87.3 kcal/mole. What is the implication regarding its stability? Explain.
16. If flasks containing two different gases at room temperature are connected so the gases mix, what kind of evidence would show that they experienced no change in energy content during the mixing?
17. How can the mixing tendency of Question 16 be explained?
18. Explain the circumstances under which an exothermic reaction does not proceed spontaneously.
19. Explain the circumstances under which an endothermic reaction is spontaneous.
20. Referring to Fig. 20-8, (*a*) how could you justify calling the reaction pathway the minimum energy pathway for reaction? (*b*) What significance is associated with the maximum energy region of this minimum energy pathway?
21. The balanced equation for a homogeneous reaction between two gases shows that 4 molecules of A react with 1 molecule of B to form 2 molecules of C and 2 molecules of D. $4A + B \rightarrow 2C + 2D$. Recognizing that the simultaneous collision of 4 molecules of one reactant with 1 molecule of the other reactant as extremely improbable, what would you infer as to the nature of the reaction mechanism for this reaction system?
22. Suppose 2 moles of hydrogen gas and 1 mole of iodine vapor are passed simultaneously into a 1-liter flask. What is the effect on the rate of the forward reaction if: (*a*) the temperature is increased; (*b*) 1 mole of iodine vapor is added; (*c*) 1 mole of hydrogen is removed; (*d*) the volume of the flask is reduced (assume this is possible); (*e*) a catalyst is introduced into the flask?

PROBLEMS

(Consult Appendix tables for essential thermochemical data.)

1. Write the thermochemical equation for the complete combustion of 1 mole of methane gas and calculate its heat of formation from the heat of reaction and product heats of formation data.
2. Write the thermochemical equation for the complete combustion of 1 mole of ethyne (acetylene) and calculate its heat of formation.
3. Write the thermochemical equation for the complete combustion of 1 mole of benzene and calculate its heat of formation.
4. Using heats of formation data, calculate the heat of combustion of 1 mole of hydrogen gas.

Chapter Twenty-one

CHEMICAL EQUILIBRIUM

1. Reversible reactions. Chemists assume that all chemical reactions are reversible—that is, the products re-form the original reactants under suitable conditions. Some reverse reactions occur less easily than others and in some cases the conditions for the reverse reactions may not be known. For example, water vapor decomposes to an appreciable extent at 3000° C. Chemists do not know how to reverse the reaction for the decomposition of $KClO_3$.

We have seen that mercury(II) oxide decomposes when heated strongly.

$$2HgO(s) \rightarrow 2Hg(l) + O_2(g)$$

However, mercury and oxygen combine to form mercury(II) oxide when heated gently.

$$2Hg(l) + O_2(g) \rightarrow 2HgO(s)$$

Suppose mercury(II) oxide is heated in a closed container from which neither the mercury nor the oxygen can escape. It is possible, once the decomposition is underway, for the mercury and oxygen that have been liberated to recombine forming mercury(II) oxide again. Thus both reactions proceed at the same time. Under just the right conditions, the rate of the composition reaction may become equal to the rate of the decomposition reaction. Mercury and oxygen combine to form mercury(II) oxide just as fast as mercury(II) oxide decomposes to form mercury and oxygen. We should then expect the amount of mercury(II) oxide, mercury, and oxygen to remain constant as long as these conditions persist. A state of *equilibrium* has been reached between the two chemical actions. *Both reactions continue but the net change is zero.* The equilibrium may be written as

$$2HgO(s) \rightleftarrows 2Hg(l) + O_2(g)$$

Chemical equilibrium is a state of balance in which the rates of opposing reactions are exactly equal.

A reaction system in equilibrium shows equal tendencies to proceed in the forward and reverse directions. In Chapter 20, Section 7, we distinguished two factors that make up the driving force for reactions, the tendency toward lowest energy and the tendency toward highest entropy. At equilibrium the driving force of the energy change accompanying a reaction is balanced by the driving force of the entropy change.

2. Equilibrium, a dynamic state. We have already discussed examples of opposing processes occurring simultaneously at the same rate. The evaporation of a liquid in a closed vessel and the condensation of its saturated vapor proceed at equal rates. The equilibrium vapor pressure established is characteristic of the liquid at the prevailing temperature.

If an excess of sugar is placed in water, sugar molecules go into solution and some of these in turn separate from solution to rejoin the crystals. At saturation, molecules of sugar are separating from solution at the same rate that other crystal molecules are going into solution. These are examples of *physical equilibria*. The opposing physical processes occur at exactly the same rate. Equilibrium is a *dynamic*

state in which two opposing processes proceed simultaneously at the same rate.

Electrovalent compounds, such as sodium chloride, are completely ionized in water solution. When an excess of sodium chloride is placed in water, a saturated solution eventually results. Equilibrium occurs as the rate of association of ions reforming the crystal equals the rate of dissociation of ions from the crystal. This is shown in the ionic equation

$$\textbf{Na}^+\textbf{Cl}^-(\textbf{s}) \rightleftarrows \textbf{Na}^+(\textbf{aq}) + \textbf{Cl}^-(\textbf{aq})$$

The dynamic character of this equilibrium system can be observed by placing an irregularly shaped crystal of sodium chloride in a saturated solution of the salt. The shape of the crystal gradually changes, becoming more regular as time passes. However, the mass of the crystal in contact with the saturated solution does not change.

Polar compounds, such as acetic acid, are quite soluble in water. Molecules of acetic acid in water solution ionize forming H_3O^+ and $C_2H_3O_2^-$ ions. However, pairs of these ions tend to rejoin, forming acetic acid molecules in the solution. This tendency is so great that equilibrium is

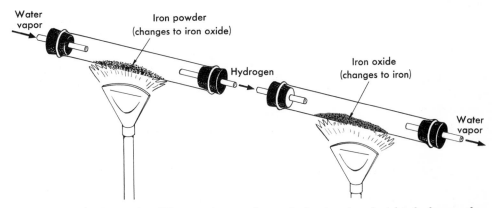

21-1 A reversible reaction. Water vapor passed over the hot iron is reduced to hydrogen, the iron having oxidized to iron(II, III) oxide. Hydrogen passed over the hot iron oxide is oxidized to water vapor and the iron oxide is reduced to iron.

quickly established between un-ionized molecules in solution and their hydrated ions, even in fairly dilute solutions. This is an example of *ionic equilibrium*. The ionic equilibrium of acetic acid in water solution may be represented by he equation

$$HC_2H_3O_2(aq) + H_2O(l) \rightleftarrows$$
$$H_3O^+(aq) + C_2H_3O_2^-(aq)$$

Many chemical reactions are noticeably reversible under ordinary conditions of temperature and concentration. They may reach a state of equilibrium unless prevented by the removal or escape of at least one of the substances involved. In some cases the forward reaction is nearly completed before the reverse reaction rate becomes high enough to establish equilibrium. *Here the products of the forward reaction* (→) *are favored.* In other cases the forward reaction is barely under way when equilibrium is established. *In these the products of the reverse reaction* (←), *the original reactants, are favored.* In still others, both the forward and reverse reactions occur to nearly the same extent before chemical equilibrium is established. *Neither reaction is favored; considerable concentrations of both reactants and products are present at equilibrium.*

Chemical reactions are employed ordinarily to convert available reactants into more desirable products. Chemists strive to produce as much of these products as possible from the reactants used. Chemical equilibrium may seriously limit the possibilities of a seemingly useful reaction. It is important to recognize the conditions which influence reaction velocities in the study of chemical equilibrium.

The significant factors which determine the rate of chemical action were discussed in Chapter 20. These are: the nature of the reactants, the temperature, the presence of a catalyst, the surface area, and the concentration of reactants.

In heterogeneous reactions, the chemical action takes place at the surfaces where the reactants in different phases meet. Here the surface area presented by solid and liquid reactants is important in rate considerations. In homogeneous reactions, those between gases and those between substances dissolved in liquid solvents, the rate is dependent on the concentration of each reactant.

The reaction rate for a simple homogeneous reaction occurring in one step follows the Law of Mass Action with respect to the concentrations of reactants. We have seen how this principle applies to the reaction between H_2 and I_2. For the general form, consider the hypothetical reversible reaction of n moles of reactant **A** and m moles of reactant **B** which form x moles of product **C** and y moles of product **D**.

$$n\mathbf{A} + m\mathbf{B} \rightleftarrows x\mathbf{C} + y\mathbf{D}$$

The rate R_1 for the forward reaction is

$$R_1 = k_1[\mathbf{A}]^n[\mathbf{B}]^m$$

Similarly, the rate R_2 for the reverse reaction is

$$R_2 = k_2[\mathbf{C}]^x[\mathbf{D}]^y$$

The coefficients of the balanced equation become the powers to which the respective molar concentrations are raised in the rate equations. Now we can restate the Law of Mass Action for homogeneous systems in its more general form: *The rate of a chemical reaction is proportional to the product of the concentrations of the reacting substances, each raised to the power corresponding to the coefficient for that substance in the balanced equation.*

As stated in Chapter 20, Section 12, many reactions do not follow a simple one-step mechanism, but may take place in several steps. Each step proceeds at its own rate. The over-all reaction can proceed no faster than the slowest step, called the rate-determining step. The correct form of the rate equation can be given for a complex reaction only if the step-by-step mechanism is known. However, in an equilibrium situation in which the rates of the forward and reverse reactions are equal, the rate equations for the over-all reactions as derived from the balanced equation are useful in defining the equilibrium state.

3. The equilibrium constant. Many chemical reactions seem to be feasible and might be expected to yield useful products. However, after they are started, they *appear* to slow down and finally stop without having run to completion. Such reactions are reversible and, under just the right conditions, *reach a state of equilibrium.* Both forward and reverse processes occur at the same rate and the concentrations of products and reactants remain constant.

The time required for reaction systems to reach equilibrium varies widely. A fraction of a second or a great many years may be required depending on the system and the conditions. Ionic reactions usually reach equilibrium very quickly.

Chemists must understand chemical equilibria in order to determine the conditions under which such reactions will yield satisfactory results. Knowledge of equilibrium enables them to predict whether certain reactions are practical. They are then able to improve the yields of desired products formed by reversible reactions.

Suppose that two substances, **A** and **B**, react to form products **C** and **D**, and that **C** and **D**, in turn, react to produce **A** and **B**. Under certain conditions equilibrium occurs in this reversible reaction. This hypothetical equilibrium reaction may be shown by the equation

$$A + B \rightleftarrows C + D$$

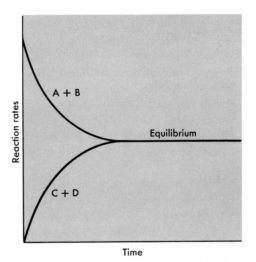

21-2 Reaction rates for the hypothetical reaction system $A + B \rightleftarrows C + D$. The rate of the forward reaction is represented by curve **A + B**. Curve **C + D** represents the rate of the reverse reaction. At equilibrium the two rates are equal.

Initially, the concentration of **C** and **D** is zero and that of **A** and **B** is maximum. In accordance with the Law of Mass Action the rate of the forward reaction *decreases* as **A** and **B** are used up. During the same time, the rate of the reverse reaction increases from its initial value of zero as **C** and **D** are formed. As these two reaction rates become equal equilibrium is established. The individual concentrations of **A, B, C,** and **D** undergo no further change as long as the same reaction conditions prevail.

At equilibrium, the rate of the product $[C] \times [D]$ *to the product* $[A] \times [B]$ *has a definite numerical value.* It is known as the **equilibrium constant** of the reaction and is designated by the letter *K*. Thus

$$\frac{[C] \times [D]}{[A] \times [B]} = K$$

Notice that the concentrations of substances on the right side of the chemical equation are given in the numerator. The concentrations of those on the left side of the chemical equation are in the denominator. Equilibrium concentrations of reactants and products are given in *moles per liter.* The constant, *K,* is independent of the initial concentrations. It is, however, dependent on the fixed temperature of the system.

The value of *K* for a given equilibrium reaction is important to the chemist because it shows him the extent to which the reactants are converted into the products of the reaction. If *K* is equal to 1, the products of the concentrations in the numerator and denominator have the same value. If the value of *K* is very small, the forward reaction occurs only very slightly before equilibrium is established. A large value of *K* indicates an equilibrium in which the original reactants are largely converted to products. If the values of *K* are known for different reaction temperatures, the chemist may select the most favorable conditions for a desired reaction. The numerical value of *K* for a particular equilibrium system is obtained by analyzing the equilibrium mixture and determining the concentrations of all substances present.

Suppose we return to the general form of a reversible reaction used in Section 2:

$$n\text{A} + m\text{B} \rightleftarrows x\text{C} + y\text{D}$$

At equilibrium, the rate of the forward reaction is equal to the rate of the reverse reaction.

$$R_1 = R_2$$

But, $$R_1 = k_1[\text{A}]^n[\text{B}]^m$$

and $$R_2 = k_2[\text{C}]^x[\text{D}]^y$$

Substituting the rate expression for each reaction:

$$k_1[\text{A}]^n[\text{B}]^m = k_2[\text{C}]^x[\text{D}]^y$$

or $$\frac{k_1}{k_2} = \frac{[\text{C}]^x[\text{D}]^y}{[\text{A}]^n[\text{B}]^m}$$

Thus, the ratio of the rate constants k_1/k_2 expresses the equilibrium constant *K* for the reaction system.

$$K = \frac{[\text{C}]^x[\text{D}]^y}{[\text{A}]^n[\text{B}]^m}$$

In the general form, the **equilibrium constant** *is the product of the concentrations of the substances produced at equilibrium divided by the product of the concentrations of the reacting substances, each concentration raised to that power which is the coefficient of the substance in the chemical equation.*

To illustrate, suppose a reaction system at equilibrium is shown by the equation

$$3\text{A} + \text{B} \rightleftarrows 2\text{C} + 3\text{D}$$

The equilibrium constant *K* would be given by the expression

$$K = \frac{[\text{C}]^2[\text{D}]^3}{[\text{A}]^3[\text{B}]}$$

The reaction between H_2 and I_2 in a closed flask is easily followed at elevated temperatures by observing the rate at which the violet color of the iodine vapor diminishes. If this reaction ran to completion with respect to iodine, the color would disappear entirely since the product hydrogen iodide is colorless.

However, the reaction is reversible and hydrogen iodide decomposes to re-form hydrogen and iodine. The rate of this reverse reaction increases as the concentration of hydrogen iodide builds up. Simultaneously, the concentrations of hydrogen and iodine diminish as they are used up and the rate of the forward reaction decreases accordingly.

As the rates of the opposing reactions

become equal, an equilibrium is established. This equilibrium mixture of hydrogen, iodine, and hydrogen iodide is indicated qualitatively by some constant level of residual iodine color. An equilibrium mixture would be similarly observed if the flask had been filled initially with hydrogen iodide. The equation for the system at equilibrium is shown as follows:

$$\mathbf{H_2(g) + I_2(g) \rightleftarrows 2HI(g)}$$

The rates of the forward and reverse reactions are respectively

$$R_1 = k_1[\mathbf{H_2}][\mathbf{I_2}]$$

and

$$R_2 = k_2[\mathbf{HI}]^2$$

At equilibrium

$$R_1 = R_2$$

and

$$k_1[\mathbf{H_2}][\mathbf{I_2}] = k_2[\mathbf{HI}]^2$$

or

$$\frac{k_1}{k_2} = \frac{[\mathbf{HI}]^2}{[\mathbf{H_2}][\mathbf{I_2}]}$$

Thus,

$$K = \frac{[\mathbf{HI}]^2}{[\mathbf{H_2}][\mathbf{I_2}]}$$

Many careful measurements of the concentrations of H_2, I_2, and HI in equilibrium mixtures of these gases at various temperatures have been made. In some experiments, the flasks were filled with hydrogen iodide at known pressure and held at fixed temperatures until equilibrium

was established. In other experiments, hydrogen and iodine were the substances introduced.

Some typical data from such experiments are shown in the table below together with the calculated values for **K**. Experiments 1 and 2 were started with hydrogen iodide. Experiments 3 and 4 were started with hydrogen and iodine. Note the close agreement obtained for numerical values of the equilibrium constant.

Once the equilibrium constant **K** for the H_2, I_2, and HI equilibrium at 425° C has been established experimentally (54.40 from the data given), this value for **K** holds for any system of H_2, I_2, and HI at equilibrium *at this temperature*. If the calculation for **K** yields a different result, either the H_2, I_2, and HI system has not reached equilibrium or the temperature of the system is not 425° C. See the Sample Problem at the top of page 360.

4. Factors that disturb equilibrium. In systems that have attained chemical equilibrium, opposing reactions occur at equal rates. Any change which alters the rate of either reaction *disturbs the equilibrium*. By displacing an equilibrium in the desired direction, chemists are often able to increase production of important industrial chemicals.

The principle of Le Chatelier provides a means of predicting the influence that disturbing factors will have on equilibrium systems. We have already made use of this important principle on several occasions.

TYPICAL EQUILIBRIUM CONCENTRATIONS OF H_2, I_2, AND HI IN MOLE/LITER AT 425° C

Exp.	$[H_2]$	$[I_2]$	$[HI]$	$K = \dfrac{[HI]^2}{[H_2][I_2]}$
(1)	0.4953×10^{-3}	0.4953×10^{-3}	3.655×10^{-3}	54.58
(2)	1.141×10^{-3}	1.141×10^{-3}	8.410×10^{-3}	54.35
(3)	3.560×10^{-3}	1.250×10^{-3}	15.59×10^{-3}	54.61
(4)	2.252×10^{-3}	2.336×10^{-3}	16.85×10^{-3}	53.97
			Average	54.40

Sample Problem

An equilibrium mixture of H_2, I_2, and HI gases at 425° C has been determined to consist of 4.5647×10^{-3} mole/liter of H_2, 0.7378×10^{-3} mole/liter of I_2, and 13.544×10^{-3} mole/liter of HI. What is the equilibrium constant for the system at this temperature?

Solution

The balanced equation for the equilibrium system is

$$H_2(g) + I_2(g) \rightleftarrows 2HI(g)$$

$$K = \frac{[HI]^2}{[H_2][I_2]}$$

$$K = \frac{[13.544 \times 10^{-3}]^2}{[4.5647 \times 10^{-3}][0.7378 \times 10^{-3}]} = 54.46$$

This value is in close agreement with the average of the four experimental values given in the table.

However, it may be helpful at this point to re-state Le Chatelier's principle: *If a system at equilibrium is subjected to a stress, the equilibrium will be displaced in the direction that relieves the stress.* This general principle holds for all kinds of dynamic equilibria, physical and ionic, as well as chemical. In applying Le Chatelier's principle to chemical equilibrium, we shall consider three important stresses.

1. Change in concentration. According to the Law of Mass Action, the reaction rate increases with an increase in the concentration of either reactant. Consider the hypothetical reaction:

$$A + B \rightleftarrows C + D$$

An increase in the concentration of **A** will displace the equilibrium to the *right*. Both **A** and **B** will be used up faster and more of **C** and **D** will be formed. The equilibrium will be reestablished with a lower concentration of **B**. *The effect has been to shift the equilibrium in such direction as to reduce the stress caused by the increase in concentration.*

Similarly, an increase in the concentration of **B** will drive the reaction to the right. An increase in either **C** or **D** will displace the equilibrium to the *left*. A *decrease* in the concentration of either **C** or **D** will have the same effect as an *increase* in the concentration of **A** or **B**—to displace the equilibrium to the *right*.

Changes in concentration have no effect on the value of the equilibrium constant. All concentrations will be readjusted, when equilibrium is reestablished, to give the same numerical ratio for the equilibrium constant. In this regard, Le Chatelier's principle leads us to the same predictions for changes in concentration as does the equilibrium constant.

2. Change in pressure. A change in pressure can affect only equilibrium systems in which *gases* are involved. According to the principle of Le Chatelier, *if the pressure on an equilibrium system is increased, the reaction is driven in the direction which relieves the pressure.*

The Haber process for the catalytic synthesis of ammonia from its elements offers an excellent illustration of the influence of pressure on an equilibrium system.

$$N_2(g) + 3H_2(g) \rightleftarrows 2NH_3(g)$$

The equation indicates that 4 molecules of the reactant gases form 2 molecules of ammonia gas. If the equilibrium mixture is subjected to an increase in pressure, the pressure can be relieved by the reaction that produces fewer gas molecules and therefore a smaller volume. Thus, the stress is lessened by the formation of ammonia and equilibrium is displaced toward the right. It is evident that *high* pressure is desirable in this industrial process (see Fig. 21-3).

In the Haber process, the ammonia produced is continuously removed by condensation to a liquid. This removes the product from the reaction environment. This change in concentration also aids in the displacement of the equilibrium to the right.

Many chemical reactions involve heterogeneous reactions in which the reactants and products are in different phases. The *concentration* of pure substances in solid and liquid states is not changed by adding or removing quantities of such substances in equilibrium systems. Since the equilibrium constant expresses a relationship between relative concentrations of reactants and products, these substances are ignored in writing the expression for the equilibrium constant.

Consider the equilibrium system represented by the equation

$$CaCO_3(s) \rightleftarrows CaO(s) + CO_2(g)$$

Carbon dioxide is the only substance in the system subject to changes in concentration. Since it is a gas, the forward (decomposition) reaction is favored by a *low* pressure.

The expression for the equilibrium constant is simply

$$K = [CO_2]$$

In the reaction,

$$CO(g) + H_2O(g) \rightleftarrows CO_2(g) + H_2(g)$$

there are equal numbers of molecules of gaseous reactants and gaseous products. Pressure could not be relieved by a shift in equilibrium. Thus, *pressure has no effect* on this equilibrium reaction.

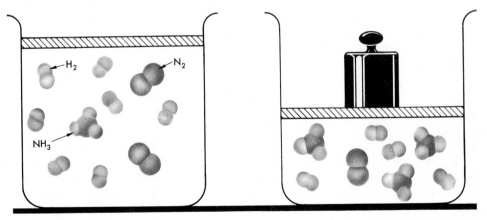

21-3 Pressure increases the yield of ammonia since the equilibrium shifts in the direction which produces fewer molecules.

Obviously an increase in pressure on confined gases amounts to an increase in the concentration of these gases. Thus, *changes in pressure do not affect the value of the equilibrium constant.*

3. *Change in temperature.* Chemical reactions are either exothermic or endothermic. Reversible reactions are exothermic in one direction and endothermic in the other. The effect of changing the temperature of an equilibrium mixture depends on which of the opposing reactions is endothermic.

The *addition* of heat, according to Le Chatelier's principle, will displace the equilibrium so that heat is absorbed. This favors the *endothermic* reaction. Conversely, the *removal* of heat favors the *exothermic* reaction. A rise in temperature increases the rate of any reaction. In an equilibrium, the rates of the opposing reactions are raised *unequally*. Thus, *the value of the equilibrium constant, for a given system, is affected by the operating temperature.*

The synthesis of ammonia is exothermic.

$$N_2(g) + 3H_2(g) \rightleftarrows 2NH_3(g) + 22 \text{ kcal}$$

Therefore, a high temperature is not desirable as it favors the decomposition of ammonia, the endothermic reaction. However, at ordinary temperatures, the forward reaction is too slow to be feasible. Fortunately, the reaction of the system may be accelerated by the use of a suitable catalyst. At moderate temperatures (about 500° C) and very high pressures, satisfactory yields of ammonia are realized.

The numerical values of equilibrium constants may range from very large to very small numbers. We have found that they are independent of changes in concentrations but not of changes in temperature. The addition of a catalyst does not affect the value of K since it accelerates both forward and reverse reactions equally.

Several equilibrium systems are listed in the following table together with numerical values of their equilibrium constants at indicated temperatures. A very small numerical constant means that the equilibrium mixture consists mainly of the substances on the left of the equation. If the value of K is large, the equilibrium mixture consists mainly of the substances on the right of the equation.

EQUILIBRIUM CONSTANTS

Equilibrium System	Value of K	Temp. °C
$N_2(g) + 3H_2(g) \rightleftarrows 2NH_3(g)$	2.66×10^{-2}	350°
$N_2(g) + 3H_2(g) \rightleftarrows 2NH_3(g)$	6.59×10^{-3}	450°
$N_2(g) + 3H_2(g) \rightleftarrows 2NH_3(g)$	2.37×10^{-3}	727°
$2H_2(g) + S_2(g) \rightleftarrows 2H_2S(g)$	9.39×10^{-5}	477°
$H_2(g) + CO_2(g) \rightleftarrows H_2O(g) + CO(g)$	4.40	1727°
$2H_2O(g) \rightleftarrows 2H_2(g) + O_2(g)$	5.31×10^{-10}	1727°
$2CO(g) + O_2(g) \rightleftarrows 2CO_2(g)$	2.24×10^{22}	727°
$H_2(g) + I_2(g) \rightleftarrows 2HI(g)$	66.9	350°
$H_2(g) + I_2(g) \rightleftarrows 2HI(g)$	54.4	425°
$H_2(g) + I_2(g) \rightleftarrows 2HI(g)$	45.9	490°
$C(s) + CO_2(g) \rightleftarrows 2CO(g)$	14.1	1123°
$Cu(s) + 2Ag^+(aq) \rightleftarrows Cu^{++}(aq) + 2Ag(s)$	2×10^{15}	25°
$I_2(g) \rightleftarrows 2I(g)$	3.76×10^{-5}	727°
$2O_3(g) \rightleftarrows 3O_2(g)$	2.54×10^{12}	1727°
$N_2(g) \rightleftarrows 2N(g)$	1.31×10^{-31}	1000°

5. Reactions that run to completion.

Many reactions are easily reversible under suitable conditions. A state of equilibrium may be established unless one or more of the products escapes or is removed. An equilibrium reaction may be driven in the preferred direction by applying the principle of Le Chatelier.

Some reactions appear to go to completion in the forward direction. No one has found a method of recombining potassium chloride and oxygen directly once potassium chlorate decomposes. Sugar may be decomposed into carbon and water by the application of heat. Yet no condition favorable for a single step recombination of these products is known.

Many compounds are formed by the interaction of ions in solutions. If solutions of two electrolytes are mixed, two pairs of ions are possible. These pairings may or may not occur. If dilute solutions of sodium chloride and potassium bromide are mixed, no reaction occurs. The resulting solution merely contains a mixture of Na^+, K^+, Cl^-, and Br^- ions. Association of ions occurs only if enough water is evaporated to cause crystals to separate. The yield would be a mixture of NaCl, KCl, NaBr, and KBr.

In some combinations of ions, reactions do occur. *Such reactions may run to completion in the sense that the ions are almost completely removed from solution.* They are referred to as *end reactions.* Chemists can predict that certain ion reactions will run to completion. The extent to which the reacting ions are removed from solution depends on *the solubility of the compound formed and the degree of ionization, if it is soluble.* Thus a product which *escapes as a gas, is precipitated as a solid,* or is *only slightly ionized,* effectively removes the reacting ions from solution. We shall consider some specific examples of the different types of end reactions.

1. Formation of a gas. Unstable substances formed as products of ionic reactions decompose spontaneously. An example is carbonic acid which yields a gas as a decomposition product.

$$H_2CO_3 \rightarrow H_2O + CO_2 \uparrow$$

Carbonic acid is produced in the reaction between sodium hydrogen carbonate and hydrochloric acid as shown by the empirical equation

$$NaHCO_3 + HCl \rightarrow NaCl + H_2CO_3$$

Since the water solution of HCl contains H_3O^+ and Cl^- ions, a closer examination of the reaction mechanism suggests that HCO_3^- ion acts as a base and acquires a proton from the H_3O^+ acid. The Na^+ and Cl^- ions are merely spectators in the water environment. Thus, the following equations may be more appropriate for this reaction.

$$H_3O^+ + HCO_3^- \rightarrow H_2O + \cancel{H_2CO_3}$$
$$\cancel{H_2CO_3} \rightarrow H_2O + CO_2 \uparrow$$

or, simply:

$$H_3O^+ + HCO_3^- \rightarrow 2H_2O + CO_2 \uparrow$$

The reaction runs to completion because one of the products escapes as a gas. Of course, the sodium ions and chloride ions would separate as sodium chloride crystals on evaporation of the water.

The reaction between iron(II) sulfide and hydrochloric acid written empirically illustrates this action more simply.

$$FeS + 2HCl \rightarrow FeCl_2 + H_2S \uparrow$$

The hydrogen sulfide formed is only moderately soluble and is given off as a gas. The iron(II) chloride is formed on evaporation of water.

2. Formation of a precipitate. When solutions of sodium chloride and silver nitrate are mixed, a white precipitate of silver chloride immediately forms.

$$Na^+ + Cl^- + Ag^+ + NO_3^- \rightarrow$$
$$Na^+ + NO_3^- + Ag^+Cl^- \downarrow$$

If chemical equivalents of the two solutes are used, only sodium ions and nitrate ions remain in solution *in quantity*. The silver ions and chloride ions, because of their very low solubility in a common solution environment, combine to form insoluble silver chloride. *The reaction runs to completion because an insoluble product is formed.*

The only reaction that occurs is between the silver ions and chloride ions. Omitting the spectator ions Na^+ and NO_3^-, the equation may be rewritten simply as

$$Ag^+ + Cl^- \rightarrow Ag^+Cl^- \downarrow$$

Crystalline sodium nitrate is recovered by evaporation of the water.

3. Formation of a slightly ionized product. Neutralization reactions occur between H_3O^+ ions formed by the ionization of acids in water and OH^- ions from basic solutions. Water molecules are formed in the process. A reaction between HCl and NaOH illustrates this.

$$HCl + H_2O \rightarrow H_3O^+ + Cl^-$$

$$Na^+OH^- \rightarrow Na^+ + OH^-$$

$$H_3O^+ + Cl^- + Na^+ + OH^- \rightarrow$$
$$Na^+ + Cl^- + 2H_2O$$

Or simply

$$H_3O^+ + OH^- \rightarrow 2H_2O$$

Water is only slightly ionized and exists essentially as covalent molecules. Thus hydronium ions and hydroxide ions are effectively removed from the solution. *The reaction runs to completion because the product is only slightly ionized.* In the reaction between hydrochloric acid and sodium hy-

droxide, sodium chloride crystallizes on evaporation of the water.

6. Common ion effect. Suppose hydrogen chloride gas is bubbled into a saturated solution of sodium chloride. As the hydrogen chloride dissolves, sodium chloride separates as a precipitate. This is an application of the *Law of Mass Action*, the chloride ion being *common* to both solutes. The concentration of chloride ions is increased while that of the sodium ions is not. As sodium chloride crystals separate, the concentration of sodium ions in the solution is lowered. Thus an increase in the concentration of chloride ions has the effect of decreasing the concentration of sodium ions in the solution. *This is known as the common ion effect.*

Of course, equilibrium will be established between the rate of dissociation of sodium chloride crystals and the rate of association of sodium and chloride ions.

$$Na^+Cl^- \rightleftarrows Na^+ + Cl^-$$

Further additions of hydrogen chloride will disturb this equilibrium and drive the reaction to the *left. By forcing* the reaction to the left, more sodium chloride is caused to separate. This further reduces the concentration of the sodium ions in solution.

The common ion effect is also observed when *one* of the ions of a weak electrolyte is added in excess to a solution. Acetic acid is such an electrolyte. A $0.1-M$ $HC_2H_3O_2$ solution is about 1.4% ionized. The ionic equilibrium may be shown by the equation

$$HC_2H_3O_2 + H_2O \rightleftarrows H_3O^+ + C_2H_3O_2^-$$

Sodium acetate is an ionic salt and is completely dissociated in water solution. Small additions of sodium acetate to a solution containing acetic acid will greatly increase the concentration of the acetate ion. The equilibrium will shift in the direction which uses acetate ions. More molecules of acetic acid are formed and the concentration of hydronium ions is reduced. In general, *the addition of a salt with an ion common to the solution of a weak electrolyte reduces the ionization of the electrolyte.* A $0.1-M$ $HC_2H_3O_2$ solution has a pH of 2.9. A solution containing $0.1-M$ concentrations of both acetic acid and sodium acetate has a pH of 4.6.

▶ **7. Ionization constant of a weak acid.** Approximately 1.4% of the solute molecules in a $0.1-M$ acetic acid solution are ionized at room temperature, and 98.6% of the $HC_2H_3O_2$ molecules remains unionized. Thus, the water solution contains three species of particles which are in equilibrium with one another, namely $HC_2H_3O_2$ molecules, H_3O^+ ions, and $C_2H_3O_2^-$ ions.

At equilibrium, the rate of the forward reaction in which $HC_2H_3O_2$ molecules ionize with H_2O to form H_3O^+ and $C_2H_3O_2^-$ ions is equal to the rate of the reverse reaction in which H_3O^+ and $C_2H_3O_2^-$ ions react to form H_2O and $HC_2H_3O_2$ molecules. The equilibrium constant for this system expresses the *equilibrium ratio of ions to molecules.*

From the equilibrium equation for the ionization of acetic acid written above,

$$K = \frac{[H_3O^+][C_2H_3O_2^-]}{[HC_2H_3O_2][H_2O]}$$

Because H_2O molecules are in such great excess at the $0.1-M$ concentration of $HC_2H_3O_2$ molecules, we may consider, without appreciable error, that the mole concentration of water H_2O remains constant. Thus,

$$K[H_2O] = \frac{[H_3O^+][C_2H_3O_2^-]}{[HC_2H_3O_2]}$$

and setting $K[H_2O] = K_a$

$$K_a = \frac{[H_3O^+][C_2H_3O_2^-]}{[HC_2H_3O_2]}$$

where K_a is called the *ionization constant of a weak acid.* Since $[H_2O]$ is about 55 moles/liter (see Section 7), K_a is about 55 times as large as the equilibrium constant K.

The expression for K_a can be written in general form for the typical weak acid **HB** from its equilibrium equation,

$$HB(aq) + H_2O(l) \rightleftharpoons H_3O^+(aq) + B^-(aq)$$

$$K_a = \frac{[H_3O^+][B^-]}{[HB]}$$

To determine the numerical value of the ionization constant K_a for acetic acid at a specific temperature, the equilibrium concentration of H_3O^+ ions, $C_2H_3O_2^-$ ions, and $HC_2H_3O_2$ molecules must be known at this temperature. Since 1 molecule of $HC_2H_3O_2$ ionizes in water to give 1 H_3O^+ ion and 1 $C_2H_3O_2^-$ ion, these concentrations can be found experimentally by measuring the pH of the solution.

Suppose that a precise electrometric experiment shows the pH of a $0.1000-M$ solution of acetic acid to be 2.876 at 25° C. The numerical value of K_a for $HC_2H_3O_2$ at 25° C may be determined as follows:

$$[H_3O^+] = [C_2H_3O_2^-] = 10^{-2.876} \text{ mole/l}$$

Antilog (-2.876) = antilog $(0.124 - 3)$
$$= 1.33 \times 10^{-3}$$

$$[H_3O^+] = [C_2H_3O_2^-] = 1.33 \times 10^{-3}$$

$$[HC_2H_3O_2] = 0.1000 - 0.00133 = 0.0987$$

$$K_a = \frac{[H_3O^+][C_2H_3O_2^-]}{[HC_2H_3O_2]}$$

$$K_a = \frac{(1.33 \times 10^{-3})^2}{9.87 \times 10^{-2}} = 1.79 \times 10^{-5}$$

Ionization data for some dilute acetic acid

IONIZATION CONSTANT OF ACETIC ACID
(25° C)

Molarity	% ionized	$[H_3O^+]$	$[HC_2H_3O_2]$	K_a
0.1000	1.35	0.00135	0.09865	1.85×10^{-5}
0.0500	1.90	0.000950	0.04905	1.84×10^{-5}
0.0100	4.16	0.000416	0.009584	1.81×10^{-5}
0.0050	5.84	0.000292	0.004708	1.81×10^{-5}
0.0010	12.48	0.000125	0.000875	1.78×10^{-5}

solutions at room temperature are given in the table above together with the ionization constant for this weak acid.

A rise in temperature will cause the equilibrium to shift according to Le Chatelier's principle and K_a will have a new value for each temperature. An increase in the concentration of $C_2H_3O_2^-$ ions, by the addition of $NaC_2H_3O_2$, disturbs the equilibrium causing a decrease in $[H_3O^+]$ and an increase in $[HC_2H_3O_2]$. Eventually the equilibrium is reestablished with the same value of K_a, but with a higher concentration of un-ionized acetic acid molecules and a lower concentration of H_3O^+ ions. The reduction in hydronium-ion concentration is accompanied by a rise in the pH of the solution.

If the proper ions are present, the pH of a weakly acidic or alkaline solution tends to remain practically constant, regardless of the addition of other ions. The concentration of hydronium ions will not vary appreciably in a solution of acetic acid containing a high concentration of sodium acetate. Similarly, the hydroxide-ion concentration in an ammonia-water solution will remain almost constant if the solution contains a high concentration of ammonium chloride. Salts used in this way are called *buffer salts*. The solutions are said to be *buffered* against changes in pH due to the addition or removal of small quantities of acids or alkalies.

Buffer action has many important applications in chemistry and physiology. The human blood is buffered so as to maintain a pH of about 7.3. Slight variations in pH are essential for the stimulation of certain physiological functions. However, pronounced changes would lead to serious disturbances of normal body functions, or even death.

8. Ionization constant of water. Pure water is a very poor conductor of electricity because it is very slightly ionized. According to the modern concept of acids and bases, some water molecules donate protons, acting as an acid. Other water molecules which accept these protons act as a base.

$$H_2O + H_2O \rightleftarrows H_3O^+ + OH^-$$

The degree of ionization is slight and equilibrium is quickly established with a very low concentration of H_3O^+ and OH^- ions.

Conductivity experiments with very pure water at room temperature show that 1 mole of H_3O^+ ions and 1 mole of OH^- ions are present in 10^7 liters. Thus $[H_3O^+]$ and $[OH^-]$ are each 10^{-7} mole per liter. The expression for the equilibrium constant is

$$K = \frac{[H_3O^+][OH^-]}{[H_2O]^2}$$

A liter of water contains

$$\frac{1000. \text{ g}}{18.0 \text{ g/mole}} = 55.5 \text{ moles}$$

and this concentration of water molecules remains substantially the same in all dilute solutions.

Thus, both $[H_2O]^2$ and K in the above equilibrium expression are constants and their product is the constant K_w, *the ion-product constant for water*. It is equal to the product of the molar concentrations of the H_3O^+ and OH^- ions.

$$K_w = [H_3O^+][OH^-]$$

At 25° C,

$$K_w = 10^{-7} \times 10^{-7} = 10^{-14}$$

The product (K_w) of the molar concentrations of H_3O^+ and OH^- has this constant value not only in pure water, but in all water solutions at 25° C. Thus an acid solution with a pH of 4 has a $[H_3O^+]$ of 10^{-4} mole per liter and a $[OH^-]$ of 10^{-10} mole per liter. An alkaline solution with a pH of 8 has a $[H_3O^+]$ of 10^{-8} mole per liter and a $[OH^-]$ of 10^{-6} mole per liter.

9. Hydrolysis of salts. In general, when normal salts are dissolved in water, we expect the solutions to remain neutral. Many salts, such as NaCl and KNO₃, behave in this way. They are formed from *strong* acids and *strong* hydroxides. Solutions of these salts have a pH of 7. When other salts are dissolved in water, solutions may be produced that are not neutral, but may be either acidic or alkaline. Such salts are said to *hydrolyze* in water solution. **Hydrolysis** *is an acid-base reaction between water and an ion of a dissolved salt.*

There are two general types of hydrolysis reactions:

1. Reactions between an anion (negative ion) base and water. Anions that are conjugate bases of weak acids, like the $CO_3^=$ and $C_2H_3O_2^-$ ions, may act as proton acceptors in water solution. Water molecules are the proton donors. The net effect is a rise in the hydroxide-ion concentration of the solution.

2. Reactions between a cation (positive ion) acid and water. Cations that contain hydro-gen like the NH_4^+ ion, and hydrated cations like the $Cu(H_2O)_4^{++}$ ion, may act as proton donors in water solution. Water molecules are the proton acceptors. The net effect is a rise in the hydronium-ion concentration of the solution.

▶ **10. Basic anion hydrolysis.** A salt whose cation is not an acid, but whose anion is a base will form solutions in water that are basic. The general reaction pattern for the basic anion B^- in water is:

$$B^-(aq) + H_2O(l) \rightleftarrows HB(aq) + OH^-(aq)$$

The basic B^- ion accepts a proton from the H_2O molecule to form the weak acid **HB** and the basic OH^- ion. The hydroxide-ion concentration $[OH^-]$ of the solution is increased as a result of the anion hydrolysis.

Referring to the general hydrolysis equation above, we can write the expression for the *hydrolysis constant K_h* as

$$K_h = \frac{[HB][OH^-]}{[B^-]}$$

This hydrolysis constant K_h may be expressed in terms of the ion product constant K_w for water and the ionization constant K_a for the weak acid.

$$K_h = \frac{K_w}{K_a}$$

Suppose we dissolve sodium carbonate in water and test it with red litmus paper. We find that the solution turns red litmus *blue*. The solution then contains an excess of OH^- ions and is basic.

The sodium ion is not an acid and does not react noticeably with water. The carbonate ion, $CO_3^=$, is a base which accepts a proton from a water molecule to form the slightly ionized bicarbonate ion, HCO_3^-.

$$CO_3^= + H_2O \rightleftarrows HCO_3^- + OH^-$$

The OH^- ion concentration builds up until equilibrium is reached. The H_3O^+ ion concentration becomes less since the product $[H_3O^+][OH^-]$ remains equal to the ionization constant of the solution, 10^{-14}. Thus the pH is *greater* than 7 and the solution is *alkaline*. In general, *salts formed from weak acids and strong hydroxides hydrolyze in water to form alkaline solutions.*

▶ **11. Acid cation hydrolysis.** A water solution of ammonium chloride, NH_4Cl, turns blue litmus *red*. This demonstrates that hydrolysis occurs and the solution contains an excess of H_3O^+ ions. Chloride ions show no noticeable tendency to react with water in solution. The ammonium ions donate protons to water molecules.

$$NH_4^+ + H_2O \rightleftarrows H_3O^+ + NH_3$$

Equilibrium is established with an increased H_3O^+ concentration. The pH is *less* than 7 and the solution is thus *acidic*.

The metallic ions of many salts are hydrated in water solution. Such hydrated ions may donate protons to water molecules and the solution becomes acidic. For example, aluminum chloride produces the hydrated cation

$$Al(H_2O)_6^{+++}$$

Copper(II) sulfate in water solution yields the light blue hydrated cation

$$Cu(H_2O)_4^{++}$$

These ions react with water to produce hydronium ions as follows:

$$Al(H_2O)_6^{+++} + H_2O \rightleftarrows$$
$$Al(H_2O)_5OH^{++} + H_3O^+$$
$$Cu(H_2O)_4^{++} + H_2O \rightleftarrows$$
$$Cu(H_2O)_3OH^+ + H_3O^+$$

Cations such as the $Cu(H_2O)_3OH^+$ ion may experience a secondary hydrolysis to a slight extent:

$$Cu(H_2O)_3OH^+ + H_2O \rightleftarrows$$
$$Cu(H_2O)_2(OH)_2 + H_3O^+$$

Expressions for the hydrolysis constant K_h for cation acids are similar to those for anion bases.

In general, salts formed from strong acids and weak hydroxides hydrolyze in water to form acidic solutions.

Aluminum sulfide, when placed in water, is observed to form both a precipitate and a gas. The reaction is

$$Al_2S_3 + 6H_2O \rightarrow 2Al(OH)_3 \downarrow + 3H_2S \uparrow$$

Both products are removed from the solution and the hydrolysis therefore runs to completion.

Both ions of a salt formed from a *weak* acid and a *weak* hydroxide will hydrolyze extensively in water. The salt may undergo complete decomposition. If both ions of the salt hydrolyze equally, the solution will be neutral. Ammonium acetate is such a salt.

Hydrolysis is often very important. Sodium carbonate, washing soda, is widely used as a cleaning agent due to the alkaline properties of its water solution. Sodium hydrogen carbonate forms a mild alkaline solution in water which has many practical uses. Through the study of hydrolysis we can see more clearly why the end-point of a neutralization reaction may occur at a pH other than 7.

▶ **12. Solubility product.** A saturated solution contains the maximum amount of solute that can be held in equilibrium with an excess of the substance at a specified temperature. The saturated solution is not necessarily a concentrated solution as we sometimes infer. The concentration will be large or small, depending on the solubility of the substance.

According to a rough rule often used to express solubilities qualitatively, a substance is said to be *soluble* if the solubility is greater than approximately 1 g per 100 g of water. It is said to be *insoluble* if the solubility is less than approximately 0.1 g per 100 g of water. Solubilities that fall in between these limits are described as *slightly soluble*.

Substances commonly referred to as insoluble are, in fact, so *sparingly soluble* that an almost negligible quantity saturates the solution. Equilibrium is then established with the undissolved excess remaining in contact with the solution. Equilibria between sparingly soluble solid substances and their saturated solutions are especially important in analytical chemistry.

We have observed that silver chloride precipitates when appreciable concentrations of Ag^+ and Cl^- ions from different sources are placed in the same solution environment. Silver chloride is a sparingly soluble salt. The solution reaches saturation at a very small concentration of its ions. All Ag^+ and Cl^- ions in excess of the

saturation concentration must normally separate as solid AgCl.

The equilibrium principles developed in this chapter can be applied to saturated solutions of such sparingly soluble salts. Suppose we consider the equilibrium system in a saturated solution of silver chloride containing an excess of the solid salt. The equilibrium equation is

$$AgCl(s) \rightleftarrows Ag^+(aq) + Cl^-(aq)$$

The equilibrium constant may be expressed as follows:

$$K = \frac{[Ag^+][Cl^-]}{[AgCl]}$$

In Section 4 we stated that the concentration of a pure substance in the solid or liquid state remains constant providing the temperature is not changed. Thus, [AgCl] in the above equation is a constant at the

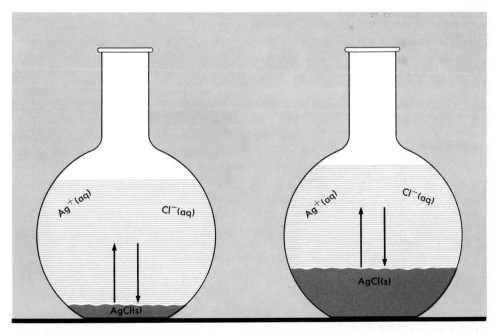

21-4   The heterogeneous equilibrium in a saturated solution is not altered by the addition of more of the solid phase.

temperature of the solution. By combining the two constants we can write

$$K[AgCl] = [Ag^+][Cl^-]$$

The product is also a constant which is called the *solubility-product constant K_{sp}*.

$$K_{sp} = K[AgCl]$$

Therefore,

$$K_{sp} = [Ag^+][Cl^-]$$

Here we see that the solubility-product constant K_{sp} of AgCl is the product of the molar concentrations of its ions in a saturated solution.

Calcium fluoride is another example of a sparingly soluble salt. A saturated solution has the solubility equilibrium according to the equation

$$CaF_2(s) \rightleftarrows Ca^{++}(aq) + 2F^-(aq)$$

The solubility-product constant is given by

$$K_{sp} = [Ca^{++}][F^-]^2$$

Observe that the solubility-product constant in this case is the product of the molar concentration of Ca^{++} ions and the molar concentration of F^- ions *squared*.

For any sparingly soluble salt having the general formula M_aX_b, the equilibrium system in a saturated solution is shown by

$$M_aX_b \rightleftarrows aM^{+b} + bX^{-a}$$

The solubility-product constant is expressed by

$$K_{sp} = [M^{+b}]^a[X^{-a}]^b$$

*The **solubility-product constant** of a substance is the product of the molar concentrations of its ions in a saturated solution, each raised to the appropriate power.*

From solubility tables we find that 1.5×10^{-4} g of AgCl saturates 100 g of water at room temperature. Since a mole of AgCl has a mass of 143.5 g, the saturation concentration (solubility) of AgCl can be expressed more appropriately in moles per liter:

$$\frac{1.5 \times 10^{-4} \text{ g}}{10^2 \text{ g}} \times \frac{10^3 \text{ g}}{\text{liter}} \times \frac{\text{mole}}{1.435 \times 10^2 \text{ g}} =$$

$$1.1 \times 10^{-5} \text{ mole/liter}$$

The equilibrium equation

$$AgCl \rightleftarrows Ag^+ + Cl^-$$

shows that 1 mole of AgCl yields 1 mole of Ag^+ ions and 1 mole of Cl^- ions in solution. Therefore, the ion concentrations in the saturated solution are

$$[Ag^+] = 1.1 \times 10^{-5}$$
$$[Cl^-] = 1.1 \times 10^{-5}$$

and

$$K_{sp} = [Ag^+][Cl^-]$$
$$K_{sp} = (1.1 \times 10^{-5})(1.1 \times 10^{-5})$$
$$K_{sp} = (1.1 \times 10^{-5})^2 = 1.2 \times 10^{-10}$$

This is the solubility-product constant of AgCl at 25° C.

The solubility of CaF_2 is given in the tables as 1.7×10^{-3} g/100 g H_2O at 25° C. Converting to a concentration expression in moles per liter as above, this becomes 2.2×10^{-4} mole/liter.

The equation for the solubility equilibrium

$$CaF_2 \rightleftarrows Ca^{++} + 2F^-$$

shows that 1 mole of CaF_2 yields 1 mole of Ca^{++} ions and 2 moles of F^- ions. The ion concentrations in the saturated solution are

$$[Ca^{++}] = 2.2 \times 10^{-4}$$
$$[F^-] = 2(2.2 \times 10^{-4})$$

and

$$K_{sp} = [Ca^{++}][F^-]^2$$
$$K_{sp} = (2.2 \times 10^{-4})(4.4 \times 10^{-4})^2$$
$$K_{sp} = (2.2 \times 10^{-4})(1.9 \times 10^{-7})$$
$$K_{sp} = 4.2 \times 10^{-11}$$

Thus, the solubility-product constant of CaF_2 is 4.2×10^{-11} at 25° C.

So long as the product $[Ca^{++}][F^-]^2$ remains less than the value for K_{sp}, the solution is *unsaturated*. If the ion product is *greater than* the value for K_{sp}, CaF_2 precipitates in order to reduce the concentrations of Ca^{++} and F^- ions. The solubility

equilibrium is then shown as

$$CaF_2(s) \rightleftarrows Ca^{++}(aq) + 2F^-(aq)$$

Because of the difficulties encountered in measuring very small concentrations of a solute with precision, solubility data from different sources may generate slightly different values of K_{sp} for a substance. Thus, calculations of K_{sp} should ordinarily be limited to two significant figures. See table below.

▶ **13. Calculating solubilities.** Solubility-product constants are computed

SOLUBILITY–PRODUCT CONSTANTS K_{sp} at 25° C

Salt	Ion Product	K_{sp}
$AgC_2H_3O_2$	$[Ag^+][C_2H_3O_2^-]$	2.5×10^{-3}
$AgBr$	$[Ag^+][Br^-]$	4.8×10^{-13}
Ag_2CO_3	$[Ag^+]^2[CO_3^=]$	8.2×10^{-12}
$AgCl$	$[Ag^+][Cl^-]$	1.2×10^{-10}
AgI	$[Ag^+][I^-]$	8.3×10^{-17}
Ag_2S	$[Ag^+]^2[S^=]$	1.6×10^{-49}
$Al(OH)_3$	$[Al^{+++}][OH^-]^3$	3×10^{-33}
$BaCO_3$	$[Ba^{++}][CO_3^=]$	4.9×10^{-9}
$BaSO_4$	$[Ba^{++}][SO_4^=]$	1.1×10^{-10}
CdS	$[Cd^{++}][S^=]$	1.0×10^{-28}
$CaCO_3$	$[Ca^{++}][CO_3^=]$	4.8×10^{-9}
CaF_2	$[Ca^{++}][F^-]^2$	4.2×10^{-11}
$Ca(OH)_2$	$[Ca^{++}][OH^-]^2$	1.3×10^{-6}
$CaSO_4$	$[Ca^{++}][SO_4^=]$	2.4×10^{-5}
$CuCl$	$[Cu^+][Cl^-]$	3.2×10^{-7}
Cu_2S	$[Cu^+]^2[S^=]$	1.6×10^{-48}
CuS	$[Cu^{++}][S^=]$	8.7×10^{-36}
FeS	$[Fe^{++}][S^=]$	3.7×10^{-19}
$Fe(OH)_3$	$[Fe^{+++}][OH^-]^3$	6.0×10^{-38}
$PbCl_2$	$[Pb^{++}][Cl^-]^2$	1.6×10^{-5}
$PbCrO_4$	$[Pb^{++}][CrO_4^=]$	1.8×10^{-14}
$PbSO_4$	$[Pb^{++}][SO_4^=]$	1.6×10^{-8}
PbS	$[Pb^{++}][S^=]$	8.4×10^{-28}
$MgCO_3$	$[Mg^{++}][CO_3^=]$	2.5×10^{-5}
MnS	$[Mn^{++}][S^=]$	1.4×10^{-15}
HgS	$[Hg^{++}][S^=]$	3×10^{-53}
NiS	$[Ni^{++}][S^=]$	1.8×10^{-21}
$SrSO_4$	$[Sr^{++}][SO_4^=]$	3.0×10^{-7}
ZnS	$[Zn^{++}][S^=]$	4.5×10^{-24}

Sample Problem

Would a precipitate be formed if 20.0 ml of 0.010–M $BaCl_2$ solution were mixed with 20.0 ml of 0.0050–M Na_2SO_4 solution?

Solution

The two possible new pairings of ions are NaCl and $BaSO_4$. Of these, $BaSO_4$ is a sparingly soluble salt. It would then precipitate from the resulting solution if the ion product $[Ba^{++}][SO_4^{-}]$ exceeded the value of the solubility-product constant K_{sp} for $BaSO_4$. From the table of solubility products, the K_{sp} is found to be 1.1×10^{-10}.

The solubility equilibrium equation is

$$BaSO_4(s) \rightleftarrows Ba^{++}(aq) + SO_4^{-}(aq)$$

and the equilibrium condition is

$$K_{sp} = [Ba^{++}][SO_4^{-}] = 1.1 \times 10^{-10}$$

If the ion product $[Ba^{++}][SO_4^{-}]$ exceeds 1.1×10^{-10}, precipitation of $BaSO_4$ is predicted.

Mole quantities of Ba^{++} and $SO_4^{=}$ ions:

$$0.020 \; 1 \times \frac{0.010 \text{ mole } Ba^{++}}{1} = 0.00020 \text{ mole } Ba^{++}$$

$$0.020 \; 1 \times \frac{0.0050 \text{ mole } SO_4^{=}}{1} = 0.00010 \text{ mole } SO_4^{=}$$

Total volume of solution containing Ba^{++} and $SO_4^{=}$ ions:

$$0.020 \; 1 + 0.020 \; 1 = 0.040 \; 1$$

Ba^{++} and $SO_4^{=}$ ion concentrations:

$$\frac{0.00020 \text{ mole } Ba^{++}}{0.040 \; 1} = 5.0 \times 10^{-3} \text{ mole } Ba^{++}/1$$

$$\frac{0.00010 \text{ mole } SO_4^{=}}{0.040 \; 1} = 2.5 \times 10^{-3} \text{ mole } SO_4^{=}/1$$

Trial value of ion product:

$$[Ba^{++}][SO_4^{=}] = (5.0 \times 10^{-3})(2.5 \times 10^{-3}) = 1.2 \times 10^{-5}$$

The ion product is much higher than K_{sp} ($K_{sp} = 1.1 \times 10^{-10}$) so precipitation will occur.

from meticulous measurements of solubilities. Once known, the solubility product provides a convenient way to determine the solubility of a sparingly soluble salt.

Suppose we wish to know how much barium carbonate, $BaCO_3$, can be dissolved in one liter of water at 25° C. From the table of solubility products we find that K_{sp} for $BaCO_3$ has the numerical value 4.9×10^{-9}. The solubility equation is written as follows:

$$BaCO_3(s) \rightleftarrows Ba^{++}(aq) + CO_3^{-}(aq)$$

Knowing the value for K_{sp}, we can write

$$K_{sp} = [Ba^{++}][CO_3^=] = 4.9 \times 10^{-9}$$

From this expression we see that $BaCO_3$ dissolves until the molar concentrations of Ba^{++} and $CO_3^=$ increase enough to make their product equal to 4.9×10^{-9}.

The solubility equilibrium equation shows that Ba^{++} ions and $CO_3^=$ ions are introduced into the solution in equal numbers as the salt dissolves. That is, 1 mole of $BaCO_3$ dissolved per liter yields 1 mole of Ba^{++} ion and 1 mole of $CO_3^=$ ion. Thus,

$$[Ba^{++}] = [CO_3^=] = [BaCO_3]\text{ dissolved}$$

$$K_{sp} = 4.9 \times 10^{-9} = [BaCO_3]^2$$

$$[BaCO_3] = \sqrt{4.9 \times 10^{-9}} = \sqrt{49 \times 10^{-10}}$$

$$[BaCO_3] = 7.0 \times 10^{-5}\text{ mole/liter}$$

The solubility of $BaCO_3$ is 7.0×10^{-5} mole/liter, giving a solution containing 7.0×10^{-5} M with respect to Ba^{++} ions and 7.0×10^{-5} M with respect to $CO_3^=$ ions.

▶ **14. Precipitation calculations.** In the example used in Section 13, the $BaCO_3$ was dissolved in water and served as the source of both Ba^{++} and $CO_3^=$ ions. Consequently the concentrations of the two ions were equal. The equilibrium system does not require the two ion concentra-

tions to be equal. It requires only that the *ion product* $[Ba^{++}][CO_3^=]$ may not exceed the value of K_{sp} for the system.

Suppose unequal amounts of $BaCl_2$ and $CaCO_3$ are added to water. A large concentration of Ba^{++} ions and a small concentration of $CO_3^=$ ions might result. If the ion product $[Ba^{++}][CO_3^=]$ exceeded the K_{sp} of $BaCO_3$, a precipitate of $BaCO_3$ would form until the ion concentrations are reduced to equilibrium values.

The solubility product may be used to predict whether a precipitate will form when two solutions are mixed. An illustration of the calculations involved in this application of the solubility product is given in the Sample Problem opposite.

The solubility-product principle can be very useful when applied to solutions of sparingly soluble substances. It cannot be applied to the solutions of moderately soluble or very soluble substances. Many solubility-product constants are known only approximately due to difficulties encountered in solubility measurements. Sometimes, as with the hydrolysis of an ion in solution, it becomes necessary to consider two equilibria simultaneously. Finally, the solubility product is sensitive to changes in solution temperature to the extent that the solubility of the dissolved substance is influenced.

REVIEW OUTLINE

Factors that disturb equilibrium (4)
 Le Chatelier's principle (4)
 Effects of concentration (4)
 Effects of pressure (4)
 Effects of temperature (4)
 End reactions (5)
 Common-ion effect (6)

Ionization constants (7)
 Weak acid (7)
 Water (8)

Hydrolysis of salts (9)
 Basic anion hydrolysis (10)
 Acid cation hydrolysis (11)

Solubility equilibria (12, 13, 14)
 Solubility-product constant (12)
 Applications in solubility (13)
 Applications in precipitation (14)

QUESTIONS

Group A

1. State three examples of physical equilibrium.
2. Write the ionic equations for three examples of ionic equilibrium.
3. What is wrong with the following statement? When equilibrium is reached, the opposing reactions stop.
4. State the Law of Mass Action.
5. An oxidation reaction proceeding in air under standard pressure is transferred to an atmosphere of pure oxygen under the same pressure. (*a*) What is the effect on the speed of the oxidation reaction? (*b*) How can you account for this effect?
6. (*a*) State the Principle of Le Chatelier. (*b*) To what kinds of equilibria does it apply?
7. (*a*) Name three factors which may disturb, or shift, an equilibrium. (*b*) Which of these affects the value of the equilibrium constant?
8. What are the three conditions under which ionic reactions involving ionic substances may run to completion? Write an equation for each.
▶ 9. What are the solubility characteristics of substances involved in solubility equilibrium systems?
▶ 10. Define the solubility-product constant.

Group B

11. The reaction between steam and iron is reversible. Steam passed over hot iron produces magnetic iron oxide (Fe_3O_4) and hydrogen. Hydrogen passed over hot magnetic iron oxide reduces it to iron and forms steam. Suggest a method by which this reversible reaction may be brought to a state of equilibrium.

12. What is the meaning of the term *dynamic* as applied to an equilibrium state?
13. Methanol is produced synthetically as a gas by the reaction between carbon monoxide and hydrogen, in the presence of a catalyst, according to the equilibrium reaction: $CO + 2H_2 \rightleftarrows CH_3OH + 24$ kcal. Write the expression for the equilibrium constant of this reaction.
14. How would you propose to regulate the temperature of the equilibrium mixture of CO, H_2, and CH_3OH of Question 13 in order to increase the yield of methanol? Explain.
15. How would you propose to regulate the pressure on the equilibrium mixture of Question 13 in order to increase the yield of methanol? Explain.
16. In the reaction, $A + B \rightleftarrows C$, the concentrations of **A, B,** and **C** in the equilibrium mixture were found to be 2.0, 3.0, and 1.0 moles per liter respectively. What is the equilibrium constant of this reaction?
17. Write the balanced ionic equations for the following reactions in water solution. If a reaction does not take place, write NO REACTION. Omit all *spectator* ions. Show precipitates by $\downarrow$ and gases by $\uparrow$. Use solubility data in the Appendix as needed. Use a separate sheet of paper. (Do not write in this book.)

(a) $BaCO_3 + HNO_3 \rightarrow$ (f) $FeS + NaCl \rightarrow$
(b) $Pb(NO_3)_2 + NaCl \rightarrow$ (g) $AgC_2H_3O_2 + HCl \rightarrow$
(c) $CuSO_4 + HCl \rightarrow$ (h) $Na_3PO_4 + CuSO_4 \rightarrow$
(d) $Ca_3(PO_4)_2 + NaNO_3 \rightarrow$ (i) $BaCl_2 + Na_2SO_4 \rightarrow$
(e) $Ba(NO_3)_2 + H_2SO_4 \rightarrow$ (j) $CuO + H_2SO_4 \rightarrow$

18. Explain why the pH of a solution containing both acetic acid and sodium acetate is higher than that of a solution containing the same concentration of acetic acid alone.
19. Complete the following table, using a separate sheet of paper. (Do not write in this book.)

pH	$[H_3O^+]$ (mole/liter)	$[OH^-]$ (mole/liter)	$[H_3O^+][OH^-]$	Property
0				
1				
3				
5				
7	$10^{-7} = 0.0000001$	$10^{-7} = 0.0000001$	10^{-14}	Neutral
9				
11				
13				
14				

20. Referring to the *Table of Equilibrium Constants*, Section 4, write the expression for the equilibrium constant for each equilibrium system listed.
21. Referring to the *Table of Typical Equilibrium Concentrations of H_2, I_2, and HI*, Section 3, explain why $[H_2] = [I_2]$ in the first two experiments.
22. What is the effect of pressure on the $H_2 + I_2 \rightleftarrows 2HI$ equilibrium? Explain.

▶ 23. (a) From the development of K_a in Section 7, show how you would express an ionization constant K_b for the weak base NH_3.
(b) In this case $K_b = 1.8 \times 10^{-5}$. What is the significance of this numerical value?

▶ 24. Given the hydrolysis reaction $B^- + H_2O \rightleftarrows HB + OH^-$, demonstrate that $K_h = K_w/K_a$.

▶ 25. The ionization constant K_a for acetic acid is 1.8×10^{-5} at 25° C. Explain the significance of this value.

PROBLEMS

▶ 1. The H_3O^+ ion concentration of a solution is 0.00040 mole per liter. This may be expressed as $H_3O^+ = 4.0 \times 10^{-4}$ mole per liter. What is the pH of the solution?

▶ 2. What is the pH of a 0.002–M solution of HCl? (At this concentration HCl is completely ionized.)

▶ 3. Find the pH of a 0.02–M solution of KOH.

4. Given a 250 ml volumetric flask, distilled water, and CP grade NaOH, (a) state how you would prepare 250 ml of 0.50–M NaOH solution. (b) What is the normality of the solution?

5. What quantity of copper(II) sulfate pentahydrate is required to prepare 750. ml of 2.00–M solution?

▶ 6. A 0.01000–N solution of acetic acid is found to have a pH of 3.3799 at 18° C. What is the ionization constant of this weak acid?

▶ 7. Ammonia is a weak base and its water solution is slightly basic due to the equilibrium reaction $NH_3 + H_2O \rightleftarrows NH_4^+ + OH^-$. The ionization constant $K_b = 1.8 \times 10^{-5}$. What is the pH of a 0.50–M NH_3 solution? (Note: Assume that the change in mole concentration of NH_3 at equilibrium is negligible.)

▶ 8. It was found by experiment that 1.3×10^{-4} g AgBr dissolved in 1 liter of water to form a saturated solution. Find K_{sp} for AgBr.

▶ 9. How many grams of $AgC_2H_3O_2$ can be dissolved in 10.0 liters of water at 25° C? (Note: The value of K_{sp} for $AgC_2H_3O_2$ can be found in the table of Section 12.)

▶ 10. If 0.0015 mole of solid $Pb(NO_3)_2$ is added to one liter of 0.0015–M H_2SO_4, (a) what substance might precipitate? (b) Will the precipitate form?

Chapter Twenty-two

OXIDATION–REDUCTION REACTIONS

1. Oxidation and reduction processes. In Chapter 6, Section 5, reactions which involved the loss of electrons by an atom or ion were defined as oxidation processes. The particles that lose the electrons are said to be *oxidized*.

The combustion of sodium in an atmosphere of chlorine illustrates this electron-transfer process. The action can be regarded as one in which a sodium atom loses an electron to a chlorine atom and becomes a sodium ion. The oxidation state of sodium has undergone a change from the zero state of the atom to the +1 state of the ion. We show this change in oxidation state by assigning the appropriate oxidation numbers.

$$Na^0 - e^- \rightarrow Na^{+1}$$

A less obvious oxidation process occurs when hydrogen burns in chlorine. Here the action is regarded as one in which the hydrogen experiences a change in the sharing of electrons. In the hydrogen molecule a pair of electrons are shared equally by the two hydrogen nuclei, hence a zero oxidation state for the hydrogen atoms.

As a result of the reaction, a hydrogen atom shares a pair of electrons with a chlorine atom. However, chlorine is the more electronegative element and the electron pair belongs less to the hydrogen atom than to the chlorine atom. This amounts to a partial transfer of electrons, a polar covalent bond. The hydrogen atom may be considered to have undergone a change from the zero to the +1 oxidation state. This again is an oxidation process.

How shall we regard the behavior of the chlorine in these reactions with sodium and hydrogen? With sodium, the result is clear. Each chlorine atom acquires an electron from a sodium atom and becomes a chloride ion. Reactions which involve the gain of electrons have been defined as *reduction* processes. The particles that gain the electrons are said to be *reduced*. The oxidation state of chlorine has undergone a change from the zero state of the chlorine atom to the −1 state of the chloride ion. For the chlorine molecule:

$$Cl_2{}^0 + 2e^- \rightarrow 2Cl^{-1}$$

The situation for chlorine is more obscure in the reaction with hydrogen. The pair of electrons shared by the hydrogen and chlorine atoms are not shared equally. They belong more to the chlorine atom because of its higher electronegativity. In this sense, the chlorine atom is considered to have experienced a change from the zero to the −1 oxidation state, a reduction process.

Thus, oxidation numbers are assigned to the atoms comprising the molecular species of covalent compounds to indicate their oxidation states. In the hydrogen chloride molecule, the oxidation number of the hydrogen atom is +1 and that of the chlorine atom is −1. The rules for assigning oxidation numbers were presented in detail in Chapter 6. They are restated here in summary form in the accompanying table.

RULES FOR ASSIGNING OXIDATION NUMBERS

1. The oxidation number of an atom of a free element is zero.
2. The oxidation number of a monatomic ion is equal to its charge.
3. The algebraic sum of the oxidation numbers of the atoms in the formula of a compound is zero.
4. The oxidation number of hydrogen is +1, except in metallic hydrides where it is −1.
5. The oxidation number of oxygen is −2. A common exception is in peroxides where it is −1. (In compounds with fluorine, the oxidation number of oxygen is +2.)
6. In combinations of nonmetals, the oxidation number of the less electronegative element is positive and of the more electronegative element is negative.
7. The algebraic sum of the oxidation numbers of the atoms in the formula of a radical is equal to its charge.

2. Oxidation and reduction occur simultaneously. It is apparent that one substance cannot gain electrons unless another substance loses electrons. If *oxidation* occurs during a chemical action, then *reduction* must occur simultaneously. If one kind of particle is oxidized, another kind of particle must be reduced *to a comparable degree.*

Any chemical process in which there is a transfer of electrons, either partial or complete, is an **oxidation-reduction reaction.** This name is often shortened to "*redox*" reaction. Most of the reactions studied in elementary chemistry are oxidation-reduction reactions. In composition reactions having ionic products, and in replacement reactions, the electron transfer is complete. In reactions which form polar covalent bonds the electron transfer is not complete. How-

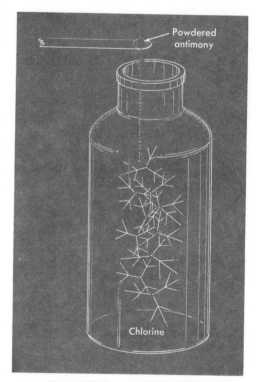

22-1   The combustion of antimony in chlorine is an oxidation-reduction reaction.

ever, in these reactions, we consider the less electronegative substance to be oxidized and the more electronegative substance to be reduced. Few covalent bonds are completely nonpolar.

Reactions in which there are no changes in oxidation state do not involve oxidation-reduction. If sodium chloride is added to the solution of silver nitrate, silver chloride precipitates.

$$Na^+ + Cl^- + Ag^+ + NO_3^- \rightarrow$$
$$Na^+ + NO_3^- + Ag^+Cl^- \downarrow$$

Or more simply,

$$Ag^+(aq) + Cl^-(aq) \rightarrow Ag^+Cl^-(s)$$

Silver chloride is an ionic compound. Note that the charge of each ion remains the same; no electrons have been transferred. This is *not* an oxidation-reduction reaction.

Oxidation-reduction reactions sometimes involve electron transfers that are not easily interpreted. For example, the *permanganate ion* in a solution of potassium permanganate has an ionic charge of -1, MnO_4^-. Under proper conditions this ion may be reduced to the *manganese(II) ion*, Mn^{++}. Under other conditions the MnO_4^- ion may be reduced to the *manganate ion*, $MnO_4^=$.

If we are to write the equation for one of these reactions, we must know the number of electrons transferred during the chemical action. The ionic charge alone is of little help if the ion consists of two or more different substances. In order to simplify the task of balancing oxidation-reduction equations, the appropriate oxidation number may be assigned to each element present in the structure. Suppose we review the assignment of oxidation numbers and their implications in the oxidation-reduction process.

Loss of electrons produces a more *positive* oxidation state, and gain of electrons

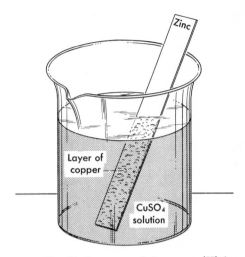

22-2   The displacement of the copper(II) ion by zinc, which happens when a clean strip of zinc is placed in a solution of copper sulfate, is a good example of a spontaneous oxidation-reduction reaction.

produces a more *negative* oxidation state. If all electrons belonging to an atom of an element are present, the oxidation state is *zero* and the atom is assigned the oxidation number 0. All atoms in their elementary form have oxidation numbers of 0. These may be written as: Na^0, K^0, Cu^0, H_2^0, and N_2^0.

In the following electronic equations the substances on the left are oxidized.

$$Na^0 - e^- \rightarrow Na^{+1}$$
$$Fe^0 - 2e^- \rightarrow Fe^{+2}$$
$$Fe^{+2} - e^- \rightarrow Fe^{+3}$$
$$2Cl^{-1} - 2e^- \rightarrow Cl_2^0$$

The superscript after each symbol is the oxidation number of that particle. The difference between oxidation numbers indicates the number of electrons lost by each atom or ion. Observe that the chloride ion has the oxidation number -1, a *negative* oxidation state. *Oxidation results in an algebraic increase in the oxidation number of a substance.* A change from -1 to 0 is an algebraic increase in the oxidation number just as is a change from 0 to +1, or +1 to +2. Each of these changes accompanies the loss of 1 electron.

In the electronic equations which follow, the substances on the left are reduced.

$$Na^{+1} + e^- \rightarrow Na^0$$
$$Cl_2{}^0 + 2e^- \rightarrow 2Cl^{-1}$$
$$Fe^{+3} + e^- \rightarrow Fe^{+2}$$
$$Cu^{+2} + 2e^- \rightarrow Cu^0$$
$$Br_2{}^0 + 2e^- \rightarrow 2Br^{-1}$$

The third equation illustrates the reduction of the iron(III) ion, oxidation number +3, to the iron(II) state, oxidation number +2. Two additional electrons would be necessary to complete the reduction of the iron(II) ion to the iron atom with oxidation number 0. *Reduction results in an algebraic decrease in the oxidation number of a substance.*

The oxidation state of each ion in a binary salt is that indicated by the ionic charge. In binary covalent compounds, shared electrons are arbitrarily assigned to the element having the greater electronegativity.

In the two ternary compounds, H_2SO_4 and H_2SO_3, oxygen is given the oxidation number -2 and hydrogen $+1$. In the H_2SO_4 molecule the total contribution of the 4 atoms of oxygen is 4 times -2, or -8. The total contribution of the two atoms of hydrogen is $2(+1) = +2$. Since the H_2SO_4 molecule is neutral, the oxidation number of the single sulfur atom must be $+6$. We may write the appropriate oxidation number adjacent to each symbol in the formula. (The numbers are usually placed above the symbols so that they may not be mistaken for an ionic charge. This practice also prevents undue spreading of the formula in a long equation.)

$$\overset{+1\ +6\ -2}{H_2SO_4}$$
$$2(+1) + 1(+6) + 4(-2) = 0$$

In the sulfurous acid molecule, H_2SO_3, the total contribution of oxygen is $3(-2) = -6$. For the hydrogen, it is $2(+1) = +2$. Thus the oxidation number of the single atom of sulfur must be $+4$.

$$\overset{+1\ +4\ -2}{H_2SO_3}$$
$$2(+1) + 1(+4) + 3(-2) = 0$$

This is seen to be a reasonable assignment of oxidation numbers by examining the electronic structures of these two molecules. The electron-dot formula of sulfuric acid is:

$$H \overset{..}{\underset{..}{O}} \overset{\overset{..}{O}}{\underset{..}{\overset{xx}{\underset{xx}{S}}}} \overset{..}{\underset{..}{O}} H$$

Oxygen is the most electronegative element present so we assign to oxygen all electrons shared with oxygen. The sulfur atom must contribute all of its electrons. Hence the oxidation number of sulfur is $+6$.

The electron-dot formula of sulfurous acid may be written:

$$H \overset{..}{\underset{..}{O}} \overset{xx}{\underset{\overset{..}{\underset{..}{O}}}{\underset{xx}{S}}} \overset{..}{\underset{..}{O}} H$$

Observe that one pair of electrons belonging to sulfur is unshared. The atom of sulfur contributes *four* electrons, hence the oxidation number is $+4$.

Suppose we apply these rules to a ternary salt. Potassium permanganate is composed of potassium ions, K^+, and the complex permanganate ion, $MnO_4{}^-$. The empirical formula is $KMnO_4$. Oxygen has the oxidation number -2 as before. The total contribution of the 4 oxygen atoms is $4(-2) = -8$. The K^+ ion is assigned the oxidation number that corresponds to its ionic charge, $+1$. The oxidation number of the manganese atom in the radical group must then be $+7$. The formula showing these oxidation states of the elements can be written:

$$K^{+1}[Mn^{+7}(O^{-2})_4]^{-1}$$

or more simply

$$\overset{+1\ +7\ -2}{KMnO_4}$$

Manganese has several important oxidation states. This oxidation number, $+7$, represents its highest oxidation state.

3. Balancing of oxidation-reduction equations. The principal use of oxidation numbers is in balancing equations for oxidation-reduction reactions. An orderly procedure is an essential part of equation writing. We must know the *facts:* what the reactants are and what the products are. We must then represent the reactants and products by their *correct formulas.* Finally, we must adjust the coefficients of all reactants and products to be in accord with the *conservation of atoms.* The method used to accomplish this third step is essentially one of trial and error.

Oxidation-reduction reactions are those in which changes in oxidation number occur. Here we must observe the *conservation of electrons,* as well as conservation of atoms, in writing equations. In all but the simplest of these reactions, trial-and-error balancing is a difficult process. This process may be simplified by *balancing the electron shift* between the particles oxidized and the particles reduced *before* adjusting the coefficients for the rest of the equation. The procedure for writing oxidation-reduction equations includes the following steps:

Step 1: Write the skeleton equation for the reaction. To do this we must know the reactants and products and represent each by the correct formula.

Step 2: Assign oxidation numbers to all elements and determine what is oxidized and what is reduced.

Step 3: Write the electronic equation for the oxidation process and the electronic equation for the reduction process.

Step 4: Adjust the coefficients in both electronic equations so that the number of electrons lost equals the number gained.

Step 5: Place these coefficients in the skeleton equation.

Step 6: Supply the proper coefficients for the rest of the equation to satisfy the conservation of atoms.

We shall illustrate the application of these steps by considering a very simple oxidation-reduction reaction. Hydrogen sulfide gas burns in air to form sulfur dioxide and water. These facts enable us to write the skeleton equation.

Step 1:

$$H_2S + O_2 \rightarrow SO_2 + H_2O$$

We now assign oxidation numbers. Changes in oxidation numbers enable us to recognize that sulfur is oxidized from the -2 state to the $+4$ state, and oxygen is reduced from the 0 state to the -2 state. The oxidation number of hydrogen remains the same; thus it plays no part in the primary action of oxidation-reduction.

Step 2:

$$\overset{+1\ -2}{H_2S} + \overset{0}{O_2} \rightarrow \overset{+4\ -2}{SO_2} + \overset{+1\ -2}{H_2O}$$

The change in the oxidation state of sulfur requires the loss of 6 electrons; $(-2) - (+4) = -6$. The change in oxidation state of the oxygen requires the gain of 2 electrons; $(0) - (-2) = +2$. The electronic equations for these two actions are:

Step 3:

$$S^{-2} - 6e^- \rightarrow S^{+4} \text{ (oxidation)}$$
$$O^0 + 2e^- \rightarrow O^{-2} \text{ (reduction)}$$

Free oxygen is diatomic, so 4 electrons must be gained during the reduction of a molecule of free oxygen.

$$O_2^0 + 4e^- \rightarrow 2O^{-2}$$

We can now adjust the coefficients of the two electronic equations so the number of electrons lost in the oxidation of sulfur equals the number gained in the reduction of oxygen. The smallest number of electrons common to both equations is 12. We can show the gain and loss of 12 electrons in the two equations by multiplying the oxidation equation by 2, and multiplying the reduction equation by 3.

Step 4:

$$2S^{-2} - 12e^- \rightarrow 2S^{+4}$$
$$3O_2^0 + 12e^- \rightarrow 6O^{-2}$$

Hence the coefficients of H_2S and SO_2 are both 2, and the coefficient of O_2 is 3. Notice that the $6O^{-2}$ is divided between the two products SO_2 and H_2O. The coefficient, 6, is accounted for with the coefficient 2 in front of each formula. These coefficients are transferred to the skeleton equation.

Step 5:

$$2H_2S + 3O_2 \rightarrow 2SO_2 + 2H_2O$$

We are ready now to adjust the coefficients of the equation in the usual way to satisfy the Law of Conservation of Atoms. In this instance no further adjustments are needed; the equation is balanced.

Step 6:

$$2H_2S + 3O_2 \rightarrow 2SO_2 + 2H_2O$$

For a second example, we will use an oxidation-reduction equation that is slightly more difficult to balance. In the reaction between manganese dioxide and hydrochloric acid, water, manganese(II) chloride, and chlorine gas are formed. The skeleton equation is:

$$\overset{+4-2}{MnO_2} + \overset{+1-1}{HCl} \rightarrow \overset{+1-2}{H_2O} + \overset{+2-1}{MnCl_2} + \overset{0}{Cl_2}$$

We assign oxidation numbers to the elements in the reaction and see that Mn^{+4} is reduced to Mn^{+2}, and some of the Cl^{-1} is oxidized to Cl^0. Hydrogen and oxygen do not take part in the primary action. The electronic equations are:

$$2Cl^{-1} - 2e^- \rightarrow Cl_2^0$$
$$Mn^{+4} + 2e^- \rightarrow Mn^{+2}$$

The number of electrons lost and gained is the same, so we transfer the coefficients to the skeleton equation, which becomes:

$$MnO_2 + 2HCl \rightarrow H_2O + MnCl_2 + Cl_2$$

The complete equation may now be balanced by inspection. Two additional molecules of HCl are required to provide the two Cl^- ions of the $MnCl_2$. This requires 2 molecules of water which then accounts for the 2 oxygens of the MnO_2. Our final equation reads:

$$MnO_2 + 4HCl \rightarrow 2H_2O + MnCl_2 + Cl_2$$

The equations for both of these illustrations can be balanced with little difficulty by trial and error. The step process is applied to a more complicated oxidation-reduction reaction in the Sample Problem at the top of page 383.

The method we have used to balance oxidation-reduction reactions is variously referred to as the *electron-shift, electron-transfer,* and *oxidation-state* method. The use of

Sample Problem

The oxidation-reduction reaction between hydrochloric acid and potassium permanganate yields the following products: water, potassium chloride, manganese(II) chloride, and chlorine gas. Write the balanced equation.

Solution

We first write the skeleton equation, being careful to show the correct formula of each reactant and each product. Appropriate oxidation numbers are placed above the symbols of the elements.

$$\overset{+1-1}{HCl} + \overset{+1+7-2}{KMnO_4} \rightarrow \overset{+1-2}{H_2O} + \overset{+1-1}{KCl} + \overset{+2-1}{MnCl_2} + \overset{0}{Cl_2}$$

We see that some chloride ions are oxidized to chlorine atoms, and the manganese of the permanganate ions is reduced to manganese(II) ions. Electronic equations are written for these two actions:

$$2Cl^{-1} - 2e^- \rightarrow Cl_2{}^0$$
$$Mn^{+7} + 5e^- \rightarrow Mn^{+2}$$

The electron shift must involve an equal number of electrons in these two equations. This number is 10. The first equation is multiplied by 5 and the second by 2. We now have:

$$10Cl^{-1} - 10e^- \rightarrow 5Cl_2{}^0$$
$$2Mn^{+7} + 10e^- \rightarrow 2Mn^{+2}$$

These coefficients are transferred to the skeleton equation, which becomes:

$$10HCl + 2KMnO_4 \rightarrow H_2O + KCl + 2MnCl_2 + 5Cl_2$$

By inspection, $2KMnO_4$ produces $2KCl$ and $8H_2O$. Now $2KCl$ and $2MnCl_2$ call for 6 additional molecules of HCl. Our balanced equation then becomes:

$$16HCl + 2KMnO_4 \rightarrow 8H_2O + 2KCl + 2MnCl_2 + 5Cl_2$$

oxidation numbers in no way implies the existence of ions. Remember that the transfer of electrons may be partial, as in polar covalent bonds, or complete, as in ionic bonds. Oxidation numbers are assigned in either case. Chemists sometimes prefer another method which differentiates between ionic and molecular equations. It is more difficult for students of elementary chemistry to use and, for this reason, has not been presented here. Either method, used properly, leads to the correctly balanced equation.

4. Oxidizing and reducing agents. An oxidizing agent takes up electrons during an oxidation-reduction reaction, and a reducing agent furnishes the electrons. It is obvious then that the substance oxidized is also the reducing agent, and the substance reduced is the oxidizing agent. An oxidized substance becomes a potential oxidizing agent. Similarly, a reduced substance is a potential reducing agent. It follows, however, that a very active reducing agent (one easily oxidized) becomes a very poor oxidizing agent, and conversely. If this seems confusing, study the table of Oxidation-Reduction Terminology at the bottom of this page.

The relatively large atoms of the Sodium Family of metals, Group I of the Periodic Table, have weak attraction for their valence electrons, form positive ions readily, and are *very active reducing agents.* The lithium atom is the most active reducing agent of all the common elements, based on electrochemical measurements. The lithium ion, on the other hand, is the weakest oxidizing agent of the common ions. The electronegativity scale suggests that the Group I metals starting with lithium should become progressively more active reducing agents. With the exception of lithium, this is the case. A possible basis for the unusual activity of lithium is discussed in Chapter 24.

Atoms of the Halogen Family, Group VII of the Periodic Table, have strong attraction for electrons. They form negative ions readily and are *very active oxidizing agents.* The fluorine atom, the most highly electronegative atom, is the most active oxidizing agent among the elements. Because of its strong attraction for electrons, the fluoride ion is the weakest reducing agent.

It is possible to arrange the elements according to their activity as oxidizing and reducing agents. (See the table at the top of the opposite page.) The left column shows the relative abilities of some metals to displace other metals from their compounds, an oxidation-reduction process. Zinc, for example, appears above copper and, as a more active reducing agent, displaces copper ions from solutions of copper compounds.

$$Zn(s) + Cu^{++}(aq) \rightarrow Zn^{++}(aq) + Cu(s)$$
$$Zn^0 - 2e^- \rightarrow Zn^{++} \text{ (oxidation)}$$
$$Cu^{++} + 2e^- \rightarrow Cu^0 \text{ (reduction)}$$

The copper(II) ion, on the other hand, is a more active oxidizing agent than the zinc ion.

Nonmetals and some important ions have been included in the series. Any reducing agent will be oxidized by oxidizing agents below it. Observe that F_2 will displace the Cl^-, Br^-, and I^- ions from their solutions. Cl_2 will displace the Br^- and I^- ions and Br_2 will displace I^- ions.

$$Cl_2 + 2Br^-(aq) \rightarrow 2Cl^-(aq) + Br_2$$
$$2Br^- - 2e^- \rightarrow Br_2^0 \text{ (oxidation)}$$
$$Cl_2^0 + 2e^- \rightarrow 2Cl^- \text{ (reduction)}$$

The permanganate, MnO_4^-, ion and the dichromate, $Cr_2O_7^=$, ion are very useful oxidizing agents. They are usually used in the form of their potassium salt. In the presence of an alkali the permanganate ion is reduced to the manganate, $MnO_4^=$, ion. In acid solutions, the permanganate ion is reduced to the manganese(II), Mn^{++}, ion. Dichromate ions, in acid solution, are reduced to chromium(III), Cr^{+++}, ions.

OXIDATION–REDUCTION TERMINOLOGY

Term	Change in Oxidation number	Change in Electron population
Oxidation	Increase	Loss of electrons
Reduction	Decrease	Gain of electrons
Oxidizing agent	Decrease	Acquires electrons
Reducing agent	Increase	Supplies electrons
Substance oxidized	Increase	Loses electrons
Substance reduced	Decrease	Gains electrons

RELATIVE STRENGTH OF OXIDIZING AND REDUCING AGENTS

	Reducing Agents	Oxidizing Agents	
Strong	Li	Li$^+$	**Weak**
	K	K$^+$	
	Ca	Ca^{++}	
	Na	Na$^+$	
	Mg	Mg^{++}	
	Al	Al^{+++}	
	Zn	Zn^{++}	
	Cr	Cr^{+++}	
	Fe	Fe^{++}	
	Ni	Ni^{++}	
	Sn	Sn^{++}	
	Pb	Pb^{++}	
	H$_2$	H$_3$O$^+$	
	H$_2$S	S	
	Cu	Cu^{++}	
	I$^-$	I$_2$	
	MnO$_4^-$	MnO$_4^-$	
	Fe^{++}	Fe^{+++}	
	Hg	Hg$_2^{++}$	
	Ag	Ag$^+$	
	NO$_2^-$	NO$_3^-$	
	Br$^-$	Br$_2$	
	Mn^{++}	MnO$_2$	
	SO$_2$	H$_2$SO$_4$ (conc.)	
	Cl$^-$	Cl$_2$	
	Cr^{+++}	Cr$_2$O$_7^=$	
	Mn^{++}	MnO$_4^-$	
Weak	F$^-$	F$_2$	**Strong**

The peroxide ion, O$_2^=$, has a single covalent bond between the two oxygens. The electronic structure may be represented as

$$\left[:\overset{..}{O} : \overset{..}{O} : \right]^=$$

The structure represents an intermediate state of oxidation between free oxygen and oxides. The oxidation number of oxygen in the peroxide form is -1.

Hydrogen peroxide, H$_2$O$_2$, has the interesting property of being able to act as both an oxidizing agent and a reducing agent. As an oxidizing agent, the oxidation number of oxygen changes from -1 to -2. As a reducing agent, the oxidation number of oxygen changes from -1 to 0.

In the decomposition of hydrogen peroxide, both water and molecular oxygen are formed.

$$\overset{-1}{H_2O_2} + \overset{-1}{H_2O_2} \rightarrow \overset{-2}{H_2O} + \overset{0}{O_2}(g)$$

The peroxide acts simultaneously as an oxidizing agent and as a reducing agent. Such a process is called *auto-oxidation*. Half of the oxygen is reduced to the oxide, forming water. The other half is oxidized to free oxygen. Impurities in a water solution of H$_2$O$_2$ act catalytically to accelerate this process.

5. Gram-equivalents of oxidizing and reducing agents. In Chapter 14, Section 14, the gram-equivalent (g-eq) of a reactant was referred to as the *mass of the substance that acquires or furnishes the Avogadro number of electrons*. This is the number of electrons that 1 mole of hydrogen atoms, the Avogadro number of hydrogen atoms, is capable of releasing or acquiring. If a reactant is oxidized, the mass required to yield the Avogadro number of electrons is the gram-equivalent of the substance. If a reactant is reduced, the mass required to take up the Avogadro number of electrons is the gram-equivalent of the substance. Thus, 1 g-eq of any reducing agent will always react with 1 g-eq of any oxidizing agent.

In the case of oxidizing and reducing agents the particular oxidation-reduction reaction must be known in order to express the quantities of reactants in terms of gram-equivalents. One atom of iron releases 2 electrons if oxidized to the iron(II) or Fe^{+2}, state and releases 3 electrons if oxidized to the iron(III), or Fe^{+3}, state. One mole of iron, 55.8 g, gives up 2 times the Avogadro number of electrons when oxidized to the +2 oxidation state. Thus the mass of iron that releases the Avogadro number of electrons in such a reaction is one-half mole; the gram-equivalent being 55.8 g Fe ÷ 2 = 27.9 g Fe. Similarly, the gram-equivalent of iron oxidized to the +3 oxidation state would be 55.8 g Fe ÷ 3 = 18.6 g Fe.

The Fe^{+++} ion in an iron(III) chloride solution is reduced to the +2 oxidation state by the addition of a tin(II) chloride solution, Sn^{++} being the reducing agent. Here 1 mole of Fe^{+++} acquires 1 Avogadro number of electrons in the reduction to Fe^{++}. The gram-equivalent of iron in this reaction is 55.8 g ÷ 1 = 55.8 g. The reducing agent Sn^{++} ions furnishes 2 times the Avogadro number of electrons. The gram-equivalent of tin in this reaction is 118.7 g ÷ 2 = 59.35 g. These relationships are readily apparent from the electronic equations for this oxidation-reduction reaction.

$$2Fe^{+3} + 2e^- \rightarrow 2Fe^{+2}$$

$$Sn^{+2} - 2e \rightarrow Sn^{+4}$$

$$\text{g-eq } Fe^{+++} = \frac{2Fe^{+++}}{e^- \text{ gained}}$$

$$= \frac{2 \times 55.8 \text{ g}}{2} = 55.8 \text{ g}$$

$$\text{g-eq } Sn^{++} = \frac{Sn^{++}}{e^- \text{ lost}}$$

$$= \frac{118.7 \text{ g}}{2} = 59.35 \text{ g}$$

6. Electrochemical reactions. *Electrochemical cells.* Oxidation-reduction reactions involve a transfer of electrons from the substance oxidized to the substance reduced. Such reactions that occur *spontaneously* can be used as a source of electric energy. If the reactants are in contact, the energy released during the electron transfer is in the form of heat. By separating the reactants in an electrolytic solution, the transfer of electrons may take place through a conducting wire connected between them. Such an arrangement is known as an **electrochemical cell**. The flow of electrons through the wire constitutes an electric current.

The dry cell is a common source of electric energy in the laboratory. Small dry cells are familiar as flashlight batteries. A zinc container serves as the negative electrode or *cathode*. A carbon rod serves as the positive electrode or *anode*. The carbon rod is surrounded by a mixture of manganese dioxide and powdered carbon. The electrolyte is a moist paste of ammonium chloride containing some zinc chloride. See Fig. 22-3 which shows these components of the dry cell in a schematic diagram.

When the external circuit is closed, *zinc atoms are oxidized at the cathode,*

$$Zn^0 - 2e^- \rightarrow Zn^{++}$$

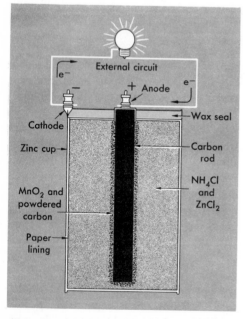

22-3 In dry cells, zinc is oxidized at the cathode and manganese(IV) is reduced to manganese(III) at the anode.

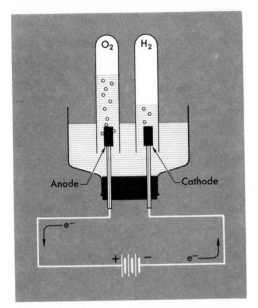

22-4 The electrolysis of water. In electrolytic cells, reduction occurs at the cathode, and oxidation occurs at the anode.

Electrons flow through the external circuit to the carbon anode. Here, if manganese dioxide were not present, hydrogen gas would be formed.

$$2NH_4^+ + 2e^- \rightarrow 2NH_3^0 + H_2 \uparrow$$

However, hydrogen is oxidized to water by the manganese dioxide, and *manganese, rather than hydrogen, is reduced at the anode.*

$$2MnO_2 + 2NH_4^+ + 2e^- \rightarrow$$
$$Mn_2O_3 + 2NH_3 + H_2O$$

The ammonia is taken up by Zn^{++} ions forming complex $Zn(NH_3)_4^{++}$ ions.

Electrolytic cells. Oxidation-reduction reactions *which are not spontaneous* may be forced to occur by means of electric energy supplied externally. The electrolysis of water is such a reaction (see Chapter 13, Section 14). The electrolytic cell for the electrolysis of water consists of two plati-num electrodes immersed in a water solution of an electrolyte such as sulfuric acid. The electrodes may be connected to dry cells, or to any other suitable source which supplies a direct current to force the decomposition reaction. An apparatus for electrolysis of water is shown in Fig. 22-4.

A current of electricity, as produced by a dry cell, is simply a stream of electrons flowing from the negative electrode of the dry cell, through the external circuit, to the positive electrode of the dry cell. The platinum electrode connected to the cathode of the dry cell acquires an excess of electrons and becomes the cathode of the electrolytic cell. The electrode connected to the anode of the dry cell loses electrons to the dry cell and becomes the anode of the electrolytic cell. *Reduction of hydronium ions occurs at the cathode in the electrolytic cell.*

$$2H_3O^+ + 2e^- \rightarrow 2H_2O + H_2^0 \uparrow$$

Oxidation of hydroxide ions takes place at the anode.

$$4OH^- - 4e^- \rightarrow 2H_2O + O_2^0 \uparrow$$

Electrolytic cells may be constructed to permit the *electroplating* of certain metals and other substances that conduct electricity. Ions of metals below hydrogen in the electrochemical series of Section 4 are readily reduced at the cathode of an *electroplating cell*. The atoms of the metal thus formed deposit as a smooth plate on the surface of the cathode.

An electroplating cell consists of a solution of a salt of the plating metal, an object to be plated (the cathode), and a piece of the plating metal (the anode). A silver-plating cell consists essentially of a solution of a soluble silver salt, a silver anode, and a cathode of the object to be plated. The silver anode is connected to the positive electrode of a battery or other source of direct current. The object to be plated

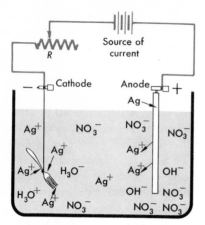

22-5 An electrolytic cell used for silver plating.

is connected to the negative electrode. *Silver ions are reduced at the cathode* of the cell when electrons flow through the circuit.

$$Ag^+ + e^- \rightarrow Ag^0$$

Silver atoms are oxidized at the anode.

$$Ag^0 - e^- \rightarrow Ag^+$$

Silver ions are removed from the solution at the cathode, being deposited as metallic silver. Metallic silver is removed from the anode as ions to maintain the Ag^+ ion concentration of the solution. Thus, in effect, silver is transferred from anode to cathode of the cell during electrolytic action.

In our discussions of electrochemical and electrolytic cells we have identified the electrodes on the basis of their *state of charge*, the negative electrode being the cathode and the positive electrode the anode. This usage is consistent with modern definitions of these electrodes in physics and electronics. Here the *electron-rich electrode defines the cathode* and the *electron-poor electrode defines the anode* in any system of which they are a part.

An older scheme for naming electrodes, still much used in electrochemistry, defines

the electrode at which oxidation occurs as the anode and the electrode at which reduction occurs as the cathode. The objection to this system lies in the fact that we must reverse the names of the electrodes with respect to their electric charge when our attention is shifted from electrochemical (spontaneous) to electrolytic (driven) cell reactions.

This electrode nomenclature becomes particularly unsatisfactory when applied to reversible cells like the automobile storage battery. In fact, it is usually abandoned as untenable since each electrode of a reversible cell would have to be both an anode and a cathode. (See the discussion of the storage battery in Section 7.)

By defining the cathode as negative and the anode as positive, we merely need to recognize that the chemical action at the cathode *is one of oxidation in electrochemical (spontaneous) cells* and *one of reduction in electrolytic (driven) cells.* Similarly, the chemical action at the anode *is one of reduction in electrochemical cells* and *one of oxidation in electrolytic cells.*

7. Lead storage battery. The basic unit of the lead storage battery is a lead(IV) oxide-lead-sulfuric acid cell. The standard twelve-volt automobile battery consists of six of these cells connected in series. As the name implies, the *storage* battery is a *storehouse* of energy. When the battery is charged, electric energy from an external source is converted to chemical energy by an oxidation-reduction reaction in which each cell acts as an *electrolytic* cell. While the battery is being discharged, the reverse oxidation-reduction reaction occurs. Chemical energy at the battery is converted to electric energy and the cells act as *electrochemical* cells.

A fully-charged lead storage cell consists of an anode of lead(IV) oxide, a cathode of spongy lead, and an electrolyte of moderately dilute sulfuric acid. During the

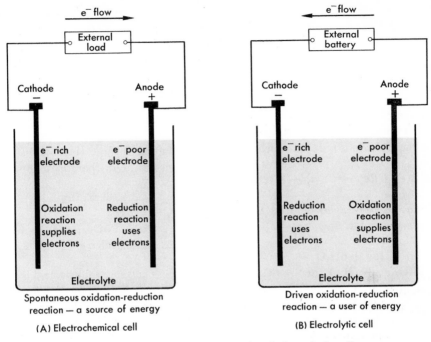

e⁻ flow →

External load

Cathode − | Anode +

e⁻ rich electrode | e⁻ poor electrode

Oxidation reaction supplies electrons | Reduction reaction uses electrons

Electrolyte

Spontaneous oxidation-reduction reaction — a source of energy

(A) Electrochemical cell

← **e⁻ flow**

External battery

Cathode − | Anode +

e⁻ rich electrode | e⁻ poor electrode

Reduction reaction uses electrons | Oxidation reaction supplies electrons

Electrolyte

Driven oxidation-reduction reaction — a user of energy

(B) Electrolytic cell

22-6   A comparison of electrochemical and electrolytic cells.

discharging cycle, the lead at the cathode is oxidized to Pb^{++} ions. Lead(II) sulfate, $PbSO_4$, is formed as a precipitate on the cathode:

$$\mathbf{Pb^0 - 2e^- \rightarrow Pb^{++}}$$

$$\mathbf{Pb^{++} + SO_4^= \rightarrow PbSO_4}$$

This oxidation may be summarized:

$$\mathbf{Pb(s) - 2e^- + SO_4^{=}(aq) \rightarrow PbSO_4(s)}$$

At the anode, H_3O^+ ions may be reduced and may then, in turn, reduce the PbO_2 to PbO forming water in the process. Reaction with sulfuric acid will then produce lead(II) sulfate and water. Lead(II) sulfate precipitates on the anode.

$$\mathbf{2H_3O^+ + 2e^- \rightarrow 2H_2O + 2H^0}$$

$$\mathbf{2H^0 + PbO_2 \rightarrow PbO + H_2O}$$

$$\mathbf{PbO + 2H_3O^+ + SO_4^= \rightarrow PbSO_4 + 3H_2O}$$

The anode reduction is not fully understood, so the above reactions may be an oversimplification of the actual reaction mechanism. The action may be summarized in the following equation

$$\mathbf{4H_3O^+(aq) + 2e^- + PbO_2(s) + SO_4^{=}(aq) \rightarrow}$$
$$\mathbf{PbSO_4(s) + 6H_2O}$$

The overall oxidation-reduction reaction of the cell during discharge is shown in the equations at the top of page 390.

During the discharging process, electrons released by oxidation at the cathode flow through the external circuit of the battery to the anode, where the reduction occurs. This constitutes an electric current capable of delivering energy to devices in this circuit.

In the discharged condition, both electrodes consist of lead(II) sulfate, and the electrolyte is more dilute. The cell may be made electrochemically active again by recharging. This is accomplished by supplying a direct current from an external

(cathode) $Pb - 2e^- + SO_4^= \rightarrow PbSO_4$
(anode) $4H_3O^+ + 2e^- + PbO_2 + SO_4^= \rightarrow PbSO_4 + 6H_2O$
(cell) $\overline{Pb + PbO_2 + 4H_3O^+ + 2SO_4^= \rightarrow 2PbSO_4 + 6H_2O}$

source in the opposite direction to the discharging current. The action at each electrode is reversed and the cell is restored to its charged condition.

During the *charging cycle*, lead(II) sulfate at the cathode is reduced to lead.

$$PbSO_4(s) + 2e^- \rightarrow Pb(s) + SO_4^=(aq)$$

Simultaneously at the anode, lead(II) sulfate is oxidized forming lead(IV) oxide.

$$PbSO_4(s) - 2e^- + 6H_2O \rightarrow$$
$$PbO_2(s) + 4H_3O^+(aq) + SO_4^=(aq)$$

The overall oxidation-reduction reaction of the lead storage cell during the charging cycle is shown in the series of equations at the top of the opposite page.

During the charging process, electrons are supplied to the cathode, and are removed from the anode, by the external source of electric energy. Electric energy is thus stored as chemical energy in the cell through the mechanism of the oxidation-reduction action. Observe that the last equation is the reverse of the overall equation for the discharging action.

$$\xrightarrow{\hspace{1cm}\text{charging}\hspace{1cm}}$$
$$2PbSO_4 + 6H_2O \rightleftarrows$$
$$Pb + PbO_2 + 4H_3O^+ + 2SO_4^=$$
$$\xleftarrow{\hspace{1cm}\text{discharging}\hspace{1cm}}$$

During charging, sulfuric acid is formed and water is decomposed. The specific gravity of the acid solution increases during charging, up to about 1.300 for a fully-charged cell. While the cell is discharging, sulfuric acid is used up and water is formed. Thus, the specific gravity of the acid is lowered during discharge. In a com-

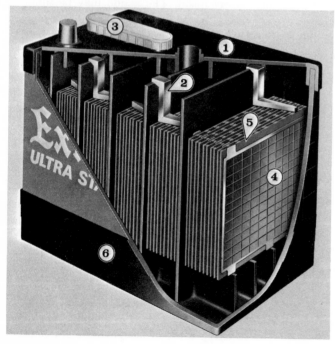

22-7   A cutaway view of an automobile storage battery. (1) Cover (2) Intercell connector (3) Vent plugs (4) Plates (5) Insulation (6) Container. (Exide)

(**cathode**)	$PbSO_4 + 2e^- \rightarrow Pb + SO_4^=$
(**anode**)	$PbSO_4 + 6H_2O - 2e^- \rightarrow PbO_2 + 4H_3O^+ + SO_4^=$
(**cell**)	$2PbSO_4 + 6H_2O \rightarrow Pb + PbO_2 + 4H_3O^+ + 2SO_4^=$

pletely discharged cell the specific gravity of the acid is about 1.100.

The principal use of the storage battery is in the automobile. It provides ignition, and operates the headlights, starting motor, and other electric equipment. A gen-erator connected with the engine charges the battery while the automobile is in op-eration. Storage batteries are also used for other purposes that require a portable source of energy, or where a source of energy is required in emergencies.

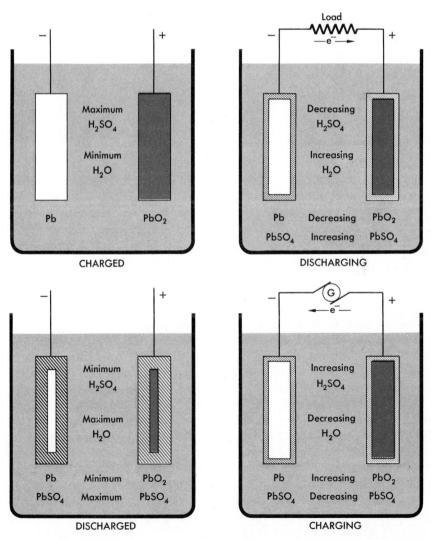

22-8 Diagrams illustrating the essential action in a storage cell.

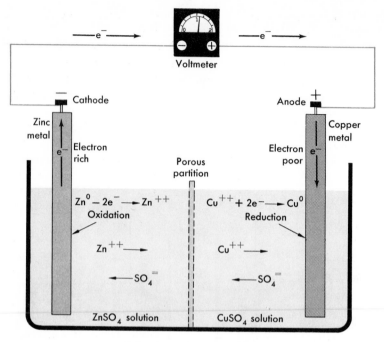

22-9 A Zn-Cu voltaic cell.

▶ **8. Oxidation potentials.** Oxidation-reduction systems are the result of two distinct reactions, oxidation in which electrons are supplied to the system, and reduction in which electrons are acquired from the system. In electrochemical cells, these reactions take place at the separate electrodes and the oxidation-reduction reaction may be thought of as the sum of these two separate reactions. As already stated, oxidation occurs at the cathode and reduction occurs at the anode in electrochemical cells.

As the cell reaction proceeds, a difference in electric potential develops between the electrodes. This potential difference can be measured by a voltmeter connected across the two electrodes. We may think of the potential difference as the sum of the potentials produced at the cathode and at the anode.

Let us consider the electrochemical cell shown in Fig. 22-9. A strip of zinc is placed

in a solution of $ZnSO_4$ and a strip of copper is placed in a solution of $CuSO_4$. The two solutions are separated by a porous partition which permits ions to pass but prevents gross mixing of the solutions. Such an arrangement is called a voltaic cell. It is capable of generating a small electron current in an external circuit connected between the electrodes.

The two electrode reactions are such that the zinc electrode acquires a negative charge with respect to the copper. The copper electrode then becomes positively charged with respect to the zinc. This shows that the zinc metal has a stronger tendency to enter the solution as ions than the copper. Zinc is said to be more active, or more easily oxidized, than copper.

The reaction at the surface of the zinc electrode is an oxidation as shown by the following equation:

$$\mathbf{Zn(s) - 2e^- \rightarrow Zn^{++}(aq)}$$

The reaction at the surface of the copper electrode is a reduction:

$$Cu^{++}(aq) + 2e^- \rightarrow Cu(s)$$

As Zn^{++} ions are formed, electrons accumulate on the zinc electrode imparting to it a negative charge. Electrons migrate through the external circuit toward the copper electrode. Here they restore the deficiency caused by removal of electrons by Cu^{++} ions undergoing reduction to metallic copper. Thus, in effect, electrons are transferred from Zn^0 atoms through the external circuit to Cu^{++} ions. The overall reaction can be written as

$$Zn^0 + Cu^{++} \rightarrow Zn^{++} + Cu^0$$

A voltmeter connected across the Cu-Zn voltaic cell will measure a potential difference of approximately 1.1 volts when the solution concentrations of Zn^{++} and Cu^{++} are each 1 M.

The portion of the voltaic cell consisting of a metal electrode in contact with its solution is called a *half-cell*. The reaction taking place at each electrode is called the *half-reaction*.

The potential difference between an electrode and its solution in a half-reaction is known as its **oxidation potential.** The sum of the oxidation potentials for the two half-reactions is approximately equal to the potential difference measured across the complete voltaic cell.

While the potential difference across a voltaic cell is easily measured, there is no way to measure an individual electrode potential. The oxidation potentials of half-reactions can be compared by using a *standard half-cell.* By assigning an arbitrary potential to the standard electrode, a specific potential can be assigned to the

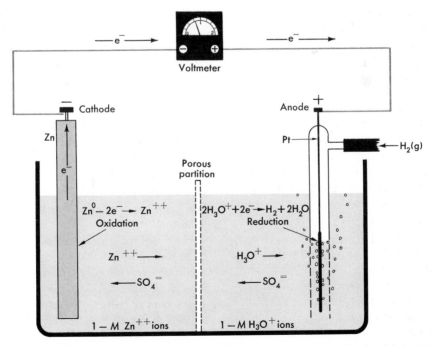

22-10   The oxidation potential of the zinc half-cell is measured by coupling it with a standard hydrogen electrode.

other electrode making up the complete cell.

Chemists use a *hydrogen electrode* immersed in a molar solution of H_3O^+ ions as a standard half-cell. (See Fig. 15-5.) It consists of a platinum electrode dipping in an acid solution of $1-M$ concentration and surrounded by hydrogen gas at 1 atmosphere pressure. *This standard hydrogen electrode is assigned an oxidation potential of zero.* The half-cell reaction is

$$H_2(g) + 2H_2O(l) \rightleftarrows 2H_3O^+(aq) + 2e^-$$

Since the potential of the hydrogen electrode is arbitrarily taken as zero, the potential difference across the whole cell is attributed entirely to whatever electrode makes up the other half-cell.

Suppose we construct a complete cell consisting of a zinc half-cell and a standard hydrogen half-cell as shown in Fig. 22-10. The potential difference E across the cell measures the oxidation potential of the zinc electrode with respect to the hydrogen electrode (the zero reference electrode) and is found to be +0.76 volt. The positive sign indicates that *zinc is more readily oxidized than hydrogen.* The half-reaction for zinc is

$$Zn \rightarrow Zn^{++} + 2e^- \quad E = +0.76\ v$$

A copper half-cell coupled with the standard hydrogen electrode gives a potential difference measurement of −0.43 volt, indicating that *copper is less readily oxidized than hydrogen.* The half-reaction for copper may be written as an oxidation reaction:

$$Cu \rightarrow Cu^{++} + 2e^- \quad E = -0.34\ v$$

From these measurements, we observe that zinc has a greater tendency to give off electrons than hydrogen by 0.76 volt while hydrogen has a greater tendency to

STANDARD OXIDATION POTENTIALS

Half-reaction	Electrode potential
$Li \rightleftarrows Li^+ + e^-$	+3.02 v
$K \rightleftarrows K^+ + e^-$	+2.92 v
$Ba \rightleftarrows Ba^{++} + 2e^-$	+2.90 v
$Ca \rightleftarrows Ca^{++} + 2e^-$	+2.87 v
$Na \rightleftarrows Na^+ + e^-$	+2.71 v
$Mg \rightleftarrows Mg^{++} + 2e^-$	+2.37 v
$Al \rightleftarrows Al^{+++} + 3e^-$	+1.67 v
$Zn \rightleftarrows Zn^{++} + 2e^-$	+0.76 v
$Cr \rightleftarrows Cr^{+++} + 3e^-$	+0.74 v
$S^= \rightleftarrows S + 2e^-$	+0.51 v
$Fe \rightleftarrows Fe^{++} + 2e^-$	+0.44 v
$Cd \rightleftarrows Cd^{++} + 2e^-$	+0.40 v
$Co \rightleftarrows Co^{++} + 2e^-$	+0.28 v
$Ni \rightleftarrows Ni^{++} + 2e^-$	+0.24 v
$Sn \rightleftarrows Sn^{++} + 2e^-$	+0.15 v
$Pb \rightleftarrows Pb^{++} + 2e^-$	+0.13 v
$H_2 + 2H_2O \rightleftarrows 2H_3O^+ + 2e^-$	0.00 v
$H_2S + 2H_2O \rightleftarrows S + 2H_3O^+ + 2e^-$	−0.14 v
$Cu^+ \rightleftarrows Cu^{++} + e^-$	−0.17 v
$Cu \rightleftarrows Cu^{++} + 2e^-$	−0.34 v
$2I^- \rightleftarrows I_2 + 2e^-$	−0.55 v
$MnO_4^= \rightleftarrows MnO_4^- + e^-$	−0.56 v
$Fe^{++} \rightleftarrows Fe^{+++} + e^-$	−0.77 v
$2Hg \rightleftarrows Hg_2^{++} + 2e^-$	−0.79 v
$Ag \rightleftarrows Ag^+ + e^-$	−0.80 v
$Hg \rightleftarrows Hg^{++} + 2e^-$	−0.85 v
$2Br^- \rightleftarrows Br_2 + 2e^-$	−1.07 v
$Mn^{++} + 6H_2O \rightleftarrows$ $MnO_2 + 4H_3O^+ + 2e^-$	−1.23 v
$2Cl^- \rightleftarrows Cl_2 + 2e^-$	−1.36 v
$Au \rightleftarrows Au^{+++} + 3e^-$	−1.48 v
$2F^- \rightleftarrows F_2 + 2e^-$	−2.87 v

give off electrons than copper by 0.34 volt. We can look upon this as indicating that zinc has a greater tendency toward oxidation than copper by 1.10 volts (0.76 v + 0.34 v).

How do the oxidation potentials for these two half-reactions with respect to the hydrogen reference electrode apply to the voltaic cell consisting of a zinc half-cell and a copper half-cell? The potential difference across the whole cell is obtained by adding the oxidation potentials of the two half-reactions (after reversing the equation for the copper half-reaction to show the reduction of the Cu^{++} ions at the anode).

$$Zn^0 \rightarrow Zn^{++} + 2e \qquad E = +0.76 \text{ v}$$
$$\underline{Cu^{++} + 2e^- \rightarrow Cu^0 \qquad E = +0.34 \text{ v}}$$
$$Zn^0 + Cu^{++} \rightarrow Zn^{++} + Cu^0 \quad E = +1.10 \text{ v}$$

The positive sign of the potential difference shows that the reaction proceeds spontaneously to the right as written, with zinc displacing copper.

Half-reactions of some common substances with standard oxidation potentials are listed in the opposite table. All half-reactions are shown as oxidation reactions. Oxidation potentials given apply to half-reactions proceeding in the forward direction shown. When the half-reaction is written in the reverse direction, the sign of the oxidation potential must be reversed. The half-reaction at the top of the list has the greatest tendency to occur in the forward direction. This tendency decreases going down the table. Such a list is often called an *electromotive series* or an *activity series*. Compare this list with the one in Section 4.

REVIEW OUTLINE

Oxidation and reduction processes (1)
    Oxidation states (1)
    Assigning oxidation numbers (1)
    Oxidation number and shared electrons (2)

Balancing oxidation-reduction equations (3)
    Meaning of conservation of electrons (3)
    Meaning of balancing electron shift (3)

Oxidizing and reducing agents (4)
    Characteristics of strong reducing agents (4)
    Characteristics of strong oxidizing agents (4)
    Relative strengths of oxidizing and reducing agents (4)
    Interpretation of relative strengths table (4)
    Determining gram-equivalents in redox reactions (5)

Electrochemical reactions (6)
    Spontaneous reactions (6)
    Applications of electrochemical cells (6)
    Driven reactions (6)
    Applications of electrolytic cells (7)
    The storage battery as a reversible cell (7)
    Reactions of the discharge cycle (7)
    Reactions of the charge cycle (7)

Oxidation potentials (8)
    Half-cell reactions (8)
    Oxidation potentials of half-reactions (8)
    Standard hydrogen reference electrode (8)
    Interpretations of standard oxidation potentials (8)

QUESTIONS

Group A

1. Differentiate between the processes of oxidation and reduction.
2. Why do oxidation and reduction occur simultaneously?
3. Particles which acquire electrons during a chemical action experience what change in oxidation state?
4. Which of the following are oxidation-reduction reactions?

   (a) $2Na + Cl_2 \rightarrow 2NaCl$
   (b) $C + O_2 \rightarrow CO_2$
   (c) $2H_2O \rightleftarrows 2H_2 + O_2$
   (d) $NaCl + AgNO_3 \rightarrow AgCl + NaNO_3$
   (e) $NH_3 + HCl \rightarrow NH_4^+ + Cl^-$
   (f) $2KClO_3 \rightarrow 2KCl + 3O_2$
   (g) $H_2 + Cl_2 \rightarrow 2HCl$
   (h) $2H_2 + O_2 \rightarrow 2H_2O$
   (i) $H_2SO_4 + 2KOH \rightarrow K_2SO_4 + 2H_2O$
   (j) $Zn + CuSO_4 \rightarrow ZnSO_4 + Cu$

5. For each oxidation-reduction reaction in Question 4 identify: (a) the substance oxidized; (b) the substance reduced; (c) the oxidizing agent; and (d) the reducing agent.
6. What is the oxidation number of each element in the following compounds: (a) $CaClO_3$; (b) Na_2HPO_4; (c) K_2SiO_3; (d) H_3PO_3; (e) $Fe(OH)_3$.
7. Assign oxidation numbers to each element in the following compounds: (a) $PbSO_4$; (b) H_2O_2; (c) $K_2Cr_2O_7$; (d) H_2SO_3; (e) $HClO_4$.
8. What constitutes the anode, cathode, and electrolyte of a fully-charged lead storage cell?
▶ 9. Define: (a) oxidation potential, (b) half-reaction, (c) half-cell.
▶ 10. Why is the standard hydrogen electrode assigned an oxidation potential of 0.00 volt?

Group B

11. What are the six steps involved in balancing oxidation-reduction equations? List them in the proper sequence.
12. Carry out the first four steps called for in Question 11 for the following:

    (a) Zinc + hydrochloric acid → zinc chloride + hydrogen.
    (b) Iron + copper(II) sulfate → iron(II) sulfate + copper.
    (c) Copper + sulfuric acid → copper(II) sulfate + sulfur dioxide + water.
    (d) Hydrochloric acid + potassium permanganate → manganese(II) chloride + potassium chloride + chlorine + water.
    (e) Bromine + water → hydrobromic acid + hypobromous acid.

13. The oxidation-reduction reaction between copper and *concentrated* nitric acid yields the following products: copper(II) nitrate, water, and nitrogen dioxide. Write the balanced equation.

14. The reaction between copper and *dilute* nitric acid yields the following products: copper(II) nitrate, water, and nitrogen monoxide. Write the balanced equation.

15. Referring to the table of Section 4, the active metals down to magnesium replace hydrogen from water. Magnesium and succeeding metals replace hydrogen from steam. Metals near the bottom of the list will not replace hydrogen from steam. How does this table help to explain this behavior?

16. Balance the oxidation-reduction equation: $K_2Cr_2O_7 + HCl \rightarrow KCl + CrCl_3 + H_2O + Cl_2$.

▶ 17. Using information from the table of Standard Oxidation Potentials in Section 8, write the equations for the half-reactions of a voltaic cell having Cu and Ag electrodes.

▶ 18. (*a*) Determine the potential difference across the voltaic cell of Question 17. (*b*) Write the equation for the overall reaction of the cell in the direction that it proceeds spontaneously.

Chapter Twenty-three

ELEMENTS OF PERIOD THREE

1. General appearance. In Chapter 5 we recognized that the chemical elements could be arranged according to increasing atomic number in a Periodic Table. In such a table, elements of a given column have similar chemical properties because of their similar outer electron arrangements. In going across a row of a Periodic Table, the properties of the elements vary considerably. The first element is a highly reactive metal. Then come other metals of decreasing activity, followed by metalloids, and then nonmetals of increasing activity. The last element in a row is a noble gas.

In this chapter we shall consider the elements in Period Three to illustrate the variation in properties which occurs as one goes across the table. In subsequent chapters, we shall be considering elements mainly within their family relationships.

Period Three is a short period containing only eight elements. The first three elements, sodium, magnesium, and aluminum, are all silvery metals with charac-

teristic metallic luster. Sodium is soft enough to be cut easily. Magnesium and aluminum are somewhat harder, but may be readily scratched with a knife. Silicon, the fourth element, is harder. It is gray, with a metallic luster. However, since silicon has properties intermediate between those of metals and nonmetals, it is classed as a metalloid. Phosphorus, the fifth element, exists commonly either as a reactive pale waxy solid, or as a more stable red powder. Phosphorus has no metallic properties—it is a nonmetal. The next two elements, sulfur and chlorine, are also nonmetals. Sulfur is a brittle yellow solid, and chlorine is a yellow-green gas. Argon, the noble gas of this period, is colorless.

2. Structure and physical properties. The following table gives melting point, boiling point, density, and color data for the elements of Period Three.

Since sodium, magnesium, and aluminum are all metals, they have certain physical properties in common. Each is a good conductor of heat and electricity, has

PHYSICAL PROPERTIES OF ELEMENTS OF PERIOD THREE

Element	Melting Point (°C)	Boiling Point (°C)	Density	Color
sodium	97.5	880	0.97 g/cm³	silver
magnesium	651	1107	1.74 g/cm³	silver
aluminum	659.7	2450	2.70 g/cm³	silver
silicon	1414	2355	2.33 g/cm³	silver-gray
phosphorus	44.1(wh)	280.5	1.82 g/cm³	waxy-white
sulfur	119	444.6	2.06 g/cm³	yellow
chlorine	− 102	− 34.5	3.21 g/l	yellow-green
argon	− 184	− 181	1.78 g/l	colorless

a silvery luster, and is ductile and malleable. Sodium and aluminum form cubic crystals, while those of magnesium are hexagonal. In each, the crystal lattice is made up of metallic ions permeated by an electron gas composed of the valence electrons. The good thermal and electric conductivity of these metals is due to the highly mobile character of these free electrons. The silvery luster of these metals can be attributed to the free electrons in the crystal surfaces. When light strikes these surfaces, the valence electrons absorb energy and are set into vibratory motions that re-radiate the energy in all directions as light. The binding force in metallic crystal lattices is the attraction between the positive ions and the negative electron gas permeating the lattice. This force is essentially uniform in all directions. Its magnitude explains the degree of hardness, ductility, and malleability of these metals. Its magnitude is further indicated by the melting and boiling points of these metals. The forces holding sodium ions in fixed positions in the crystal lattice are weaker than those of magnesium and aluminum. This accounts for its lower melting point and its softness. The forces holding the mobile ions together in the liquid state are evidently quite high, as shown by the rather wide temperature range over which these metals are liquids. The increase in density is explained by the progressively heavier, yet smaller atoms, as we go from sodium, to magnesium, to aluminum. Since the atoms are smaller they may be packed closer and closer together.

Silicon exists as macromolecules having cubic crystal structure. The pattern of atomic arrangement in the crystal is identical with diamond (see Fig. 16-4), except that the internuclear distance is greater, 2.35 Å in silicon compared to 1.54 Å in diamond. You recall that the electron configuration of carbon is $1s^22s^22p^2$ and that hybridization produces four equivalent sp^3 orbitals. Consequently carbon atoms form four equivalent covalent bonds in the diamond structure. The electron configuration of silicon is analogous; $1s^22s^22p^63s^23p^2$. In similar fashion hybridization occurs in the third energy level, forming four equivalent sp^3 orbitals, and hence four equivalent covalent bonds. The change from metallic to macromolecular structure between aluminum and silicon accounts for the great difference in melting points between these two consecutive elements. The less compact structure accounts for the decrease in density, even though silicon atoms are smaller and heavier than aluminum atoms. Unlike diamond, some of the valence electrons in silicon crystals are free to move, giving silicon a low electric conductivity. Such substances with low electric conductivity are called *semiconductors*.

Phosphorus has the electron configuration $1s^22s^22p^63s^23p^3$. With its three half-filled $3p$ orbitals, a phosphorus atom is capable of forming three covalent bonds. Elementary yellow phosphorus exists as discrete P_4 molecules, each atom of which forms three covalent bonds. See Fig. 23-1. The low melting and boiling points of yellow phosphorus together with its brittleness indicates that there are only weak van der Waals forces between the P_4 molecules. With no free electrons, yellow phosphorus has no luster, is a poor conductor of heat, and is a nonconductor of electricity. These are all typical properties of nonmetals.

The electron configuration of sulfur is $1s^22s^22p^63s^23p^4$. Hence sulfur atoms have two half-filled $3p$ orbitals and should form two covalent bonds. This they do in elementary sulfur, but the molecule consists of eight atoms joined together in a puckered ring, as shown in Fig. 23-2. The relatively low melting point and brittleness of sulfur may be attributed to the weak van der Waals forces between the S_8 molecules. Sulfur has the common nonmetallic properties: no luster, poor thermal conductivity, and nonconduction of electricity.

We have already seen (Chapter 6) that chlorine exists as diatomic molecules, Cl_2, with a single covalent bond joining the two atoms. The van der Waals forces between chlorine molecules are very weak, hence

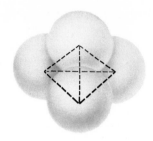

23-1 The structure of P_4 molecules of phosphorus.

the element is a gas at room temperature.

Argon exists as single atoms since it has no half-filled orbitals to use in bond formation. The van der Waals forces between argon atoms are very weak indeed. This is evident from the very low boiling point of this gas.

3. Electron configurations, ionization energies, and oxidation states. The table below lists the electron configuration, ionization energy, oxidation states, and atomic radius for each of the Period Three elements.

In our earlier discussion of ionization energy (Chapter 5), it was pointed out that as one goes across a period, the ionization energy generally increases because of the increasing nuclear charge. However, decreases are noted in Period Three when the first electron enters the $3p$ sublevel (at aluminum), and when pairing begins to occur in the $3p$ sublevel (at sulfur). These

ATOMIC STRUCTURE AND RELATED PROPERTIES OF ELEMENTS OF PERIOD THREE

Element	Electron Configuration	Ionization Energy (ev)	Principal Oxidation States	Atomic Radius (Å)
sodium	$1s^22s^22p^63s^1$	5.15	+1	1.57
magnesium	$1s^22s^22p^63s^2$	7.64	+2	1.36
aluminum	$1s^22s^22p^63s^23p^1$	5.96	+3	1.25
silicon	$1s^22s^22p^63s^23p^2$	8.15	+4	1.17
phosphorus	$1s^22s^22p^63s^23p^3$	11.0	+3, +5	1.10
sulfur	$1s^22s^22p^63s^23p^4$	10.36	−2, +4, +6	1.04
chlorine	$1s^22s^22p^63s^23p^5$	13.01	−1, +5, +7	0.99
argon	$1s^22s^22p^63s^23p^6$	15.76	0	1.54

decreases are to be expected. The decrease between magnesium and aluminum occurs because the outer $3p$ sublevel electron in aluminum has higher energy than an outer $3s$ sublevel electron in magnesium and thus requires less energy to remove from the atom. The decrease between phosphorus and sulfur occurs because a half-filled $3p$ sublevel with three singly occupied orbitals is a more stable electron configuration (has lower energy) than a $3p$ sublevel with one filled and two singly occupied orbitals.

The covalent radius decreases gradually across the period with one exception. There is a significant increase in radius upon completion of the octet in the element argon. This general decrease is due to electrons entering the same energy level at about the same distance from the nucleus. Yet the nuclear charge becomes successively greater and tends to pull the electrons closer to the nucleus. The relationship between atomic radius and ionic radius for sodium, magnesium, aluminum, sulfur, and chlorine was described in Chapter 6, Section 8.

The oxidation states of sodium, $+1$, magnesium, $+2$, and aluminum, $+3$, have already been explained. Sodium has one electron which may be removed at low energy. Magnesium has two, and aluminum three such electrons. (See Chapter 5, Section 9.) The $+4$ oxidation state of silicon is explained by its formation of four covalent bonds with sp^3 hybridization. Phosphorus, which has an electron-dot symbol $\cdot \overset{\cdot}{P} :$ may add three electrons, forming the $P^{\equiv}$ ion, as in the compounds of phosphorus known as phosphides. It is also possible for this atom to share three or five electrons in forming covalent bonds, giving it oxidation numbers of $+3$ or $+5$.

The electron-dot symbol of sulfur is $\cdot \overset{\cdot\cdot}{\underset{\cdot}{S}} :$. Sulfur may add two electrons, forming

the sulfide ion, $S^=$, oxidation number -2. Sulfur may also share two, four, or six electrons, giving oxidation states of $+2$, $+4$, or $+6$.

Chlorine, with the electron-dot symbol $: \overset{\cdot\cdot}{Cl} :$, commonly adds one electron, forming the chloride ion. Here chlorine has the oxidation number -1. However, it is also possible for chlorine to share 1, 3, 5, or all 7 electrons in covalent bonding. In such cases the oxidation numbers are $+1$, $+3$, $+5$, or $+7$.

Argon, since this noble gas forms no compounds, always has an oxidation number of zero.

4. Properties of oxides of Period Three elements. The elements of Period Three form a great variety of compounds with oxygen. Some such as sodium, phosphorus, sulfur, and chlorine form two or more oxides. For our purpose it will be sufficient to describe the properties of only one oxide per element.

Sodium oxide, Na_2O, and magnesium oxide, MgO, are white solids. The reaction of sodium with oxygen usually yields sodium peroxide, Na_2O_2. However, some sodium oxide may be prepared by heating sodium at about $180°$ C in a limited amount of dry oxygen. Magnesium oxide is produced by burning magnesium in pure oxygen. Both sodium oxide and magnesium oxide are ionic compounds. Sodium

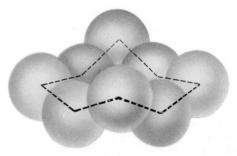

23-2 The structure of S_8 molecules of sulfur.

OXIDES OF PERIOD THREE ELEMENTS

Oxide	Melting Point (°C)	Boiling Point (°C)	Type of Compound	Nature of Reaction with Water
Na_2O	subl. 1275		ionic	Forms OH^-
MgO	2800	3600	ionic	Forms OH^-
Al_2O_3	2050	2250	ionic	None; hydroxide is amphiprotic
SiO_2	1710	2230	macromolecular	None
P_4O_{10}	subl. 347		molecular	Forms H_3O^+
SO_2	−75	−10.	molecular	Forms H_3O^+
Cl_2O	−20	4	molecular	Forms H_3O^+

oxide readily dissolves in water, forming a basic solution which contains Na^+ and OH^- ions.

$$Na_2O + H_2O \rightarrow 2Na^+ + 2OH^-$$

Magnesium oxide is only slightly soluble in water, but it, too, forms a basic solution.

$$MgO + H_2O \rightarrow Mg^{++} + 2OH^-$$

Aluminum oxide, Al_2O_3, is a white ionic compound which is usually prepared by heating aluminum hydroxide or the hydrated oxides of aluminum. Aluminum oxide is virtually insoluble in water, so this dehydration reaction is not reversible. Aluminum hydroxide, a white, insoluble, gelatinous substance, must be prepared indirectly from aluminum oxide. Aluminum hydroxide is an amphiprotic substance, reacting as a base in the presence of hydronium ion, and as an acid in the presence of hydroxide ion.

$$Al(OH)_3 + 3H_3O^+ \rightarrow Al(H_2O)_6^{+++}$$
$$Al(OH)_3 + 3OH^- \rightarrow AlO_3^{\equiv} + 3H_2O$$

Silicon dioxide, SiO_2, is widely distributed in nature as quartz. White sand is principally silicon dioxide. Silicon dioxide is macromolecular in structure. It consists of silicon atoms tetrahedrally bonded to four oxygen atoms, each of which is, in turn, bonded to another silicon atom tetrahedrally bonded to four oxygen atoms. This structure extends indefinitely. It is believed that all the silicon-oxygen bond distances are equal in length. The silicon-oxygen bonds are further believed to be covalent, but with an appreciable degree of ionic character.

Silicon dioxide is practically insoluble in water. It acts as an acid with hot, concentrated solutions containing hydroxide ion.

$$SiO_2 + 4OH^- \rightarrow SiO_4^{-4} + 2H_2O$$

Silicon dioxide does not react with common acids, but acts as a base with hydrofluoric acid.

$$SiO_2 + 4HF \rightarrow SiF_4 + 2H_2O$$

In an abundant supply of oxygen, phosphorus burns to form diphosphorus pentoxide, P_4O_{10}. (The formula given is believed to be the correct molecular formula. The name is that of the corresponding empirical formula.) P_4O_{10} is a white molecular solid. It reacts rapidly with water, forming a solution containing phosphoric acid, H_3PO_4.

$$P_4O_{10} + 10H_2O \rightarrow 4H_3O^+ + 4H_2PO_4^-$$

Phosphoric acid is a moderately strong acid. The equilibrium constant for its first ionization is of the order of 10^{-2}.

Sulfur burns in air or oxygen to form sulfur dioxide, SO_2. This compound is molecular, and at room temperature is a colorless gas with a choking odor. Sulfur dioxide readily dissolves in and reacts with water, forming a solution containing sulfurous acid, H_2SO_3.

$$SO_2 + 2H_2O \rightarrow H_3O^+ + HSO_3^-$$

This acid is also moderately strong. The equilibrium constant for its first ionization is of the order of 10^{-2}.

Dichlorine monoxide, Cl_2O, is prepared by the moderate oxidation of chlorine with mercury(II) oxide.

$$2Cl_2 + HgO \rightarrow HgCl_2 + Cl_2O$$

This compound is an unstable yellow gas which reacts with water to give a solution containing hypochlorous acid, HClO.

$$Cl_2O + 2H_2O \rightarrow 2HClO$$
$$2HClO + 2H_2O \rightleftharpoons 2H_3O^+ + 2ClO^-$$

Hypochlorous acid is a very weak acid, which exists only in water solution. Its ionization constant is of the order of 10^{-8}.

5. **Properties of the binary hydrogen compounds of Period Three elements.** Each of the elements of Period Three forms at least one binary compound with hydrogen. Silicon, phosphorus, and sulfur each form two or more binary hydrogen compounds. However, as with the oxides, we shall describe the properties of only one binary hydrogen compound of each of the Period Three elements.

Sodium hydride, NaH, is formed by direct union of sodium and hydrogen at moderately elevated temperatures. It is an ionic compound, crystallizing in the cubic system like sodium chloride, but with hydride ion, H^-, as the negative ion. It reacts vigorously with water, yielding hydrogen and hydroxide ion.

$$NaH + H_2O \rightarrow H_2 + Na^+ + OH^-$$

Magnesium hydride, MgH_2, a less stable compound than sodium hydride, was first prepared about 1950. It may be made by direct union by heating the elements under high pressure in the presence of magnesium iodide. Complex indirect methods are more satisfactory, however. Magnesium hydride is a nonvolatile, colorless solid which reacts violently with water.

$$MgH_2 + 2H_2O \rightarrow Mg(OH)_2 + 2H_2$$

In a vacuum magnesium hydride is stable to about 300° C. Above this temperature it decomposes into its constituent elements. The structure of magnesium hydride is believed to be polymeric, with MgH_2 units bonded together as $(MgH_2)_x$ in which x is unknown.

Aluminum hydride, known only since the 1940's, may be made by the action of lithium hydride on aluminum chloride in ether solution.

$$3LiH + AlCl_3 \xrightarrow[\text{solution)}]{\text{(ether}} AlH_3 + 3LiCl$$

Aluminum hydride is a white amorphous solid of unknown (probably highly polymerized) structure, $(AlH_3)_x$. It is stable in a vacuum up to 100° C. At higher temperatures it decomposes into aluminum and hydrogen.

Monosilane, SiH_4, is a colorless, stable, but readily flammable gas consisting of nonpolar covalent molecules. It, along with other silicon hydrides, is produced when magnesium silicide is treated with dilute hydrochloric acid.

$$Mg_2Si + 4H_3O^+ \rightarrow$$
$$2Mg^{++} + SiH_4 \uparrow + 4H_2O$$

Monosilane reacts very readily with water to yield hydrogen and silicon dioxide.

HYDRIDES OF PERIOD THREE ELEMENTS

Hydride	Melting Point (°C)	Boiling Point (°C)	Type of Compound	Nature of Reaction with Water
NaH	d. 800		ionic	Forms OH^- + H_2
$(MgH_2)_x$	d. 300		polymeric	Forms OH^- + H_2
$(AlH_3)_x$	d. 100		polymeric	
SiH_4	−185	−112	molecular	Forms SiO_2 + H_2
PH_3	−134	−88	molecular	None
H_2S	−83	−62	molecular	Forms H_3O^+
HCl	−112	−84	molecular	Forms H_3O^+

$$SiH_4 + 2H_2O \rightarrow SiO_2 + 4H_2$$

Other known silicon hydrides are: Si_2H_6, Si_3H_8, Si_4H_{10}, Si_5H_{12}, and Si_6H_{14}. Notice the similarity of these formulas to those of the alkanes. These compounds are much more reactive than the alkanes because silicon-silicon bonds and silicon-hydrogen bonds are weaker than the corresponding carbon-carbon and carbon-hydrogen bonds in the alkanes.

Phosphine, PH_3, one of two or three known binary phosphorus-hydrogen compounds, is a molecular substance in which the atoms are covalently bonded in an ammonia-type structure. At room temperature it is a colorless gas with an unpleasant odor resembling that of rotten fish. Phosphine is very poisonous and flammable. The simplest method of preparing phosphine is by treating calcium phosphide with water.

$$Ca_3P_2 + 6H_2O \rightarrow$$
$$3Ca^{++} + 6OH^- + 2PH_3 \uparrow$$

Phosphine dissolves in water producing a solution which is essentially neutral.

Hydrogen sulfide, H_2S, is a colorless, foul-smelling and very poisonous gas, with an odor resembling decaying eggs. It is a molecular compound, with slightly polar covalent bonding within the molecule. Hydrogen sulfide is usually prepared in the laboratory by the action of dilute hydrochloric acid on iron(II) sulfide.

$$FeS + 2H_3O^+ \rightarrow Fe^{++} + 2H_2O + H_2S \uparrow$$

Hydrogen sulfide is flammable. The products of combustion are water vapor and sulfur or sulfur dioxide, depending on the combustion conditions.

Hydrogen sulfide dissolves in and reacts with water, forming a weakly acid solution of hydrosulfuric acid. The first ionization constant of hydrosulfuric acid is of the order of 10^{-7}.

$$H_2S + H_2O \rightleftarrows H_3O^+ + HS^-$$

The binary hydrogen compound of chlorine is the colorless, sharp-odored, poisonous gas, hydrogen chloride, HCl. Hydrogen chloride consists of highly polar covalent molecules. Hydrogen chloride may be prepared by the direct combination of its elements, or by heating sodium chloride with moderately concentrated sulfuric acid.

$$H_2 + Cl_2 \rightarrow 2HCl \uparrow$$
$$NaCl + H_2SO_4 \rightarrow HCl \uparrow + NaHSO_4$$

Hydrogen chloride is very soluble in water. It is completely ionized by the water, yielding hydronium ions and chloride ions.

$$HCl + H_2O \rightarrow H_3O^+ + Cl^-$$

This solution, called hydrochloric acid, is a strong acid.

REVIEW OUTLINE

General appearance of Period Three elements (1)
    Metal—metalloid—nonmetal—noble gas (1)

Physical properties (2)
    Physical state (2)
    Color (2)
    Crystalline or molecular structure (2)
    Binding forces (2)
    Density (2)
    Hardness (2)
    Conductivity of heat and electricity (2)
    Ductility (2)
    Malleability (2)

Chemical properties (3)
    Electron configuration (3)
    Ionization energy (3)
    Oxidation states (3)
    Atomic radius (3)

Properties of oxides of Period Three elements (4)
    Preparation of oxide (4)
    Structure of oxide (4)
    Reaction of oxide with water (4)

Properties of hydrides (5)
    Preparation of hydride (5)
    Structure of hydride (5)
    Reaction of hydride with water (5)

QUESTIONS

Group A

1. (*a*) Describe the variation in metallic-nonmetallic properties as one goes across Period Three. (*b*) Relate this to the variation in number of outer-shell electrons.
2. (*a*) What physical properties do metals have in common? (*b*) What physical properties do nonmetals have in common?
3. Describe the nature of the binding force between (*a*) atoms of sodium; (*b*) atoms of silicon; (*c*) atoms of chlorine; (*d*) molecules of chlorine; (*e*) atoms of argon.
4. Why is the melting point of silicon so much higher than the melting point of aluminum when these are consecutive elements?
5. What difference is there in the interatomic forces of elements which are malleable and of those which are brittle?
6. Why is the sodium ion so much smaller than the sodium atom?

7. Why is the chloride ion somewhat larger than the chlorine atom?
8. Compare the reactions of Na_2O, SiO_2, and Cl_2O with water.
9. Compare the reactions of NaH, SiH_4, and HCl with water.
10. Why are the silicon hydrides much more reactive than the alkanes?

Group B

11. What accounts for the silvery luster of metals?
12. Why is the density increase between sodium and aluminum proportionally greater than the atomic weight increase?
13. Compare the magnitude of the binding force between atoms of liquid argon and atoms of liquid aluminum.
14. Explain why diamond is a nonconductor and silicon a semiconductor, when both have the same crystal structure and types of bonding.
15. Phosphorus atoms form three covalent bonds, sulfur atoms form two covalent bonds, and chlorine atoms form one covalent bond; yet phosphorus molecules are tetratomic, sulfur molecules are octatomic, and chlorine molecules are diatomic. Explain.
16. Explain the observed decrease in ionization energy between magnesium and aluminum and between phosphorus and sulfur.
17. (a) Draw electron-dot symbols for the elements of Period Three. (b) Using these symbols explain how the common oxidation states for each element are attained.
18. Relate electronegativity differences to the type of bonding observed in the (a) oxides of the elements of Period Three; (b) hydrides of the elements of Period Three.
19. Compare the structure of silicon dioxide with that of elementary silicon.
20. Compare the structures of (a) NH_3 and PH_3; (b) H_2S and H_2O. In your comparison include molecular shape and size, and type of bonding.

Chapter Twenty-four

THE METALS OF GROUP I

1. Sodium Family. The first group of elements on the left of the Periodic Table includes the chemically active metals lithium, sodium, potassium, rubidium, cesium, and francium. They are commonly known as the Sodium Family of elements. Some important properties of these Group I metals are listed in the table at the top of the next page.

Each element in the family has one electron in its outermost shell. The next-to-outermost shell consists of eight electrons. An outer octet is easily attained in each case by the removal of a single electron. Thus, the ion formed by the loss of one electron has the stable electronic configuration of the preceding noble gas. For example, the sodium ion has the electron configuration 2–8, the same as that of the neon atom. The electron configuration of the potassium ion, 2–8–8, is the same as that of the argon atom.

The Group I elements form hydroxides that are strongly basic, and thus are commonly referred to as the *alkali* metals.

They possess certain metallic characteristics to a high degree. Each has a silvery luster, is a good conductor of electricity and heat, and is ductile and malleable. These metals are relatively soft and can be cut with a knife. The properties of the Group I metals can be related to their characteristic crystalline lattice structures.

The crystal lattice of the alkali metals is generated by a body centered cubic unit cell made up of metallic ions with a +1 charge. The valence electrons compose a cloud of electron gas that permeates the lattice structure. (See Chapter 11, Section 14.) The high heat and electric conductivity is due to the mobile character of these free electrons.

The silvery luster of the Group I metals can be attributed to the free electrons in the crystal surfaces. When light falls on these surfaces the valence electrons absorb energy and are set into vibratory motion re-radiating the energy in all directions as light.

The binding force in the metallic crystal

PROPERTIES OF GROUP I ATOMS

Element	Atomic Number	Atomic Weight	Electron Configuration	Oxidation Number	Melting Point °C	Boiling Point °C	Density g/cm³	Metallic Radius Å	Ionic Radius Å
lithium	3	6.939	2, 1	+1	186	1336	0.53	1.23	0.60
sodium	11	22.9898	2, 8, 1	+1	97.5	880	0.97	1.57	0.95
potassium	19	39.102	2, 8, 8, 1	+1	62.3	760	0.86	2.02	1.33
rubidium	37	85.47	2, 8, 18, 8, 1	+1	38.5	700	1.53	2.16	1.48
cesium	55	132.905	2, 8, 18, 18, 8, 1	+1	28.5	670	1.87	2.35	1.69
francium	87	[223]	2, 8, 18, 32, 18, 8, 1	+1	....	....	....	....	....

lattice is the attraction between the positive ions and the negative electron cloud permeating the lattice. This force is essentially uniform in all directions, explaining the softness, ductility, and malleability of the alkali metals. Little energy is required to cut these metals or change their shape.

The Group I metals are characterized by low ionization potentials (see Chapter 5, Section 8). The ionization potential decreases as the atom size increases going down the group. As would be expected, they are vigorous reducing agents. The lithium atom, probably because of the exceptional hydration tendency of its ion, is the strongest reducing agent even though other members of the family have lower ionization potentials. Ionization energy measures the tendency of an isolated atom to hold a valence electron, whereas the oxidation potential measures the tendency of the metal to form ions in aqueous solution.

Electrons which absorb energy from a suitable source become excited, or stepped up to higher energy levels. When excited electrons fall back to their normal energy levels in an atom structure the extra energy is emitted, sometimes as visible light, producing a spectrum characteristic of that atom. Electrons of the Group I metals are quite easily excited to higher energy states. The energy supplied by a Bunsen flame is sufficient to accomplish this. Compounds of these metals impart characteristic colors to flames. The flame colors serve as the basis for simple identification tests (known as *flame tests*) for the metallic elements. Lithium compounds produce a carmine (red) flame; sodium, yellow; potassium, violet; rubidium and cesium, reddish violet (magenta).

Many difficulties are encountered in handling and storing the alkali metals because of their chemical activity. They are usually stored under kerosene or some other liquid hydrocarbon because they react so vigorously with water. In reaction with water, they release hydrogen and form solutions that are strongly basic. The metals do not exist free in nature, but are found only in combined form.

All of the ordinary compounds of the alkali metals are ionic, including their hydrides. Only lithium forms the oxide directly with oxygen. Sodium forms the

GROUP I METALS AS REDUCING AGENTS

Element	Oxidation potential (volts)	Ionization energy (ev)
Li	+3.05	5.39
Na	+2.71	5.14
K	+2.92	4.34
Rb	+2.93	4.18
Cs	+2.92	3.89
Fr	....	....

24-1 Potassium, a Group I metal, reacts vigorously with water like other members of this group. The light for this photograph was produced by dropping a small amount of pure potassium into a beaker of water. (B. M. Shaub)

that Robert W. Bunsen and Augustus Matthiessen succeeded in isolating the metal. Lithium, the metal of lowest density, is prepared by electrolyzing fused lithium chloride.

Lithium finds many uses in metallurgical processes. Its compounds are used in ceramics, welding, drugs, the manufacture of chemicals, and the synthesis of organic compounds. It dissolves in liquid ammonia, as do the other alkali metals.

When it is alloyed, lithium loses most of its reactivity. Lithium-magnesium alloys have the highest strength-to-weight ratio of all structural materials. The high strength and low weight per unit volume make these alloys important in aircraft and spacecraft design.

The element in gross quantity consists of a mixture of two isotopes, lithium-6 and lithium-7. The mixture occurs in the ratio of about 7.4 parts lithium-6 to 92.6 parts lithium-7. Lithium-6 plays a key role in

peroxide instead and rubidium and cesium form the "superoxides." However, the ordinary oxides can be prepared indirectly. These oxides are basic anhydrides and react with water to form the hydroxides.

Nearly all of the compounds of the alkali metals are quite soluble in water. The alkali-metal ions are colorless. They have a negligible tendency to hydrolyze in water solution or to form complex ions.

LITHIUM

2. Lithium and its compounds. Lithium is a fairly common element occurring in nature as Li^+ ions in several types of rocks of very complex composition. This element was discovered in 1817 by Johan Arfvedson (1792–1841), a student of Berzelius. It was not until 1855

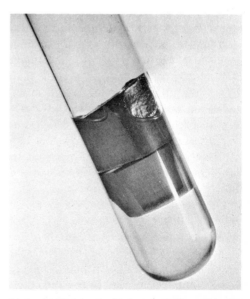

24-2 Lithium, the lightest of the solid elements, is shown in this photograph immersed in an inert oil in order to prevent it from coming into contact with water. (B. M. Shaub)

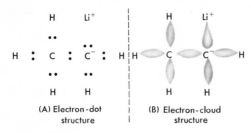

$$H \quad Li^+$$

$$H : C : C^- : H$$

$$H \quad H$$

(A) Electron-dot structure

(B) Electron-cloud structure

24-3 The carbon-lithium bond in C_2H_5Li. (A) Shared pair of electrons shown nearer carbon giving it a slight negative charge. (B) Shared electrons shown spending most time near carbon (where the cloud is thickest).

thermonuclear (hydrogen bomb) technology in the form of the solid compound lithium-6 deuteride.

Lithium reacts with oxygen, the halogens, hydrogen, and water forming ionic compounds. The chemical reactivity derives from its electronic structure and the density of the positive charge on its nucleus. When the valence electron has been removed, the positive charge on the ion is "dense" because it is shielded only by a single electron shell as compared to two and three shells for sodium and potassium ions.

Lithium chloride demonstrates the high charge density of the Li^+ ion and its strong hydration tendency. Crystalline LiCl is a vigorous dehydrating agent. It takes water vapor from the air and quickly goes into solution in the water it removes. On the other hand, pure sodium chloride is not hygroscopic even in damp weather.

Organometallic compounds formed with lithium metal have properties typical of molecules rather than ions. In these instances lithium behavior departs from that which is characteristic of the other alkali metals. The organometal compound ethyl-sodium C_2H_5Na, for example, resembles NaCl in that it has a high melting point, high electric conductivity, and low solubility in organic solvents. These are the

properties of an ionically bonded salt and suggest the structure $Na^+C_2H_5^-$.

Ethyl-lithium C_2H_5Li, on the other hand, has a low melting point, low electric conductivity, and good solubility in organic solvents. These properties suggest molecules rather than ions. The lithium atom is assumed to be covalently bonded to a carbon atom as shown in Fig. 24-3.

A flame test of lithium salts reveals a carmine-red coloration characteristic of lithium. This serves as an identification test for lithium. Strontium salts produce a scarlet-red flame and calcium salts give a yellowish-red flame.

SODIUM

3. Occurrence of sodium. Metallic sodium is never found free in nature. However, compounds containing the Na^+ ion and sodium complexes are widely distributed in soil, natural waters, and in plants and animals. Sodium is such an abundant element that it is difficult to find an absolutely sodium-free material.

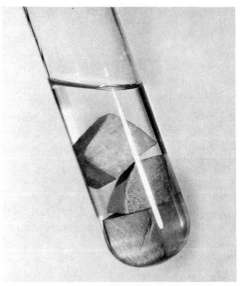

24-4 Sodium, the sixth most abundant element, is stored under kerosene. (B. M. Shaub)

4. The preparation of sodium. Sir Humphry Davy first prepared metallic sodium in 1807 by the electrolysis of moist sodium hydroxide. The metal is prepared today by the electrolysis of fused sodium chloride in an apparatus called the *Downs cell* (see Fig. 24-5). Since sodium chloride has such a high melting point (801° C), calcium chloride is mixed with it to lower the melting point to 580° C. The molten sodium is collected under oil. The chlorine produced simultaneously is a very valuable by-product.

$$2NaCl \xrightarrow{\text{(elect)}} 2Na + Cl_2 \uparrow$$

The recovery of sodium is accomplished by reducing the Na^+ ion. This occurs at the cathode of the Downs cell.

$$Na^+ + e^- \rightarrow Na^0$$

The Cl^- ion is oxidized at the anode and the two products, chlorine gas and sodium metal, are kept separated by an iron-gauze diaphragm. Chemical reduction of sodium ions, as well as the other alkali-metal ions, would not appear to be feasible since the alkali metals themselves are the strongest reducing agents. However, chemical reduction of some of the rarer alkali-metal ions can be carried out under suitable temperature conditions. See Section 12.

5. Properties of sodium. Sodium is a silvery-white, lustrous metal that tarnishes rapidly when exposed to air. It is very soft, has a lower density than water, and a low melting point. When a pellet of sodium is dropped into water, it melts from the heat of the reaction.

$$2Na + 2H_2O \rightarrow 2NaOH + H_2 \uparrow$$

When exposed to air, sodium unites with the oxygen to form sodium peroxide, Na_2O_2. By maintaining sodium in excess, some Na_2O can be produced along with

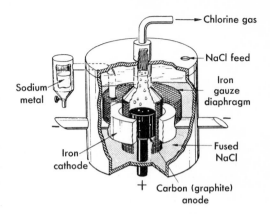

Chlorine gas
NaCl feed
Iron gauze diaphragm
Sodium metal
Fused NaCl
Iron cathode
Carbon (graphite) anode

24-5 Elementary sodium is produced by the electrolysis of fused sodium chloride in a Downs cell. Chlorine is a valuable by-product.

the bulk product Na_2O_2. This may be due to the strong reducing character of the sodium atom. Of the alkali metals, only lithium reacts directly with oxygen to form the normal oxide. The normal oxide of sodium, Na_2O, can be formed by heating NaOH with sodium.

$$2NaOH + 2Na \rightarrow 2Na_2O + H_2 \uparrow$$

The remaining alkali metals react directly with oxygen to form superoxides of the type $M^+O_2^-$, in which the oxygen atoms may be considered to have an oxidation number of $-\frac{1}{2}$. The superoxide of sodium, NaO_2, can be prepared indirectly.

Sodium reacts with all ordinary acids. It burns in an atmosphere of chlorine gas, uniting directly with the chlorine to form sodium chloride.

A flame test of sodium compounds reveals a strong yellow coloration characteristic of vaporized sodium atoms. This is a common identification test for sodium.

6. Uses of sodium. Most of the sodium produced in the United States is used in the production of tetraethyl lead, the antiknock additive for gasoline. It is used as a heat-transfer agent, in the preparation of dyes and other organic compounds, and in sodium vapor lamps.

Important new uses of sodium are continuously being developed, particularly as a chemical reducing agent. Titanium, zirconium, niobium, and tantalum are produced from their fused salts by reduction, using sodium as the reducing agent.

7. Sodium chloride. Sodium chloride is found in sea water, in salt wells, and in deposits of rock salt. Rock salt is mined in many places in the world.

Pure sodium chloride is not deliquescent. However, magnesium chloride, which is very deliquescent, is usually present in the sodium salt as an impurity. This explains why common salt becomes wet and sticky in damp weather. Sodium chloride crystallizes in a cubic pattern. See Fig. 24-6.

Sodium chloride is essential in the diet of man and animals and is present in certain body fluids. Perspiration contains considerable amounts of it. Consequently, those who perspire freely in hot weather often find it advisable to increase their salt intake by the use of salt tablets.

Since sodium chloride is the cheapest compound of sodium, we find it used as a starting material for the production of many other sodium compounds. Some sodium compounds are most easily prepared directly from metallic sodium, however. Essentially all sodium metal production utilizes sodium chloride as the raw material.

Fused salt mixtures containing sodium chloride are being used in numerous processes in connection with atomic fuels. For example, a molten mixture of sodium chloride, potassium chloride, and zinc chloride is used to produce electro-refined thorium from spent atomic fuel. With the fused salt mixture as the electrolyte and the spent-fuel alloy as the anode, the operating voltage of the cell is adjusted to deposit thorium at the cathode. Anode elements less positive than thorium settle

out as an insoluble anode sludge. Those more positive than thorium remain in solution.

8. Sodium hydroxide. Most commercial sodium hydroxide comes as a by-product from the electrolysis of sodium chloride solution.

$$2NaCl + 2H_2O \xrightarrow{\text{(elect)}} 2NaOH + Cl_2 + H_2 \uparrow$$

Considerable amounts are also made by adding calcium hydroxide (slaked lime) to sodium carbonate solution.

$$Na_2CO_3 + Ca(OH)_2 \rightarrow 2NaOH + CaCO_3 \downarrow$$

The precipitated calcium carbonate is filtered off, and the remaining solution of sodium hydroxide is concentrated by evaporation.

Sodium hydroxide converts some types of animal and vegetable matter into solu-

24-6 Native crystals of sodium chloride, known as halite, recovered from the Mojave Desert in California. (B. M. Shaub)

ble materials by chemical action. It is described as a very *caustic* substance because of its destructive effect on skin, hair, and wool.

Sodium hydroxide is a white crystalline solid that is marketed in the form of flakes, pellets, and sticks. It is very deliquescent, and reacts with water and carbon dioxide from the air, finally producing sodium carbonate. Its water solution is strongly basic.

Sodium hydroxide reacts with fats, forming soap and glycerol. Thus, one of its important uses is for making soap. Sodium hydroxide is also used in the production of rayon and cellulose film, in petroleum refining, and in the production of paper. A commercial grade of sodium hydroxide is sold under the name of lye, or caustic soda.

9. The Solvay process. The great bulk of the sodium carbonate and sodium hydrogen carbonate produced in this country and abroad is manufactured by

the **Solvay process.** It was developed in 1864 by Ernest Solvay (1838–1922), a Belgian, and is presented as a classical illustration of efficiency in chemical production.

The raw materials for the Solvay process are salt, limestone, and coal. The salt is pumped as brine from nearby salt wells. Limestone is strongly heated to yield the carbon dioxide and calcium oxide needed in the process:

Equation 1:

$$CaCO_3 \rightarrow CaO + CO_2 \uparrow$$

Coal is converted into coke, gas, coal tar, and ammonia by destructive distillation. The coke and gas are used as fuel in the plant, the coal tar is sold as a useful by-product, and the ammonia is used in the process.

In operation, a cold saturated solution of sodium chloride is treated with ammonia and carbon dioxide. The ammonia dis-

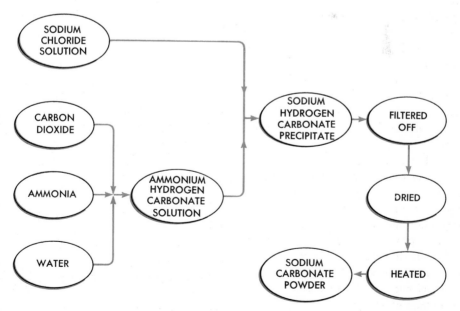

24-7 A flow diagram of the main reactions in the Solvay process. The success of the process depends on the re-use of the by-products, which for simplicity have been omitted here.

solves in the water and combines with the carbon dioxide to form ammonium hydrogen carbonate.

Equation 2:

$$NH_3 + H_2O + CO_2 \rightarrow NH_4HCO_3$$

The sodium chloride then reacts with the ammonium hydrogen carbonate and forms sodium hydrogen carbonate (sodium bicarbonate) and ammonium chloride. Sodium hydrogen carbonate is only slightly soluble in this solution and precipitates.

Equation 3:

$$NaCl + NH_4HCO_3 \rightarrow$$
$$NaHCO_3 \downarrow + NH_4Cl$$

The precipitated sodium hydrogen carbonate of Equation 3 is filtered off, dried, and heated to convert it into sodium carbonate.

Equation 4:

$$2NaHCO_3 \rightarrow Na_2CO_3 + H_2O \uparrow + CO_2 \uparrow$$

The dried sodium carbonate is packaged and sold. Pure baking soda (sodium hydrogen carbonate) is prepared by dissolving the sodium carbonate in water, and then forcing in carbon dioxide gas under pressure. The reaction is just the reverse of Equation 4 above.

Equation 5:

$$Na_2CO + H_2O + CO_2 \rightarrow 2NaHCO_3$$

The ammonia used in the process is more valuable than the sodium carbonate or sodium hydrogen carbonate. Hence it must be recovered and used over again if the process is to be profitable. The calcium oxide produced in Equation 1 above is slaked by adding water to form calcium hydroxide.

Equation 6:

$$CaO + H_2O \rightarrow Ca(OH)_2$$

The calcium hydroxide reacts with the ammonium chloride that was produced in Equation 3 above.

Equation 7:

$$Ca(OH)_2 + 2NH_4Cl \rightarrow$$
$$CaCl_2 + 2H_2O + 2NH_3 \uparrow$$

The ammonia gas is used over again as shown in Equation 2. Calcium chloride produced in Equation 7 is a by-product that finds some use because it is hygroscopic and inexpensive. However, the supply generally exceeds the demand.

10. Other compounds of sodium. Sodium compounds are widely used because they are usually cheap, and because common sodium compounds are soluble in water. The accompanying table gives characteristics of some additional familiar sodium compounds.

POTASSIUM

11. Occurrence of potassium. Combined potassium is widely distributed in nature but it is not easily available. This is so because most deposits of potassium compounds, in the form of feldspar rocks, are insoluble and weather slowly. Large deposits of potassium chloride, crystallized with magnesium and calcium compounds as complex salts, are found in Texas and New Mexico. Some potassium compounds are extracted from Searles Lake in California.

12. Preparation of potassium. Potassium was first prepared by Sir Humphry Davy in 1807 by the electrolysis of fused potassium hydroxide. Potassium can be prepared commercially by electrolyzing fused potassium chloride.

$$2KCl \rightarrow 2K + Cl_2 \uparrow$$

IMPORTANT SODIUM COMPOUNDS

Chemical Name	Common Name	Formula	Color	Uses
sodium carbonate	washing soda	$Na_2CO_3 \cdot 10H_2O$	white	In laundry; in glass making.
sodium hydrogen carbonate	baking soda	$NaHCO_3$	white	As leavening agent in baking.
sodium hydride	none	NaH	white	In cleaning scale and rust from steel forgings and castings.
sodium nitrate	Chile saltpeter	$NaNO_3$	white, or colorless	As fertilizer; in making nitric acid.
sodium sulfate	Glauber's salt	$Na_2SO_4 \cdot 10H_2O$	white, or colorless	In making glass; as a cathartic in medicine.
sodium peroxide	none	Na_2O_2	yellowish white	As oxidizing and bleaching agent; as source of oxygen.
sodium thiosulfate	hypo	$Na_2S_2O_3 \cdot 5H_2O$	white, or colorless	As fixer in photography; as antichlor.
sodium cyanide (CAUTION: very poisonous.)	prussiate of soda	$NaCN$	white	To destroy vermin; to extract gold from ores; in silver and gold plating; in case-hardening of steel.
sodium tetraborate	borax	$Na_2B_4O_7 \cdot 10H_2O$	white	As a flux; in making glass; as a water softener.
sodium phosphate (normal)	TSP	$Na_3PO_4 \cdot 10H_2O$	white	As a cleaning agent; as a water softener.
sodium sulfide	none	Na_2S	colorless	In the preparation of sulfur dyes; for dyeing cotton; to remove hair from hides.

However, there are few uses for which potassium is preferable to the cheaper sodium. The small annual production of potassium today is by the reaction

$$KCl + Na \rightarrow NaCl + K$$

The reaction proceeds to the right and equilibrium is prevented because of the lower boiling point of potassium.

13. Properties of potassium. Potassium metal is soft, of low density, and has a silvery luster that quickly acquires a bluish-gray tarnish when it is exposed to air. It is more active than sodium, floats on water, and as it reacts with the water it burns with a violet flame.

Potassium can be identified by the transient violet to reddish violet color imparted to a Bunsen flame by the vaporizing potassium atoms. However, the presence of sodium masks the violet color of potassium in the flame. Potassium can be detected in a mixture of sodium and potassium compounds by observing the colored flame through cobalt-blue glass. This glass filters out the yellow sodium flame and permits observation of the potassium flame.

24-8 Potassium, the seventh most abundant element, shown crystallized in a sealed tube. (B. M. Shaub)

14. Compounds of potassium. All common potassium compounds are soluble in water. Potassium hydroxide is prepared by the electrolysis of a solution of potassium chloride. It has the properties of a typical strong alkali. Potassium nitrate is made by mixing hot, concentrated solutions of potassium chloride and sodium nitrate.

$$KCl + NaNO_3 \rightarrow KNO_3 + NaCl \downarrow$$

When the solutions are mixed, sodium chloride, being the least soluble of the four salts, precipitates and is removed. Then as the solution cools, the potassium nitrate crystallizes from the saturated sodium chloride solution.

The table on the opposite page lists a few of the more important potassium compounds.

Sodium compounds can often be used instead of potassium compounds. Sodium chlorate is as satisfactory as potassium chlorate for many uses. Sodium hydroxide is as useful for most purposes as potassium hydroxide. It is not only cheaper, but also furnishes more hydroxide ions per gram. Sodium has an atomic weight of 23, and potassium an atomic weight of 39. Thus 56 grams of KOH are needed to furnish 1 mole (17 g) of hydroxide ions, but only 40 grams of NaOH are needed to furnish the same quantity of hydroxide ions. Sodium carbonate is used most often for making glass, but potassium carbonate yields a more lustrous glass that is preferred for optical uses. Potassium nitrate is used instead of sodium nitrate for making black gunpowder because it is not hygroscopic.

There is one very important use for potassium compounds for which there is no substitution. Green plants must have these compounds to grow properly. Therefore, complete chemical fertilizers always contain a substantial percentage of this necessary element.

RUBIDIUM, CESIUM, AND FRANCIUM

15. Rubidium and cesium. Rubidium and cesium were discovered in 1860 by Bunsen, who examined their spectra with the newly invented spectroscope. Because of the great chemical activity of these alkali metals, chemical reduction of the Rb⁺ and Cs⁺ ions would not seem to be possible. However, the reduction of the Rb⁺ ion in fused RbCl with calcium is possible because, at the elevated temperature, rubidium escapes from the reaction environment as a gas.

$$Ca + 2RbCl \rightarrow CaCl_2 + 2Rb \uparrow$$

Of course, these metals can be produced by the electrolysis of their fused chlorides or hydroxides.

Rubidium and cesium are used in pho-

IMPORTANT POTASSIUM COMPOUNDS

Chemical Name	Common Name	Formula	Color	Uses
potassium hydroxide	caustic potash	KOH	white	In making soft soap; in the Edison battery.
potassium chloride	none	KCl	white	As source of potassium; as a fertilizer.
potassium sulfate	none	K_2SO_4	white	As source of potassium; as a fertilizer.
potassium carbonate	potash	K_2CO_3	white	In making glass; in making soap.
potassium chlorate	none	$KClO_3$	white	As oxidizing agent; in fireworks; in explosives.
potassium nitrate	saltpeter	KNO_3	white	In black gunpowder; in fireworks; in curing meats.
potassium bromide	none	KBr	white	As a sedative; in photography.
potassium iodide	none	KI	white	In medicine; in iodized salt; in photography.
potassium permanganate	none	$KMnO_4$	purple	As a germicide; as an oxidizing agent.

toelectric cells, and to remove the last traces of oxygen from other electronic tubes. Of all the metals, electrons are ejected most easily from cesium by light falling on the metal. This phenomenon is known as the *photoelectric effect*. Rubidium and cesium are used in photoelectric cells sensitive to visible light because only these are photosensitive over the full range of the visible spectrum.

16. Francium. Francium was discovered by Mlle. M. Perey in 1937, and named for her native country, France. It is a radioactive element formed by the disintegration of an isotope of actinium. Francium has been produced only in trace quantities and little is known of its properties except as they are indicated by its position in the Periodic Table.

SPECTROSCOPY

17. Use of a spectroscope. One type of *spectroscope* consists of a glass prism, a collimator tube to focus a narrow beam of light rays upon the prism, and a small

telescope for examining the light which passes through the prism. When white light is passed through a triangular prism, a band of colors called a *continuous spectrum* is produced due to the unequal bending of light of different wavelengths.

Examination of a sodium flame by

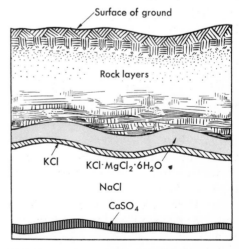

24-9   A cross-section of a salt deposit, showing how the different minerals were deposited as the sea water evaporated.

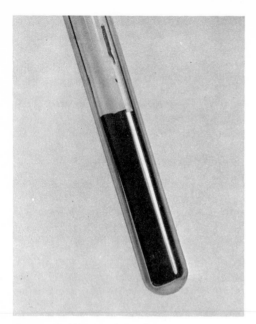

24-10 Rubidium, shown here in a sealed ampule, is very slightly radioactive. (B. M. Shaub)

means of a spectroscope reveals a characteristic bright-yellow line. Since this yellow line is always in the same relative place in the spectrum, it serves to identify sodium. Potassium produces both red and violet spectral lines. The spectrum chart, Color Plate II, Chapter 14, shows the characteristic color lines of several elements and also the continuous spectrum of white light produced by an incandescent solid.

18.   Origin of spectral lines.   A platinum wire held in a Bunsen flame becomes white hot, or incandescent, and emits white light. When the incandescent wire is viewed through a spectroscope, a continuous spectrum of colors is observed. The energy of the white light is distributed over a continuous range of light frequencies that includes the entire visible spectrum. Light energy of the shortest wavelength (highest frequency) is bent most to yield the deep violet color char-

acteristic of one extremity of the visible spectrum. Light energy of the longest wavelength (lowest frequency) is bent least to yield the deep red color characteristic of the other extremity of the visible spectrum. Between these two extremities there is a gradual blending from one color to the next making it possible to recognize six elementary colors: red, orange, yellow, green, blue, and violet. In general, incandescent solids and gases under high pressure give continuous spectra.

Luminous gases and vapors under low pressure give discontinuous spectra called *bright line spectra.* These consist of narrow lines of color which correspond to light energy of certain wavelengths. Atoms of different elements produce their own characteristic line spectra.

Electrons in atoms are restricted to energies of only certain values, as discussed in Chapter 4. In normal atoms, electrons occupy the lowest energy levels

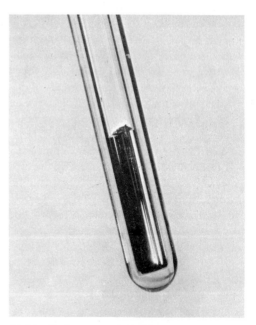

24-11 Cesium, an extremely active member of the Sodium Family, is sealed in a glass ampule. (B. M. Shaub)

available to them. The energy of an electron can be changed only as it moves from one discrete energy level to another. A certain amount of energy is absorbed with each jump to a higher energy level, or is emitted with each jump to a lower level. The quantity of energy in each change is equal to the difference between the discrete energy levels involved.

When substances are vaporized in a flame, electrons are raised to higher energy levels by heat energy. When these electrons fall back into the lower energy levels available to them, energy is emitted producing spectral lines characteristic of the wavelengths of the energy emitted. Thus, vaporized sodium atoms produce a spectrum consisting of two narrow yellow lines very close together (seen in the ordinary spectroscope as a single yellow line). Potassium atoms produce two red lines and a violet line. Lithium atoms yield intense red and yellow lines and weak blue and violet lines. Excited atoms produce spectra which serve as "fingerprints" that enable chemists to identify them by the use of a spectroscope.

Bright lines in the visible portion of the spectrum account for the flame coloration produced by certain metals. The color seen is the combination of light energies of the different wavelengths emitted. Spectral lines produced by excited atoms that fall outside the range of visible wavelengths may be photographed even though they cannot be seen with the unaided eye.

REVIEW OUTLINE

Group I Elements
    General properties of Group I elements (1)
    Crystal structure of Group I elements (1)
    Ionization potentials of Group I elements (1)

Lithium
    Occurrence and discovery of lithium (2)
    Uses of lithium (2)
    Unusual properties of lithium (2)
    Identification test for lithium (2)
    Compounds of lithium (2)

Sodium
    Occurrence of sodium (3)
    Discovery and preparation of sodium (4)
    Properties of sodium (5)
    Uses of sodium (6)
    Sodium chloride: properties and uses (7)
    Sodium hydroxide: properties and uses (8)
    Solvay process (9)
    Other compounds of sodium (10)

Potassium
    Occurrence of potassium (11)
    Discovery and preparation of potassium (12)
    Properties of potassium (13)
    Compounds of potassium (14)

Rubidium, cesium, and francium
    Discovery and uses of rubidium and cesium (15)
    Discovery of francium (16)

Spectroscopy
    Description and use of the spectroscope (17)
    Origin of spectral lines (18)

QUESTIONS

Group A

1. Describe the electron configuration of the atoms and ions of the elements in Group I.
2. Compare the methods of preparing lithium, sodium, and potassium.
3. List three uses for metallic sodium.
4. Distinguish between the terms *caustic* and *corrosive*.
5. (*a*) What are the raw materials for the Solvay process? (*b*) What are the products and by-products?
6. (*a*) What is caustic soda? (*b*) Washing soda? (*c*) Baking soda?
7. Why do molasses and baking soda have a leavening action in cookies?
8. What are the sources of potassium compounds in the United States?
9. (*a*) How are sodium and potassium stored in the laboratory stockroom? (*b*) Why must they be stored in this fashion?
10. Write the balanced formula equation for the reaction of potassium and water.
11. Describe the flame tests for lithium, sodium, and potassium.
12. Why are rubidium and cesium preferred over the other alkali metals for use in ordinary photoelectric cells?
13. Write three equations to show how sodium carbonate can be produced in the Solvay process.
14. Write three equations for the recovery of ammonia in the Solvay process.

Group B

15. Why are the members of the Sodium Family soft, malleable metals with low melting points and low boiling points?
16. Why is NaCl necessary in the diet of many animals and man?
17. Why is sodium chloride used as a starting material for preparing metallic sodium and other compounds of sodium?
18. (*a*) Why are sodium compounds more frequently used than potassium compounds? (*b*) For what purpose can sodium compounds not be substituted for potassium compounds?
19. What by-product of the Solvay process has such limited use and yet is produced in such quantity that disposal of it is actually a problem to the manufacturers?
20. For what purposes are spectroscopes used in chemical analysis?
21. Why does table salt become sticky in damp weather when pure sodium chloride is not deliquescent?

22. Explain why potassium has a lower density than sodium, although it consists of heavier atoms.
23. Write a balanced chemical equation for the reaction which occurs when sodium hydroxide is exposed to the air.
24. In the Solvay process, why does the reaction between sodium chloride and ammonium hydrogen carbonate run to completion?
25. Why does a solution of sodium carbonate in water turn red litmus paper blue?
26. Suppose you had a tremendous quantity of acid that had to be neutralized, and that NaOH, KOH, and LiOH were all available at the same price per pound. Which of these three would you use? Why?

PROBLEMS

1. (*a*) How many grams of sulfuric acid in water solution can be neutralized by 10.0 g of sodium hydroxide? (*b*) 10.0 g of potassium hydroxide?
2. If you have 1.00 kg of sodium nitrate and 1.00 kg of potassium chloride, how much potassium nitrate can you make by reacting these two substances, assuming that all the potassium nitrate can be recovered?
3. If crystallized sodium carbonate, $Na_2CO_3 \cdot 10H_2O$ sells for 5 cents a pound, what is anhydrous sodium carbonate worth per pound?
4. How many liters of carbon dioxide can be liberated from 50.0 g of each of the following: (*a*) Na_2CO_3; (*b*) $NaHCO_3$; (*c*) K_2CO_3; (*d*) $KHCO_3$?
5. How many pounds of sodium chloride and how many cubic feet of carbon dioxide (at S.T.P.) are required to produce a ton of anhydrous sodium carbonate?

Chapter Twenty-five

THE METALS OF GROUP II

1. Calcium Family. The elements of Group II of the Periodic Table are members of the Calcium Family and consist of the metals beryllium, magnesium, calcium, strontium, barium, and radium. They are often called the *alkaline-earth metals*.

Beryllium and magnesium, like aluminum of Group III and the transition metal titanium, are commercially important light metals. They follow the corresponding alkali metals lithium and sodium in their chemical behavior. Radium is important because it is radioactive. Radioactivity and the properties of radium will be described in Chapter 31. The remaining three elements, calcium, strontium, and barium, have similar properties and are typical members of the Calcium Family.

Each alkaline-earth element has two valence electrons and forms doubly charged ions of the M^{++} type. There is a stronger force of attraction between the metal ions and the electron cloud of the metallic crystals. Consequently, these metals are more dense, harder, and have higher melting and boiling points than the corresponding members of the Sodium Family.

The atoms and ions of the members of the Calcium Family are smaller than those of the corresponding members of the Sodium Family because of their higher nuclear charge. For example, the magnesium ion Mg^{++} has the same electron configuration as the corresponding Group I ion Na^+, $1s^2 2s^2 2p^6$. However, Mg^{++} has a nuclear charge of $+12$ and Na^+ has a nuclear charge of $+11$. The higher nuclear charge of the Mg^{++} ion produces a stronger attraction for electrons resulting in smaller K and L shells.

The alkaline-earth metals form hydrides, oxides or peroxides, hydroxides, and halogenides with general similarities to those of the alkali metals. The hydrides of the alkaline-earth metals are ionic and contain the H^- ion. They react with water to liberate hydrogen gas and form basic hydroxide solutions. In fact, calcium hydride is frequently used as a convenient source of hydrogen.

PROPERTIES OF GROUP II ATOMS

Element	Atomic Number	Atomic Weight	Electron Configuration	Oxidation Number	Melting Point °C	Boiling Point °C	Density g/cm³	Metallic Radius Å	Ionic Radius Å
beryllium	4	9.0122	2, 2	+2	1280	2970	1.85	0.889	0.31
magnesium	12	24.312	2, 8, 2	+2	651	1107	1.74	1.364	0.65
calcium	20	40.08	2, 8, 8, 2	+2	842	1240	1.55	1.736	0.99
strontium	38	87.62	2, 8, 18, 8, 2	+2	800	1150	2.54	1.914	1.13
barium	56	137.34	2, 8, 18, 18, 8, 2	+2	850	1140	3.78	1.981	1.35
radium	88	[226]	2, 8, 18, 32, 18, 8, 2	+2	700	1140	5(?)	.....	....

The oxides of beryllium, magnesium, and calcium have very high melting points and CaO and MgO are used as refractory materials. They are considered to be ionic but are more covalent than alkali-metal oxides. Strontium and barium form peroxides with oxygen, probably because of the large size of their ions.

The hydroxides are formed by adding water to the oxides. Except for Be(OH)₂ which is amphiprotic, the hydroxides are completely dissociated in water solution yielding OH⁻ ions. Those above barium are only slightly soluble in water, the solubility increasing with the size of the metallic ion. These hydroxide solutions have low concentrations of OH⁻ ions. They are weakly basic because of their slight solubility in water and not because of a lack of ionic character.

BERYLLIUM

2. Preparation and properties. Beryllium is not a common element. It occurs in the mineral beryl, $Be_3Al_2Si_6O_{18}$. The *aquamarine* and *emerald* are varieties of beryl which are prized as gems. Beryllium can be isolated by the electrolysis of a fused mixture of sodium and beryllium chlorides. It is a very hard silvery-white metal which has a specific gravity of 1.85.

Beryllium, with copper, forms nonsparking alloys that are used for electric switches and for tools. Beryllium-copper springs are practically unbreakable. Beryllium is used for making windows for X-ray tubes because these rays readily pass through elements with low atomic numbers. Of the low-atomic-number elements, beryllium can be best fabricated for this purpose. The addition of beryllium to light-metal alloys makes them easier to work. Beryllium oxide, BeO, is used in the nuclear reactors in which plutonium is made.

Beryllium compounds are somewhat covalent. This is an important difference be-

25-1 Fused pellets of beryllium. This metal produces alloys that are extremely elastic. (B. M. Shaub)

tween beryllium compounds and the compounds of the other members of Group II. Furthermore, beryllium salts are extensively hydrolyzed in water. These characteristics show that nonmetallic properties begin to appear in the Period 2 elements even near the extreme left of the Periodic Table. Beryllium and its compounds are exceedingly poisonous.

MAGNESIUM

3. Occurrence of magnesium. Magnesium compounds are widely distributed on land and in the sea. Magnesium sulfate is found in the ground in many places, but notably in British Columbia and the State of Washington. A double chloride of potassium and magnesium is mined from the potash deposits of Texas and New Mexico. Sea water contains a significant quantity of magnesium compounds.

25-2 Feathery crystals shown here are composed of magnesium, the eighth most abundant element. (B. M. Shaub)

Dolomite, $CaCO_3 \cdot MgCO_3$, is a double carbonate of magnesium and calcium which is often found in the United States and Europe. It is an excellent building stone, and is useful for lining steel furnaces. Pulverized dolomite neutralizes soil acids and also supplies magnesium for the growth of plants.

Talc and asbestos are silicates of magnesium. Asbestos, which is mined in Ontario and Quebec, Canada, is a remarkable mineral. It has a high melting point, is nonflammable, and is a good heat insulator. Its fibrous structure permits the mineral to be spun into threads and woven into cloth. It is mixed with cement for making asbestos shingles. With magnesium oxide it is used for covering steam pipes and furnaces. Asbestos is also used for making automobile brake linings, fireproof curtains and clothing, and as an electric insulator.

Elementary magnesium was first prepared by Davy in 1807, in the series of experiments which resulted in the isolation of sodium, calcium, and similar active metals.

4. Extraction of magnesium. *From magnesium chloride.* Most of the magnesium of commerce is obtained from sea water. The first step in obtaining magnesium from sea water is to treat it with lime made from oyster shells, which are inexpensive and readily available. This treatment causes the magnesium ions to be precipitated as magnesium hydroxide.

$$Mg^{++} + 2OH^- \rightarrow Mg(OH)_2 \downarrow$$

The magnesium hydroxide is separated from the water by filtration. The addition of hydrochloric acid converts the magnesium hydroxide to magnesium chloride.

$$Mg(OH)_2 + 2HCl \rightarrow MgCl_2 + 2H_2O$$

Magnesium is recovered by electrolysis of fused magnesium chloride.

$$MgCl_2 \xrightarrow{\text{(elect)}} Mg + Cl_2 \uparrow$$

Magnesium can be recovered in another process by electrolyzing a fused mixture of magnesium chloride, calcium chloride, and sodium chloride at about 700° to 750° C.

From magnesium oxide. In the United States some magnesium of high purity is prepared from magnesium oxide by reducing it with ferrosilicon, an alloy of iron and silicon. The reduction is carried out at a temperature of about 1150° C in a vacuum. At this high temperature and low pressure, the magnesium evaporates, is condensed, and cast into molds.

5. Properties of magnesium. Magnesium is a silver-white metal with a specific gravity of 1.74. When heated, it becomes ductile and malleable. Its tensile strength is not quite as great as that of aluminum.

Magnesium is not acted upon by dry air, but in moist air a coating of basic magnesium carbonate forms on its surface. Because this coating is not porous, it protects the metal underneath from further tarnishing. *A metal which forms a nonporous, nonscaling coat of tarnish is said to be a **self-protective metal**.*

When heated in air to the kindling point, magnesium burns with an intensely hot flame and gives off a dazzling white light. The products of the combustion are magnesium oxide, MgO, and magnesium nitride, Mg_3N_2. Magnesium is one of the few metals which combines directly with nitrogen. Boiling water reacts with magnesium slowly to form the hydroxide and hydrogen is set free. All the common acids react with it.

Once ignited, magnesium burns in water, in carbon dioxide, and in nitrogen. These reactions are shown by the equations:

$$Mg + H_2O \rightarrow MgO + H_2$$

$$2Mg + CO_2 \rightarrow 2MgO + C$$

$$3Mg + N_2 \rightarrow Mg_3N_2$$

At a temperature of about 800° C, mag-

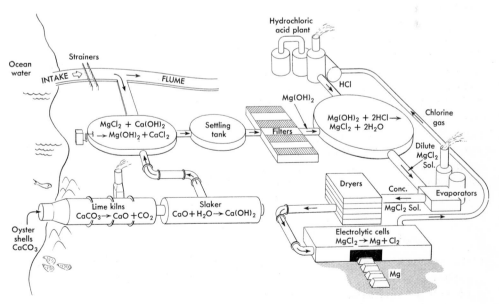

25-3   Diagram of a plant for the production of magnesium from sea water.

COMMON MAGNESIUM COMPOUNDS

Chemical Name	Common Name	Formula	Appearance	Uses
magnesium carbonate	none	$MgCO_3$	white, usually fluffy	For lining furnaces; in making the oxide.
basic magnesium carbonate	magnesia alba	$Mg_4(OH)_2(CO_3)_3 \cdot 3H_2O$	soft, white powder	In tooth cleansers; for pipe coverings.
magnesium oxide	magnesia	MgO	white powder	As refractory; for lining furnaces.
magnesium chloride	none	$MgCl_2$	white, crystalline solid	With asbestos for stone flooring.
magnesium sulfate	Epsom salts	$MgSO_4 \cdot 7H_2O$	white, crystalline solid	In laxatives, cathartics; in dye industry.
magnesium hydroxide	milk of magnesia	$Mg(OH)_2$	white, milky suspension	As antacid; in laxatives.

nesium carbonate decomposes to *light* magnesium oxide and carbon dioxide. Further heating to above 1400° C converts the light oxide to *dense* MgO, a refractory material having a melting point above 2800° C.

6. Uses of magnesium. The brilliant white light produced by burning magnesium makes it useful for flares and fireworks. Magnesium forms light, strong alloys with aluminum, such as magnalium and Dowmetal. Other alloying metals are lithium, thorium, zinc, and manganese. Magnesium alloys are used for making tools and fixtures, for the beams of delicate chemical balances, and for automobile and airplane parts. The growth of the aircraft and aerospace industries has produced a much greater demand for magnesium. The table at the top of the page lists a few of the more common magnesium compounds.

CALCIUM

7. Distribution of calcium. Calcium ranks fifth in abundance by weight among the elements in the earth's crust, atmosphere, and surface waters. It is widely distributed over the earth's surface in many rock and mineral forms.

The best known of these mineral forms are the carbonate and sulfate. Calcium carbonate occurs principally as limestone, marble, and calcite. Other forms are coral, pearls, and oyster shells. Calcium sulfate occurs as gypsum, $CaSO_4 \cdot 2H_2O$, and the anhydride, $CaSO_4$.

Calcium was first isolated by Davy in 1808. He prepared metallic calcium by electrolyzing a moist mixture of calcium oxide and mercury(II) oxide, and then distilling the mercury from the resulting calcium-mercury amalgam.

8. Preparation of calcium. Since calcium occurs as Ca^{++} ions, the metal must be recovered by reduction. Electrolytic reduction may be accomplished using fused calcium chloride.

$$CaCl_2 \xrightarrow{\text{(elect)}} Ca + Cl_2 \uparrow$$

A graphite crucible, which also serves as the anode, holds the fused chloride. An iron cathode dips into the fused salt. As metallic calcium forms on the end of the cathode, it is slowly raised from the mass. In this way an irregular-shaped rod of metallic calcium is produced.

25-4 Calcium, the fifth most abundant element. (B. M. Shaub)

Chemical reduction is generally employed today for recovering calcium. Calcium oxide is heated with aluminum in a vacuum retort.

$$3CaO + 2Al \rightarrow Al_2O_3 + 3Ca \uparrow$$

The reaction proceeds because the calcium metal is distilled off as a gas at the reaction temperature.

9. Properties of calcium. Metallic calcium is silver-white in color, but a freshly-cut piece tarnishes to a bluish-gray surface within a few hours. It is somewhat harder than lead, but it is only about one-eighth as dense. If a piece of calcium is added to water, it reacts with the water and liberates hydrogen slowly.

$$Ca + 2H_2O \rightarrow Ca(OH)_2 + H_2$$

Since calcium has a greater electrochemical activity than sodium, we should expect this reaction to proceed more violently. However, the reaction is much less violent than that of sodium and potassium with water. The calcium hydroxide produced in this reaction is only slightly soluble and

coats the surface of the calcium. This coating protects the metal from the rapid interaction with the water.

Calcium is a good reducing agent. It burns with a bright, yellowish-red flame in oxygen. It also unites directly with chlorine. Calcium salts yield the yellowish-red color in flame tests. Sodium contamination often alters the color to orange-yellow. The flame color becomes greenish through cobalt-blue glass and is masked by the yellowish-green flame of the barium salts. Consequently, the flame test must be used with caution.

Calcium is used in small amounts to reduce uranium and to deoxidize copper. Some alloy steels contain small quantities of calcium. Lead-calcium alloys are used for bearings in machines. Calcium is also used to harden lead for cables and storage battery grids.

25-5 Marble is an excellent stone for the construction of buildings and monuments. Here it is shown being quarried in Vermont. (Paul Conklin-PIX)

10. Calcium carbonate. Calcium carbonate, $CaCO_3$, is an abundant mineral found in a number of different forms.

1. Limestone. This is the most common form of calcium carbonate. It was formed in past geologic ages from the accumulations of the shells of clams, oysters, and other marine animals. Limestone occurs in layers as a *sedimentary rock*, and is quarried in varying amounts in almost every state in the country. Pure calcium carbonate is white, or colorless, when crystalline. Most deposits, however, are gray because of impurities.

Limestone is used for making glass, as a flux in mak ng iron and steel, and as a source of carbon dioxide. It is used as a building stone, and considerable quantities are used for making roads. Powdered or pulverized limestone is used to neutralize acid soils. It is heated to produce calcium oxide, CaO. Calcium oxide, called *quicklime*, is one of the largest tonnage chemicals in industry.

A mixture of limestone and clay is converted to *cement* by heating strongly in a rotary kiln. Sometimes limestone deposits have clay already mixed with the calcium carbonate in about the right proportions for making cement. Such deposits are called *natural cement*.

2. Calcite. The clear, crystalline form of calcium carbonate is known as calcite. Transparent, colorless specimens are called *Iceland spar.*

3. Marble. This rock was originally deposited as limestone, and later changed by heat and pressure into marble with a resulting increase in the size of the calcium carbonate crystals. Hence it is classed as a *metamorphic rock.*

4. Shells. The shells of such animals as snails, clams, and oysters consist largely of calcium carbonate. In some places, large masses of such shells have become cemented together to form rock called *co-quina* (koh-*kee*-nuh). It is used as a building stone in the southern states. Tiny marine animals, called *polyps*, deposit limestone as they build coral reefs. Chalk, such as that of the chalk cliffs of England, consists of the microscopic shells of small marine animals. Blackboard "chalk," however, contains some claylike material mixed with calcium carbonate, and should not be confused with natural chalk.

5. Precipitated chalk. This form of calcium carbonate is made by the reaction of sodium carbonate and calcium chloride.

$$Na_2CO_3 + CaCl_2 \rightarrow CaCO_3 \downarrow + 2NaCl$$

It is soft and finely divided. Thus it forms a nongritty scouring powder that is suitable for tooth pastes and tooth powders. Under the name of *whiting* it is used as a filler for paints. When it is ground with linseed oil, it forms putty.

11. Hardness in water. Rainwater falling on the earth usually contains carbon dioxide in solution. As it soaks through the ground, it reaches deposits of limestone or dolomite. Some of the calcium carbonate and magnesium carbonate in these rocks is converted to the soluble bicarbonates of these metals. This water, which contains Ca^{++} ions and Mg^{++} ions in solution, is called "*hard water.*" This term indicates that it is "hard" to get a lather when soap is added to such water. Conversely, a water that lathers readily with soap is called "soft" water. The terms are not precise, but they are in common usage. Deposits of iron and other heavy metals in the ground may also produce hard water.

Water hardness is of two types: *temporary hardness* in which HCO_3^- ions are present along with the metal ions; and *permanent hardness* in which other negative ions (usually $SO_4^=$) more stable than the HCO_3^- ion are present along with the metal ions.

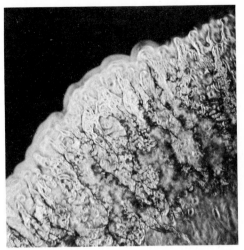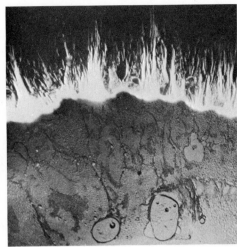

25-6 Photomicrographs of soap in the process of dissolving in hard water (left) and in soft water (right). In hard water the solution process is inhibited by a barrier of sticky soap curd, but in soft water soap streamers extend into the water, forming a clear solution. (Permutit)

The principal component of ordinary soap is water-soluble sodium stearate, $NaC_{18}H_{35}O_2$. When soap is added to water containing Ca^{++} ions, the large $C_{18}H_{35}O_2^-$ ions react with the Ca^{++} ions to form the insoluble stearate, $Ca(C_{18}H_{35}O_2)_2$, which deposits as a gray scum.

$$Ca^{++} + 2C_{18}H_{35}O_2^- \rightarrow Ca(C_{18}H_{35}O_2)_2 \downarrow$$

The metal ions in hard water react with the soap to form precipitates until all of these ions are removed. Until this occurs, no lasting lather will be produced. Soft water does not contain the ions of these troublesome metals and therefore lathers easily when soap is added.

12. Softening of hard water. Hard water is a nuisance in laundering because the sticky precipitate wastes soap and collects on the fibers of the garments being laundered. In bathing, the hard water does not lather freely, and the precipitate forms a scum on the bathtub. In steam boilers, temporary hard water containing the HCO_3^- ions has a still more serious fault. When this water is boiled, calcium

carbonate collects as a hard scale inside the boiler and the steam pipes. It may form a thick crust on these surfaces, acting as a heat insulator and preventing efficient transfer of heat. Thus, for most purposes, hard water should be softened before it is used.

There are several practical methods of softening water. Generally, the nature of the hardness and the quantity of soft water required determine the most economical and effective method.

1. Boiling (for temporary hardness). Hard water containing HCO_3^- ions may be softened by boiling. The metal ions precipitate as carbonates according to the following typical reaction:

$$Ca^{++} + 2HCO_3^- \rightarrow$$
$$CaCO_3 \downarrow + H_2O + CO_2 \uparrow$$

This reaction is reversible except for the fact that boiling removes the CO_2 and drives the reaction to the right.

2. Precipitation. When sodium carbonate, Na_2CO_3, is added to hard water, precipitates of Ca^{++} and Mg^{++} ions are formed as insoluble carbonates. The Na^+ ions added to the water, of course, cause no difficulties with soap.

$$Ca^{++} + CO_3^{=} \rightarrow CaCO_3 \downarrow$$
$$Mg^{++} + CO_3^{=} \rightarrow MgCO_3 \downarrow$$

The addition of a basic solution such as NH_3-Aq or limewater to temporary hard water supplies OH^- ions which neutralize the HCO_3^- ions and precipitate the objectionable metal ions as carbonates.

$$Ca^{++} + HCO_3^- + OH^- \rightarrow CaCO_3 \downarrow + H_2O$$
$$Mg^{++} + HCO_3^- + OH^- \rightarrow$$
$$MgCO_3 \downarrow + H_2O$$

Other precipitating agents such as borax and trisodium phosphate are sometimes used. Both produce basic solutions by hydrolysis and the phosphate salts of calcium and magnesium are insoluble.

3. Ion exchange. Certain natural minerals, known as *zeolites*, have porous, three-dimensional networks of silicate-aluminate groups that act as large fixed ions carrying negative charges. Metallic ions such as Na^+ are attached to these complexes to form giant molecules. If hard water is allowed to stand in contact with sodium zeolite, Ca^{++} and Mg^{++} ions replace the Na^+ ions. Since the zeolite ions are immobile, the objectionable metal ions are given up by the water, being exchanged for Na^+ ions.

$$Ca^{++} + Na_2 \text{ zeolite} \rightarrow Ca \text{ zeolite} + 2Na^+$$

An application of the Law of Mass Action enables the exhausted zeolite to be regenerated and used over and over again. By immersing Ca zeolite in a concentrated sodium chloride solution (high Na^+ concentration), the Ca^{++} ions are replaced. This is a reversal of the above equation.

$$2Na^+ + Ca \text{ zeolite} \rightarrow Na_2 \text{ zeolite} + Ca^{++}$$

A synthetic zeolite, known as *permutit*,

25-7 The scale of calcium carbonate which has collected on the inside of this pipe cuts down the flow of steam through it and acts as an insulator. Thus, the scale prevents efficient transfer of heat. (Permutit)

acts more rapidly than natural zeolites and is commonly used today in most household water softeners. Sodium chloride, the cheapest of all sources of Na^+ ions, is used to regenerate the water-softening agent in the softener.

Important recent advances in the field of synthetic ion exchanges have enabled chemists to develop ion-exchange resins far superior to the zeolites. One type of resin, called an *acid-exchange resin* or a *cation exchanger*, has large negatively charged organic units whose neutralizing ions in water are H_3O^+ ions. A second type of resin, called a *base-exchange resin* or *anion exchanger*, has large positively charged organic units whose neutralizing ions in water are OH^- ions.

Combinations of the two types of ion-exchange resins make possible the removal of both positive and negative ions in solution in water. Hard water passed through the cation exchanger has the metallic ions (cations) removed and replaced by H_3O^+ ions. The water then passed through the anion exchanger has the negative ions (anions) removed and replaced by OH⁻ ions. The H_3O^+ and OH^- ions form water by neutralization.

Natural water or a water solution of salts treated by combinations of ion-exchange resins is rendered *ion-free* except for the small equilibrium quantities of H_3O^+ and OH^- ions and is called *deionized* or *demineralized water*. Deionized water is now being used for many processes that formerly required distilled water. In fact, deionized water is as free of ions as the most carefully distilled water, although it may contain some dissolved carbon dioxide.

An acid-exchange resin can be regenerated by running a strong acid such as sulfuric acid through it. Similarly, a base-exchange resin can be regenerated using a basic solution.

13. Calcium oxide. Calcium oxide is a white, ionic solid with a cubic structure. It is refractory since it does not melt or vaporize below the temperature of the electric arc. It unites chemically with water to form calcium hydroxide.

$$CaO + H_2O \rightarrow Ca(OH)_2$$

During this process, called *slaking*, the mass swells and large quantities of heat are evolved.

If a lump of quicklime is exposed to air, it gradually absorbs water, swells decidedly, cracks, and crumbles to a powder. It first forms calcium hydroxide, and then slowly unites with carbon dioxide from air to form calcium carbonate. Thus a mixture of calcium hydroxide and calcium carbonate is formed. Such a mixture is valuable for liming soils, but air slaking ruins lime for making mortar and plaster.

Calcium oxide is produced by heating calcium carbonate to a high temperature in a rotary kiln.

$$CaCO_3 \rightarrow CaO + CO_2 \uparrow$$

A high concentration of carbon dioxide in the kiln would drive the reaction in the reverse direction according to Le Chatelier's principle. An equilibrium is avoided by removing the carbon dioxide from the kiln as it is formed.

14. Calcium hydroxide. Calcium hydroxide, or *slaked lime*, is a white solid which is sparingly soluble in water. Its water solution, called *limewater*, has basic properties. A suspension of calcium hydroxide in water is known as milk of lime. Mixed with flour paste or glue, it makes whitewash.

Calcium hydroxide is the cheapest of the hydroxides. It is used to remove hair from hides before they are tanned, or converted into leather. It is useful for liming soils, for liberating ammonia from ammonium compounds, and for softening temporary hard water. Large quantities are used for making mortar and plaster.

Lime mortar consists of slaked lime, sand, and water. Although mortar of this general composition has been used for many centuries, the process by which it sets to a hard mass is still not fully understood. The first step in the setting is loss of water by evaporation. It appears that the lime and sand slowly react according to the equation:

$$Ca(OH)_2 + SiO_2 \rightarrow CaSiO_3 + H_2O$$

Carbon dioxide from the air reacts with the lime also, as follows:

$$Ca(OH)_2 + CO_2 \rightarrow CaCO_3 + H_2O$$

Mortar becomes harder over a period of many years as chemical changes occur in the center of the mass.

15. Calcium sulfate. Calcium sulfate occurs as the mineral *gypsum*. Trans-

25-8 Strontium. Radioactive strontium 90 is present in atomic fallout. (B. M. Shaub)

parent crystals of gypsum are called *selenite*.

When gypsum is heated gently, it partially dehydrates and forms a white powder known as plaster of Paris according to the equation:

$$2CaSO_4 \cdot 2H_2O \rightarrow$$
$$(CaSO_4)_2 \cdot H_2O + 3H_2O \uparrow$$

When plaster of Paris is mixed with water, it forms a paste useful in making molds and casts which set rapidly by uniting with water, the reverse of the above reaction. Gypsum is mixed with lime to make the finish coat of plaster. Large quantities are used in making wallboard or plasterboard.

STRONTIUM AND BARIUM

16. Strontium compounds. The sulfate and the carbonate are the chief strontium minerals. Since all the compounds

of strontium impart a beautiful scarlet color to a flame, they are used in fireworks displays.

Strontium nitrate, $Sr(NO_3)_2$, when mixed with powdered shellac, makes a red light for fireworks and flares. Strontium salts give an intense scarlet color in flame tests, but the color is not easily obtained with dilute solutions. The inexperienced observer usually has difficulty in distinguishing between lithium and strontium flames.

17. Compounds of barium. Both the sulfate and carbonate of barium are found in nature. The compounds of barium are similar in chemical characteristics to the compounds of calcium. The following are most widely used.

Barium sulfate, $BaSO_4$, is a dense white

25-9 Barium, a dense metal. The sample shown is submerged in oil to prevent oxidation. (B. M. Shaub)

solid which is used as a filler in making heavy paper and also in paints. It gives more body to paper and makes it less transparent. It increases the durability of paint.

Barium peroxide, BaO_2, is used in fireworks, as a vigorous oxidizing agent, and to some extent for making hydrogen peroxide.

Barium nitrate, $Ba(NO_3)_2$, is a white crystalline solid. All barium compounds impart a yellowish-green color to a flame. This color, however, may be obscured by sodium impurities and may, in turn, obscure the calcium flame. The nitrate is generally used in making flares and fireworks.

The oxides of both barium and strontium are used to coat the filaments of vacuum tubes. A single layer of barium atoms on the surface of the filament is said to multiply the yield of electrons given off by the filament more than one hundred million times.

REVIEW OUTLINE

Group II Elements: the Calcium Family
  General properties of Group II elements (1)
  Ionic nature of Group II elements (1)
  Oxides and hydroxides of Calcium Family (1)

Beryllium
  Preparation and properties of beryllium (2)
  Uses of beryllium (2)

Magnesium
  Occurrence of magnesium (3)
  Extraction of magnesium from sea water (4)
  Extraction of magnesium from magnesium oxide (4)
  Properties of magnesium (5)
  Uses of magnesium and magnesium alloys (6)

Calcium
  Occurrence of calcium (7)
  Preparation of calcium (8)
  Properties and uses of calcium (9)
  Test for calcium (9)
  Calcium carbonate (10)
  Hard water: causes and types (11)
  Methods of softening hard water (12)
  Preparation and uses of calcium oxide (13)
  Preparation and uses of calcium hydroxide (14)
  Occurrence and uses of calcium sulfate (15)

Strontium and barium
  Compounds of strontium (16)
  Test for strontium (16)
  Compounds of barium: occurrence and uses (17)

QUESTIONS

Group A

1. What useful alloy is made from beryllium and a heavy metal?
2. List some of the common uses for asbestos.
3. (*a*) What is dolomite? (*b*) For what purposes is it used?
4. Since magnesium is an active metal, why is it that objects made from it do not corrode rapidly as iron does?
5. Compare the preparation of elementary calcium with that of elementary sodium.
6. What are the important uses for metallic calcium?
7. In what forms is calcium carbonate found in nature?
8. (*a*) What does the term *hard water* mean? (*b*) What does the term *soft water* mean? (*c*) What is the difference between temporary and permanent hardness of water?
9. What principle is employed to regenerate a zeolite water softener?
10. Distinguish: (*a*) limestone; (*b*) quicklime; (*c*) slaked lime; (*d*) lime; (*e*) hydrated lime.
11. For what gas is limewater used as a test solution?
12. How could you demonstrate that a piece of coral is a carbonate?
13. Write an equation to show the action of water containing dissolved carbon dioxide on limestone.
14. How is cement manufactured from clay and limestone?
15. How are "red fire" and "green fire" made for fireworks?

Group B

16. Write three balanced equations to show the steps in the preparation of magnesium from sea water.
17. Why must the reduction of magnesium oxide by ferrosilicon be carried out in a vacuum?
18. How do beryllium compounds differ from those of the other Group II elements?
19. Why are the members of the Calcium Family denser and harder than the corresponding members of the Sodium Family?
20. Why does calcium chloride exist as a hydrate, $CaCl_2 \cdot 2H_2O$, while sodium chloride does not occur as a hydrate?
21. Give two reasons why the reaction of calcium with water is not as vigorous as that of potassium and water.
22. (*a*) What metallic ions cause water to be hard? (*b*) What negative ion causes temporary hardness? (*c*) What negative ion causes permanent hardness?
23. What type of chemical reaction occurs between soap and hard water?
24. Write an empirical equation to show the softening action of sodium carbonate on hard water containing: (*a*) calcium sulfate; (*b*) magnesium bicarbonate.
25. What are some uses for calcium chloride which is produced in large quantities as a by-product of the manufacture of Solvay soda?
26. (*a*) How is plaster of Paris made? (*b*) Why does it harden?
27. What are the uses for barium sulfate?

28. (*a*) What impurity may still remain in water that has been passed through both an acid exchange resin and a base exchange resin? (*b*) For what kind of solutions would such water be objectionable?

29. How can you account for the fact that temporary hard water containing Ca^{++} ions can be softened by the addition of limewater, a solution containing Ca^{++} ions and OH^- ions?

PROBLEMS

1. How many kilograms of calcium oxide can be produced from 1.00 metric ton of limestone which contains 12.5% of impurities?

2. How much mass will 86.0 kg of gypsum lose when it is converted into plaster of Paris?

3. Calculate the percentage of beryllium in beryl, $Be_3Al_2Si_6O_{18}$.

4. What quantity of magnesium can be prepared from a metric ton of magnesium oxide, MgO?

5. A cubic mile of sea water contains in solution enough minerals to form about 35 million pounds of magnesium chloride. How much metallic magnesium could be obtained from this?

6. If dolomite is 95.0% a double carbonate of calcium and magnesium, together with 5.0% of impurities such as iron and silica, what is the percentage of magnesium in the sample? (Compute to 3 significant figures.)

7. How many pounds of carbon dioxide can be obtained from a ton of oyster shells that are 81.0% calcium carbonate?

8. How many liters will the carbon dioxide produced in Problem 7 occupy at S.T.P.?

9. If the carbon dioxide of Problem 8 is measured at 720. mm pressure and 20.° C, what volume does it occupy?

Chapter Twenty-six

THE TRANSITION METALS

1. Transition subgroups. The transition elements are unique among the chemical elements because of the *inner building*, or belated filling of the next-to-outermost energy level of the atoms. In the fourth period beyond calcium (at. no. 20) the inner $3d$ sublevel is filled before the filling of the $4s$ and $4p$ sublevels is resumed. In the fifth period there is an inner building of the $4d$ sublevel following strontium (at. no. 38) before the filling of the $5s$ and $5p$ sublevels is resumed.

The filling of the $5d$ sublevel following barium (at. no. 56) in the sixth period is interrupted by still another inner building of the $4f$ sublevel which greatly complicates this period. There are *seven* $4f$ orbitals which can accommodate 14 electrons. Their filling gives rise to the *Lanthanide Series* of rare earth elements which have almost identical properties.

In the seventh period, the filling of the $6d$ sublevel is similarly interrupted by an inner building of the $5f$ sublevel which appears to be characteristic of the *Actinide Series* of rare earth elements. The placement of lawrencium (at. no. 103) in the scandium subgroup seems to mark the resumption of the $6d$ inner building. If chemists succeed in producing element 104, we may assume that it will resemble hafnium (at. no. 72) and be placed in the titanium subgroup.

The transition elements are responsible for the long periods of the Periodic Table as it is arranged in Chapter 5. The choice of the initial and final elements in the transition series depends somewhat on the definition used. Based on electron populations, they are most conveniently considered to consist of the ten subgroups interposed between Group II and Group III beginning with the fourth period. The first-row transition elements are of greatest importance since they are the most abundant. Their electronic configurations are shown in the table opposite.

2. General properties of transition elements. We have stated that the transition elements are characterized by the belated filling of the *d* sublevel in the next-to-outermost shell. This phenomenon is responsible for several unique properties among the transition elements. Important among these are their *distinctly metallic character, variable oxidation states, strong color, tendency to form complex ions,* and *attraction into a magnetic field.*

3. Metallic character. All transition elements are distinctly metallic due to the small number of electrons in the outermost shell. This number does not exceed two. The atoms are small compared to the Group I and Group II metals and show some tendency toward covalent bonding among their particles. Thus, with a few notable exceptions, they are hard and brittle. Their melting points are generally higher than those of other metals.

4. Oxidation states. The transition metals form compounds in which they exhibit several oxidation states. The energy levels of the outermost *d* and *s* electrons do not differ greatly and the ionization energies of these electrons are relatively low.

The *d* sublevel has five available orbitals which can accommodate ten electrons when all are filled. The *s* sublevel has one orbital which can accommodate two electrons when filled. We may expect electrons to occupy the *d* orbitals singly as long as unoccupied orbitals of similar energy are available. The *s* electrons and one or more *d* electrons can be used in chemical bonding.

In the first-row transition metals several $4s$ and $3d$ electrons are available to be transferred to or shared with other substances. Thus several oxidation states become possible (the maximum oxidation state is limited by the total number of $4s$ and $3d$ electrons present).

The common oxidation states of these transition metals are given in the table (page 438) together with their $3d$ and $4s$ electron populations using the orbital notation introduced in Chapter 4. Recall that $\bigcirc$ represents an unoccupied orbital, $\bigotimes$ represents an orbital occupied by one electron, and $\otimes$ represents an orbital occupied by an electron pair.

Observe that the maximum oxidation state increases to +7 for manganese and then decreases. The difficulty of forming the higher oxidation states increases toward the end of the row due to the general increase in ionization energy with atomic number. The higher oxidation states generally involve covalent bonding.

Manganese loses its two $4s$ electrons to become the Mn^{+2} ion. Higher oxidation

ELECTRONIC CONFIGURATIONS OF FIRST–ROW TRANSITION ELEMENTS

Name	Symbol	Atomic Number	1s	2s	2p	3s	3p	3d	4s
scandium	Sc	21	2	2	6	2	6	1	2
titanium	Ti	22	2	2	6	2	6	2	2
vanadium	V	23	2	2	6	2	6	3	2
chromium	Cr	24	2	2	6	2	6	5	1
manganese	Mn	25	2	2	6	2	6	5	2
iron	Fe	26	2	2	6	2	6	6	2
cobalt	Co	27	2	2	6	2	6	7	2
nickel	Ni	28	2	2	6	2	6	8	2
copper	Cu	29	2	2	6	2	6	10	1
zinc	Zn	30	2	2	6	2	6	10	2

OXIDATION STATES OF FIRST-ROW TRANSITION ELEMENTS

Element	Electron Populations			Common Oxidation States
	$1s^2 2s^2 2p^6 3s^2 3p^6$	3d	4s	
scandium	Each			+3
titanium	transition			+2, +3, +4
vanadium	element			+2, +3, +4, +5
chromium	has			+2, +3, +6
manganese	all			+2, +3, +4, +6, +7
iron	of			+2, +3
cobalt	these			+2, +3
nickel	sublevels			+2, +3
copper	filled			+1, +2
zinc				+2

states involve one or more of the $3d$ electrons. In the permanganate ion, MnO_4^-, manganese exhibits the +7 oxidation state. It is covalently bonded with the oxygen atoms.

In general, when the electronic configuration of an atom includes both $3d$ and $4s$ valence electrons, the $3d$ electrons are lower in energy than the $4s$ electrons. Thus, the first electron removed in an ionizing reaction will be the one most loosely held, a $4s$ electron. This is illustrated by the stepwise ionization of titanium. The ground-state configurations of the valence electrons are as follows:

$$Ti^0 \text{ —— } 3d^2 4s^2$$
$$Ti^{+1} \text{ —— } 3d^2 4s^1$$
$$Ti^{+2} \text{ —— } 3d^2 4s^0$$
$$Ti^{+3} \text{ —— } 3d^1$$
$$Ti^{+4} \text{ —— } 3d^0$$

5. Color. The color of the transition metals and their compounds is attributed to the presence of $3d$ electrons in their structure. We know that the electrons of an atom can acquire energy only in discrete quantities. The energy associated with certain wavelengths of light is just the amount needed to raise a $3d$ electron to a higher energy state. When white light illuminates the substance, these wavelength components are absorbed and the remaining light is reflected. It is no longer white light because of the missing components, but is a color which is the complement of the light removed.

6. The formation of complex ions. The NO_3^- ion, $SO_4^=$ ion, and NH_4^+ ion are complex to the extent that they are charged particles made up of more than a single atom. These familiar ions are covalent structures whose net ionic charge is the algebraic sum of the oxidation numbers of all the atoms present. Because of their small size and their stability, the common complex ions behave just like single-atom ions and do not themselves ionize to form simpler particles.

The transition metals have a marked tendency to form complex ions which do ionize slightly into simpler fragments. Because this ionization is slight, an equilibrium is quickly established between complex ion and its component ions.

Complex-ion formation with ammonia (NH_3), cyanide ions (CN^-), thiosulfate ions ($S_2O_3^=$), and thiocyanate ions (SCN^-) are common. In each case the transition metal is the central atom. The number of groups attached to, or *coordinated* with, the central atom is called the *coordination number*. Some complex ions formed by transition metals are given in the table opposite.

When silver nitrate and ammonia-water solutions are mixed, a silver-ammonia complex is formed.

$$Ag^+ + 2NH_3 \rightarrow Ag(NH_3)_2^+$$

$$Ag^+ + 2 : \overset{\displaystyle H}{\underset{\displaystyle \ddot{H}}{\ddot{N}}} : H \rightarrow \left[H : \overset{\displaystyle H}{\ddot{N}} : Ag : \overset{\displaystyle H}{\ddot{N}} : H \right]^+$$

The equilibrium between the silver-ammonia complex, silver ion, and ammonia molecule is established with an ionization constant K_i of approximately 6×10^{-8}.

$$Ag(NH_3)_2^+ \rightleftarrows Ag^+ + 2NH_3$$

$$K_i = \frac{[Ag^+][NH_3]^2}{[Ag(NH_3)_2^+]} = 6 \times 10^{-8}$$

Further additions of NH_3 will reduce the Ag^+ ion concentration according to Le Chatelier's principle.

The formation of complex ions leads to an increase in the solubility of the metal ion by taking it into a complex and thus, in effect removing it from solution as a simple ion. It is possible to increase the solubility of a precipitate by transforming the cation into a complex ion.

The formation of chloride complexes may lead to an increase in solubility where, by common-ion effect, a decrease in solubility would be expected. As an example, let us consider the equilibrium of sparingly soluble AgCl.

$$AgCl(s) \rightleftarrows Ag^+(aq) + Cl^-(aq)$$

A small addition of Cl^- ion does, in fact, shift the equilibrium to the left and lower the solubility as indicated by the common-ion effect. If a large concentration of Cl^- ion is used, *the solid AgCl dissolves.* This anomaly is explained by the formation of the soluble $AgCl_2^-$ complex ion.

The very limited ionization of complex ions is indicated by the small values for the ionization constants K_i given in the table on page 440. The smaller the value for K_i, the more stable is the complex ion and the more effectively it ties up the simple metal ions as part of the soluble complex.

7. Paramagnetism. *Substances that are attracted into a magnetic field are said to be* **paramagnetic.** Paramagnetism among elements and their compounds is associated with the presence of unpaired electrons in the structure. Some transition metals have unpaired *d* electrons.

SOME COMMON COMPLEX IONS

Coordinating Atom	Coordinating Group	Typical Complex ions	Color
N	$\overset{\displaystyle H}{\underset{\displaystyle H}{\circ \ddot{N} : H}}$	$Ag(NH_3)_2^+$ $Ni(NH_3)_4^{++}$ $Co(NH_3)_6^{+++}$	—— blue blue
C	$\circ \ddot{C} ::: N :^-$	$Fe(CN)_6^{=}$ $Fe(CN)_6^{---}$	yellow red
S	$\overset{\displaystyle :\ddot{O}:}{\underset{\displaystyle :\ddot{O}:}{\circ \ddot{S} : \ddot{S} : \ddot{O}:}} =$	$Ag(S_2O_3)_2^{---}$	——
S	$\circ \ddot{S} : C ::: N :^-$	$FeSCN^{++}$	red

IONIZATION OF COMPLEX IONS

Complex ion	Equilibrium reaction	K_i
$Ag(NH_3)_2^+$	$Ag(NH_3)_2^+ \rightleftarrows Ag^+ + 2NH_3$	6×10^{-8}
$Co(NH_3)_6^{++}$	$Co(NH_3)_6^{++} \rightleftarrows Co^{++} + 6NH_3$	1×10^{-5}
$Co(NH_3)_6^{+++}$	$Co(NH_3)_6^{+++} \rightleftarrows Co^{+++} + 6NH_3$	2×10^{-34}
$Cu(NH_3)_4^{++}$	$Cu(NH_3)_4^{++} \rightleftarrows Cu^{++} + 4NH_3$	5×10^{-14}
$Ag(CN)_2^-$	$Ag(CN)_2^- \rightleftarrows Ag^+ + 2CN^-$	2×10^{-19}
$Au(CN)_2^-$	$Au(CN)_2^- \rightleftarrows Au^+ + 2CN^-$	5×10^{-39}
$Cu(CN)_3^-$	$Cu(CN)_3^- \rightleftarrows Cu^+ + 3CN^-$	1×10^{-35}
$Fe(CN)_6^{--}$	$Fe(CN)_6^{--} \rightleftarrows Fe^{++} + 6CN^-$	1×10^{-35}
$Fe(CN)_6^{---}$	$Fe(CN)_6^{---} \rightleftarrows Fe^{+++} + 6CN^-$	1×10^{-42}
$Fe(SCN)^{++}$	$Fe(SCN)^{++} \rightleftarrows Fe^{+++} + SCN^-$	8×10^{-3}
$Ag(S_2O_3)_2^{---}$	$Ag(S_2O_3)_2^{---} \rightleftarrows Ag^+ + 2S_2O_3^=$	6×10^{-14}

Manganese, for example, has 5 unpaired $3d$ electrons as does the Mn^{++} ion. Electron sharing in covalent complexes may reduce the number of unpaired electrons to the point where the substance is not paramagnetic. Most of the compounds of transition metals in all but the highest oxidation states are paramagnetic.

8. Transition metal similarities. The electron population in the outermost shell of the transition elements remains fairly constant, never exceeding two electrons, as the progressive inner building proceeds across a period. It is not surprising to observe a marked similarity of properties within a horizontal sequence as well as down through a subgroup.

In the first five subgroups, those headed by Sc, Ti, V, Cr, and Mn, the most significant similarities appear within each subgroup. However, within the 6th, 7th, and 8th subgroups headed by Fe, Co, and Ni, the similarities across each period are more pronounced than those down each subgroup. This is to say that iron, cobalt, and nickel resemble each other more than do iron, ruthenium, and osmium, the members of the iron subgroup.

In the 9th and 10th subgroups headed by Cu and Zn, we again find the greatest similarity within each subgroup. We shall next examine in some detail some of the most common, and most important, transition metals within the framework of their similarities just stated.

THE IRON FAMILY

9. Members of the Iron Family. The Iron Family consists of the heavy metals *iron, cobalt,* and *nickel.* They are in the fourth period and each is the first member of the subgroup of transition metals that bears its name. The iron subgroup includes *iron* (at. no. 26) in the fourth period, *ruthenium* (at. no. 44) in the fifth period, and *osmium* (at. no. 76) in the sixth

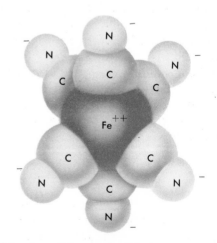

26-1 A possible space model of a complex ion, the hexacyanoferrate(II) ion $Fe(CN)_6^{-4}$.

period. The cobalt subgroup includes *cobalt* (at. no. 27) in the fourth period, *rhodium* (at. no. 45) in the fifth period, and *iridium* (at. no. 77) in the sixth period. The nickel subgroup includes *nickel* (at. no. 28) in the fourth period, *palladium* (at. no. 46) in the fifth period, and *platinum* (at. no. 78) in the sixth period.

As stated in Section 8, the similarities between iron, cobalt, and nickel are more pronounced than those within each of the three subgroups they head. The remaining six members of these three subgroups have properties similar to platinum and may be considered to be members of the *Platinum Family*. They are noble metals—rare and expensive.

Iron is by far the most important member of the Iron Family. Alloys of iron, cobalt, and nickel are important structural metals. Significant properties of the metals of the Iron Family are listed in the table at the bottom of the page.

The Iron Family is located in the midst of the transition elements where atoms have less than the maximum number of $3d$ electrons. Each member exhibits the $+2$ and $+3$ oxidation states. The $+3$ oxidation state of iron tends generally to be more stable than the $+2$ state. This tendency decreases through cobalt to nickel, the latter occurring only rarely in the $+3$ oxidation state. The electron population of iron, cobalt, and nickel sublevels is shown in the accompanying table in which paired and unpaired electrons of the $3d$ and $4s$ sublevels are represented by paired and unpaired dots.

ELECTRON POPULATION OF THE IRON FAMILY

Sublevel	1s	2s	2p	3s	3p	3d	4s
Maximum population	2	2	6	2	6	10	2
iron	2	2	6	2	6	:	:
cobalt	2	2	6	2	6	: : . . .	:
nickel	2	2	6	2	6	: : : . .	:

The two $4s$ electrons are removed with the relative ease characteristic of metals to form the Fe^{++}, Co^{++}, or Ni^{++} ion. In the case of iron, one $3d$ electron is also easily removed to form the Fe^{+++} ion since the five remaining $3d$ electrons constitute a half-filled sublevel. (Recall that filled and half-filled sublevels have extra stability.) It becomes progressively more difficult to remove a $3d$ electron from cobalt and nickel to form the Co^{+++} and Ni^{+++} ions. This is possibly because of the increasing nuclear charge of these atoms and the fact that neither a half-filled nor filled sublevel is left.

All three metals of the Iron Family have a strong magnetic property commonly referred to as *ferromagnetism* because of the unusual extent to which it is possessed by iron. Cobalt is strongly magnetic; nickel is the least magnetic of the group. The ferromagnetic nature of iron, cobalt, and nickel is considered to be related to the similarities in the spin orientation of their unpaired $3d$ electrons.

Each spinning electron is a tiny magnet. Electron pairs are formed by two electrons spinning in opposite directions. The electronic magnetisms of such a pair of elec-

THE IRON FAMILY

Element	Atomic Number	Atomic Weight	Electron Configuration	Oxidation Numbers	Melting Point, °C	Boiling Point, °C	Density, g/cm³
iron	26	55.847	2, 8, 14, 2	$+2, +3$	1535	3000	7.86
cobalt	27	58.9332	2, 8, 15, 2	$+2, +3$	1495	2900	8.90
nickel	28	58.71	2, 8, 16, 2	$+2, +3$	1455	2900	8.90

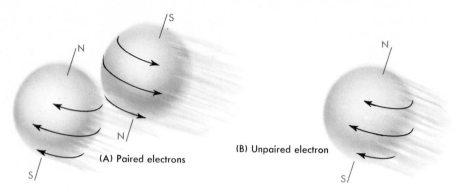

(A) Paired electrons

(B) Unpaired electron

26-2 Magnetism in matter stems basically from the spin of electrons.

trons neutralize each other. In the metals of the Iron Family, groups of atoms may be so aligned as to form a small magnetized region, called a *domain*. Ordinarily magnetic domains with the metallic crystals point in random directions and cancel one another so that the net magnetism is zero. A piece of iron becomes magnetized when an outside force aligns the domains in the same direction. Refer to Fig. 26-2 which illustrates the mechanism of electron spin for paired and unpaired electrons.

10. Occurrence of iron. Iron is the fourth element in abundance by weight in the earth's crust. Nearly 5% of this crust consists of iron. It is the second most abundant metal, being surpassed only by aluminum. Meteors are known to contain iron. This fact, together with the knowledge of the magnetic nature of the earth itself, suggests that the core of the earth may be composed mainly of iron.

Unfortunately, much of the iron in the crust of the earth cannot be removed profitably. Only those iron-bearing minerals from which the iron can be recovered by a practical and profitable method are considered to be iron ores.

The most abundant ore is *hematite*, Fe_2O_3, a reddish-brown substance. *Limonite*, $2Fe_2O_3 \cdot 3H_2O$, is a hydrated oxide which yields a yellow powder when it is

crushed. Magnetite, Fe_3O_4, is a magnetic ore which is rich in iron. Pieces of magnetite will attract iron filings like an ordinary magnet. These were the lodestones of ancient times. *Siderite*, $FeCO_3$, is a carbonate of iron that is also mined as an ore. *Pyrite*, FeS_2, called fool's gold, is an abundant iron mineral used in the production of sulfuric acid. It is of minor importance as an iron ore.

The largest deposits of iron ore in the world are those of hematite in the Lake Superior region of the United States. However, these deposits are rapidly being depleted.

In addition to the high-grade hematite deposits of the Lake Superior region, there is an abundance of low-grade ore, *taconite*, which is a mixture of hematite and magnetite in a matrix of rock. The proportions are two parts magnetite to one part hematite.

The rapid depletion of hematite has stimulated the development of processes for upgrading the taconite deposits into a profitable source of iron. The taconite may be roasted in a reduction furnace to convert the hematite to magnetite. This reduction reaction is shown in the following equation.

$$6Fe_2O_3 + C \rightarrow 4Fe_3O_4 + CO_2$$

The magnetite can be concentrated by magnetic separation to provide a satisfactory substitute for the high-grade hematite as a source of iron.

The process by which low-grade ores are enriched or concentrated is called *beneficiation*. This is a general term applied to any process, physical or chemical, which renders the ore more suitable for reduction to the metal. The magnetic separation of magnetite from low-grade ores is an example of *physical beneficiation*. The roasting of hematite in a reducing atmosphere to convert it to magnetite is an example of *chemical beneficiation*.

11. The blast furnace. Iron oxide is reduced to iron in a giant structure called a *blast furnace*. See Fig. 26-3. A blast of hot air, sometimes enriched with oxygen in the most modern furnaces, is forced into the base of the furnace through blowpipes called *tuyères* (twee-*yair*).

The charge placed in the blast furnace consists of iron oxide, coke, and a flux, in the proper proportions as calculated from an analysis of the raw materials. Usually the flux is limestone, because silica or sand is the most common impurity in the iron ore. Some iron ores contain limestone as an impurity and, in such cases, the flux added is sand.

12. Chemical reactions within the blast furnace. The blast furnace reduces the iron ore to iron and removes the earthy gangue as slag. Coke is required for the first function and the limestone for the second. The products of the blast furnace are *pig iron*, *slag*, and *flue gas*.

The actual chemical changes which occur are complex and still somewhat obscure. The coke is ignited by the blast of hot air and some of it burns forming carbon dioxide.

$$C + O_2 \rightarrow CO_2 \uparrow$$

As the carbon dioxide which is formed just above the tuyères rises through the furnace, it comes in contact with hot coke and is reduced to carbon monoxide.

26-3 The largest and most modern blast furnace, the "Amanda," at Ashland, Ky. (Armco Steel Corporation)

$$CO_2 + C \rightarrow 2CO \uparrow$$

The carbon monoxide thus formed is actually the reducing agent that reduces the iron oxide to metallic iron.

$$Fe_2O_3 + 3CO \rightarrow 2Fe + 3CO_2 \uparrow$$

This reduction probably occurs in steps as temperature increases toward the bottom of the furnace. Possible steps are

$$Fe_2O_3 \rightarrow Fe_3O_4 \rightarrow FeO \rightarrow Fe$$

To prevent the possibility of any reversal of the reactions, the operation is so controlled that there will be a large excess of carbon monoxide. For that reason, the exhaust gases contain from 20 to 30% carbon monoxide.

The white-hot liquid iron collects in the bottom of the furnace. Every 4 or 5 hours it is tapped off. It may be cast into molds to form *pig iron*, or it may be converted directly into steel.

In the middle region of the furnace, the limestone decomposes into calcium oxide and carbon dioxide.

$$CaCO_3 \rightarrow CaO + CO_2 \uparrow$$

The calcium oxide combines with silica to form a calcium silicate slag which is more readily fused than silica.

$$CaO + SiO_2 \rightarrow CaSiO_3$$

This glassy slag also collects in a pool at the bottom of the furnace. Since it has a much lower density than liquid iron, it floats on top of the melted iron and prevents the re-oxidation of the iron. The melted slag is tapped off every few hours. Usually the slag is thrown away, although it is sometimes used for making Portland cement.

13. The properties of wrought iron. *Wrought iron,* the purest form of iron used

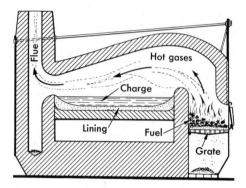

26-4 In the reverberatory furnace the hot gases are deflected down on the charge in the bed of the furnace.

commercially, is made by heating cast iron in a furnace lined with iron oxide. The oxygen from the iron oxide lining unites with the excess carbon in the cast iron, and the oxides of carbon escape. Other impurities in the cast iron are similarly oxidized and form a slag. As the purity of the iron increases, the melting point rises, and the iron is collected as a pasty mass. Most of the slag is removed by hammering the iron while still plastic.

14. Steel production. The relatively high carbon content of cast iron makes it very hard and brittle. It is very brittle at low temperatures due to the presence of phosphorus. It is also very brittle at high temperatures due to the presence of sulfur.

The conversion of cast iron to steel is essentially a purification process in which the impurities are removed by oxidation. Near the end of the process the proper amounts of carbon and selected alloying substances are added to give the desired properties to the steel.

Despite large imports from Japan and Western Europe, steel production in the United States has been well in excess of 100 million tons per year since 1963. Present technological developments in the industry are concerned primarily with improvements in steel quality and efficiency in production methods rather than increased outputs.

The most important producer of steel in the United States today, in terms of quantity, is the *open-hearth process*. Some very high quality steels are made by the *electric-furnace process*. Iron(III) oxide is used as the oxidizing agent in both of these furnaces.

A new process, representing perhaps the most significant technological advance in steelmaking since the end of World War II, is presently exerting a major influence in the steel industry. This is the *basic-oxygen process*, initially developed in Austria as a method of producing small quantities of high quality steel. In this process pure oxygen, delivered at a tremendous rate through a water-cooled lance, is used as the oxidizing agent.

The Jones and Laughlin Steel Corporation was the first major American producer to install a large scale basic-oxygen furnace. By this process a vessel can turn out 300 tons of high quality steel in 50 minutes, eight times faster than the traditional open-hearth furnace.

The impact of the basic-oxygen process can be visualized from the fact that two recently installed basic-oxygen furnaces, each rated at 250 tons and both having an annual capacity of 2.2 million tons, have replaced a 14-furnace open-hearth shop which had a capacity of 1.9 million tons. Steel production experts have predicted that no more open-hearth furnaces will be built.

Other recent technological advances of great importance in steel production are:

Continuous casting, in which freshly made liquid steel is cast directly into slabs ready for the rolling mills. Several conventional steps in steelmaking are by-passed in this process.

Vacuum degassing, in which steel is melted by either an electric arc or induction heating in a high vacuum. Unwanted gases are removed and the purity and uniformity of the metal are improved by this process.

15. Open-hearth process.

1. The furnace. The open-hearth furnace holds a pool of molten steel 30 to 80 feet in length, 12 to 15 feet in width, and about 2 feet in depth. From 50 to 200 tons are made in one batch. The furnace is built of steel plates covered with a thick lining of either limestone or silica. The choice of the lining depends on whether the cast iron has acid or basic impurities.

2. The heating system. A high temperature is necessary to burn out the impurities from the cast iron, and to melt the steel

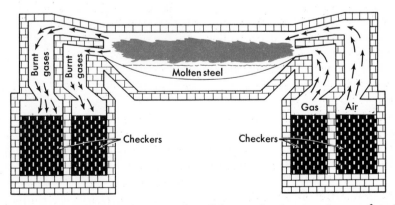

26-5 Sectional diagram of an open-hearth furnace for the manufacture of steel.

26-6 The electric furnace pictured here is tilted while a heat of high grade steel is being tapped. These furnaces may draw 12,000 amperes at 40 volts to produce the heat required to make stainless steel and other alloy steels. (Armco Steel Corporation)

scrap which forms part of the charge. Producer gas is used as the fuel. Both the gas and the air for its combustion are preheated before entering the furnace.

3. The charge. The charge for an open-hearth furnace consists of molten iron from the blast furnace, scrap steel, iron ore, and limestone. The iron ore supplies oxygen to unite with the carbon in the liquid iron from the blast furnace. The limestone unites with impurities to form a slag which is drained off. Scrap "steel" may form as much as 50% of the charge.

The impurities in the pig iron are oxidized in the following way:

$$3C + Fe_2O_3 \rightarrow 3CO \uparrow + 2Fe$$
$$3Mn + Fe_2O_3 \rightarrow 3MnO + 2Fe$$
$$12P + 10Fe_2O_3 \rightarrow 3P_4O_{10} + 20Fe$$
$$3Si + 2Fe_2O_3 \rightarrow 3SiO_2 + 4Fe$$
$$3S + 2Fe_2O_3 \rightarrow 3SO_2 \uparrow + 4Fe$$

The limestone flux decomposes as in the blast furnace:

$$CaCO_3 \rightarrow CaO + CO_2 \uparrow$$

Calcium oxide and the oxides of impurities, except those of carbon and sulfur which escape as gases, react to form slag:

$$P_4O_{10} + 6CaO \rightarrow 2Ca_3(PO_4)_2$$
$$SiO_2 + CaO \rightarrow CaSiO_3$$
$$MnO + SiO_2 \rightarrow MnSiO_3$$

16. The electric-furnace process. In one common type of electric furnace for making steel, large carbon electrodes extend through the top of the furnace (see Fig. 26-6). The furnace is lined with dolomite. The charge usually consists of scrap steel, cast iron, and iron ore.

When the electric current is turned on, an arc forms through the charge between the electrodes, producing the heat necessary to carry out the process. There is no electrolysis. This process produces high grade steel. It allows for testing of the steel at various intervals before it is finished. Purer raw materials are also used in the charge. Furthermore, the operation is carried on in a reducing atmosphere, which prevents oxidation of the steel.

26-7 Charging a basic-oxygen furnace with molten iron. (Jones & Laughlin Steel Corp.)

26-8 The oxygen lance delivering pure oxygen into a basic-oxygen furnace at a speed of Mach 2. (Jones & Laughlin Steel Corp.)

17. Basic-oxygen process. The basic-oxygen furnace consists of a refractory lined vessel open at the top and capable of being rotated through 360° for charging, tapping, and relining. The furnace may be charged with scrap, molten iron, lime, limestone, and iron ore as required.

A water-cooled lance is inserted from above to a predetermined position over the charge and oxygen is blown in at a speed of Mach 2 (2 times the speed of sound). A tremendous turbulence is produced by the oxygen crashing into the molten metal at this speed. The oxygen is delivered for 20 minutes to oxidize the carbon and refine the steel. The total operational time is about 50 minutes per batch. The finished steel is poured into ingot molds or delivered directly to a continuous casting unit for immediate working.

18. Vacuum-degassing   processes. The exacting requirements placed on

special steels for gas turbine blades, rocket motor cases, and parts for spacecraft place these metals in a "superalloy" category. Gases such as hydrogen, nitrogen, and oxygen retained in steel cause the center of the solidified metal to be porous and contribute to its lack of structural uniformity.

Two highly successful methods have been developed to remove the unwanted gases in steel under vacuum conditions. By these *vacuum-degassing processes* special steel alloys of the highest quality are produced. They differ simply in the manner of melting the steel; the metal is heated by *induction* or an *electric arc*.

1. Vacuum-induction process. The steel is melted and refined in a crucible surrounded by an electric coil. A secondary current is induced in the steel to provide the melting heat. The entire furnace is contained in a highly evacuated chamber. The vacuum pumps remove the offending gases. Alloy additions are made through vacuum locks. The final product is cast into ingots under vacuum conditions also.

2. Vacuum-arc process. The steel to be melted serves as one electrode and an

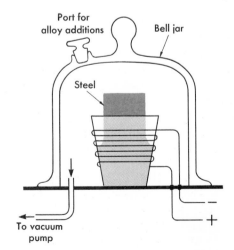

26-9 Vacuum degassing by induction-melting.

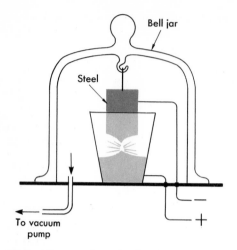

26-10   Vacuum degassing by electric-arc process.

evacuated crucible serves as the other electrode. An electric arc between the two electrodes causes the steel to melt into the crucible. Gaseous impurities are removed by the vacuum pumps and the crucible serves as an ingot mold to allow the metal to solidify under high-vacuum conditions.

19. Pure iron. Pure iron is a metal that is seldom seen. It is silver-white, soft, ductile, tough, and does not tarnish readily. It melts at 1535° C. Commercial iron contains carbon and other impurities that alter its properties. Cast iron melts at about 1150° C. All forms of iron corrode, or rust, in moist air, so it is not a self-protective metal. The rust that forms is brittle and scales off, leaving the metal underneath exposed to corrosion.

In many cases the corrosion of iron seems to be an electrochemical process. A carbon particle in contact with a piece of moist iron causes the iron to rust rapidly. The carbon acts as the positive element of a miniature electrochemical cell, and the iron becomes the negative element (see Fig. 26-12). Rain water containing dissolved carbon dioxide enhances the action. Merely a difference in the amount of

oxygen over the surface of wet iron will result in rusting. A single drop of rain containing dissolved carbon dioxide sets up a tiny cell between the iron at the center of the drop and the iron around the edge. Iron(II) hydroxide is formed and is readily converted to iron(III) hydroxide. By loss of water the familiar red rust, $Fe_2O_3 \cdot XH_2O$ is formed.

Dilute acids generally act readily on iron, but alkalies do not react with it. Concentrated nitric acid does not react with iron. In fact, dipping iron into concentrated nitric acid renders the iron *passive*, or *inactive*, with respect to its behavior toward other chemicals. Concentrated sulfuric acid has little effect on iron.

20. Three oxides of iron. Of the three oxides of iron, *iron(II) oxide*, FeO, is of little importance since it oxidizes rapidly when exposed to the air forming *iron(III) oxide*, Fe_2O_3. This oxide is the important ore of iron. It is used as a cheap red paint pigment known as red ocher, Venetian red, or Indian red. It is also used for grinding and polishing glass lenses and mirrors. When used for this purpose it is referred to as *rouge*.

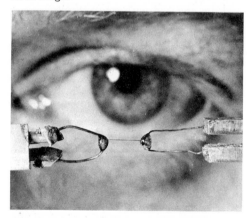

26-11   A tiny "whisker" of pure iron, free of the structural imperfections of the ordinary metal, provides scientists with a means of studying the nature of the enormous forces which bind atoms tightly together. (Westinghouse)

Limonite is a natural *hydrated iron(III) oxide* which is pulverized and used as a pigment called yellow ocher. When it is heated or roasted, it forms pigments known as *siennas* and *umbers*. *Magnetic iron oxide*, Fe_3O_4, is an important ore. It is composed of Fe_2O_3 and FeO, and may be considered to be iron(II, III) oxide.

21. Reactions of the Fe^{++} ion. Hydrated iron(II) sulfate, $FeSO_4 \cdot 7H_2O$ is the most important compound of iron in the +2 oxidation state. It is commonly called *green vitriol* or *copperas*. It is used to form a mordant, and for making blue-black inks. Iron(II) sulfate may be prepared by the action of dilute sulfuric acid on iron. The crystalline hydrate, on exposure to air, loses water of hydration and turns brown due to oxidation. Iron(II) sulfate in solution is gradually oxidized to the iron(III) state by dissolved oxygen. The formation of a brown precipitate of basic iron(III) sulfate is evidence of this change.

$$4FeSO_4 + O_2 + 2H_2O \rightarrow 4Fe(OH)SO_4 \downarrow$$

By making the solution acidic with sulfuric acid and adding a small amount of metallic iron, the Fe^{++} ion may be readily maintained in the reduced state. Hydrated iron(II) ammonium sulfate, $Fe(NH_4)_2(SO_4)_2 \cdot 6H_2O$, is a better source of Fe^{++} ions in the laboratory because it is stable in contact with air.

Iron(II) salts are readily oxidized to iron(III) salts by use of the corresponding acid and an oxidizing agent. In the case of the nitrate, nitric acid meets both requirements.

$$3Fe(NO_3)_2 + 4HNO_3 \rightarrow$$
$$3Fe(NO_3)_3 + NO \uparrow + 2H_2O$$

Crystals of hydrated iron(II) chloride, $FeCl_2 \cdot 2H_2O$, are blue as long as the reduced state is maintained. Gradual oxi-

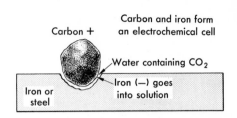

26-12 Iron and steel contain impurities and corrode readily unless covered by a protective coating. The miniature electrochemical cell formed between the carbon and iron surfaces speeds up the rusting action.

dation to the iron(III) state is evident as a green color develops. Iron(II) chloride may be prepared by the action of hydrochloric acid on iron.

Iron(II) hydroxide is formed as a white precipitate when sodium hydroxide is added to a solution of an iron(II) salt. The precipitate is first green, in the presence of air, and finally brown as the iron(III) hydroxide is formed.

We may show the oxidation of the Fe^{++} ion in the use of an iron ink (ordinary blue-black ink). If a freshly prepared solution of iron(II) sulfate is added to a solution of tannic acid, the nearly colorless compound, *iron(II) tannate*, is formed. It slowly oxidizes to form the black compound, *iron(III) tannate*. Usually a blue dye is added to an iron ink, which also contains dextrin to make it wet the pen and the paper.

Iron inks are easily removed by the use of a reducing agent, such as oxalic acid, or salt and lemon juice. Skimmed milk applied at once to fresh ink stains, and then followed by cold water, will usually remove nearly all the stain.

22. Reactions of the Fe^{+++} ion. Iron(III) chloride, $FeCl_3 \cdot 6H_2O$, is the most important compound of iron in the +3 oxidation state. The anhydrous salt may be recovered as black crystals in the composition reaction between iron and chlorine. The hydrated Fe^{+++} ion,

$Fe(H_2O)_6^{+++}$, imparts a pale violet color which usually is not seen because of hydrolysis. Hydrated iron(III) chloride has a yellow-brown color.

The Fe^{+++} ion undergoes hydrolysis in water solutions of iron(III) salts. The solutions are acidic.

$$Fe^{+++} + 2H_2O \rightleftarrows FeOH^{++} + H_3O^+$$
$$FeOH^{++} + 2H_2O \rightleftarrows Fe(OH)_2^+ + H_3O^+$$
$$Fe(OH)_2^+ + 2H_2O \rightleftarrows Fe(OH)_3 + H_3O^+$$

The hydrolysis is extensive when it occurs in boiling water and the blood-red colloidal suspension of iron(III) hydroxide is formed.

Iron(III) ions are removed from solution by the addition of a solution containing hydroxide ions. A red-brown gelatinous precipitate of iron(III) hydroxide is formed. By evaporating the water, red Fe_2O_3 remains. It is the Venetian red pigment, or the rouge polishing powder referred to in Section 20.

$$Fe^{+++} + 3OH^- \rightarrow Fe(OH)_3 \downarrow$$

23. Tests for the iron ions. Potassium hexacyanoferrate(II), $K_4Fe(CN)_6$ (also called potassium ferrocyanide), is a light yellow crystalline salt containing the complex hexacyanoferrate(II) ion (ferrocyanide ion), $Fe(CN)_6^{--}$. The iron is in the +2 oxidation state. It may be formed by adding an excess of cyanide ions to a solution of an iron(II) salt.

> **CAUTION:** *Solutions containing the cyanide ion are deadly poisons and should never be handled by inexperienced chemistry students.*

$$6KCN + FeCl_2 \rightarrow K_4Fe(CN)_6 + 2KCl$$

The iron of the $Fe(CN)_6^{--}$ ion may be oxidized by chlorine to the +3 state to form the hexacyanoferrate(III) ion (ferricyanide ion) $Fe(CN)_6^{\equiv}$.

$$2K_4Fe(CN)_6 + Cl_2 \rightarrow 2K_3Fe(CN)_6 + 2KCl$$

The oxidation of the iron from the +2 state to the +3 state is accompanied by the reduction of the chlorine from the 0 to the -1 state. Potassium hexacyanoferrate(III), $K_3Fe(CN)_6$ (known also as potassium ferricyanide), is a dark red crystalline salt.

When Fe^{++} ions and $Fe(CN)_6^{\equiv}$ ions are brought together a deep blue precipitate forms. *The pigment color is due to the presence of iron in two different oxidation states.* This insoluble substance is called Turnbull's blue, and is now considered to have the composition $KFeFe(CN)_6 \cdot H_2O$.

$$FeSO_4 + K_3Fe(CN)_6 + H_2O \rightarrow$$
$$KFeFe(CN)_6 \cdot H_2O \downarrow + K_2SO_4$$

or simply

$$Fe^{++} + K^+ + Fe(CN)_6^{\equiv} + H_2O \rightarrow$$
$$KFeFe(CN)_6 \cdot H_2O \downarrow$$

Similarly, Fe^{+++} ions and $Fe(CN)_6^{--}$ ions form a deep blue precipitate. Again the color is a pigment color and is due to the presence of *two different* oxidation states of iron. The precipitate is called Prussian blue, and is now recognized as having the same composition as Turnbull's blue, $KFeFe(CN)_6 \cdot H_2O$.

$$Fe^{+++} + K^+ + Fe(CN)_6^{--} + H_2O \rightarrow$$
$$KFeFe(CN)_6 \cdot H_2O \downarrow$$

Fe^{++} ions and $Fe(CN)_6^{--}$ ions form a white precipitate of $K_2FeFe(CN)_6$, if precautions have been taken to prevent the oxidation of any Fe^{++} ions. Of course, on exposure to air, it begins to turn blue due to oxidation. Fe^{+++} ions and $Fe(CN)_6^{--}$ ions give only a brown solution. From these reactions it is evident that we have a means of detecting the presence of the two oxidation states of iron.

1. *Test for the Fe⁺⁺ ion.* Suppose a few drops of $K_3Fe(CN)_6$ solution are added to a solution of iron(II) sulfate (or iron(II) ammonium sulfate). The characteristic dark blue precipitate, $KFeFe(CN)_6 \cdot H_2O$ forms.

$$Fe^{++}+SO_4^{=}+3K^{+}+Fe(CN)_6^{\equiv}+H_2O \rightarrow$$
$$KFeFe(CN)_6 \cdot H_2O \downarrow + 2K^{+} + SO_4^{=}$$

The two potassium ions and the sulfate ion are merely spectator ions in this reaction. *The formation of a blue precipitate when $K_3Fe(CN)_6$ is added to a solution suspected of containing the iron(II) ion serves as a test for the Fe⁺⁺ ion.*

2. *Test for the Fe⁺⁺⁺ ion.* Suppose a few drops of $K_4Fe(CN)_6$ solution is added to a solution of iron(III) chloride, the characteristic blue precipitate, $KFeFe(CN)_6 \cdot H_2O$, forms.

$$Fe^{+++}+3Cl^{-}+4K^{+}+Fe(CN)_6^{==}+H_2O \rightarrow$$
$$KFeFe(CN)_6 \cdot H_2O \downarrow + 3K^{+} + 3Cl^{-}$$

Three potassium ions and three chloride ions are spectators in this reaction. *The formation of a blue precipitate when $K_4Fe(CN)_6$ is added to a solution suspected of containing iron(III) ions serves as a test for the Fe⁺⁺⁺ ion.*

Potassium thiocyanate, KSCN, provides another excellent test for the Fe⁺⁺⁺ ion. It is often used to confirm the $K_4Fe(CN)_6$ test. A blood-red solution results from the formation of the complex $FeSCN^{++}$ ion.

24. Cobalt. Cobalt is found in nature in numerous minerals, together with iron, nickel, copper, silver, and arsenic. It is ordinarily recovered as a by-product of the smelting of various ores. Both cobalt and nickel often remain as oxides after the roasting and reduction processes. Cobalt is usually found combined with arsenic and sulfur. The principal ores are *cobaltite*, CoAsS; *smaltite*, $CoAs_2$; and *linnalite*, Co_3S_4. Metallic cobalt is produced by the reduction of its oxide with aluminum.

This metal so closely resembles nickel that the two metals are often spoken of as "twins." Cobalt has been used to plate iron, but its most important uses are in the making of alloys.

Stellite, a very hard alloy of cobalt and chromium, is used for making metal-cutting lathe tools. *Carboloy* is made by combining cobalt with a carbide of tungsten. It is one of the hardest materials manufactured. It is a tough alloy, not easily broken, and is used for high-speed cutting tools. *Alnico* is a very strongly ferromagnetic alloy composed of aluminum, cobalt, iron, and nickel. It is used extensively for making small permanent magnets used in loudspeakers, telephones, and hearing aids.

25. Compounds of cobalt. Cobalt forms cobalt(II) and cobalt(III) compounds, in which the oxidation numbers are +2 and +3, respectively. The cobalt(II) compounds, which exist as red crystals and form pink-colored solutions, are more common than cobalt(III) compounds.

Cobalt(II) chloride, $CoCl_2 \cdot 6H_2O$, is red when it exists as the hydrate, but turns

26-13 Fused pellets of cobalt. For centuries its salts have given color to porcelains. (B. M. Shaub)

blue when dehydrated. Paper covered with a solution of cobalt(II) chloride may be used as a crude *hygrometer* to tell how much moisture the air contains. In damp weather, the paper appears pink, changing to violet, and then to blue, as the air becomes less moist.

Cobalt(II) nitrate, $Co(NO_3)_2$, is used to some extent in analytical work. Cobalt compounds impart a blue color to glass. This metal can be made radioactive and is used in treating the victims of certain types of cancer.

26. Cobalt nitrate tests. Cobalt(II) nitrate provides a test for the identification of aluminum, magnesium, and zinc by a method of blowpipe analysis. The test is based on the fact that the nitrate, when heated strongly, decomposes to the oxide and combines with the oxides of these metals to form distinctly colored complexes. A compound of the unknown metal is first heated in the oxidizing flame of the blowpipe on charcoal or plaster of Paris. A drop of cobalt(II) nitrate is then added and the mass is heated again. If *aluminum* is present, a blue coloration develops. *Magnesium* yields a pink-colored mass. *Zinc* produces a green color.

27. Nickel. Nickel is a hard, silver-white metal, capable of taking a high polish. It does not tarnish easily. Its chemical properties resemble those of iron, although it is less active.

Nickel is used for toughening steel, for nickel-plating, and as a catalyst for hardening oils. It is used also in several alloys. The *coin nickel* used in the United States is composed of 25% nickel and 75% copper. *Monel metal* contains about 67% nickel, 28% copper, and small quantities of iron and manganese. It is made directly from a complex ore of nickel and copper, from which neither metal can be satisfactorily extracted. This alloy is strong and tough, and it resists the action of air, sea water,

and acids. Monel metal is used in making valves for steam engines, decorative metal trimmings, and for other purposes requiring a metal that does not tarnish easily. *Nichrome*, an alloy of nickel, chromium, iron, and manganese, melts at a high temperature, and has a high resistance to the passage of an electric current. It is used in making the heating units for electric irons, toasters, and other heating appliances.

28. Compounds of nickel. Nickel forms nickel(II) and (rarely) nickel(III) salts, in which the oxidation numbers are +2 and +3, respectively. Nickel(II) salts, which are more common, usually crystallize as beautiful green crystals. The most common salts are nickel(II) chloride, nickel(II) nitrate, and nickel(II) sulfate. Nickel(II) sulfide, when prepared by precipitation, is a black, amorphous powder. Nickel flake and nickel(II) oxide are used for making the active mixture inside the positive plates of the Edison storage battery. When such a battery is charged, *the nickel(II) compound is oxidized to the*

26-14   Pure nickel squares sheared from an electrolytically refined nickel cathode. (The International Nickel Co., Inc.)

nickel(III) compound, being reduced again as the battery is discharged. Nickel(II) ammonium sulfate, a double salt, is used as the electrolyte for nickel plating. A piece of pure nickel is used as the anode of the plating cell, and the object to be plated is the cathode.

THE COPPER FAMILY

29. Members of the Copper Family. The Copper Family consists of *copper*, *silver*, and *gold*, the copper subgroup of transition metals. All three metals appear below hydrogen in the electrochemical series. They are not easily oxidized and may be found in nature in the free, or native, state. Because of their pleasing appearance, durability, and relative scarcity, these metals have been used for ornamental and coinage purposes since the time of their discovery.

The atoms of copper, silver, and gold have a single electron in their outermost energy levels. Thus they form compounds in which they exhibit the +1 oxidation state. To this extent, they resemble the Group I metals of the Sodium Family.

Each metal of the Copper Family has 18 electrons in the next-to-outermost shell and, because the *d* electrons in this shell have energies that differ only slightly from the energy of the outer *s* electron, one or two of these electrons can be removed with comparative ease. Thus, copper and gold commonly form compounds in which they exhibit respectively the +2 and +3 oxida-

tion states. In the case of silver the +2 oxidation state has been achieved only under extreme oxidizing conditions.

Copper, silver, and gold are very dense, ductile, and malleable. They are classed as heavy metals along with the other transition metals in the central region of the Periodic Table. Some important properties of each metal are shown in the table at the bottom of the page.

30. Copper and its recovery. Copper, alloyed with tin in the form of bronze, has been in use for over 5000 years. Native copper deposits lie deep underground and are difficult to mine.

Sulfide ores of copper yield most of our supplies of this metal. *Chalcocite*, Cu_2S, *chalcopyrite*, $CuFeS_2$, and *bornite*, Cu_3FeS_3, are the principal sulfide ores. The beautiful minerals *malachite*, $Cu_2(OH)_2CO_3$, and *azurite*, $Cu_3(OH)_2(CO_3)_2$, are basic carbonates of copper. Malachite is a rich green, and azurite is a deep blue. Besides serving as ores of copper, fine specimens of these minerals are sometimes polished for ornamental purposes or for use in the making of jewelry.

The carbonate ores of copper are leached with dilute sulfuric acid forming a solution of copper(II) sulfate. The copper is then recovered by electrolysis. High grade carbonate ores may be roasted to convert them into copper(II) oxide, the oxide then being reduced with coke to yield the metallic copper.

The sulfide ores are usually low-grade and require concentrating before they

THE COPPER FAMILY

Element	Atomic Number	Atomic Weight	Electron Configuration	Oxidation Numbers	Melting Point, °C	Boiling Point, °C	Density g/cm³
copper	29	63.54	2, 8, 18, 1	+1, +2	1083	2336	8.9
silver	47	107.870	2, 8, 18, 18, 1	+1	960.8	1950	10.5
gold	79	196.967	2, 8, 18, 32, 18, 1	+1, +3	1063	2600	19.3

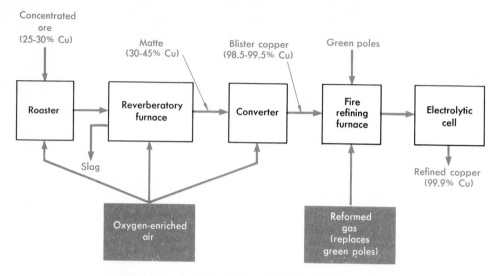

26-15   New technology in the copper refining process.

can be smelted profitably. The concentration is accomplished by oil-flotation. Earthy gangue is wetted by water and the ore is wetted by oil. A froth is produced and the oil-wetted ore is floated to the surface of the flotation cell in the froth. (See Chapter 15, Section 14, for a detailed description of the flotation process.) This treatment changes the concentration of the ore from 1 to 2% content of copper to a concentration which may be as high as 25 to 30% copper.

The concentrated ore is partially roasted to form a mixture of Cu_2S, FeS, FeO, and SiO_2 known as *calcine*. The roasting process using oxygen-enriched air yields sulfur dioxide of high quality which is converted directly into sulfuric acid. Calcine is fused with limestone as a flux in a furnace. Part of the iron is removed as a silicate slag, while the rest of the iron, together with the copper, forms a mixture of sulfides which is commonly referred to as *matte*. Copper matte is processed in the reverberatory furnace and the end product contains approximately 40% copper.

The melted matte is then refined in a converter supplied with oxygen-enriched air as the oxidizing agent. Sulfur from the sulfides, as well as arsenic and antimony impurities, are removed as volatile oxides. Most of the iron is removed as a slag. Some of the copper(I) sulfide is converted into copper(I) oxide which then reacts with more copper(I) sulfide to form metallic copper and sulfur dioxide. The following equations show the chemical reactions involved in this process.

$$2Cu_2S + 3O_2 \rightarrow 2Cu_2O + 2SO_2 \uparrow$$
$$2Cu_2O + Cu_2S \rightarrow 6Cu + SO_2 \uparrow$$

The molten copper is cast as *blister* copper of 98.5 to 99.5% purity. As the copper cools, dissolved gases escape forming blisters, hence the name. Impurities remaining are iron, silver, gold, and perhaps zinc. In the fourth step of the copper-refining process blister copper is further purified in a fire-refining furnace.

31.   Electrolytic refining of copper. Since crude copper contains appreciable amounts of silver and gold, the cost of its refining is offset by the recovery of these precious metals. Copper is largely used for making electric conductors, and very small amounts of impurities greatly increase the electric resistance.

In electrolytic refining, sheets of pure copper are used as the cathodes in electrolytic cells, and large plates of impure copper are used as the anodes. The electrolyte is a solution of copper(II) sulfate in sulfuric acid. A direct current at low voltage is used to operate the cell. During the electrolysis, copper and other metals above it in the electrochemical series, which compose the anode, are oxidized and enter the solution as ions.

$$Cu^0 - 2e^- \rightarrow Cu^{++}$$
$$Fe^0 - 2e^- \rightarrow Fe^{++}$$
$$Zn^0 - 2e^- \rightarrow Zn^{++}$$

At the low voltages used, the less active silver and gold are not oxidized and so do not go into solution. As the anode is used up they fall to the bottom of the cell as a sludge, from which they are easily recovered.

We might expect the various positive ions of the electrolyte to be reduced at the cathode. However, H_3O^+ ions, Fe^{++} ions, and Zn^{++} ions all require higher voltages than Cu^{++} ions to be discharged. At the low potential maintained across the cell, only Cu^{++} ions are reduced at the cathode.

$$Cu^{++} + 2e^- \rightarrow Cu^0$$

Thus of all the metals present, only copper plates out on the cathode. Electrolytic copper is over 99.9% pure.

32. Properties of copper. Copper is a soft, ductile, malleable, red metal with a specific gravity of 8.9. Next to silver, it is the best conductor of electricity.

Heated in air, copper forms a black coating of copper(II) oxide, CuO. A copper wire, and most copper compounds, color a Bunsen flame green.

Copper forms copper(II) salts which dissociate in water to form blue solutions. The color is characteristic of the hydrated copper(II) ion, $Cu(H_2O)_4{}^{++}$. The addition of an excess of ammonia to solutions containing this ion produces the deeper blue, complex $Cu(NH_3)_4{}^{++}$ ion.

An excess of sulfur vapor forms a blue-black coating of copper(I) sulfide on hot copper. In moist air, copper tarnishes and forms a protective coating of a green basic carbonate, $Cu_2(OH)_2CO_3$. Sulfur dioxide in the air may also combine with copper to produce a green basic sulfate, $Cu_4(OH)_6SO_4$. The green color seen on copper roofs is due to the formation of these compounds.

Both copper(I) and copper(II) compounds are known, although copper(II) compounds are much more common. Copper(II) oxide is used in current rectifiers to change alternating current to direct current. It is also used as an oxidizing agent in chemical laboratories.

Hydrated copper(II) sulfate, $CuSO_4 \cdot 5H_2O$, commonly called *blue vitriol*, is an important copper compound. It is used in electroplating, to kill algae in reservoirs,

26-16 The principle of electrolytic refining of copper is illustrated by the action in this simple electroplating cell. (Fritz Goro, Life Magazine)

to make the agricultural spray known as Bordeaux mixture, and to prepare other copper compounds.

Because copper stands below hydrogen in the replacement series, it does not replace hydrogen from acids. Thus it is not acted on by nonoxidizing acids such as hydrochloric and dilute sulfuric except very slowly when oxygen is present. The oxidizing acids, nitric and hot concentrated sulfuric, react vigorously with copper to produce the corresponding copper(II) salts. These are typical oxidation-reduction reactions.

CAUTION: *All the soluble compounds of copper are poisonous.*

33. Tests for the Cu^{++} ion. A dilute solution of a copper(II) salt changes to a very deep-blue color when ammonia is added. This is caused by the formation of the complex Cu(NH$_3$)$_4$$^{++}$ ion. The addition of K$_4$Fe(CN)$_6$ to a solution containing the Cu^{++} ion produces a red precipitate of Cu$_2$Fe(CN)$_6$, copper(II) hexacyanoferrate(II), also known as copper(II) ferrocyanide. If copper is present in a borax bead formed in an *oxidizing* flame, a clear blue color appears on cooling. The hot bead is green. A bead formed in a *reducing* flame is colorless while hot, and an opaque red when cool.

34. Silver and its recovery. Silver is obtained as a by-product in the refining of silver-bearing lead and copper ores. Silver is also found free in nature. Silver sulfide, Ag$_2$S, and silver chloride, AgCl, are common silver ores.

Extraction processes are the following:

1. By-product silver. The residue that falls to the bottom of the electrolytic tank in which copper is refined is treated with dilute sulfuric acid to remove impurities more active than silver. By treating the residue with concentrated sulfuric acid, the silver is separated from the gold as

silver sulfate. Scrap copper is then added to the silver sulfate solution to precipitate the silver.

$$Ag_2SO_4 + Cu \rightarrow CuSO_4 + 2Ag \downarrow$$

2. Cyanide process. Crushed silver ore is roasted with common salt to convert the silver to silver chloride. This sparingly soluble salt ($K_{sp} = 1.2 \times 10^{-10}$) is added to a dilute solution of NaCN and, on standing, soluble complex Ag(CN)$_2$$^-$ ions are formed.

$$Ag^+ + 2CN^- \rightarrow Ag(CN)_2^-$$

Silver is precipitated from the filtered sodium argenticyanide solution by adding metallic zinc:

$$2Ag(CN)_2^- + Zn \rightarrow Zn(CN)_4^- + 2Ag \downarrow$$

3. Parkes process. Crude lead which contains silver and gold as impurities is melted in a large kettle. Zinc is then added, and the mixture is stirred. Both silver and gold are much more soluble in molten zinc than in lead. The zinc rises to the surface, carrying with it almost all of the silver and gold. The zinc alloy is scraped off, and the zinc is vaporized in a retort. The residue which is left consists of silver, gold, and a little lead. It is heated in a crucible made of bone ash, called a *cupel*. The lead oxidizes, and the lead oxide is absorbed by the cupel, leaving a button of silver and gold. Nitric acid reacts with silver but does not react with gold. In this way, the silver is separated from the gold.

35. Properties and uses of silver. Silver is a soft, white, lustrous metal. Its specific gravity is 10.5. It is the best conductor of heat and electricity known.

Silver is an inactive metal. It does not unite with oxygen in the air, even at elevated temperatures. Traces of hydrogen sulfide in the air cause a brownish-black coating of silver sulfide to form on the surface of silver. The sulfur compounds present in such foods as mustard and eggs cause silverware to tarnish readily.

Silver reacts readily with oxidizing acids such as nitric acid and hot concentrated sulfuric acid. Hydrochloric acid does not react with it, nor does fused sodium hydroxide or potassium hydroxide.

United States silver coins have traditionally contained 90% silver and 10% copper. Since 1965, half dollars containing 40% silver and quarters and dimes with no silver have been minted. These silverless coins consist of a copper-nickel alloy bonded to a core of pure copper. In silvering mirrors, a solution of a silver compound mixed with a reducing agent such as formaldehyde is poured on the clean glass. A film of metallic silver is deposited on the glass as the reduction occurs. Next to coinage, the principal use for silver is in photography.

The halogen compounds of silver— silver chloride, $AgCl$; silver bromide, $AgBr$; and silver iodide, AgI—are sensitive to light, especially if organic matter is present. The chemical action which occurs is one of reduction. A black, finely divided deposit of silver is formed. Silver bromide is the most light sensitive of the halogen compounds of silver. However, all three are used in photography.

Silver nitrate, $AgNO_3$, crystallizes in colorless scales. It is sometimes used, under the name *lunar caustic*, for cauterizing wounds and bites. *Argyrol* is a compound of silver with a protein, silver vitellin, that is used in medicine as an antiseptic.

36. Test for the silver ion. Certain solubility characteristics of the silver, Ag^+, ion enable us to recognize its presence in solutions. The chlorides of silver, mercury(I), and lead are very slightly soluble. If a soluble chloride is added to a test solution containing silver ions, silver chloride forms as a white precipitate. If lead and

26-17   Ancient silver coins. (Life Magazine)

mercury(I) ions are present, they too precipitate as chlorides. Certain other metallic oxy-chloride complexes, which otherwise might precipitate, may be prevented from doing so by first making the test solution acid with HNO_3.

Since lead chloride is soluble in hot water, it may be removed from the precipitate by washing with hot water. The silver chloride can be separated from the mercury(I) chloride in the precipitate by washing it with an ammonia-water solution. This produces the soluble complex $Ag(NH_3)_2^+$ ion. The basic filtrate contains these silver-ammonia ions and chloride ions. By neutralizing the hydroxide ions of the basic filtrate with nitric acid, silver chloride again precipitates. *The formation of a white precipitate when this filtrate is made acidic in the manner described indicates the presence of silver.*

37. Gold and its recovery. Gold was probably the first metal known to man. Primitive people collected gold for its ornamental value before any metallurgical processes were known.

Gold occurs in *alluvial* deposits as fine particles mixed with sand. It is also found in veins mixed with quartz. While it is usually found as the native metal, compounds of gold with tellurium sometimes occur. Sea water contains 0.1 to 0.2 mg per metric ton, but it would cost many times its value to extract it.

The gold from low-grade ores is recovered by a cyanide process similar to that used for silver. The soluble complex $Au(CN)_2^-$ ion is formed.

$$Au^+ + 2CN^- \rightarrow Au(CN)_2^-$$

Metallic zinc is used to precipitate the gold.

$$2Au(CN)_2^- + Zn \rightarrow Zn(CN)_4^= + 2Au \downarrow$$

Gold is sometimes extracted from pulverized ore with moist chlorine gas. Gold unites with the chlorine to form gold(III) chloride, $AuCl_3$, which is soluble in water. The solution of gold(III) chloride is reduced by iron(II) sulfate to metallic gold, which precipitates.

38. Properties and uses of gold. Gold is a soft, yellow metal that is very ductile. It is so malleable that it can be hammered into sheets so that 250 of them would be required to equal the thickness of this page. Gold is an excellent conductor of heat and electricity. It has a specific gravity of 19.3.

Gold does not tarnish when exposed to the air, even at elevated temperatures. Hydrofluoric acid reacts with it slowly. Such strong acids as hydrochloric, nitric, and sulfuric do not react with it when used separately, but *aqua regia* ($HNO_3 + 3HCl$) does react with it readily forming gold(III) chloride.

In some compounds gold exhibits the +1 oxidation state, but those with gold in the +3 oxidation state are more common. Gold(III) chloride is used in photography to give prints of a more pleasing shade. The complex $Au(CN)_2^-$ ion as $NaAu(CN)_2$ is used for gold plating.

Colloidal gold may be produced by the electric-arc method or by the reduction of gold(III) chloride. If a solution of tin(II) chloride and stannic acid is added to a dilute solution of gold(III) chloride, the gold is reduced to the free metal by tin(II) chloride. Colloidal stannic acid may be formed by heating the mixture, and the gold particles are adsorbed on the stannic acid dispersion. A purple structural color results which is known as *purple of Cassius*.

THE ZINC SUBGROUP

39. Metals of the zinc subgroup. The last subgroup of transition elements is composed of the metals *zinc, cadmium,* and *mercury.* Like the metals of the copper subgroup and a few other transition metals, these metals have 18 electrons in their next-to-outermost shells. Zinc and

26-18   Gold, the most malleable metal. (B. M. Shaub)

cadmium form ions in which they exhibit the +2 oxidation state. Mercury exhibits both the +1 and +2 oxidation states. The mercury(I) ion is known to have the $(Hg:Hg)^{++}$ structure rather than Hg^+ as it is commonly written in empirical formulas. The Hg^+ ion has a single electron remaining in the valence shell. Two such ions share their odd electrons to form a covalent bond and attain greater stability, resulting in the structure Hg_2^{++}.

Ions of mercury are much more difficult to form than those of zinc and cadmium. In fact, mercury has a strong tendency to form covalent bonds. In some respects it resembles metals of the Copper Family more closely than zinc and cadmium. Properties of the metals of the zinc subgroup are listed in the table at the bottom of the page.

40. Zinc and its recovery. Zinc ores were used for making brass centuries before the discovery of zinc as a metal. It is thought to have been produced first in 1746 from a silicate ore by heating the ore with charcoal.

Zinc does not occur as the native metal because of its chemical activity. The principal ore is *sphalerite*, ZnS, also called *zinc blende*. *Zincite*, ZnO, and *smithsonite*, $ZnCO_3$, are also important ores. *Willemite*, Zn_2SiO_4, and *calamine*, $Zn_2SiO_4 \cdot H_2O$, are silicate ores of zinc. The mineral *franklinite*, a complex mixture of oxides of zinc, iron, and manganese, is found at Franklin, New Jersey.

Two methods are used to recover zinc.

By reduction with coal. The zinc ores are first roasted to convert them into oxides.

$$2ZnS + 3O_2 \rightarrow 2ZnO + 2SO_2 \uparrow$$

The oxides are mixed with powdered coal and heated in earthenware retorts.

$$ZnO + C \rightarrow Zn + CO \uparrow$$

Because of the low boiling point of zinc (907° C) it is distilled from the retorts as a vapor. It is then condensed in iron or earthenware receivers. Some of the zinc is deposited as *zinc dust* in the upper part of the receivers. Liquid zinc collects at the bottom of the receivers where it is drawn off and cast in molds. Such *spelter*, as it is called, may contain arsenic, cadmium, and carbon as impurities, but may be purified by redistillation.

By electrolysis. In the newer electrolytic process, the ore is first roasted, and then extracted with sulfuric acid to produce a solution of zinc sulfate. Iron and manganese are removed as impurities by adding lime and blowing air through the solution. Sheets of aluminum are used as cathodes in the electrolytic cells. By passing an electric current through the cell, zinc ions are reduced at the cathode and metallic zinc plates out on the aluminum. Zinc that is 99.9% pure is then stripped off the cathodes. Electrolytic zinc is now preferred for making brass and other alloys because of its higher purity.

THE ZINC SUBGROUP OF TRANSITION ELEMENTS

Element	Atomic Number	Atomic Weight	Electron Configuration	Oxidation Numbers	Melting Point, °C	Boiling Point, °C	Density g/cm³
zinc	30	65.37	2, 8, 18, 2	+2	419.5	907	7.14
cadmium	48	112.40	2, 8, 18, 18, 2	+2	320.9	767	8.64
mercury	80	200.59	2, 8, 18, 32, 18, 2	+1, +2	−38.87	356.6	13.55

41. Properties and uses of zinc.
Metallic zinc is bluish-white in color. At room temperature it is somewhat brittle, but at about 100° C it becomes malleable and ductile. It is a moderately hard metal, slightly less dense than iron.

Zinc burns in air with a bluish-white flame and forms white clouds of zinc oxide. At room temperature dry air does not affect zinc, but moist air reacts with it and forms a coating of basic zinc carbonate, $Zn_2(OH)_2CO_3$. The tarnish which forms is adherent and somewhat impervious. Hence zinc is a self-protective metal.

Zinc stands well above hydrogen in the electrochemical series and may be expected to react readily with acids replacing the hydrogen. *Mossy* zinc, produced by pouring molten zinc dropwise into water, is commonly used in the laboratory to displace hydrogen from nonoxidizing acids. It is found, however, that pure zinc reacts only very slowly with acids. Thus spelter, rather than electrolytic zinc, is preferred for preparing mossy zinc.

The active hydroxides, such as sodium hydroxide, react with zinc and set free hydrogen gas. Soluble zincates, which may be considered as the salts of zincic acid, are formed.

$$Zn + 2NaOH \rightarrow Na_2ZnO_2 + H_2 \uparrow$$

From this behavior, it is evident that the hydroxide of zinc is amphiprotic. It acts as the hydroxide, $Zn(OH)_2$, in the presence of a strong acid, but acts as the acid, H_2ZnO_2, in the presence of a strong hydroxide. Thus:

$$HCl + Zn(OH)_2 \rightarrow ZnCl_2 + 2H_2O$$
$$2NaOH + H_2ZnO_2 \rightarrow Na_2ZnO_2 + 2H_2O$$

Zinc hydroxide dissolves readily in ammonia water because of the strong tendency of zinc to form complex ions, a common property of transition metals.

With NH_3-Aq, a stable zinc-ammonia complex, $Zn(NH_3)_4^{++}$, is formed. Similarly, with cyanide solutions, a very stable zinc-cyanide complex, $Zn(CN)_4^=$, is formed.

$$Zn^{++} + 4NH_3 \rightleftarrows Zn(NH_3)_4^{++}$$
$$Zn^{++} + 4CN^- \rightleftarrows Zn(CN)_4^=$$

Large quantities of zinc are used for galvanizing iron. A thin protective covering of zinc is placed over the iron by dipping, electroplating, or by condensing of zinc vapor on the surface of the iron.

CAUTION: *All soluble salts of zinc are poisonous. Acid foods are never stored in galvanized iron containers.*

From the electrochemical series, it is evident that zinc is a strong reducing agent and is well suited for use as the negative electrode in an electrochemical cell. Here electrolytic zinc is preferred, because particles of carbon in the cathode cause local electrochemical action between the impurity and the zinc.

The most important alloy of zinc is *brass*, which contains zinc and copper. The proportions vary, but ordinary brass contains about 60% copper and 40% zinc. *Bronze* contains copper and tin; usually some zinc is added.

German silver is an alloy containing copper, nickel, and zinc. The name *silver* is a misnomer, since there is no silver in the alloy.

42. Cobalt nitrate test for zinc. To test for zinc, a slight depression is made in a block of charcoal or plaster of Paris. The metal, or its compound, is then placed in this depression and heated strongly with the oxidizing flame of a blowpipe. If zinc is present, its oxide will be canary yellow when hot, and white when cold. The residue is then moistened with a drop or two of cobalt nitrate solution, and again heated. If the residue is *dark green*, the presence of zinc is indicated. When tested in the same manner, magnesium compounds give a delicate *flesh (pink)* color, whereas aluminum compounds give a *blue* color.

43. Cadmium and its uses. Cadmium was discovered in 1817 as an impurity in zinc carbonate. It is usually found in nature associated with zinc. It also occurs as the sulfide, CdS, in the rather rare mineral known as *greenockite*. It is a bluish-white metal which resembles zinc and magnesium in its chemical properties. Cadmium is used in making some fusible alloys. It forms a more durable coating for iron and steel than zinc does. For that reason, a considerable amount of cadmium is used for plating screws, nuts, bolts, and other objects made of iron or steel. Cadmium metal is used for making the negative plates of the *nickel-cadmium* storage battery. Cadmium sulfide is a fine yellow pigment used as an artist's color called cadmium yellow. *The soluble salts of cadmium are poisonous.*

Cadmium is becoming increasingly important industrially. Because of its low coefficient of friction and resistance to fatigue, it is used in bearing alloys. Production of cadmium in the United States has been stimulated by its use in control rods for nuclear reactors.

44. Mercury and its uses. Mercury was known in ancient China and India. It has been found in the tombs of Egypt built nearly 3500 years ago.

The bulk of the world's supply of mercury comes from California and Texas, and from Spain and Italy. It may occur as tiny globules scattered through rock, although the chief ore of mercury is a red mineral known as cinnabar, mercury(II) sulfide. The metal can be obtained by simply heating the ore:

$$HgS + O_2 \rightarrow Hg + SO_2 \uparrow$$

26-19 Cadmium. It is found in nature with zinc. (B. M. Shaub)

Mercury is the only metal that is a liquid at room temperatures, although gallium metal has a melting point of 29.8° C. It is silver-white, lustrous, and about 13.6 times as dense as water. It freezes to a hard, brittle solid at approximately −39° C, and boils at a temperature of nearly 357° C.

If heated in air, mercury slowly changes to a red oxide, HgO. Hydrochloric acid does not react with mercury since hydrogen is above mercury in the replacement series. Nitric and hot concentrated sulfuric acids, however, react with it to form mercury(II) nitrate and mercury(II) sulfate, respectively, in typical oxidation-reduction reactions.

Mercury is found far down in the electrochemical series. Thus most metals replace it from its compounds. It is a poor reducing agent, which accounts for its reluctance to combine with oxygen and its inability to displace hydrogen from nonoxidizing acids.

An alloy of mercury with one or more other metals is known as an *amalgam*. Mercury forms amalgams with most metals, although platinum and iron are exceptions. An amalgam consisting of silver, tin, zinc, and mercury is used for fillings in teeth. When freshly prepared, it is soft enough to be pressed into the cavity of a tooth, but it hardens in a very short time.

45. Compounds of mercury. Mercury forms two series of compounds, one in which the oxidation number is +1 and the other in which the oxidation number is +2.

Mercury(I) chloride, a white solid with the molecular formula Hg_2Cl_2, is insoluble in water. It is used in medicine as a laxative under the name of *calomel*. Exposure to sunlight causes mercury(I) chloride to change slowly to mercury and mercury(II) chloride:

$$Hg_2Cl_2 \rightarrow Hg + HgCl_2$$

Mercury(I) nitrate, $Hg_2(NO_3)_2$, is fairly soluble in water. Mercury(I) chloride is precipitated when chloride ions are added to a solution of mercury(I) nitrate. Ammonia reacts with this precipitate forming the insoluble white mercury(II) complex, $HgNH_2Cl$, and metallic mercury as a black dispersion. *The mixture of these two products gives a gray residue which serves as a test for the Hg_2^{++} ion.*

$$Hg_2Cl_2 + 2NH_3 \rightarrow$$
$$HgNH_2Cl \downarrow + Hg \downarrow + NH_4Cl$$
white   black

CAUTION: *All the soluble salts of mercury are extremely poisonous.*

The white of eggs, or milk, may be used as an antidote because the albumin in egg whites or milk forms an insoluble mercury albuminate. The use of Hg_2Cl_2 (calomel) in medicine is safe even though the Hg_2^{++} ion is very poisonous, because the compound is only very slightly soluble.

Mercury(II) chloride is commonly called bichloride of mercury or corrosive sublimate. It is essentially covalent and has the molecular formula $HgCl_2$. It forms white crystals that can be purified by sublimation. It is extremely poisonous.

Mercury(II) oxide, HgO, is used as an antiseptic under the name red precipitate. Priestley obtained oxygen by heating this compound. Sublimed *mercury(II) sulfide*, HgS, forms a red pigment known as vermilion. It is used as a paint to retard the growth of barnacles on ships.

REVIEW OUTLINE

Transition subgroups of the Periodic Table
Inner building of *d* sublevels (1)
Inner building of *f* sublevels (1)
General properties of transition elements (2)
Metallic character (3)
Oxidation states (4)
Color (5)
Complex ions and solubility (6)
Paramagnetism (7)

The Iron Family
Members of the Iron Family (9)
Sources of iron (10)
Recovery of iron from its ores (11, 12, 13)

QUESTIONS

Group A

1. What structural similarity determines the metallic character of transition elements?
2. Which process is most used for making steel in this country?
3. Explain why iron inks write blue and dry black.

4. List five points of similarity between copper, silver, and gold.
5. A gold ring is stamped 14K. What does this mean?
6. (*a*) What is blister copper? (*b*) How did it get its name?
7. How is copper obtained from the native ore?
8. (*a*) Have you ever seen any silver oxide? (*b*) What is the tarnish on a piece of old silverware?
9. Why does the copper trim on roofs frequently acquire a green surface?
10. What are three methods of protecting sheet iron with zinc?
11. What are some uses for the metal cadmium?
12. Starting with zinc sulfide, how is metallic zinc obtained?
13. What is an amalgam?
14. How is the mercury recovered from the amalgam formed in the amalgamation process?

Group B

15. Why does impure iron rust more rapidly than pure iron?
16. How can you detect an iron(II) and an iron(III) compound, if both are present in the same solution?
17. Identify three significant factors which make the basic oxygen process attractive in steel production.
18. Why did man have some metals in very early times, yet many metals have been obtained only within the last century?
19. Suppose you have a powdered mixture that contained 90% gold and 10% silver. How could you obtain pure gold from such a mixture?
20. How can silver be obtained from the *anode mud* that collects in a tank used for the electrolysis of copper?
21. What metals are alloyed in German silver?
22. How may lead chloride be separated from silver chloride?
23. Why does it usually pay to refine copper by electrolysis?
24. What is the cyanide process of extracting gold?
25. Describe the cyanide process of extracting silver from silver ore.
26. Would galvanized iron containers be suitable for holding milk and other dairy products? Explain.
27. What is meant when we say that zinc hydroxide is amphiprotic?

PROBLEMS

1. How much iron(II) chloride can be made by adding 165 g of iron to an excess of hydrochloric acid? Compute to 3 significant figures.
2. How much iron(III) chloride can be prepared from the iron(II) chloride in the preceding problem if more hydrochloric acid is added and air is blown through the solution?
3. What is the percentage of iron in a sample of limonite, $2Fe_2O_3 \cdot 3H_2O$?
4. How many grams of silver nitrate can be obtained by adding 100. g of pure silver to an excess of nitric acid?
5. A sample of hematite ore contains Fe_2O_3 87.0%, silica 8.0%, moisture 4.0%, other impurities 1.0%. What is the percentage of iron in the ore?

6. What will be the loss in mass when 1.0×10^6 metric tons of the ore in the preceding problem are heated to 200° C?

7. How much limestone will be needed to combine with the silica in 1.0×10^6 metric tons of the ore of Problem 5?

8. (*a*) How much carbon monoxide is required to reduce 1.0×10^6 metric tons of the ore of Problem 5? (*b*) How much coke must be supplied to meet this requirement? (Assume the coke to be 100% carbon.)

9. Iron(II) sulfate is oxidized to iron(III) sulfate in the presence of sulfuric acid using nitric acid as the oxidizing agent. Nitrogen monoxide and water are also formed. Balance the equation.

10. Silver reacts with dilute nitric acid to form silver nitrate, water, and nitrogen monoxide. Balance the equation.

11. Copper reacts with hot concentrated sulfuric acid to form copper(II) sulfate, sulfur dioxide, and water. Balance the equation.

Chapter Twenty-seven

ALUMINUM AND THE METALLOIDS

1. Nature of metalloids. The elements with properties that are intermediate between metallic and nonmetallic are called *metalloids* or *semimetals*. They exemplify the transition from metals to nonmetals and occupy a diagonal region in the Periodic Table extending from the upper center toward the lower right. See Fig. 27-1.

The metalloids include the elements *boron, silicon, germanium, arsenic, antimony,* *tellurium,* and *polonium.* Aluminum is included in this chapter because of its unique position in the Periodic Table with respect to the metalloids.

Aluminum is distinctly metallic and it is by the familiar properties of metals that we generally recognize it. However, aluminum can appear with oxygen in negative aluminate ions, its hydroxide is amphiprotic, its oxide is probably macromolecular, and its hydride is polymeric. These

PROPERTIES OF ALUMINUM AND METALLOIDS

Element	Atomic Number	Electron Configuration	Oxidation States	Melting Point (°C)	Boiling Point (°C)	Density (g/cm³)	Atomic Radius Å	Ionization Energy (ev)
boron	5	2, 3	+3	2300	2550	2.34	0.80	8.3
aluminum	13	2, 8, 3	+3	660	2057	2.70	1.25	6.0
silicon	14	2, 8, 4	+2, +4, −4	1420	2355	2.42	1.17	8.1
germanium	32	2, 8, 18, 4	+2, +4, −4	959	2700(?)	5.35	1.22	8.1
arsenic	33	2, 8, 18, 5	+3, +5, −3	sublimes		5.73	1.21	10.5
antimony	51	2, 8, 18, 18, 5	+3, +5, −3	631	1380	6.68	1.39	8.6
tellurium	52	2, 8, 18, 18, 6	+2, +4, +6, −2	452	1390	6.25	1.37	9.0
polonium	84	2, 8, 18, 32, 18, 6	───	───	───	───	───	───

characteristics, taken collectively, tend to place aluminum in the realm of the metalloids.

Boron, silicon, arsenic, and antimony are typical of metalloidal behavior and will be considered separately as representative elements. Some of their important properties, together with those of aluminum and the other metalloids named above, are listed in the table on the opposite page.

Germanium is a moderately rare element whose compounds have been of little importance. With the development of the transistor, germanium has become important as a semiconductor material. It is chemically similar to silicon which stands above it in Group IV. Germanium is more metallic than arsenic which is its neighboring element to the right in the fifth period. The major oxidation state of germanium is +4.

Tellurium, a semiconductor, is most stable in a hexagonal metallic-like form. Its chemistry is typically metalloid. It appears with oxygen in both tellurite and tellurate ions showing respectively the +4 and +6 oxidation states. It combines covalently with the more electronegative oxygen and halogens in which the +2, +4, and +6 oxidation states are observed. It forms tellurides (−2 oxidation state) with such elements as gold, hydrogen, and lead. In fact, tellurium is the only element combined with gold in nature. Tellurium is out of step in the Periodic Table to the extent that it has a lower atomic number but higher atomic weight than iodine.

27-1 The metalloids exemplify the transition from metals to nonmetals.

Polonium is a dangerously radioactive element used as a source of alpha particles. It was discovered by Pierre and Marie Curie in 1898 just prior to their discovery of radium. Little is known of its chemistry but it appears to be more metallic than tellurium.

ALUMINUM

2. Aluminum as a light metal. Aluminum, atomic number 13, is the second member of Group III which is headed by boron and includes gallium, indium, and thallium. All are typically metallic except boron which is classed as a metalloid. Boron as an element and in compounds differs from aluminum and the other Group III elements primarily because of the small size of its atom. Its chemistry resembles that of silicon and germanium more than it does aluminum.

Aluminum is a low-density metal used structurally both as the pure metal and alloyed with other light metals or with heavy metals such as copper and iron. Aluminum follows its corresponding alkaline-earth metal, magnesium, in chemical behavior. However, the Group III metals below aluminum are separated from their Group II counterparts by the intervening transition metals.

3. Occurrence of aluminum. Aluminum is the most abundant metal in the earth's crust. It is found in many clays, rocks, and other minerals. While the aluminum industry is working on processes by which aluminum may be economically extracted from clay, none has yet proved successful. Such a process would make the United States less dependent on foreign sources of aluminum ore. At present, bauxite, an impure aluminum oxide ore, is imported from Jamaica, Surinam, and British Guiana. It is also mined in Georgia, Alabama, Tennessee, and Arkansas.

4. Discovery of aluminum. Friedrich Wöhler, the German chemist, first isolated aluminum. As late as 1855 aluminum sold at $90 per pound; but by 1870 the price had fallen to $12 per pound. In 1886 a newer process of reduction by sodium lowered the price of aluminum to about $2 per pound. This was still too expensive to enable its full development as a structural and household metal.

It remained for a young American, Charles Martin Hall, to develop a cheap practical method of aluminum production. While still a student at Oberlin College, Hall discovered that aluminum could be separated from its oxide by electrolysis. His process, commercialized in 1889, reduced the price of aluminum to about 20¢ per pound. Today aluminum is one of our most widely used metals.

5. Recovery of aluminum. Fused salt electrolysis has great commercial significance, being used to produce alkali and alkaline-earth metals as well as aluminum and related metals in huge quantities.

Aluminum is extracted by electrolyzing aluminum oxide (refined bauxite) dissolved in molten cryolite, Na_3AlF_6, at a temperature slightly below 1000° C. The process was developed in 1886 by Charles Martin Hall (1863–1914) and independently in France in the same year by Paul Héroult.

The electrolytic cell, shown in Fig. 27-2, consists of an iron box lined with graphite which serves as a cathode. Graphite rods serve as the anode, and cryolite-aluminum oxide is the electrolyte. Heat is produced by the large current in the cell to melt the cryolite which dissolves the aluminum oxide. This heat is great enough to maintain the aluminum metal in the bottom of the cell in a molten state for convenient removal.

The electrode reactions are complex and are not understood completely. Aluminum is reduced at the cathode, possibly from a complex ion structure composed of aluminum, oxygen, and fluorine. Carbon dioxide is the major product at the anode, which is gradually consumed. This suggests that oxygen is formed at the anode by oxidation of the $O^=$ ion or some complex containing oxygen in the negative oxidation state. The following electrode reactions are probably oversimplifications of the reaction mechanism, but serve to summarize the oxidation-reduction processes.

Cathode: $4Al^{+3} + 12e^- \rightarrow 4Al^0$

Anode: $6O^{-2} - 12e^- \rightarrow 3O_2^0$

$3C + 3O_2 \rightarrow 3CO_2 \uparrow$

6. Properties of aluminum. Aluminum has a specific gravity of 2.7. It is ductile and malleable, but is not as tenacious as brass, copper, or steel. It ranks with the best conductors of electricity, being surpassed only by silver, copper, and gold. Aluminum can be welded, cast, or spun, but it can be soldered only by the use of a special solder.

Aluminum takes a high polish, but soon becomes covered with a thin layer of aluminum oxide. This oxide layer is adherent and impervious; hence aluminum is a self-protective metal. Hydrochloric and sul-furic acids react readily with aluminum and form salts of the respective acids. Nitric acid hardly affects aluminum at all. Salt water corrodes it rapidly, especially when it is hot. A strong alkali like sodium hydroxide reacts with aluminum forming sodium aluminate and liberating hydrogen.

$$2Al + 6NaOH \rightarrow 2Na_3AlO_3 + 3H_2 \uparrow$$

Aluminum is an excellent reducing agent although it is not as active as the Group I and Group II metals.

$$Al^0 \rightarrow Al^{+3} + 3e^-$$

The Al^{+3} ion is quite small and carries a large positive charge. The ion hydrates vigorously in water solution and is usually written $Al(H_2O)_6^{+++}$. Water solutions of aluminum salts are generally acidic due to hydrolysis of the Al^{+3} ion.

7. The thermite reaction. A mixture of powdered aluminum and iron oxide, raised to a high enough temperature to start the reaction, produces a tremendous amount of heat. Such a reaction between aluminum and the oxide of a less active metal is called the *thermite reaction.*

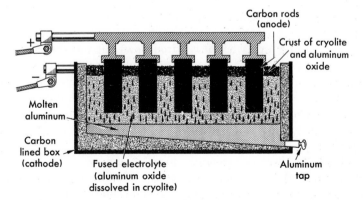

27-2 Aluminum is produced by electrolysis. Purified aluminum oxide is dissolved in melted cryolite, sodium aluminum fluoride.

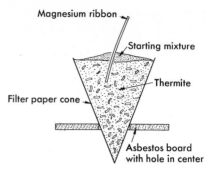

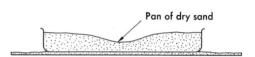

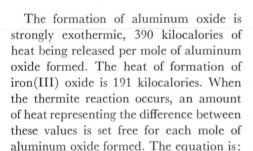

27-3 The thermite reaction. Dry sand protects the table top. Spectators must stand at a safe distance. Sharp black and white contrast shows the brilliance of the molten iron.

The formation of aluminum oxide is strongly exothermic, 390 kilocalories of heat being released per mole of aluminum oxide formed. The heat of formation of iron(III) oxide is 191 kilocalories. When the thermite reaction occurs, an amount of heat representing the difference between these values is set free for each mole of aluminum oxide formed. The equation is:

$$2Al + Fe_2O_3 \rightarrow Al_2O_3 + 2Fe + 199\,kcal$$

The sudden liberation of such a large quantity of heat energy produces a very high temperature, estimated at 3500° C.

It is not practical to use aluminum to reduce cheaper metals. However, the thermite reaction may be used when it is desirable to produce a small quantity of carbon-free metal. A more important use of this reaction is to reduce metallic oxides which are not readily reduced with carbon. Chromium, manganese, titanium, tungsten, and molybdenum may be extracted from their oxides by the thermite reaction. All these metals are used in making alloy steels. Uranium, used to produce nuclear energy, may also be reduced by the thermite reaction.

8. Thermite welding. The very high temperature produced by the thermite reaction makes it possible to use such a mixture for welding. Massive steel parts, such as propeller shafts and rudder posts on a ship, or the crankshafts of heavy machinery, can be repaired quickly by means of thermite. A mixture of powdered aluminum and either Fe_2O_3 or Fe_3O_4 is placed in a cone-shaped crucible above the metals to be welded. A little starting mixture consisting of barium peroxide and powdered magnesium is placed in a slight depression in the top of the mixture. Within a few seconds after the starting mixture is ignited, the white-hot molten iron flows out through the bottom of the cone and welds the broken ends.

9. Uses of aluminum oxide. Bauxite, the chief ore of aluminum, is an oxide of aluminum. Corundum and emery are also natural oxides of this metal, and are used as abrasives. Emery is used in the form of emery paper, emery cloth, or emery grinding wheels.

Rubies and sapphires are aluminum oxide colored by traces of metallic oxides. Synthetic rubies and sapphires are made by fusing pure aluminum oxide in the flame of an oxyhydrogen blowtorch. In making clear sapphires, no coloring matter is added. Synthetic rubies are colored by adding a tiny amount of chromium.

Alundum is an oxide of aluminum made by fusing bauxite. It is used for making grinding wheels and other abrasives, crucibles, funnels, tubing, and other pieces of laboratory apparatus.

10. Aluminum hydroxide. If a little sodium hydroxide solution is added to a solution of an aluminum salt, such as aluminum chloride, a white gelatinous precipitate of aluminum hydroxide is formed.

$$AlCl_3 + 3NaOH \rightarrow Al(OH)_3\downarrow + 3NaCl$$

Aluminum hydroxide is insoluble in water, but if an excess of sodium hydroxide is added, soluble sodium aluminate is formed. In this reaction aluminum hydroxide acts as an acid, H_3AlO_3.

$$H_3AlO_3 + 3NaOH \rightarrow Na_3AlO_3 + 3H_2O$$

If, on the other hand, hydrochloric acid is added to aluminum hydroxide, the aluminum hydroxide acts as a hydroxide, $Al(OH)_3$.

$$Al(OH)_3 + 3HCl \rightarrow AlCl_3 + 3H_2O$$

These reactions show the amphiprotic nature of aluminum hydroxide.

Aluminum hydroxide is so weakly basic that its salts with weak acids are almost completely hydrolyzed. If sodium carbonate is added to a solution of aluminum chloride, aluminum carbonate might be expected to precipitate. It is possible that aluminum carbonate may be first formed, but, if so, it immediately hydrolyzes and forms aluminum hydroxide. A precipitate of aluminum hydroxide is always formed when a soluble carbonate, or even a soluble sulfide, is added to a solution of an aluminum salt.

Aluminum hydroxide may be used to remove suspended matter from drinking water. It also finds use as a mordant, an insoluble gelatinous material used to impregnate cotton fabrics in the dyeing process. Aluminum hydroxide is usually precipitated on the fibers before they are dyed.

Colored pigments for use in the paint industry are sometimes made by precipitating a dye with aluminum hydroxide in a large vat. The insoluble compound, which contains the dye, is then filtered off. Such pigments are known as *lakes*.

11. Double salts of aluminum. If solutions of potassium sulfate and aluminum sulfate are mixed, the double salt $KAl(SO_4)_2 \cdot 12H_2O$ crystallizes when some of the water is evaporated. A double sulfate formed in such a manner and having similar properties is called an *alum*.

Instead of potassium sulfate, either ammonium sulfate or sodium sulfate may be used. The sulfates of such trivalent metals as chromium or iron may be used instead

27-4 These crucibles are made of Alundum, an artificial oxide of aluminum. (The Norton Co.)

of aluminum sulfate. The general formula, $M^+M^{+++}(SO_4)_2 \cdot 12H_2O$, in which M^+ is some univalent element or radical, and M^{+++} is some trivalent metal, is used to represent the alums. The different alums are used to form mordants.

12. Some silicates of aluminum. Fuller's earth is a silicate of aluminum which is a good absorbent. It is used for clarifying oils by filtration and for removing spots and stains from textile fabrics.

Mica is a potassium aluminum silicate which is translucent and infusible. It is used for the translucent tops of fuse plugs. As an electric insulator, it is used in the commutators of motors and dynamos.

The feldspars are complex silicates which usually contain aluminum silicate with the silicates of either sodium or potassium. They fuse rather easily. When water or carbon dioxide brings about the weathering of the feldspars, the alkalies are leached out as the soluble silicates or carbonates. Hence the disintegration of a feldspar may add potassium to the soil. The insoluble portion is a fine white clay, or hydrated aluminum silicate, known as kaolin. Colored clays usually owe their color to traces of iron compounds.

BORON

13. Boron as a metalloid. The first member of a periodic group often exhibits properties somewhat different from those of the remaining elements of the group. These elements are in the second period across the Periodic Table and have only the K shell containing 2 electrons beneath their valence shell. All elements below this series have their valence electrons backed up by a shell population of at least 8 electrons. The beryllium atom is quite small and the 2 valence electrons are held rather firmly. Bonds formed by beryllium with other substances tend to be more co-

27-5 Boron, a metalloid, is best known as a constituent of borax. (B. M. Shaub)

valent than ionic. Lithium is a stronger reducing agent than its position in Group I would suggest. Boron is a metalloid while all other Group III elements are metals. Nitrogen, oxygen, and fluorine likewise differ in important ways from the other members of their respective groups.

Boron atoms are small, their atomic radius being only 0.80Å. Their valence electrons are quite tightly bound, giving boron a relatively high ionization energy for a Group III element. Boron also has the highest electronegativity of any element in Group III. A consideration of these characteristics indicates that boron is a metalloid which forms only covalent bonds with other atoms. At low temperatures boron is a poor conductor of electricity; but as the temperature is raised its electrons have more kinetic energy, and the conductivity of boron increases. This behavior is typical of a semiconductor.

14. Recovery of boron. Boron is not found as the free element. It can be isolated in reasonably pure form by reducing boron trichloride with hydrogen at a high temperature. Elementary boron has little commercial value; hence chemists seldom separate it from its compounds.

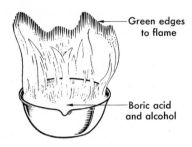

Green edges to flame

Boric acid and alcohol

27-6 An alcohol flame has green edges when boric acid is present. This serves as a test for boric acid.

Colemanite, a hydrated borate of calcium which is given the formula $Ca_2B_6O_{11} \cdot 5H_2O$, is found in the desert regions of California and Nevada. Sodium tetraborate, $Na_2B_4O_6 \cdot 4H_2O$, is found as the mineral *kernite* in California, also. The salt brines of Searles Lake, California, yield most of the commercial supply of boron compounds today. When calcium borate is treated with sodium carbonate, sodium tetraborate, or *borax*, is produced. Some hot springs contain small amounts of boric acid, H_3BO_3, in solution.

15. Useful compounds of boron. Boron carbide, B_4C, known as Norbide, is an extremely hard abrasive made by combining boron with carbon in an electric furnace. The form of boron nitride called Borazon, made by combining boron and nitrogen under extreme heat and pressure, is the hardest synthetic material known. Alloys of boron with iron or manganese are used to increase the hardness of steel.

Boric acid can be prepared by adding sulfuric acid to a concentrated solution of sodium tetraborate in water. The acid is only moderately soluble and separates as colorless, lustrous scales. It is such a weak acid that 4% solutions of it may be used to wash the eye with safety. It is a mild antiseptic. *A test for boric acid depends on the fact that boric acid colors an alcohol flame green* (see Fig. 27-6).

Borax is sodium tetraborate with the formula $Na_2B_4O_7 \cdot 10H_2O$. It is used alone and in washing powders as a water softener. Because it dissolves metallic oxides leaving a clean metallic surface, it is also used as a *flux* for welding metals. The borates of certain metals are used in making glazes and enamels. Large amounts of boron compounds are used to make borosilicate glass, of which Pyrex is an example.

Boron combines with hydrogen to form several boron hydrides such as B_2H_6, diborane, and B_4H_{10}, tetraborane. Methyl and ethyl groups may be substituted for the hydrogen atoms in these compounds. These boron compounds have positive heats of formation. Thus, when they are oxidized, they liberate unusually large amounts of energy.

16. Borax bead tests. If a platinum wire with a loop on one end is dipped in powdered borax and held in a flame, the borax swells and then fuses to form a clear, glass-like bead. If such a bead is further heated in an oxidizing blowpipe flame with a tiny speck of metal or metallic compound, the metallic oxide formed reacts with the borax bead, and may impart to the bead a characteristic color. The color depends on the kind of metal used. For example, cobalt colors such a bead *blue;* chromium produces a *green* bead; and nickel yields a *brown* bead. This borax bead test is useful in identifying certain metals. The chemical reactions involved and the structure of the colored compounds formed are not well understood.

SILICON

17. Silicon as a metalloid. Silicon atoms, with four valence electrons, crystallize with a tetrahedral bond arrangement similar to that of carbon atoms in diamond. Atoms of silicon also have small atomic radii and tightly held electrons.

27-7 Silicon, the second most abundant element. (B. M. Shaub)

Consequently their ionization energy and electronegativity are fairly high. Silicon is a metalloid which forms covalent bonds when combining with all other elements, except possibly the halogens. The electric conductivity of silicon is similar to that of boron; it, too, is a semiconductor. Unlike carbon, silicon forms only single bonds, and forms silicon-oxygen bonds in preference to silicon-silicon or silicon-hydrogen bonds. However, much of its chemistry is similar to that of carbon. Silicon has much the same role in mineral chemistry as carbon has in organic chemistry.

The somewhat similar small radii of the atoms of boron and silicon enable them to be used interchangeably in glass even though boron is a member of Group III and silicon belongs in Group IV.

18. Silicon and its compounds. Silicon ranks second in abundance by weight among the elements of the earth's crust; but, as in the case of boron, it does not occur free in nature. Silicon of high purity can be produced by the reduction of silicon dioxide, SiO_2, with magnesium.

The chief use for elementary silicon is in an alloy with iron, called *ferrosilicon*, for making silicon steel. The ferrosilicon may be prepared directly by the reduction of a mixture of silicon dioxide and iron oxide with carbon. Silicon is used in the production of silicones. Specially purified silicon is used in transistors and other semiconductor devices.

The compounds of silicon, such as sand, sandstone, quartz, and many different silicate rocks are widely distributed in nature. It is the abundance of these compounds that gives silicon its high rank among the elements of the earth's crust.

Silicon dioxide, SiO_2, commonly called *silica*, is one of the most widely distributed mineral compounds in the world. It is found in many forms, four of which are given below.

1. As sand. Ordinary sand is silicon dioxide. Great quantities of sand are used in making glass. It is mixed with lime and water to make mortar, and with crushed stone and cement in making concrete.

2. In the mineral sandstone. This mineral is a sedimentary rock formed under water by particles of sand which are bound together by a kind of natural cement. It is used as a building stone.

3. As quartz. The transparent crystalline variety of silica is known as quartz. Quartz crystals consist of tetrahedra with a central silicon atom bonded to four oxygen atoms at the corners. Each oxygen atom serves as the corner of two such tetrahedra. Quartz is a fairly hard mineral because in order to break it, some strong silicon-oxygen bonds must be broken. Pure *rock crystal* is colorless, but traces of impurities impart different colors to such forms of quartz as amethyst, smoky quartz, rose quartz, and milky quartz.

Quartz may be softened in an oxyhydrogen blowtorch and fashioned into tubing, crucibles, and other laboratory apparatus. It is also melted in a graphite crucible in an electric furnace and then extruded from the furnace under high pressure. This material is no longer crystalline because the regularity of the silicon-oxygen tetrahedra has been somewhat disturbed by the heating. The randomness of this arrangement resembles that of a liquid. Fused quartz of this type is a super-cooled liquid, or a glass.

Quartz transmits ultraviolet rays much better than glass does. It is not as easily acted upon by acids and alkalies as ordinary glassware. Because it has a very low coefficient of expansion, about one-eighteenth that of glass, it is not likely to break even if it is heated or cooled suddenly.

4. As amorphous silica. Such common minerals as flint, jasper, chalcedony, sard, carnelian, onyx, and agate consist largely of silica. Onyx and agate are made up of bands of different colors. Fine specimens of crystallized and amorphous silica are used as semiprecious gems.

Silicon dioxide is insoluble in water and ordinary acids, but hydrofluoric acid reacts with it, as follows:

$$SiO_2 + 2H_2F_2 \rightarrow SiF_4 \uparrow + 2H_2O$$

The silicon tetrafluoride, SiF_4, which is formed by the reaction, is volatile and escapes into the air. Sodium carbonate reacts with silica at high temperatures and forms sodium silicate.

$$Na_2CO_3 + SiO_2 \rightarrow Na_2SiO_3 + CO_2 \uparrow$$

Silicon carbide, SiC, is made by heating sand and coke in an electric furnace. Salt is usually added to the mixture to facilitate fusion, and sawdust is used to make it more porous. The main reaction is:

$$SiO_2 + 3C \rightarrow SiC + 2CO \uparrow$$

On cooling, crystals of silicon carbide, called *carborundum*, are formed surrounding the central core. The crystals are crushed, graded to size by sifting through fine sieves, mixed with a binder, and manufactured into grinding wheels and sharpening stones. Silicon carbide has a structure resembling diamond but with alternate carbon atoms replaced by silicon atoms. The rigid structure and strong covalent bonds give it great hardness.

19. Silicones. Silicon resembles carbon in the ability of its atoms to link together to form chains. A group of compounds, called *silicones*, has alternate silicon and oxygen atoms, with hydrocarbon groups attached to the silicon atoms. Thus the silicones are part organic and part inorganic. By using different hydrocarbon groups, a variety of silicones can be produced. One silicone chain has the structure

$$\left[\begin{array}{ccc} & H & & H \\ & | & & | \\ H-C-H & & H-C-H \\ & | & & | \\ -Si & -O- & Si & -O- \\ & | & & | \\ H-C-H & & H-C-H \\ & | & & | \\ & H & & H \end{array} \right]_x$$

The silicones are not much affected by heat, have excellent electric insulating properties, and are water repellents. Some silicones are oils or greases which may be used as lubricants. Silicon varnishes are used to coat wires for the windings of elec-

27-8   Crystals of silicon carbide. (B.M.Shaub)

tric motors. This permits the electric motor to operate at high temperatures without short circuits. Cloth that has been treated with a silicone repels water. Silicones are used in automobile and furniture polishes.

20. Manufacture of glass. Glass was made by the Egyptians many centuries before the Christian era. It is hard and very brittle when cold but softens when heated. It becomes so plastic when very hot that it can be blown, rolled, or pressed into any shape. It is transparent and almost entirely insoluble in water.

Ordinary glass is composed of the silicates of sodium and calcium. It is probably a solid solution of these silicates in each other. In making the many different kinds of glass, potassium may be substituted for sodium. Barium, lead, aluminum, boron, and even zinc may be substituted for all or part of the calcium or silicon.

For making *ordinary glass*, the raw materials are sand, limestone, and sodium carbonate. A certain proportion of old, broken glass is added to make the whole batch melt more rapidly. The mixture is heated in a long, tanklike furnace to a temperature of about 1400° C by the combustion of fuel gas. The process is continuous, raw materials being dumped in at one end, and liquid glass being withdrawn from the opposite end.

Some of the sand reacts with the limestone forming calcium silicate and carbon dioxide, as follows:

$$CaCO_3 + SiO_2 \rightarrow CaSiO_3 + CO_2 \uparrow$$

The rest of the sand reacts with the sodium carbonate according to the following equation:

$$Na_2CO_3 + SiO_2 \rightarrow Na_2SiO_3 + CO_2 \uparrow$$

Optical glass is made by heating sand, potassium carbonate, and lead oxide in pots made of fire clay. Such glass is made in small batches of a few hundred pounds each. Glass for cut glass tableware is also made in small batches from the same raw materials in a fire-clay pot.

Pyrex glass is made in a tank furnace by fusing sand, borax, and aluminum oxide. It is a sodium aluminum borosilicate glass and has a coefficient of expansion only one-third that of ordinary, soda-lime glass.

27-9 A convertible rear window made of flexible glass. (Corning Glass Works)

While soda-lime glass may be softened in a Bunsen burner flame, Pyrex glass has a much higher softening temperature and can be worked only in the flame of a blast lamp.

Extensive research in glass-making processes since the end of World War II has produced several new kinds of glass with improved strength and flexibility and with unusual properties. Among these are:

1. Glass-ceramic materials having unusual thermal shock resistance and high mechanical strength. These are important as nose cones for rockets and cooking ware for kitchens.

2. Chemically strengthened glass having flexibility in sheet form. Such special sheet glass may be found in the rear windows of convertible tops for automobiles in place of the conventional vinyl windows.

3. Glass fibers having very high strength. Their use improves the structural performance of glass fiber-reinforced plastics by 50%.

4. Photosensitive glass in which an image can be developed by heating.

5. Glass with special optical and radiation-absorbing properties for many specialized technical services.

After glass has been formed into a finished article, it is cooled very slowly to prevent brittleness. The slow cooling process is called *annealing.* It is accomplished by passing the glass through a long narrow chamber. The temperature in the chamber is regulated carefully so that it is hot at one end and room temperature at the other.

Metals impart colors to glass. Even a small quantity of iron compounds as impurities in sand impart a pale-green color to finished glass. Consequently, glass makers try to secure as pure sand as possible. Manganese gives an amethyst or red color when added to glass. Small quantities of a manganese compound are sometimes added to a batch of glass to neutralize the pale-green color imparted by iron compounds. Chromium in glass gives it a deep-green color. Cobalt produces a deep blue. Silver is used to make yellow glass. Selenium is added to the batch to make red glass. White, or opalescent, glass is made by adding calcium fluoride to the raw materials.

ARSENIC

21. The recovery of arsenic. Some arsenic is found uncombined in nature. It is also found in ores combined with sulfur. It is prepared from these sulfide ores by roasting them to form oxides which are then reduced with carbon to obtain elementary arsenic. Arsenic is also present as an impurity in many metallic ores. It is recovered from the chimney stacks of the smelters when these ores are processed. This is the most important source of arsenic in the United States.

22. Properties and uses of arsenic. Metallic arsenic is a brittle, gray solid. When freshly cut, it has a bright metallic luster which rapidly tarnishes in moist air. It exists in three allotropic forms. Chemically it may act as a metal and form oxides and chlorides. It may also act as a nonmetal and form acids. When heated, arsenic sublimes and forms a yellow vapor, As_4, which has the odor of garlic.

When ignited, arsenic burns with a pale-blue flame and forms diarsenic trioxide, As_4O_6. (The name corresponds to the empirical formula, even though the molecular formula is As_4O_6.) Arsenic unites indirectly with hydrogen to form arsine, AsH_3, a compound analogous to ammonia. It is a deadly poisonous gas. Metallic arsenic is little used.

Diarsenic trioxide is used in producing other compounds of arsenic and in making some kinds of glass. Another use is as a preservative of animal skins that are to be mounted. Some medicines contain small quantities of arsenic compounds.

CAUTION: *While very small amounts of arsenic have medicinal value, larger quantities are extremely poisonous.*

Arsenic compounds make excellent insecticides. Paris green, a compound of copper and arsenic, is used to destroy certain beetles and other insect pests. However, it is now being replaced by the arsenates of lead and calcium. Enormous quantities of lead arsenate, $Pb_3(AsO_4)_2$, are used every year for spraying fruit trees and other plants. Calcium arsenate, $Ca_3(AsO_4)_2$, is also used as an insecticide.

ANTIMONY

23. Recovery of antimony. Some antimony is found free in nature. Its most important ore is *stibnite*, a sulfide of antimony, Sb_2S_3. Antimony is usually prepared from stibnite by reduction with iron. While China has been the chief source of antimony, deposits in Bolivia and Mexico are now being developed. Very little antimony is found in the United States; most of it is imported.

24. Properties and uses of antimony. Antimony is a dense, brittle, silver-white metalloid with a bright metallic luster. It is less active than arsenic, and exists in several allotropic forms. When strongly heated in air, antimony forms a white oxide, diantimony trioxide, Sb_4O_6. (Again the name corresponds to the empirical formula, not the molecular formula.) This compound is amphiprotic. It reacts with hydroxides to form antimony(III) salts. Pure antimony is not affected by hydrochloric acid, but reacts readily in aqua regia and forms antimony pentachloride, $SbCl_5$. Antimonates, which are compounds analogous to the phosphates and arsenates, are also known.

Type metal contains antimony, tin, and lead. Antimony is an important constituent because it causes this alloy to expand when it solidifies. Hence the edges of the type which is cast from this alloy are sharp and distinct.

An antifriction alloy of lead and antimony is used between the bearing surfaces of the moving parts of machinery. The friction of steel sliding over this antifriction alloy is much less than the friction of steel sliding over steel.

An alloy of lead and antimony is used for the plates in storage batteries. This alloy is stronger and more resistant to acids than is lead alone. Thus battery plates made from the alloy are more durable.

Only a few of the compounds of antimony are used extensively. The sulfides are used in matches, and as pigments. Red rubber contains diantimony trisulfide. Tartar emetic, potassium antimonyl tartrate, $KSbOC_4H_4O_6$, is used as a mordant in the dyeing of cotton goods.

CAUTION: *The soluble compounds of antimony are nearly as poisonous as the compounds of arsenic.*

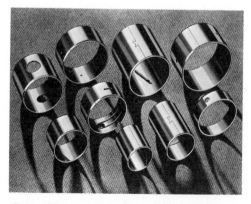

27-10   The bearings shown here are made of antifriction alloy to help reduce friction produced when a shaft turns inside them. (Clevite Corporation)

REVIEW OUTLINE

The metalloid elements
    Periodic order of the metalloids (1)
    Relation of aluminum to the metalloids (1)
    Properties of metalloids (1)

Aluminum
    Periodic relation of aluminum to other light metals (2)
    Occurrence of aluminum (3)
    Discovery of aluminum (4)
    Recovery of aluminum (5)
    Properties and uses of aluminum (6)
    Thermite process (7)
    Thermite welding (8)
    Compounds of aluminum
        Aluminum oxide (9)
        Aluminum hydroxide (10)
        Double salts of aluminum (11)
        Silicates of aluminum (12)

Boron
    Boron as a metalloid (13)
    Occurrence and recovery of boron (14)
    Compounds of boron (15)
    Borax bead tests for metals (16)

Silicon
    Silicon as a metalloid (17)
    Occurrence and recovery of silicon (18)
    Compounds of silicon (18)
    The structure of silicones (19)
    The manufacture of glass (20)
        Composition of different kinds of glass (20)
        Annealing process (20)
        Colors in glass (20)

Arsenic
    Occurrence and recovery of arsenic (21)
    Properties and uses of arsenic (21)
    Compounds of arsenic (22)

Antimony
    Occurrence and recovery of antimony (23)
    Properties and uses of antimony (24)
    Compounds of antimony (24)

QUESTIONS

Group A

1. In what materials does aluminum occur in nature?
2. What are the important physical properties of aluminum?
3. What is the chemical nature of corundum and emery?
4. Why must aluminum oxide be dissolved in fused cryolite before it can be decomposed by electricity?
5. Why are certain metallic oxides reduced with aluminum rather than with carbon?
6. Write the chemical formulas for four different alums.
7. What is the main source of boron compounds in the United States?
8. Why may borax be used as a flux in welding metals?
9. Name some of the varieties of amorphous silica.
10. (*a*) How does silicon rank in abundance among the elements? (*b*) What accounts for this rank?
11. (*a*) From what raw materials is silicon carbide made? (*b*) Write the equation for the reaction by which it is prepared.
12. (*a*) Of what is ordinary glass composed? (*b*) How are these materials believed to be related in glass?
13. What are the raw materials used in making ordinary glass?
14. (*a*) How does Pyrex glass differ in composition from ordinary glass? (*b*) How does it differ in properties?
15. Should the preparation of arsenic be classed as a product or a by-product of smelting operations?
16. Why must extreme care be used in handling arsenic and its compounds?

Group B

17. What reaction occurs when aluminum is placed in: (*a*) hydrochloric acid solution; (*b*) sodium hydroxide solution?
18. Write equations to show the net anode and cathode reactions during the electrolysis of aluminum oxide.
19. Write balanced equations to show the amphiprotic nature of aluminum hydroxide.
20. Why do we import bauxite from the West Indies and South America when almost any clay bank in the United States contains aluminum?
21. What geographic conditions affect the location of plants for the production of aluminum from purified bauxite?
22. Describe the properties characteristic of metalloids such as boron and silicon in terms of (*a*) atomic radius; (*b*) ionization energy; (*c*) electronegativity; (*d*) type of bonds formed; (*e*) electric conductivity.
23. Explain how the test for boric acid is performed.
24. (*a*) What is the structure of a quartz crystal? (*b*) What characteristic of this structure gives quartz its hardness? (*c*) How does fused quartz differ in structure from quartz crystals?

25. (*a*) What is a silicone? (*b*) What are some of the important uses for silicones?
26. Compare the structure of silicon carbide and diamond.
27. Why is sand of very high purity desired by glass manufacturers?
28. How is glass of different colors obtained for use in "stained glass" windows in churches and public buildings?
29. Why is quartz not damaged by rapid temperature changes?
30. When a red crystalline compound was tested by means of a borax bead, the bead turned blue. What metal was probably present in the compound?
31. Boron nitride and diamond have similar crystal structures. Is there any relationship between this fact and the similarity of their hardness?
32. (*a*) In what form does boric acid principally exist in water solution, as molecules, or as hydronium and borate ions? (*b*) What experimental evidence supports your answer?
33. Why is silicon dioxide usually not classified as an acid anhydride?
34. Why would you expect silicones to be water repellent?

PROBLEMS

1. How much aluminum and how much iron(III) oxide must be used in a thermite mixture to produce 10.0 kg of iron for a welding job?
2. What is the percentage of aluminum in sodium alum which crystallizes with 12 molecules of water of hydration?
3. How many liters of hydrogen can be prepared by the reaction of 50. g of aluminum and 100. g of sodium hydroxide in solution?
4. Calculate the percentage of boron in colemanite, $Ca_2B_6O_{11} \cdot 5H_2O$.
5. How many grams of sodium silicate can be prepared from 1.000 kg of sodium carbonate by reacting it with an excess of silica?
6. How many liters of carbon dioxide are liberated in Problem 5?
7. How many grams of $SbCl_3$ can be prepared by the reaction of 10.0 g of antimony with chlorine?
8. A compound contains 96.15% arsenic and 3.85% hydrogen. Its vapor has a specific gravity, air standard, of 2.695. What is the molecular formula of the compound? Use precise atomic weights.
9. Boric acid, H_3BO_3, is produced when sulfuric acid is added to a water solution of borax, $Na_2B_4O_7$. How much boric acid can be prepared from 5.00 lb of borax?
10. What weight of silicon dioxide and what weight of carbon are needed in order to prepare 1.00 ton of silicon carbide in an electric furnace?

Chapter Twenty-eight

NITROGEN AND ITS COMPOUNDS

NITROGEN

1. Occurrence of nitrogen. About four-fifths of the atmosphere by volume is elementary nitrogen. Combined nitrogen is also widely distributed. It is found in the proteins of both plants and animals. Natural deposits of both potassium nitrate and sodium nitrate are raw materials for the production of other nitrogen compounds.

2. Discovery of nitrogen. In 1772 Daniel Rutherford (1749–1819), a Scottish physician, published a study of the respiration products of small animals in a closed vessel. After he had separated the gas which we know as carbon dioxide from the exhaled air, he found that a colorless gas remained. This remaining gas would support neither life nor burning. This was the first separation of relatively pure nitrogen from the air.

3. Preparation of nitrogen.

1. By fractional distillation of liquid air. Air will condense to a liquid if it is cooled sufficiently. Small amounts of liquid air

were first produced in France in 1877. Today it is produced in large amounts as a preliminary step in separating the components of the atmosphere.

Figure 28-1 is a simplified diagram of a liquid air machine. By means of a compressor, the air is first put under a pressure of from 3000 to 4000 lb/in². This hot compressed air then flows through a coiled pipe in a condenser through which water circulates to absorb the heat of compression. In the liquefier, the gas flows out through a needle valve, and expands rapidly. This expansion cools the gas. The cool gas then flows back through the outer of the two pipes of the liquefier, cooling still further the gas in the inner tube of the liquefier. The expanded gas is recycled. The continuous expansion of cooler and cooler gas in the liquefier finally produces a low enough temperature to liquefy some of the gas. The liquid air collects in the reservoir at the bottom of the liquefier.

Liquid air resembles water in appear-

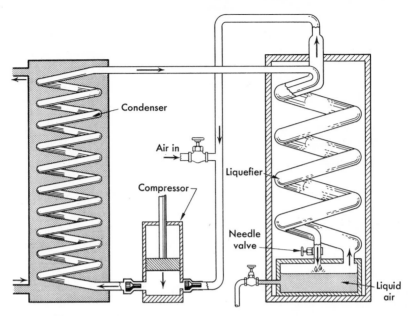

28-1 This diagram shows how a liquid air machine operates.

ance. Under ordinary atmospheric pressure, liquid air boils at a temperature of about $-190°$ C. Its boiling temperature is not constant, because liquid air is essentially a mixture of liquid nitrogen which boils at $-195.8°$ C, and liquid oxygen which boils at $-182.7°$ C. Fractional distillation of liquid air is the commercial method for producing nitrogen, oxygen, and the noble gases (except helium).

2. By decomposing ammonium nitrite. Pure nitrogen can be prepared in the laboratory by gently heating ammonium nitrite, NH_4NO_2.

$$NH_4NO_2 \rightarrow N_2 \uparrow + 2H_2O$$

Ammonium nitrite is too unstable to store in the laboratory. Usually, it is prepared by heating gently a mixture of ammonium chloride and sodium nitrite solutions. The ions form ammonium nitrite which then decomposes to yield nitrogen.

$$NH_4Cl + NaNO_2 \rightarrow NH_4NO_2 + NaCl$$
$$\searrow N_2 \uparrow + 2H_2O$$

4. Physical properties of nitrogen. Nitrogen is a colorless, odorless, and tasteless gas. It is slightly less dense than air, and is only slightly soluble in water. Its density shows that its molecules are diatomic, N_2. Nitrogen condenses to a colorless liquid at $-195.8°$ C and freezes to a white solid at $-209.9°$ C.

5. Chemical properties of nitrogen. Nitrogen atoms have the electron configuration $1s^2 2s^2 2p^3$. Nitrogen atoms share $2p$ electrons and form diatomic molecules containing a triple covalent bond.

$$\overset{\circ}{_{\circ}}N \overset{\circ\circ}{_{\circ\circ}} N \overset{\bullet}{_{\bullet}}$$

This triple covalent bond (unlike those between carbon atoms) is very strong. As a result, elementary nitrogen is rather inactive. It unites with other elements with difficulty.

Nitrogen does not burn in oxygen. However, when a lightning discharge passes through the air, or when nitrogen and oxygen are passed through an electric arc, nitrogen monoxide, NO, is formed.

By the use of a catalyst, nitrogen can be made to combine with hydrogen to form ammonia, NH_3. This method of making ammonia will be described later in Section 10.

At a high temperature, nitrogen combines directly with such metals as magnesium, titanium, and aluminum to form nitrides.

6. Uses of elementary nitrogen. Substances burn rapidly in pure oxygen. Nitrogen, on the other hand, does not support combustion. Therefore, nitrogen in the air serves as a diluting agent and effectively reduces the rate of combustion.

Because of its inertness, nitrogen is used as a blanketing atmosphere during the processing of food. It prevents oxidation which would cause food to spoil or which would affect its natural taste. It is used by chemical, petroleum, and paint industries in a similar fashion to prevent fires or explosions. Nitrogen is used with argon for filling electric lamps. It is also used in metalworking operations to control furnace atmospheres. Large amounts of atmospheric nitrogen are used to make ammonia, nitric acid, and other nitrogen compounds.

7. Test for nitrogen. The best test for nitrogen depends on the fact that magnesium combines with it when heated and forms magnesium nitride, Mg_3N_2. If water is added to magnesium nitride, ammonia is produced and can be detected by its odor.

$$Mg_3N_2 + 6H_2O \rightarrow 3Mg(OH)_2 + 2NH_3 \uparrow$$

8. Nitrogen fixation. All living organisms contain nitrogen compounds. The nitrogen in these compounds is called *combined* or *fixed* nitrogen. *Any process that converts free nitrogen into nitrogen compounds is called* **nitrogen fixation.** Such processes are

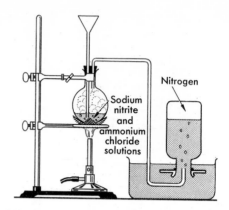

28-2 Pure nitrogen can be prepared by the decomposition of ammonium nitrite in solution. The flask must be heated gently to prevent too rapid decomposition.

important because nitrogen compounds in the soil make it possible to grow plants. Two natural and two artificial methods of nitrogen fixation are described below.

1. One natural method is to grow certain crops which will put nitrogen compounds into the soil. Most crops remove nitrogen compounds from the soil rapidly. On the other hand, certain types of crop plants, belonging to the bean and pea family, return rather large amounts of nitrogen compounds to the soil. These plants have small *nodules*, or swellings, on their roots in which organisms known as **nitrogen-fixing bacteria** grow. If the soil is alkaline, these bacteria have the ability to take free nitrogen from the air and convert it into nitrogen compounds which the plants can use.

2. Another *natural method* of nitrogen fixation occurs during electric storms. Lightning discharges furnish sufficient energy to cause some of the nitrogen and oxygen of the air to unite, forming an oxide of nitrogen. After a series of changes, nitrogen compounds are washed down into the soil in the ensuing rain.

3. The chief *artificial method* of nitrogen fixation is the manufacture of ammonia from a mixture of nitrogen and hydrogen. This ammonia can then be oxidized to nitric acid. The nitric acid, in turn, can be converted into nitrates suitable for fertilizer.

4. Another *artificial method* is the manufacture of calcium cyanamid, $CaCN_2$. In this process, nitrogen is passed over white-hot calcium carbide.

$$CaC_2 + N_2 \rightarrow CaCN_2 + C$$

The cyanamid may be used directly as a nitrogen fertilizer, or it may be converted into ammonia by superheated steam.

$$CaCN_2 + 3H_2O \rightarrow CaCO_3 + 2NH_3 \uparrow$$

The ammonia may then be converted to suitable nitrates.

AMMONIA AND AMMONIUM COMPOUNDS

9. Occurrence of ammonia. Very small traces of ammonia, NH_3, are found in the air. Decomposition of the complex proteins in the bodies of dead plants and animals produces some of this. An odor of ammonia is always noticeable around buildings where animals are housed. Bacteria break down the nitrogen compounds in manures to form this ammonia.

10. Preparation of ammonia.

1. By decomposing ammonium compounds. In the laboratory, ammonia is prepared by heating a mixture of calcium hydroxide and an ammonium compound. Usually ammonium chloride or ammonium sulfate is the compound used.

$$Ca(OH)_2 + 2NH_4Cl \rightarrow$$
$$CaCl_2 + 2NH_3 \uparrow + 2H_2O$$
$$Ca(OH)_2 + (NH_4)_2SO_4 \rightarrow$$
$$CaSO_4 + 2NH_3 \uparrow + 2H_2O$$

The mixture may be heated in a test tube fitted with an L-shaped delivery tube, as shown in Fig. 28-3. Ammonia is so soluble in water that it cannot be collected by water displacement. It can be collected by downward displacement of air in an inverted container.

In either reaction, the ammonium ion, NH_4^+, from the ammonium salt, reacts with the hydroxide ion, OH^-, from the calcium hydroxide, to form ammonia and water.

$$NH_4^+ + OH^- \rightarrow NH_3 \uparrow + H_2O$$

Heating drives the reaction to the right since ammonia is a gas.

Any strong hydroxide may be used instead of calcium hydroxide. For example:

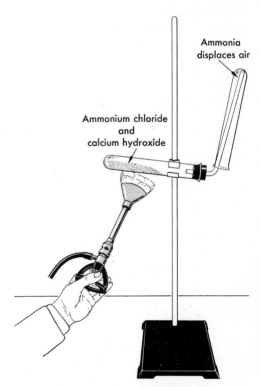

Ammonia displaces air

Ammonium chloride and calcium hydroxide

28-3 When the mixture of ammonium chloride and calcium hydroxide in the test tube is heated, ammonia is evolved.

$$NaOH + NH_4Cl \rightarrow$$
$$NaCl + NH_3 \uparrow + H_2O$$

2. By destructive distillation of bituminous coal. When bituminous coal is heated in a closed container without access to air, ammonia is one of the gaseous products. The ammonia from this reaction is then converted to ammonium sulfate by treatment with sulfuric acid.

$$2NH_3 + H_2SO_4 \rightarrow (NH_4)_2SO_4$$

3. By the Haber process. Chemists have long known that ammonia can be prepared by passing an electric spark through a mixture of nitrogen and hydrogen. But the reaction is reversible:

$$N_2 + 3H_2 \rightleftarrows 2NH_3 + 22 \text{ kcal}$$

Only a very small percentage of ammonia

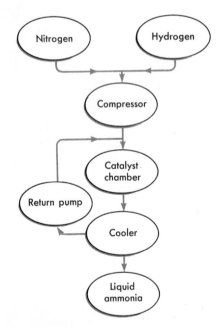

28-4 A flow diagram of the Haber process. Ammonia gas produced in the catalyst chamber is condensed into a liquid in the cooler. The uncombined nitrogen and hydrogen are recirculated through the catalyst chamber.

is produced. The problem of increasing that percentage was solved in 1913 by Fritz Haber (1868–1934), a German chemist.

The reaction between nitrogen and hydrogen is exothermic. Thus higher temperatures, desirable for increasing the rate at which the molecules of nitrogen and hydrogen react, shift this equilibrium toward the left. However, four volumes of reactants produce only two volumes of products, so increased pressure shifts the equilibrium toward the right. Haber found that by using a catalyst to increase the speed of reaction, and by using a temperature of about 600° C at a pressure of about 200 atmospheres, he could obtain a yield of about 8% ammonia.

Today, the yield from the Haber process has been improved to about 40%. This was brought about by using pressures as high as 1000 atmospheres, and an improved catalyst, a mixture of porous iron and the oxides of potassium and aluminum.

The ammonia is produced in special chrome-vanadium steel bombs which withstand the tremendous pressure. It is separated from the unreacted nitrogen and hydrogen by being dissolved in water, or by being cooled until it liquefies. The uncombined gases are returned to the bombs to be exposed again to the action of the catalyst.

11. Physical properties of ammonia. Ammonia is a colorless gas with a characteristic, penetrating odor. It is less dense than air and is easily liquefied when sufficiently cooled. Liquid ammonia, which has a boiling point of −34° C at atmospheric pressure, is sold in steel cylinders.

One of the unusual properties of ammonia is its great solubility in water. One liter of water at 20° C dissolves about 700 liters of ammonia. At 0° C nearly 1200 volumes of ammonia can be dissolved in one volume of water.

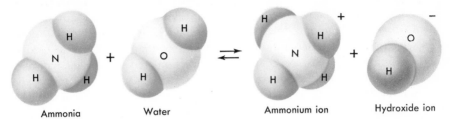

28-5 Ammonia reacts with water to form ammonium ion and hydroxide ion. In this reaction water acts as an acid (proton donor) and the ammonia acts as a base (proton acceptor).

The structural formula for ammonia is:

$$\text{H} \overset{\circ\circ}{\underset{\underset{\text{H}}{\circ\circ}}{\text{N}}} \text{H}$$

The hydrogen atoms covalently bond to the nitrogen atom by having the $1s$ hydrogen electrons occupy the half-filled $2p$ nitrogen orbitals.

For a compound with such a simple molecular structure and low molecular weight, ammonia has an unusually high melting point and a high boiling point. You will remember from the study of Chapter 11 that water shows these properties to an even greater degree. Just as in the case of water, the high melting point and high boiling point are explained by the formation of hydrogen bonds between molecules of ammonia when in the solid and liquid states. The three hydrogen atoms are not symmetrically bonded to the nitrogen atom. Consequently, ammonia molecules are polar molecules. Hydrogen atoms from one ammonia molecule form hydrogen bonds to the nitrogen atom in adjacent ammonia molecules. The polar nature of both water and ammonia molecules is also believed to be the reason for the high solubility of ammonia in water.

12. Chemical properties of ammonia. Gaseous ammonia does not support ordinary combustion or burn in air, but it will burn in pure oxygen. At ordinary tempera-

tures it is a stable compound, although it is decomposed into nitrogen and hydrogen at high temperatures. When ammonia is dissolved in water, most of the ammonia forms a simple solution. A small part of the ammonia reacts with water and ionizes, according to the reaction:

$$NH_3 + H_2O \rightleftarrows NH_4^+ + OH^-$$
$$K_i = 1.8 \times 10^{-5}$$

This mixture of molecules and ions is commonly called *ammonium hydroxide;* a better name is *ammonia-water solution.* Ammonia-water solution is weakly basic.

Do not confuse the *ammonium ion*, NH_4^+, with the *ammonia molecule.* While the ammonium ion may act like a metallic ion in its compounds, it cannot be isolated as NH_4^+. All attempts to separate ammonium from ammonium compounds result in the decomposition of the compound into ammonia and other products. The ammonium ion has a tetrahedral structure like methane because the hydrogen atoms are linked to the central nitrogen by s-sp^3 hybrid bonds.

13. Uses of ammonia and ammonium compounds.

1. As fertilizers. Ammonium compounds have long been used to supply nitrogen to the soil for growing plants. Recently, techniques have been worked out to use ammonia directly as a fertilizer.

2. As a cleaning agent. Ammonia-water solution makes a good cleaning agent because it is weakly basic, emulsifies grease, and leaves no residue to be wiped up.

3. As a refrigerant. Ammonia is used in factories which make ice. A compressor is used to liquefy ammonia gas, as shown in Fig. 28-6. The heat liberated during the compression of the gas is absorbed by water which flows down over the cooling and condensing coils. At this high pressure and lowered temperature, the ammonia liquefies. The cold, liquid ammonia then flows to a tank of brine in which are suspended the cans of fresh water to be frozen. As the liquid ammonia passes through a needle valve into coils of pipe immersed in the brine where reduced pressure is maintained, it evaporates and expands. This cools the brine to a temperature of about −10° C, well below the freezing point of fresh water.

In cold storage rooms, frozen food locker plants, or ice cream plants, brine is cooled by the evaporation of liquid ammonia as in the making of ice. Then the cold brine is pumped through coils of pipes to the freezing and storage rooms.

4. For making other compounds. Great quantities of ammonia are oxidized to make nitric acid, as explained in Section 15 of this chapter. It is also used in the production of nylon and one type of rayon, and as a catalyst in the preparation of several types of plastics. Ammonia is used in the synthesis of sulfa drugs, vitamins, and antimalarials. It is also used as a neutralizing agent by the petroleum industry, and in the rubber industry to prevent the coagulation of latex during transportation.

▶ **14. Hydrazine: another compound of nitrogen and hydrogen.** Hydrazine, N_2H_4, is produced by oxidizing ammonia-water solution with sodium hypochlorite. It burns readily, and finds considerable use as a fuel for rockets. It also serves as a strong reducing agent.

NITRIC ACID

15. Preparation of nitric acid. Two methods are commonly used to prepare this important acid.

1. From nitrates. Small amounts of nitric

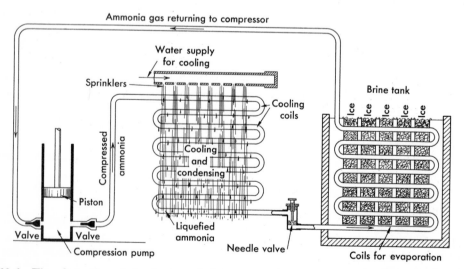

28-6 The absorption of the heat needed to evaporate and expand the liquid ammonia lowers the temperature of the fresh water until it freezes into ice.

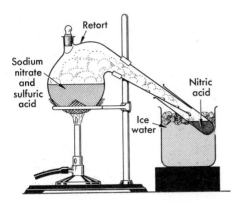

28-7 Nitric acid may be prepared in the laboratory by the action of sulfuric acid on sodium nitrate.

acid may be prepared in the laboratory by heating a nitrate with sulfuric acid. The reaction is carried out in a glass-stoppered retort because of the corrosive action of nitric acid on apparatus with rubber stoppers or rubber connectors.

$$NaNO_3 + H_2SO_4 \rightarrow NaHSO_4 + HNO_3 \uparrow$$

The nitric acid vapor is condensed in the side arm of the retort and collected in the receiver.

2. From ammonia. Wilhelm Ostwald (1853–1933), a German chemist, learned how to oxidize ammonia to nitric acid with the aid of a catalyst at about the same time that Haber developed the process for the synthesis of ammonia. These two processes fit together perfectly. Ammonia is made by synthesis from nitrogen and hydrogen. The ammonia is then oxidized to nitric acid in another part of the same plant. Some of the nitric acid may be neutralized with additional ammonia producing ammonium nitrate. This compound is a useful fertilizer and an ingredient in making explosives.

In the Ostwald process, a mixture of ammonia and air is heated to a tempera-

ture of 600° C. It is then passed through a tube containing platinum gauze, which serves as the contact catalyst. On the surface of the platinum, the ammonia is oxidized to nitrogen monoxide, NO.

$$4NH_3 + 5O_2 \rightarrow 4NO + 6H_2O$$

This reaction is exothermic and raises the temperature of the mixture of gases to about 1000° C. Then more air is mixed with the nitrogen monoxide to oxidize it to nitrogen dioxide, NO_2.

$$2NO + O_2 \rightarrow 2NO_2$$

The nitrogen dioxide is cooled and absorbed in water, forming nitric acid.

$$3NO_2 + H_2O \rightarrow 2HNO_3 + NO \uparrow$$

The nitrogen monoxide produced in this reaction is also oxidized to nitrogen dioxide and absorbed in water.

Today almost all of the nitric acid used in industry is made by the oxidation of ammonia.

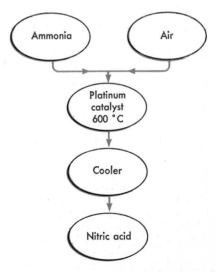

28-8 Flow diagram of the Ostwald process for the oxidation of ammonia into nitric acid.

16. Physical properties of nitric acid. Pure HNO_3 is a colorless liquid, about 1.5 times as dense as water. It fumes in moist air and boils at 86° C Pure HNO_3 is unstable, and for that reason, the concentrated nitric acid of commerce is a 68% solution of HNO_3 in water. It boils at 120° C.

17. Chemical properties of nitric acid.

1. Stability. Nitric acid is not very stable. When boiled, or even when exposed to sunlight, it decomposes to some extent. Water and nitrogen dioxide are two products of its decomposition. The deep yellow color of concentrated nitric acid stored in laboratory bottles is caused by small amounts of dissolved nitrogen dioxide formed when the acid is exposed to light. In more dilute water solution, HNO_3 is more stable.

2. Acid properties. Dilute nitric acid has the usual properties of acids. It reacts with metals, metallic oxides, and metallic hydroxides, forming salts known as *nitrates.*

Nitric acid stains the skin yellow, forming xanthoproteic (zan-thoh-proh-*tee*-ik) acid. It produces the same effect with many proteins, and for that reason is used as a *test* for proteins. (See Chapter 19, Section 17.)

3. As an oxidizing agent. Nitric acid molecules furnish oxygen which unites with various materials that may be in contact with it. Nitric acid is a powerful oxidizing agent.

Nitric acid may react in a variety of ways. The concentration of the acid, the activity of the reducing agent that is mixed with it, and the temperature at which the reaction is carried out determine what products are formed. Under ordinary conditions, moderately dilute nitric acid is reduced to nitrogen monoxide. If concentrated nitric acid is reduced, nitrogen dioxide is the product.

With other reducing agents and different conditions for the reaction, such other reduction products as N_2O, N_2, and NH_3 may be formed. N_2O, dinitrogen monoxide, is more commonly called nitrous oxide.

4. Action with metals. Nitric acid is such a vigorous oxidizing agent that hydrogen gas is *not usually* set free when this acid is added to common metals. *Very dilute nitric acid* reacts with such active metals as sodium, calcium, or magnesium, forming a nitrate and setting hydrogen free.

$$Mg + 2HNO_3 \rightarrow Mg(NO_3)_2 + H_2 \uparrow$$

In reactions with less active metals such as zinc and copper, the hydrogen appears in the water product and the nitrogen of the nitric acid is reduced. Copper reacts with cold, dilute nitric acid according to the equation:

$$3Cu + 8HNO_3 \rightarrow$$
$$3Cu(NO_3)_2 + 2NO \uparrow + 4H_2O$$

With concentrated nitric acid, copper reacts as follows:

$$Cu + 4HNO_3 \rightarrow$$
$$Cu(NO_3)_2 + 2NO_2 \uparrow + 2H_2O$$

Nitric acid does not react with gold or platinum because of the stability of these metals. It reacts with aluminum and iron very slowly, probably because of the formation of semi-protective surface coatings. When nitric acid reacts with a metal, the nitrate of that metal is usually formed. The nitrates of the various metals are crystalline compounds which are readily soluble in water.

18. Test for a nitrate. To several milliliters of the solution to be tested in a test tube, an equal volume of a solution of iron(II) sulfate, $FeSO_4$, is added. With the test tube held in an inclined position, a few milliliters of concentrated sulfuric acid is added slowly, so that it runs down the inclined wall of the test tube very gradually and settles to the bottom, not mixing with the other mixture in the tube. If the solution tested does contain a nitrate, a *brown layer* containing nitrosyl iron(II) sulfate, $Fe(NO)SO_4$, forms at the junction of the acid and the other mixture (Fig. 28-9).

19. Uses of nitric acid.

1. For making fertilizers. About 75% of the nitric acid produced in the United States is used in the manufacture of fertilizers. Ammonium nitrate is the most important nitrate so used, and is readily manufactured in plants using the combined Haber-Ostwald processes. Sodium nitrate and potassium nitrate are also used as fertilizer ingredients.

2. For making explosives. Many modern explosives are made directly or indirectly from nitric acid. The acid itself is not an explosive, but many of the compounds derived from it form the most violent explosives known. Among these are nitroglycerin, smokeless powder, and TNT.

3. For making dyes. Nitric acid reacts with several products obtained from coal tar, forming *nitro compounds.* One of these coal tar products, benzene, reacts with nitric acid to form nitrobenzene, $C_6H_5NO_2$. (See Chapter 17, Section 19.) Aniline,

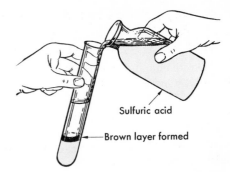

Sulfuric acid

Brown layer formed

28-9 The brown layer formed when sulfuric acid is added slowly to a solution of iron(II) sulfate containing nitrate ions serves as a test for the nitrate ion.

$C_6H_5NH_2$, a compound used in making different dyes, is made by reducing nitrobenzene with hydrogen.

4. For making plastics. Cotton, which consists mainly of cellulose, $(C_6H_{10}O_5)_n$, is treated with a mixture of nitric acid and sulfuric acid to make nitrocellulose plastics. (See Chapter 19, Section 11.) A variety of products is formed, depending on the amount of nitric acid used, the temperature, and the length of time the acid is allowed to act on the cellulose. Manufacturers use sulfuric acid to absorb the water that is formed in the reaction. Celluloid, pyroxylins, photographic film, and many other products are made from such nitrocellulose plastics.

REVIEW OUTLINE

QUESTIONS

Group A

1. (*a*) Where are large quantities of elementary nitrogen found? (*b*) In what kinds of compounds does combined nitrogen occur naturally?
2. (*a*) Who first isolated relatively pure nitrogen? (*b*) How was this done?
3. (*a*) Which has the higher boiling point, liquid nitrogen or liquid oxygen? (*b*) What practical use is made of this difference in boiling points?
4. (*a*) Write the balanced equation for the production of nitrogen from ammonium chloride and sodium nitrite. (*b*) Of what type of reaction is this an example?
5. How can you test a bottle of colorless gas to determine whether or not it is nitrogen?
6. What is meant by *nitrogen fixation?*
7. (*a*) What are two natural methods of nitrogen fixation? (*b*) Name two artificial methods.
8. (*a*) What is the purpose of high pressure in the Haber process? (*b*) What is the function of the catalyst?
9. Why is *ammonia-water solution* a better name for the solution of ammonia in water than *ammonium hydroxide?*
10. Give two reasons why ammonia-water solution makes an excellent window cleaner.
11. Why is a glass-stoppered retort used for the laboratory preparation of nitric acid?

12. What condition must be met for the reaction between sodium nitrate and sulfuric acid to run to completion?
13. Write three equations to show the steps in the production of nitric acid from ammonia.
14. Why does concentrated nitric acid turn yellow in the laboratory?

Group B

15. (*a*) Why does compressing a gas raise its temperature? (*b*) Why does a gas become colder when it is allowed to expand?
16. What structural feature of the nitrogen molecule accounts for the stability of this element?
17. (*a*) Name three uses for nitrogen. (*b*) For each use, give the related physical or chemical property of nitrogen which makes the use possible.
18. What must be the condition of the soil for nitrogen-fixing bacteria to be most effective?
19. (*a*) Write the balanced equation for the reaction between calcium hydroxide and ammonium nitrate for producing ammonia. (*b*) Write the net ionic equation for this reaction. (*c*) How does the net ionic equation for this reaction compare with the net ionic equations for the reactions between calcium hydroxide and ammonium chloride, and between sodium hydroxide and ammonium sulfate?
20. Why is the boiling point of ammonia, $-34°$ C, so much higher than the boiling point of methane, $-162°$ C, when they both consist of molecules of nearly the same molecular weight?
21. Why is ammonia so soluble in water, yet methane is nearly insoluble in water?
22. Why may zinc be used with either hydrochloric or sulfuric acids for producing hydrogen, but not with nitric acid?
23. You are given a colorless solution of a salt. Tell how you would test it to determine whether the salt is a nitrate or not.
24. Why might a farmer alternate crops of corn and lima beans on one of his fields in successive years?
25. The equation for the reaction of copper and dilute nitric acid indicates that colorless nitrogen monoxide gas is one of the products. Yet when we carry out this reaction in an evaporating dish, dense reddish-brown nitrogen dioxide gas billows over the rim of the dish. Explain.
26. What is the oxidation number of nitrogen in (*a*) NH_3; (*b*) N_2H_4; (*c*) N_2; (*d*) HNO_2; (*e*) HNO_3?

PROBLEMS

Group A

1. How many grams of ammonia will be produced by the reaction of steam on 160. g of calcium cyanamid?
2. How many liters of nitrogen and hydrogen are required for the preparation of 200. liters of ammonia?
3. If 15 g of HNO_3 is needed for a laboratory experiment, what mass of sodium nitrate is required for its preparation?

Group B

4. What volume, in liters, of nitrogen at S.T.P. can be prepared from a mixture of 10. g of NH_4Cl and 10. g of $NaNO_2$?

5. How many grams of nitric acid can be prepared from 50.0 g of potassium nitrate of 80.0% purity?

6. (*a*) What mass of copper(II) nitrate may be prepared from 254 g of copper by reaction with nitric acid? (*b*) How many liters of nitrogen monoxide at S.T.P. are also produced?

Chapter Twenty-nine

SULFUR AND ITS COMPOUNDS

SULFUR

1. Occurrence of sulfur. Sulfur is one of the elements known since ancient times. It occurs in nature as the free element or combined with other elements in sulfides and sulfates. Sulfur is naturally associated with volcanic regions and considerable amounts are mined in regions where volcanoes were formerly active. The sulfur mines in Sicily are of this type and have been worked for centuries.

The United States is the greatest producer of sulfur. Immense deposits of nearly pure sulfur occur about 500 feet below the surface of the ground in Texas and Louisiana, near the Gulf of Mexico in a nonvolcanic region. These deposits are now the world's greatest source of sulfur.

2. The mining of sulfur. The sulfur beds in Texas and Louisiana are as much as 200 feet thick. Between the surface of the ground and the sulfur there is a layer of quicksand. This makes it difficult to sink a shaft to the sulfur so that it can be mined by the common methods.

Herman Frasch (1852–1914), an American chemist, devised a method of obtaining the sulfur without sinking a shaft. This is done by a complex system of pipes by which superheated water (170° C, under pressure) is pumped into the sulfur deposits. The hot water melts the sulfur which is then forced to the surface by hot air. See Fig. 29-1. The melted sulfur may be shipped in the molten state in tank cars or ocean-going tankers. Or it may be allowed to solidify in large wooden molds, and then be broken into pieces for shipment. See Fig. 29-2.

3. Physical properties of sulfur. Common sulfur is a yellow, *odorless* solid which is practically insoluble in water and is twice as dense as water. It dissolves readily in carbon disulfide and in carbon tetrachloride.

Sulfur melts at a temperature of 114.5° C, forming a pale-yellow mobile liquid. When it is heated to a still higher temperature, instead of becoming more

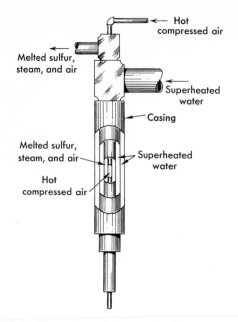

29-1 The system of concentric pipes used in the Frasch process of mining sulfur.

mobile, as liquids usually do, it becomes thicker (more viscous) and does not flow freely. At a temperature of about 250° C, the melted sulfur becomes so thick that it hardly flows from an inverted tube. As the temperature rises, the color changes from a light yellow to a reddish-brown, and then almost to black. Near the boiling point the fluidity increases and the liquid again flows freely. Sulfur boils at 445° C. This unusual behavior is due to the existence of different allotropic forms of liquid sulfur.

4. Allotropic forms of sulfur. Sulfur exists in several different solid and liquid allotropic forms. These are produced by different arrangements of groups of sulfur atoms.

1. Rhombic sulfur. This form of solid sulfur is stable at ordinary temperatures. It consists of eight-membered puckered rings of sulfur atoms connected in these rings by single covalent bonds. See Fig. 29-3. Crystals of rhombic sulfur may be prepared by dissolving roll sulfur in carbon disulfide, and then allowing the solvent to evaporate slowly. The specific gravity of rhombic sulfur is 2.06.

2. Monoclinic sulfur. Sulfur can also be crystallized in the form of long needle-like monoclinic crystals. This allotropic form can be prepared by first melting some sulfur in a crucible at as low a temperature

29-2 Crude sulfur being loaded for shipment. (Texas Gulf Sulfur Co.)

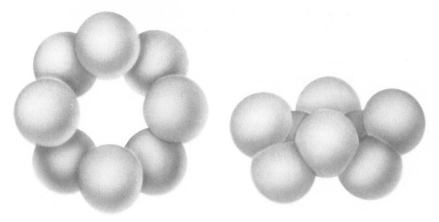

29-3   The structure of S_8 molecules of sulfur.

as possible. It is next allowed to cool slowly until a crust just begins to form. If the crust is then broken and the liquid sulfur remaining poured off, a mass of monoclinic crystals will be found lining the walls of the crucible. Heat energy must be added to form this type of sulfur, and when such crystals cool below 95° C they gradually change back into the rhombic form. However, monoclinic sulfur still consists of eight-membered rings of sulfur atoms but in a different crystalline arrangement. The specific gravity of monoclinic sulfur is 1.96.

3. λ-sulfur. (Lambda-sulfur.) This is the liquid allotropic form of sulfur which is produced at temperatures just above the melting point of sulfur. It is quite fluid and has a straw-yellow color. It, too, consists of eight-membered rings of sulfur atoms. The almost spherical shape of these S_8 mole-

cules enables them to roll over one another easily, and gives this form of sulfur its fluidity.

4. μ-sulfur. (Mu-sulfur.) If λ-sulfur is heated to about 200° C, it darkens to a reddish, and then almost black liquid. The molten sulfur becomes so viscous that it will not flow. The heating imparts enough energy to the sulfur atoms to open some of the eight-membered rings. When a ring of sulfur atoms breaks open, the sulfur atoms on either side of the break are each left with an unshared electron. These sulfur atoms form bonds with similar sulfur atoms from other open rings, and produce long chains. These chains are another allotropic form of sulfur, μ-sulfur. The color of μ-sulfur arises from the greater absorption of light by electrons which formerly completed the ring structure but which are now free to migrate along the chain

29-4   A chain of sulfur atoms as found in mu-sulfur.

structure. The high viscosity of μ-sulfur is caused by the tangling of the chains of sulfur atoms. However, as the temperature is raised still further, these chains break up into smaller groups of atoms and the fluidity of the mass increases. The color becomes still darker because the breaking-up of the chains produces more free electrons.

Sulfur vapor, produced when sulfur boils at 445° C, consists again of S_8 molecules. If sulfur vapor is heated to a higher temperature, these molecules gradually dissociate into S_2 molecules. Monatomic molecules of sulfur are produced at very high temperatures.

5. Amorphous sulfur. Amorphous sulfur is a rubbery, plastic mass made by pouring boiling sulfur into cold water. It is dark-brown, or even black in color, and is elastic, like rubber. At the boiling point

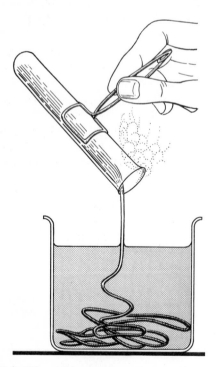

29-5 The sudden cooling of mu-sulfur produces amorphous sulfur.

of sulfur, the long enmeshed chains have largely broken down, and the sulfur is fluid again. Eight-membered rings of sulfur atoms and chains are now in equilibrium. The S_8 rings are evaporating. When this boiling mixture is suddenly cooled, the chains of μ-sulfur have no time to re-form into rings, and amorphous sulfur is produced. A mass of amorphous sulfur soon loses its elasticity, becoming hard and brittle. In the cooler amorphous sulfur the transformations into successive allotropic forms proceed in reverse order. Finally, it once again becomes the S_8 ring configuration of the stable rhombic variety. Amorphous sulfur is insoluble in carbon disulfide.

5. Chemical properties of sulfur. At room temperature, sulfur is not very active chemically. When heated, it unites with oxygen to produce sulfur dioxide.

$$S + O_2 \rightarrow SO_2 \uparrow$$

Traces of sulfur trioxide, SO_3, are also formed when sulfur burns in air. Sulfur can be made to combine with nonmetals such as hydrogen, carbon, and chlorine; but such compounds are formed with some difficulty, and are not very stable. The differences in electronegativity between sulfur and hydrogen, carbon, and chlorine are so small that the bonding in such compounds is predominantly covalent.

From the formulas SO_3, SO_2, and H_2S, we see that sulfur may have an oxidation number of $+6$, or $+4$ when it combines with oxygen, and of -2 when it combines with hydrogen. Electron-dot formulas for these compounds are shown on the opposite page. Notice that the actual molecules of sulfur trioxide and sulfur dioxide are resonance hybrids of the possible structures given. Sulfur is similar to oxygen in the manner in which it combines with other elements. This can be seen from the

SIMILARITIES BETWEEN SULFUR AND OXYGEN

hydrogen sulfide	H_2S	hydrogen oxide	H_2O
carbon disulfide	CS_2	carbon dioxide	CO_2
copper(I) sulfide	Cu_2S	copper(I) oxide	Cu_2O
copper(II) sulfide	CuS	copper(II) oxide	CuO
mercury(II) sulfide	HgS	mercury(II) oxide	HgO
zinc sulfide	ZnS	zinc oxide	ZnO

Sulfur trioxide

Sulfur dioxide   Hydrogen sulfide

table at the top of the page.

Powdered zinc and sulfur combine vigorously. The heat produced when iron filings and sulfur unite causes the whole mass to be heated to incandescence. Copper unites with the vapor of boiling sulfur to form copper(I) sulfide. If the oxide of any metal is insoluble in water, as a rule the sulfide of that metal is insoluble in water also.

6. Uses of sulfur. Sulfur is used in making sulfur dioxide, carbon disulfide, sulfuric acid, and other sulfur compounds. Several million tons are used annually in the manufacture of sulfuric acid. Matches, fireworks, and black gunpowder all contain either sulfur or sulfur compounds. Sulfur is also used in the preparation of certain dyes, medicines, and fungicides. It is also used in the vulcanization of rubber. (See Chapter 17, Section 22.)

HYDROGEN SULFIDE

7. Hydrogen sulfide formed by natural processes. When sulfur-containing proteins decay, hydrogen sulfide is one of the products formed. The odor of decayed eggs is due to the formation of hydrogen sulfide. Coal is seldom entirely free from sulfur. When it burns, sulfur dioxide and some traces of hydrogen sulfide pass off into the air. Some mineral waters also contain hydrogen sulfide.

8. Preparation of hydrogen sulfide. A metallic sulfide and either hydrochloric or sulfuric acid may be used to prepare hydrogen sulfide. Iron(II) sulfide, FeS, is suitable for the purpose. Exchange reactions occur when these acids are used.

$$FeS + 2HCl \rightarrow FeCl_2 + H_2S \uparrow$$
$$FeS + H_2SO_4 \rightarrow FeSO_4 + H_2S \uparrow$$

Hydrogen sulfide is a gas, and the exchange reactions go to completion. The gas is usually collected by upward displacement of air since it is denser than air and moderately soluble in water.

9. Physical properties of hydrogen sulfide. The gas is colorless, and has the very disagreeable odor of decayed

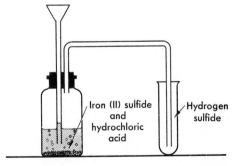

29-6 The laboratory method of preparing hydrogen sulfide.

eggs. *Hydrogen sulfide is poisonous.* In co⌐-centrated form, it is a violent poison, which may cause death if inhaled. When diluted with air, it causes nausea, headache, and dizziness.

10. Chemical properties of hydrogen sulfide.

1. Hydrogen sulfide burns. The products formed depend on the relative amounts of hydrogen sulfide and oxygen present. If an abundance of oxygen is available, 2 volumes of hydrogen sulfide rⁿacts with 3 volumes of oxygen.

$$2H_2S + 3O_2 \rightarrow 2SO_2 \uparrow + 2H_2O \uparrow$$

When 2 volumes of hydrogen sulfide reacts with 2 volumes of oxygen, half the sulfur does not burn.

$$2H_2S + 2O_2 \rightarrow 2H_2O \uparrow + SO_2 \uparrow + S \downarrow$$

If only 1 volume of oxygen is available for burning 2 volumes of hydrogen sulfide, the hydrogen combines with the oxygen, and all the sulfur is set free.

$$2H_2S + O_2 \rightarrow 2H_2O \uparrow + 2S \downarrow$$

2. Hydrogen sulfide is a good reducing agent. Sulfide ions in hydrogen sulfide give up their electrons readily to oxidizing agents. To show its properties as a reducing agent, hydrogen sulfide may be bubbled through a solution of hydrogen peroxide. The oxygen in hydrogen peroxide is reduced from peroxide to oxide, while the sulfide ions are oxidized to sulfur in the form of a fine white powder which remains suspended in the water.

$$H_2O_2 + H_2S \rightarrow 2H_2O + S \downarrow$$

3. Hydrogen sulfide forms a weak acid. Dissolved in water, hydrogen sulfide forms a weak diprotic acid called hydrosulfuric acid.

$$H_2S + H_2O \rightleftarrows H_3O^+ + HS^-$$
$$HS^- + H_2O \rightleftarrows H_3O^+ + S^=$$

This weak acid turns blue litmus red, and reacts with hydroxides to form sulfides and water.

$$Cu(OH)_2 + H_2S \rightarrow CuS \downarrow + 2H_2O$$

▶ For the two stages of ionization of hydrogen sulfide solution, the ionization constants are:

$$K_{ion\,1} = \frac{[H_3O^+][HS^-]}{[H_2S]} = 5.7 \times 10^{-8}$$

$$K_{ion\,2} = \frac{[H_3O^+][S^=]}{[HS^-]} = 1.2 \times 10^{-15}$$

To show the relationship between $[S^=]$ and $[H_3O^+]$ in such solutions, we may multiply

$$K = K_{ion\,1} \times K_{ion\,2}$$
$$K = \frac{[H_3O^+][HS^-][H_3O^+][S^=]}{[H_2S][HS^-]}$$
$$K = 5.7 \times 10^{-8} \times 1.2 \times 10^{-15}$$
$$K = 6.8 \times 10^{-23}$$

or

$$K = \frac{[H_3O^+]^2[S^=]}{[H_2S]} = 6.8 \times 10^{-23}$$

Saturated solutions of H_2S in water are approximately 0.1M with respect to H_2S. Hence we may substitute $[H_2S] = 10^{-1}$,

$$\frac{[H_3O^+]^2[S^=]}{10^{-1}} = 6.8 \times 10^{-23}$$

and then

$$[S^=] = \frac{6.8 \times 10^{-24}}{[H_3O^+]^2}$$

This indicates that the sulfide ion concentration in hydrogen sulfide solutions varies inversely as the square of the hydronium ion concentration. The following table gives sulfide ion concentrations in mole/liter for various hydronium ion concentrations, also in mole/liter.

SULFIDE ION CONCENTRATIONS IN HYDROGEN SULFIDE SOLUTIONS

$[H_3O^+]$	pH	$[S^=]$
10^{-1}	1	6.8×10^{-22}
10^{-3}	3	6.8×10^{-18}
10^{-5}	5	6.8×10^{-14}
10^{-7}	7	6.8×10^{-10}
10^{-9}	9	6.8×10^{-6}
10^{-11}	11	6.8×10^{-2}

Thus, it is possible to vary the sulfide ion concentration in solutions of H₂S, by adjusting the pH to an appropriate value.

4. Hydrogen sulfide acts on metals. The tarnishing of some metals is due to the formation of a coating of a sulfide of the metal. Such foods as eggs and mustard form enough hydrogen sulfide to produce a tarnish of black silver sulfide on silver tableware.

11. Tests for the presence of a sulfide. Any soluble sulfide furnishes sulfide, S⁼, ions in solution. Such ions unite with silver, lead, or copper to form black precipitates. A drop of a soluble sulfide solution applied to a silver coin forms a brownish-black stain.

When hydrochloric acid is added to a moderately insoluble sulfide, hydrogen sulfide is set free. It can usually be recognized by its odor.

A strip of filter paper moistened with a solution of lead acetate, Pb(C₂H₃O₂)₂, quickly turns brownish-black when exposed to hydrogen sulfide in water solution or as a gas.

$Pb(C_2H_3O_2)_2 + H_2S \rightarrow PbS\downarrow + 2HC_2H_3O_2$

▶ **12. Hydrogen sulfide in chemical analysis.** Hydrogen sulfide may be used to analyze minerals or metals. When it is added to a solution containing the ions of certain metals, insoluble sulfides of those metals are precipitated. The table below lists common sulfides, together with their color and solubility product constant, where available.

The listing is in the *experimental* order in which sulfides may be precipitated by H₂S from solutions containing the metallic ion as the hydronium ion concentrations decrease. The solubility product constants for the sulfides are not very reliable, but roughly, it is observed that the solubility product constants increase as one goes down the table.

PROPERTIES OF COMMON SULFIDES

Compound	Color	K_{sp}
As₂S₃	yellow	
As₂S₅	yellow	
HgS	black	3×10^{-53}
CuS	black	8.7×10^{-36}
Sb₂S₃	orange	
Sb₂S₅	orange	
Bi₂S₃	brown-black	1×10^{-70}
SnS₂	yellow	
CdS	yellow	1×10^{-28}
PbS	black	8.4×10^{-28}
ZnS	white	4.5×10^{-24}
CoS	black	5×10^{-22}
NiS	black	1.8×10^{-21}
FeS	brown-black	3.7×10^{-19}
MnS	pink	1.4×10^{-15}

In the classical scheme of analysis, the sulfides listed are divided into two groups by sulfide precipitations under different pH conditions: the sulfides of arsenic through lead are precipitated at pH = 1; the sulfides of zinc through manganese are precipitated at pH = 9.

Two sample calculations will show why this separation is possible. Suppose in the same solution we have [Pb⁺⁺] = 0.001 *M* and [Zn⁺⁺] = 0.001 *M*. We acidify with HCl until [H₃O⁺] = 10⁻¹ *M*, and pass in H₂S until the solution is saturated. At this [H₃O⁺], [S⁼] = 6.8 × 10⁻²². (See Section 10.) Then $[Pb^{++}][S^=] = 10^{-3} \times 6.8 \times 10^{-22} = 6.8 \times 10^{-25}$. The K_{sp} of PbS is exceeded; PbS precipitates. But $[Zn^{++}][S^=] = 10^{-3} \times 6.8 \times 10^{-22} = 6.8 \times 10^{-25}$ also. However, the K_{sp} of ZnS is not exceeded, and Zn^{++} remains in solution.

Since the sulfides listed above lead sulfide all have smaller solubility products, these sulfides will be precipitated by H_2S in a solution where pH = 1. The sulfides listed below zinc sulfide have solubility products which are larger than that of zinc sulfide. Hence none of these will be precipitated by H_2S in a solution having pH = 1. The theoretical pH conditions for separating any pair of sulfides with suitably different solubility products may be determined by similar computations.

OTHER SULFIDES

13. Metallic sulfides found in nature. Many important ores are found in nature as sulfides. Large quantities of copper sulfide are found in Montana. Zinc sulfide is one of the important sources of zinc. Nearly all of our lead comes from lead sulfide. The sulfides of such metals as silver, nickel, arsenic, antimony, and iron are found in nature. Sulfides of iron are a profitable source of sulfur and sulfur compounds, but are not important as a source of iron.

▶ **14. Preparation and properties of carbon disulfide.** When sulfur vapor is passed over heated charcoal in an electric furnace, carbon and sulfur unite to form a vapor which condenses to an almost colorless liquid. Its formula is CS_2, analogous to that of carbon dioxide. The commercial product has a disagreeable odor, somewhat resembling boiled cabbage. The liquid does not dissolve in water. It has a very low kindling temperature and burns rapidly. Its vapor burns explosively when mixed with air.

$$CS_2 + 3O_2 \rightarrow CO_2 \uparrow + 2SO_2 \uparrow$$

Carbon disulfide is a good solvent for rubber, phosphorus, waxes, and resins. It is used in the manufacture of varnishes and matches, and in one step of the process of manufacturing viscose rayon. It is also used in the preparation of carbon tetrachloride.

THE OXIDES OF SULFUR

15. Occurrence of sulfur dioxide. Traces of sulfur dioxide may be found in the air for several reasons. Sulfur dioxide occurs in some volcanic gases and in some mineral waters. Coal contains sulfur as an impurity, and, as coal is burned, the sulfur is burned to sulfur dioxide. The roasting of sulfide ores converts the sulfur of the ore into sulfur dioxide. The sulfur dioxide is sometimes expelled into the air, although modern smelting plants convert it into sulfuric acid.

16. Preparation of sulfur dioxide.

1. By burning sulfur. The simplest way to prepare sulfur dioxide is to burn sulfur in air or in pure oxygen.

$$S + O_2 \rightarrow SO_2 \uparrow$$

The gas produced by burning sulfur in air is mixed with nitrogen, but this is not objectionable for many operations.

2. By roasting sulfides. Enormous quantities of sulfur dioxide are produced when sulfide ores are roasted. The roasting of *sphalerite*, ZnS, is typical.

$$2ZnS + 3O_2 \rightarrow 2ZnO + 2SO_2 \uparrow$$

Sulfur dioxide is a by-product in this operation. Iron pyrites, FeS_2, is roasted to produce sulfur dioxide for making sulfuric acid.

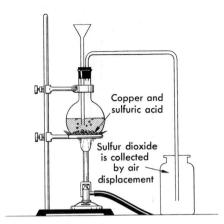

29-7 Sulfur dioxide may be prepared in the laboratory by reducing hot, concentrated sulfuric acid with copper.

3. By the reduction of sulfuric acid. In one of the laboratory methods of preparing this gas, copper is heated with concentrated sulfuric acid (see Fig. 29-7). The hot, concentrated acid is a vigorous oxidizing agent. The copper is oxidized and the sulfur in sulfuric acid is reduced.

$$Cu + 2H_2SO_4 \rightarrow CuSO_4 + 2H_2O + SO_2 \uparrow$$

4. By the decomposition of sulfites. In this second laboratory method, pure sulfur dioxide may be prepared by the action of a strong acid on a sulfite. When sodium sulfite reacts with sulfuric acid, the following reaction occurs:

$$Na_2SO_3 + H_2SO_4 \rightarrow$$
$$Na_2SO_4 + H_2O + SO_2 \uparrow$$

Sulfurous acid, H_2SO_3, is first formed; it then decomposes into water and sulfur dioxide (see Fig. 29-8).

17. Physical properties of sulfur dioxide. Pure sulfur dioxide is a colorless gas with a suffocating, choking odor. It is more than twice as dense as air, and is very soluble in water. It is one of the easiest gases to liquefy, since it becomes liquid at room temperature under a pressure of about two atmospheres. Liquid

sulfur dioxide is commercially available in steel cylinders.

18. Chemical properties of sulfur dioxide.

1. It is an acid anhydride. Sulfur dioxide is the anhydride of sulfurous acid. As it dissolves in water, it also reacts with the water:

$$H_2O + SO_2 \rightleftarrows H_2SO_3$$

This accounts, in part at least, for the high solubility of sulfur dioxide in water. Sulfurous acid is a weak acid, which will turn litmus paper red, neutralize hydroxides, and form hydrogen sulfites and sulfites.

$$H_2SO_3 + H_2O \rightleftarrows H_3O^+ + HSO_3^-$$
$$K_i = 1.2 \times 10^{-2}$$
$$HSO_3^- + H_2O \rightleftarrows H_3O^+ + SO_3^=$$
$$K_i = 5.6 \times 10^{-8}$$

Both of these reactions are reversible, and the acid decomposes into water and sulfur dioxide again when the water solution is warmed. A solution of sulfurous acid, if exposed to the air, will react slowly with oxygen and form sulfuric acid.

2. It is a stable gas. Sulfur dioxide does

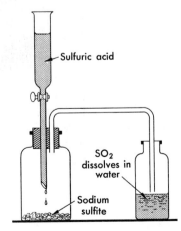

29-8 An acid added to a sulfite forms unstable sulfurous acid which decomposes into sulfur dioxide and water.

not burn. In the presence of a suitable catalyst, it may be oxidized to sulfur trioxide.

$$2SO_2 + O_2 \rightleftarrows 2SO_3$$

19. Uses for sulfur dioxide and sulfurous acid.

1. For making sulfuric acid. Tremendous quantities of sulfur dioxide are oxidized to form sulfur trioxide which is then combined with water to form sulfuric acid. (See Section 21.)

2. As a preservative. Dried fruits, such as apricots and prunes, are treated with sulfur dioxide which acts as a preservative.

3. In the petroleum industry. Liquid sulfur dioxide is used in the treatment of kerosene and light lubricating oils.

4. For making sulfites. Sulfurous acid is diprotic and reacts with hydroxides to form hydrogen sulfites and sulfites.

5. For bleaching. Sulfurous acid does not harm the fibers of wool, silk, straw, and paper, and can be used to bleach them. It is believed that the sulfurous acid converts the colored compounds in these materials to white sulfites. The bleaching is not permanent and the natural yellow color of the fiber reappears after some time.

6. In preparing paper pulp. Sulfurous acid reacts with limestone to form calcium hydrogen sulfite, $Ca(HSO_3)_2$. When wood chips are heated in calcium hydrogen sulfite solution, the lignin which binds the cellulose fibers together is dissolved, leaving the fibers unchanged. The fibers are then processed to form **paper.**

20. Sulfur trioxide.
Sulfur trioxide is the anhydride of sulfuric acid. It is an intermediate product in the manufacture of sulfuric acid. Sulfur trioxide is a white, crystalline solid at room temperature. It reacts with water to form sulfuric acid:

$$SO_3 + H_2O \rightarrow H_2SO_4$$

SULFURIC ACID

21. Preparation of sulfuric acid.
Most of the sulfuric acid produced in the United States today is made by the contact process. In this process, sulfur dioxide is prepared by burning sulfur or by roasting iron pyrites, FeS_2. Impurities which might combine with the catalyst and "poison" it are then removed from the gas. The purified sulfur dioxide is mixed with air, and passed through heated iron pipes which contain the catalyst, usually divanadium

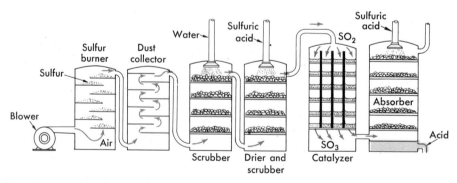

29-9   In making sulfuric acid by the contact process, sulfur is burned to form sulfur dioxide. The gas is freed from dust, scrubbed, dried, and passed through a catalyst where it is converted into sulfur trioxide. The sulfur trioxide is then absorbed in 97% sulfuric acid in which it is readily soluble.

pentoxide, V_2O_5. This close "contact" of the sulfur dioxide and the catalyst gives the *contact process* its name. While sulfur dioxide and oxygen of the air are both adsorbed on the surface of the catalyst, they react to form sulfur trioxide. See Fig. 29-9.

Although the oxidation of sulfur dioxide is an exothermic process, it is carried out at about 400° C. This temperature is high enough to cause the reaction to proceed at a practical rate. The heat evolved by the reaction is used to preheat the entering reactants. This prevents the temperature in the catalyzer from becoming high enough to promote excessive decomposition of the sulfur trioxide produced. ·

Gaseous sulfur trioxide does not dissolve in or unite readily with pure water. Consequently, sulfur trioxide is absorbed in 97% sulfuric acid, in which it is readily soluble. The sulfur trioxide combines with the 3% water and forms 100% sulfuric acid. Part of this may be drawn off, and the remainder diluted with water to make 97% acid for the absorption of more sulfur trioxide. Very pure, highly concentrated sulfuric acid is produced by the contact process.

22. Physical properties of sulfuric acid. Concentrated sulfuric acid is a dense, oily liquid. It contains only about 2% water, and has a specific gravity of about 1.84 and a boiling point of 338° C. Pure sulfuric acid is colorless. Commercial acid may be yellow or brown or almost black because of the presence of impurities, especially organic matter.

When sulfuric acid is added to water (*you must never add water to sulfuric acid*) a great deal of heat is evolved because of the formation of the hydrates $H_2SO_4 \cdot H_2O$ and $H_2SO_4 \cdot 2H_2O$.

23. Chemical properties of sulfuric acid.

1. Its acid properties. Sulfuric acid, being a diprotic acid, ionizes in dilute water solution in two stages:

$$H_2SO_4 + H_2O \rightleftarrows H_3O^+ + HSO_4^-$$
$$HSO_4^- + H_2O \rightleftarrows H_3O^+ + SO_4^=$$
$$K_i = 1.26 \times 10^{-2}$$

At 18° C, 0.1 N H_2SO_4 is 90% ionized in the first stage and 60% ionized in the second stage. Sulfuric acid can react with hydroxides to form hydrogen sulfates and sulfates. It reacts with metals and with the oxides of metals. Because it is more highly ionized, *dilute* sulfuric acid reacts with metals above hydrogen in the oxidizing and reducing agents series more vigorously than *cold, concentrated* sulfuric acid does. See Chapter 22 for this series.

2. Its oxidizing properties. Hot, concentrated sulfuric acid is a vigorous oxidizing agent. The sulfur is reduced from the +6 oxidation state to the +4 or −2 oxidation state depending on the strength of the acid and the reducing agent with which it reacts. Thus with copper, sulfur dioxide is produced (see Section 16). With zinc and hot, slightly diluted acid, hydrogen sulfide is the gaseous product.

$$4Zn + 5H_2SO_4 \rightarrow$$
$$4ZnSO_4 + H_2S \uparrow + 4H_2O$$

3. Its dehydrating properties. The strong affinity of sulfuric acid for water makes it an excellent *dehydrating* agent. Gases may be dried by bubbling them through concentrated sulfuric acid. Lumps of pumice stone soaked in sulfuric acid may be used in the lower part of a desiccator. In fact, sulfuric acid is such an active dehydrating agent that it will take hydrogen and oxygen, in the proportion needed to form water, from such substances as sucrose, $C_{12}H_{22}O_{11}$, or cellulose, $(C_6H_{10}O_5)_n$, leaving the carbon uncombined. The equation for this process is as follows:

$$C_{12}H_{22}O_{11} + 11H_2SO_4 \rightarrow$$
$$12C + 11H_2SO_4 \cdot H_2O$$

In the same manner, concentrated sulfuric acid chars wood, paper, cotton, starch, and other organic compounds.

In making some products commercially, water is formed as a by-product. Let us illustrate this with the reaction for making nitroglycerin, $C_3H_5(NO_3)_3$.

$$C_3H_5(OH)_3 + 3HNO_3 \rightarrow$$
$$C_3H_5(NO_3)_3 + 3H_2O$$

In the manufacture of this explosive, concentrated nitric acid is used. Since the nitric acid is reacting with a nonelectrolyte, the reaction is slow. To prevent dilution of the acid, which would cause the reaction to proceed still more slowly, sulfuric acid is always mixed with the nitric acid. The sulfuric acid acts as a dehydrating agent. It absorbs the water as fast as it is formed and thus maintains the rate of the reaction.

In the laboratory preparation of carbon monoxide, sulfuric acid is used to dehydrate formic acid (see Chapter 16).

> **CAUTION:** *Sulfuric acid burns the flesh severely.* Great care must be used in the handling of sulfuric acid so that it does not come in contact with the skin.

24. Uses of sulfuric acid. Calcium phosphate, $Ca_3(PO_4)_2$, is quarried in great amounts in Florida, Tennessee, and other states. This rock phosphate is treated with sulfuric acid (about 4 million tons/year) to convert it to a more soluble form for use as *superphosphate* fertilizer.

Sulfuric acid is used also in the preparation of other acids and various sulfates. Many other chemicals are made from sulfuric acid.

The iron and steel industries use large quantities of sulfuric acid to remove a coating of oxide from the surface of iron or steel before the metal is plated, or before it is coated with an enamel.

Sulfuric acid is used in the refining of petroleum products to remove certain organic impurities. The electrolyte in lead storage batteries is dilute sulfuric acid.

Sulfuric acid serves as a dehydrating agent in the production of smokeless powder and nitroglycerin. It is used in the manufacture of photographic film, in making nitrocellulose plastics, in manufacturing rayon, paints and pigments, cellophane, and in innumerable articles of commerce.

25. Importance of some sulfates. Sulfuric acid reacts with many metals to form sulfates. Some of the most important sulfates are those of copper, iron, zinc, calcium, barium, and aluminum. Copper(II) sulfate is used in copper plating and to produce mordants in dyeing. Iron(II) sulfate finds use in water purification and in the manufacture of ink. Zinc sulfate is used to make lithopone, a white paint pigment. Hydrated calcium sulfate

29-10 When a white precipitate that is insoluble in hydrochloric acid is formed after the addition of barium chloride solution, the presence of a sulfate is indicated.

is the mineral gypsum. Barium sulfate and aluminum sulfate are used in preparing other compounds of these elements. Nearly all sulfates are soluble in water, those of calcium, strontium, barium, and lead(II) being the chief exceptions. The hydrogen sulfates are not very important.

26. Test for a sulfate. When a solution of barium chloride is added to sulfuric acid or to any soluble sulfate, a white precipitate of barium sulfate is formed.

$$Ba^{++} + SO_4^= \rightarrow BaSO_4 \downarrow$$

Barium sulfate is insoluble in hydrochloric acid. White precipitates of barium oxalate, barium carbonate, barium sulfite, or barium phosphate which might be confused with the barium sulfate precipitate are all soluble in hydrochloric acid. Thus the addition of hydrochloric acid when performing the test prevents the formation of these interfering precipitates.

REVIEW OUTLINE

Sulfur
>   Occurrence (1)
>   Mining—Frasch process (2)
>   Physical properties (3)
>   Allotropic forms (4)
>   Rhombic sulfur (4)
>   Monoclinic sulfur (4)
>   Lambda sulfur (4)
>   Mu sulfur (4)
>   Amorphous sulfur (4)
>   Chemical properties (5)
>   Uses of sulfur (6)

Hydrogen sulfide
>   Occurrence (7)
>   Preparation (8)
>   Physical properties (9)
>   Chemical properties—relationship of [S$^=$] and [H$_3$O$^+$] in H$_2$S solutions (10)
>   Test for sulfide (11)
>   Uses of hydrogen sulfide—sulfide precipitation (12)

Other sulfides
>   Metallic sulfides (13)
>   Carbon disulfide (14)

Oxides of sulfur
>   Sulfur dioxide (15)
>   Occurrence (15)
>   Preparation—roasting (16)
>   Physical properties (17)
>   Chemical properties (18)
>   Uses of sulfur dioxide (19)
>   Uses of sulfurous acid (19)

Sulfur trioxide (20)

Sulfuric acid
> Preparation—contact process (21)
> Physical properties (22)
> Chemical properties (23)
> Uses of sulfuric acid (24)
> Importance of sulfates (25)
> Test for sulfate ions (26)

QUESTIONS

Group A

1. Where are sulfur deposits located in the United States?
2. (*a*) What is the function of the superheated water in the Frasch process? (*b*) The function of the compressed air? (*c*) Why is this process used instead of more conventional mining methods?
3. (*a*) What is the odor of sulfur? (*b*) Of hydrogen sulfide? (*c*) Of sulfur dioxide?
4. A pupil prepared some nearly black amorphous sulfur in the laboratory. The next week when he examined it, it had become brittle and much lighter in color. Explain.
5. What are the uses of elementary sulfur?
6. Write the formulas for: (*a*) iron(III) sulfide; (*b*) diarsenic pentasulfide; (*c*) copper(II) sulfide; (*d*) mercury(II) sulfide; (*e*) silver sulfide; (*f*) tin(IV) sulfide; (*g*) diantimony trisulfide.
7. Describe two natural processes which release hydrogen sulfide into the air.
▶8. (*a*) Give several uses for carbon disulfide. (*b*) What property of carbon disulfide is involved in each case?
9. (*a*) Write balanced formula equations to show the reactions between hydrogen sulfide and solutions of the chlorides of mercury(II), lead(II), and antimony(III). (*b*) Write the net ionic equations for these reactions.
10. What metals have important sulfide ores?
11. Sulfur dioxide may be found as an impurity in the air. From what sources does it come?
12. Write balanced formula equations for: (*a*) a commercial preparation of sulfur dioxide; (*b*) a laboratory preparation of sulfur dioxide.
13. (*a*) What method of gas collection is used in a laboratory preparation of sulfur dioxide? (*b*) What properties of sulfur dioxide determine this choice?
14. What is the principal use for sulfur dioxide?
15. Why is the contact process for producing sulfuric acid so named?
16. What is the proper method of diluting sulfuric acid?
17. Why are large quantities of sulfuric acid used in the iron and steel industry?
18. Name four important sulfates and give their uses.
19. Why is a mixture of nitric acid *and sulfuric acid* used in making nitrocellulose?
20. Write balanced chemical equations to show the formation from sulfurous acid and sodium hydroxide of: (*a*) sodium hydrogen sulfite; (*b*) sodium sulfite.

21. How can you test a soluble salt to determine whether it is (*a*) a sulfide; (*b*) a sulfate?
22. What is the purpose of the concentrated hydrochloric acid in the test for a soluble sulfate?

Group B

23. (*a*) What is the molecular formula for rhombic sulfur? (*b*) Why is this molecular formula not usually used in equations?
24. Explain the changes in color and fluidity of sulfur between its melting point and boiling point.
25. Is the change from rhombic sulfur to monoclinic sulfur exothermic or endothermic? Explain.
26. (*a*) Write a formula equation for the laboratory preparation of hydrogen sulfide. (*b*) What type of chemical reaction is this? (*c*) Write the net ionic equation for the reaction. (*d*) Write a different formula equation for this preparation which has this same net ionic reaction.
27. How are the products of combustion of hydrogen sulfide related to the amount of oxygen available?
28. Balance the equation for the oxidation of hydrogen sulfide by hydrogen peroxide using the electron transfer method.
29. Draw electron dot formulas to show the resonance structure of sulfur dioxide.
30. In the contact process, why is sulfur trioxide absorbed in 97% sulfuric acid rather than in water?
31. Give two reasons why boiling concentrated sulfuric acid burns the flesh so badly.
32. Is sulfur dioxide easy to liquefy? Explain.
33. Why is sulfur dioxide so soluble in water?
34. Explain the heat exchange needed in the catalyst chamber of a contact sulfuric acid plant.
35. Balance the following oxidation-reduction equations:
    (*a*) $Hg + H_2SO_4 \rightarrow HgSO_4 + SO_2 \uparrow + H_2O$; (*b*) $Cu_2S + O_2 \rightarrow Cu_2O + SO_2 \uparrow$.
36. What test might be applied to determine whether a white crystalline powder is a sulfite or a hydrogen sulfite?

PROBLEMS

Group A

1. How many kilograms of sulfur dioxide may be produced by burning 1.0 kg of pure sulfur?
2. (*a*) What volume of oxygen is required for the complete combustion of 5.0 liters of hydrogen sulfide? (*b*) Assuming the air to be 21% oxygen, what volume of air is required?
3. Calculate the percentage composition of lead sulfide, PbS.

4. How many liters of carbon dioxide at S.T.P. are formed by burning 39.0 g of carbon disulfide?
5. What is the percentage composition of H_2SO_4?
6. How many grams of sodium sulfite are required for the production of 1.00 liter of sulfur dioxide by reaction with sulfuric acid?
7. A lead smelter processes 500. metric tons of zinc sulfide, ZnS, each day. If no sulfur dioxide is lost, how many kilograms of sulfuric acid could be made in the plant daily?

Group B

8. Calculate the mass in grams of 500. ml of hydrogen sulfide measured at 27° C and 740. mm pressure.
9. How many kilograms of sulfuric acid can be prepared from 5.00 kg of sulfur that is 99.5% pure?
10. How many liters of sulfur dioxide at 25° C and 740. mm pressure may be produced by the roasting of 1200. kg of iron pyrites, FeS_2?
11. (*a*) If 140. kg of scrap iron is added to a large vat of dilute sulfuric acid, how many kilograms of iron(II) sulfate can be produced? (*b*) How many kilograms of 95% sulfuric acid are required?
12. How many liters of sulfur dioxide can be prepared from a mixture of 100. g of copper and 100. g of H_2SO_4?
▶13. Calculate the sulfide ion concentration in saturated hydrogen sulfide solutions in water when the pH is 2, 4, 6, 8, and 10.
▶14. What must be the pH of the solution in order to separate the following pairs of ions in 0.01M solutions as sulfides by precipitation with hydrogen sulfide? (*a*) Hg^{++} and Fe^{++}; (*b*) Bi^{+++} and Zn^{++}; (*c*) Co^{++} and Ni^{++}.
▶15. If a barium chloride solution is 0.01M, what is the smallest sulfate ion concentration which may be detected by precipitation? K_{sp} $BaSO_4$ = 1.5 × 10⁻⁹.
▶16. If a lead acetate solution is 0.01M, what is the smallest sulfide ion concentration which may be detected by precipitation?

Chapter Thirty

THE HALOGEN FAMILY

1. The Halogen Family: Group VII of the Periodic Table. The Halogen Family consists of the nonmetallic elements fluorine, chlorine, bromine, iodine, and astatine. See the table at the bottom of this page.

From this table we see that each of these elements has seven electrons in the outermost shell. In order to attain an outer octet of electrons, a halogen atom must acquire one electron. Since the atoms of these elements are so strongly electronegative, they are all active elements which have never been found free in nature. In the elementary state they exist as covalent diatomic molecules. Fluorine, having the smallest atoms and the greatest affinity for electrons, is the most highly electronegative element. Fluorine, consequently, cannot be prepared from its

THE HALOGEN FAMILY

Element	Atomic Number	Atomic Weight	Electron Configuration	Principal Oxidation Number	Melting Point, °C	Boiling Point, °C	Color	Density, 10° C	Atomic Radius Å	Ionic Radius Å
fluorine	9	18.9984	2, 7	−1	−223	−187	pale-yellow gas	1.69 g/l	0.64	1.36
chlorine	17	35.453	2, 8, 7	−1	−101.6	−34.6	greenish-yellow gas	3.207 g/l	0.99	1.81
bromine	35	79.909	2, 8, 18, 7	−1	−7.2	58.78	reddish-brown liquid	3.12 g/ml	1.14	1.95
iodine	53	126.9044	2, 8, 18, 18, 7	−1	113.5	184.35	grayish-black crystals	4.93 g/ml	1.33	2.16
astatine	85	210.	2, 8, 18, 32, 18, 7							

compounds by any purely chemical reduction. The other halogens, with increasingly larger atoms, are less electronegative than fluorine. As a result, the smaller, lighter halogens are able to replace and oxidize the larger, heavier halogens from their compounds. Astatine is a synthetic radioactive halogen produced in 1940 at the University of California by Corson, Mackenzie, and Segré.

It is evident from the table that there is a regular change in properties shown by the members of this family, proceeding from the smallest and lightest to the largest and heaviest. Refer also to the charts showing ionization energy and electronegativity in Chapters 5 and 6.

Each of the halogens combines with hydrogen. Hydrogen fluoride molecules, because of the great electronegativity difference between hydrogen and fluorine, are so polar that they associate by hydrogen bonding. The remaining hydrogen halogenides with smaller electronegativity differences do not show this property. Each of the hydrogen halogenides is a colorless gas which is ionized in water solution. With the exception of hydrofluoric acid, these acids are highly ionized and are strong acids.

Each of the halogens forms ionic salts with metals. Hence the name *halogens*, which means "salt producers."

FLUORINE

2. Preparation of fluorine. Fluorine was first prepared in 1886 by Henri Moissan (1852–1907). He electrolyzed a solution of potassium hydrogen fluoride, KHF_2, in liquid anhydrous hydrogen fluoride in a platinum tube, using platinum-iridium electrodes. Today it is prepared by electrolyzing a mixture of potassium fluoride and hydrogen fluoride in a stainless steel or copper electrolytic cell with a graphite anode. The fluoride coating protects these metals from further attack.

3. Properties of fluorine. Fluorine is the most active nonmetallic element. A fluorine atom, with seven electrons in its outer L shell, has a great affinity for an additional electron to complete its octet. An acquired electron is very strongly attracted by the positively charged nucleus due to the small size of the fluorine atom. This accounts for its extreme electronegativity. It unites with hydrogen explosively, even in the dark. It forms compounds with all elements except helium, neon, and argon. There are no known positive oxidation states of fluorine. It forms salts known as *fluorides*. Fluorine reacts with gold and platinum slowly. Special carbon steel containers are used to transport fluorine. These become coated with iron fluoride which resists further action.

4. Usefulness of fluorine compounds. The mineral fluorspar, CaF_2, is used in preparing most fluorine compounds. Sodium fluoride is used as a poison for destroying roaches and vermin. A trace of sodium fluoride, or the cheaper sodium silico-fluoride, is added to the drinking water of many communities because fluorides help prevent tooth decay. Fluorides have also been added to some tooth pastes to help prevent tooth decay.

Dichlorodifluoromethane, commercially called "Freon," CCl_2F_2, is used as a refrigerant. It is odorless, nonflammable, and nontoxic. It is also used as the propellant in spray cans of insecticides. In the production of aluminum, melted cryolite, $AlF_3 \cdot 3NaF$, is used as a solvent for aluminum oxide. Uranium is converted to the gaseous uranium hexafluoride, UF_6, for separating the uranium isotopes.

Fluorine combines with the noble gases krypton, xenon, and radon. The extreme radioactivity of radon coupled with its short half-life has made experiments with radon fluorides very difficult to perform. Two fluorides of krypton, KrF_2 and KrF_4, have been prepared by passing electric discharges through krypton-fluorine mixtures cooled to the temperature of liquid nitrogen. These krypton fluorides are not stable at room temperature, and decompose into their constituent elements.

Three fluorides of xenon, XeF_2, XeF_4, and XeF_6, have been made by successive additions of fluorine to the xenon atom. All are white solids at ordinary temperatures; XeF_6 is the most highly reactive. The three compounds each react with hydrogen, producing elementary xenon and hydrogen fluoride. With water, XeF_2 produces xenon, oxygen, and hydrogen fluoride. The other two fluorides react with water to yield xenon trioxide, XeO_3, a colorless, highly explosive solid. Xenon trioxide dissolves in water to form a stable solution which is a very strong oxidizing agent. It is believed that the xenon fluorides will find use as fluorinating agents.

5. Preparation and properties of hydrogen fluoride. This compound, HF, is prepared by treating calcium fluoride with concentrated sulfuric acid.

$$CaF_2 + H_2SO_4 \rightarrow CaSO_4 + 2HF \uparrow$$

30-1   Crystals of xenon tetrafluoride.

The colorless gas which is set free by the reaction fumes strongly in moist air. It dissolves in water and forms hydrofluoric acid. This acid is very corrosive, attacking the flesh and forming painful sores which heal slowly. The vapor is very dangerous if inhaled. Hydrofluoric acid reacts with most substances. Wax, lead, platinum, and certain plastics are important exceptions.

At ordinary room temperature, the molar volume of hydrogen fluoride has a

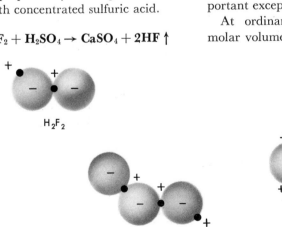

30-2   Among the molecules found in hydrogen fluoride at room temperature are H_2F_2, H_3F_3, and H_6F_6 molecules.

mass of about 50. g; thus hydrogen fluoride has an average molecular weight of 50. Since the molecular weight of an HF molecule is only 20., this indicates that hydrogen fluoride contains some molecules more complex than HF. Some scientists believe that gaseous hydrogen fluoride is an approximately equal mixture of H_2F_2 and H_3F_3 molecules, having molecular weights of 40. and 60. respectively. There is some evidence, however, for the existence of even more complex molecules up to and including H_6F_6 in gaseous hydrogen fluoride. At higher temperatures, the molar volume of the gas has a mass of only 20. g, showing that the gas dissociates into HF molecules. The association of hydrogen fluoride molecules is an example of hydrogen bonding, due to the high electronegativity of fluorine and the resulting polarity of hydrogen fluoride molecules.

The hydrogen-fluorine bond is estimated to have about 50 percent ionic character.

Water dipoles can cause some of the H_2F_2 molecules present in hydrofluoric acid at room temperature to ionize as follows:

$$H_2O + H_2F_2 \rightleftarrows H_3O^+ + HF_2^-$$

The hydrogen difluoride ion, HF_2^-, contains the strongest hydrogen bond known; even stronger than the hydrogen bonds in molecules like H_2F_2 and H_3F_3. Because of its slight ionization, hydrofluoric acid is a weak acid. Being a diprotic acid, it forms both acid and normal salts.

$$H_2F_2 + KOH \rightarrow KHF_2 + H_2O$$
$$H_2F_2 + 2KOH \rightarrow 2KF + 2H_2O$$

6. Uses of hydrofluoric acid. The chief uses of hydrofluoric acid are as a catalyst in the manufacture of high-octane

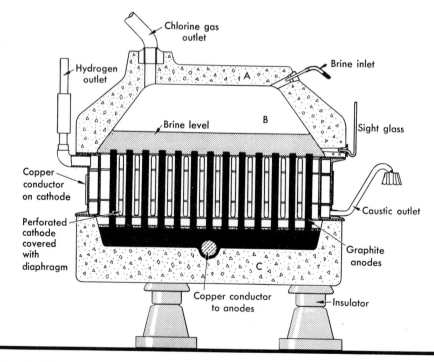

30-3   The Hooker cell is used for preparing chlorine by the electrolysis of a solution of sodium chloride.

gasoline, and in the manufacture of synthetic cryolite for aluminum production.

For many years hydrofluoric acid has been used for etching glass. Electric light bulbs may be frosted by exposing the inside surface of the bulb to the fumes of hydrogen fluoride.

CHLORINE

7. Wide occurrence of compounds. Because chlorine is a strongly electronegative element, it never occurs free or uncombined in nature. It is found rather abundantly in the form of chlorides of sodium, potassium, and magnesium. Common table salt, sodium chloride, is widely distributed in sea water, in salt brines underground, and in rock salt deposits. Sodium chloride is the commercial source for the preparation of chlorine.

8. Preparation of chlorine. The element chlorine was first isolated in 1774 by Scheele. There are various ways to prepare it; we shall discuss three.

1. By the electrolysis of sodium chloride. Chlorine is commonly prepared by the electrolysis of sodium chloride in water solution. The concentration of the solution is such that hydrogen from the water is liberated at the cathode, and chlorine gas is set free at the anode. The gases, hydrogen and chlorine, are kept separate from each other and from the solution by asbestos diaphragms. The sodium and hydroxide ions remaining in the solution are recovered as sodium hydroxide.

$$2NaCl + 2H_2O \xrightarrow{\text{(elect)}} 2NaOH + H_2\uparrow + Cl_2\uparrow$$

A small amount of chlorine is prepared by electrolysis of fused sodium chloride, as a by-product of sodium production.

2. By the oxidation of hydrogen chloride. When a mixture of manganese dioxide

and hydrochloric acid is heated, the manganese oxidizes half of the chloride ions in the reacting HCl to chlorine atoms. Manganese is reduced during the reaction from the +4 oxidation state to the +2 state.

$$MnO_2 + 4HCl \rightarrow MnCl_2 + 2H_2O + Cl_2\uparrow$$

This is the method that was used by Scheele in first preparing chlorine. It is a useful laboratory preparation.

In an alternative procedure, manganese dioxide is mixed with sodium chloride and sulfuric acid, and heated. The sodium chloride and sulfuric acid react to form hydrogen chloride.

$$2NaCl + H_2SO_4 \rightarrow Na_2SO_4 + 2HCl$$

The chloride ions are oxidized by the manganese of the manganese dioxide and free chlorine is liberated.

$$2HCl + MnO_2 + H_2SO_4 \rightarrow MnSO_4 + 2H_2O + Cl_2\uparrow$$

Combining the two preceding equations gives the following equation for the overall reaction.

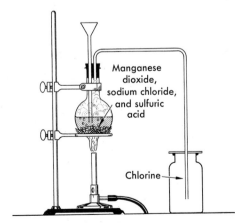

30-4 One method of preparing chlorine in the laboratory is by heating a mixture of manganese dioxide, sodium chloride, and sulfuric acid.

$$2NaCl + 2H_2SO_4 + MnO_2 \rightarrow$$
$$Na_2SO_4 + MnSO_4 + 2H_2O + Cl_2 \uparrow$$

3. *By the action of hydrochloric acid on calcium hypochlorite.* This is a convenient laboratory method for the preparation of chlorine, since heat is not needed. Furthermore, the chlorine can be produced in small quantities as required. Hydrochloric acid is allowed to drop onto calcium hypochlorite powder. Chlorine is liberated and calcium chloride and water are formed.

$$4HCl + Ca(ClO)_2 \rightarrow$$
$$CaCl_2 + 2Cl_2 \uparrow + 2H_2O$$

9. Physical properties of chlorine. At room temperature chlorine is a greenish-yellow gas, which has a disagreeable, suffocating odor. It is about 2.5 times as dense as air, and is moderately soluble in water, forming a pale-yellow solution. Chlorine is easily liquefied and is usually marketed in steel cylinders.

When inhaled in small quantities, chlorine affects the mucous membranes of the nose and throat, producing about the same symptoms as a bad head cold. If inhaled in larger quantities, chlorine is so toxic that it causes death. The bad effects from breathing chlorine are partly alleviated by inhaling either alcohol or ammonia.

10. Chemical properties of chlorine. The outer shell of a chlorine atom contains seven electrons. Chlorine undergoes many reactions as it acquires the additional electron to complete the octet. Its chemical properties will be discussed under the following subtopics.

1. *Action with metals.* When powdered antimony is sprinkled into a jar of moist chlorine, the two elements unite spontaneously, emitting a shower of sparks. Antimony trichloride is formed.

$$2Sb + 3Cl_2 \rightarrow 2SbCl_3$$

In a similar manner, hot metallic sodium burns in chlorine and forms sodium chloride. Chlorine combines directly with such metals as copper, iron, zinc, and arsenic, if they are heated slightly.

2. *Action with hydrogen.* If hydrogen and chlorine are mixed in the dark, no reaction occurs. But such a mixture explodes violently if it is heated, or if it is exposed to sunlight. The heat or sunlight provides the activation energy. A jet of hydrogen, burning in air, will continue to burn if it is introduced into a bottle of chlorine.

$$H_2 + Cl_2 \rightarrow 2HCl \uparrow$$

This is an example of combustion without the presence of oxygen.

Chlorine has such a great affinity for hydrogen that it can take hydrogen from some of its compounds. Chlorine does not support the combustion of wood or paper. A paraffin candle, however, continues to burn in chlorine with a smoky flame. In this reaction the hydrogen of the paraffin unites with the chlorine forming hydrogen chloride, and the carbon is left uncombined. Turpentine is a hydrocarbon with the formula $C_{10}H_{16}$. A strip of filter paper moistened with hot turpentine and suspended in a jar of chlorine burns with a sooty flame. Hydrogen chloride is formed, and a dense cloud of soot is set free:

$$C_{10}H_{16} + 8Cl_2 \rightarrow 10C + 16HCl \uparrow$$

3. *Action with water.* A freshly prepared solution of chlorine in water is yellow-green in color. If such a solution stands in sunlight for a few days, both the yellow-green color and the pronounced odor of the chlorine disappear. The chlorine unites with the water to form hypochlorous acid and hydrochloric acid. Hypochlorous acid is unstable and decomposes into hydrochloric acid giving off oxygen.

$$2H_2O + 2Cl_2 \rightarrow 2HClO + 2HCl$$
$$\searrow 2HCl + O_2$$

Because of this reaction, chlorine water is a good oxidizing agent.

If no oxidizable material is in contact with hypochlorous acid, its decomposition produces molecules of oxygen as shown by the above equation. However, if an oxidizable material is in contact with the hypochlorous acid, the liberated oxygen combines directly with the oxidizable material. In bleaching, the oxygen combines with the dye. If the dye can be oxidized to a colorless compound, it will be bleached successfully. However, if the dye cannot be oxidized to a colorless compound, it will not be bleached. Hypochlorous acid will not bleach all dyes or destroy all colors. Many dyestuffs are not affected by it at all. Hypochlorous acid usually removes natural colors. It bleaches ordinary ink spots because the resulting compounds are white or pale-colored oxides. It does not affect printer's ink because it cannot oxidize the carbon in it.

11. Uses of chlorine.

1. For bleaching. Bleaching solutions are generally solutions of sodium hypochlorite. They are made by electrolyzing sodium chloride, and allowing the liberated chlorine to mix with the sodium hydroxide being produced. They may also be made by the reaction between chlorine and sodium carbonate. Dry powdered chlorine bleaches are also available. They generally contain sodium hypochlorite also.

CAUTION: Chlorine destroys silk or wool fibers. *Commercial bleaches containing hypochlorites must never be used on silk or wool.*

2. As a disinfectant. Since moist chlorine is a good oxidizing agent, it destroys bacteria. Large quantities of chloride of lime, $Ca(ClO)Cl$, are used as a disinfectant.

In city water systems, billions of gallons of water are treated with chlorine to kill disease-producing bacteria. The water in swimming pools is usually treated with chlorine to insure its safety for bathing. Chlorine is also sometimes used to kill bacteria in sewage before it is discharged into lakes or rivers, so the contamination from this source will be at a minimum.

3. For making compounds. Because chlorine combines directly with many metals and nonmetals it is used to produce many chlorides. Among these are chloroform, $CHCl_3$; carbon tetrachloride, CCl_4; aluminum chloride, Al_2Cl_6; and disulfur dichloride, S_2Cl_2.

12. Preparation of hydrogen chloride.

In the laboratory, hydrogen chloride can be prepared by treating sodium chloride with sulfuric acid.

$$NaCl + H_2SO_4 \rightarrow NaHSO_4 + HCl \uparrow$$

This same reaction is used commercially, but it is carried out at a higher temperature. Under this condition, a second molecule of HCl may be produced if more NaCl is used.

$$2NaCl + H_2SO_4 \rightarrow Na_2SO_4 + 2HCl \uparrow$$

Hydrogen chloride is also prepared commercially by the direct union of hydrogen and chlorine which are both obtained by the electrolysis of concentrated sodium chloride solution (see Section 8 of this chapter).

Hydrogen chloride is dissolved in pure water, and sold under the name of hydrochloric acid.

13. Physical properties of hydrogen chloride.

This gas is colorless, and has a sharp, penetrating odor. It is denser than air and extremely soluble in water. One volume of water at $0°$ C will dissolve more than 500 volumes of the gas at standard pressure. Hydrogen chloride fumes in moist air. It is so soluble that it condenses water vapor from the air into minute drops of hydrochloric acid.

14. Chemical properties of hydrogen chloride. Hydrogen chloride is a stable compound which does not burn. Some vigorous oxidizing agents react with it to form water and chlorine.

Hydrogen chloride gas does not act as an acid except in the sense that it may be a proton donor. This is also true of the liquid which is formed by compressing and cooling the gas. However, a water solution of the gas is a strong acid known as *hydrochloric acid*. Hydrogen chloride is a polar covalent compound, but when it is dissolved in water the water dipoles cause it to ionize extensively, forming hydronium ions and chloride ions. Thus the solution has acid properties. The concentrated acid contains about 38% hydrogen chloride by weight, and is about 1.2 times as dense as water. Hydrochloric acid is a typical non-oxidizing acid. It reacts with many metals and oxides of metals, and neutralizes hydroxides, forming salts and water.

15. Uses of hydrochloric acid. This acid is used in preparing certain chlorides and in cleaning metals. Many metals must be freed from their oxides and other forms of tarnish before they can be galvanized, enameled, tinned, or plated with other metals.

Some hydrochloric acid is essential in the process of digestion.

16. Abundance of chlorides. Theoretically, it is possible to form a chloride of almost any metal. The metallic chlorides form an important group of salts. Nearly all of them are crystalline compounds, and most of them are soluble in water. The chlorides of lead, silver, and mercury(I) are insoluble. Sodium chloride is used for food preservation and seasoning. It is also a very important chemical raw material. Aluminum chloride is

employed as a catalyst in the "cracking" of petroleum to increase the yield of gasoline. Chlorides of carbon, sulfur, and phosphorus have some important applications.

17. Test for a chloride. The test for a soluble chloride is based on the insolubility of silver chloride. Silver nitrate is added to the solution to be tested for chloride ions. The formation of a white precipitate which is soluble in ammonia-water solution, but is reprecipitated when excess nitric acid is added, is a test for the chloride ion.

The ionic equations for the reactions involved in the test for the chloride ion are:

1. Forming the white silver chloride precipitate:

$$Ag^+ + Cl^- \rightarrow Ag^+Cl^- \downarrow$$

2. Dissolving the silver chloride in ammonia-water solution:

$$Ag^+Cl^- + 2NH_3 \rightarrow Ag(NH_3)_2^+ + Cl^-$$

3. Reprecipitating the silver chloride by adding nitric acid:

$$Ag(NH_3)_2^+ + Cl^- + 2H_3O^+ + 2NO_3^- \rightarrow$$
$$Ag^+Cl^- \downarrow + 2NH_4^+ + 2NO_3^- + 2H_2O$$

BROMINE

18. Occurrence and discovery of bromine. Several bromides, particularly those of sodium and magnesium, are found in nature. For many years the chief source of bromine was the mother liquor left after sodium chloride had been extracted from the brine of salt wells. Now, however, there is such a great demand for bromine in manufacturing antiknock fluids for gasoline that processes have been developed to extract it from sea water.

Bromine was discovered in 1826 by the French chemist Antoine-Jerome Balard (1802–1876). He produced bromine by treating the mother liquor of a natural brine with chlorine gas.

19. Bromine from bromides. In the laboratory bromine can be prepared by using manganese dioxide, sulfuric acid, and sodium bromide.

$$2NaBr + MnO_2 + 2H_2SO_4 \rightarrow$$
$$Na_2SO_4 + MnSO_4 + 2H_2O + Br_2 \uparrow$$

This method is exactly analogous to that for preparing chlorine.

The commercial extraction of bromine from sea water depends on the ability of chlorine to displace bromide ions from solution, as chlorine is more highly electronegative than bromine.

$$2Br^- + Cl_2 \rightarrow 2Cl^- + Br_2$$

Large quantities of acidified sea water are treated with chlorine. Bromine is liberated and then blown out of the solution by steam or air. It can be condensed directly, or it may be absorbed in sodium carbonate solution, from which it can be recovered by treatment with sulfuric acid. A similar reaction is used to extract bromine from bromides found in salt wells of Michigan, Ohio, and West Virginia. Bromine may also be prepared by electrolysis of soluble bromides.

20. Physical properties of bromine. Bromine is a dark-red liquid which is about three times as dense as water. It evaporates readily, forming a vapor which is very irritating to the eyes and throat and has a very disagreeable odor. Bromine is moderately soluble in water. Its reddish-brown solution is used in the laboratory under the name of bromine water. It is readily soluble in carbon tetrachloride, carbon disulfide, and in water solutions of bromides.

> **CAUTION:** *Great care must be used in handling bromine;* it burns the flesh and forms wounds which heal slowly.

21. Chemical properties of bromine. Bromine is not as electronegative as chlorine. It unites with hydrogen with difficulty to form hydrogen bromide. It combines with some metals to form bromides. When it is moist, it is a good bleaching agent. Its water solution is a good oxidizing agent, and forms hydrobromic acid and oxygen in the presence of sunlight.

22. Uses of bromides. The bromides of sodium and potassium are employed in medicine as sedatives but they should not be used unless prescribed by a physician. Silver bromide, AgBr, is a yellowish solid which is extensively used as the sensitive salt for making photographic films or plates. Ethylene bromide, $C_2H_4Br_2$, is used to increase the efficiency of lead tetraethyl, $Pb(C_2H_5)_4$, in antiknock gasoline. The combustion of lead tetraethyl produces lead oxide which is harmful to automobile cylinder walls and exhaust lines. The addition of ethylene bromide permits lead bromide to be formed instead. Lead bromide is volatile enough to go off with the exhaust gases. Other organic bromine

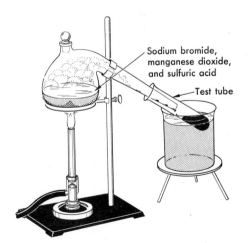

Sodium bromide, manganese dioxide, and sulfuric acid

Test tube

30-5 Bromine may be prepared in the laboratory by heating a mixture of sodium bromide, manganese dioxide, and sulfuric acid in a glass-stoppered retort.

compounds are used in the manufacture of dyestuffs.

23. Test for a soluble bromide. Two facts are used in testing for soluble bromides. First, that bromine is very soluble in carbon tetrachloride, to which it imparts an orange-red color. Second, that chlorine will displace bromine from a bromide.

To the solution to be tested for a bromide, carbon tetrachloride and several milliliters of chlorine water are added, and the mixture is shaken vigorously. If *bromide* ions are present, *bromine* molecules are set free by the chlorine. The bromine, being much more soluble in carbon tetrachloride than it is in water, is extracted by the carbon tetrachloride to which it imparts an orange-red color. The carbon tetrachloride does not mix with the water, but forms a separate layer below the water. While it is *Br₂ molecules* which color the carbon tetrachloride when the test is positive, the only form in which bromine could have existed and be oxidized to free bromine by chlorine was as *Br⁻ ions*. Therefore, a positive test indicates the presence of bromide ions in the original solution.

IODINE

24. Discovery and occurrence of iodine. The element iodine was discovered in 1811 by Bernard Courtois (1777–1838), a French chemist. He noticed the purplish vapor of iodine while investigating the ashes from seaweeds. For many years nearly all iodine was extracted from seaweeds.

At present, the most important domestic source of iodine is the iodides found in California oil well brines. The iodine is liberated from the brine by treatment with chlorine. Some iodine is obtained from Chile, where it is found in the nitrate deposits as sodium iodate, $NaIO_3$.

25. Preparation of iodine. The laboratory preparation of iodine is similar to that of chlorine and bromine. An iodide is heated with manganese dioxide and sulfuric acid.

$$2NaI + MnO_2 + 2H_2SO_4 \rightarrow$$
$$Na_2SO_4 + MnSO_4 + 2H_2O + I_2 \uparrow$$

The iodine is driven off as a vapor. It may be condensed as a solid upon the walls of a cold dish or beaker.

Either chlorine or bromine may be used to displace iodine from a soluble iodide.

$$2NaI + Cl_2 \rightarrow 2NaCl + I_2$$
$$2NaI + Br_2 \rightarrow 2NaBr + I_2$$

26. Physical properties of iodine. Iodine is a steel-gray solid. When heated, it sublimes (vaporizes without melting) and produces a beautiful violet-colored vapor. The odor of this vapor is irritating, resembling that of chlorine.

Iodine is very slightly soluble in water, but it is much more soluble in water solutions of sodium or potassium iodide with which it forms the complex I_3^- ion. It dissolves readily in alcohol, forming a dark-brown solution. It is very soluble in carbon disulfide and carbon tetrachloride, to which it imparts a rich purple color. Free iodine colors starch paste blue. This

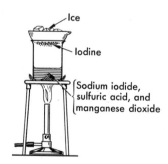

30-6 Iodine is prepared in the laboratory by heating sodium iodide and manganese dioxide with sulfuric acid.

color change, caused by some of the iodine being adsorbed on the surface of the starch particles, serves as a test for free iodine. Conversely, an iodine solution may be used to test for starch.

27. Chemical properties of iodine. Iodine is active chemically, though less so than either bromine or chlorine. It combines with metals to form iodides, and it may also unite with some nonmetals. If a crystal of iodine is placed on a small piece of white phosphorus, the two elements unite spontaneously with the liberation of light and heat.

28. Uses for iodine. Iodine is used for making certain iodides, especially AgI which is used in photography. It is also used as an antiseptic for cuts and open wounds. Surgeons sometimes use a tincture of iodine to sterilize the skin before making an incision during an operation.

> **CAUTION:** *Iodine is poisonous if taken internally. Starch paste or starchy foods may be used as an antidote.*

If a bottle containing tincture of iodine is left unstoppered, some of the solvent will evaporate. The more concentrated tincture which is left may blister the skin. Blistering may also result if a bandage or dressing is placed on the skin after the iodine is applied, or if a second application is used.

29. Uses of iodides. Potassium iodide, KI, finds some use in medicine. Iodine is present in the thyroid gland of the body. The thyroid manufactures the iodine-containing compound, *thyroxine*, which controls the rate at which the body uses food energy. If the diet is deficient in iodine, the thyroid gland may become enlarged. This condition is known as simple goiter. Iodine compounds may be added to the water in certain localities where simple goiter is common. Either sodium iodide, NaI, or potassium iodide, KI, is added to common salt to make *iodized salt*. Silver iodide, AgI, finds some use in photography.

30. Test for soluble iodides. To the solution to be tested, a few milliliters of carbon tetrachloride and a few milliliters of chlorine water are added, and the mixture is shaken vigorously. If an iodide was present, the carbon tetrachloride globule which sinks to the bottom is colored purple due to the presence of free iodine. Here again, as in the test for bromides, the liberation of the *free halogen* constitutes a positive test for the presence of the corresponding *halogenide ion* in the solution tested.

REVIEW OUTLINE

Halogen family: General characteristics (1)

Fluorine
    Preparation (2)
    Properties (3)
    Compounds—noble gas compounds (4)
    Hydrogen fluoride—hydrogen bonding (5)
    Uses of hydrofluoric acid (6)

Chlorine
    Occurrence (7)
    Preparation (8)
    Physical properties—bleaching action (9)

Chemical properties (10)
Uses of chlorine (11)
Preparation of hydrogen chloride (12)
Physical properties of hydrogen chloride (13)
Chemical properties of hydrogen chloride (14)
Uses of hydrochloric acid (15)
Uses of chlorides (16)
Test for chlorides (17)

Bromine
Occurrence (18)
Preparation (19)
Physical properties (20)
Chemical properties (21)
Uses of bromides (22)
Test for bromine ion (23)

Iodine
Occurrence (24)
Preparation (25)
Physical properties (26)
Chemical properties (27)
Uses of iodine (28)
Uses of iodides (29)
Test for iodide ion (30)

QUESTIONS

Group A

1. Why are the halogens never found in nature as free elements?
2. List the halogens in order of increasing activity.
3. What does the term *halogen* mean?
4. (*a*) What kind of container must be used for fluorine? (*b*) For hydrofluoric acid?
5. Write balanced formula equations for the stepwise fluorination of xenon to XeF_2, XeF_4, and XeF_6.
6. What are the most important uses for hydrofluoric acid?
7. (*a*) What compound is the commercial source of chlorine? (*b*) For what other element is this compound the commercial source?
8. (*a*) Write the equation for the laboratory preparation of chlorine from manganese dioxide and hydrochloric acid. (*b*) Assign oxidation numbers and tell which element is oxidized and which element is reduced.
9. Describe the physiological effects of chlorine.
10. (*a*) List the physical and chemical properties of hydrogen chloride which must be considered in choosing a method of collecting this gas in the laboratory. (*b*) Which method of collection is necessitated by this combination of properties?

11. How could you test an unknown solution to determine if there are any chloride ions present in it?
12. Why is bromine produced in large quantities today?
13. (*a*) Write the ionic equation for the reaction involved in extracting bromine from sea water. (*b*) What type of reaction is this?
14. List the important physical properties of bromine.
15. What is the most important source of iodine in the United States?
16. What is the danger of using tincture of iodine that has been in the medicine cabinet for several years?
17. (*a*) For what purpose does the body require iodine? (*b*) From what sources may it be obtained?

Group B

18. Fluorine does not exhibit any positive oxidation state. Why?
19. Water reacts with xenon difluoride to yield xenon, oxygen, and hydrogen fluoride. (*a*) Write the equation for this reaction. (*b*) Assign oxidation numbers to each element, and balance the equation by a method appropriate to an oxidation-reduction equation.
20. What properties does "Freon" have which makes it useful as the propellant in aerosol spray cans?
21. Why do hydrogen fluoride molecules exhibit hydrogen bonding?
22. Why must the hydrogen, chlorine, and sodium hydroxide produced in a Hooker cell be kept separated from each other?
23. (*a*) For which does chlorine have greater affinity, carbon or hydrogen? (*b*) What experimental evidence can you give to support your answer?
24. (*a*) Why is freshly prepared chlorine water yellow-green in color? (*b*) Why does it become colorless after standing in sunlight?
25. When chlorine is added to water for bleaching purposes, what element is responsible for the bleaching effect?
26. Is liquid hydrogen chloride an acid? Explain.
27. What constitutes a positive test for bromide ions in a solution?
28. Compare the colors of: (*a*) solid iodine; (*b*) iodine in alcohol; (*c*) iodine in carbon tetrachloride; (*d*) iodine vapor.
29. Hydrogen forms binary compounds with each of the four common halogens. (*a*) Write the formulas you would expect for these compounds. (*b*) From electronegativity differences, compare the ionic characters of the bonds in each of these compounds. (*c*) Write equations for the reactions you would expect each to have with water.
30. The reactions between water molecules and molecules of the hydrogen halogenides (Question 29) are reversible. (*a*) Qualitatively, at equilibrium, what are the relative concentrations of the particles involved? (*b*) What does this indicate about the relative stability of the hydrogen halogenide molecules compared with the stability of the ions which can be formed from them?
31. Why are sodium chloride and calcium chloride ionic salts, while aluminum chloride is molecular?

PROBLEMS

Group A

1. What mass of sodium hydroxide is formed during the production of 710. kg of chlorine by the electrolysis of sodium chloride?
2. Bromine (10.0 g) is needed for an experiment. How many grams of sodium bromide are required to produce this bromine?
3. Chlorine reacts with calcium hydroxide to produce bleaching powder, $Ca(ClO)Cl$, and water. (*a*) What mass of calcium hydroxide is required for making 250. g of bleaching powder? (*b*) What mass of chlorine is also required?
4. How many grams of zinc chloride may be produced from 11.2 liters of chlorine at S.T.P.?

Group B

5. How many grams of hydrogen fluoride can be obtained when 600. g of 95% sulfuric acid acts on 390. g of calcium fluoride?
6. What is the percentage of bromine in ethylene bromide, $C_2H_4Br_2$?
7. How many liters of chlorine at S.T.P. can be obtained from 468 g of sodium chloride by electrolysis?
8. A laboratory experiment requires five 250.-ml bottles of chlorine, measured at 27° C and 750. mm pressure. What volume of 38% hydrochloric acid (density 1.20 g/ml) and what mass of manganese dioxide will be required?

Chapter Thirty-one

RADIOACTIVITY

NATURAL RADIOACTIVITY

1. Discovery of radioactivity. In 1896 the French scientist Henri Becquerel (bek-*rel*) (1852–1908) was studying the properties of certain minerals. He was particularly interested in their ability to *fluoresce*, or give off visible light, after they had been exposed to sunlight. Among these minerals was a sample of uranium ore. By accident, Becquerel found that uranium ore gives off certain invisible rays. He discovered that these rays penetrated the light-proof covering of a photographic plate and affected the film as if it had been exposed to light rays directly. Substances which emit such invisible rays are *radioactive,* and the property is called *radioactivity.*

2. Discovery of radium. Becquerel was intensely interested in the source of radioactivity. At his suggestion, Pierre Curie (1859–1906) and his wife Marie (1867–1934) started to investigate the properties of uranium and its ores. They soon learned that uranium and uranium compounds are mildly radioactive, but that one uranium ore (pitchblende) had unexpected properties. It was four times more radioactive than the amount of uranium warranted.

It was a tremendous task to process several tons of pitchblende, but in 1898 the Curies discovered in it two new radioactive metallic elements, *polonium* and *radium*. These accounted for the unexpected radioactivity of pitchblende. The Curies separated only a few milligrams of radium chloride, $RaCl_2$. Even this tiny amount involved more than 10,000 crystallizations and recrystallizations. Radium is more than 1,000,000 times as radioactive as the same mass of uranium.

Elementary radium was not isolated by Madame Curie until 1910. What is marketed as radium usually consists of one of its salts, the bromide, the chloride, or the carbonate. The radioactivity of an element is not affected by chemical combination.

3. Sources of radium. Radium is always found in uranium ores. However, it cannot occur in such ores in a greater proportion than 1 part of radium to 3,000,000 parts of uranium. The reason for these conditions will be explained in Section 8. The extraction of radium is a long, tedious, and costly procedure. Formerly, ores from Europe and Africa were used. Now, however, ore deposits near Great Bear Lake in northern Canada are utilized for the production of radium.

4. Properties of radium. Radium is the element of highest atomic weight in Group II of the Periodic Table. Its physical properties were listed in the table at the beginning of Chapter 25. It is the least electronegative member of its group, with chemical properties similar to those of barium.

Radium is an important element not because of its physical or chemical properties, but because of its radioactivity. It is one of the most highly radioactive elements known. Because of this radioactivity, radium and radium compounds have several unusual properties which are also observed in other radioactive materials.

1. It affects the light-sensitive emulsion on a photographic plate. Even though a photographic plate is wrapped in heavy black paper and kept in the dark, radiations from radioactive materials penetrate the wrapping and affect the plate in the same way that light does when the plate is exposed to it. When the plate is developed, a black spot shows up on the negative where the invisible radiation struck it. The rays from radioactive materials penetrate paper, wood, flesh, and *thin* sheets of metal.

2. Radium and its compounds discharge an electroscope and affect a Geiger counter. The radiation from radium ionizes the molecules of the gases in the air. These ionized molecules conduct the electric charge away from the knob of an electroscope discharging it in the process. The activity of a sample of a radium compound may be measured by the speed with which it discharges an electroscope. In a similar way, the radiation given off by radium ionizes

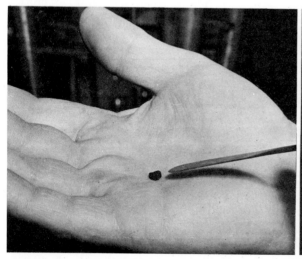 

31-1 Left, a fragment of metallic uranium, one of the radioactive elements; and right, a photograph produced when radiation from the same fragment of uranium penetrated the light-tight wrappings of a photographic plate. (Matt Grimaldi and Mark Schupack)

Metal disk
Metal stem
Insulator
Metal case
Glass window
Gold foil leaves

31-2 An electroscope may be used to detect and measure radioactivity.

the low pressure gas in the tube of a Geiger counter. Electricity can thus momentarily pass through the tube. The passage of electricity may be registered as a "click" by a loudspeaker.

3. Radium compounds produce fluorescence with certain other compounds. A small quantity of radium bromide added to zinc sulfide causes the zinc sulfide to glow. Since the glow is visible in the dark, the mixture is used in making luminous paint.

4. The physiological effects of radium. The radiation from radium may destroy the germinating power of seeds, kill bacteria, or other larger animals. Those who work with radium may be severely burned by the rays which it emits. Such burns require a long time to heal, and may sometimes prove fatal. Because the radiations from radium often destroy cancerous cells more readily than normal cells, they are used in the treatment of cancer and certain skin diseases.

5. Radium atoms undergo radioactive decay. Radium atoms continually decay into simpler atoms and simultaneously emit radiation. One half of any number of radium atoms will decay into simpler atoms in 1620 years. One half of what remains, or one-fourth of the original atoms, will decay in the next 1620 years. One half of

what is left, or one-eighth of the original atoms, will decay in the next 1620 years, and so on. This period of 1620 years is called the *half-life of radium*. Each radioactive isotope has its own characteristic half-life.

5. Other natural radioactive elements. The radioactive elements known to Becquerel were uranium and thorium. We have already learned how the Curies discovered two more, polonium and radium. Since that time, several more natural radioactive elements have been discovered. All the elements beyond bismuth in the Periodic Table are radioactive. Several artificial radioactive elements have also been prepared. One of the important natural radioactive elements is the noble gas *radon*, which is given off when radium atoms decay. It is collected in tubes and used in place of radium for the treatment of disease.

6. Nature of radioactivity. The radiation emitted by such radioactive elements as uranium, thorium, and radium has been carefully studied. Sir Ernest Rutherford discovered that such radiation is complex, consisting of three distinct types of emissions.

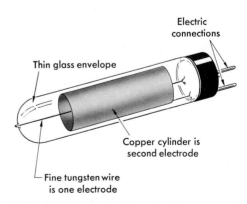

Electric connections
Thin glass envelope
Copper cylinder is second electrode
Fine tungsten wire is one electrode

31-3 A diagram showing the construction of a Geiger-Müller counter tube. Radiation passing through the tube ionizes the gas it contains and enables current to flow.

1. The α (alpha) particles are helium nuclei. Their mass is nearly four times that of the protium atom. They have a +2 charge, and move at speeds that are near one-tenth the speed of light. They have low penetrating power primarily because of their relatively large mass. A thin sheet of aluminum foil or of paper will stop them. However, they burn flesh and ionize air quickly.

2. The β (beta) particles are electrons. They travel at speeds near the speed of light, and their penetrating power is much greater than that of alpha particles.

3. The γ (gamma) rays are high-energy electromagnetic waves—the same kind of radiation as visible light, but of much shorter wavelength and higher frequency. Gamma rays are produced by transitions in energy levels in the nucleus. They are the most penetrating of the radiations given off by radioactive elements.

Fig. 31-4 shows the effect of a powerful magnetic field, perpendicular to the plane of the paper, on the complex radia-

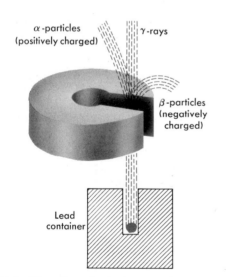

31-4 The effect of a magnet on the different types of radiations. The north pole of the magnet is toward the reader and the south pole is away from the reader.

tion emitted from a small particle of radioactive material. The heavy alpha particles are deflected slightly in one direction. The lighter beta particles are deflected more markedly in the opposite direction. The gamma rays, being uncharged, are not affected by the magnet. By the use of such a magnetic field, Rutherford learned much about radiation from radioactive material.

7. Decay of atoms of radioactive elements. Radioactive atoms decay spontaneously, yielding energy. At first it was believed that they did not lose mass and would give off energy forever. However, more careful investigation shows that radioactive materials do lose mass slowly.

A long series of experiments has shown that the source of this energy is the decay of nuclei of radium and other radioactive elements. The alpha and beta particles are the products of such nuclear decay. Spontaneously, certain heavy nuclei break down into simpler and lighter nuclei, releasing enormous quantities of energy by this decay.

8. A series of related radioactive elements. All naturally occurring radioactive elements belong to one of three series of related elements. The heaviest or "parent" elements of these series are the uranium isotope with mass number 238, the uranium isotope with mass number 235, and the thorium isotope with mass number 232. Since radium is in the family which has the uranium isotope with mass number 238 as its parent, let us trace this decay series.

The nucleus of a uranium atom contains 92 protons, indicated by its atomic number 92, and has a mass number of 238. As this nucleus decays, it ejects an alpha particle which becomes an atom of helium when its positive charge is neutralized. An alpha particle has a mass number of 4. Since it contains two protons, it has an atomic number of 2. The residue left from

THE URANIUM DECAY SERIES

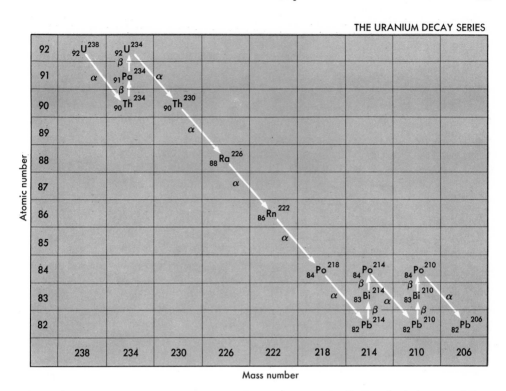

31-5 The parent element of the Uranium Decay Series is $_{92}U^{238}$. The final element of the series is $_{82}Pb^{206}$.

the uranium nucleus will thus have an atomic number of 90 and a mass number of 234. It is an isotope of thorium, sometimes designated Uranium X_1. The *nuclear equation* for this transmutation reaction may be written:

$$_{92}U^{238} \rightarrow {}_{90}Th^{234} + {}_2He^4$$

A *transmutation* is the change in the identity of a nucleus because of a change in the number of its protons. Since the above equation is a nuclear equation, only nuclei are represented. The superscript is the mass number. The subscript is the atomic number. Alpha particles are represented as helium nuclei, $_2He^4$. The total of the mass numbers on the left must equal the total of the mass numbers on the right. The total of the atomic numbers on both sides of the equation must also be equal.

The half-life of Uranium X_1 is about 24 days. It decays by emitting a beta particle. The loss of a beta particle from the nucleus increases the number of positive charges in the nucleus, the atomic number, by one. The beta particle is believed to be formed by the transformation of a neutron into a proton and beta particle (electron). Since the mass of the lost beta particle is negligible, the mass number of the resulting atom stays the same.

$$_{90}Th^{234} \rightarrow {}_{91}Pa^{234} + {}_{-1}e^0$$

The symbol $_{-1}e^0$ represents an electron with an atomic number of -1 and a mass number of 0. $_{91}Pa^{234}$ is an isotope of protactinium, sometimes designated Uranium X_2. This isotope decays by emitting a beta particle and producing $_{92}U^{234}$, sometimes designated Uranium II.

$$_{91}Pa^{234} \rightarrow {}_{92}U^{234} + {}_{-1}e^0$$

The decay of Uranium II is by alpha particle emission.

$$_{92}U^{234} \rightarrow {}_{90}Th^{230} + {}_2He^4$$

The isotope of thorium produced also emits an alpha particle, forming the element radium.

$$_{90}Th^{230} \rightarrow {}_{88}Ra^{226} + {}_2He^4$$

Now we can see why ores of uranium must contain radium, since radium is one of the products of the decay of uranium atoms. The rates of decay of $_{92}U^{238}$, the intervening elements, and of radium itself, determine the proportion of uranium atoms to radium atoms which is found in uranium ores.

The decay of radium proceeds according to the chart shown in Fig. 31-5. Radium decays by the emission of an alpha particle forming radon as shown by the nuclear equation:

$$_{88}Ra^{226} \rightarrow {}_{86}Rn^{222} + {}_2He^4$$

Radon nuclei are unstable and have a half-life of about four days. They decay by alpha particle emission.

$$_{86}Rn^{222} \rightarrow {}_{84}Po^{218} + {}_2He^4$$

You should be able to explain the remaining atomic number and mass number changes shown on the decay chart in terms of the emitted particles. When Radium F, an isotope of polonium, loses an alpha particle, it forms an element with atomic number 82 and mass number 206. This is a stable, nonradioactive, isotope of lead. These spontaneous transmutations, beginning with $_{92}U^{238}$, passing through $_{88}Ra^{226}$, on down to $_{82}Pb^{206}$, occur continuously at rates which scientists have never been able to alter.

9. Applications of natural radioactivity. The age of minerals containing radioactive substances can be estimated. Since radioactive substances decay at known rates, an analysis of the mineral is made to determine the amount of long-lived "parent" element and the amounts of the "descendent" elements in the sample. Then by calculation, scientists can determine how long it must have taken for these amounts of "descendent" elements to be produced. This is assumed to be the age of the mineral. By this method one of the oldest minerals has been estimated to be about three billion years old.

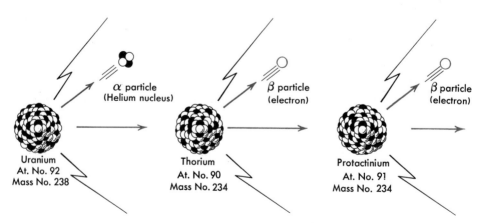

31-6 This diagram shows successive alpha and beta particle emissions in the decay of $_{92}U^{238}$.

Some carbon atoms involved in the oxygen-carbon dioxide cycle of living plants and animals are radioactive because of the continuous production of radioactive $_6C^{14}$ from $_7N^{14}$ atoms in the atmosphere. This change is brought about by the action of cosmic rays. (Cosmic rays are protons and other heavy nuclei of very high energy which come to the earth from outer space.) When living things die, the oxygen-carbon dioxide cycle no longer operates in them. They no longer replace carbon atoms in their cells with other carbon atoms. Thus the level of radioactivity produced by the radioactive carbon in a given amount of nonliving material slowly diminishes.

Carbon from a wooden beam taken from the tomb of an Egyptian pharaoh yields about half the radiation level of carbon in the wood of living trees. Since the half-life of a $_6C^{14}$ atom is 5770 years, the age of wood with half the radioactivity of currently living wood is about 5770 years. Objects up to about 30,000 years old have been dated by this method.

ARTIFICIAL RADIOACTIVITY

10. Stability of a nucleus. On the atomic mass scale, the isotope of carbon with six protons and six neutrons in its nucleus is defined as having an *atomic mass* of exactly 12 (see Chapter 3, Section 11). On this scale, a $_2He^4$ nucleus has a mass of 4.0015, while the mass of a proton is 1.0073 and the mass of a neutron is 1.0087. Since a $_2He^4$ nucleus contains two protons and two neutrons, we might expect its mass to be the combined mass of these four particles, 4.0320. [2(1.0073) + 2(1.0087) = 4.0320.] Note that there is a difference of 0.0305 atomic mass unit between the actual mass, 4.0015, and the calculated mass, 4.0320, of a $_2He^4$ nucleus. *This difference in mass is called the* **nuclear mass defect.** *The mass defect, converted according to Einstein's equation, $E = mc^2$ (see Chapter 1, Section 11), is the energy released when a nucleus is formed from its component particles. This energy is generally referred to as the* **binding energy.**

If the binding energies of the atoms of the elements are calculated, it is found that the lightest and the heaviest elements have the smallest binding energies per nuclear particle while the elements of intermediate atomic weights have the greatest binding energies per nuclear particle. The elements with the greatest binding energies are the ones with the most stable nuclei. Therefore, we see that the nuclei of the lightest and heaviest atoms are less stable than the nuclei of the elements of intermediate atomic weight.

There are factors other than mass that are associated with the stability of atomic nuclei. These are the ratio of neutrons to protons and the even-odd nature of the number of neutrons and protons.

Many properties of nuclear particles indicate the existence of energy levels in the atomic nucleus. Of atoms having similar masses, the most stable nuclei are those whose ratio of protons to neutrons is 1:1. Nuclei with a greater number of neutrons than protons have lower binding energy and are less stable. In nuclei with an equal number of protons and neutrons, these particles apparently occupy the lowest energy levels in the nucleus and thereby give it stability. However, in nuclei that contain an excess of neutrons over protons, some of the neutrons seem to occupy higher energy levels, reducing the binding energy and consequently lowering the stability of the nucleus.

The even-odd relationship of the number of protons to the number of neutrons affects the stability of a nucleus. By far the greatest number of stable nuclei have even numbers of both protons and neutrons. Less frequent in occurrence are stable nuclei with an even number of protons and an odd number of neutrons, or vice versa. Only a few stable nuclei are known which have odd numbers of both protons and neutrons.

Because of the difference in stability of different nuclei, there are four types of nuclear reactions in which nuclear energy is liberated. In each case a small amount of the mass of the reactants is converted into energy and products of greater stability result.

1. A nucleus undergoes *radioactive decay,* forming a slightly lighter, more stable nucleus, and emitting an alpha or beta particle, and gamma rays.

2. A nucleus is bombarded with alpha particles, protons, deuterons (deuterium nuclei, $_1H^2$), neutrons, etc. The unstable nucleus that is formed emits a proton or a neutron and becomes more stable. This is called *nuclear disintegration.*

3. A very heavy nucleus splits and forms medium-weight nuclei. This process is known as *fission.*

4. Light-weight nuclei combine to form heavier, more stable nuclei. This process is known as *fusion.*

11. Stable nuclei from radioactive decay. The emission of an alpha particle from a radioactive nucleus decreases the mass of the nucleus. The resulting nucleus of lower mass has a higher binding energy, and is more stable.

Alpha particle emission decreases the number of protons and neutrons in a nucleus equally and also by an even number. Beta particle emission, by transforming a neutron into a proton, brings the neutron-proton ratio nearer to 1:1. Both of these changes thus promote an increase in the stability of the nucleus undergoing such change.

12. The first nuclear disintegration. When scientists discovered how uranium and radium undergo natural decay and transmutation, they wondered if man-made transmutations could be produced by adding extra protons to the nucleus to make new elements. In 1919 Rutherford produced the first nuclear disintegration by bombarding nitrogen with alpha particles from radium. He obtained protons (hydrogen nuclei) and a stable isotope of oxygen. This first nuclear disintegration may be represented by the following equation:

$$_7N^{14} + _2He^4 \rightarrow _8O^{17} + _1H^1$$

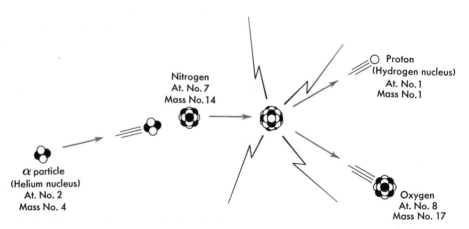

31-7   This diagram shows the historic nuclear disintegration performed by Rutherford.

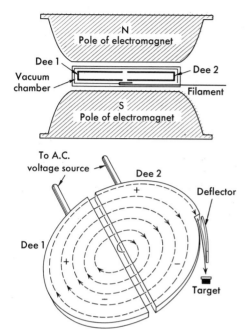

31-8 A diagram of the cyclotron used to produce "atomic bullets" of very high energy.

13. Verification of Einstein's equation. In 1932 two English scientists, J. D. Cockcroft (1897–   ), and E. T. S. Walton (1903–   ), experimentally verified Einstein's equation, $E = mc^2$. They bombarded lithium with high speed protons. Alpha particles and a very large amount of energy were produced.

$$_3\text{Li}^7 + {_1}\text{H}^1 \rightarrow {_2}\text{He}^4 + {_2}\text{He}^4 + \text{energy}$$

There is a loss of matter in this reaction. One lithium nucleus, having a mass of 7.0143, was hit by a proton having a mass of 1.0073. These formed two alpha particles (helium nuclei) each having a mass of 4.0015. Calculation, $(7.0143 + 1.0073) - 2(4.0015)$, shows that there is a loss of 0.0186 atomic mass unit. Cockcroft and Walton found that the energy emitted in the reaction agreed very well with that predicted by Einstein for such a loss in mass. Subsequent experiments have offered further support for Einstein's equa-

tion for the conversion of matter into energy.

14. Neutron emission in some nuclear disintegrations. We have already stated that neutrons were discovered by Chadwick in 1932. He first detected them during the bombardment of beryllium by alpha particles:

$$_4\text{Be}^9 + {_2}\text{He}^4 \rightarrow {_6}\text{C}^{12} + {_0}\text{n}^1$$

The symbol for a neutron is $_0\text{n}^1$, indicating a particle with zero atomic number (no protons) and a mass number of 1. This reaction proved that neutrons were a second type of particle in the nuclei of atoms.

▶**15. The cyclotron and other "atom smashers."** Radium, the natural source of alpha particles used in many early experiments, is rather inefficient in producing nuclear changes. As a result, scientists sought more efficient ways of producing high-energy particles for nuclear bombardment. This search resulted in the development of many large electric devices for the acceleration of charged particles.

The **cyclotron** is the invention of Dr. E. O. Lawrence (1901–1958) of the University of California. It consists of a cylindrical box placed between the poles of a huge electromagnet and exhausted until a high vacuum is produced. The "bullets" used to bombard nuclei are usually protons or deuterons. They are introduced into the cylindrical box through its center.

Inside the box are two hollow, D-shaped electrodes called *dees*. These are connected to a source of very high voltage through an oscillator. When the cyclotron is in operation, the electric charge on these dees is reversed very rapidly by the oscillator. The combination of the high voltage alternating potential and the action of the field of the electromagnet causes the protons or deuterons inside to move in a spiral course. They move faster and faster as

31-9   The 60-inch cyclotron of the Brookhaven National Laboratory. (Brookhaven National Laboratory)

they near the outside of the box and acquire more and more energy. When they reach the outer rim of the box, they are deflected toward the target. The energy of the particles accelerated in a cyclotron may reach 15,000,000 electron-volts. This is the energy an electron would have if it were accelerated across a potential difference of 15,000,000 volts. By studying the fragments of atoms formed by bombardment, scientists have learned a great deal about atomic structure. They also have discovered much about the disintegration products of atoms. Other machines for bombarding atomic nuclei are the *synchrotron*, the *betatron*, and the *linear accelerator*.

The synchrotron operates in principle like the cyclotron. By varying both the oscillating voltage and the magnetic field, the particles can be accelerated in a narrow circular path rather than in a spiral path. A synchrotron can impart an energy

31-10 A portion of the huge synchrotron at the Brookhaven National Laboratory. (Brookhaven National Laboratory)

of more than 30 billion electron-volts to the protons which it accelerates. The betatron is a device which accelerates electrons rather than positively charged particles. The accelerated electrons may be used as "bullets" for bombardment, or for producing high-energy X rays. Still another type of particle accelerator is the linear accelerator. In this device the particles travel in a straight line through many stages of potential difference which act to accelerate the particles.

16. Neutrons as "bullets." Prior to the discovery of neutrons in 1932, alpha particles and protons were used in studying atomic nuclei. However, alpha particles and protons are charged particles. It requires great quantities of energy, such as are imparted to these particles by cyclotrons and synchrotrons to "fire" these charged "bullets" into a nucleus. Their positive charge causes them to be repelled by the positive nuclear charge.

Neutrons are produced when accelerated positively charged particles from an atom smasher strike a target material, usually beryllium. Since neutrons have no charge, they can easily penetrate the nucleus of an atom because there is no force of repulsion. Fast neutrons may go right through an atom without causing any change in it. Some fast neutrons, however, may produce the disintegration of a nucleus. Slow neutrons, on the other hand, are sometimes trapped by a nucleus. This nucleus then becomes unstable, and may disintegrate. Fast neutrons may be slowed down by passage through materials composed of elements of low atomic weight such as deuterium oxide or graphite.

17. Man-made elements from neutron bombardment. When $_{92}U^{238}$, the most plentiful isotope of uranium, is bombarded with slow neutrons, a $_{92}U^{238}$ nucleus may capture a neutron. An unstable isotope of uranium, $_{92}U^{239}$, is formed. This

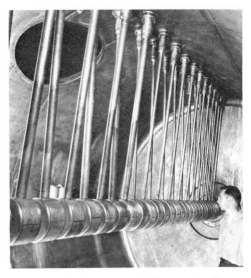

31-11 The interior of the heavy ion linear accelerator or "Hilac" at the University of California Radiation Laboratory. (University of California)

emits a beta particle and forms a man-made radioactive element, neptunium. Neptunium has atomic number 93.

$$_{92}U^{238} + _{0}n^{1} \rightarrow _{92}U^{239}$$
$$_{92}U^{239} \rightarrow _{93}Np^{239} + _{-1}e^{0}$$

Neptunium is an unstable element also. Its nucleus ejects a beta particle, forming still another man-made element, plutonium, atomic number 94.

$$_{93}Np^{239} \rightarrow _{94}Pu^{239} + _{-1}e^{0}$$

Neptunium and plutonium were the first man-made *transuranium* elements. *Transuranium elements* are those with more than 92 protons in their nuclei. As this is written, there are twelve reported artificially prepared transuranium elements. In addition to neptunium and plutonium, there are americium, curium, berkelium, californium, einsteinium, fermium, mendelevium, element 102, lawrencium, and element 104.

These have been prepared by bombard-

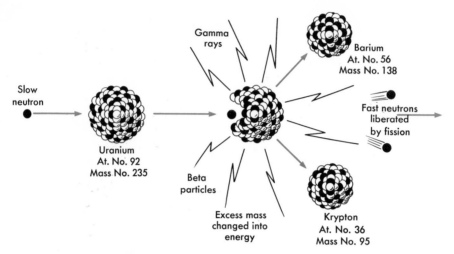

31-12   Neutrons from fission of a $_{92}U^{235}$ nucleus, when slowed down by a carbon moderator,

ment of the nuclei of uranium or more complex elements with neutrons, alpha particles, or other "nuclear bullets."

18. Artificial radioactive atoms. In 1934 Madame Curie's daughter Irène (1897–1956), working with her husband, Frédéric Joliot (1900–1958), discovered that stable atoms can be made artificially radioactive. This occurs when they are bombarded with deuterons or neutrons. Now radioactive isotopes of all the elements have been prepared. Many new radioactive isotopes are manufactured by slow-neutron bombardment in the nuclear reactor at Oak Ridge, Tennessee. The equation for the formation of radioactive $_{27}Co^{60}$ from natural nonradioactive $_{27}Co^{59}$ by slow-neutron bombardment is:

$$_{27}Co^{59} + _{0}n^{1} \rightarrow _{27}Co^{60}$$

The radiation from $_{27}Co^{60}$ consists of beta particles and gamma rays.

Radioactive $_{15}P^{32}$ is prepared by bombardment of $_{16}S^{32}$ with slow neutrons:

$$_{16}S^{32} + _{0}n^{1} \rightarrow _{15}P^{32} + _{1}H^{1}$$

The radiation from $_{15}P^{32}$ consists only of beta particles.

Radioactive phosphorus and radioactive cobalt, as well as other radioactive elements, are used in the treatment of various forms of cancer. Also, many radioactive isotopes are used as tracers to determine the course of chemical reactions, the wearing ability of various products, the efficiency of fertilizers, and the flow of fluids through pipelines.

19. Fission of $_{92}U^{235}$. The element uranium exists as three naturally occurring isotopes, $_{92}U^{238}$, $_{92}U^{235}$, and $_{92}U^{234}$. Most uranium is the isotope $_{92}U^{238}$. Only 0.7% of natural uranium is $_{92}U^{235}$. $_{92}U^{234}$ is found only in insignificant traces. We have already stated that transuranium elements may be produced when $_{92}U^{238}$ is bombarded with slow neutrons. However, when $_{92}U^{235}$ is bombarded with slow neutrons, each atom may capture one of the neutrons. This additional neutron in the nucleus makes it very unstable. Instead of emitting an alpha or beta particle, as in other radioactive changes, the nucleus splits into medium-weight parts. Neutrons are usually produced during this fission. There is a small loss of mass, which appears as a great amount of energy. One equation

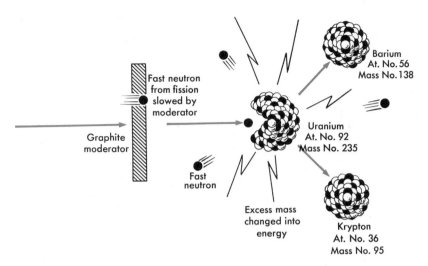

can cause fission in a second $_{92}U^{235}$ nucleus. This process makes a chain reaction possible.

for the fission of $_{92}U^{235}$ is written as follows:

$$_{92}U^{235} + _0n^1 \rightarrow$$
$$_{56}Ba^{138} + _{36}Kr^{95} + 3_0n^1 + \text{energy}$$

The atomic mass of $_{92}U^{235}$ is slightly greater than 235. The atomic masses of the unstable isotopes of barium and krypton are slightly less than 138 and 95 respectively. So instead of the masses of the reactants equalling the masses of the products, there is a conversion of about 0.2 atomic mass unit into energy during the fission process. Plutonium, made from $_{92}U^{238}$, also undergoes fission and produces more neutrons when bombarded with slow neutrons.

20. Nuclear chain reaction. *A chain reaction is one in which the material or energy which initiates the reaction is also one of the products.* The fissions of $_{92}U^{235}$ and $_{94}Pu^{239}$ can produce chain reactions. One neutron initiates the fission of one $_{92}U^{235}$ nucleus. Two or three neutrons are given out when this fission occurs. These neutrons can start the fission of other $_{92}U^{235}$ nuclei. Again neutrons are emitted. These can

cause the fission of still other $_{92}U^{235}$ nuclei. This is a chain reaction. It will continue until all the $_{92}U^{235}$ atoms have split or until the neutrons fail to strike $_{92}U^{235}$ nuclei. This is what happens in an uncontrolled chain reaction such as the explosion of a nuclear warhead.

21. Action in a nuclear reactor. *A nuclear reactor is a device in which the controlled fission of radioactive material produces new radioactive substances and energy.* One of the earliest types built at Oak Ridge, Tennessee, in 1943, contains natural uranium. It has a lattice-type construction with blocks of graphite forming the framework. Spaced between the blocks of graphite are rods of uranium, encased in aluminum cans for protection. *Control rods* of neutron-absorbing boron steel are inserted into the lattice to regulate the number of free neutrons. This reactor is air cooled.

The rods of uranium or uranium oxide are the *nuclear fuel* for the reactor, since the energy released in the reactor comes from changes in the uranium nuclei. Graphite is said to be the *moderator*, because it slows down the fast neutrons produced by fission and makes them more effective for producing additional nuclear changes. The amount of uranium in such a reactor is important. Enough uranium must be present to sustain a chain reaction. This quantity of uranium is called the *critical size.*

Two types of reactions occur in the fuel in such a reactor. Neutrons cause the nuclei of $_{92}U^{235}$ to undergo fission. The fast neutrons from this fission are slowed down by passage through the graphite. Some strike other $_{92}U^{235}$ nuclei and continue the chain reaction. Other neutrons strike $_{92}U^{238}$ nuclei, and initiate the changes which finally produce plutonium. Great quantities of energy are liberated so the reactor has to be cooled continuously by blowing air through tubes in the lattice. The rate of the reaction is controlled by the insertion or removal of the neutron-absorbing control rods. This type of reactor is now being used to produce radioactive isotopes.

22. Fusion reactions. We have already indicated that increased nuclear stability could be produced by combining light-weight nuclei to form heavier nuclei. This process was defined as *fusion.*

Fusion reactions are the source of the sun's energy. It is believed that there are two series of such reactions going on in the sun, one at the very hot central region of the sun's interior, and another in the outer portion of the sun which is at a slightly lower temperature. Although these two reactions have a different sequence of intermediate reactions, their net effect is the combination of four hydrogen nuclei to form a helium nucleus, with a loss of mass and corresponding production of energy.

The thermonuclear bomb, sometimes called the hydrogen bomb, or H-bomb, produces energy by a fusion reaction. It can be made much more destructive than an atomic bomb because more energy is liberated per gram of fuel in a fusion reaction than in a fission reaction. Also, the quantities of reacting materials may be made much larger; in fact they are theoretically unlimited. Fusion reactions do not require a critical size of reacting materials; they are not chain reactions.

One possible reaction in a hydrogen

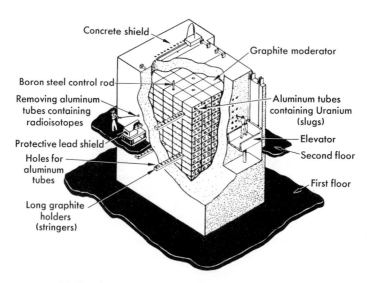

31-13   A cutaway view of the Oak Ridge reactor.

bomb is the formation of alpha particles and tremendous energy from a compound of lithium and hydrogen. This compound may be formed of the particular isotopes $_3Li^6$ and $_1H^2$ and have the formula $_3Li^6_1H^2$. Such a fusion reaction can be started only by subjecting $_3Li^6_1H^2$ to extremely high temperature and pressure. These conditions are met by using an atomic bomb as the detonator to set off the hydrogen bomb.

Current research indicates that fusion reactions may be controlled. If so, this may be another possible source of energy for power generation.

REVIEW OUTLINE

Natural radioactivity
    Discovery of radioactivity (1)
    Discovery of radium (2)
    Properties of radioactive materials (4)
        Electroscope (4)
        Geiger counter (4)
        Half-life (4)
    Nature of radioactivity (6)
        Alpha particles (6)
        Beta particles (6)
        Gamma rays (6)
    Radioactive decay series (7)
        Parent element (8)
        Nuclear equation (8)
        Transmutation reaction (8)
    Applications of natural radioactivity (9)

Artificial radioactivity
    Nuclear stability (10, 11)
        Nuclear mass defect (10)
        Binding energy (10)
        Nuclear reactions (10)
            Radioactive decay (10)
            Nuclear disintegration (10, 12)
            Fission (10)
            Fusion (10)
    Acceleration of charged particles
        Cyclotron (15)
        Synchrotron (15)
        Betatron (15)
        Linear accelerator (15)
    Neutron bombardment (16)
        Transuranium elements (17)
        Artificial radioactivity (18)
    Nuclear chain reaction (20)

Nuclear reactor
>   Control rod (21)
>   Nuclear fuel (21)
>   Moderator (21)
>   Critical size (21)
> Fusion reactions (22)

QUESTIONS

Group A

1. (*a*) Who discovered radioactivity? (*b*) How was the discovery made?
2. What evidence led Pierre and Marie Curie to suspect that there were radioactive elements other than uranium in pitchblende?
3. How does the radioactivity of radium compare with that of uranium?
4. What practical use is made of the fluorescence produced in zinc sulfide by a radium compound?
5. What is meant by the *half-life* of a radioactive element?
6. From what part of a radioactive atom do the alpha and beta particles come?
7. What change in identity and mass number occurs when a radioactive atom gives off an alpha particle?
8. What change in identity and mass number occurs when a radioactive atom gives off a beta particle?
9. How is the age of a radioactive mineral estimated?
10. Name the four types of nuclear reactions which produce more stable nuclei.
11. In what ways does natural radioactive decay produce more stable nuclei?
12. How were neutrons first detected as nuclear particles?
13. Why are neutrons better particles than protons or alpha particles for bombarding atomic nuclei?
14. What may happen to a neutron that is fired at the nucleus of an atom?
15. For what purposes are radioactive isotopes used?
16. (*a*) What are the naturally occurring isotopes of uranium? (*b*) What is their relative abundance?
17. (*a*) What is fission? (*b*) How is it produced in $_{92}U^{235}$?
18. What is meant by the *critical size* of a reactor?
19. Why must a nuclear reactor be continually cooled?
20. (*a*) What reaction produces the sun's energy? (*b*) To what man-made reaction is this similar?

Group B

21. Why is radium studied separately rather than with the other elements of Group II?
22. Is the radioactivity of an element affected by the other elements with which it may be chemically combined?

23. Why can the radiation from a radioactive material affect photographic film, even though the film is well wrapped in black paper?
24. How does a radioactive material affect the rate of discharge of an electroscope?
25. Where are most of the natural radioactive elements found in the Periodic Table?
26. Give the mass, nature, and speed range of: (*a*) alpha particles; (*b*) beta particles.
27. What do scientists believe gamma rays to be?
28. Write the nuclear equation for the emission of an alpha particle by $_{88}Ra^{226}$.
29. Write the nuclear equation for the emission of a beta particle by $_{82}Pb^{214}$.
30. Write nuclear equations for successive emissions of an alpha particle and a beta particle from $_{84}Po^{214}$.
31. (*a*) Which kinds of elements have the smallest binding energy? (*b*) Which kind has the largest binding energy? (*c*) How does the binding energy affect the stability of a nucleus?
32. What factors affect the stability of a nucleus?
33. How does each type of nuclear reaction produce more stable nuclei?
34. (*a*) Who produced the first nuclear disintegration? (*b*) Write the equation for this reaction.
35. How was Einstein's equation for the relationship between matter and energy, $E = mc^2$, proved to be correct?
▶36. (*a*) Describe the path of the accelerated particles in a cyclotron. (*b*) What causes them to take this path?
37. Explain the changes occurring in the nucleus by which $_{94}Pu^{239}$ is produced from $_{92}U^{238}$.
38. (*a*) How are artificially radioactive isotopes prepared? (*b*) Write a nuclear equation to show the preparation of such an atom. (*c*) What use is made of the atom whose preparation you have shown in this nuclear equation?
39. (*a*) Describe a chain reaction. (*b*) How does the fission of $_{92}U^{235}$ produce a chain reaction?
40. How is a uranium-graphite reactor constructed?

GLOSSARY

GLOSSARY

absolute deviation. See *deviation, absolute*.

absolute zero. The lowest possible temperature, 0° K or −273.15° C.

accelerator. A substance that speeds up a chemical reaction by acting as a positive catalyst.

accuracy. The nearness of a measurement to its accepted value.

acid. A substance which gives up protons to another substance.

acid, amino. An organic acid characterized by both —N and —C groups

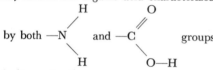

in the molecule.

acid anhydride. An oxide that reacts with water to form an acid, or that is formed by the removal of water from an acid.

acid, conjugate. The structure formed when a base acquires a proton.

actinide series. Rare earth elements of the seventh period following radium, in which the transitional inner building of the 6*d* sublevel is interrupted by the inner building of the 5*f* sublevel.

activated. Pertaining to an adsorbent, the surface of which has been freed of adsorbed gases by heating.

activated complex. The transitional structure resulting from an effective collision of reactant particles and persisting while old bonds are breaking and new bonds are forming.

activation energy. See *energy, activation*.

activity (electromotive) series. A table of metals or nonmetals arranged in order of descending activities.

addition. A reaction in which atoms are added to an unsaturated organic molecule.

adsorbate. A material adsorbed on the surface of another.

adsorbent. A material upon whose surface adsorption occurs.

adsorption. The concentration of a gas, liquid, or solid on the surface of a solid or liquid.

aerosol. A suspensoid in which a gas is the dispersing medium.

alcohol. A compound containing a hydrocarbon group and one or more —OH, hydroxyl, groups.

aldehyde. A compound which has a hydrocarbon group and one or more —C $\overset{O}{\underset{H}{\diagup\!\!\diagup}}$, formyl, groups.

alkadiene. A straight- or branched-chain hydrocarbon with two double covalent bonds between carbon atoms.

alkali. The hydroxide (or carbonate) of a Group I metal.

alkali metal. See *metal, alkali*.

alkaline-earth metal. See *metal, alkaline-earth*.

alkane. A straight- or branched-chain hydrocarbon in which the carbon atoms are connected by only single covalent bonds; a member of the paraffin series.

alkene. A straight- or branched-chain hydrocarbon in which two carbon atoms are connected by a double bond; a member of the olefin series.

alkyl group. A group derived from an alkane by the loss of a hydrogen atom; frequently symbolized by R—.

alkyl halogenide. An alkane in which one or more halogen atoms is substituted for a like number of hydrogen atoms.

alkyne. A straight- or branched-chain hydrocarbon in which two carbon atoms are connected by a triple covalent bond; a member of the acetylene series.

allotrope. One of the two or more different forms of an element in the same physical state.

allotropy. The existence of an element in two or more forms in the same physical state.

alloy. A material composed of two or more metals.

alloy, anti-friction. An alloy which reduces friction.

alloy, fusible. An alloy which has a low melting temperature.

alluvial. Pertaining to soil, sand, or gravel deposited by running water.

alnico. A strongly ferromagnetic alloy composed of aluminum, cobalt, iron, and nickel.

alpha particle. A helium nucleus emitted from the nucleus of a radioactive element.

alum. A double salt that is a sulfate of a monovalent and a trivalent metal.

amalgam. An alloy of mercury with one or more other metals.

amide. A derivative of ammonia in which one of the hydrogen atoms has been replaced by an RCO— group and the other two hydrogen atoms possibly have been replaced by alkyl groups.

amine. A derivative of ammonia in which one, two, or all three hydrogen atoms have been replaced by alkyl groups.

amino acid. See *acid, amino.*

amorphous. Without definite shape.

amphiprotic. Capable of acting either as an acid or as a base.

amphoteric. See *amphiprotic.*

analysis. The separation of a material into its component parts to determine its composition.

Ångström. A unit of linear measure; 1×10^{-8} cm.

anhydrous. Without water of crystallization.

anion. An ion attracted to the anode of an electrolytic cell; a negative ion.

anion hydrolysis. See *hydrolysis, anion.*

annealing. The process of heating a material to above a certain temperature and then slowly cooling it in order to decrease its hardness and brittleness.

anode. A positively charged, or electron-poor, electrode.

anti-friction alloy. See *alloy, anti-friction.*

anti-oxidant. A substance which retards oxidation.

arc-type furnace. A furnace in which the heat is produced by an electric arc between carbon electrodes.

aromatic hydrocarbon. See *hydrocarbon, aromatic.*

atom. The smallest particle of an element that can exist either alone or in combination with other atoms of the same or of another element.

atom, excited. An atom which has absorbed a photon.

atomic mass. See *mass, atomic.*

atomic number. The number of protons in the nucleus of an atom.

atomic theory. See *theory, atomic.*

atomic weight. See *weight, atomic.*

Avogadro number. The number of carbon-12 atoms in exactly 12 grams of this isotope; 6.02252×10^{23}.

baking soda. Sodium hydrogen carbonate, $NaHCO_3$.

barometer. An apparatus for measuring atmospheric pressure.

base. A substance which acquires protons from another substance.

base, conjugate. The part of an acid that is left after it has donated a proton.

basic anhydride. An oxide which reacts with water to form a solution containing OH^- ions.

beneficiation. Any physical or chemical process by which low-grade ores are concentrated.

beta particle. An electron emitted from the nucleus of a radioactive element.

betatron. A device for accelerating electrons.

binary. Pertaining to compounds made up of two elements.

binary compound. See *compound, binary.*

binding energy. See *energy, binding.*

biocolloid. A lyophilic colloidal system existing within plant and animal organisms.

blast furnace. A tall cylindrical chamber in which iron oxide is reduced using coke, limestone, and a blast of hot air.

bleaching. The operation by which color is partially or wholly removed from a colored material.

blister copper. Crude copper as produced in a reverberatory furnace.

blue vitriol. Hydrated copper(II) sulfate, $CuSO_4 \cdot 5H_2O$.

boiling point. The temperature at which the equilibrium vapor pressure of a liquid is equal to the prevailing atmospheric pressure.

borax. Sodium tetraborate, $Na_2B_4O_7 \cdot 10H_2O$.

borazon. A crystalline form of boron nitride. The hardest synthetic material known.

brass. An alloy of copper and zinc.

bright-line spectrum. See *spectrum, bright-line.*

bronze. An alloy of copper and tin.

Brownian movement. The haphazard motion of colloidally dispersed particles as a result of collisions with the molecules of the dispersing medium.

buffer. A substance which, when added to a solution, causes a resistance to any change in pH.

buffered solution. See *solution, buffered.*

calcine. A partially roasted copper ore.

calorie. A unit of heat; the heat required to raise the temperature of 1 gram of water through 1 Celsius degree.

carbohydrate. A compound of carbon, hydrogen, and oxygen, such as a sugar, a starch, or a cellulose, formed by green plants and used as a source of food.

carboloy. An extremely hard alloy of cobalt and tungsten carbide.

carbonyl group. The $\diagdown \!\! C \!\! = \!\! O$ group.

Carborundum. Silicon carbide, SiC.

carboxyl group. The $-C \diagup\!\!\!\!\!\overset{\displaystyle O}{\diagdown \atop O-H}$ group.

catalyst. An agent which affects the rate of a chemical action without itself being permanently altered.

catalyst, contact. A catalytic agent which influences the speed of a reaction by altering the contact efficiency between the particles of the reactants.

catalyst, heterogeneous. A catalyst introduced into a reaction system in a different phase from that of the reactants.

catalyst, homogeneous. A catalyst introduced into a reaction system in the same phase as all reactants and products.

catalytic agent. See *catalyst.*

catalytic poison. A specific material which when preferentially adsorbed on the surface of a contact catalyst retards or stops the catalytic action.

cathode. A negatively charged, or electron-rich, electrode.

cation. An ion attracted to the cathode of an electrolytic cell; a positive ion.

cation hydrolysis. See *hydrolysis, cation.*

caustic. (*1*) Capable of converting some types of animal and vegetable matter into soluble materials by chemical action; (*2*) a substance with such properties.

caustic, lunar. Silver nitrate, $AgNO_3$.

Celsius temperature. See *temperature, Celsius.*

cement. A substance made from limestone and clay which, after mixing with water, sets to a hard mass.

centi-. Metric prefix meaning 0.01.

centigrade scale. The Celsius temperature scale.

chain reaction. A reaction in which the material or energy which initiates the reaction is also one of the products.

chemical bond. The linkage between atoms produced by transfer or sharing of electrons.

chemical change. A change in which new substances with new properties are formed.

chemical equilibrium. See *equilibrium, chemical.*

chemical formula. See *formula, chemical.*

chemical kinetics. The branch of chemistry concerned with the sequence of steps by which chemical reactions occur and the rate at which they proceed.

chemical properties. Those properties which pertain to the behavior of a material in changes in which its identity is altered.

chemical symbol. Either a single capital letter, or a capital letter and a small letter used together, as an abbreviation for (*1*) an element; (*2*) an atom of an element; (*3*) a mole of atoms of an element.

chemistry. The science dealing with the structure and composition of substances and the changes in composition which these substances undergo.

chemistry, organic. The chemistry of carbon compounds.

colloidal state. A state of subdivision of matter ranging between the dimensions of ordinary molecules and microscopic particles.

colloidal suspension. A two-phase system having dispersed particles suspended in a dispersing medium.

combustion. Any chemical action which occurs so rapidly that both noticeable heat and light are produced.

combustion, heat of. The heat of reaction evolved by the complete combustion of one mole of a substance.

common-ion effect. The shift in equilibrium which occurs when a substance is added to a solution of a second substance with which it has a common ion, the volume being kept constant.

complex ion. A charged particle made up of a group of atoms.

compound. A substance which can be decomposed into two or more simpler substances by ordinary chemical means.

compound, binary. A compound consisting of only two elements.

compound, stable. A compound that does not decompose easily.

compound, unstable. A compound that decomposes easily.

concentrated. Containing a relatively large amount of solute.

condensation. (1) The process of converting a gas into a liquid or solid. (2) Increasing the size of very small particles up to colloidal size.

condensation temperature. See *temperature, condensation.*

conjugate acid. See *acid, conjugate.*

conjugate base. See *base, conjugate.*

constant. A magnitude that does not change in value.

constant, equilibrium. The product of the concentrations of the substances produced at equilibrium divided by the product of the concentrations of reactants, each concentration raised to that power which is the coefficient of the substance in the chemical equation.

constant, gas. The value of the quotient pV/nT; 0.082057 l-atm/mole-°K.

constant, hydrolysis. The equilibrium constant of a reversible reaction between an ion of a dissolved salt and water.

constant, ionization. The equilibrium constant of a reversible reaction by which ions are produced from molecules.

constant, rate. The rate of a reaction, at a fixed temperature, in which the concentration of each reactant is one mole per liter.

constant, solubility-product. The product of the molar concentrations of the ions of a sparingly soluble substance in a saturated solution, each concentration raised to the appropriate power.

contact agent. See *catalyst, contact.*

contact catalyst. See *catalyst, contact.*

control rod. A rod of neutron-absorbing material used in regulating the reaction in a nuclear reactor.

coordination number. The number of molecules or ions attached to a central metallic atom.

corrode. (1) To disintegrate slowly. (2) To waste away by chemical action, especially the action of an acid on a metal.

covalence. Covalent bonding.

covalent bonding. Bonding in which atoms share electrons.

covalent crystal. See *crystal, covalent.*

cracking. A process of breaking down complex organic molecules by the action of heat or a catalyst or both.

critical pressure. See *pressure, critical.*

critical size. The amount of radioactive material required to sustain a chain reaction.

critical temperature. See *temperature, critical.*

critical volume. The volume occupied by one mole of a gas at its critical temperature and critical pressure.

crystal. A homogeneous portion of a substance bounded by plane surfaces making definite angles with each other, giving a regular geometric form.

crystal, covalent. A crystal consisting of an array of atoms that share electrons with their neighboring atoms and form a giant, compact, interlocking structure.

crystal, ionic. A crystal consisting of ions arranged in a systematic order.

crystal lattice. The pattern of points which describe the arrangement of particles in a crystal structure.

crystal, metallic. A crystal lattice consisting of positive ions permeated by a cloud of valence electrons.

crystal, molecular. A crystal consisting of molecules arranged in a systematic order.

crystalline. Consisting of or made of crystals.

cupel. A porous crucible or dish of bone ash.

cyclotron. An electromagnetic device for accelerating protons or deuterons in a spiral path.

data. A group of facts or statistics.

dehydrating agent. A substance which removes water from a material.

dehydration. The removal of oxygen and hydrogen atoms from a substance in the form of water.

deliquescence. The property of certain substances to take up water from the air to form a solution.

density. The mass per unit volume of a material.

destructive distillation. See *distillation, destructive.*

detergent. A substance which removes dirt.

deuterium. The isotope of hydrogen having one proton and one neutron in the nucleus.

deviation. An expression denoting the limitation in precision of a measurement.

deviation, absolute. The difference between an individual measurement and the average for a set of several identical measurements.

deviation, relative. The percentage average deviation based on the average value for a set of identical measurements.

diatomic. Consisting of two atoms.

diffusion. The process of spreading out spontaneously to fill a space uniformly; the intermingling of the particles of substances.

dilute. Containing a relatively small amount of solute.

dimension. The unit structure of a measured quantity.

dimer. A compound formed by two simpler molecules or radicals.

dimeric. Capable of forming twofold polymers.

dipole. A polar molecule, one region of which is positive and the other negative.

diprotic. Referring to an acid capable of donating two protons per molecule.

disaccharide. A carbohydrate which yields two monosaccharide units on dilute acid hydrolysis.

dispersion. A scattering, or state of being scattered.

dissociation. The separation of the ions of an electrovalent substance during the solution process.

distillation. The process of evaporation followed by condensation of the vapors in a separate vessel.

distillation, destructive. The process of decomposing materials by heating them in a closed vessel without access to air or oxygen.

distillation, fractional. The separation of the components of a mixture which have different boiling points by controlled vaporization.

domain. Small magnetized regions formed by groups of properly aligned atoms of ferromagnetic substances.

ductile. Capable of being drawn into a wire.

effervescence. The rapid evolution of a gas from a liquid in which it is dissolved.

efflorescence. The property of hydrated crystals to lose water of crystallization when exposed to the air.

elastic collision. A collision in which there is no loss of energy.

electrochemical. Pertaining to spontaneous oxidation-reduction reactions used as a source of electric energy.

electrochemical cell. An apparatus which enables an electrochemical reaction to be used as a source of electric energy.

electrochemical reaction. A spontaneous oxidation-reduction reaction in which chemical energy is transformed into electric energy.

electrode. A conductor by which an electric current either enters or leaves an electrolyte, cell, or other apparatus.

electrolysis. Separation of a compound into simpler substances by electricity.

electrolyte. A substance whose water solution conducts an electric current.

electrolytic. Pertaining to driven oxidation-reduction reactions which utilize electric energy from an external source.

electrolytic cell. An apparatus which enables electric energy to be changed into chemical energy by electrolytic action.

electrolytic reaction. A driven oxidation-reduction reaction in which electric energy is transformed into chemical energy.

electromagnetic radiation. A form of energy, such as light, X rays, or radio waves, which travels through space as waves at the rate of 3.00×10^8 m/sec.

electromotive series. See *activity series.*

electron. A negatively charged particle found in an atom. It has $\frac{1}{1837}$ of the mass of the protium (hydrogen) atom.

electron affinity. The energy released when an electron is added to a neutral atom.

electron cloud. The portion of space about a nucleus in which the electrons may most probably be found.

electron pair. Two electrons of opposite spin in the same space orbital.

electron, valence. One of the electrons in an incomplete outer shell of an atom.

electron-volt. The energy required to move an electron across a potential difference of one volt.

electronegative element. See *element, electronegative.*

electronegativity. The property of an atom of attracting the shared electrons forming a bond between it and another atom.

electroplating. Deposition of a metal on a surface by means of an electric current.

electropositive element. See *element, electropositive.*

electroscope. A device for determining the presence of electric charge.

electrovalence. Ionic bonding.

element. A substance which cannot be further decomposed by ordinary chemical means.

element, electronegative. An element having a relatively strong attraction for valence electrons.

element, electropositive. An element having a relatively weak attraction for valence electrons.

element, parent. The heaviest, most complex, naturally occurring element in a decay series of radioactive elements.

element, rare earth. An element which usually differs in electronic configuration from that of next lower or higher atomic number only in the number of electrons in the second-from-outside shell.

element, transition. An element which usually differs in electronic configuration from that of next lower or higher atomic number only in the number of electrons in the next-to-the-outside shell.

element, transuranium. An element with a higher atomic number than uranium.

empirical formula. See *formula, empirical.*

emulsion. See *emulsoid.*

emulsoid. A colloidal system in which there is a strong attraction between the dispersed substance and the dispersing liquid.

end point. That point reached in titration in which the quantities of acid and hydroxide present are chemically equivalent. Also called the equivalence point.

end reaction. A reaction between certain ions which runs to completion in the sense that the ions are almost completely removed from solution.

endothermic. Pertaining to a reaction which occurs with the absorption of heat.

energy. The capacity for doing work.

energy, activation. Energy required to transform reactants into an activated complex.

energy, binding. The energy released when a nucleus is formed from its component particles.

energy, heat. The energy transferred between two systems that is associated exclusively with the difference in temperature between the two systems.

energy, ionization. The energy required to remove an electron from an atom.

energy, kinetic. Energy of motion.

energy level. A region about the nucleus of an atom in which electrons move. A shell.

energy, potential. Energy of position.

entropy. That property which describes the disorder of a system.

enzyme. A catalyst which is produced by living cells.

equilibrium. A dynamic state in which two opposing processes take place at the same time and at the same rate.

equilibrium, chemical. The state of balance attained in a reversible chemical action in which the rates of the opposing reactions are equal.

equilibrium constant. See *constant, equilibrium.*

equilibrium, ionic. The state of balance attained in a reversible ionization action between un-ionized molecules in solution and their hydrated ions.

equilibrium, physical. A dynamic state in which two opposing physical processes in the same system proceed at equal rates.

equilibrium, solution. The physical state attained in which the opposing processes of dissolving and crystallizing of a solute occur at equal rates.

equilibrium vapor pressure. See *pressure, equilibrium vapor.*

equivalence point. See *end point.*

error. An expression denoting the limitation in accuracy of a measurement.

error, experimental. The absolute error in an experimental measurement.

error, percentage. The relative error in an experimental measurement.

ester. A compound formed by the reaction between an acid and an alcohol.

esterification. The process of producing an ester by reaction of an acid with an alcohol.

ether. An organic oxide.

eudiometer. A gas-measuring tube.

evaporation. The escape of molecules from the surface of liquids and solids.

excited atom. See *atom, excited.*

exothermic. Pertaining to a reaction which occurs with the evolution of heat.

experimental error. See *error, experimental.*

exponential notation. A system of writing large and small numbers using the form $M \times 10^n$, where M is a number between 1 and 10 having a single digit to the left of the decimal point, and n is a positive or negative integer.

external phase. The dispersing medium of a colloidal suspension.

fat. An ester of glycerol and long carbon chain acids.

feldspar. A complex silicate, usually aluminum silicate with either sodium or potassium silicate.

fermentation. A chemical change produced by the action of an enzyme.

ferromagnetism. The property of certain metals whereby they are strongly attracted by a magnet.

ferrosilicon. An alloy of iron and silicon.

filtration. The process of removing suspended material from a liquid by allowing the liquid to pass through a porous material such as filter paper or a layer of sand.

fission. The break-up of a nucleus into medium-weight parts.

flame test. A test to determine the identity of an element in a compound by the color which the compound imparts to a flame.

flotation. The process by which low-grade ores are separated from gangue as a result of preferential wetting action.

fluid. A material which flows; a liquid or gas.

flux. (*1*) A material used to promote the fusion of minerals. (*2*) A substance used to remove the oxide coating from a metallic surface prior to soldering or welding.

formal solution. See *solution, formal*.

formality. The concentration of a solution expressed in gram-formula weights per liter of solution.

formula. A shorthand method of representing the composition of substances using chemical symbols and numerical subscripts.

formula, chemical. A shorthand notation using chemical symbols and numerical subscripts to represent the composition of a substance.

formula, empirical. A chemical formula which denotes the constituent elements of a substance and the simplest relative number of atoms of each.

formula equation. A concise symbolized picture of a chemical change.

formula, molecular. A chemical formula which denotes the constituent elements of a molecular substance and the number of atoms of each composing one molecule.

formula, simplest. See *formula, empirical*.

formula, structural. A formula which indicates kind, number, arrangement, and valence bonds of the atoms in a molecule.

formula weight. See *weight, formula*.

formyl group. The $-C\begin{subarray}{l}\ \\ \diagdown\end{subarray}\begin{subarray}{l}O\\ \diagup\!\!\!/\\ \\ H\end{subarray}$ group.

fractional distillation. See *distillation, fractional*.

free-energy change. The net driving force of a reaction system; the difference between the change in heat content and the change in entropy occurring in a reaction system.

freezing. The process of converting a liquid into a solid.

fungicide. A chemical material that kills nongreen plants known as fungi.

fusible alloy. See *alloy, fusible*.

fusion. The combination of light-weight nuclei to form a heavier, more stable nucleus.

galvanize. To coat iron or steel with zinc.

gamma ray. A high-energy electromagnetic wave emitted from the nucleus of a radioactive element.

gangue. Worthless rock or soil in which valuable minerals occur.

gas. The state of matter characterized by neither a definite volume nor a definite shape.

gas constant. See *constant, gas*.

gas, ideal. A perfect gas; one which conforms exactly to the Gas Laws.

gas, water. A fuel gas made by blowing a blast of steam through a bed of red-hot coke.

Geiger counter. A device for determining the presence of radiation from radioactive materials.

gel. A jelly-like mass consisting of a colloidal suspension of a liquid in a solid.

generator. In chemistry, the vessel in which a reaction occurs to produce a desired gaseous product.

German silver. An alloy of copper, zinc, and nickel.

glass. An amorphous material, usually transparent, consisting ordinarily of a mixture of silicates.

gram. A metric unit of mass equal to one thousandth of the standard kilogram.

gram-atomic weight. See *weight, gram-atomic*.

gram-equivalent. (*1*) The mass of a reactant in grams which contains, replaces, or reacts with (directly or indirectly) the Avogadro number of hydrogen atoms. (*2*) The mass of a substance that acquires or furnishes the Avogadro number of electrons.

gram-formula weight. See *weight, gram-formula.*

gram-molecular weight. See *weight, gram-molecular.*

Grignard reagent. A compound of the type RMgX.

ground state. The most stable state of an atom.

group. A vertical column of elements in the Periodic Table.

half-cell. The portion of a voltaic cell consisting of a metal electrode in contact with its solution.

half-life. The length of time required for the decay of one-half of a given number of atoms of a radioactive element.

half-reaction. The reaction taking place at the electrode of a half-cell.

halogen. The name given to the family of elements having seven valence electrons.

hard water. Water containing ions such as calcium and magnesium which form precipitates with soap.

heat energy. See *energy, heat.*

heat of combustion. See *combustion, heat of.*

heat of formation. The heat of reaction evolved or absorbed when one mole of a compound is formed from its constituent elements.

heat of reaction. The quantity of heat evolved or absorbed during a chemical reaction.

heat of solution. See *solution, heat of.*

heavy water. Water containing deuterium atoms in place of ordinary hydrogen atoms.

heterogeneous. Having parts with different properties.

heterogeneous catalyst. See *catalyst, heterogeneous.*

heterogeneous reaction. A reaction system in which reactants and products are present in different phases.

hexagonal. A crystalline system in which three equilateral axes intersect at angles of 60° and with a vertical axis of variable length at right angles.

homogeneous. Having similar properties throughout.

homogeneous catalyst. See *catalyst, homogeneous.*

homogeneous reaction. A reaction system in which all reactants and products are in the same phase.

homologous series. A series of similar compounds which conform to a general formula.

hybridization. The combining of two or more orbitals of the same energy level but different sublevels into new orbitals of equal energy.

hydrate. A crystallized substance that contains water of crystallization.

hydrated ion. See *ion, hydrated.*

hydration. (*1*) The attachment of water molecules to particles of the solute. (*2*) The solvation process in which water is the solvent. (*3*) The addition of hydrogen and oxygen atoms to a substance in the proportion in which they occur in water.

hydride. A compound of hydrogen and at least one other element of lower electronegativity.

hydrocarbon. A compound containing hydrogen and carbon.

hydrocarbon, aromatic. A hydrocarbon which has alternating single and double covalent bonds in six-membered carbon rings.

hydrogen bond. A weak chemical bond between a hydrogen atom in one polar molecule and the more electronegative atom in a second polar molecule of the same substance.

hydrogenation. The addition of hydrogen to a material.

hydrolysis. (*1*) An acid-base reaction between water and an ion of a dissolved salt. (*2*) A chemical reaction which involves the splitting of a bond and addition of hydrogen and oxygen in the proportions in which they occur in water.

hydrolysis, anion. Hydrolysis reaction in which an anion base accepts a proton from a water molecule, increasing the OH^- ion concentration of the solution.

hydrolysis, cation. Hydrolysis reaction in which a cation acid donates a proton to a water molecule, increasing the H_3O^+ ion concentration of the solution.

hydrolysis constant. See *constant, hydrolysis.*

hydronium ion. See *ion, hydronium.*

hydrosol. A suspensoid in which water is the dispersing medium.

hydrous oxide. See *oxide, hydrous.*

hygroscopic. Absorbing and retaining moisture from the atmosphere.

hypothesis. A possible or tentative explanation.

ice point. 0° C.

ideal gas. See *gas, ideal.*

immiscible. Not capable of being mixed.

indicator. A substance which changes in color on the passage from acidity to alkalinity, or the reverse.

inertia. Resistance of matter to change in position or motion.

ingot. A molded block of metal.

inhibitor. A substance which hinders catalytic action. See *catalytic poison.*

inorganic. Pertaining to materials which are not hydrocarbons or their derivatives.

insoluble. (*1*) Not soluble. (*2*) So sparingly soluble as to be considered, in the usual sense, not soluble.

internal phase. The dispersed particles of a colloidal suspension.

ion. An atom or group of atoms with an unbalanced electrostatic charge.

ion-exchange resin. A resin which can exchange hydronium ions for positive ions; or one which can exchange hydroxide ions for negative ions.

ion, hydrated. An ion of a solute to which molecules of water are attached.

ion, hydronium. A hydrated proton; the H_3O^+ ion.

ion, spectator. An ion in a reaction system which takes no part in the chemical action.

ionic bonding. Bonding in which one or more electrons are transferred from one atom to another.

ionic crystal. See *crystal, ionic.*

ionic equilibrium. See *equilibrium, ionic.*

ionization. The formation of ions from polar solute molecules by the action of the solvent.

ionization constant. See *constant, ionization.*

ionization energy. See *energy, ionization.*

isomer. One of two or more compounds having the same molecular formula, but different structures.

isometric. A crystalline system in which the three axes are at right angles, as in a cube, and are equal in length.

isotope. One of two or more forms of atoms with the same atomic number but with different atomic masses.

kaolin. A fine white clay composed of hydrated aluminum silicate.

Kelvin temperature. See *temperature, Kelvin.*

kernel. The portion of an atom excluding the valence electrons.

ketone. An organic compound that contains the $C\!\!=\!\!O$, carbonyl, group.

kiln. A furnace used for producing quicklime, making glass, baking pottery, etc.

kilo-. Metric prefix meaning 1000.

kilocalorie. The quantity of heat required to raise the temperature of one kilogram of water one Celsius degree.

kinetic energy. See *energy, kinetic.*

kinetic theory. See *theory, kinetic.*

lake. A pigment made by precipitating a dye with aluminum hydroxide.

lanthanide series. Rare earth elements of the sixth period, following barium, in which the transitional inner building of the 5*d* sublevel is interrupted by the inner building of the 4*f* sublevel.

law. A generalization which describes behavior in nature.

leavening agent. A substance which releases carbon dioxide in a dough or batter.

lime. Calcium oxide, CaO; also called quicklime.

lime, slaked. A common name for calcium hydroxide, $Ca(OH)_2$.

limewater. A water solution of calcium hydroxide.

linear accelerator. A particle accelerator in which the particles travel in a straight line through many stages of potential difference.

lipid. An organic compound found in plant and animal tissue which is insoluble in water, but soluble in nonpolar solvents.

liquefaction. The process of converting a gas or solid to a liquid.

liquid. The state of matter characterized by a definite volume, but an indefinite shape.

liter. The metric unit of capacity; a cubic decimeter.

litmus. A dye extracted from lichens, used as an indicator.

lunar caustic. See *caustic, lunar.*

lye. A commercial grade of either sodium hydroxide or potassium hydroxide.

lyophilic. Pertaining to a colloidal system of the emulsoid type.

lyophobic. Pertaining to a colloidal system of the suspensoid type.

macromolecular crystal. See *crystal. covalent.*

magnetic quantum number. See *quantum number, magnetic.*

malleable. Capable of being shaped by hammering or rolling.

mass. The quantity of matter which a body possesses; a measure of the inertia of a body.

mass, atomic. The mass of an atom relative to the carbon-12 = exactly 12 scale.

mass defect. See *nuclear mass defect*.

mass number. (*1*) The integer closest to the atomic mass of an atom. (*2*) The sum of the number of protons and neutrons in the nucleus of an atom.

matte. A partially refined copper ore consisting of a mixture of the sulfides of iron and copper.

matter. Anything which occupies space and has mass.

melting. The process of converting a solid into a liquid.

melting point. The temperature at which a solid changes to a liquid.

metal. One of a class of elements which show a luster, are good conductors of heat and electricity, and are electropositive.

metal, alkali. An element of Group I of the Periodic Table.

metal, alkaline-earth. An element of Group II of the Periodic Table.

metal, Monel. An alloy of nickel and copper that is highly resistant to corrosion.

metal, self-protective. A metal which forms a nonporous, nonscaling coat of tarnish.

metal, type. An alloy of antimony, tin, and lead.

metallic crystal. See *crystal, metallic*.

metalloid. An element having certain properties characteristic of a metal, but which is generally classed as a nonmetal.

metamorphic. Pertains to rocks that have undergone a change in form due to heat or pressure.

meter. The metric unit of length.

metric system. A decimal system of measurement.

milli-. Metric prefix meaning 0.001.

miscible. Capable of being mixed.

mixture. A material composed of two or more substances each of which retains its own characteristics.

moderator. A material which slows down neutrons.

molal solution. See *solution, molal*.

molality. The concentration of a solution expressed in moles of solute per 1000 grams of solvent.

molar heat of fusion. The heat energy required to melt one mole of solid at its melting point.

molar heat of vaporization. See *standard molar heat of vaporization*.

molar solution. See *solution, molar*.

molar volume. The volume, in liters, of one mole of a gas at S.T.P.; taken as 22.4 liters for ordinary gases, precisely 22.414 liters for an ideal gas.

molarity. The concentration of a solution expressed in moles of solute per liter of solution.

mole. The amount of substance containing the Avogadro number of any kind of chemical unit. In practice, the gram-atomic weight of an element represented as monatomic; the gram-molecular weight of a molecular substance; the gram-formula weight of a nonmolecular substance; and the gram-ionic weight of an ion.

molecular crystal. See *crystal, molecular*.

molecular formula. See *formula, molecular*.

molecular weight. See *weight, molecular*.

molecule. The smallest chemical unit of a substance which is capable of stable independent existence.

molecule, polar. A molecule containing one or more unsymmetrically arranged polar covalent bonds, and as a whole having regions of positive and negative charge.

monatomic. Consisting of one atom.

Monel metal. See *metal, Monel*.

monoclinic. A crystalline system in which there are three unequal axes with one oblique intersection.

monomer. A simple molecule, or single unit of a polymer.

monoprotic. Referring to an acid capable of donating one proton per molecule.

monosaccharide. A carbohydrate which cannot be simplified by dilute acid hydrolysis.

mordant. A substance which, by combining with a dye, produces a fast color in a textile fiber.

mortar. A mixture of lime, sand, and water, which sets to a hard mass.

mother liquor. The saturated solution remaining after crystals have separated from a solution.

neutralization. The reaction between hydronium ions and hydroxide ions to form water.

neutron. A neutral particle found in the nucleus of an atom. It has about the same mass as a proton.

nichrome. An alloy of nickel, chromium, iron, and manganese.

nitride. A compound of nitrogen and a less electronegative element.

nitrile. An alkyl derivative of hydrogen cyanide having the general formula RCN.

nitrogen fixation. The process of converting elementary nitrogen into nitrogen compounds.

nodule. A knob-like swelling on the roots of plants of the bean and pea family in which nitrogen-fixing bacteria grow.

nonelectrolyte. A substance whose water solution does not conduct an electric current appreciably.

nonmetal. One of a class of elements which are usually poor conductors of heat and electricity and are electronegative.

nonpolar bond. A covalent bond between atoms with negligible difference in electronegativity.

normal solution. See *solution, normal.*

normality. The concentration of a solution expressed in gram-equivalents of solute per liter of solution.

nuclear change. Formation of a new substance through changes in the identity of atoms.

nuclear disintegration. The emission of a proton or neutron from a nucleus as a result of bombarding the nucleus with alpha particles, protons, deuterons, neutrons, etc.

nuclear equation. An equation representing changes in the nuclei of atoms.

nuclear mass defect. The difference between the mass of a nucleus and the sum of the masses of its constituent particles.

nuclear reactor. A device in which the controlled fission of radioactive material produces new radioactive substances and energy.

nucleus. The positively charged, dense, central part of an atom.

occlusion. The adsorption of a gas on a solid.

octet. An outer shell of an atom having s and p orbitals filled with eight electrons.

open-hearth. A large furnace in which steel is made in a shallow pool.

orbital. See *space orbital.*

ore. A mineral containing an element that can be extracted profitably.

organic. Pertaining to carbon compounds, particularly hydrocarbons and their derivatives.

organic chemistry. See *chemistry, organic.*

organosol. A suspensoid in which an organic liquid is the dispersing medium.

orthorhombic. A crystalline system in which there are three unequal axes at right angles.

oxidation. (*1*) Any chemical reaction which involves the loss of one or more electrons by an atom or an ion. (*2*) An algebraic increase in the oxidation number of a substance.

oxidation number. A number assigned to each element to indicate the number of electrons assumed to be gained, lost, or shared in compound formation.

oxidation potential. The potential difference between an electrode and its solution in a half-reaction.

oxidation-reduction reaction. Any chemical process in which there is a transfer of electrons, either partial or complete.

oxidation state. See *oxidation number.*

oxide. A compound consisting of oxygen and usually one other element.

oxide, hydrous. A hydrated metallic oxide.

oxidizing agent. The atom or ion which takes up electrons during an oxidation-reduction reaction.

paramagnetism. The property of a substance whereby it is attracted into a magnetic field.

parent element. See *element, parent.*

Paris green. A compound of copper and arsenic.

partial pressure. See *pressure, partial.*

peptide. A compound consisting of amino acid groups joined by the peptide linkage.

peptide linkage. The
$$-\overset{\text{O}}{\overset{\|}{\text{C}}}-\overset{\text{H}}{\overset{|}{\text{N}}}-$$
linkage.

peptization. The process of preparing colloidal suspensions by the addition of a substance which reduces suspended particles to colloidal dimensions.

peptizing agent. A substance which when added to a suspension causes peptization.

percentage error. See *error, percentage.*

period. A horizontal row of elements in the Periodic Table.

Periodic Table. A tabular arrangement of the chemical elements based on their atomic structure.

permanent hardness. Hardness in water caused by the sulfates of calcium and magnesium, which can be removed by precipitation or ion-exchange methods.

permutit. A synthetic zeolite used in softening water.

pH. Hydronium ion index; the common logarithm of the reciprocal of the hydronium ion concentration.

phenolphthalein. An indicator which is colorless in the presence of excess H_3O^+ ions and red in the presence of excess OH^- ions.

phenomenon. An event or situation of scientific interest susceptible of scientific description and explanation.

photoelectric effect. The emission of electrons by a substance when exposed to light.

photon. A quantum (unit) of electromagnetic radiation energy.

photosynthesis. The process by which plants manufacture carbohydrates with the aid of sunlight, using carbon dioxide and water as the raw materials, and chlorophyll as the catalyst.

physical change. A change in which the identifying properties of a substance remain unchanged.

physical equilibrium. See *equilibrium, physical.*

physical properties. Those properties which can be determined without causing a change in the identity of a material.

pigment color. Color due to the absorption by pigments of some portions of white light.

plaster of Paris. A form of calcium sulfate, $(CaSO_4)_2 \cdot H_2O$, produced by partially dehydrating gypsum.

plastic. A natural or synthetic material which can be shaped while soft into a required form and then hardened to produce a durable finished article.

polar covalent bond. A covalent bond in which there is an unequal attraction for the shared electrons and a resulting unbalanced distribution of charge.

polar molecule. See *molecule, polar.*

polymer. A compound formed by two or more simpler molecules or radicals with repeating structural units.

polymeric. Capable of polymerization.

polymerization. A union of two or more similar structures in which the atoms remain in similar relative position.

polysaccharide. A carbohydrate which yields many monosaccharide units on dilute acid hydrolysis.

potential energy. See *energy, potential.*

precipitate. (1) A substance, usually a solid, which separates from a solution as a result of some physical or chemical change. (2) To produce such a substance.

precipitation. The separation of a solid from a solution.

precision. The agreement between the numerical values of two or more measurements made in the same way. The reproducibility of measured data.

pressure. Force per unit area.

pressure, critical. The pressure required to liquefy a gas at its critical temperature.

pressure, equilibrium vapor. The pressure of a vapor in equilibrium with its liquid.

pressure, partial. The pressure each gas of a gaseous mixture would exert if it alone were present.

pressure, standard. The pressure exerted by a column of mercury 760 mm high at $0°$ C.

pressure, vapor. Pressure due to the vapor of confined liquids and solids.

principal quantum number. See *quantum number, principal.*

product. An element or compound resulting from chemical action.

product, substitution. A compound in which various atoms or groups have been substituted for one or more atoms or groups.

promoter. A substance which increases the activity of a catalyst when introduced in trace quantities.

proportion. The relation of one portion to another; the equality between ratios.

protective agent. A colloidal substance which, when adsorbed on suspended particles, stabilizes the system.

protein. A high molecular weight complex amide containing carbon, hydrogen, oxygen, and nitrogen.

protium. The isotope of hydrogen having one proton and no neutrons in the nucleus.

protolysis. Proton-transfer reactions.

proton. A positively charged particle found in the nucleus of an atom. It has $\frac{1836}{1837}$ of the mass of the protium (hydrogen) atom.

proton acceptor. A base according to the Brønsted concept.

proton donor. An acid according to the Brønsted concept.

quantum number, magnetic. The quantum number which indicates the orientation in space of an orbital.

quantum number, principal. The quantum number which indicates the average distance of an orbital from the nucleus of an atom.

quantum number, secondary. The quantum number which indicates the shape of an orbital.

quantum number, spin. The quantum number which indicates the direction of spin of an electron.

quantum numbers. The numbers which describe the position with respect to the nucleus, shape, and spatial orientation of an orbital, as well as the spin and energy of the electron(s) in each orbital.

quicklime. A common name for calcium oxide, CaO. Also called lime.

radical. A charged group of covalently bonded atoms.

radioactive. Having the property of radioactivity.

radioactive decay. A radioactive change in which a nucleus emits a particle and rays, forming a slightly lighter, more stable nucleus.

radioactive tracer. A radioactive element introduced in small quantities to determine the behavior of chemically similar non-radioactive atoms in various physical or chemical changes.

radioactivity. The spontaneous, uncontrollable decay of the nucleus of an atom with the emission of particles and rays.

rare earth element. See *element, rare earth.*

rate constant. See *constant, rate.*

rate-determining step. The slowest of a sequence of steps along a reaction pathway.

reactant. An element or compound entering into a chemical action.

reaction mechanism. The pathway of a chemical reaction; the sequence of steps by which a reaction occurs.

reaction velocity. Pertains to the rate at which a reaction proceeds.

redox. Pertaining to oxidation-reduction reactions.

reducing agent. The atom or ion which supplies electrons during an oxidation-reduction reaction.

reduction. (*1*) Any chemical reaction which involves the gain of one or more electrons by an atom or an ion. (*2*) An algebraic decrease in the oxidation number of a substance.

refractory. (*1*) Not readily melted. (*2*) A substance which is not readily melted.

relative deviation. See *deviation, relative.*

resistance furnace. A furnace in which heat is produced by the electric resistance of loose pieces of coke.

resonance. The nature of the bonding in substances when combination of two or more valence bond structures is required.

resonance hybrid. A substance whose properties show that its structure resonates among several possible valence bond structures.

respiration. The process by which a plant or animal absorbs oxygen and gives off products of oxidation in the tissues, especially carbon dioxide.

reversible reaction. A chemical reaction in which the products re-form the original reactants under suitable conditions.

rhombic. See *orthorhombic.*

roasting. Heating in the presence of air.

S.T.P. The abbreviation for "standard temperature and pressure."

salt. A compound composed of positive ions of a metal or radical and negative ions produced when certain acids transfer protons to a base.

salting out. The precipitation of a colloidal dispersion by the addition of a soluble salt.

saponification. The process of making a soap by hydrolysis of an ester with a strong hydroxide.

saturated. (*1*) Pertaining to a solution in which the concentration of solute is the maximum possible under existing conditions. (*2*) Pertaining to an organic compound which has only single covalent bonds between carbon atoms.

scattering. The deflection or dispersion of rays of light by particles of suspended matter.

science. A body of systematized knowledge.

secondary quantum number. See *quantum number, secondary.*

sedimentary. Pertains to rocks formed from sediment that has been deposited in layers.

self-protective metal. See *metal, self-protective.*

semiconductor. A substance, such as silicon or germanium, which has low electric conductivity.

shell. A region surrounding the nucleus of an atom in which electrons move. An energy level.

sherardize. To galvanize by the condensation of zinc vapor on a ferrous metal surface.

significant figures. The digits in a measurement which represent the number of units counted with reasonable assurance.

silica. Silicon dioxide, SiO_2.

silicone. One of a group of compounds containing a chain of alternate silicon and oxygen atoms, with hydrocarbon groups attached to the silicon atoms.

simplest formula. See *formula, empirical.*

slag. An easily melted product of the reaction between the flux and the impurities of an ore.

slaked lime. See *lime, slaked.*

slaking. The addition of water to quicklime, CaO, to produce hydrated (slaked) lime, $Ca(OH)_2$.

slurry. A watery mixture.

soft water. (*1*) Water that lathers readily with soap. (*2*) Water that is free of hardening agents, or from which these agents have been removed.

solid. The state of matter characterized by a definite shape.

solubility. The amount of a solute dissolved in a given amount of solvent, at equilibrium, under specified conditions.

solubility-product constant. See *constant, solubility-product.*

soluble. Capable of being dissolved.

solute. The dissolved substance in a solution.

solution. A homogeneous mixture of two or more substances, the composition of which may be varied within definite limits.

solution, buffered. A solution containing a relatively high concentration of a buffer salt which tends to maintain a constant pH.

solution equilibrium. See *equilibrium, solution.*

solution, formal. A solution containing one gram-formula weight of solute per liter of solution.

solution, heat of. The difference between the heat content of a solution and the heat content of its components.

solution, molal. A solution containing one mole of solute per 1000 grams of solvent.

solution, molar. A solution containing one mole of solute per liter of solution.

solution, normal. A solution containing one gram-equivalent of solute per liter of solution.

solution, standard. A solution that contains a precisely known concentration of solute.

solvation. The clustering of solvent particles about the particles of solute.

solvent. The dissolving medium in a solution.

space orbital. A highly probable location about a nucleus in which an electron may be found.

specific gravity. The ratio of the density of a substance to the density of a standard of reference. Solids and liquids are referred to water; gases are commonly referred to air.

specific surface. The ratio of the surface area of particles to their volume.

spectator ion. See *ion, spectator.*

spectroscope. An optical instrument consisting of a collimator tube, a glass prism, and a telescope, used for producing and viewing spectra.

spectrum. The pattern of colors formed by passing light through a prism.

spectrum, bright-line. A spectrum consisting of a series of bright lines having frequencies characteristic of the atoms present.

spelter. Commercial zinc.

spin quantum number. See *quantum number, spin.*

stable compound. See *compound, stable.*

standard molar heat of vaporization. The heat energy required to vaporize one mole of liquid at its standard boiling point.

standard pressure. See *pressure, standard.*

standard solution. See *solution, standard.*

standard temperature. See *temperature, standard.*

steam point. 100° C.

steelite. A hard alloy made up of cobalt and chromium.

sterling. Pertaining to silver which contains 7.5% copper.

stoichiometry. The branch of chemistry pertaining to the numerical relationships of chemical elements and compounds and the mathematical proportions of reactants and products in chemical transformations.

structural color. Color due to the scattering of white light by colloidally suspended particles.

structural formula. See *formula, structural.*

sublimation. The change of state from a solid to a vapor.

sublime. To pass from the solid to the gaseous state without liquefying.

subscript. A number written below and to the side of a symbol. If at the left, it represents the atomic number; if at the right, it represents the number of atoms of the element.

substance. A homogeneous material which is composed of one particular kind of matter.

substitution. A reaction in which one or more atoms are substituted for hydrogen atoms in a hydrocarbon.

substitution product. See *product, substitution.*

superheated water. Water heated under pressure to a temperature above its normal boiling point.

supersaturated. Pertaining to a solution which contains an amount of solute in excess of that normally possible under existing conditions.

superscript. A number written above and to the side of a symbol. If at the right, it represents the mass number of the atom represented by the symbol.

suspension. See *suspensoid.*

suspensoid. A colloidal suspension in which there is little attraction between the dispersed substance and the dispersing liquid.

synchrotron. A particle accelerator in which particles move in a circular path due to variation of the oscillating voltage and the magnetic field.

synthesis. The composition or combination of simple substances to make a more complex substance.

synthetic. Man-made. Artificial.

tartar emetic. Potassium antimonyl tartrate, $KSbOC_4H_4O_6$.

temperature. A measure of the ability of a system to transfer heat to, or acquire heat from other systems.

temperature, Celsius. Temperature on the Celsius scale which has two fixed points, the freezing point and the steam point of water, as $0°$ and $100°$.

temperature, condensation. The lowest temperature at which a substance may exist as a gas at atmospheric pressure.

temperature, critical. The highest temperature at which it is possible to liquefy a gas with any amount of pressure.

temperature, Kelvin. Temperature on the Kelvin scale which is numerically $273°$ higher than that on the Celsius scale.

temperature, standard. $0°$ Celsius.

temporary hardness. Hardness in water caused by the presence of hydrogen carbonates of calcium and magnesium, which can be removed by boiling.

ternary. Composed of three elements.

tetragonal. A crystalline system in which the three axes are at right angles, but only the two lateral axes are equal.

theory. A plausible explanation of a natural phenomenon in terms of a simple model which has familiar properties.

theory, atomic. A theory which includes information concerning the structure and properties of atoms, the kinds of reactions they undergo, the kinds of compounds they form, and the properties of these compounds. It also includes information about the mass, volume, and energy relationships in reactions between atoms.

theory, kinetic. A theory pertaining to the motion of the ultimate particles of substances and, in particular, of the molecules of gases.

thermite reaction. The reaction by which a metal is prepared from its oxide by reduction with aluminum.

titration. The process by which the capacity of a solution of unknown concentration to combine with one of known concentration is measured.

total charge. The product of the charge of an ion by the number of that ion taken.

toxic. Poisonous.

transition. Pertaining to subgroups of elements characterized by the belated filling of the next-to-outermost energy level of the atoms.

transition element. See *element, transition.*

transmutation reaction. A reaction in which the nucleus of an atom undergoes a change in its positive charge, and consequently in its identity.

transuranium element. See *element, transuranium.*

triad. A group of three similar elements, the second of which has an atomic weight approximately equal to the average of the atomic weights of the others.

triclinic. A crystalline system in which there are three unequal axes and oblique intersections.

triple point. A single condition of temperature and pressure at which the solid, liquid, and gaseous states of a substance can exist simultaneously in equilibrium.

triprotic. Referring to an acid capable of donating three protons per molecule.

tritium. The isotope of hydrogen having one proton and two neutrons in the nucleus.

tuyère. A blowpipe in the base of a blast furnace.

Tyndall effect. The dispersion or scattering of light by colloidal particles.

type metal. See *metal, type*.

ultramicroscope. A microscope in which the object is illuminated at right angles to the optical axis of the microscope.

unit cell. The smallest portion of the crystal lattice which determines the pattern of the lattice structure.

unsaturated. An organic compound with a double or triple bond between two carbon atoms.

unstable compound. See *compound, unstable*.

valence electron. See *electron, valence*.

van der Waals forces. Forces of attraction between nonpolar covalent molecules dependent on the number of electrons in the molecules and the tightness with which they are held.

vapor. The gaseous state of substances which normally exist as liquids or solids.

vapor pressure. See *pressure, vapor*.

vapor pressure, equilibrium. See *pressure, equilibrium vapor*.

vinyl group. The CH_2=CH— group.

volatile. Easily vaporized.

vulcanization. The heating of rubber with other materials to improve its properties.

water gas. See *gas, water*.

water glass. A water solution of sodium silicate.

water of crystallization. Water that has united with some compounds as they crystallize from solution.

water of hydration. See *water of crystallization*.

water softener. A chemical substance which removes hardness from water.

weight. The measure of the earth's gravitational attraction for a body.

weight, atomic. The average relative mass of the naturally occurring atoms of an element on the carbon-12 = exactly 12 scale.

weight, formula. The sum of the atomic weights of all the atoms present in a chemical formula.

weight, gram-atomic. The mass in grams of one mole of naturally occurring atoms of an element.

weight, gram-formula. The mass of a substance in grams equal to its formula weight; one mole of the substance.

weight, gram-molecular. The mass of a molecular substance in grams equal to its molecular weight; one mole of molecules of the substance.

weight, molecular. The formula weight of a molecular substance.

word equation. A brief statement which identifies by name the reactants entering into chemical action and the products formed.

X rays. Electromagnetic radiations of high frequency and short wavelength.

zeolite. A natural mineral, sodium silico-aluminate, used to soften water.

zwitterion. A dipolar ion having an —NH_3^+ group at one end and a —COO^- group at the other.

APPENDIX

APPENDIX

TABLE 1.—METRIC–ENGLISH EQUIVALENTS

1 inch = 2.54 centimeters.	1 meter = 39.37 inches.
1 quart (U.S. liquid) = 0.946 liter.	1 liter = 1.06 quarts (U.S. liquid).
1 ounce = 28.35 grams.	1 gram = 0.035 ounce.
1 pound = 453.6 grams.	1 kilogram = 2.2 pounds.
1 ton = 0.907 metric ton.	1 metric ton = 1.10 tons.

TABLE 2.—ISOTOPES OF SOME ELEMENTS

(Naturally occurring nonradioactive isotopes are given in ordinary type. Naturally occurring radioactive isotopes are in bold-face italics. All other radioactive isotopes are in italics. Naturally occurring isotopes are listed in order of their abundance. All other isotopes are listed in order of length of half-life.)

Elements	Mass Numbers of Isotopes
H	1, 2, 3
He	4, 3, *6, 7, 5*
Li	7, 6, *8, 9, 5*
Be	9, *10, 7, 11, 8, 6*
B	11, 10, *8, 13, 12, 9*
C	12, 13, *14, 11, 10, 15, 16*
N	14, 15, *13, 16, 17, 12*
O	16, 18, 17, *15, 14, 19, 20*
F	19, *18, 17, 20, 21, 16*
Ne	20, 22, 21, *24, 23, 19, 18*
Na	23, *22, 24, 25, 21, 26, 20*
Mg	24, 26, 25, *28, 27, 23*
Al	27, *26, 28, 29, 25, 30, 24, 23*
Si	28, 29, 30, *32, 31, 27, 26*
P	31, *33, 32, 30, 34, 29, 28*
S	32, 34, 33, 36, *35, 38, 37, 31, 30*
Cl	35, 37, *36, 39, 38, 40, 33, 34, 32*
Ar	40, 36, 38, *39, 42, 37, 41, 35*
K	39, 41, **40**, *43, 42, 44, 45, 38, 37*
Ca	40, 44, 42, 48, 43, **46**, *41, 45, 47, 49, 39, 38*
Cr	52, 53, 50, 54, *51, 48, 49, 56, 55, 46, 47*
Fe	56, 54, 57, 58, *60, 55, 59, 52, 53, 61*
Ni	58, 60, 62, 61, 64, *59, 63, 66, 57, 56, 65*
Cu	63, 65, *67, 64, 61, 62, 66, 60, 59, 68, 58*
Zn	64, 66, 68, 67, 70, *65, 72, 62, 69, 63, 71, 60, 61*
Br	79, 81, *77, 82, 83, 76, 75, 74, 84, 80, 78, 85, 88, 87, 89, 90*
Sr	88, 87, 86, 84, *90, 85, 89, 82, 83, 91, 92, 80, 81, 93, 94, 95*
Ag	107, 109, *105, 111, 113, 112, 104, 103, 106, 115, 102, 116, 108, 117, 110, 114*
Sn	120, 118, 116, 119, 117, 124, 122, 112, 114, 115, *126, 113, 125, 121, 110, 127, 123, 111, 109, 108, 129, 128, 130, 132*

TABLE 2.—ISOTOPES OF SOME ELEMENTS (cont'd)

I	127, *129, 125, 126, 131, 124, 133, 123, 130, 135, 132, 121, 120, 134, 128, 119, 118, 117, 122, 136, 137, 138, 139*
Ba	138, 137, 136, 135, 134, 130, 132, *133, 140, 131, 128, 129, 126, 139, 141, 127, 142, 143*
W	184, 186, 182, 183, 180, *181, 185, 188, 178, 187, 177, 176, 179*
Pt	195, 194, 196, 198, **192, 190,** *193, 188, 191, 197, 200, 189, 184, 186, 187, 199*
Pb	208, 206, 207, **204,** *205, 202, 210, 203, 200, 212, 201, 209, 198, 199, 196, 211, 214, 195, 194*
Bi	209, *208, 207, 205, 206, 210, 203, 204, 202, 201, 212, 213, 200, 199, 214, 215, 196, 211*
Rn	222, *211, 224, 210, 209, 221, 212, 208, 223, 207, 206, 204, 215, 220, 219, 218, 217, 216*
Ra	
	226, 228, 225, 223, 224, 230, 227, 229, 222, 221, 220
U	**238, 235, 234,** *236, 233, 232, 230, 237, 231, 229, 239, 228, 227*
Np	*237, 236, 235, 234, 239, 238, 240, 231, 233, 241, 232*
Pu	*244, 242, 240, 239, 236, 238, 241, 237, 245, 234, 243, 232, 235, 233*
Am	*243, 241, 245, 240, 242, 239, 238, 237, 244, 246*
Cm	*247, 248, 250, 245, 246, 243, 244, 242, 241, 240, 239, 238, 249*
Bk	*247, 249, 245, 246, 248, 243, 244, 250*
Cf	*251, 249, 250, 252, 248, 254, 253, 246, 247, 245, 244*
Es	*254, 252, 255, 253, 250, 249, 248, 246*
Fm	*253, 252, 255, 251, 254, 256, 250, 249, 248*
Md	*256, 255*
(102)	*253, 255, 254*
Lw	*257*

TABLE 3.—THE ELEMENTS, THEIR SYMBOLS, ATOMIC NUMBERS, AND ATOMIC WEIGHTS

The more important elements are printed in color.

Name of element	Symbol	Atomic number	Atomic weight	Name of element	Symbol	Atomic number	Atomic weight
Actinium	Ac	89	[227]	Mercury	Hg	80	200.59
Aluminum	Al	13	26.9815	Molybdenum	Mo	42	95.94
Americium	Am	95	[243]	Neodymium	Nd	60	144.24
Antimony	Sb	51	121.75	Neon	Ne	10	20.183
Argon	Ar	18	39.948	Neptunium	Np	93	[237]
Arsenic	As	33	74.9216	Nickel	Ni	28	58.71
Astatine	At	85	[210]	Niobium	Nb	41	92.906
Barium	Ba	56	137.34	Nitrogen	N	7	14.0067
Berkelium	Bk	97	[249*]	(Nobelium)	(No)	102	[254]
Beryllium	Be	4	9.0122	Osmium	Os	76	190.2
Bismuth	Bi	83	208.980	Oxygen	O	8	15.9994
Boron	B	5	10.811	Palladium	Pd	46	106.4
Bromine	Br	35	79.909	Phosphorus	P	15	30.9738
Cadmium	Cd	48	112.40	Platinum	Pt	78	195.09
Calcium	Ca	20	40.08	Plutonium	Pu	94	[242]
Californium	Cf	98	[251*]	Polonium	Po	84	[210*]
Carbon	C	6	12.01115	Potassium	K	19	39.102
Cerium	Ce	58	140.12	Praseodymium	Pr	59	140.907
Cesium	Cs	55	132.905	Promethium	Pm	61	[147*]
Chlorine	Cl	17	35.453	Protactinium	Pa	91	[231]
Chromium	Cr	24	51.996	Radium	Ra	88	[226]
Cobalt	Co	27	58.9332	Radon	Rn	86	[222]
Copper	Cu	29	63.54	Rhenium	Re	75	186.2
Curium	Cm	96	[247]	Rhodium	Rh	45	102.905
Dysprosium	Dy	66	162.50	Rubidium	Rb	37	85.47
Einsteinium	Es	99	[254]	Ruthenium	Ru	44	101.07
Erbium	Er	68	167.26	Samarium	Sm	62	150.35
Europium	Eu	63	151.96	Scandium	Sc	21	44.956
Fermium	Fm	100	[253]	Selenium	Se	34	78.96
Fluorine	F	9	18.9984	Silicon	Si	14	28.086
Francium	Fr	87	[223]	Silver	Ag	47	107.870
Gadolinium	Gd	64	157.25	Sodium	Na	11	22.9898
Gallium	Ga	31	69.72	Strontium	Sr	38	87.62
Germanium	Ge	32	72.59	Sulfur	S	16	32.064
Gold	Au	79	196.967	Tantalum	Ta	73	180.948
Hafnium	Hf	72	178.49	Technetium	Tc	43	[99*]
Helium	He	2	4.0026	Tellurium	Te	52	127.60
Holmium	Ho	67	164.930	Terbium	Tb	65	158.924
Hydrogen	H	1	1.00797	Thallium	Tl	81	204.37
Indium	In	49	114.82	Thorium	Th	90	232.038
Iodine	I	53	126.9044	Thulium	Tm	69	168.934
Iridium	Ir	77	192.2	Tin	Sn	50	118.69
Iron	Fe	26	55.847	Titanium	Ti	22	47.90
Krypton	Kr	36	83.80	Tungsten	W	74	183.85
Lanthanum	La	57	138.91	Uranium	U	92	238.03
Lawrencium	Lw	103	[257]	Vanadium	V	23	50.942
Lead	Pb	82	207.19	Xenon	Xe	54	131.30
Lithium	Li	3	6.939	Ytterbium	Yb	70	173.04
Lutetium	Lu	71	174.97	Yttrium	Y	39	88.905
Magnesium	Mg	12	24.312	Zinc	Zn	30	65.37
Manganese	Mn	25	54.9380	Zirconium	Zr	40	91.22
Mendelevium	Md	101	[256]				

A value given in brackets denotes the mass number of the isotope of longest known half-life, or for those marked with an asterisk, a better known one. The atomic weights of most of these elements are believed to have no error greater than ±0.5 of the last digit given.

TABLE 4.—COMMON ELEMENTS

Name	Symbol	Approx. At. Wt.	Common Ox. Nos.	Name	Symbol	Approx. At. Wt.	Common Ox. Nos.
Aluminum	Al	27.0	+3	Magnesium	Mg	24.3	+2
Antimony	Sb	121.8	+3,+5	Manganese	Mn	54.9	+2,+4,+7
Arsenic	As	74.9	+3,+5	Mercury	Hg	200.6	+1,+2
Barium	Ba	137.3	+2	Nickel	Ni	58.7	+2
Bismuth	Bi	209.0	+3	Nitrogen	N	14.0	−3,+3,+5
Bromine	Br	79.9	−1,+5	Oxygen	O	16.0	−2
Calcium	Ca	40.1	+2	Phosphorus	P	31.0	+3,+5
Carbon	C	12.0	+2,+4	Platinum	Pt	195.1	+2,+4
Chlorine	Cl	35.5	−1,+5,+7	Potassium	K	39.1	+1
Chromium	Cr	52.0	+2,+3,+6	Silicon	Si	28.1	+4
Cobalt	Co	58.9	+2,+3	Silver	Ag	107.9	+1
Copper	Cu	63.5	+1,+2	Sodium	Na	23.0	+1
Fluorine	F	19.0	−1	Strontium	Sr	87.6	+2
Gold	Au	197.0	0,+3	Sulfur	S	32.1	−2,+4,+6
Hydrogen	H	1.0	−1,+1	Tin	Sn	118.7	+2,+4
Iodine	I	126.9	−1,+5	Titanium	Ti	47.9	+3,+4
Iron	Fe	55.8	+2,+3	Tungsten	W	183.8	+6
Lead	Pb	207.2	+2,+4	Zinc	Zn	65.4	+2

TABLE 5.—COMMON IONS AND THEIR CHARGES

Name	Symbol	Charge	Name	Symbol	Charge
Aluminum	Al^{+++}	+3	Lead(II)	Pb^{++}	+2
Ammonium	NH_4^+	+1	Magnesium	Mg^{++}	+2
Barium	Ba^{++}	+2	Mercury(I)	Hg_2^{++}	+1
Calcium	Ca^{++}	+2	Mercury(II)	Hg^{++}	+2
Chromium(III)	Cr^{+++}	+3	Nickel(II)	Ni^{++}	+2
Cobalt(II)	Co^{++}	+2	Potassium	K^+	+1
Copper(I)	Cu^+	+1	Silver	Ag^+	+1
Copper(II)	Cu^{++}	+2	Sodium	Na^+	+1
Hydronium	H_3O^+	+1	Tin(II)	Sn^{++}	+2
Iron(II)	Fe^{++}	+2	Tin(IV)	Sn^{++++}	+4
Iron(III)	Fe^{+++}	+3	Zinc	Zn^{++}	+2
Acetate	$C_2H_3O_2^-$	−1	Hydroxide	OH^-	−1
Bromide	Br^-	−1	Hypochlorite	ClO^-	−1
Carbonate	$CO_3^=$	−2	Iodide	I^-	−1
Chlorate	ClO_3^-	−1	Nitrate	NO_3^-	−1
Chloride	Cl^-	−1	Nitrite	NO_2^-	−1
Chromate	$CrO_4^=$	−2	Oxide	$O^=$	−2
Fluoride	F^-	−1	Permanganate	MnO_4^-	−1
Hexacyanoferrate(II)	$Fe(CN)_6^{\equiv}$	−4	Peroxide	$O_2^=$	−2
Hexacyanoferrate(III)	$Fe(CN)_6^{\equiv}$	−3	Phosphate	$PO_4^{\equiv}$	−3
Hydride	H^-	−1	Sulfate	$SO_4^=$	−2
Hydrogen carbonate	HCO_3^-	−1	Sulfide	$S^=$	−2
Hydrogen sulfate	HSO_4^-	−1	Sulfite	$SO_3^=$	−2

TABLE 6.—ELECTRONIC ARRANGEMENT OF THE ELEMENTS

Shells	K	L		M			N				O				P				Q
Sub-Levels	$1s$	$2s$	$2p$	$3s$	$3p$	$3d$	$4s$	$4p$	$4d$	$4f$	$5s$	$5p$	$5d$	$5f$	$6s$	$6p$	$6d$	$6f$	$7s$
1 Hydrogen	1																		
2 Helium	2																		
3 Lithium	2	1																	
4 Beryllium	2	2																	
5 Boron	2	2	1																
5 Carbon	2	2	2																
7 Nitrogen	2	2	3																
8 Oxygen	2	2	4																
9 Fluorine	2	2	5																
10 Neon	2	2	6																
11 Sodium	2	2	6	1															
12 Magnesium	2	2	6	2															
13 Aluminum	2	2	6	2	1														
14 Silicon	2	2	6	2	2														
15 Phosphorus	2	2	6	2	3														
16 Sulfur	2	2	6	2	4														
17 Chlorine	2	2	6	2	5														
18 Argon	2	2	6	2	6														
19 Potassium	2	2	6	2	6		1												
20 Calcium	2	2	6	2	6		2												
21 Scandium	2	2	6	2	6	1	2												
22 Titanium	2	2	6	2	6	2	2												
23 Vanadium	2	2	6	2	6	3	2												
24 Chromium	2	2	6	2	6	5	1												
25 Manganese	2	2	6	2	6	5	2												
26 Iron	2	2	6	2	6	6	2												
27 Cobalt	2	2	6	2	6	7	2												
28 Nickel	2	2	6	2	6	8	2												
29 Copper	2	2	6	2	6	10	1												
30 Zinc	2	2	6	2	6	10	2												
31 Gallium	2	2	6	2	6	10	2	1											
32 Germanium	2	2	6	2	6	10	2	2											
33 Arsenic	2	2	6	2	6	10	2	3											
34 Selenium	2	2	6	2	6	10	2	4											
35 Bromine	2	2	6	2	6	10	2	5											
36 Krypton	2	2	6	2	6	10	2	6											
37 Rubidium	2	2	6	2	6	10	2	6			1								
38 Strontium	2	2	6	2	6	10	2	6			2								
39 Yttrium	2	2	6	2	6	10	2	6	1		2								
40 Zirconium	2	2	6	2	6	10	2	6	2		2								
41 Niobium	2	2	6	2	6	10	2	6	4		1								
42 Molybdenum	2	2	6	2	6	10	2	6	5		1								
43 Technetium	2	2	6	2	6	10	2	6	6		1								
43 Ruthenium	2	2	6	2	6	10	2	6	7		1								
45 Rhodium	2	2	6	2	6	10	2	6	8		1								
46 Palladium	2	2	6	2	6	10	2	6	10										
47 Silver	2	2	6	2	6	10	2	6	10		1								
48 Cadmium	2	2	6	2	6	10	2	6	10		2								
49 Indium	2	2	6	2	6	10	2	6	10		1	2							
50 Tin	2	2	6	2	6	10	2	6	10		2	2							
51 Antimony	2	2	6	2	6	10	2	6	10		2	3							
52 Tellurium	2	2	6	2	6	10	2	6	10		2	4							

TABLE 6.—ELECTRONIC ARRANGEMENT OF THE ELEMENTS (cont'd)

	Shells	K	L		M			N				O				P				Q
	Sub-Levels	1s	2s	2p	3s	3p	3d	4s	4p	4d	4f	5s	5p	5d	5f	6s	6p	6d	6f	7s
53	Iodine	2	2	6	2	6	10	2	6	10		2	5							
54	Xenon	2	2	6	2	6	10	2	6	10		2	6							
55	Cesium	2	2	6	2	6	10	2	6	10		2	6			1				
56	Barium	2	2	6	2	6	10	2	6	10		2	6			2				
57	Lanthanum	2	2	6	2	6	10	2	6	10		2	6	1		2				
58	Cerium	2	2	6	2	6	10	2	6	10	2	2	6			2				
59	Praseodymium	2	2	6	2	6	10	2	6	10	3	2	6			2				
60	Neodymium	2	2	6	2	6	10	2	6	10	4	2	6			2				
61	Promethium	2	2	6	2	6	10	2	6	10	5	2	6			2				
62	Samarium	2	2	6	2	6	10	2	6	10	6	2	6			2				
63	Europium	2	2	6	2	6	10	2	6	10	7	2	6			2				
64	Gadolinium	2	2	6	2	6	10	2	6	10	7	2	6	1		2				
65	Terbium	2	2	6	2	6	10	2	6	10	9	2	6			2				
66	Dysprosium	2	2	6	2	6	10	2	6	10	10	2	6			2				
67	Holmium	2	2	6	2	6	10	2	6	10	11	2	6			2				
68	Erbium	2	2	6	2	6	10	2	6	10	12	2	6			2				
69	Thulium	2	2	6	2	6	10	2	6	10	13	2	6			2				
70	Ytterbium	2	2	6	2	6	10	2	6	10	14	2	6			2				
71	Lutetium	2	2	6	2	6	10	2	6	10	14	2	6	1		2				
72	Hafnium	2	2	6	2	6	10	2	6	10	14	2	6	2		2				
73	Tantalum	2	2	6	2	6	10	2	6	10	14	2	6	3		2				
74	Tungsten	2	2	6	2	6	10	2	6	10	14	2	6	4		2				
75	Rhenium	2	2	6	2	6	10	2	6	10	14	2	6	5		2				
76	Osmium	2	2	6	2	6	10	2	6	10	14	2	6	6		2				
77	Iridium	2	2	6	2	6	10	2	6	10	14	2	6	9						
78	Platinum	2	2	6	2	6	10	2	6	10	14	2	6	9		1				
79	Gold	2	2	6	2	6	10	2	6	10	14	2	6	10		1				
80	Mercury	2	2	6	2	6	10	2	6	10	14	2	6	10		2				
81	Thallium	2	2	6	2	6	10	2	6	10	14	2	6	10		2	1			
82	Lead	2	2	6	2	6	10	2	6	10	14	2	6	10		2	2			
83	Bismuth	2	2	6	2	6	10	2	6	10	14	2	6	10		2	3			
84	Polonium	2	2	6	2	6	10	2	6	10	14	2	6	10		2	4			
85	Astatine	2	2	6	2	6	10	2	6	10	14	2	6	10		2	5			
86	Radon	2	2	6	2	6	10	2	6	10	14	2	6	10		2	6			
87	Francium	2	2	6	2	6	10	2	6	10	14	2	6	10		2	6			1
88	Radium	2	2	6	2	6	10	2	6	10	14	2	6	10		2	6			2
89	Actinium	2	2	6	2	6	10	2	6	10	14	2	6	10		2	6	1		2
90	Thorium	2	2	6	2	6	10	2	6	10	14	2	6	10		2	6	2		2
91	Protactinium	2	2	6	2	6	10	2	6	10	14	2	6	10	2	2	6	1		2
92	Uranium	2	2	6	2	6	10	2	6	10	14	2	6	10	3	2	6	1		2
93	Neptunium	2	2	6	2	6	10	2	6	10	14	2	6	10	5	2	6			2
94	Plutonium	2	2	6	2	6	10	2	6	10	14	2	6	10	6	2	6			2
95	Americium	2	2	6	2	6	10	2	6	10	14	2	6	10	7	2	6			2
96	Curium	2	2	6	2	6	10	2	6	10	14	2	6	10	7	2	6	1		2
97	Berkelium	2	2	6	2	6	10	2	6	10	14	2	6	10	8	2	6	1		2
98	Californium	2	2	6	2	6	10	2	6	10	14	2	6	10	10	2	6			2
99	Einsteinium	2	2	6	2	6	10	2	6	10	14	2	6	10	10	2	6	1		2
100	Fermium	2	2	6	2	6	10	2	6	10	14	2	6	10	11	2	6	1		2
101	Mendelevium	2	2	6	2	6	10	2	6	10	14	2	6	10	12	2	6	1		2
102		2	2	6	2	6	10	2	6	10	14	2	6	10	13	2	6	1		2
103	Lawrencium	2	2	6	2	6	10	2	6	10	14	2	6	10	14	2	6	1		2

TABLE 7.—PRESSURE OF WATER VAPOR IN MILLIMETERS OF MERCURY

° C	mm	° C	mm	° C	mm	° C	mm
0.0	4.6	17.5	15.0	22.5	20.4	30.0	31.8
5.0	6.5	18.0	15.5	23.0	21.1	35.0	42.2
7.5	7.8	18.5	16.0	23.5	21.7	40.0	55.3
10.0	9.2	19.0	16.5	24.0	22.4	50.0	92.5
12.5	10.9	19.5	17.0	24.5	23.1	60.0	149.4
15.0	12.8	20.0	17.5	25.0	23.8	70.0	233.7
15.5	13.2	20.5	18.1	26.0	25.2	80.0	355.1
16.0	13.6	21.0	18.6	27.0	26.7	90.0	525.8
16.5	14.1	21.5	19.2	28.0	28.3	95.0	633.9
17.0	14.5	22.0	19.8	29.0	30.0	100.0	760.0

TABLE 8.—DENSITY AND SPECIFIC GRAVITY OF GASES

Gas	Density Grams per Liter S.T.P.	Specific Gravity Air Standard	Gas	Density Grams per Liter S.T.P.	Specific Gravity Air Standard
Ammonia	0.771	0.597	Hydrogen chloride	1.636	1.268
Carbon dioxide	1.977	1.529	Hydrogen sulfide	1.539	1.190
Carbon monoxide	1.250	0.968	Methane	0.714	0.554
Chlorine	3.214	2.486	Nitrogen	1.251	0.964
Dinitrogen monoxide	1.977	1.530	Nitrogen monoxide	1.340	1.037
Ethyne (acetylene)	1.169	0.906	Oxygen	1.429	1.105
Hydrogen	0.0899	0.0695	Sulfur dioxide	2.927	2.264

TABLE 9.—SOLUBILITY OF GASES IN WATER

Volume of gas (reduced to S.T.P.) that can be dissolved in 1 volume of water.

Gas	0° C	10° C	20° C
Air	0.0292	0.0228	0.0187
Ammonia	1298.9	910.4	710.6
Carbon dioxide	1.713	1.194	0.878
Chlorine	4.54	3.148	2.299
Hydrogen	0.0215	0.0196	0.0182
Hydrogen chloride	506.7	473.9	442.0
Hydrogen sulfide	4.670	3.399	2.582
Nitrogen	0.0235	0.0186	0.0155
Oxygen	0.0489	0.0380	0.0310
Sulfur dioxide	79.79	56.65	39.37

TABLE 10.—SOLUBILITIES

S, soluble in water. A, soluble in acids, insoluble in water. P, partially soluble in water, soluble in dilute acids. I, insoluble in dilute acids and in water. a, slightly soluble in acids, insoluble in water. d, decomposes in water.

	Acetate	Bromide	Carbonate	Chlorate	Chloride	Chromate	Hydroxide	Iodide	Nitrate	Oxide	Phosphate	Silicate	Sulfate	Sulfide
Aluminum	S	S	—	S	S	—	A	S	S	a	A	I	S	d
Ammonium	S	S	S	S	S	S	—	S	S	—	S	—	S	S
Barium	S	S	P	S	S	A	S	S	S	S	A	S	a	d
Calcium	S	S	P	S	S	S	S	S	S	P	P	P	P	P
Copper(II)	S	S	—	S	S	—	A	—	S	A	A	A	S	A
Iron(II)	S	S	P	S	S	—	A	S	S	A	A	—	S	A
Iron(III)	S	S	—	S	S	A	A	S	S	A	P	—	P	d
Lead(II)	S	S	A	S	S	A	P	P	S	P	A	A	P	A
Magnesium	S	S	P	S	S	S	A	S	S	A	P	A	S	d
Manganese(II)	S	S	P	S	S	—	A	S	S	A	P	I	S	A
Mercury(I)	P	A	A	S	a	P	—	A	S	A	A	—	P	I
Mercury(II)	S	S	—	S	S	P	A	P	S	P	A	—	d	I
Potassium	S	S	S	S	S	S	S	S	S	S	S	S	S	S
Silver	P	a	A	S	a	P	—	I	S	P	A	—	P	A
Sodium	S	S	S	S	S	S	S	S	S	S	S	S	S	S
Strontium	S	S	P	S	S	P	S	S	S	S	A	A	P	S
Tin(II)	d	S	—	S	S	A	A	S	d	A	A	—	S	A
Tin(IV)	S	S	—	—	S	S	P	d	—	A	—	—	S	A
Zinc	S	S	P	S	S	P	A	S	S	P	A	A	S	A

TABLE 11.—SOLUBILITY OF COMPOUNDS

Solubilities given in grams of anhydrous compound that can be dissolved in 100 grams of water at the indicated temperatures.

Compound	0° C	20° C	60° C	100° C
Ammonium chloride	29.4	37.2	55.2	77.3
Ammonium nitrate	118.3	192	421.0	871.0
Barium hydroxide	1.67	3.89	20.94	101.40$^{80°}$
Calcium hydroxide	0.19	0.17	0.12	0.08
Calcium sulfate (gypsum)	0.18	0.19	0.20	0.16
Cerium sulfate	17.35	9.16	3.73	
Copper(II) sulfate	14.3	20.7	40.0	75.4
Lead(II) chloride	0.67	0.99	1.98	3.34
Lead(II) nitrate	38.8	56.5	95	138.8
Mercury(II) chloride	3.5	6.1	14	38
Potassium bromide	53.5	65.2	85.5	104.0
Potassium chlorate	3.3	7.4	24.5	57.0
Potassium chloride	27.6	34.0	45.5	56.7
Potassium iodide	127.5	144	176	208
Potassium nitrate	13.3	31.6	110.0	246.0
Potassium sulfate	7.4	11.1	18.2	24.1
Silver nitrate	122	222	525	952
Sodium acetate	119	123.5	139.5	170
Sodium chloride	35.7	36.0	37.3	39.8
Sodium nitrate	73.0	88.0	124.0	180.0
Sugar (sucrose)	179.2	203.9	287.3	487.2

TABLE 12.—HEAT OF FORMATION

ΔH_f = heat of formation of the given substance from its elements. All values of ΔH_f are expressed as kcal/mole at 25° C. Negative values of ΔH_f indicate exothermic reactions. State of substance: s = solid, l = liquid, g = gaseous.

Substance	State	ΔH_f	Substance	State	ΔH_f
Aluminum oxide	s	−399.09	Iron(II,III) oxide	s	−267.0
Ammonia	g	−11.04	Iron(III) oxide	s	−196.5
Barium sulfate	s	−350.2	Lead(II) oxide	s	−52.07
Benzene	g	+19.82	Lead(II) nitrate	s	−107.35
Benzene	l	+11.72	Lead(II) sulfide	s	−22.54
Calcium chloride	s	−190.0	Magnesium chloride	s	−153.40
Calcium hydroxide	s	−235.80	Magnesium oxide	s	−143.84
Calcium oxide	s	−151.9	Mercury(II) chloride	s	−55.0
Carbon (diamond)	s	+0.45	Mercury(II) fulminate	s	+64
Carbon (graphite)	s	0.00	Mercury (II) nitrate	s	−93.0
Carbon dioxide	g	−94.05	Mercury(II) oxide	s	−21.68
Carbon disulfide	g	+27.55	Methane	g	−17.89
Carbon disulfide	l	+21.0	Nitrogen dioxide	g	+8.09
Carbon monoxide	g	−26.42	Nitrogen monoxide	g	+21.60
Carbon tetrachloride	g	−25.5	Oxygen (O_2)	g	0.00
Carbon tetrachloride	l	−33.3	Ozone (O_3)	g	+34.00
Copper(II) nitrate	s	−73.4	Potassium bromide	s	−93.73
Copper(II) oxide	s	−37.1	Potassium chloride	s	−104.18
Copper(II) sulfate	s	−184.00	Potassium hydroxide	s	−101.78
Dinitrogen monoxide	g	+19.49	Potassium nitrate	s	−117.76
Dinitrogen pentoxide	g	+3.6	Potassium sulfate	s	−342.66
Dinitrogen pentoxide	s	−10.0	Silver chloride	s	−30.36
Dinitrogen tetroxide	g	+2.31	Silver nitrate	s	−29.43
Diphosphorus pentoxide	s	−360.0	Silver sulfide	s	−7.60
Ethyne (acetylene)	g	+54.19	Sodium bromide	s	−86.03
Hydrogen (H_2)	g	0.00	Sodium chloride	s	−98.23
Hydrogen bromide	g	−8.66	Sodium hydroxide	s	−101.99
Hydrogen chloride	g	−22.06	Sodium nitrate	s	−101.54
Hydrogen fluoride	g	−64.2	Sodium sulfate	s	−330.90
Hydrogen iodide	g	+6.20	Sulfur dioxide	g	−70.96
Hydrogen oxide (water)	g	−57.80	Sulfur trioxide	g	−94.45
Hydrogen oxide (water)	l	−68.32	Tin(IV) chloride	l	−130.3
Hydrogen peroxide	g	−31.83	Zinc nitrate	s	−115.12
Hydrogen peroxide	l	−44.84	Zinc oxide	s	−83.17
Hydrogen sulfide	g	−4.82	Zinc sulfate	s	−233.88
Iron(II) sulfate	s	−220.5	Zinc sulfide	s	−14.0

TABLE 13.—HEAT OF COMBUSTION

ΔH_c = heat of combustion of the given substance. All values of ΔH_c are expressed as kcal/mole of substance oxidized to $H_2O(l)$ and/or $CO_2(g)$ at constant pressure and 25° C. State of substance: s = solid, l = liquid, g = gaseous.

Substance	Formula	State	ΔH_c
Hydrogen	H_2	g	−68.52
Graphite	C	s	−94.05
Carbon monoxide	CO	g	−67.64
Methane	CH_4	g	−212.80
Ethane	C_2H_6	g	−372.82
Propane	C_3H_8	g	−530.60
Butane	C_4H_{10}	g	−687.98
Pentane	C_5H_{12}	g	−845.16
Hexane	C_6H_{14}	l	−995.01
Heptane	C_7H_{16}	l	−1151.27
Octane	C_8H_{18}	l	−1307.53
Ethene (ethylene)	C_2H_4	g	−337.23
Propene (propylene)	C_3H_6	g	−491.99
Ethyne (acetylene)	C_2H_2	g	−310.62
Benzene	C_6H_6	l	−780.98
Toluene	C_7H_8	l	−934.50

TABLE 14.—PROPERTIES OF IMPORTANT ELEMENTS

Name	Specific Gravity		Melting Point ° C	Boiling Point ° C	Common Oxidation Numbers
	Water Std.	Air Std.			
Aluminum	2.70		660	2057	+3
Antimony	6.68		631	1380	+3, +5
Arsenic	5.73		(sublimes)	(sublimes)	+3, +5
Barium	3.78		850	1140	+2
Bismuth	9.75		271.3	1560	+3
Boron	2.34		2300	2550 (sublimes)	+3
Bromine	3.12		−7.2	58.8	−1, +5
Calcium	1.55		842	1240	+2
Carbon	1.7–3.5		(sublimes above 3500° C)	4200	+2, +4
Chlorine		2.486	−101.6	−34.6	−1, +5, +7
Chromium	7.14		1890	2482	+2, +3, +6
Cobalt	8.90		1495	2900	+2, +3
Copper	8.9		1083	2336	+1, +2
Fluorine		1.312	−223	−187	−1
Gold	19.3		1063	2600	0, +3
Hydrogen		0.0695	−259	−253	−1, +1
Iodine	4.93		113.5	184.4	−1, +5
Iron	7.86		1535	3000	+2, +3
Lead	11.34		327.5	1750	+2, +4
Magnesium	1.74		651	1107	+2
Manganese	7.3		1244	2097	+2, +4, +7
Mercury	13.55		−38.9	356.6	+1, +2
Nickel	8.90		1455	2900	+2
Nitrogen		0.964	−209.9	−195.8	−3, +3, +5
Oxygen		1.105	−218	−183	−2
Phosphorus	1.8–2.3		44.1	280	+3, +5
Platinum	21.45		1769.3	3825	+2, +4
Potassium	0.86		62.3	760	+1
Radium	5 (?)		700	1140	+2
Silicon	2.42		1420	2355	+4
Silver	10.5		960.8	1950	+1
Sodium	0.97		97.5	880	+1
Strontium	2.54		800	1150	+2
Sulfur	2.0		114.5	444.6	−2, +4, +6
Tin	7.31		231.9	2270	+2, +4
Titanium	4.5		1677	3277(?)	+3, +4
Tungsten	19.3		3410	5927	+6
Zinc	7.14		419.5	907	+2

TABLE 15.—FOUR–PLACE LOGARITHMS OF NUMBERS

n	0	1	2	3	4	5	6	7	8	9
10	0000	0043	0086	0128	0170	0212	0253	0294	0334	0374
11	0414	0453	0492	0531	0569	0607	0645	0682	0719	0755
12	0792	0828	0864	0899	0934	0969	1004	1038	1072	1106
13	1139	1173	1206	1239	1271	1303	1335	1367	1399	1430
14	1461	1492	1523	1553	1584	1614	1644	1673	1703	1732
15	1761	1790	1818	1847	1875	1903	1931	1959	1987	2014
16	2041	2068	2095	2122	2148	2175	2201	2227	2253	2279
17	2304	2330	2355	2380	2405	2430	2455	2480	2504	2529
18	2553	2577	2601	2625	2648	2672	2695	2718	2742	2765
19	2788	2810	2833	2856	2878	2900	2923	2945	2967	2989
20	3010	3032	3054	3075	3096	3118	3139	3160	3181	3201
21	3222	3243	3263	3284	3304	3324	3345	3365	3385	3404
22	3424	3444	3464	3483	3502	3522	3541	3560	3579	3598
23	3617	3636	3655	3674	3692	3711	3729	3747	3766	3784
24	3802	3820	3838	3856	3874	3892	3909	3927	3945	3962
25	3979	3997	4014	4031	4048	4065	4082	4099	4116	4133
26	4150	4166	4183	4200	4216	4232	4249	4265	4281	4298
27	4314	4330	4346	4362	4378	4393	4409	4425	4440	4456
28	4472	4487	4502	4518	4533	4548	4564	4579	4594	4609
29	4624	4639	4654	4669	4683	4698	4713	4728	4742	4757
30	4771	4786	4800	4814	4829	4843	4857	4871	4886	4900
31	4914	4928	4942	4955	4969	4983	4997	5011	5024	5038
32	5051	5065	5079	5092	5105	5119	5132	5145	5159	5172
33	5185	5198	5211	5224	5237	5250	5263	5276	5289	5302
34	5315	5328	5340	5353	5366	5378	5391	5403	5416	5428
35	5441	5453	5465	5478	5490	5502	5514	5527	5539	5551
36	5563	5575	5587	5599	5611	5623	5635	5647	5658	5670
37	5682	5694	5705	5717	5729	5740	5752	5763	5775	5786
38	5798	5809	5821	5832	5843	5855	5866	5877	5888	5899
39	5911	5922	5933	5944	5955	5966	5977	5988	5999	6010
40	6021	6031	6042	6053	6064	6075	6085	6096	6107	6117
41	6128	6138	6149	6160	6170	6180	6191	6201	6212	6222
42	6232	6243	6253	6263	6274	6284	6294	6304	6314	6325
43	6335	6345	6355	6365	6375	6385	6395	6405	6415	6425
44	6435	6444	6454	6464	6474	6484	6493	6503	6513	6522
45	6532	6542	6551	6561	6571	6580	6590	6599	6609	6618
46	6628	6637	6646	6656	6665	6675	6684	6693	6702	6712
47	6721	6730	6739	6749	6758	6767	6776	6785	6794	6803
48	6812	6821	6830	6839	6848	6857	6866	6875	6884	6893
49	6902	6911	6920	6928	6937	6946	6955	6964	6972	6981
50	6990	6998	7007	7016	7024	7033	7042	7050	7059	7067
51	7076	7084	7093	7101	7110	7118	7126	7135	7143	7152
52	7160	7168	7177	7185	7193	7202	7210	7218	7226	7235
53	7243	7251	7259	7267	7275	7284	7292	7300	7308	7316
54	7324	7332	7340	7348	7356	7364	7372	7380	7388	7396

TABLE 15.—FOUR-PLACE LOGARITHMS OF NUMBERS (cont'd)

n	0	1	2	3	4	5	6	7	8	9
55	7404	7412	7419	7427	7435	7443	7451	7459	7466	7474
56	7482	7490	7497	7505	7513	7520	7528	7536	7543	7551
57	7559	7566	7574	7582	7589	7597	7604	7612	7619	7627
58	7634	7642	7649	7657	7664	7672	7679	7686	7694	7701
59	7709	7716	7723	7731	7738	7745	7752	7760	7767	7774
60	7782	7789	7796	7803	7810	7818	7825	7832	7839	7846
61	7853	7860	7868	7875	7882	7889	7896	7903	7910	7917
62	7924	7931	7938	7945	7952	7959	7966	7973	7980	7987
63	7993	8000	8007	8014	8021	8028	8035	8041	8048	8055
64	8062	8069	8075	8082	8089	8096	8102	8109	8116	8122
65	8129	8136	8142	8149	8156	8162	8169	8176	8182	8189
66	8195	8202	8209	8215	8222	8228	8235	8241	8248	8254
67	8261	8267	8274	8280	8287	8293	8299	8306	8312	8319
68	8325	8331	8338	8344	8351	8357	8363	8370	8376	8382
69	8388	8395	8401	8407	8414	8420	8426	8432	8439	8445
70	8451	8457	8463	8470	8476	8482	8488	8494	8500	8506
71	8513	8519	8525	8531	8537	8543	8549	8555	8561	8567
72	8573	8579	8585	8591	8597	8603	8609	8615	8621	8627
73	8633	8639	8645	8651	8657	8663	8669	8675	8681	8686
74	8692	8698	8704	8710	8716	8722	8727	8733	8739	8745
75	8751	8756	8762	8768	8774	8779	8785	8791	8797	8802
76	8808	8814	8820	8825	8831	8837	8842	8848	8854	8859
77	8865	8871	8876	8882	8887	8893	8899	8904	8910	8915
78	8921	8927	8932	8938	8943	8949	8954	8960	8965	8971
79	8976	8982	8987	8993	8998	9004	9009	9015	9020	9025
80	9031	9036	9042	9047	9053	9058	9063	9069	9074	9079
81	9085	9090	9096	9101	9106	9112	9117	9122	9128	9133
82	9138	9143	9149	9154	9159	9165	9170	9175	9180	9186
83	9191	9196	9201	9206	9212	9217	9222	9227	9232	9238
84	9243	9248	9253	9258	9263	9269	9274	9279	9284	9289
85	9294	9299	9304	9309	9315	9320	9325	9330	9335	9340
86	9345	9350	9355	9360	9365	9370	9375	9380	9385	9390
87	9395	9400	9405	9410	9415	9420	9425	9430	9435	9440
88	9445	9450	9455	9460	9465	9469	9474	9479	9484	9489
89	9494	9499	9504	9509	9513	9518	9523	9528	9533	9538
90	9542	9547	9552	9557	9562	9566	9571	9576	9581	9586
91	9590	9595	9600	9605	9609	9614	9619	9624	9628	9633
92	9638	9643	9647	9652	9657	9661	9666	9671	9675	9680
93	9685	9689	9694	9699	9703	9708	9713	9717	9722	9727
94	9731	9736	9741	9745	9750	9754	9759	9763	9768	9773
95	9777	9782	9786	9791	9795	9800	9805	9809	9814	9818
96	9823	9827	9832	9836	9841	9845	9850	9854	9859	9863
97	9868	9872	9877	9881	9886	9890	9894	9899	9903	9908
98	9912	9917	9921	9926	9930	9934	9939	9943	9948	9952
99	9956	9961	9965	9969	9974	9978	9983	9987	9991	9996

PERIODIC TABLE

METALS

TRANSITION ELEMENTS

	I	II								

1 — H, 1.00797, atomic number 1

Period 2 — I: Li 6.939 (2,1) #3; II: Be 9.0122 (2,2) #4

Period 3 — I: Na 22.9898 (2,8,1) #11; II: Mg 24.312 (2,8,2) #12

Period 4
- K 39.102 (2,8,8,1) #19
- Ca 40.08 (2,8,8,2) #20
- Sc 44.956 (2,8,9,2) #21
- Ti 47.90 (2,8,10,2) #22
- V 50.942 (2,8,11,2) #23
- Cr 51.996 (2,8,13,1) #24
- Mn 54.9380 (2,8,13,2) #25
- Fe 55.847 (2,8,14,2) #26
- Co 58.9332 (2,8,15,2) #27

Period 5
- Rb 85.47 (2,8,18,8,1) #37
- Sr 87.62 (2,8,18,8,2) #38
- Y 88.905 (2,8,18,9,2) #39
- Zr 91.22 (2,8,18,10,2) #40
- Nb 92.906 (2,8,18,12,1) #41
- Mo 95.94 (2,8,18,13,1) #42
- Tc [99*] (2,8,18,14,1) #43
- Ru 101.07 (2,8,18,15,1) #44
- Rh 102.905 (2,8,18,16,1) #45

Period 6
- Cs 132.905 (2,8,18,18,8,1) #55
- Ba 137.34 (2,8,18,18,8,2) #56
- Lanthanide Series
- Lu 174.97 (2,8,18,32,9,2) #71
- Hf 178.49 (2,8,18,32,10,2) #72
- Ta 180.948 (2,8,18,32,11,2) #73
- W 183.85 (2,8,18,32,12,2) #74
- Re 186.2 (2,8,18,32,13,2) #75
- Os 190.2 (2,8,18,32,14,2) #76
- Ir 192.2 (2,8,18,32,17,0) #77

Period 7
- Fr [223] (2,8,18,32,18,8,1) #87
- Ra [226] (2,8,18,32,18,8,2) #88
- Actinide Series
- Lw [257] (2,8,18,32,32,9,2) #103

Lanthanide Series
- La 138.91 (2,8,18,18,9,2) #57
- Ce 140.12 (2,8,18,20,8,2) #58
- Pr 140.907 (2,8,18,21,8,2) #59
- Nd 144.24 (2,8,18,22,8,2) #60
- Pm [147*] (2,8,18,23,8,2) #61
- Sm 150.35 (2,8,18,24,8,2) #62
- Eu 151.96 (2,8,18,25,8,2) #63

Actinide Series
- Ac [227] (2,8,18,32,18,9,2) #89
- Th 232.038 (2,8,18,32,18,10,2) #90
- Pa [231] (2,8,18,32,20,9,2) #91
- U 238.03 (2,8,18,32,21,9,2) #92
- Np [237] (2,8,18,32,23,8,2) #93
- Pu [242] (2,8,18,32,24,8,2) #94
- Am [243] (2,8,18,32,25,8,2) #95

OF THE ELEMENTS

Noble gases

VIII

NONMETALS

III	IV	V	VI	VII	Noble gases VIII
					4.0026 **He** 2 — (2)
10.811 **B** 5 — (2,3)	12.01115 **C** 6 — (2,4)	14.0067 **N** 7 — (2,5)	15.9994 **O** 8 — (2,6)	18.9984 **F** 9 — (2,7)	20.183 **Ne** 10 — (2,8)
26.9815 **Al** 13 — (2,8,3)	28.086 **Si** 14 — (2,8,4)	30.9738 **P** 15 — (2,8,5)	32.064 **S** 16 — (2,8,6)	35.453 **Cl** 17 — (2,8,7)	39.948 **Ar** 18 — (2,8,8)

	III	IV	V	VI	VII	VIII
58.71 **Ni** 28 (2,8,16,2)	63.54 **Cu** 29 (2,8,18,1)	65.37 **Zn** 30 (2,8,18,2)	69.72 **Ga** 31 (2,8,18,3)	72.59 **Ge** 32 (2,8,18,4)	74.9216 **As** 33 (2,8,18,5)	78.96 **Se** 34 (2,8,18,6) / 79.909 **Br** 35 (2,8,18,7) / 83.80 **Kr** 36 (2,8,18,8)
106.4 **Pd** 46 (2,8,18,18,0)	107.870 **Ag** 47 (2,8,18,18,1)	112.40 **Cd** 48 (2,8,18,18,2)	114.82 **In** 49 (2,8,18,18,3)	118.69 **Sn** 50 (2,8,18,18,4)	121.75 **Sb** 51 (2,8,18,18,5)	127.60 **Te** 52 (2,8,18,18,6) / 126.9044 **I** 53 (2,8,18,18,7) / 131.30 **Xe** 54 (2,8,18,18,8)
195.09 **Pt** 78 (2,8,18,32,17,1)	196.967 **Au** 79 (2,8,18,32,18,1)	200.59 **Hg** 80 (2,8,18,32,18,2)	204.37 **Tl** 81 (2,8,18,32,18,3)	207.19 **Pb** 82 (2,8,18,32,18,4)	208.980 **Bi** 83 (2,8,18,32,18,5)	[210*] **Po** 84 (2,8,18,32,18,6) / [210] **At** 85 (2,8,18,32,18,7) / [222] **Rn** 86 (2,8,18,32,18,8)

RARE EARTH ELEMENTS

157.25 **Gd** 64 (2,8,18,25,9,2)	158.924 **Tb** 65 (2,8,18,27,8,2)	162.50 **Dy** 66 (2,8,18,28,8,2)	164.930 **Ho** 67 (2,8,18,29,8,2)	167.26 **Er** 68 (2,8,18,30,8,2)	168.934 **Tm** 69 (2,8,18,31,8,2)	173.04 **Yb** 70 (2,8,18,32,8,2)

[247] **Cm** 96 (2,8,18,32,25,9,2)	[249*] **Bk** 97 (2,8,18,32,26,9,2)	[251*] **Cf** 98 (2,8,18,32,28,8,2)	[254] **Es** 99 (2,8,18,32,28,9,2)	[253] **Fm** 100 (2,8,18,32,29,9,2)	[256] **Md** 101 (2,8,18,32,30,9,2)	[254] **102** (2,8,18,32,31,9,2)

A value given in brackets denotes the mass number of the isotope of longest known half-life, or for those marked with an asterisk, a better known one.

RELATIVE SIZES OF ATOMS AND

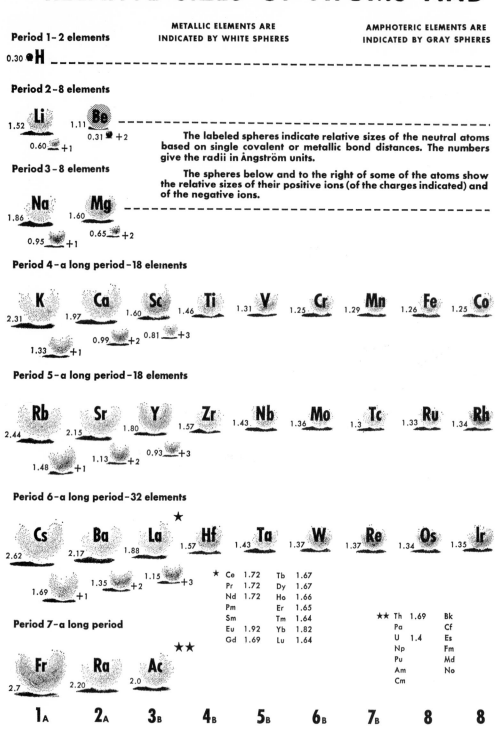

Period 1-2 elements

METALLIC ELEMENTS ARE
INDICATED BY WHITE SPHERES

AMPHOTERIC ELEMENTS ARE
INDICATED BY GRAY SPHERES

0.30 H

Period 2-8 elements

Li 1.52
Be 1.11
0.31 +2
0.60 +1

The labeled spheres indicate relative sizes of the neutral atoms based on single covalent or metallic bond distances. The numbers give the radii in Ångström units.

The spheres below and to the right of some of the atoms show the relative sizes of their positive ions (of the charges indicated) and of the negative ions.

Period 3-8 elements

Na 1.86
Mg 1.60
0.65 +2
0.95 +1

Period 4-a long period-18 elements

K 2.31
Ca 1.97
Sc 1.60
Ti 1.46
V 1.31
Cr 1.25
Mn 1.29
Fe 1.26
Co 1.25

1.33 +1
0.99 +2
0.81 +3

Period 5-a long period-18 elements

Rb 2.44
Sr 2.15
Y 1.80
Zr 1.57
Nb 1.43
Mo 1.36
Tc 1.3
Ru 1.33
Rh 1.34

1.48 +1
1.13 +2
0.93 +3

Period 6-a long period-32 elements

★

Cs 2.62
Ba 2.17
La 1.88
Hf 1.57
Ta 1.43
W 1.37
Re 1.37
Os 1.34
Ir 1.35

1.69 +1
1.35 +2
1.15 +3

★			
Ce	1.72	Tb	1.67
Pr	1.72	Dy	1.67
Nd	1.72	Ho	1.66
Pm		Er	1.65
Sm		Tm	1.64
Eu	1.92	Yb	1.82
Gd	1.69	Lu	1.64

Period 7-a long period

★★

Fr 2.7
Ra 2.20
Ac 2.0

★★			
Th	1.69	Bk	
Pa		Cf	
U	1.4	Es	
Np		Fm	
Pu		Md	
Am		No	
Cm			

| 1A | 2A | 3B | 4B | 5B | 6B | 7B | 8 | 8 |

IONS IN THE PERIODIC TABLE

NON METALLIC ELEMENTS ARE INDICATED BY BLACK SPHERES

Based on an arrangement by Dr. J. A. Campbell
Harvey Mudd College, Claremont, California

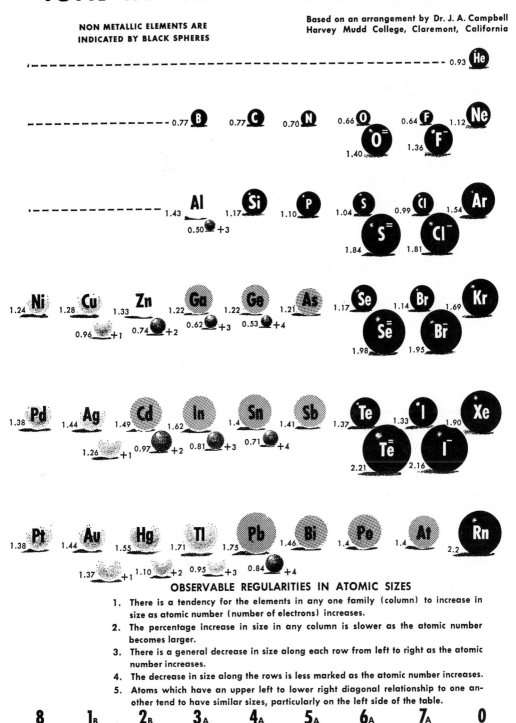

OBSERVABLE REGULARITIES IN ATOMIC SIZES

1. There is a tendency for the elements in any one family (column) to increase in size as atomic number (number of electrons) increases.
2. The percentage increase in size in any column is slower as the atomic number becomes larger.
3. There is a general decrease in size along each row from left to right as the atomic number increases.
4. The decrease in size along the rows is less marked as the atomic number increases.
5. Atoms which have an upper left to lower right diagonal relationship to one another tend to have similar sizes, particularly on the left side of the table.

| **8** | **1**B | **2**B | **3**A | **4**A | **5**A | **6**A | **7**A | **0** |

Published by The Welch Scientific Company, 1515 Sedgwick St., Chicago 10, Illinois, U. S. A.

INDEX

INDEX

Page references for illustrations are printed in **boldface.**

THE ELEMENTS, THEIR SYMBOLS, ATOMIC NUMBERS, AND ATOMIC WEIGHTS

The more important elements are printed in color.

Name of element	Symbol	Atomic number	Atomic weight	Name of element	Symbol	Atomic number	Atomic weight
Actinium	Ac	89	[227]	Mercury	Hg	80	200.59
Aluminum	Al	13	26.9815	Molybdenum	Mo	42	95.94
Americium	Am	95	[243]	Neodymium	Nd	60	144.24
Antimony	Sb	51	121.75	Neon	Ne	10	20.183
Argon	Ar	18	39.948	Neptunium	Np	93	[237]
Arsenic	As	33	74.9216	Nickel	Ni	28	58.71
Astatine	At	85	[210]	Niobium	Nb	41	92.906
Barium	Ba	56	137.34	Nitrogen	N	7	14.0067
Berkelium	Bk	97	[249*]	(Nobelium)	(No)	102	[254]
Beryllium	Be	4	9.0122	Osmium	Os	76	190.2
Bismuth	Bi	83	208.980	Oxygen	O	8	15.9994
Boron	B	5	10.811	Palladium	Pd	46	106.4
Bromine	Br	35	79.909	Phosphorus	P	15	30.9738
Cadmium	Cd	48	112.40	Platinum	Pt	78	195.09
Calcium	Ca	20	40.08	Plutonium	Pu	94	[242]
Californium	Cf	98	[251*]	Polonium	Po	84	[210*]
Carbon	C	6	12.01115	Potassium	K	19	39.102
Cerium	Ce	58	140.12	Praseodymium	Pr	59	140.907
Cesium	Cs	55	132.905	Promethium	Pm	61	[147*]
Chlorine	Cl	17	35.453	Protactinium	Pa	91	[231]
Chromium	Cr	24	51.996	Radium	Ra	88	[226]
Cobalt	Co	27	58.9332	Radon	Rn	86	[222]
Copper	Cu	29	63.54	Rhenium	Re	75	186.2
Curium	Cm	96	[247]	Rhodium	Rh	45	102.905
Dysprosium	Dy	66	162.50	Rubidium	Rb	37	85.47
Einsteinium	Es	99	[254]	Ruthenium	Ru	44	101.07
Erbium	Er	68	167.26	Samarium	Sm	62	150.35
Europium	Eu	63	151.96	Scandium	Sc	21	44.956
Fermium	Fm	100	[253]	Selenium	Se	34	78.96
Fluorine	F	9	18.9984	Silicon	Si	14	28.086
Francium	Fr	87	[223]	Silver	Ag	47	107.870
Gadolinium	Gd	64	157.25	Sodium	Na	11	22.9898
Gallium	Ga	31	69.72	Strontium	Sr	38	87.62
Germanium	Ge	32	72.59	Sulfur	S	16	32.064
Gold	Au	79	196.967	Tantalum	Ta	73	180.948
Hafnium	Hf	72	178.49	Technetium	Tc	43	[99*]
Helium	He	2	4.0026	Tellurium	Te	52	127.60
Holmium	Ho	67	164.930	Terbium	Tb	65	158.924
Hydrogen	H	1	1.00797	Thallium	Tl	81	204.37
Indium	In	49	114.82	Thorium	Th	90	232.038
Iodine	I	53	126.9044	Thulium	Tm	69	168.934
Iridium	Ir	77	192.2	Tin	Sn	50	118.69
Iron	Fe	26	55.847	Titanium	Ti	22	47.90
Krypton	Kr	36	83.80	Tungsten	W	74	183.85
Lanthanum	La	57	138.91	Uranium	U	92	238.03
Lawrencium	Lw	103	[257]	Vanadium	V	23	50.942
Lead	Pb	82	207.19	Xenon	Xe	54	131.30
Lithium	Li	3	6.939	Ytterbium	Yb	70	173.04
Lutetium	Lu	71	174.97	Yttrium	Y	39	88.905
Magnesium	Mg	12	24.312	Zinc	Zn	30	65.37
Manganese	Mn	25	54.9380	Zirconium	Zr	40	91.22
Mendelevium	Md	101	[256]				

A value given in brackets denotes the mass number of the isotope of longest known half-life, or for those marked with an asterisk, a better known one. The atomic weights of most of these elements are believed to have no error greater than ±0.5 of the last digit given.